ARMCHAIR GENERAL

ARMCHAIR GENERAL

A Calendar Year of British Battles, Sieges,
Atrocities and Heroics

Stuart Thresher

UNIFORM

Published by Uniform
An imprint of Unicorn Publishing Group
5 Newburgh Street
London W1F 7RG

www.unicornpublishing.org

Second revised edition 2018, 2019

A catalogue record for this book is available from
the British Library

5 4 3 2

ISBN 978-1-911604-80-8

Cover design Unicorn Publishing Group
Typeset by Vivian@Bookscribe

Printed and bound in the UK

"All a man can do, our fellows will do..."

FIELD MARSHAL SIR JOHN FRENCH, PARIS, 1914

For

Great Grandpa William
who charged with the Queen's Lifeguards
at Paardeberg 1900

Great Uncle Albert
who gave as much as a man can at Vimy Ridge 1917

Grandpa Leslie
who won the Military Medal at 's-Hertogenbosch 1944

Uncle Tim
who served in Northern Ireland, fought in the Gulf and
Iraq 1991-93, Bosnia 1995 and Afghanistan 2003

and

Cousins Steve and Delia
who served in Afghanistan 2010 & 2014

Chronology

YEAR	DATE	PLACE

Marian Civil War

YEAR	DATE	PLACE
1568	13 May	Langside

Anglo-Spanish Wars

YEAR	DATE	PLACE
1568	23 September	San Juan de Ulua
1574	29 January	Reimersvaal
1579	1 March	Nuestra Señora de la Concepcíon
1586	1 January	Santo Domingo o.s
1586	9 February	Cartagena o.s
1587	19 April	Cadiz o.s
1588	29 July	Gravelines o.s

Anglo-Scottish Wars

YEAR	DATE	PLACE
1594	3 October	Glenlivet o.s

Ireland

YEAR	DATE	PLACE
1595	25 May	Crossdall & Clontibret o.s
1601	24 December	Kinsale o.s

Wars of the Three Kingdoms

YEAR	DATE	PLACE
1642	23 October	Edgehill
1643	19 January	Braddock Down
1643	18 March	New Ross
1643	19 March	Hopton Heath
1643	30 June	Adwalton Moor
1643	5 June	Lansdowne Hill
1643	13 July	Roundway Down
1643	20 September	Newbury
1644	25 January	Nantwich
1644	29 June	Cropredy Bridge
1644	2 July	Marston Moor
1644	27 October	2nd Newbury
1645	14 June	Naseby
1645	24 September	Rowton Heath
1645	26 November	Newark
1646	16 February	Torrington
1648	8 May	St Fagan's
1649	2 August	Rathmines
1649	2 October	Wexford
1649	6 December	Lisnagarvey
1651	3 September	Worcester

Anglo-Dutch Wars

YEAR	DATE	PLACE
1652	19 May	Goodwin Sands o.s
1652	28 September	Kentish Knock o.s
1652	30 November	Dungeness o.s
1653	20 February	Portland o.s
1653	2 June	Gabbard o.s
1653	29 July	Sheveningen o.s

Cromwell's Western Design

YEAR	DATE	PLACE
1658	25 June	Jamaica o.s

Anglo-Dutch Wars

YEAR	DATE	PLACE
1665	3 June	Lowestoft o.s
1666	25 July	North Foreland o.s
1667	9 June	River Medway o.s
1673	4 June	Schooneveld o.s
1673	11 August	Texel o.s

Pirates and Privateers

YEAR	DATE	PLACE
1668	29 May	St Augustine o.s
1669	27 April	Maracaibo o.s
1671	18 January	Panama City o.s

Nine Years War

YEAR	DATE	PLACE
1689	25 August	Walcourt n.s
1692	3 August	Steenkerque n.s

Williamite War

YEAR	DATE	PLACE
1690	30 April	Cromdale n.s
1690/1691	12 July (Celebrated)	Boyne/ Augrim n.s/ o.s

War of the Spanish Succession

YEAR	DATE	PLACE
1704	13 August	Blenheim n.s
1706	23 May	Ramillies n.s
1706	6 November	Santa Cruz de Tenerife n.s
1707	25 April	Almansa n.s
1708	11 July	Oudenaarde n.s
1709	7 May	La Gudina n.s
1709	11 September	Malplaquet n.s
1710	20 August	Zaragoza n.s

Jacobite Rebellions

YEAR	DATE	PLACE
1719	10 June	Glenshiel o.s
1745	21 September	Prestonpans o.s
1746	16 April	Culloden o.s

War of Jenkins Ear

YEAR	DATE	PLACE
1739	22 November	Portobello n.s
1740	26 June	Fort Mose n.s

YEAR	DATE	PLACE
1743	2 March	La Guaira n.s

War of the Austrian Succession

YEAR	DATE	PLACE
1743	27 June	Dettingen n.s
1744	22 Feb	Toulon n.s
1744	20 April	Villafranca n.s
1745	11 May	Fontenoy n.s

India, Persia, Afghanistan

YEAR	DATE	PLACE
1751	3 December	Arnee
1757	23 March	Chandannagar
1757	23 June	Plassey
1759	25 November	Chinsurah
1764	22 October	Buxar

French and Indian War

YEAR	DATE	PLACE
1755	9 July	Monongahela
1755	8 September	Lake George
1756	27 March	Fort Bull
1757	9 August	Fort William Henry
1758	8 July	Fort Carillon
1759	13 September	Plains of Abraham (Quebec)
1760	28 April	Sainte Foy

Seven Years War

YEAR	DATE	PLACE
1759	1 August	Minden
1761	15 July	Villinghausen

American War of Independence

YEAR	DATE	PLACE
1775	19 April	Lexington and Concord
1775	17 June	Bunker Hill
1775	31 December	Quebec
1776	17 March	Boston
1776	27 August	Long Island
1776	16 September	Harlem Heights
1776	11 October	Valcour Island
1776	28 October	White Plains
1776	16 November	Fort Washington
1777	3 January	Princeton
1777	7 July	Hubbardton
1777	4 October	Germantown
1777	7 October	Bemis Heights
1777	5 December	White Marsh
1778	28 June	Monmouth
1778	29 August	Rhode Island
1779	23 February	Vincennes
1779	16 July	Stony Point

YEAR	DATE	PLACE
1780	17 April	Martinique
1780	12 May	Charleston
1780	16 August	Camden
1781	6 January	Jersey
1781	1 February	McCowan's Ford
1781	15 March	Guildford Court House
1781	16 March	Cape Henry
1781	29 April	Fort Royal, Martinique
1781	5 September	Chesapeake bay
1781	16 October	Yorktown
1782	12 April	Providien
1782	12 April	Saintes

French Revolutionary War

YEAR	DATE	PLACE
1794	1 June	Glorious First of June
1795	5 January	Guadeloupe
1797	14 January	Droits de l'Homme
1797	26 April	Cadiz

Ireland

YEAR	DATE	PLACE
1798	12 June	Ballynahinch

French Revolutionary War

YEAR	DATE	PLACE
1798	1 August	The Nile
1799	28 February	River Hooghly
1799	20 March	Acre

India, Persia, Afghanistan

YEAR	DATE	PLACE
1799	5 April	Seringapatam

French Revolutionary War

YEAR	DATE	PLACE
1801	21 March	Alexandria
1801	2 April	Copenhagen

India, Persia, Afghanistan

YEAR	DATE	PLACE
1803	23 September	Assaye

Napoleonic Wars

YEAR	DATE	PLACE
1804	5 October	Cape Santa Maria
1805	21 October	Trafalgar
1805	4 November	Ortegal
1806	8 January	Blaauwberg
1806	6 February	Santo Domingo
1807	3 February	Montevideo
1807	2 September	Copenhagen
1808	21 August	Vimeiro
1809	16 January	Corunna

YEAR	DATE	PLACE
1809	28 July	Talavera
1809	30 July	Walcheren
1810	27 September	Bussaco
1810	15 October	Fuengirola
1811	5 March	Barrosa
1811	14 March	Casal Novo
1811	3 May	Fuentes de Oñoro
1811	16 May	Albuera
1812	20 January	Ciudad Rodrigo
1812	6 April	Badajoz
1812	22 July	Salamanca
1813	21 June	Vitoria
1813	31 August	San Sebastián
1813	10 November	Nivelle
1815	16 June	Quatre Bras
1815	18 June	Waterloo

American War of 1812

YEAR	DATE	PLACE
1812	13 October	Queenston Heights
1814	6 September	Plattsburgh
1814	14 December	Lake Borgne
1814	27 December	USS Carolina, New Orleans
1815	15 January	USS President

Anglo-Ashanti Wars

YEAR	DATE	PLACE
1826	7 August	Dodowa
1874	31 January	Amoafo

India, Persia, Afghanistan

YEAR	DATE	PLACE
1839	23 July	Ghazni
1842	13 January	Gandamack
1845	18 December	Mudki
1845	21 December	Ferozeshah
1846	28 January	Aliwal
1846	10 February	Sobraon
1849	21 February	Gujrat

Maori Flagstaff Wars

YEAR	DATE	PLACE
1846	11 January	Ruapekapeka Pa

Crimean War

YEAR	DATE	PLACE
1854	20 September	Alma
1854	25 October	Balaclava
1854	5 November	Inkerman

India, Persia, Afghanistan

YEAR	DATE	PLACE
1857	7 February	Khushab
1857	18 November	Lucknow

Abyssinian Campaign

YEAR	DATE	PLACE
1868	10 April	Amba Magdala

Zulu War

YEAR	DATE	PLACE
1879	22 January	Isandlwana
1879	22/23 January	Rorke's Drift
1879	12 March	Intombe River
1879	29 March	Khambula
1879	4 July	Ulundi

India, Persia, Afghanistan

YEAR	DATE	PLACE
1879	6 October	Charasiab
1879	23 December	Kabul
1880	27 July	Maiwand
1880	1 September	Kandahar

First Boer War

YEAR	DATE	PLACE
1880	20 December	Bronkhorstspruit
1881	8 February	Ingogo
1881	27 February	Majuba Hill

Egypt, Sudan

YEAR	DATE	PLACE
1882	13 September	Tel-El-Kebir
1883	3 November	El Obeid
1884	4 February	El Teb
1884	29 February	2nd El Teb
1884	13 March	Tamai
1885	17 January	Abu Klea
1885	26 January	Khartoum

Matabele War

YEAR	DATE	PLACE
1893	1 November	Bembesi
1893	4 December	Shangani Patrol

Jameson Raid

YEAR	DATE	PLACE
1896	2 January	Doornkop

North West Frontier

YEAR	DATE	PLACE
1897	12 September	Saragarhi

Egypt, Sudan

YEAR	DATE	PLACE
1896	7 June	Ferkeh
1898	8 April	Atbara
1898	2 September	Omdurman

Second Boer War

YEAR	DATE	PLACE
1899	19 October	Talana Hill

YEAR	DATE	PLACE
1899	24 October	Rietfontein
1899	30 October	Ladysmith
1899	15 November	Chieveley
1899	23 November	Belmont
1899	28 November	Modder River
1899	10 December	Stormberg
1899	11 December	Magersfontein
1899	15 December	Colenso
1900	24 January	Spion Kop
1900	5 February	Vaal Krantz
1900	14 February	Tugela Heights
1900	18 February	Paardeberg
1900	7 November	Leliefontein
1900	29 November	Rhenosterkop
1902	7 March	Tweebosch
1902	11 April	Rooiwal

The Great War

YEAR	DATE	PLACE
1914	23 August	Mons
1914	28 August	Heligoland Bight
1914	6 September	Marne
1914	10 October	La Bassée
1914	19 October	Ypres
1914	29 October	Gheluvelt
1914	2 November	Tanga
1914	8 December	Falkland Islands
1914	16 December	Scarborough, Hartlepool, Whitby
1915	19 February	Dardanelles
1915	10 March	Neuve Chapelle
1915	25 April	Gallipoli
1915	9 May	Aubers Ridge
1915	6 August	Sari Bair
1915	21 August	Scimitar Hill, Hill 60
1915	25 September	Loos
1915	26 December	Lake Tanganyika
1916	21 January	Hanna
1916	11 March	Latema-Reata Nek
1916	31 May	Jutland
1916	1 July	Somme
1916	14 July	Bazentin Ridge
1916	26 September	Thiepval Ridge
1916	1 October	Ancre Heights
1917	9 January	Rafa
1917	9 April	Arras
1917	7 June	Messines

YEAR	DATE	PLACE
1917	6 July	Aqaba
1917	31 July	Third Ypres
1917	9 October	Poelcapelle
1917	26 October	Passchendaele
1917	31 October	Beersheba
1917	13 November	El Mughar
1917	19 November	Jerusalem
1917	20 November	Cambrai
1917	22 December	Jaffa
1918	21 March	Kaiserschlacht
1918	7 April	Lys
1918	21 April	Red Baron
1918	23 April	Zeebrugge
1918	8 August	Amiens
1918	18 September	Epehy

Ireland

YEAR	DATE	PLACE
1916	24 April	Dublin, Easter Rising
1920	21 November	Dublin, Bloody Sunday
1921	25 February	Coolavokig
1921	25 May	Dublin Custom House

India, Persia, Afghanistan

YEAR	DATE	PLACE
1919	13 April	Amritsar

Second World War

YEAR	DATE	PLACE
1939	13 December	River Plate
1940	21 May	Arras
1940	26 May	Dunkirk
1940	3 July	Mers El Kebir
1940	15 September	Finest Hour
1940	11 November	Taranto
1940	14 November	Coventry
1940	27 November	Cape Spartivento
1940	9 December	Sidi Barrani
1940	29 December	London
1941	10 January	HMS *Illustrious*, Malta
1941	4 March	Lofoten Islands
1941	20 May	Crete
1941	24 May	Denmark Strait
1941	27 May	*Bismarck*
1941	12 December	Jitra
1941	17 December	Gulf of Sirte
1941	19 December	Alexandria
1941	25 December	Hong Kong

YEAR	DATE	PLACE
1942	7 January	Slim River
1942	14 January	Muar River
1942	27 January	Endau
1942	11 February	English Channel
1942	15 February	Singapore
1942	3 March	Pegu
1942	28 March	St Nazaire
1942	5 May	Madagascar
1942	19 August	Dieppe
1942	30 August	Alam El Halfa
1942	23 October	El Alamein
1942	17 November	Tunisia
1942	7 December	Bordeaux
1943	17 May	Great Dams of Germany
1943	30 May	Cologne
1943	24 July	Hamburg
1943	2 December	Bari
1943	26 December	North Cape
1943	28 December	Bay of Biscay
1944	8 March	Imphal
1944	24 March	Stalag Luft III
1944	31 March	Nuremberg
1944	4 April	Kohima
1944	18 May	Monte Cassino
1944	5/6 June	Pegasus Bridge
1944	6 June	Normandy
1944	17 November	Arnhem
1944	8 November	Scheldt Estuary
1944	12 November	Tirpitz
1945	12 January	Bergen Harbour
1945	13 February	Dresden
1945	18 April	Hamburg

Korean War

YEAR	DATE	PLACE
1951	22 April	Imjin River
1951	8 October	Maryangsan

Cyprus Emergency

YEAR	DATE	PLACE
1955	1 April	Cyprus

The Troubles

YEAR	DATE	PLACE
1969	12 August	Derry, Belfast
1972	30 January	Derry, Bloody Sunday
1979	27 August	Mullaghmore, Warrenpoint

Falkland Islands

YEAR	DATE	PLACE
1982	2 April	Port Stanley
1982	1 May	Black Buck One
1982	2 May	ARA General Belgrano
1982	28 May	Goose Green
1982	11 June	Mount Longdon
1982	13 June	Mount Tumbledown

Gulf War

YEAR	DATE	PLACE
1991	26 February	7 Easting, Norfolk

War on Terror

YEAR	DATE	PLACE
2007	7 December	Musa Qala

Dates, Old Style Julian or New Style Gregorian?

Since 45 BC the western world had lived by the Julian Calendar, a reform originally proposed by Julius Ceasar from the previously used Roman Calendar. That Britain was barely trading with the Roman Empire at the time meant the event likely went unquestioned in these islands despite the fact that Julius had made a mistake. It was some time until this mistake was picked up however, something like 1621 years in fact when around 1576 Aloysius Lilius, an astronomer and chronographer, found himself struggling with the timing of the northern vernal equinox and Easter. Basically Aloysius realised that the calendar year was in fact 10 minutes and 48 seconds shorter than previously thought. His mathematics was then backed up after his death by Pope Gregory XIII who introduced a new calendar in 1582 named after himself, the Gregorian Calendar.

Whilst most of Europe immediately adopted the New Style Calendar upon Gregory's papal bull, *Inter gravissimas*, there were some who were none too enamoured by any directive issued by a pope, in particular Protestant Englishmen. Queen Elizabeth I of England did briefly consider adopting Gregory's New Style Calendar but quickly abandoned the idea so that in 1588 off the south coast of England a Catholic Armada was sighted by Englishmen ten days before any Spaniards arrived. Or if that's not clear, a few days later the Battle of Gravelines was fought simultaneously by the English on 29 July and by the Spanish on 8 August.

The disparity in dates continued, even the Protestant Dutch Republic changed in 1582 so that seven decades later they were fighting the English ten days apart. Not until 1752 was the unpopular, popish, New Style Gregorian Calendar introduced to bring Great Britain in line with the rest of Europe by which time the Old Style Julian Calendar was not just ten days behind but eleven. Indeed when it was announced in Britain that Wednesday 2 September 1752 would be followed by Thursday 14 September rioting occurred in several towns as an angry population, whose lives had been unfairly shortened, cried 'Give us back our eleven days!'.

As far as *Armchair General* is concerned I have stayed true to the Old Style Julian Calendar up to the end of the Seventeenth Century Dutch Wars since these were the dates that the British, whether fighting against Spaniards, Dutchmen or each other, believed themselves to be fighting on. The Nine Years War and Williamite Wars are slightly more confusing since the Dutch led (King William III) British were largely fighting with Dutchmen against Frenchmen and Catholic Irish all of whom had been, or would have been had they been allowed, living their entire lives under the Gregorian New Style Calendar. I've dated them accordingly. Continuing on, the Eighteenth Century Wars of Succession were fought by an even greater multitude of nations all of whom bar Great Britain were adhering to the Gregorian Calendar and so since in 1752, the British concluded Gregory had been right all along, their constituent battles have been dated New Style Gregorian. In the middle of these altercations of course, the British found time to fight amongst themselves, the Jacobite Wars, internal affairs which since all the combatants were fighting by the Julian Calendar, are recorded on an Old Style date. After 1752 there are no more headaches, we're Gregorian all the way. I hope that clears things up!

Introduction

I remember there was always a ripple of excitement around the primary school classroom whenever my headmaster began drawing a battlefield on the blackboard. It seems from an early age there is something that gets the attention of the British when there is a good fight to be had, usually, but not always, just as long as we are not personally involved. Unfortunately for me though, that primary school excitement was lost at secondary school despite the fact that I was lucky enough to attend a very good one, Sevenoaks. For our first two years instead of history and geography we were offered 'predicament, experience and belief', or PEB for short. Of course, there was some history involved but whatever it was it didn't seem to bear any relevance to my limited daily thought processes and as soon as I had the choice it went out with the dirty laundry, rugby and cricket taking preference. It was a colossal mistake and I blame Sevenoaks School entirely for having given me the choice!

Winston Churchill once remarked, 'the farther back you can look, the farther forward you are likely to see' and so I left Sevenoaks unable to see very far at all, leaving my reawakening for near twenty years later and a three week holiday to Cyprus with the wife and kids. My eureka moment came in the Heathrow Terminal lounge when it suddenly occurred to me that three weeks under a burning Mediterranean sun was going to be a long time and so I decided to visit the airport bookshop where I found the exact same book my South African boss had been reading for the past few weeks, Thomas Pakenham's masterpiece *The Scramble For Africa*. It's a near 700-page house brick of a book but very readable even for someone with as short an attention span as me although I must confess it took me more than three weeks to read. Intrigued, I was out of the blocks, needing to know more, book after book came and went on the 17.44 train from Cannon Street to Sevenoaks as I became a Forrest Gump of British Military History – I just kept going.

Working in the City I thought I was reasonably savvy but what amazed me was how much I didn't know about the amazing journey the British people have been on and how much almost everyone else I knew didn't know about it either. Indeed a straw poll amongst my colleagues had the Boer War fought in the Middle East and England playing no part in the Hundred Years War, even Ralf from Swiss Bank was more knowledgable. Be sure I am not talking about ignorant people here, these were sharp minds working in a highly pressurised environment who just did not have the time or inclination to read a 600 pager but...but...but... they were vaguely interested.

What *Armchair General* is then is a stop-gapper, a very basic, five minute daily history that capitalises on the recent trend of anniversary celebrations, not just for the Great War but almost all British wars and conflicts. Be warned though, all I am giving here are the basics, if you want more and that's partly the aim of the book, there are many outstanding authors producing outstanding pieces of work, many of them covered in my bibliography. If I am to mention a few that have influenced *Armchair General* more than most they would be Alfred Burne's *The Hundred Years War*, Jonathan Sumption's *Trial by Battle* and *Trial by Fire*, John Sugden's *Sir Francis Drake*, C.V Wedgewood's *The King's War*, Mark Urban's *Fusiliers: How the British Army Lost America but Learn How To Fight*, Gregory Fremont Barnes and Todd Fisher's *The Napoleonic Wars*, both Thomas Pakenham's masterpieces *The Boer War* and *The Scramble for Africa* and Gary Sheffield's *Forgotten Victory, The First World War; Myths and Realities*. I should also mention two background works, Simon Schama's *A History of Britain*, all three volumes, and Allan Mallinson's *The Making of the British Army: From the English Civil War to the War on Terror*. These books should take prime position in your book case whereas *Armchair General* is possibly for your downstairs toilet, if it makes your coffee table that would be great, should it enhance your next trip to Yorkshire, France, Spain, Portugal, South Africa, America or wherever I'll be delighted – after all there are not many places the British have not left a footprint.

From the 793 sack of Lindisfarne to the 2007 Battle of Musa Qala, 395 battles on all 366 days of the year, across all five continents, all the famous battles are there, their backgrounds, their events and their consequences, short term or long. Surely no other nation has the propensity for a fight like the British, either the naked aggression of the distant past or the stubborn defence of the more recent. Disasters and atrocities there have been aplenty but no doubt many more victories and heroics. How the British have won so many, as you will discover, has often been nothing short of miraculous. No doubt the good fortune to live on an island ranks high, luck often mixing with astonishing bravery, considerable ingenuity and that noted national trait, sheer bloody mindedness. I hope you do not need any of those qualities to enjoy this book.

Stuart Thresher

January

"We've got the old fox safe now, we'll go over and bag him in the morning."

LIEUTENANT GENERAL CHARLES,
LORD CORNWALLIS, TRENTON, 1777

1 January 1586

Anglo-Spanish Wars
Battle of Santo Domingo

KING PHILIP II of Spain had been Lord of the Seventeen Provinces of the Netherlands since 1555 but, largely due to his repression of the developing Protestant faith, the Dutch revolted in 1568. Philip considered himself the defender of the Catholic faith and although he would spend his entire life campaigning against Dutch heresy, by the 1580s the powerful Spanish were already getting much the better of the Dutch revolters. In 1584 Philip then signed the Treaty of Joinville with the Catholic League raising the spectre of a Franco-Spanish Catholic alliance that would not only crush Protestantism in Holland but more than likely also in England. Queen Elizabeth I of England retorted by signing the Treaty of Nonsuch with the Dutch and began sending her Protestant allies military support. Although undeclared, a state of war thus existed between Spain and England with the Queen's Secretary, Sir Francis Walsingham, authorising Sir Francis Drake to raid the Spanish mainland and New World in an effort to both hamper Spanish efforts against the Netherlands and provide a boost to England's own treasury. Drake enjoyed nothing more than attacking the Spanish after treachery at San Juan de Ulua in 1568, having made a piratical return to the Caribbean in 1572–73 and a state sponsored round the world privateering raid in 1577–80.

On 14 September 1585 Drake sailed from Plymouth in his flagship, the 600-ton *Elizabeth Bonaventure*, the greatest warship in the world, accompanied by more than thirty-five heavily armed ships, the most powerful fleet that had ever left English shores. Drake had left in a hurry, ridding himself of unwanted nobles but was consequently now in need of additional supplies, resolving his problem by intercepting a Biscayan trawler before threatening Vigo in Spain where the terrified governor humiliatingly allowed the English fleet to provision itself. Drake then sailed for Cape Verde, destroying the town of Santiago and nearby villages when they declined to pay a ransom before sailing west for the uninhabited Caribbean island of St Kitts, en route putting down a near mutiny led by Francis Knollys whilst also suffering several hundred deaths amongst his crews likely to typhus. Recuperating on St Kitts, Drake resolved to attack the former centre of the Spanish bullion route, Santo Domingo, Hispaniola (Haiti, Domincan Republic)

On 'New Year's Day'* 1586, the residents of Santo Domingo awoke to the horrifying sight of English sails, that is if they had slept at all. Letters from King Philip warning of 'El Draques' approach had been intercepted by Drake himself but the Governor of the city, Licentiate Christobal de Ovalle, had been forewarned the day before and had gathered a 1,500 strong militia, sunk three ships across the harbour bar, repositioned an unseaworthy but armed galley and built earthworks fortified with cannon astride the town. That these obstacles were of little concern to a man like Drake was not lost on many more townsfolk who departed during the night. Soon arriving however, having landed ashore six miles to the west through coral reefs at the mouth of the River Hayna, were 800 men under Drake's Lieutenant General Christopher Carleill who approached the city through thick jungle. Meanwhile Drake began exchanging fire with the galley and forts around the harbour, a cannonball crashing through the *Elizabeth Bonaventure* but the poor quality of Spanish powder leaving most of their shot to fall short. The English warships then pounded the waterfront whilst the advancing Carleill drove off a detachment of spanish cavalry, skirmishers and stampeding cattle with heavy arquebus fire before engaging 200 defenders at the two western gates with pike and lance. On overwhelming the defenders Carleill's men then stormed into the city, Ovalle, whose performance had been questionable, fleeing with many others but leaving behind his wife and nieces. By nightfall all of Santo Domingo bar the main fort had fallen.

Drake's sea dogs now desecrated the housing, monasteries and cathedrals of Santo Domingo. Having emptied the treasury Drake then sought to ransom the city from further destruction, burning a church at a time and hanging two Dominican Friars in revenge for the murder of his black messenger boy before receiving 25,000 Ducats a month later. A third of Santo Domingo was in ruins but the haul had been poor, Drake therefore sought another target, no less than the principal city on the Spanish Main, Cartagena, Colombia.

---

* Between the years 1155 and 1752 1 January was often considered New Year's Day although officially, 25 March held the honour. On the British introduction of the Gregorian Calendar 1 January again officially became New Year's Day whilst 25 March plus the eleven days missed by the Julian Calendar, ie 6 April, became the Legal and Civil New Year's Day.

2 January 1896

Jameson Raid
Battle of Doornkop

DIAMONDS, IN CONJUNCTION with developing German imperialism, had prompted Britain to annex the Boer Republic of the Transvaal in 1877 with the Orange Free State likely to follow. The aim was to create a British South African Confederation but defeat in the 1880–81 First Boer War left British Prime Minister William Gladstone conceding independence under British suzerainty to Transvaal President, Paul Kruger. Five years later the world's greatest reserves of gold were then discovered at Witwatersrand prompting another influx of largely British *Uitlanders* (foreigners), the outnumbered Boers, again in fear of losing their independence, responded by protecting their rights (including mining franchises) by denying them to the new immigrants.

In 1890 the arch imperialist Prime Minister of the British Cape Colony Cecil Rhodes sent an expedition north of the Transvaal to create South Zambezia (what would become Rhodesia/Zimbabwe) but also with large mining interests on the Rand (De Beers Mining Corporation) Rhodes was also seeking to gain further control of the Transvaal mining industry. By 1895 both Rhodes and fellow diamond magnate Alfred Beit believed that not just the Transvaal but the whole of British South Africa was at stake if foreign powers, particularly America and Germany, gained the Rand rather than Great Britain. To achieve another 'British' annexation Rhodes decided to prompt a rebellion of disgruntled *Uitlanders* in Johannesburg with an armed invasion of the Transvaal from Rhodesia.

In London, Colonial Secretary Joseph Chamberlain was sympathetic but uncomfortable with Rhodes' venture, eventually undermining the whole project by messaging leaders in Johannesburg to refrain from taking part; already waiting for the starting gun on the Transvaal/ Bechuanaland (Botswana) border, however, was Rhodes' right hand man Doctor Leander Starr Jameson and a force of 400 armed Rhodesian Police. Telegrams reaching the raiders all told of relative *Uitlander* disinterest in Johannesburg but Jameson, a veteran of the 1893 First Matabele War and a noted risk taker took the decision to start the rebellion himself. Cabling Rhodes in Cape Town to warn him of his intentions, Jameson received no reply before, on 29 December 1895, marching for Johannesburg. The Jameson Raid first headed south to meet another 120 men near Mafeking, Cape Colony before continuing east toward Johannesburg with six Maxim guns, two 7-pounder guns, a 12-pounder and several crates of Champagne. Due to the Pitsani/ Cape Town telegraph wire being cut but not the Pitsani/ Pretoria wire the Boers were fully aware of Jameson's movements the moment he stepped out of Pitsani and consequently shadowed him across the Highveld, several skirmishes resulting in minimal British and Boer casualties despite the use of the Maxims. More importantly no one rode out from Johannesburg to join Jameson except two bicyclists who informed him that no one had or was likely to rebel.

On the morning of 2 January 1896 the Jameson Raid reached Doornkop just two hours from Johannesburg. The night before, Jameson had encountered substantial Boer resistance but pressed on, his advance, however, was now blocked by overwhelming numbers of Boers in well-entrenched positions, expert marksmen to a man. A fierce firefight raged with British casualties mounting but the Maxim guns kept the Boers at bay as Jameson kept faith for an *Uitlander* uprising. After several hours of fighting, Boer artillery, a shortage of water and ammunition, jamming Maxims and sixty-five casualties forced Jameson's hand, he surrendered. It had been a fiasco, Jameson was marched off to jail in Pretoria expecting to be shot.

To the embarrassment of Prime Minister Robert Gascoyne-Cecil, Lord Salisbury, Kruger sent Jameson for trial in London but Kruger himself would in turn be embarrassed when news broke of a congratulatory telegram he had received from Germany's Kaiser Wilhelm II. Suddenly a hero, Jameson became the inspiration behind Rudyard Kipling's poem 'If' and later returned as Prime Minister of the Cape Colony, a position from which Cecil Rhodes now resigned. Two months later Rhodes had another headache, the loss of his police with Jameson led to a Second Matabele War in Rhodesia, Boy Scouting born from the bloodshed as thousands paid with their lives. In 1899 the British Army would again try to annex the Boer Republics, this time in unprecedented strength.

3 January 1777

American War of Independence Battle of Princeton

THE AMERICAN CONTINENTAL Army of General George Washington had only known retreat since the British Army's evacuation of Boston had prompted renewed offensives in New York City and south from Quebec City down the length of Lake Champlain in the Hudson Valley. Howe's tacit victories in New York were followed up by General Henry Clinton taking Rhode Island in early December while Lieutenant General Charles, Lord Cornwallis harassed the American retreat through the open country of New Jersey across the River Delaware to Pennsylvania. The Americans were short on morale and consequently suffering high levels of desertion but British General William Howe's inability to inflict a decisive defeat upon them was about to bite him back.

Although his army was still in tact Washington's position looked desperate, Congress had evacuated Philadelphia in fear of a British attack and many of his men were struck with sickness when the bitterly cold winter set in. Worse, many commissions of those both sick and healthy were about to expire at the end of the year reducing American numbers even further. But just as it looked likely King George III would regain control of his thirteen colonies Washington chose to return to the offensive. On Christmas Day night 1776 the 2,000-strong Continental Army crossed back over the freezing Delaware to attack and surprise the advanced 1,500-strong Hessian garrison under Johann Rall at Trenton. Victory was complete but greater than the strategic success was the impact on American morale which now soared enabling Washington to renew commissions and dramatically increase recruitment.

Cornwallis and 7,000 British Redcoats were, however, advancing toward Princeton a mere eleven miles to the north of Trenton, Washington preparing to defend the town just a week after he had taken it but now with more than double his original force. Leaving a 1,200-man garrison in Princeton under Lieutenant Colonel Charles Mahwood, Cornwallis advanced with 5,000 Redcoats toward

Washington's defences but ran into determined skirmishing along the route which severely delayed him. Bringing their cannon to bear the Redcoats eventually reached the bridge in Trenton where a bloody battle took place before night fell. With astonishing confidence that he now had Washington trapped and against the advice of his Quartermaster, Cornwallis, however, would not press the attack in the dark claiming 'we've got the old fox safe now, we'll go over and bag him in the morning'. True to form, when Cornwallis again arrived outside Trenton on 3 January 1777 the 'old fox' Washington was not there but behind him about to attack Mahwood's garrison at Princeton.

Washington had left 500 men in Trenton but only to give Cornwallis the impression the Americans were digging in. By 08.00 the remainder of the Continental Army had negotiated a difficult march through woods around Cornwallis and were now just two miles from Princeton. An American column under Brigadier General Hugh Mercer and Colonel John Cadwalader now turned west to destroy a bridge over the Stoneybrook stream, hampering any Cornwallis recovery but met with Mahwood and a British column of reinforcements leaving Princeton for Trenton. Mahwood fell back to an orchard where a fierce gun battle raged before Mahwood ordered a bayonet charge. Having failed to surrender, Mercer was personally on the receiving end of the British charge before Cadwalader's brigade came up in support to again force Mahwood back. This time the British artillery came to Mahwood's rescue with grapeshot devastating the oncoming Americans before Washington and Brigadier General John Sullivan brought up further reinforcements of Virginians, Rhode Islanders and Pennsylvanians who turned the tide of the battle decisively with a series of musket volleys. Mahwood and a few British escaped to Trenton courtesy of another bayonet charge whilst others retreated back into Princeton where they were captured or escaped to New Brunswick.

After looting British supplies, Washington then left Princeton before Cornwallis could bring up the main British Army. The three consecutive American victories at Trenton and Princeton left Cornwallis to retreat from New Jersey for the winter giving time and space to the exhausted Continental Army. Worse, France and Spain were becoming aware that American Independence at British expense may well be a cause worth fighting for.

4 January 871

Viking
Battle of Reading

PAGAN VIKINGS BEGAN appearing off British shores toward the end of the eighth century, in 793 shocking the whole of Europe with a violent sack of the defenceless monastery on the holy island of Lindisfarne. Violent raids on the wealth of the Anglo-Saxon population and in particular the Christian Church became common place over the next few decades as Vikings took full advantage of a country divided into so many kingdoms that any concerted defence was well-nigh impossible. Gradually, however, through conquest, intermarriage and alliance the old tribal divides began to disappear leaving four major Anglo-Saxon Kingdoms, Northumbria, Mercia (the late eighth century King Offa, as bretwalda (overlord), being the nearest man to a king of all England), East Anglia and Wessex to defend against Viking raids of increasing size and duration that by the mid ninth century reached as far south as Kent. In 850 a Viking fleet of 350 ships captured London and Canterbury, killing the Mercian King Berhrtwulf before, in 865, a Great Heathen Army of Danes led by Ivar the Boneless landed in East Anglia. Paid to go in peace by King Edmund the Martyr, the Heathen Army then marched north to capture York in Northumbria, the city becoming the Viking capital for the next century. The violence continued when the Great Heathen Army marched back south to Nottingham in Mercia where it was attacked and forced back to York by a combined Mercian and Wessex Army. In 869 Ivar and his pagan warriors then returned to East Anglia, this time Edmund bravely making a stand only to pay dearly, earning his epithet when brutally executed after refusing to renounce his Christian faith.

In late December 870 the Heathen Army, now under Ivar's brother Halfdan Ragnarsson (both were sons of the seemingly immortal Ragnar Lodbrok), joined with that of the Great Summer Army under Bagsecg to continue on a destructive path south toward the Kingdom of Wessex (an area stretching across England south of the Thames). Three days after building a fortified camp at Reading a force of

Danes advanced on Englefield (English Field) where a Saxon *fyrd* (militia) had formed under the Ealdorman of the Shire Aethelwulf. In a bloody shield wall battle of swords, spears, battle axes and stone hammers the *fyrd* miraculously drove the Vikings back behind their pallisades at Reading.

Aethulwulf was then joined by the King of the West Saxons, Aethelred and his brother Alfred. Four days later on 4 January 871 the combined Saxon *fyrds* attacked the Vikings at Reading. Numbers and details are scant but a fierce fight developed, the Anglo-Saxon Chronicle states 'much slaughter on either hand, Ealdorman Aethulwulf among the slain'. Several Saxon attacks were repulsed before the Vikings then went on the offensive themselves, forcing the *fyrd* to retreat to Ashdown on the Berkshire Downs where Alfred reputedly blew 'the Blowing Stone' (a perforated Sandstone block which still exists at Kingstone Lisle) to signal the alarm.

The Heathen Army continued on, approaching Ashdown on 8 January 871 as it split into two columns on high ground, one under Ragnarsson and one under Bacsecg whilst the Saxon *fyrd* did likewise under Aethelred and Alfred. Alfred was anxious to attack rather than fight a defensive battle but the pious Aethelred remained in prayer within his tent, refusing to emerge despite several pleas from his brother. Alfred attacked regardless to initiate a violent all-day clash of shield walls that left many dead, including Bagsecg, before the Heathen Army again retreated to Reading.

The Vikings would regroup under Ragnarsson to fight Aethelred again two weeks later at Basing, this time victorious but indecisively so and again similarly two months later at Marton (Wiltshire or Dorset). When Aethelred died in April 871, possibly from wounds received in these battles, Alfred became King of Wessex, initially paying the Danish warlord Guthrum to depart (Ragnarsson had marched north to consolidate his brothers earlier conquests) before the latter's treachery reopened hostilities in 876. A Saxon coup using overwhelming Viking strength then forced Alfred to take refuge in the Athelney marshes where a vision of Saint Cuthbert provided inspiration. The decisive battle would come at Edington in 878, a battle that would lay the foundations for Alfred to become Great and his son and grandson to unite England under one crown. Edmund the Martyr became the first Patron Saint of England and was later venerated even by Vikings, including King Canute. His remains were housed in the church at Bury St Edmunds.

5 January 1795

French Revolutionary War
Battle of Guadeloupe

ANY BRITISH EMPATHY for the French Revolution was lost on 21 January 1793 when King Louis XVI of France was guillotined at the Place de la Révolution, now Place de la Concorde. Even before then the revolution had provoked fear in Britain largely due to the prophetic writings of Edmund Burke who correctly predicted the course of global violence that events in France would inflict. Just over a decade earlier, at crippling expense to themselves, the French nation had enabled the Americans to win independence from British imperialism and now the National Constituent Assembly ruling France pledged their support for any other people attempting to gain liberty, an undertaking appreciated by black slaves on French plantations in the West Indies but not by Europeans who saw it as a cynical attempt to incite civil unrest in their own lands. To spread their ideology France declared war on all of Europe with an army of enormous strength boosted by fervent nationalism and a levée en masse declared by the Committee of Public Safety.

The tiny British Army, derided throughout Europe following the American War, could not hope to match the French and after a debacle in Flanders in which Lieutenant Colonel Arthur Wellesley learnt the valuable lesson of what not to do, left Continental operations to their partners of the First Coalition, primarily Austria and Prussia. Whilst Wellesley would soon head for India, Prime Minister William Pitt, the Royal Navy and a few marines then turned their attention to the wealthy French islands of the Caribbean. In 1789 British exports were worth £14 million and her West Indian colonies £4.5 million but French West Indian exports, mainly sugar, cocoa and coffee, were worth double and also served to further stimulate the economies of both countries in the production of related goods and materials. By an aggressive policy in the Caribbean Britain could thus fund its war effort at the expense of France but, out of necessity, Pitt and Secretary for War Henry Dundas, Viscount Melville split the fleets of the Royal Navy throughout the East Indies, the Mediterranean and the West Indies leaving Vice Admiral John Jervis, commanding a bare strength Leeward Island Station, to target Tobago, Martinique, St Lucia, Guadeloupe and French Guiana.

Jervis took Martinique in March 1794 followed by St Lucia, Tobago and Guadeloupe with troops under General Sir Charles Grey but yellow fever and a French counter-attack under Victor Hugues ousted the British from Guadeloupe in December. Hugues then freed the slaves of Guadeloupe who would obviously fight to retain control of the island, leaving any British counter-invasion temporarily impossible. Instead the 32-gun frigate HMS *Blanche* under Captain Robert Faulknor patrolled off the island of Désirade, ten miles west.

Faulknor soon became aware that the French 38-gun frigate *Pique* under Captain Conseil was refitting at Pointe á Pitre, Guadeloupe and blockaded the harbour until *Pique* emerged on 4 January 1795. Despite superior gunnery *Pique* was initially reluctant to engage HMS *Blanche*, both ships manoeuvring to gain the weather gauge but only closing to exchange broadsides in the early hours of 5 January 1795. The fight was immediately ferocious as cannonballs ripped through the decks and rigging causing *Blanche* to lose her main and mizzen masts before *Pique* turned to ram the port side of the stricken British ship. French sailors and marines now tried to board *Blanche* with repeated assaults and musket volleys as the British desperately tried to lash *Pique*'s bowsprit to the capstan, their only chance. Faulknor was killed by a musket ball to the heart before *Pique* broke away, rounding *Blanche*'s stern and ramming her starboard but this time successfully lashed to the remnants of *Blanche*'s main mast. Unable to bring her guns to bear whilst under a terrible fire from *Blanche*'s guns raking both port and starboard, the completely dismasted *Pique* surrendered with 186 men dead and wounded. HMS *Blanche* had lost twenty-nine dead and wounded during the five-hour battle. Assisted by HMS *Veteran*, HMS *Blanche* towed *Pique* to port where she was pressed into British service.

Hugues continued to incite rebellions in the British West Indies. In 1802 Guadeloupe was seized from her former slaves by a French invasion ordered by Napoleon Bonaparte. Britain regained the island in 1810 but it was returned to France by the 1814 Treaty of Paris, confirmed by the 1815 Treaty of Vienna.

6 January 1781

American War of Independence
Battle of Jersey

THE AMERICAN WAR of Independence had erupted at Lexington and Concord back in 1775. Since then British fortunes had oscillated from a humiliating siege in Boston to determined advances in New York and New Jersey (named after the island of Jersey) before a lack of strategic command both in London and in North America led to a disastrous surrender at Saratoga, Upstate New York. The Saratoga capitulation coupled with determined American resistance in New Jersey was bad enough on its own for British interests but, far worse, it also encouraged France and Spain to join the war on the side of the American cause.

General Henry Clinton replaced General William Howe as British Commander-in-Chief North America and initially opted for a war of attrition but both King George III and Secretary of State for the Colonies, George Germain, Lord Sackville demanded a more vigorous prosecution. As Howe had switched the main theatre south from Boston to New York with a left hook in 1777 so too did Clinton from New York to Virginia, Georgia and the Carolinas in 1780. Whilst in 1777 Howe had only to reckon with General George Washington's Continental Army, however, Clinton and Royal Navy Vice Admiral Marriot Arbuthnot now had to additionally contend with a French fleet under Rear Admiral Charles René, Chevalier Destouches and French troops under Jean Baptiste de Vimeur, Comte de Rochambeau. After losing New France (Canada, American Mid West) to Britain two decades previous, the French were eager to deny the British influence across the Atlantic and indeed in Europe where they signed the Treaty of Aranjuez with Spain as a joint policy to recover lost territories, including British-held Gibraltar which was besieged from mid-1779 onwards. In turn, the British threat to French reinforcements sailing to North America was not just from the Royal Navy but also from privateers operating from western British ports, the Caribbean, America itself and particularly from the island of Jersey, just fourteen miles off the French mainland.

France had already failed to take Jersey in 1779 as part of a general threat to invade Britain but now they would make another attempt. Since the island was heavily defended by a series of forts, redoubts, gun batteries and round towers manned by the Royal Militia of Jersey, three infantry regiments and a naval squadron the task would be no pushover despite her proximity. Indeed, the French Army was decidedly unenthusiastic, doubting whether the island could be held even if it could be taken in the first place so the whole operation was handed to Colonel Phillippe de Rullecourt, a participant in the previous failure but now fully sponsored by King Louis XVI who was willing to throw in the rank of General should Rullecourt succeed in taking Jersey's capital, Saint Helier.

Rullecourt and 800 French troops landed at La Roque on the south-east tip of Jersey as planned on the night of 5 January and were joined early the following morning by another 200. Of another 1,000 French troops there was no sign but an undeterred Rullecourt evaded drunk British sentries to enter Saint Helier where his troops barricaded the main square. As the town slept, ready to celebrate Old Christmas, the Day of the Epiphany, 6 January 1781, the Governor of Jersey, Major Moses Corbet, received his own epiphany in the form of Rullecourt who surprised him at Government House requesting his surrender. Believing the French to be in force and since Rullecourt was being urged by his second in command, Mir Sayyad, to murder the inhabitants and burn the town, Corbet duly did surrender (an offence for which he would later face a Court Martial). Meanwhile, outside, command of British forces fell to Major Francis Peirson who collected 2,000 men to attack what he correctly suspected to be a weak French force. Advancing from the heights above, down into the narrow streets of St Helier, most of the British troops could not get near the French such was the crush, a well and truly trapped Rullecourt using Corbet as a human shield. A fierce firefight nevertheless broke out with Rullecourt falling mortally wounded within seconds. Many French attempted to flee whilst others fought on from houses around the square but the battle was over within minutes, Peirson victorious but tragically not before he had received a musket ball to the heart.

A public house in Pierson's name, pockmarked by musket balls, still stands in the Royal Square, St Helier.

7 January 1942

Second World War
Battle of Slim River

JAPANESE DETERMINATION TO create a new order in South East Asia by breaking the trading domination of the western imperial powers, Great Britain, Holland and the United States of America, had led to simultaneous December 1941 attacks on Pearl Harbor, Hawaii, Siam (Thailand), British Hong Kong, British Malaya and the Dutch East Indies. The right-wing government of Thailand led by Major General Plaek Phibunsongkhram quickly signed an armistice which then allowed the Japanese 5th Infantry Division (15,000 men) of Lieutenant General Takuro Matsui to invade North West Malaya whilst the 18th Infantry Division (22,000 men) under Lieutenant General Renya Mutaguchi advanced down the east coast. The defence of the Malayan Peninsular was in the hands of General Officer Commanding Lieutenant General Arthur Percival whose principal task was to defend Singapore. Percival proposed to do this at sea with Royal Navy Force Z under Admiral Thomas Phillips and in North Malaya with the 9th and 11th Indian Infantry Divisions using delaying tactics with Royal Air Force support until reinforcements arrived in Singapore. Percival's strategy began disintegrating almost immediately, however, when Phillips and Force Z steamed north without an aircraft carrier to attack the Imperial Japanese Navy. Neither did Philips request air cover from the Royal Australian Air Force until too late, paying for his folly by going down with HMS *Prince of Wales* and HMS *Repulse*, both sunk by Japanese bombers and torpedo bombers. Percival now faced complete Japanese air, naval and armoured superiority, his forces possessing not a single tank to combat the two hundred Japanese. The British Indian divisions consequently fell back delaying the enemy barely at all, the 11th Indian defeated at Jitra and Gurun before successfully holding a line at Kampar in a bitter four-day jungle battle which at least allowed the 9th Indian to retreat down the east coast. The fighting of these successive actions shattered the 11th Indian but with no reserve and more Japanese landings to their south they retreated again for another defence at Trolak, five miles north of the Slim River, sixty miles north of Kuala Lumpur.

The Japanese spearhead of twenty light tanks under Major Toyosaku Shimada supported by an infantry battalion of the 42nd Regiment under Colonel Tadao Ando were now to advance through a British defensive gauntlet down the new main Penang-Kuala Lumpur Road with thick jungle on either side (two infantry battalions were flanking but could not keep pace with Shimada). At 03.30 on 7 January 1942 Ando's infantry rained down mortar fire on forward companies of Hyderabadis as Shimada's armour pressed on, firing through the darkness using the old road to increase the Japanese frontage and scatter the defenders. As rain fell, the Hyderabadis retreated through Punjabis who put up stiffer resistance with mines and anti-tank guns, knocking out the lead Japanese tank to expose those queuing behind to artillery fire that never came. Instead Shimada's tanks moved around the stricken vehicle to scatter the Punjabis in a two-hour fight before advancing on a line of Argyll and Sutherland Highlanders specifically trained in the art of jungle warfare. The Highlanders were completely taken by surprise, however, allowing four Japanese tanks led by Lieutenant Sadanobu Watanabe to drive straight though them before fierce fighting developed with Shimada's remaining armour and Ando's infantry who were following on bicycles. In the fighting, the Highlanders lost half their strength with many men lost in the jungle for months if not years. More Punjabis under Lieutenant Colonel Cyril Stokes then marched up the road to support the Highlanders but were caught in close column and devastated by Watanabe's machine guns. Watanabe's trail of destruction continued, catching Gurkhas under Lieutenant Colonel Jack Fulton in a similar predicament as he sped on to capture the Slim River road bridge in tact, cutting the demolition charges himself before British engineers could blow it.

The 11th Indian Division, now scattered across miles of jungle, was largely mopped up by the following Japanese 42nd Regiment often suffering brutal atrocities. Kuala Lumpur fell four days later. As the Japanese advance on Singapore continued apace, Percival prepared an ambush at Muar.

8 January 1806

Napoleonic Wars
Battle of Blaauwberg

THE CAPE OF Good Hope, South Africa had first been sighted by the Portuguese Bartholomew Diaz in 1488 but was settled by Europeans only in 1652 when the Dutch East India Company established a shipping station en route to the Dutch East Indies. The colony remained Dutch up until just prior to the turn of the nineteenth century and the French Revolutionary Wars during which the Dutch Republic became a 'sister republic' to France. The Cape Colony was therefore by extension controlled by Revolutionary France as part of the now Batavian Republic, a development that consequently threatened British shipping to the East and particularly India as it passed around the Cape of Good Hope. In 1795, following the battle of Muizenberg, the Cape was captured by Britain only to be returned to the Dutch/French by the 1802 Peace Treaty of Amiens. When Napoleon then transgressed the terms of Amiens to begin the Napoleonic Wars just a year later the renewed French threat to British East Indiamen prompted another British Naval expedition.

In Autumn 1805 a Royal Navy fleet of over sixty ships under the command of Commodore Sir Home Popham transported two brigades of infantry under Major General David Baird south via Madeira, spending several months at sea and hence with no knowledge of Vice Admiral Horatio Nelson's victory over the Spanish and French fleet at Trafalgar. The Cape of Good Hope was defended by approximately 2,000 men of various races including Batavian and French marines, German and Hungarian mercenaries, Hottentots and Javanese all supported by any number of slaves and commanded by Dutch Lieutenant General Jan Janssens who was fully expectant of an imminent confrontation with the British.

On 4 January 1806 Janssens' warning guns on Signal Hill brought him the news he had been dreading, immediately alerting his militias as the Royal Navy sailed into Table Bay between Robben Island and Blaauwberg (Blue Mountain). Baird was unable to land troops in Camps Bay and was reluctant to land further north at Saldanha Bay which would have necessitated a long march back south through the stifling heat of a South African summer. On 6 January, however, the strong winds hampering Baird's initial plans subsided allowing landings to begin at Losperd Bay just north of Cape Town against a token Dutch force led by Colonel Frans Le Seuer. When the winds suddenly increased, however, further landings became impossible leaving those already ashore badly isolated but crucially Janssens had halted at Rietvlei. The following day more British troops resumed the landings, Baird immediately marching south in sweltering heat toward Cape Town expecting to find Janssens on the edge of the town in defensive positions strengthened by British forces during their previous occupation. Instead Janssens was now on the plain east of Blaauwberg Mountain and Kleinberg Hill (possibly attempting to deny the British water) so that when Baird arrived at Blaauwberg on 8 January 1806 he found the 5,000-strong Batavian force blocking his path on a 1,600 yard front, infantry in the centre with mounted *Burghers* (locals) on both flanks. Proceedings commenced with an artillery duel as Baird set about clearing the Batavian Scouts on the Kleinberg Hill before Scottish Highlanders advanced with bagpipes in full cry on the Batavian centre. Firing a volley at distance, the Highlanders then charged with the bayonet, the sound and sight of them too much for the German mercenaries who turned and ran. Janssens' position was already perilous but his well-trained African troops and French marines began to fill the gaps and return fire. Batavian problems were far from over though as doubt began to spread through their troops, in particular the flanks which wavered just as soon as Baird pressed another attack. Despite heavy casualties the French centre held firm until the realistic Janssens ordered a retreat covered by horsemen and Hottentot light infantry. The Batavians had suffered over 300 casualties but had kept their guns in tact, retreating inland while Baird entered Cape Town.

Janssens' position was hopeless but he avoided an unconditional surrender. Unhappy under British occupation many Dutch would make the 1835 Great Trek inland across the Orange and Vaal Rivers to again form their own Republics. Even there seventy-one years later their independence would again be challenged by the British.

9 January 1917

The Great War
Battle of Rafa

THE 1914 ENTRY of Turkey (Ottoman Empire) into the Great War on the side of the Central Powers presented a large threat to British interests in the Middle East, predominantly the Anglo-Persian Oil Company supplying the Royal Navy and the Suez Canal – the short route to British India. German diplomacy promised the restoration of Turkish territories lost in the Russo-Turkish War of 1877–78 but German ambition was also to use the Ottoman Empire to strengthen their own hand throughout the Levant, India, the Far East, and East and North Africa largely at British expense.

In late 1914 the British sent Indian Expeditionary Force D to successfully protect the Persian oil refineries but a further advance into Mesopotamia (Iraq) ended in early 1916 with the surrender at Kut of 13,000 British and Indian troops under Major General Charles Townshend, at the time the worst capitulation in the history of the British Army. Whilst the British had been invading Ottoman Mesopotamia, Turkey invaded what was technically a British territory to the south-west of Palestine, the Sinai Peninsular, Egypt (before 1914 Britain had ruled Egypt (and the Sudan) on behalf of the Khedivate of Egypt, a vassal of the Ottoman Sultan in Constantinople (Istanbul)). German Colonel Friedrich von Kressentein with 20,000 Turkish troops was looking to attack the Suez Canal but had been tracked across the desert by British aircraft before being repulsed near Ismailia by British, Indian, Gurkha, Egyptian, Australian and New Zealand troops under Major General John Maxwell who had additionally benefited from Royal Navy support.

The British 1915 offensive on the Gallipoli Peninsular then drained troops from both armies, Kressenstein maintaining outposts across the Sinai, raiding the Suez Canal and attempting to raise an Egyptian revolt against British rule. In return, the British were largely unable to trouble Kressentein but once Gallipoli had been miraculously evacuated (the one true success of the campaign) the Egyptian Expeditionary Force (EEF) was formed under Lieutenant General Archibald

Murray only to then be weakened by calls from the Western Front. Nevertheless Murray sent an archaeologist, Thomas Lawrence into the Arabian Hejaz to persuade Arab irregulars under Emir Faisal to fight a guerrilla war against the Turks whilst the EEF successfully counter-attacked at Romani. Lieutenant General Philip Chetwode and Australian Major General Harry Chauvel then led a 6,000-strong mounted (including six Ford cars) EEF Desert Column across the Sinai for an attack on the Turkish El Arish garrison which had taken up a defensive position at Magdaba, the British advance supported by the construction of a railway, roads and water pipes stretching 300 miles from the Nile Delta. Victory at Magdaba then enabled the Royal Navy to supply Chetwode at El Arish before taking the war into Ottoman Palestine at Rafa.

After an overnight march of twenty-nine miles, Chetwode's Desert Column began an encirclement of Rafa, cutting communications with stronger Turkish garrisons further east at Gaza and Beersheba before the Honourable Artillery Company commenced proceedings at 07.00 on 9 January 1917. As the shelling intensified troops of the 5th Mounted Infantry Brigade, the Anzac Mounted Division and the Imperial Camel Corps moved up on foot to attack the three Turkish redoubts from west to east A, B and C but all encountered heavy machine-gun fire and artillery across 2,000 yards of open ground from lines of trenches manned by 2,000 Turks around the central hill of El Magruntein. After exchanging fire for nearly ten hours north of Rafa, the New Zealand Mounted Rifles had closed to within 600 yards but with ammunition and water running low and Turkish reinforcements close by, Chetwode called off the attack only for the New Zealanders to suddenly cover the final yards, breaking into the Turkish defences to capture the central Turkish redoubt B with the bayonet. Chetwode now pressed the attack, light horse, cameliers and yeomanry successfully storming the remaining redoubts.

Rafa had cost 500 British casualties and was followed by an advance on Gaza where Turkish reinforcements inflicted 10,000 more amidst two successive defeats, Murray was recalled. In July good news would come from the south when Lawrence arrived back in Cairo from Aqaba.

10 January 1941

Second World War
Attack on HMS *Illustrious*, Malta

ITALIAN DICTATOR, BENITO Mussolini had belatedly joined the Second World War with his Axis partner Germany on the point of victory over France and Great Britain. Mussolini had always been intent on building a new 'Roman Empire' for Italy in the Mediterranean and North Africa and did not want to miss out on the spoils. Adding to his previous conquests of Abyssinia (Ethiopia) and Libya he was now successful in Somaliland as well as in British Egypt where he advanced as far as Sidi Barrani (with further outposts at Mersa Matruh) directly threatening Cairo and the Suez Canal. At the time, German Chancellor Adolf Hitler had been content to allow Mussolini his day in the sun while the *Luftwaffe* sought to conquer British airspace prior to a cross Channel invasion of the British Isles, Operation Sea Lion. By the end of 1940, however, Sea Lion was a distant memory, Reichsmarschal Herman Goring commanding the *Luftwaffe* now trying to bomb the British into submission whilst Hitler prepared to invade his ideological enemy, Bolshevik Russia.

Though fully stretched just defending Britain, Prime Minister Winston Churchill was also determined to defend British interests in the Mediterranean, the Italian Navy suffering at the hands of British Fairey Swordfish biplanes at Taranto and running for cover at Spartivento. In Egypt too, General Rodolpho Graziani and the Italian 10th Army were soon in headlong retreat from Sidi Barrani back past Tobruk, Libya following a counter-attack from Major General Richard O'Connor and the Western Desert Force. In Greece, the Italians had also been repulsed by spirited Greek resistance that had surprised everyone and were now back in Albania. Mussolini's dreams of empire already seemed to be on the point of collapse, British optimism in the Eastern Mediterranean and North Africa increasing accordingly but Churchill was aware via Ultra intercepts that Hitler was not about to allow his Italian Ally to collapse. As confirmation arrived that German forces were building in the Balkans for an invasion of Yugoslavia and Greece, Churchill's Mediterranean fleet was receiving confirmation of its own that German Forces had arrived in southern Italy prior to a landing in Libya.

On 10 January 1941 Force A from Alexandria, Egypt, consisting of armoured aircraft carrier HMS *Illustrious*, the battleships HMS *Warspite* and *Valiant* and seven destroyers, had escorted convoy MW5 to Malta before turning back for Alexandria protecting ME6, a nine-freighter military convoy. At midday *Illustrious* had five Fairey Fulmar fighters in the air engaging five Italian Savoia-Marchetti 79s. Two Fulmars returned to Malta and one back to Illustrious whilst the other two chased two SM 79s away from the battle zone, it was however, a deliberate Axis decoy. *Illustrious'* Captain Denis Boyd had been deceived and was attempting to launch another four Fulmars when he was suddenly attacked by nearly forty German Junkers 87 bombers and Junkers 88 'Stuka' dive bombers from Sturmkampfgeschwader 1 and 2. Opening the German account over the Mediterranean, the Stukas screamed down on *Illustrious* for a seven-minute attack, immediately scoring a direct hit with a 1,100 pound bomb near the aft lift, knocking out a Fulmar but courtesy of the armoured deck not the ship itself. The next hit, however, dropped into the aft lift exploding in the hangar, blowing the lift out of the well, crippling the sprinkler system and the steering gear. As fire raged below decks another Stuka crashed onto the deck and another three bombs scored direct hits, one piercing the deck and hull causing flood and fire as aviation fuel ignited. At 13.30 another wave of thirteen Stukas attacked but now harassed by Fulmars scored only one direct hit with several near misses. In all *Illustrious* had been hit six times and was still on fire as Boyd steered back to Valetta, Malta using just the ship's engines. He had lost ten Fairey Swordfish, five Fulmars and over 200 men.

Illustrious would come under further attack at Malta, the bombardment of which would intensify. Rommel would shortly land in Libya and advance across the Western Desert. The German 12th Army of Field Marshal Wilhelm List was also just three months away from invading Greece. In 1942 Malta was awarded the George Cross, the civilian equivalent to the Victoria Cross, by King George VI. The award appears on the Maltese national flag.

11 January 1846

Maori Wars
Battle of Ruapekapeka Pa

POLYNESIAN MAORI BEGAN populating New Zealand only as late as the thirteenth century and only in 1642 were the islands sighted by the Dutchman Abel Tasman. In 1769 the British Captain James Cook mapped the islands which in 1788 then came under the jurisdiction of the British penal colony of New South Wales. By then Cook had been killed in Hawaii by Polynesian cousins of the Maori who, in New Zealand, now traded with European and American whalers for muskets used in bloody internal conflicts. The London-based New Zealand Company headed by MP George Lambton and later the New Zealand Association headed by Edward Wakefield, sought to exploit these Maori conflicts by buying land (with muskets) which was then to be sold on to European settlers at a healthy profit. In 1839, as Maori violence increased both internally and against Europeans, the British Government yielded to church protestations and decided to intervene, Wakefield accelerating land purchases with increasing recklessness before the new Lieutenant Governor William Hobson froze all land transactions leaving him unable to satisfy arriving immigrants. Hobson's 1840 Treaty of Waitangi respected Maori land rights in return for sovereignty under Queen Victoria but grievances soon arose from nine inaccurate translations of the treaty.

Among the first to object was Hone Heke, a *Rangatira* (man of wisdom) of the Ngapuhi, who resented the capital moving to Auckland, customs taxes and continued governmental control of land sales. Heke's vexation was also exacerbated by American Captain William Mayhew's tales of American independence from British rule (also largely due to taxes) and the British execution of an eighteen-year-old Ngapuhi boy for murder. Heke gathered allies, four times within a year cutting down the British flagstaff on Maiki Hill, Kororareka (Russell), the last of which saw an aggressive attack on British forces and destroyed the town. Heke was pursued inland by British and Maori loyal to the Crown, defending a *Pa* (fortified hill) at Puketutu before being soundly beaten at Te Ahuahu by a smaller

Loyalist Maori force under Tamati Waka Nene, Heke wounded. The struggle was then continued by Te Ruki Kawiti at Ohaeawai Pa, an ingenius earth fortification where 300 Maori resisted the cannon of 800 British and Loyalist Maori before retreating to an even more impressive Pa at Ruapekapeka (the Bat's Nest).

Lieutenant Colonel Henry Despard led 1,100 British, 450 Loyalist Maori and seven cannon up the River Kawakawa and a fifteen mile march to Ruapekapeka Pa 1,000 feet above sea level. Amongst the troops was the new British Governor of New Zealand Captain George Grey who attached himself to the artillery which began shelling the Pa at 1,200 yards on 27 December 1845. One of Kawiti's two cannon was knocked out immediately but the intense two-week-long bombardment did little damage to the impressive earthworks beneath which sheltered 300 Maori. From the Pa, the world's first defensive trench system, Kawiti launched several sorties in an attempt to prevent the increasing proximity of Despard's cannon. On 10 January however, as Heke joined Kawiti, Despard upped his game, heavy cannon smashing the huge wooden stockades to create a breach but still he refrained from storming, continuing the bombardment through the night as Heke tried to persuade Kawiti to retreat into the forest behind. On the following morning 11 January 1846, Despard's Loyalist Maori approached the Pa to find no defenders (accounts differ, Kawiti may have taken Heke's advice or since it was a Sunday he may have been in prayer behind the Pa). Reinforcing British troops then quickly entered from the front only to be hit by a volley of muskets from rebel Maoris reentering the back. A musket battle then raged, Kawiti drawing Despard out toward the forest behind the Pa where, in a four hour battle, the British were hit by more volleys from concealed positions, losing over forty men dead and wounded but inflicting similar casualties on Heke and Kawiti who were sent into a full retreat.

Honi Heke and Te Ruki Kawiti were pardoned by Grey as the Flagstaff War ended. From 1853 the Colonial Government of New Zealand began to direct land sales to European settlers for farming, rebelling Maoris then subject to widespread confiscations from 1863 onwards sparking further conflict across much of the country. Maori grievances against these confiscations have only recently been addressed.

12 January 1945

Second World War Bombing of Bergen Harbour

THE ALLIED OFFENSIVE from D-Day 6 June 1944 to the borders of the German Third Reich had been conducted by Supreme Headquarters Allied Expeditionary Force commander Dwight D. Eisenhower on a broad front strategy that had placed huge stress on Allied logistics especially until a major port had been captured. British Field Marshal Bernard Montgomery's inspired but ultimately flawed Operation Market Garden could have precipitated an early German collapse but despite heroics at Arnhem the Operation had failed. The difficult Montgomery then answered British Admiral Bertram Ramsay's appeal for the British 21st Army Group, on the left flank of the Allied advance, to clear the Scheldt Estuary and open the massive port of Antwerp, an accomplishment that put an end to Allied supply problems. German chances of avoiding an invasion of the Reich had now seemingly ended but Chancellor Adolf Hitler was prepared for a desperate last gamble, an armoured counter-offensive through the Ardennes against the United States First Army followed by a drive to Antwerp that would split Allied forces, deny them the port, encircle and destroy them. If successful the Wehrmacht could then concentrate on defending Germany from the Soviet Red Army on the Eastern Front and perhaps agree an armistice.

The shock of the German attack rocked the Americans, the British playing only a minor part, but in grim winter-fighting German supply problems, Allied air superiority and dogged American resistance on the ground had halted the German advance by the year end. Still Hitler was not finished, launching two further attacks on New Year's Day 1945 but for most of the German High Command all hope of capturing Antwerp was now lost. With Germany's surface fleet weakened by the loss of all four major battleships, *Tirpitz* having been sunk in November, disruption of Allied logistics across the English Channel and North Sea was left almost entirely to the U-boat fleet of Grand Admiral Karl Donitz. Despite U-boat bases on the French coast, protected by concrete up to eight metres thick to withstand Allied bombing (the towns around them had been devastated, Lorient and St Nazaire in particular) Donitz had, however, transferred much of his U-boat fleet to Norway.

RAF Bomber Command had first targeted the equally well-protected U-boat bunkers at Bergen with 140 Lancasters and Halifaxes on 4 October 1944. The raid was a disaster, although just one Lancaster was lost, the bombing had hit the town killing and wounding 273 civilians including sixty-one children in Laksevaag School. The bombers returned on 29 October, 237 Lancasters and seven Mosquitos, again hitting the town (fifty-two civilians killed) whilst barely scratching the bunkers. On 12 January 1945, following their success in sinking the *Tirpitz* in Kaafjord, thirty-two Lancasters of Nos 9 and 617 'Dambusters' Squadron each carrying a Barnes Wallis 'Tallboy' earthquake 12,000lb bomb flew from RAF Woodhall Spa led by a solitary Mosquito. The flight under Canadian Group Captain John Fauquier encountered *Luftwaffe* Focke Wulf 190s off the coast of Norway losing a Lancaster but over Bergen Harbour vastly improved bomb aiming meant three Tallboys hit the bunker, one penetrating the roof, destroying workshops and damaging two U-boats killing twenty-six Germans but mercifully no Norwegians. Other Lancasters attacked shipping in the harbour sinking a minelayer and damaging a cargo ship but with the loss of another Lancaster.

On the day of the Bergen Raid the Soviet Army launched a two-million-strong Vistula-Oder offensive into Poland that within a month would reach within forty-three miles of Berlin. The twenty-six German divisions left on the Western Front were also badly defeated on the west bank of the River Rhine after Hitler had denied Field Marshal Albert Kesselring a withdrawal. US forces then first crossed the Rhine at Remagen on 7 March. Donitz' U-boats continued to sail until May 1945, by then 3,500 Allied ships had been sunk for the loss of 783 U-boats. Donitz succeeded Hitler as President of Germany and Supreme Commander of Armed Forces, determined that Germany surrender to Britain and the United States rather than the Russians. He was tried for war crimes at Nuremburg and served ten years' imprisonment at Spandau Prison.

13 January 1842

Afghan Wars
Battle of Gandamack

BY 1839 GOVERNOR General of India George Eden, Lord Auckland believed three decades of Russian expansion in Central Asia and the erratic behaviour of the Emir of Afghanistan, Dost Mohammed Khan had become such a threat to British India that he ordered a British invasion of Afghanistan. A division of the British East India Company's Bengal Army marched through the Bolan Pass to Quetta whilst a division of the Bombay Army sailed into the River Indus, marching the remaining distance before combining to successfully storm the Fortress at Ghazni just over one hundred miles short of Kabul. On learning of defeat at Ghazni, Dost Mohammed asked for terms of surrender but unable to countenance the exile insisted upon by British Lieutenant General John Keane, instead fled into the Hindu Kush mountains. The British marched into Kabul on 6 August 1839, setting up a military cantonment outside the city whilst Shah Shuja Durrani, the new puppet emir set up his court inside Kabul at the Fortress of Bala Hissar. With Kabul seemingly under control, all but 8,000 British troops then returned to India. Travelling in the opposite direction were families of the soldiers who remained, life in Kabul taking on a more British feel with theatre, cricket, horse racing and dinner parties. Perceiving the British Army to now be one of occupation and Durrani to be tyrannical, Afghans began rebelling under the guerrilla style leadership of Wazir Akbar Khan, a son of Dost Mohammed. As tension in Kabul increased, Auckland in Simla, India, then replaced the Kabul Garrison Commander General Sir Willoughby Cotton, with an unfit, fifty-nine-year-old veteran of Waterloo, Major General William Elphinstone.

In November 1841, a general uprising in Kabul began with the murder of the original 1836 British peace envoy to Dost Mohammad, Sir Alexander Burnes. Elphinstone looked south to Kandahar for reinforcements but General Sir William Nott was unable to march through the Afghan winter snows. Elphinstone's lack of reprisals then led to increased Afghan confidence and, on 23 November 1841, an artillery bombardment of the British cantonment. A month later, civil servant Sir William Macnaghten was then invited to discuss the situation over tea with Akbar Khan, the trusting Macnaghten then murdered before being dragged through the streets and hung in the Bazaar. As law and order in Kabul and within the British Army began to disintegrate, Elphinstone struck a catastrophic deal with the treacherous Akbar Khan – that on surrendering his artillery he would be allowed free passage to retreat from Kabul back to the British fort at Jallalabad ninety miles away through the freezing mountains of Eastern Afghanistan.

The artillery-free British column of 4,500 troops and 12,000 women, children and servants began the daunting march on 6 January 1842, the first few yards exposing Elphinstone's folly as those left behind were murdered or enslaved. Major Edward Pottinger was soon pleading with Elphinstone to head for Durrani's nearby Fort of Bala Hissar but Elphinstone fatefully pressed on, the terrified civilians, especially stragglers, becoming victim to increasing opportunist attacks from Gilzai warriors in the surrounding hills. Constant skirmishing ensued as the column crawled on through thick snow. After three days and having covered just twenty-five miles, 3,000 were already dead, those that made a run of their own cut down by Afghan tribesmen. By 12 January the death toll had risen to 12,000, Elphinstone taken prisoner (he would die a captive) leaving Brigadier Thomas Anquetil with just sixty-five men of the 44th Regiment of Foot with negligible ammunition surrounded with other survivors at Gandamack. On 13 January 1842, Anquetil refused to surrender and, with his men, was massacred.

Just one man, Doctor William Brydon, missing part of his skull, made it to Jallalabad, which, under the command of Colonel Robert 'Fighting Bob' Sale, the hero of Ghazni, would defy a siege at incredible odds for another three months. Auckland suffered a stroke on receiving news of Elphinstone's retreat, whilst back in Kabul, Durrani was assassinated. Field Marshal Sir George Pollock with Nott led a punitive expedition back to Kabul in September 1842, liberating over 100 prisoners as well as rescuing 2,000 Indian sepoys before destroying the Bazaar and withdrawing. The British Army would return in force thirty-six years later.

14 January 1942
Second World War
Battle of Muar

JAPANESE EFFORTS TO create a new order in South East Asia had met stunning initial success. A surprise attack on the United States Pacific Fleet at Pearl Harbor, Hawaii on 7 December 1941 coinciding with invasions across Asia. Thailand signed an armistice almost immediately, Hong Kong fell on Christmas Day 1941, Manila on 2 January 1942 and Kuala Lumpur on 11 January as the British were forced out of North Malaya following a crushing defeat at the Slim River. As British resistance collapsed (the Indian 11th Army no longer an effective fighting unit) General Archibald Wavell arrived in Singapore to take command of ABDA (American, British, Dutch, Australian), immediately ordering Lieutenant General Arthur Percival to withdraw to Johore, South Malaya specifically to defend Singapore. Percival assigned the defence of Muar, from the mountain jungles to the Mallacca Straits to 'Westforce' (Australian 8th Division and Indian 45th Brigade) commanded by General Gordon Bennett with the battered remnants of the Indian III Corps under Lieutenant General Lewis Heath holding a line further south. Bereft of tanks and air cover and having been outmanoeuvred through 'impenetrable' jungle down the Malay Peninsular by the Japanese 25th Army of Lieutenant General Tomoyuki Yamashita, Percival now changed tactics, setting up an ambush at Gemensah Bridge and a defence of Muar Town, Bakri and Parit Sulong.

At 16.00 on 14 January 1942 the relentless Japanese advance reached the area of Tampin, splitting south to Muar and east to Gemensah and Gemas. Hundreds of Japanese moving east, many on bicycle began crossing the Gemensah Bridge as the Australian 2/30th Battalion under Lieutenant Colonel Frederick Gallegan watched on. As the main 'peloton' crossed the bridge, Gallegan ordered charges underneath be detonated before opening fire on the hapless Japanese now trapped on the far side. Unable to call in artillery when Japanese further on cut their telegraph wire, the Australians nevertheless inflicted several hundred casualties before withdrawing to Gemas. The Gemensah Bridge was, however, repaired within hours allowing

Japanese light tanks to advance on Gemas where Gallegan's Australians put up another spirited defence in two days of bitter close quarter fighting, knocking out several tanks before withdrawing once again into Segamat. Meanwhile to the southwest a battalion of the Japanese Imperial Guards under Colonel Masakazu Ogaki advanced by sea whilst the 4th and 5th Guards Regiments under General Takuma Nishimura advanced on land along the coast toward Muar. At Muar awaited the Indian 45th Infantry Brigade with the British 53rd Infantry Brigade behind in support but in no condition to fight having just spent three months at sea. As reinforcements were arriving in Singapore it was vital the Japanese be delayed but the 45th were caught by surprise when Nishimura and Ogaki crossed the River Muar by barge. Immediately the Rajputana and Garhwal Rifles were overrun as aircraft from the Japanese Army and Navy Air Service added to the onslaught destroying the 45th's Headquarters, Commander Brigadier Herbert Duncan surviving but not the majority of his staff. Australian artillery briefly checked the Japanese advance but, Muar fell within twenty-four hours leaving Nishimura to press on to Bakri. Again Australians checked the advance with the British 53rd desperately protecting the retreat of the Indian 45th. Duncan now launched several unsuccessful counter-attacks at Bakri and Yong Peng, getting himself killed before a surrounded Lieutenant Colonel Charles Anderson broke out with the remnants of the Australian 2/29th Battalion, the Indian 45th Brigade and supporting Jats for Parit Sulong. Anderson's small force fought through fifteen miles of jungle, abandoning their wounded en route but just 900 men successfully evaded capture, Anderson winning the Victoria Cross.

Almost the entire 45th Indian Brigade was lost at Muar. Anderson's wounded were massacred at Parit Sulong, Nishimura perhaps unjustly executed for the crime in 1951. With Malaya lost, 85,000 British and Commonwealth troops prepared to defend Singapore against 30,000 Japanese.

14 January 1797

French Revolutionary War
Pursuit of the Droits de l'Homme

 REVOLUTION HAD SWEPT through France in 1789 as commoners exerted their new powers through a National Assembly granted by King Louis XVI. But as King Charles I of England had paid a heavy price for recalling Parliament in 1640 so too now did Louis and his Queen Marie Antoinette, both meeting their end by guillotine within six months of each other in 1793. France was engulfed by a rebellion based on the philosophies of Montesquieu, Rousseau and Voltaire, embodied by the Declaration of Rights of Man and the Citizen (les droits de l'homme et du citoyen), itself based on the 1776 American Declaration of Independence for which the French had fought. The revolutionaries also looked to spread their ideology beyond France, pledging support for any people seeking liberty, including their own black slaves in the West Indies and Indian Ocean, but though viewed with considerable scepticism by monarchic Europe there was one particular corner of Europe where the bells of *Liberté, Equalité* and *Fraternité* offered by a French supported revolution rang loud – Ireland.

After the 1791 wide circulation of Thomas Paine's *Rights of Ma*n, the Society of United Irishmen was formed by Theobald Wolfe Tone calling for Catholic emancipation or better, an end to British rule in Ireland altogether. The United Irishmen had been gaining in strength until France declared war on Britain in 1793 when they were summarily banned. Living in the United States Tone then requested the ruling French Directory under Paul Barras support an insurrection in Ireland against the British as they had in America twenty years previous. Since Prussia had withdrawn from the First Coalition in 1795, Austria was now firmly on the defensive (largely due to a brilliant Corsican General advancing through Italy by the name of Napoleon Bonaparte) and the Royal Navy was struggling with sickness and insubordination Barras and the Directory agreed to send 15,000 French troops in forty-four ships under Vice Admiral Morard de Galles, General Lazare Hoche and Tone himself.

Aboard *Fraternité,* Galles' fleet sailed on 16 December 1796 from Brest confronted only by Commodore Sir Edward Pellew on the 44-gun HMS *Indefatigable.* By the morning Galles' fleet had been scattered by rough seas, high winds and heavy fog but continued on toward Bantry Bay. Bad weather had spared Britain invasion before and Galles' now joined the long list, the French fleet battered en route and in the bay before the entire expedition was abandoned to run what was now a gauntlet of British warships back to Brest. The weather did not relent, the *Mutine* was blown to Tenerife, and by 13 January the 74-gun *Droits de l'Homme* captained by Jean Baptiste de Lacrosse with 1,300 men aboard was still only off Ushant, spotted by Pellew and Captain Robert Reynolds on the 36-gun HMS *Amazon.* Concerned at the condition of his ship, Lacrosse steered south-east for the French coast attempting to outrun Pellew despite his massive advantage in gunnery. With the loss of her top masts causing *Droits de l'Homme* to roll in the high seas which in turn prevented an opening of her lower gun ports, Lacrosse was attacked by Pellew from the rear, cannonballs raking both port and starboard. The 800 soldiers aboard *Indefatigable* then added volleys of musketry to the cannon fire as the British ship pulled ahead. Both ships now broadsided in gale force winds before *Amazon* closed to increase the weight of British shot. Lacrosse was in no mood to surrender, however, the foundering *Droits de l'Homme* now short of her mizzen mast with ammunition nearly exhausted and casualties increasing but continuing to fight through the darkness into the early hours of 14 January 1797. As all three ships foundered in the high seas, guns breaking loose from their breeching tackle, they were blown towards shore at Plozevet. *Indefatigable* veered south but remained afloat whilst *Amazon* sailed north where she was sand-banked but upright in the Bay of Audierne. Nearby *Droits de l'Homme* was also sand-banked but keeling over in the pounding surf. A three-day operation in appalling weather rescued only 300 men.

That the French had made Bantry Bay at all shook the British public enough to cause a run on the banks. Without French assistance, the United Irishmen would rebel against British rule a year later in another bloody episode in the history of the two nations. Edward Pellew would become Commander-in-Chief of the Mediterranean Fleet by the end of the Napoleonic Wars.

15 January 1815

American War of 1812
Capture of the USS *President*

SINCE 1792 THE United Kingdom of Great Britain and Ireland had been preoccupied fighting Revolutionary France and her Emperor Napoleon Bonaparte but on 18 June 1812, six days before 600,000 men of the *Grande Armée* crossed the Nieman River for what would turn out to be a disastrous French invasion of Russia, the President of the United States of America, James Madison declared war on Britain. American grievances largely centered around a British trade embargo against France that also adversely affected their thirty-year-old nation, Madison believing he could rid North America of the British entirely by invading poorly defended Canada. The north-eastern states of the US were, however, wholly unsupportive, their banks refused to provide finance and the consequently small US invasion force was driven back into Upper New York State and Vermont. Madison was then soon on the defensive when Napoleon abdicated in 1814 allowing 16,000 battle-hardened British troops to attempt to regain territories lost in the War of American Independence. However, after burning Washington DC (including the White House), a British attempt to seize strategic Baltimore failed before an invasion of Upper New York State also met defeat at Plattsburgh on Lake Champlain. Two years of war had achieved nothing notable for either side except an American national anthem born from the 'Star Spangled Banner' that had flown above Fort McHenry, Baltimore. Since the defeat of France meant the British embargo was now defunct, the main catalyst for the war had disappeared and both sides began months of peace talks, at last signing the Treaty of Ghent on 24 December 1814.

Across the Atlantic, unaware that the war had ended, Vice Admiral Alexander Cochrane and Major General Edward Pakenham would continue with the siege of New Orleans until 18 January 1815, Pakenham, brother-in-law of Field Marshal Sir Arthur Wellesley, Duke of Wellington, needlessly killed before the British were forced into retreating by future US President Andrew Jackson. Meanwhile on the eastern US seaboard the Royal Navy continued to press a blockade, including the Bay of New York where four US warships headed by the 44-gun frigate USS *President*, named by the First President of the United States, George Washington, and one of the original six ships of the US Navy, had been trapped for over a year.

On 14 January 1815 a snow storm blew in from the north-west, driving the British blockading fleet of HMS *Endymion*, *Majestic*, *Pomone* and *Tenedos* off their station allowing Commodore Stephen Decateur commanding *President*, to make a run for the open sea and the South Atlantic. Disaster struck Decateur immediately, however, when his pilots failed to locate New York's sandbars, the grounded *President* taking a pounding in the surf and gale force winds for two hours before breaking free with significant damage to her hull and masts. Unable to return to port against the wind, Decateur sailed south along the coast of Long Island when on the morning of 15 January 1815 a British squadron under Captain John Hayes on *Majestic* regathered and located *President* sailing south-east. The chase wore on into the afternoon, the faster *Endymion* captained by Henry Hope catching *President*, the pair now sailing east with *Endymion* soon firing from her bow on *President's* aft. *Endymion* then moved up to broadside *President's* starboard with the US ship only able to partially return fire. Decateur then turned *President* to starboard across *Endymion's* bow but Hope also turned, both ships now parallel exchanging broadsides, *President* firing at *Endymion's* rigging with chain-shot knowing that the three other British vessels were close behind. By 20.00 Decateur, with 105 casualties, struck his colours but with *Endymion* in difficulty escaped half-an-hour later only to be again caught by *Pomone*.

USS *President* became HMS *President* on arrival at Spithead. The Treaty of Ghent saw no gains for either side, both nations entering what would become over two hundred years of friendship. The national identities of Canada and the United States had, however, been greatly enhanced.

16 January 1809

Napoleonic Wars
Battle of Corunna

POST REVOLUTION, FRANCE and their Emperor Napoleon Bonaparte had defeated all European continental opposition by 1808. The sea, however, still belonged to the United Kingdom of Great Britain and Ireland forcing Napoleon into a desperate attempt to defeat the one nation that had consistently opposed him from day one by banning all trade with Britain from Russia to Italy, the Continental System. British goods manufactured at the beginning of the Industrial Revolution were, however, in high demand and the system leaked, provoking a French invasion of Portugal before Napoleon increased his ambition to dominate the whole of the Iberian Peninsular, deposing King Charles IV of Spain and his son, Crown Prince Ferdinand in favour of his own brother Joseph. After twelve unhappy years in an alliance with France, almost the whole of Spain now revolted, forcing the French *Grande Armée* back across the River Ebro to leave the 12–15,000 strong army of General Jean Junot isolated in Lisbon, Portugal.

After sixteen years fighting a war of self preservation the British Government of William Cavendish-Bentinck, Duke of Portland recognised that the turmoil in Spain at last presented an opportunity to take the war to France on European soil. Indeed, Lieutenant General Arthur Wellesley had returned from his empire – building exploits in India and had successfully relieved Denmark of her navy in 1807, now he was redirected to Portugal from Cork, Ireland with 15,000 British troops.

Wellesley defeated Junot at Vimeiro in August 1808 but his superior, Lieutenant General Hew Dalrymple had then arrived to agree the Convention of Cintra, shipping home Junot's army fully equipped, both he and Wellesley recalled to answer before an enquiry. Replacing Dalrymple, Lieutenant General Sir John Moore commanding the now 30,000 British troops in Lisbon, marched 15,000 of them, minus their artillery, into Spain to unite with 15,000 from Corunna under Major General Sir David Baird and patriot Spanish forces at Burgos. The regional

Spanish armies, however, were ragged, poorly trained, poorly armed and very poorly led. Worse, unknown to Moore, Napoleon himself was entering Spain with 125,000 French reinforcements to deal with the 'hideous Leopard [England] that contaminates… Spain and Portugal' intent on carrying his 'victorious eagles to the Pillars of Hercules [Gibraltar]'.

The *Grande Armée* swept into Madrid as Moore, learning of Spanish collapses but not of Napoleon's presence, pressed on past Salamanca intent on attacking a 16,000-strong French Army at Carrion under Marshal Nicolas Jean de Dieu Soult. Moore united with Baird but then suddenly aghast at the proximity of Napoleon, ordered a desperate retreat to Corunna 300 miles away across the snowbound Galicean mountains. After seventeen days of failing discipline, drunken disorder, roads strewn with dead soldiers, women, children, horses and discarded equipment with the light infantry under Brigadier Robert Craufurd and Hussars under Major General Edward Paget in the rear fighting off Soult's vanguard (Napoleon had returned to Paris), Moore's pitiful army reached Corunna only to find an absence of transport in the harbour.

The pursuing Soult arrived outside Corunna three days later with 12,000 men but in just as poor a state of health and crucially unable to resupply whereas Moore had just received the additional morale boost of two-hundred-and-fifty transports arriving. To cover the British evacuation Moore formed a defensive perimeter south of Corunna centered around Elvina, inviting an attack which Soult duly delivered at 14.00 on 16 January 1809. To the east of Elvina, skirmishing held the British left whilst on the high ground to the west Soult launched artillery bombardments and infantry attacks supported by flanking cavalry in an attempt to cut off Moore's access to the harbour. Elvina fell to the French, Baird losing an arm in the process, before Moore counter-attacked with the Queen's Own and Highlander Infantry supported by the cavalry under Lieutenant General Henry Paget (brother), retaking the village only for Soult to take and lose Elvina once more. Defending Elvina with the Guards the heroic Moore was mortally wounded by a cannonball but survived long enough to see the French repulsed. By nightfall Soult could only skirmish across the difficult terrain allowing the British to embark their transports.

The retreat to Corunna had nevertheless been a disaster, 8,000 casualties, but in Lisbon the British were still 15,000 strong and the most famous general of his day, Wellesley, was returning to lead them back into Spain where resistance, symbolised by the siege of Zaragoza, was stiffening.

17 January 1885

Mahdist War
Battle of Abu Klea

BRITISH RESPONSIBILITY FOR the Sudan came with suzerainty over Egypt and the Suez Canal following the 1882 Battle of Tel El-Kebir which crushed an Egyptian military coup protesting at foreign involvement in Egyptian affairs. Egyptian debts had originally forced French and British financial involvement but once the security of the Suez Canal was threatened even the normally anti-imperialist British Prime Minister William Gladstone had been happy to intervene. Though the Egyptian revolt had been defeated, a concurrent Islamic uprising was very much ongoing in the Sudan where Muhammed Ahmed, the Mahdi (guided one) had been gaining an *Ansar* (following) since 1881. Anglo-Egyptian defeats to the Mahdi at El Obeid and El Teb were countered by victories at the 2nd Battle of El Teb and Tamai, efforts which meant the Red Sea ports were accessible to Major General Charles 'Chinese' Gordon (sent to Khartoum with serious reservations by Gladstone) for an evacuation of Egyptian and loyal Sudanese garrisons. Much loved by Queen Victoria and the British public, Gordon had previously been a Governor General of the Sudan for the Ottoman Empire and had developed an attachment to the people he was now asked to forsake, disobeying orders on arrival in Khartoum he began by upgrading the city's defences rather than conducting a large-scale evacuation. Just weeks later, Khartoum had been invested by the *Ansar* ending any hope of Gordon completing his mission.

Though Khartoum was partially defended by the White and Blue River Niles, Gordon had just 8,000 Egyptian and Sudanese soldiers to protect a further fifteen miles of perimeter and a population of 35,000 but, rather than storm the city, the Mahdi sat down to starve Gordon into submission. Suspicious that Gordon's subsequent pleas for reinforcements were a ploy to involve Britain in a war against the Mahdi, an unsympathetic Gladstone then faced public outcry that Gordon must be saved. Following months of indecision in Westminster, General Garnet Wolseley began to assemble a 5,400 man military expedition at Wadi Halfa on the

Egypt/Sudan border before sailing up the Nile and its great cataracts in steamers and Royal Navy whalers piloted by Canadian voyageurs. As all eyes in Khartoum searched the northern horizon for smoke from the steamers Wolseley did not hurry before, in a sudden quest for haste, splitting his force in two at Korti – a River Column continuing up the Nile whilst a Desert Column dashed across the great bend of the Nile for Metemma. Wolseley believed that just the sight of a few British Redcoats would be enough to frighten the Mahdi into lifting the siege of Khartoum.

The Desert Column commanded by Major General Sir Herbert Stewart arrived at the oasis of Abu Klea on 16 January where it constructed a thorn bush defensive Zeriba. On the morning of 17 January 1885 Stewart divided the column, leaving a defence of the Zeriba while 1,400 men formed square and advanced with skirmishers to the fore, ammunition and camels in the centre. The square was changing formation just as it approached a large Wadi (ravine) with camels lagging behind and sailors bringing up a naval gun but awaiting in the Wadi were 10,000 of the Mahdi's dervishes, the sudden sight of which caused panic within the square. Colonel Fred Burnaby rode out to restore order but the dervishes saw their chance and charged in column from several hundred yards. The British skirmishers ran for the cover of the square obstructing their comrade's field of fire with many British Martini Henry rifles also jamming through dust. Still in formation, the dervishes wheeled around their own dead comrades before crashing into the rear of the square, breaking it to earn the eternal admiration of the British soldier. As the front of the square turned inward to fire, several British officers were killed before a hand-to-hand fight raged, revolvers and swords against spears as the square closed up again. All dervishes inside the square were cut down with the fight finished inside fifteen minutes, the Desert Column suffering 150 casualties including Burnaby, the dervishes over 1,000.

Stewart resumed the advance on Khartoum, defeating the dervishes again at Abu Kru, himself mortally wounded. Colonel Charles Wilson assumed command, meeting Gordon's steamers at Metemma but delayed his departure just as the Mahdi was preparing to assault Khartoum. 'Play up! Play up! and Play the game!', the Battle of Abu Klea is celebrated by Sir Henry Newbolt's poem *Vitae Lampada*.

18 January 1671 o.s

Anglo-Spanish Wars
Raid on Panama City

AFTER RAIDING MARACAIBO on the Spanish Main in 1669 Captain Henry Morgan returned to Port Royal, Jamaica where he went unpunished by the Governor Sir Thomas Modyford who recognised that England needed an occasional show of strength in the Caribbean despite no state of war existing with Spain. Morgan had attacked Maracaibo in response to Spanish raids on English possessions, deliberately calculating that further Spanish reprisals would keep he and his buccaneers in business for some time to come. He was not wrong, having retired to his plantation the Spanish reacted to such a degree that both he and Modyford were soon of the opinion that another large scale English operation was requisite.

In August 1670, just a month after Spain and England had confirmed peace in the Caribbean by signing the Treaty of Madrid, Morgan put out a call to arms for another attack on the Spanish Main. Assembling a thirty-eight-strong fleet loaded with over two thousand men of dubious character eager for plunder, Morgan sailed from Isla Vaca, Hispaniola (Haiti, Dominican Republic) for San Lorenzo on the River Chagres, Panama. On 17 December 1670 the buccaneers succeeded in capturing San Lorenzo castle with a bloody frontal assault that killed most of the Spanish garrison. Morgan then installed his own garrison before sailing 1,200 buccaneers up river for a torturous trek through the Panamanian jungle to Panama City on the Pacific coast. The Spanish had guessed Morgan's intended target and had adopted a scorched earth policy but as the buccaneers approached the great treasure city, Morgan discovered horses and cattle that hd been overlooked by the defenders. Fully refreshed the buccaneers were, however, still short of information on Panama's defences since prisoners there were none, all adversaries having fled before them on their departure from the Caribbean coast. There could, however, be no turning back, Morgan would not survive ten more days in the jungle and no doubt he and his men would be harassed all the way back to San Lorenzo.

On 18 January 1671, Morgan's buccaneers marched onto the plain in front of Panama City to be faced by 3,600 Spaniards under the President of Panama, Don Juan Perez de Guzman who also sent a detachment of cavalry to cut off Morgan's retreat. The Spanish immediately launched a frontal cavalry attack but heavy ground and the deadly accurate musket fire of the buccaneers forced them back. The Spanish then speculatively tried to stampede a herd of cattle most of which were shot before the Spanish cavalry again attacked, this time departing altogether once they had been strongly repulsed. The Spanish infantry had so far been unable to match the musketry of the buccaneers and took a lead from their cavalry by also departing. The buccaneers now ran amok, pressing home their attack before launching an attack on Panama City itself which still contained over 2,000 Spanish troops and artillery. After several hours of fighting the defenders broke, Morgan entering the city and immediately putting it to the sack, torturing and robbing the inhabitants for over a month.

The buccaneers, however, had missed the opportunity to attack the Spanish galleon, *Santisima Trinidad*, which had been in the Bay of Panama laden with treasure at the time of the initial assault. Wary of being a long way from reinforcements, Morgan ordered his men to refrain from alcohol in case of counter-attack and also destroyed moored Spanish shipping so that his own men could not desert with their captured wealth. Panama burned for four weeks as Morgan exhausted its wealth before returning to San Lorenzo across the Panama isthmus with a baggage train of 175 mules laden with treasure. Here he ordered that the castle be demolished during the progress of which he reputedly slipped back to Jamaica with the proceeds of his expedition, abandoning many of his men to their fate.

On returning to Port Royal, Jamaica though, Morgan was promptly arrested as a pirate and sent back for trial in England where he denied all knowledge of the Treaty of Madrid. As England and a furious Spain descended into acrimony once again Morgan became a celebrated figure, knighted by King Charles II, he returned to Jamaica as Lieutenant Governor in 1674.

19 January 1419

Hundred Years' War
Siege of Rouen

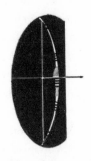THE CONFLICT BETWEEN the French House of Orléans (Armagnac) and Burgundy had been instrumental in the success of King of England Henry V's 1417 conquest of Lower Normandy. Henry, however, sought nothing less than the French Crown itself and the hand of Catherine of Valois, the daughter of the present French King Charles VI, a marriage that would cement his future position as both King of France and England. Henry's ally by a common enemy, John 'the fearless' Duke of Burgundy, had also benefited from English exertions, not least from the 1415 defeat of the largely Orléanist French Army at Agincourt, an event to which Duke John had been summoned by the French king but had conspicuously failed to attend. France began to recover militarily under Bernard, Count of Armagnac but as Henry invaded Normandy, Duke John advanced on Paris forcing Armagnac to return there to protect his king's court, including Queen Isabelle and their fifth son, the Dauphin Charles (the other four being deceased). When Armagnac was then murdered by the pro Burgundy Parisian mob and, since King Charles was mad, Duke John and Queen Isabelle became de facto heads of state.

Meanwhile in Lower Normandy Armagnac's enforced absence had given Henry's armies more or less a free hand, Caen, Falaise, Alençon, Bayeux, Lisieux, Exmes, Sees, Argentan, Saint Lo, Coutances, Carentan, Valognes, Evreux, Louviers had all been reduced whilst Cherbourg was besieged. Henry now marched towards the greatest prize of all, the mighty city of Rouen but the success of Duke John's diplomacy with Queen Isabelle meant the Anglo-Burgundian alliance was in considerable doubt. An English herald was sent to Burgundy asking whether treaties would be honoured but if there was anyone the pro Burgundian Parisians hated more than the Armagnacs it was the English and they now expected Duke John to defend France. John could not simply abandon Paris for Rouen however, the Dauphin was at large and his supporters (for Armagnac now read Dauphinist) were to be reckoned with. Duke John stayed put.

After a two-week struggle to cross the River Seine at Pont de L'Arche, Henry and the English Army arrived before the gates of Rouen on 31 July 1418. The 70,000 inhabitants had destroyed everything outside the walls within a distance of four miles whilst the walls themselves were dominated by sixty towers, lined with cannon and in the case of the south wall protected by 300 yards of the River Seine. Just five gates permitted an entry whilst 16,000 French troops under Guy Le Bouteiller were present to prevent one. Henry had likely a similar number of English troops outside in four camps connected by trenches and portable bridges, all supplied by his Navy which dragged ships overland to avoid the French at Caudebec. Henry's impressive array of cannon and siege engines now pounded Rouen but, rather than storming, the English king waited for hunger to take its inevitable toll. By October cats and rats had become delicacies in the beleaguered city from which desperate French sorties were resolutely defeated whilst their heightening pleas for relief fell on the deaf ears of Burgundians and Dauphinists alike. In December Bouteiller then expelled 12,000 *bouches inutiles* (useless mouths) but Henry would not let them pass. Bouteiller, however, would not take them back, the pity of even the toughest medieval soldier tested as *les bouches* remained stranded in a ditch under the city walls as the winter temperatures plummeted. Henry argued with French ambassadors that its was not he who had put them there whilst his soldiers passed them what they could, Henry even giving them a Christmas meal before they again returned to die in the ditch. On 19 January 1419, after more than five months of misery, Bouteiller finally surrendered, many French citizens changing allegiance as he did so, disgusted at the ruling French classes.

Henry gave thanks in the Notre Dame Cathedral the following day, it was the supreme moment of his life. All of Normandy save Mont St Michel had now fallen to the English king who then took Duke John's Pontoise in a coup de main. Forced to seek a truce with the Dauphin, John met his duplicitous match at Montereau where he was murdered. With France in chaos and the English Army outside Paris, Queen Isabelle, who wished for her daughter Catherine to sit on the French throne rather than her son, the Dauphin, sought help from Henry. Thousands of Parisians lined the city walls as the great English warrior king passed by for Troyes. There he would become heir to the Kingdom of France on King Charles' death and win the hand of Catherine of Valois. The dispossessed Dauphin would now wage war against the English and his parents, calling on the 'Auld Alliance' with Scotland to do so. The Siege of Rouen is commemorated in a fifteenth century, 1,300-line poem, written by the little known John Page.

19 January 1643

English Civil Wars
Battle of Braddock Down

IN APRIL 1640 King Charles I of England, Scotland and Ireland (Wales was part of England) recalled Parliament after an eleven year break and immediately regretted it. Instead of receiving funding for an invasion of Scotland, which he had sent into revolt with his new *Book of Common Prayer*, Charles received a long list of grievances accumulated over his fourteen-year reign. Parliament arguments against Charles were not so much whether or not he ruled but how, from his governance of the Church of England to his foreign policy with Catholic Spain and the economy of his Three Kingdoms. This *Short Parliament* lasted a little more than three weeks but it reconvened six months later again at Charles behest, this time a *Long Parliament* of twenty years with accordingly magnified grievances leading to a transfer of army command from the Crown to Parliament and moves made to prevent Bishops, loyal to Charles, from voting in the House of Commons. Charles attempted to remove this threat to his authority by personally arresting the Puritan Leader of the House, John Pym, and four other Members of Parliament only to find on arrival at Westminster that his 'birds had flown'. Having failed so publicly, Civil War between the king and his Parliament was now inevitable, both sides hurriedly raising forces, the king largely in the North (Cavaliers), raising the Royal Standard at Nottingham before marching south to Edgehill for an October 1642 undisciplined, indecisive battle against Robert Devereux, Earl of Essex and his London Trained Bands (Roundheads).

Over the following winter a propaganda war then began in London with Parliamentary news sheets answered by those of the Royalist Mercurius Aulicus smuggled in from Royalist Oxford. The Commons soon began to divide between hardliners and a peace party whilst the citizens outside suffered from a lack of coal from besieged Newcastle and the demands of extra taxation to pay for Parliamentary troops. At sea, the English Channel was full of French privateers supplying Irish Catholic insurgents, not friends of Charles but, in the Protestant London Parliament, possessing a common enemy.

In the South West of England and the islands off shore, the Scilly Isles, Lundy, the Isle of Man, Jersey and Guernsey, Charles enjoyed considerable support. By mid January 1643 Royalists Sir Ralph Hopton and Sir John Berkeley had raised 5,000 men in Cornwall ready to resist a Parliamentary attack from Devon. Short on supplies, food and ammunition, their initial plan rather optimistically relied on buying French arms in exchange for Cornish tin but luck favoured them when four Parliament cargo ships were blown inshore near Falmouth. Sir Nicholas Slanning hurried out in smaller vessels to harass whilst John Arundel peppered them with cannon fire from Pendennis Castle. The Parliament ships then took cover in Falmouth Harbour where Hopton and a boarding party relieved them of their much desired cargo.

Hopton was now able to confront two Parliamentary forces that were approaching from Devon, one under William, Lord Ruthin and another under Henry Grey, Earl of Stamford. Hopton ideally wanted to prevent Ruthin and Stamford from uniting and moved to confront Ruthin's 4,000 men at Braddock Down, Bodmin Moor on 19 January 1643. On the broken ground of the Down, Hopton hid most of his force, deceiving Ruthin into attacking what he thought were stragglers. As Ruthin charged he was, however, met not only by volleys of musket fire but also a blast from six cannon that Hopton had also held back. The nasty surprise stopped the Parliament charge in its tracks, Ruthin bitterly regretting his decision to attack without waiting for his own cannon or Stamford's arrival. Hopton's Cavaliers now emerged from the gorse to take full advantage of Roundhead discomfort, pressing a counter-attack vigorously. A sharp Parliament retreat back to Lostwithiel ensued with the Parliament cavalry running down many of their own infantry in the panic. Even in Lostwithiel there was no let up for the Parliamentarians who were then set upon by the townsfolk.

Hopton had killed 200 and captured 1,500 Parliamentarians along with nearly 1,000 muskets, four cannon and wagon loads of money. Cornwall was now secure whilst Charles' formidable Queen Henrietta had also drummed up Spanish, French, Dutch and Scottish support. The king's cause would suffer a reverse at Lichfield but in March, Spencer Compton, Earl of Northampton would look to recover the town on nearby Hopton Heath.

20 January 1812

Napoleonic Wars
Storming of Ciudad Rodrigo

 IN JUNE 1807 the Emperor of the French, Napoleon Bonaparte, had crushed a Russian Army under Count Levin von Bennigsen at Friedland leaving Tsar Alexander I little choice but to become a French ally in the face of an all conquering *Grande Armée*. Indeed Napoleon now had virtually no European opposition as the Fourth Coalition collapsed, Prussia having been defeated the year before at Jena-Auerstadt and Austria, as part of the Third Coalition, having been defeated at Ulm in 1805. In opposition to the ambitions of the French Emperor only Great Britain again remained, the defeat of whom Napoleon could only effect by means of the Continental System, an embargo on all British trade with Europe, since the British Isles were otherwise untouchable behind the 'wooden walls' of the Royal Navy. However, by 1811 the system was hurting Russian trade more than its intended target since British goods at the onset of the Industrial Revolution were very much in demand. The Tsar infuriated Napoleon by turning a blind eye to smuggling as well as refusing him the hand in marriage of his sister Anna, he also fumed at the lack of French assistance in his war with Turkey and at Napoleon's marriage to Austrian Duchess, Marie Louise of Parma. In return Napoleon fumed at Alexander's duplicity. Despite his attempts to enforce the Continental System in Portugal having stirring up a hornets' nest of British, Portuguese and Spanish resistance throughout the Iberian Peninsular, Napoleon now prepared to do exactly the same in Russia with 600,000 men, half of them Prussian and Austrian.

In the Iberian Peninsular meanwhile, the Anglo-Portuguese Army under General Sir Arthur Wellesley, Viscount Wellington had forced the French out of Portugal whilst the Spanish were improving in battle and their *Guerrilleros* harassed the French with horrific violence. Napoleon still required 30,000 additional men for Russia and Marshal Louis Suchet required another 10,000 in Valencia leaving Marshal Auguste Marmont in northern and Marshal Jean de Dieu Soult in southern Spain under even greater pressure. Wellington was not to miss such an opportunity and duly began an offensive on the Spain/Portugal border fortress towns of Ciudad Rodrigo and Badajoz the capture of which would give him free movement in to and out of Spain.

Wellington began the decisive year of 1812 on 8 January by moving 11,000 men and thirty-eight cannon through heavy snows to besiege Ciudad Rodrigo, immediately storming the Grand Teson Redoubt to the north overlooking the city walls. Trenches and emplacements were then dug into the frozen soil protected further by gabions of earth carried up by troops under fire of grapeshot. The Santa Cruz Convent to the west and the San Francisco Convent to the north of the fortress were then stormed as British siege batteries began pounding the walls of Ciudad Rodrigo itself. A desperate sortie from the undermanned 2,000-strong French garrison of Brigadier Jean Barrie was then also repulsed. Over the next five days the British gun batteries moved closer, firing nearly 10,000 balls to create two breaches, the 'Great' on the north-west corner and the 'Lesser' on the north tower which, though not ideal, Wellington decided to storm immediately concerned at the proximity of Marmont's Army. At nightfall on 19 January, after crossing the River Agueda, an initial British attack was made on the south-west wall, scaling the outworks before working around to the 'Great' breach which was assaulted against intense musket fire by the 94th Regiment of Foot under Major Generals Henry Campbell and Henry Mackinnon. At the top of the breach, the 94th were hit by volleys of grapeshot from two French 24-pounders, the survivors descending the rubble to rush the guns with fixed bayonets while their comrades behind rushed the ramparts. As the fighting raged the French then exploded a mine under the breach, killing Mackinnon amongst many others. At the 'Lesser' breach light infantry under Major General Robert Craufurd also broke into the town, joining those flooding in from the north-west as French resistance crumbled. Fighting continued into the morning of 20 January 1812 becoming an orgy of violence as the British infantry, furious at 1,700 casualties which also included Craufurd, ran amok despite the inhabitants being British allies.

The French hold on northern Spain was badly shaken, it would soon be shaken further at Badajoz to where the soon to be Earl of Wellington, Duke of Ciudad Rodrigo now marched for a siege of even greater ferocity.

21 January 1916
The Great War
Battle of Hanna

THE UNITED KINGDOM of Great Britain and Ireland had supported the Ottoman Empire (Turkey) throughout the nineteenth century as a bulwark against Russian expansion into the Mediterranean, the Middle East and South Asia as well as to protect British interests against Mahdism in North Africa, including the finances of Egypt and the Suez Canal. German diplomacy at the beginning of the twentieth century, however, promised Turkey assistance in regaining territories in the Caucasus, Balkans and Persia lost to Russia in the Russo-Turkish War of 1876–78 so that when the Great War broke out in August 1914 the pro German, Turkish Minister for War, Ismail Enver Pasha, signed a secret alliance with the Central Powers. For their part the Germans, as had Russia, were looking to build influence through Anatolia, the Middle East, East Africa and India by using the Muslim Ottoman Empire to disrupt British interests in Muslim Persia (Iran) and Mesopotamia (Iraq), particularly the Anglo-Persian Oil Company supplying the Royal Navy who at the time were in the process of switching to oil from coal power.

To protect their Middle East interests, the British Government of Herbert Asquith launched the Mesopotamia Campaign, sending the Indian Expeditionary Force D (IEFD) comprised solely of the 6th (Poona) Infantry Division, 11,000 troops under Lieutenant General Arthur Barrett to the mouth of the River Shatt al-Arab, taking Fao Fortress on 8 November 1914. Aided by Sheikh Mubarak Al-Sabah of Kuwait (which came under British protection), Barrett had already accomplished his basic mission to safeguard the Persian Gulf oil facilities but nevertheless advanced north to Basra, countering an Ottoman advance on 21 November before Major General Charles Fry, commanding the 104th Wellesley Rifles and the 110th Mahratta Light Infantry, advanced on Qurna at the confluence of the Rivers Tigris and Euphrates. Fry could not force a crossing of the Euphrates but British gunboats secured an Ottoman surrender in December. Major General Charles Mellis then held off an Ottoman counter-attack at Shaiba.

The IEFD was now reorganised into a corps commanded by Lieutenant General John Nixon who ordered the sick Barrett's replacement, Major General Charles Townshend, to press on up the Tigris to Kut Al Amara and Baghdad accompanied by two gunboats. Turkish troops had been tied down on the Gallipoli Peninsular for much of 1915 but not now, an unhappy Townshend halted at Ctesiphon outside Baghdad in November after a five day battle with 18,000 Turks under Colonel Nureddin Pasha. Townshend retreated back to Kut pursued by Nureddin who besieged him there on 7 December 1915. Nixon ordered Townshend to maintain a defence whilst he assembled a 20,000-strong relief expedition, the Tigris Corps, under Lieutenant General Fenton Aylmer which left Basra on 3rd January 1916 for the 300-mile advance. On 6 January, as the 12th Indian Infantry Division made a diversion, 13,000 men of the 7th (Meerut) Infantry Division assaulted the Turkish defences first at Sheik Saad and again, reinforced by 3rd (Lahore) Infantry Division (both Indian Divisions had fought on the Western Front only a few months previous) at Wadi, on both occasions with heavy losses that reduced the Tigris Corps to just half the original strength. Regardless, Nixon ordered Aylmer on up the Tigris but blocking him at the Hanna Defile were 30,000 troops of the Turkish 6th Army under Khalil Pasha. On 21 January 1916, after a dismal bombardment 4,000 Meerutis charged across 600 yards of flooded marshland against Ottoman lines defended by astutely placed machine-guns and artillery. Meeruti casualties quickly mounted with the ground providing no cover but on the left a handful of men made the Turkish front line only to be 'bombed' (hand grenaded) by Turkish counter-attacks and forced to withdraw. Despite the total failure of the morning's attack, Aylmer decided on another that afternoon over ground ever more difficult to return the same abject result, many of the 2,700 casualties left in agony in the freezing marsh overnight.

At Dujaila in March, and despite two more battalions of Kitchener's Volunteers, Aylmer would again fail to relieve Kut, Townshend's subsequent surrender on 29 April 1916, at the time, being the worst capitulation in the history of the British Army. In 1917 the Mesopotamian Campaign would resume in conjunction with a British advance from the Sinai Peninsular, Egypt.

22 January 1879

Zulu War
Battle of Isandlwana

THE LONDON MISSIONARY Society had many missionaries in Africa but none more reknowned than Dr David Livingstone. Famously found at Ujiji in 1871 by explorer Henry Stanley, Livingstone had died in 1873, his body carried back for burial in Westminster Abbey by his faithful African servant Jacob but his ambition to bring the three Cs of Commerce, Christianity and Civilisation to Africa would live on. The imminent Scramble for Africa that followed on the heels of Livingstone's death would, however, be driven by the first of these, a race for the resources of the untamed continent by the great military powers of Europe, none more so than Great Britain.

By 1877 Britain had annexed the South African Boer Republic of the Transvaal with the Orange Free State sure to follow, the Dutch speaking Boers satisfied by the protection provided by the British military against their traditional enemy, the Zulu. Two subsequent years of increasing Zulu violence across the Zululand/ Transvaal border then squared nicely with the increasing imperial ambition of the British High Commissioner for southern Africa, Henry Bartle Frere (who along with John Kirk had previously closed the Zanzibar slave market, completing Livingstone's dream of extinguishing slavery in the region), and the Administrator of the Transvaal, Theophilius Shepstone, who despite protestations from Zulu King Cetshwayo deemed an annexation of the previously British friendly Zululand necessary by force (Shepstone himself had crowned Cetshwayo in 1873).

Lieutenant General Frederick Thesiger, Lord Chelmsford's central column of three, crossed the Buffalo River on 11 January 1879 leaving behind a support column under Brevet Colonel Anthony Durnford at the Rorke's Drift mission station. The 5,000 British Redcoats and African troops with a six-piece artillery train continued slowly on up to make camp under the rock promontary of Isandlwana from where, with rumours of Zulus ever closer, reconnoitring forces and pickets were immediately sent out. At 01.30 on the morning of 22 January 1879 one of these pickets under Major John Dartnell reported the presence of a large body of Zulu and requested reinforcements. Despite Boer warnings not to divide his forces against such a mobile enemy, Chelmsford himself led 2,500 men out the Isandlwana camp at first light to support Dartnell whilst issuing orders for Durnford to move up from Rorke's Drift, the camp meanwhile under the temporary command of Brevet Lieutenant Colonel Henry Pulleine. The Zulus for whom Dartnell and Chelmsford were now searching had disappeared whilst back at Isandlwana the arriving Durnford decided to conduct a sweep of the Inyoni Mountains to protect Chelmsford's rear rather than assume command of the camp. In giving chase to a handful of Zulu during this sweep Lieutenant Charles Raw rode over a ridge to find to his horror, sitting in silence in the valley below, the main Zulu Impi of 24,000 highly disciplined warriors who realised immediately that the hour had come and attacked. Raw and Durnford began a fighting retreat whilst sending to Pulleine for reinforcements, Pulleine ignoring previous orders which prioritised a defence of the camp by obliging Durnford with an infantry company even though Zulus were already appearing on the hills around him. With the British split in three by their own doing, Pulleine was also receiving orders to strike camp from a blissfully unaware Chelmsford who in turn completely failed to appreciate the gravity of the situation once developments had been reported to him.

Although a militia armed mainly with assegais, knobkerries and cowhide shields, the Zulu were no average fighting force. Under the command of Chief Nshingwayo Kamahole the well-trained, exceptionally brave warriors now attacked in the classic Zulu formation of a chest and horns. The Zulu attack momentarily stalled against the heavy fire of Pulleine's defenders with Durnford falling back in good order but all the time Pulleine's right was being outflanked by the Zulu left horn, the gap between he and Durnford soon infiltrated with Zulus. Worse, Durnford withdrew further, further exposing Pulliene's right flank from which the Natal Native Contingent now fled. Durnford rode back into camp to discuss the deteriorating situation with Pulleine who sounded a general retreat to shorten the British perimeter and increase firepower but it was too late, the Zulu chest rallied and charged, entering the camp simultaneously with many of the retreating British. The British position now collapsed, against impossible odds Redcoats fighting back to back in isolated groups on the slopes of Isandlwana with bayonet and rifle butt once their ammunition had been exhausted, a solar eclipse adding to the terror.

No less than 1,300 British troops, including Durnford and Pulleine, lost their lives but the nightmare was not over, smoke was already rising from Rorke's Drift.

22/23 January 1879

Zulu War
Battle of Rorke's Drift

IN 1879 THE British High Commissioner for Southern Africa, Henry Bartle Frere, and the Administrator of the Transvaal, Theophilius Shepstone, had engineered a war against King Cetshwayo of the Zulu in an attempt to increase British imperialism in South Africa having already annexed the Boer Republic of the Transvaal two years before. The British advance from Natal into Zululand was, however, soon in trouble when, on 22 January 1879, Lieutenant General Frederick Thesiger, Lord Chelmsford had ignored local advice by dividing the strength of his central column at Isandlwana, the camp of which under Brevet Colonel Anthony Durnford and Brevet Lieutenant Colonel Pulleine was now on the point of being overrun by 24,000 Zulus under Chief Nshingwayo Kamahole. Whilst the ultimate price for Chelmsford's complacency was being paid by 1,300 men at Isandlwana the 4,000 strong Zulu Reserve Impi under the King's brother Prince Dabulamansi KaMpande had swung right heading for the Buffalo River. Preferring to maintain the moral high ground against naked British aggression, Cetshwayo had forbade any Zulu crossing of the Buffalo but KaMpande had so far missed the glory and ignored orders to approach, at 15.30, the main British supply depot, the mission station at KwaJimu (Jim's land), Rorke's Drift.

The station was garrisoned by a single company of the Warwickshire 24th Regiment of Foot under Lieutenant Gonville Bromhead and by a poorly-armed company of the Natal Native Contingent (NNC) under Captain William Stevenson. Royal Engineers who had been manning pontoons over the river had unfortunately just moved up to Isandlwana to be caught in the unfolding maelstrom but their commanding officer, Lieutenant John Chard, had just arrived back. The defence of Rorke's Drift was then bolstered by the retreating (from Isandlwana) Natal Native Horse (NNH) under Lieutenant Alfred Henderson who set up a picket on the far side of Shiyane Hill directly in the path of the KaMpande's Zulu. In overall command of the station was Major Henry Spalding but Spalding now hotfooted to Helpmekaar for another company of the 24th Foot, leaving Chard in command but assuring him that nothing was about to happen. Wisely Chard began using mealie bags and biscuit tins to build connecting walls between the two buildings of the station, the storehouse and the hospital, in an attempt to give the 500 defenders some cover. On the approach of the Zulu, however, Henderson's NNH fled for the second time that day, their example in following Spalding to Helpmekaar demoralising the NNC sufficiently enough to follow suit. Chard was now left with just 156 men to defend Rorke's Drift, half of them sick in the hospital.

The 24th was still busy shortening the perimeter when 600 Zulu suddenly appeared from the south and attacked on the run into heavy British fire, finally checked only when they ran into a cross fire from the storehouse. Several Zulu now took cover to begin firing with obsolete rifles on the south wall whilst the majority rounded the hospital and attacked the north-west wall, again driven back by disciplined fire and the bayonet. The main body of Zulu now followed, a covering fire from the south and west allowing them to move up under the British defensive walls where continued attacks were held, bayonet against assegai. Although poor shots the Zulu then began firing on the north wall forcing Chard to retreat behind another line of biscuit tins which exposed the hospital. The roof ablaze, the hospital was then defended room by room whilst the sick were removed, a now fully surrounded Chard ordering mealie bags to be used for a redoubt giving an extra line of fire which duly decimated further Zulu attacks. As the night drew on, the British occupied just the storehouse and a few yards in front but helped by the light of the burning hospital fired over 20,000 rounds of ammunition in repelling continuous Zulu attacks. Zulu attacks were maintained all night, but by first light on 23 January 1879 they were gone. Close to exhaustion both in effort and ammunition the British repaired the walls only for a huge force of Zulu to reappear opposite on the KwaSinqindi Hill but they too were spent, as Chard prepared to receive another attack the Zulu retreated back across the Buffalo River.

The heroic defence of Rorke's Drift was widely publicised to cover up the disaster at Isandlwana, eleven Victoria Crosses awarded including Chard and Bromhead. The Battles of Isandlwana and Rorke's Drift are commemorated respectively in the 1979 Arrow film *Zulu Dawn* and the 1964 MGM film *Zulu*. The sacked Chelmsford would now hastily attempt to defeat the Zulu before the arrival of his replacement Lieutenant General Garnet Wolseley.

24 January 1900

Second Boer War
Battle of Spion Kop

THE THREE SUCCESSIVE British defeats suffered during 'Black Week' in December 1899 had lowered faith in Commander in Chief South Africa General Sir Redvers Buller to an all time low. 'Poor Buller' had arrived in South Africa to find British commanders already in Natal had ignored his instructions and were now suffering the consequences. The lists of British casualties were bad enough but abject defeats at Nicholson's Nek, Stormberg, Magersfontein and Colenso against Boer militias were unforgivable in a Victorian Britain raised on a diet of comfortable victories in colonial warfare. Buller's suggestion to 'let go' Ladysmith, where Lieutenant General Sir George White and 13,000 British troops had been besieged since early November, then led to Secretary of State for War Henry Petty-Fitzmaurice, Lord Lansdowne appointing Field Marshal Lord Frederick Roberts as his replacement, a man who ironically suggested that not only Ladysmith be let go but also Kimberley and Mafeking in Cape Colony. On his arrival Roberts also retained the same strategy as Buller, a two-pronged advance through the Orange Free State and Natal, himself commanding the former, Buller the latter.

Meanwhile Transvaal President Paul Kruger had been urging Boer offensives, particularly into Natal but, content to maintain the moral high ground, all his generals had refused. Kruger's ambassador in the Hague, Netherlands was also rallying anti British sentiment when suddenly the more aggressive Free State General Louis Botha launched an aggressive attack on Ladysmith, White holding him off but hardly comfortably. Ladysmith would surely fall if Buller did not soon resume British offensives and so he returned to the flanking plan which had been ditched in December in favour of the fiasco of the frontal attack at Colenso. This time Buller would move around the Boer defences further west by crossing the Tugela River at Potgieter's and Trichardt's Drifts.

After a march through storms, mud and blistering heat, Buller crossed the Tugela at Potgieters whilst Lieutenant General Sir Charles Warren, 10,600 infantry, 2,200 cavalry and thirty-six guns crossed further to the west at Trichardt's intending to strike before Botha could reinforce. So slow was Warren, however, that Buller issued him an ultimatum, Warren then resolving to attack the critical point in the Boer defences at Spion Kop, a task so tough that Botha was not bothering to defend it.

On 24 January 1900, after a night march, Major General Edward Woodgate's Lancashires and Lieutenant Colonel Alec Thorneycroft's Irregular Mounted Infantry, 2,000 men, climbed the rocky slopes of Spion Kop, overwhelming a lone Boer picket. Under cover of darkness and an early morning mist they then half-heartedly dug into stony ground believing they commanded all around. Botha, however, soon began shelling the plateau with two Boer gun batteries on the Tabanyama Plateau whilst Burghers from the Pretoria and Carolina Commandos began to scale the north slope. As the mist lifted the full horror of the British position now became evident – too shallow, the trench was overlooked to the front by Conical Hill and to the right by Aloe Knoll, Boers now enfilading the trenches whilst shrapnel shells continued to sweep the entire British position. Woodgate was soon mortally wounded as the British became hopelessly pinned down, Thorneycroft rallying forty survivors for a bayonet charge on the far crest which claimed the lives of almost all but not the formidable Thorneycroft. Watching on from Mount Alice five miles away Buller immediately promoted Thorneycroft to Brigadier General, the fighting intensifying through the heat of the day, close range rifle fire, bayonet charges and hand-to-hand combat with both Buller and Warren failing to launch a diversion until 17.00. When they did, two infantry battalions under Lieutenant Colonel Robert Riddell successfully scaled Twin Peaks a mile to the east before, in a brilliant feat of arms, sending General Schalk Burger and his Lydenburg Commando into a full retreat leaving Botha isolated at Spion Kop. Still on the plateau Thorneycroft was shattered, physically and mentally, and he too retreated despite Winston Churchill, now of the South African Light Horse, advising him of imminent reinforcements. The following morning Botha retook Spion Kop without firing a shot.

In memory of the 1,500 casualties, terracing at many British football grounds, notably Liverpool, was named after Spion Kop. Surviving the battle that day was a Natal Indian Ambulance Corps stretcher bearer who fifty years later would lead his country to independence from British rule, Mohandas Gandhi. Buller was at least learning how to unlock the Boer defences, he would try again at Vaal Krantz in three weeks time.

25 January 1644

English Civil Wars
Battle of Nantwich

KING CHARLES I of the Three Kingdoms of England, Scotland and Ireland had been staring at victory after only a year of fighting since the 1642 outbreak of the English Civil War. It was exactly the position he had hoped, limitations of money and men that fought out of loyalty to the king rather than for the Parliament cause of democracy, economics, politics and religion meant Charles required a quick victory or likely he would not have one at all. Defeated in battle, Parliament disarray both in the field and in the House of Commons, Westminster was illustrated by protests in the streets in daily expectation of the king's advance on London. Political factions argued over suing for peace while two senior commanders, Robert Devereux, Earl of Essex and Sir William Waller were at enmity following a debacle at Roundway Down, Wiltshire. Adding to Parliament's problems their figurehead, the Leader of the House of Commons, John Pym, died in December 1643. Only in the Eastern Counties had Edward Montagu, Earl of Manchester and Oliver Cromwell held a crumbling Parliament front.

Charles' casualties and consequent failure to march on London, however, bought Parliament time and also unearthed an inspirational figure in Edward Massey, the young Governor of Gloucester who, with his Puritan citizens, resisted seemingly impossible odds when the king invested his town. From Gloucester back to Newbury, Alton and Arundel, Essex' Army then inflicted further damaging losses on Charles' battle weary Royalist recruits, both sides now recruiting from the king's other two realms, the Royalists from both Ireland and Scotland, Parliament from just Scotland.

Lancashire and Cheshire had so far largely been under the king's command but exceptions at Manchester and Nantwich meant Parliament were able to launch attacks into Royalist North Wales. To date these attacks had been defeated by Charles, Lord Capel but Capel was unable to rid himself entirely of the menace and was replaced by John, Lord Byron. With Royalist reinforcements from Ireland,

Byron was immediately successful, defeating William Brereton at Middlewich before marching south on Nantwich, garrisoned by 2,000 Parliamentarians under George Booth. On 18 January 1644 Booth repulsed Byron's 5,000-strong Royalist Army with heavy losses before a siege in the snow developed. In response, having escaped the Royalist siege of Hull for a successful campaign in Lincolnshire with Oliver Cromwell, Thomas Fairfax crossed the Pennines to join the bruised Brereton for a relief of Nantwich.

Fairfax' 5,000 Parliamentarians were in poor health but approached Nantwich on 24 January just as the frozen countryside began thawing. Meanwhile Byron, his own numbers dwindling due to casualties, sickness and disease, began moving his Royalist infantry and cannon west over the River Weaver toward drier ground near Acton. So sharp though was the thaw that the Beam Bridge was swept away by a raging torrent leaving Byron and 1,800 cavalry stranded on the east bank. In pouring rain at 14.00 on 25 January 1644 Fairfax attacked Royalist forces under Richard Gibson west of the Weaver. Supported by cannon from St Mary's Churchyard, Acton, Gibson held Fairfax' initial assault before the Parliament cavalry of William Fairfax (brother) forced back his right wing. Byron now approached from the north-east after a six mile ride to the nearest bridge, threatening William Fairfax and the Parliament left. Thomas Fairfax posted two infantry regiments with cavalry support to hold Byron while desperate fighting continued in the centre – cannon, muskets, sword and pike in a muddy mêlée across ditches and hedges. Booth then led a Parliament sortie of musketeers from the Nantwich garrison into the Royalist rear which was protected by Sir Fulk Hunke's local militia. Booth overran Hunke before attacking Gibson's gunners in the churchyard whilst in the centre, Fairfax' main assault broke the Royalist Irish Regiment under Henry Warren, just the flanks now fighting on. After two hours the battle was over, 1,500 Royalists surrendering and defecting to Parliament.

Unable to reach Gibson, Byron retreated to Chester having lost almost his entire army. Nantwich temporarily ended Charles' hopes of securing the North which would come under increasing pressure from Parliament forces notably three months later at York and, six months later, on the Moor outside Long Marston.

26 January 1885

Mahdist Wars
Siege of Khartoum

IN THE EARLY 1880s Britain became involved in Egypt and by extension the Sudan to protect their financial investments and the Suez Canal. Western involvement led to an Egyptian revolt which was crushed at Tel El Kebir in 1882 but in the Sudan an Islamic uprising led by Mohammed Ahmed, the Mahdi had gained momentum. The anti-imperialist British Government of William Gladstone was reluctant to involve itself in a war with the Mahdi but would if necessary defend Egypt and the Red Sea ports. To this effect Major General Charles Gordon was sent to Khartoum to evacuate Egyptian garrisons and any Europeans who wanted to depart. Gordon, a favourite of Queen Victoria, had served the Khedive of Egypt as Governor General of the Sudan but it was precisely this experience that meant he was less likely to abandon Khartoum than a neutral. So anxious were those that appointed Gordon that the policy of withdrawal was again hammered into him by the British envoy in Cairo, Sir Evelyn Baring, but on arrival in Khartoum Gordon set about administering the city and opened a dialogue with the Mahdi, inadvertently offending him by sending a scarlet cloak and a Tarboush, two distinct symbols of the hated Ottoman rule. The Mahdi, who respected Gordon, politely declined and sent by return a patched Jibbah and straw skull cap, the identifiable garments of Mahdism.

A furious Gordon now began asking for reinforcements while both Britain and Turkey still firmly pressed for a withdrawal. The *Ansar* (Mahdi following) then besieged Khartoum on 13 March 1884, trapping Gordon who possessed 8,000 Egyptians and Bashi-Bazouks to defend a fifteen-mile perimeter between the Blue and White Niles which surround the rest of the city. Inside Khartoum were also 35,000 civilians with food for six months. A masterful soldier, Gordon led a vigorous resistance with many sorties usually by paddle steamer but he could not afford any heavy losses. As the Nile waters rose in early summer and the *Ansar* wearied, escape was again urged by the British Government but still Gordon refused to abandon the people of Khartoum, his pleas for assistance ever more desperate. Now the British public clamoured for a relief army to be sent, Gladstone's worst nightmare was being realised but, after weeks of delay, General Garnet Wolseley was charged with leading one.

Assembling his force at Wadi Halfa, Wolseley crucially chose to advance up over the great cataracts of the Nile rather than overland from Suakin on the Red Sea. British progress was painfully slow but Gordon was aware of its existence, searching the horizon every day for the next few months in the desperate hope of seeing black smoke from Wolseley's steamers. By November the relief column was still only at Korti (300 miles north of Khartoum) where, to save time, Wolseley split his force – a River Column continuing upstream and a Desert Column cutting across the great bend of the Nile to Metemma from where it could make contact with Gordon just a hundred miles further south. General Herbert Stewart led the Desert Column deeper into the hostile desert wastes fighting two sharp engagements at Abu Klea and Abu Kru, himself mortally wounded at the latter. General Sir Charles Wilson then assumed command, arriving in Metemma on 21 January before crucially delaying for three days to service Gordon's awaiting steamers.

Meanwhile in Khartoum the population was dying of malnutrition and dysentery, the Mahdi had requested Gordon surrender, avoid bloodshed and had offered him safe passage, but on 26 January 1885, no doubt aware of Wilson's presence, he gave the order for 60,000 dervishes to assault the city. Assisted by the low level of the Nile they stormed over Gordon's defences meeting scant resistance. The entire Anglo-Egyptian-Sudanese garrison was wiped out and a further 4,000 civilians killed. Despite orders that he be spared, Gordon was shot and speared before his head was delivered in a leather bag to the Mahdi.

Just two days later Wilson's steamer, the Bordein with twenty Redcoats and 240 Egyptians aboard, came within sight of the burning Khartoum. Queen Victoria, greatly distressed at 'this fearful news', blamed Gladstone and his Cabinet which duly fell. The British public bristled with indignation but Gordon would not be forgotten; thirteen years later another Anglo-Egyptian-Sudanese Army under Sirdar Horatio Herbert Kitchener would seek revenge.

Gordon is still remembered in the Promenade Gardens, Gravesend, in the Victoria Embankment Gardens, Westminster and by the pupils of Gordon School, Woking who march in his memory through Whitehall every year.

27 January 1942

Second World War
Battle of Endau

JAPAN'S DRAMATIC ENTRY into the Second World War at Pearl Harbor, Hawaii on 7 December 1941 coincided with invasions throughout South East Asia. Already masters of coastal China and with forces in Vichy French Indo-China (Vietnam, Cambodia), Japan had advanced into Thailand, the Philippines, Dutch East Indies (Indonesia), British Borneo and Malaya. Defending North Malaya, the III Indian Corps under Lieutenant General Lewis Heath, subordinate to General Officer Commanding Lieutenant General Arthur Percival, had been outmanoeuvred the length of the Peninsular by the Japanese 25th Army of Tomoyuki Yamashita, Japanese air and naval superiority adding to 200 light tanks, thousands of bicycles and flanking attacks through supposed impenetrable jungle. Percival was desperately trying to delay the Japanese advance on Singapore, the 'Gibraltar in the East', to where British and Australian reinforcements were being shipped from Ceylon (Sri Lanka). After the fall of Kuala Lumpur, Percival sent the Australian 8th Infantry Division to relieve the battered Indian 11th on the west coast, inflicting heavy casualties at Gemensah Bridge and Gemas but the Australians were unable to hold the position when Japanese Imperial Guards defeated the Indian 45th and British 53rd Brigades at Muar, Bakri and Parit Sulong. Meanwhile on the east coast the Indian 9th Division under Major General Arthur Barstow had been able to fight a more measured retreat but were now in danger of becoming isolated by Yamashita's rapid western advance into the southernmost state of Johore.

In Cam Rahn Bay, Indo-China, infantry of the Japanese 18th Division under Lieutenant General Renya Mutaguchi now boarded eleven troop ships destined for Thailand and British Burma (Myanmar). Escorted by seventeen warships under the command of Rear Admiral Shintaro Hashimoto, Mutaguchi was also to support Japanese efforts in Malaya by isolating Barstow's Indian 9th Division from Singapore and seize airfields at Kahang and Kluang with troops landed by two of the Japanese ships at Endau, Johore.

Early on 26 January 1942, the Japanese convoy was spotted twenty miles off Endau by two British Lockheed Hudsons. That afternoon the Royal Air Force and Royal Australian Air Force launched twelve Vildebeest biplane torpedo bombers and nine Hudsons with twelve Brewster Buffalos and nine Hurricanes following in support. The obsolete Vildebeests were, however, badly mauled at the hands of twenty Nakajima fighters as a second wave of nine Vildebeest and three Albacores set off from Singapore, again mauled before their fighter escort arrived. Undeterred a third wave of six Hudsons and a fourth of five Blenheims arrived but only added to the British death toll, fifteen aircraft and their crews having now failed to return.

Simultaneously Rear Admiral Ernest Spooner, commanding British naval forces in Singapore, ordered his only two available but ageing destroyers HMS *Vampire* and HMS *Thanet* to sea. After the loss of the battleships HMS *Prince of Wales* and *Repulse* in December 1941 and with many vessels involved in convoys from Ceylon and evacuations from Singapore, it was all Spooner had. In the early morning darkness of 27 January 1942 *Vampire* and *Thanet* approached Endau searching for Mutaguchi's troopships. Sighting a Japanese destroyer, Captain William Moran on *Vampire* deliberately failed to engage before mistakenly attacking a minesweeper. Moran missed with two torpedoes but was not countered before turning south-east at 03.13. Another five minutes and Moran sighted the Japanese destroyer *Shirayuki*, turning with *Thanet* he fired five torpedoes all of which missed. *Shirayuki* returned fire at 03.30 by searchlight but through a smokescreen, initiating an artillery duel in which *Thanet* was hit within minutes by *Yugiri*. Having lost all steam and electrical power *Thanet* was doomed, the destroyers *Amagiri, Hatsuyuki and Sendai* now joining *Shirayuki* and *Yugiri* as *Vampire* fled. HMS *Thanet* sank at 04.18, with the loss of twelve men, thirty-one picked up by Shirayuki and sixty-six escaping ashore.

Thanet's survivors picked up by *Shirayuki* were never returned but the sixty-six escapees did regain Singapore. Their relief would not last as all British troops soon crossed back into Singapore. Under instruction from Prime Minister Winston Churchill, Percival prepared to make a final stand.

28 January 1846

Sikh Wars
Battle of Aliwal

FOR SEVERAL DECADES since the 1803 Battle of Assaye the British had little interest in further expansion out of North West India across the River Sutlej into the Sikh Empire. The power of the British-friendly Sikh Army, the Khalsa, was a deterrent in itself to British imperial design but also served to allay British concern at Russian ambition toward India and South Asia. Increasing Russian influence in Persia, however, led to an ultimately disastrous 1839 British invasion of Afghanistan whilst that same year the death of Sikh Maharajah Ranjit Singh, would lead to a power vacuum in the Punjab that gave the ever more powerful Khalsa uncertain leadership. As the instability of the region again raised British concern, the increase in British forces south of the Sutlej in turn raised concern within the Punjab, the Khalsa ever more paranoid of a British invasion. The First Anglo-Sikh War erupted when the Khalsa crossed the Sutlej in December 1845 only to be defeated at Mudki and Ferozeshah, the British East India Company's Bengal Army winning both encounters largely thanks to lamentable leadership on the part of the Sikh Sirdars Tej and Lal Singh, both of whom were in thrall to Maharani Jindan Singh, acting regent of the Sikh Empire who had vowed vengeance on the Khalsa following the murder of her brother Wazir Jawahir Singh.

Both sides had suffered heavy casualties, especially at Ferozeshah, the Khalsa retreating back across the Sutlej with the British unable to pursue but by early January both were receiving reinforcements. The Sikhs also built a pontoon bridge back over the Sutlej at Sobraon from where they were launching raids into British territory, particularly towards Ludhiana which was being reinforced with Gurkhas, Indian sepoys and cavalry. In mid January British Commander in Chief Sir Hugh Gough received information that Sirdar Ranjur Singh had crossed the Sutlej further east with 10,000 men and forty guns heading for Buddowal directly threatening British supply lines at Ludhiana. Gough ordered Lieutenant General Sir Harry

Smith, a veteran of the Napoleonic Wars, with 10,000 men and thirty-two guns to cut off the Sikh advance, the two armies coming into contact at Buddowal where Smith decided to march around Ranjur to Ludhiana. Hampered by sandy terrain Smith's men laboured under heavy gunfire before checking the Sikh attack with their own heavy gunfire, Smith finally relieving Ludhiana, albeit exhausted. Ranjur then abandoned Buddowal and retreated north-west back to Aliwal where he was further reinforced by 4,000 Sikhs and twelve guns formerly trained by General Paolo Avitabile, an Italian mercenary. The Sikhs entrenched in a three-mile fronted semicircle from Aliwal west to Bhundri with their backs to the Sutlej.

Smith advanced to occupy Buddowal before on the morning of 28 January 1846 advancing six miles toward Aliwal, cavalry and horse artillery to the front with infantry in column behind ready to deploy. The Sikhs opened the battle of Aliwal at 10.00 as expected with an artillery barrage but the unperturbed Smith brought up two brigades of infantry under Brigadiers Christopher Godby and George Hicks to attack the village of Aliwal which, when taken, would give an enfilading fire down a dry nullah (river bed) into the Sikh centre. Godby and Hicks were supported by a general advance in the centre and a cavalry charge commanded by Brigadier Charles Cureton, supported by Shekhawati Infantry on their right. Godby and Hicks successfully took Aliwal to leave Ranjur Singh under increasing pressure in his centre and on his left. Ranjur sent his own cavalry further west, to the right of Bhundri, to attack the British left but was met by the 16th Queens Lancers under Major John Smyth and Bengal Light Cavalry under Major John Angelo. Smyth and Angelo checked the Sikh cavalry before the 53rd Regiment of Foot under Brigadier R.W. Wilson took Bhundri with the bayonet. The Sikhs, backs against the River Sutlej, desperately formed into squares for protection against further British cavalry charges but were pounded by the Bengal Horse Artillery. Defeated, they were soon routed, fleeing back across the river losing their entire artillery train of sixty seven guns as well as leaving 2,000 dead and wounded on the field and in the Sutlej.

Smith had achieved a victory through brilliant tactics at a cost of 600 casualties. The bridgehead at Sobraon was the Khalsa's only foothold left in British territory. The conclusion to the First Sikh War would come there on 10 February 1846.

29 January 1574

Anglo-Spanish Wars
Battle of Reimersvaal

 CATHOLIC KING PHILIP of Spain was already, by right of his wife Queen Mary I, King of England and Ireland when, in 1556, he inherited the Spanish throne from his father Charles V, Holy Roman Emperor. The Spanish Kingdom included the Netherlands and Italy but not the remainder of the vast Habsburg Empire (Austria, Switzerland, Hungary, Czech Republic, Croatia, Bavaria, Slovenia) which was ruled from Vienna by his father until 1558, uncle until 1564 and cousin until 1576. Philip's Spain benefited from riches exported from the Spanish Main but suffered from debts incurred by Charles' Italian Wars against both France and the Ottoman Empire. The finances were not helped when Queen Mary died in 1558, Philip instantly losing his English and Irish titles to Queen Elizabeth I who declined his hand in marriage and, as Supreme Governor of the Church of England, pursued a conservative Protestant policy. Philip's own Spanish Netherlands (Holland, Belgium and Luxembourg), a vibrant but heavily taxed economy (by both Charles and Philip) was also coming to support the Protestant Reformation, support which in 1566 alongside grievances against Spanish rule erupted into the Beeldenstorm, a violent revolt against Catholicism that spread from the south to the north of the country. Viewing himself as the protector of the Catholic faith, Philip crushed heretics in his own country with the Spanish Inquisition and now in the Spanish Netherlands by military force; 10,000 men under the ruthless Fernando de Toledo, Duke of Alba but his troubles were just beginning.

On the Spanish Main, the exploits of English Captains John Hawkins and Francis Drake were encouraging increasing piracy and state-sponsored privateering whilst the Ridolfi Plot, Philip's plan to assassinate Elizabeth, had also been uncovered by Hawkins. Anglo-Spanish relations deteriorated but Elizabeth was still unwilling to risk outright war with Philip and attempted to appease him in 1572 by expelling Dutch 'Sea Beggars' from English ports. The gesture, however, merely forced the Sea Beggars across the North Sea where they captured the ports of Brielle and

Vlissingen (Flushing), joining the revolt of William I, Prince of Orange who, with a few exceptions dominated the northern Netherlands particularly Holland and Zeeland. Philip replaced Alba with Luis de Requesens y Zuniga, Governor of the Duchy of Milan.

On the island of Walcheren, commanding the Scheldt Estuary and the port of Antwerp (a busy trading city where the worlds first stock exchange had opened (the Dutch Revolt partly led to the opening of the London Stock Exchange in 1571)), only the Spanish garrisons at Middelburg and Arnemuiden held out after spending a year besieged by Dutch and English troops under Colonel Thomas Morgan. Since the Spanish relief of Middelburg had already been thwarted three times by the combined Beggar fleets of Lodiwijk van Boisot and Joos de Moor, Zuniga appointed Captain Don Julian de Romero alongside Flemish Admiral Gerard de Glimes for a fourth attempt. The Beggars in turn reinforced their sixty-four ships with Morgan's besieging English troops.

On 29 January 1574, the Spanish fleet sailed into the Scheldt Estuary, spotting the Anglo-Dutch rebels off Reimerswaal. Against De Glimes' advice Romero closed delivering broadsides that were returned by Boisot who lost an eye in the exchange. The Anglo-Dutch then gained the upper hand grappling the smaller Spanish ships which could not extricate themselves in the narrow estuary. A terrific close quarter fight then developed across decks for two hours, De Glimes' ship grounding on a sandbank to be attacked on all sides and set ablaze by Morgan. Romero was in error again sailing to assist De Glimes, his effort merely succeeding in setting his own ship ablaze. As the Anglo-Dutch ran amok over his burning decks, Romero then jumped from a porthole to swim ashore. The Spanish fleet was routed losing fifteen ships and 1,200 men. Middelburg surrendered to William nine days later.

The Dutch Revolt against Spain, otherwise known as the Eighty Years War (1568–1648), continued with English support until the English Civil War broke out in 1642. The Dutch Navy finished Spain as a naval power in 1639 but growing prosperity as a global trading nation would then lead the Dutch Republic into three bitter naval wars with former ally, England.

30 January 1972
The Troubles
Derry, Bloody Sunday

VIOLENCE HAD INCREASED across Northern Ireland since 1956 when the Irish Republican Army (IRA) began Operation Harvest to end the partition of Ireland. Catholic discontent voiced in demonstrations held by the Northern Ireland Civil Rights Association (NICRA) unsettled Loyalist Protestants but in Derry the discontent was somewhat justified, the city was comfortably Catholic yet gerrymandering had given Loyalist Protestants control of the council, employment and housing. However, since the Republic of Ireland was dominated by the Roman Catholic Church (the Pope had witnessed the drafting of the Constitution), Protestants in Northern Ireland feared absorption and were consequently in no mood to grant concessions to Catholic dissenters. Sectarianism in both states had effectively become firmly entrenched.

By 1969, Catholics in Bogside had barricaded themselves into an area known as Free Derry with vigilantes resisting any incursion by the Royal Ulster Constabulary. Province-wide rioting then accompanied the marches of the Protestant Orangemen and Apprentice Boys of Derry until the British Army restored order, but the welcome granted to British soldiers did not last, Catholics soon retreated once again behind their barricades and resisted any incursions with violence. RUC and British Army stop-and-search tactics successful in Malaya and Cyprus then alienated Catholics further, in particular the July 1970 Falls Curfew Operation which resulted in a four hour battle, a thirty-six hour curfew and over 300 arrests.

By 1971 the IRA was beginning to mount offensive operations against the RUC and the British Army – bombings, ambushes, off-duty shootings and honeytraps that prompted the Governments of Northern Ireland and Britain to reintroduce internment (detention without trial of terrorist suspects) leading to more riots as the effort degenerated into a public relations disaster. IRA and Protestant Ulster Volunteer Force paramilitary activity escalated (not without loss to themselves, home-made bombs being highly unstable) until on 18 January 1972 all marches and parades were banned by the Prime Minister of Northern Ireland Brian

Faulkner. But just four days later Catholic protesters marched on the internment camp at Magilligan, Derry, achieving another public relations coup for the IRA by deliberately provoking the Parachute Regiment. Following this success NICRA decided to march the following week, this time on the centre of Derry.

At 14.45 on 30 January 1972 as many as 15,000 Catholic protestors set off down Creggan Road and William Street for the Guildhall but aware of military barricades turned right at 'Aggro Corner' to march down Rossville Street. Several agitators, however, continued along both William Street and Little James Street for a confrontation with the Royal Green Jackets and 1st Battalion, Parachute Regiment who replied with rubber bullets, water cannon and CS gas. Lieutenant Colonel Derek Wilford commanding 1 Para then requested an advance to arrest the troublemakers but the consenting order was deliberately delayed by Brigadier Pat Maclellan at Brigade HQ to achieve a separation between violent and non-violent protestors. Because of the delay Wilford then chased the demonstrators down Rossville Street with more than the one company permitted. Several shots rang out on William Street, both IRA and 1 Para, wounding two protestors as two armoured personnel carriers continued along Rossville Street to Eden Place and the Rossville Flats where the Paras disembarked to make arrests amongst a rapidly dispersing crowd. At Eden Place the Paras, under the impression they were about to be attacked, fired several live rounds over the heads of the crowd but at the rubble barricade in Rossville Street, the Rossville Flats and at Kells Walk, Paratroop fire hit thirteen protestors. Four of these troops then advanced into Glenfada Park North shooting a further six protestors, in Abbey Park another two and on exiting Glenfada Park North another four. Of the twenty-seven casualties, thirteen lost their lives.

The immediate Widgery Report stated the Paras believed they had been under fire but the Saville Report, published thirty-eight years later, stated all casualties had been unarmed. Coroner Major (retd) Hubert O'Neill described it as 'sheer, unadulterated murder'. The 'Troubles' continued with bombings, assassinations and ambushes, none worse than on another shocking day in August 1979 when the IRA would gain revenge on the Paras at Warrenpoint.

31 January 1874
Anglo-Ashanti Wars
Battle of Amoafo

THE PORTUGUESE HAD led the late medieval world in oceanic voyaging but their feats had been followed upon by several western European nations including the Dutch Republic and Great Britain. Having discovered a source of the valuable gold, ivory and slave trades at Elmina (Ghana) in the Gulf of Guinea in 1471 the Portuguese traded with the local tribes of the Gold Coast for the next 166 years before losing Elmina to the Dutch, the now dominant western European sea power who were handed the remaining Portuguese Forts for good measure. The Dutch traded alongside their fellow Europeans, first paying tribute to the Denkyira but then to the more powerful Ashanti who in 1807 moved against the British-backed Fante to protect their access to the sea. At virtually the same time both the British and the Dutch banned slave trading, a valuable Ashanti commerce, but the trade continued until 1821 when the British Government relieved the African Company of Merchants of direct control of the British Gold Coast. The move led to the British Gold Coast becoming a protectorate, the near extinction of the slave trade and the First Anglo-Ashanti War in which the angry Ashanti were defeated by Edward Purdon at Dodowa.

The Dutch and British then began buying out the interests of the other before exchanging forts, the Dutch owning those west of Elmina, the British those east. The Dutch, however, found the Fante so difficult that they sold out to Britain in 1872 leaving the Ashanti landlocked by virtue of their continued poor relationship with the British. Again 12,000 unhappy Ashanti invaded the new, enlarged, British Gold Coast with a British led Fante force holding Elmina only with Royal Navy assistance until the arrival of Sir Garnet Wolseley, a veteran of the Crimea and the Indian Mutiny. Although the Ashanti were now in retreat, Wolseley resolved to lead a punitive expedition of 2,500 British and West Indians, 1,000 Fante and 3,000 porters into the West African bush intent on capturing the Ashanti capital Kumasi and its ruler, the Asantehene, Kofi Karakari.

On 19 January 1874 Wolseley crossed the River Pra to trek through mountain forests and burnt villages, the jungle paths littered with skeletons and evidence of human sacrifice (the Ashanti were nevertheless a highly developed society). At Fomena, regretting previous actions, Karakari asked to negotiate but Wolseley's demands were deliberately outrageous and the British advance continued. His pleas for peace exhausted, Karakari looked to surprise Wolseley but Ashanti command was racked with dissent, the King of Dwaben furiously leading away half the 20,000 warriors when Asamoa Nkwanta and Karakari himself insisted on a traditional front and flank attack rather than an overwhelming full frontal.

When British scouts under Edric, Lord Gifford were attacked, Wolseley formed his column into a 400 yard wide by two mile long infantry square which continued early the following day, 31 January 1874. Advancing into a wooded ravine outside Amoafo, the Black Watch, complete with bagpipes, were struck by a terrific musket volley fired from the bush. Highlanders then joined their compatriots, moving across the ravine firing at five times the rate of the Ashanti with accurate Snider-Enfield breech loading rifles. More British engaged before British Hausa artillery advanced to fire at the still invisible enemy before the Black Watch launched a bayonet charge. The Ashanti reeled back to a ridge where they again suffered from the Hausa artillery and more Black Watch & Highlander bayonet charges. Ashanti counter-attacks then began to strike the British flanks, Wolseley maintaining the advance to take Amoafo but still subjected to attack. After six hours of fierce fighting the battle paused but the Ashanti were now moving to attack the five mile long supply column in the British rear. West Indians and Fante held this attack with help from the Rifle Brigade. With heavy casualties Karakari retreated beyond Kumasi.

Greeted by the stench of mass executions and more human sacrifice, Wolseley burnt Kumasi before retreating to avoid the heavy rains, Karakari suddenly agreeing to his terms. Britain formally annexed Ashanti in 1896 with the British Gold Coast becoming Ghana in 1957. Reporting on Wolseley's expedition was the explorer Henry Stanley, he would shortly set out to discover Lake Victoria as the source of the River Nile.

February

"We could stay here forever."

MAJOR GENERAL GEORGE POMEROY COLLEY,
MAJUBA HILL, 1881

1 February 1781

American War of Independence Battle of McCowan's Ford

 THE INITIALLY PROMISING 1777 British offensives into New York State, New Jersey and the Hudson Valley had eventually met with disaster after serious failures of command in both London and on the spot in North America. Commander-in-Chief North America General William Howe had been replaced by General Henry Clinton but British prospects at preventing American independence received a further blow when France (and Spain) seized the opportunity to avenge their own North American losses suffered during the French and Indian War just two decades previous. In Europe, British-held Gibraltar was soon in the midst of a three-and-a-half year Spanish siege and the British island of Jersey was subjected to two, albeit half-hearted French invasions. The ideology of a liberated, self governing people was a developing philosophy in a France dominated throughout the eighteenth century by an absolutist monarchy but their successes gained freeing North America from British rule would, by the end of the decade, contribute to the downfall of their own King Louis XVI.

Though British prospects in North America now looked bleak both King George III and his Secretary of State for the Colonies, George Germain, Lord Sackville desired a more vigorous prosecution of the war. By 1780 Clinton had little option but to repeat Howe's left hook of 1777 this time further south into Georgia and South Carolina, specifically the port of Charleston. Having taken the wooden town by siege and the firing of red hot shot, 6,000 American Patriots surrendered allowing a considerably wealthier Clinton to return to New York whilst Lieutenant General Charles, Lord Cornwallis gained mastery of the huge mosquito and snake infested hinterland of South Carolina over the stifling summer. Having added local loyalists to the regulars for a drive into North Carolina, the 5,000 strong sickness and disease struck British Army then successfully drew American Major General Horatio Gates south to comprehensively defeat him at Camden.

The disgraced Gates was replaced by Major General Nathanael Greene whose ruthless discipline restored the remnants of the Southern Continental Army whilst Cornwallis continued to struggle with losses of his own at the end of a 100-mile-long supply line that was harassed constantly by Patriot partisans under Brigadier Generals Thomas 'the Carolina Gamecock' Sumpter and Francis 'the Swamp Fox' Marion. Only the ingenuity of Lieutenant Colonel Nisbet Balfour, Commandant of Charleston, kept the British Army in the field at all. Cornwallis knew he must advance to the promised better climate of North Carolina or his army would suffer further, perhaps catastrophically. The initial British advance, however, soon met with disaster in October 1780 when 1,000 loyalist militia under Major Patrick Ferguson were annihilated at King's Mountain. Cornwallis then retired back to Camden for the winter before additional reinforcements and supplies warranted another advance in January 1781 in which cavalry commander Colonel Banastre Tarleton was immediately defeated at Cowpens. Cornwallis and the bruised Tarleton pressed on, increasing their speed by marching as light infantry and limiting numbers of black servants but with partisans and now Greene's militia's eroding their strength every step of the way to the River Catawba where they intended to force a crossing at McCowan's Ford (now Cowan's).

As the rain fell at 01.00 on 1 February 1781, Cornwallis sent Lieutenant Colonel James Webster to make a show at Beattie's Ford whilst six miles downstream at McCowan's Ford he began an artillery bombardment of Patriot positions held by 300 North Carolina Militia under Brigadier General William Lee Davidson. At daybreak British Guards then entered the water for the half-mile crossing against water soon waist high, many men behind hanging on to gun carriages for dear life whilst keeping their cartridges above the water line. Well within range Davidson's militia opened fire, raking Redcoats who struggled through to shallow water before returning fire. When they did Davidson was soon dead, shot from his horse as the Guards, Grenadiers and Royal Welch, stormed ashore to clear the far bank with a bayonet charge.

Greene had been at McCowan's Ford only a day before but he would now attempt to draw Cornwallis further north to the border of Virginia, extending British supply lines beyond breaking point. Cornwallis was no fool, Greene would have to turn back south for the decisive battle of the campaign at Guildford Court House.

2 February 1461

Wars of the Roses
Battle of Mortimer's Cross

THE WEAK RULE of England's King Henry VI had led to a peasants revolt in 1450 before rioting mercers protesting at foreign competition besieged the Tower of London in 1456. Dissatisfaction at losses in France at the end of the Hundred Years' War added to general acrimony creating a state of near chaos in which a feud between Richard Plantagenet, Duke of York and Edmund Beaufort, Duke of Somerset had erupted in violence at St Albans in 1455. Both men had been seeking favour at each other's expense from a king prone to bouts of insanity but within five years both were dead, Somerset at St Albans and more recently York at Wakefield, the latter's head now on display at Micklegate Bar, the western gate of the town of York. York had always sworn allegiance to his king but after Henry's 1460 defeat at Northampton and subsequent imprisonment he had returned from exile to unnerve even his own support by claiming the throne of England for himself. York's subsequent death at Wakefield five months later had therefore been sweet revenge for Henry's French Queen Margaret of Anjou, who now rode south at the head of a Lancastrian Army of rampaging Northerners. Londoners who just months earlier had been more than happy at the prospect of Yorkist rule trembled with fear.

Richard Neville, Earl of Warwick had been left to defend London when York and Richard Neville (father), Earl of Salisbury had gone north to their deaths at Wakefield whilst York's son, Edward, Earl of March had also departed, marching west to resist Lancastrian forces developing in Wales. On hearing of his father's defeat and death, March anticipated Margaret's advance on London and decided on a return to reinforce Warwick but news then arrived that Sir Owen Tudor, married to King Henry V's widow Catherine of Valois (mother of King Henry VI), their son Jasper Tudor, Earl of Pembroke (half brother to the king) and James Butler, Earl of Wiltshire had landed in Wales with a French and Irish Army and were now recruiting Welshmen to the Lancastrian cause. March would have to make an about turn and defeat the Tudors and Wiltshire in quick time if he was to assist Warwick in London. The only good news for March was that his loyal servant and old friend William Hastings, Squire of Burton Hastings, a grandson of Thomas, Lord Camoys who had commanded Henry V's left at Agincourt and a son of Leonard Hastings who had also fought at Agincourt was about to join him at Shrewsbury. A fine soldier in his own right, Hastings arrived with every man he could muster bringing Yorkist strength up to possibly 5,000 (accounts of the battle are almost non-existent), slightly more than the Lancastrians.

The two armies met at Mortimer's Cross by the River Lugg near Hereford on 2 February 1461 but before battle commenced three suns were seen rising in the sky (the phenomenon of Parhelion) terrifying the Yorkists (it was important to have God on your side in a medieval battle with anything unusual likely to be considered a bad omen). However, once March had assured his superstitious men that it was in fact a clear sign that God was on their side the Yorkists blocked the Lancastrian advance across the Lugg. Pembroke and Wiltshire approached in column but likely deployed across the front before, at around midday, Wiltshire engaged the Yorkist right which retreated. Meanwhile, Pembroke attacked the Yorkist centre which held before Owen Tudor attempted to outflank the Yorkist left only to be decisively defeated. After routing Tudor, March's Yorkists on the left then turned on Pembroke's centre causing the whole Lancastrian Army to break. In the manner of the Wars of the Roses the subsequent seventeen-mile pursuit was merciless as Yorkists brutally avenged Wakefield.

Pembroke and Wiltshire escaped but Owen Tudor was captured and taken to Haverford West where he was beheaded with ten others in the market place. Edward, Earl of March had won a great victory but the delay incurred meant he could not now support Warwick who was about to advance up Watling Street to where the wars had started six years previous, St Albans. There he would face Queen Margaret's Northerners alone on Shrove Tuesday 1461.

3 February 1807

Napoleonic Wars
Battle of Montevideo

 AT THE BEGINNING of the Napoleonic Wars the Third Coalition of Austria, Russia and Great Britain had been crushed with frightening efficiency by the Emperor of the French Napoleon Bonaparte, the Austrians at Ulm and the Russians at Austerlitz. In 1805 Austria then signed the Peace of Pressburg, withdrawing from the war whilst the Russians withdrew from Europe. A peace deal now would have retained Napoleon his territorial gains across virtually all western and southern Europe but the British Prime Minister Henry Petty, Lord Lansdowne and his King, George III, the Elector of Hanover could not countenance Napoleon's authority over the German state of Hanover. In consolidating his power across the River Rhine, Napoleon formed a confederation of sixteen German states formally part of the Holy Roman Empire (Austria) but in so doing posed a direct threat to the peace loving King Frederick William III of Prussia. On the advice of his Queen Louisa, Frederick brought Prussia back into the conflict for the first time in over a decade by joining a Fourth Coalition with Russia, Britain and Sweden, confident Prussia could succeed where the more powerful Austria had failed.

Perhaps distracted by Queen Louisa dressed as an amazon, however, the Prussian Army was routed by the French *Grande Armée* at the October 1806 battle of Jena-Auerstadt. While just Russia (and a defensive Sweden) now opposed the all-powerful Napoleon on land, so too did Britain at sea where over the past year Vice Admiral Horatio, Lord Nelson, Rear Admiral Richard Strachan and Vice Admiral Thomas Duckworth had shattered Franco-Spanish fleets at Trafalgar, Ortegal and in the Caribbean respectively. To further secure the sea lanes, especially those to India, British Rear Admiral Home Riggs Popham had also ferried two brigades of infantry under Lieutenant General Sir David Baird to the Cape of Good Hope, South Africa defeating the Franco-Dutch Batavian Republic at Blaauwberg. Now all-powerful at sea, the British looked to extend their Cape success across the South Atlantic to Spanish South America.

Riggs Popham had not the strength for a general invasion but was looking to seize strategic points in an effort to open Spanish markets to British competition. A force of 1,500 men under General William, Lord Beresford transferred from the Cape to take Rio de la Plata (Argentina) and its capital Buenos Aires almost unopposed in June 1806, Beresford fortunate that Viceroy Rafael de Sobremento had refused to arm the local Creoles and had sent his main force across the River Plate to Montevideo (Uruguay). Beresford's occupation, however, was highly unpopular, lasting just forty-six days before suffering defeat in a street fight to 1,200 men under Santiago de Liniers. While Beresford now languished in a Buenos Aires jail the British planned another expedition, this time with 6,000 men under Brigadier General Sir Samuel Auchmuty and a Royal Navy squadron under Rear Admiral Charles Stirling.

Initially landing at Maldonado, Auchmuty reembarked under the noses of threatening Gauchos to sail nine miles west of Montevideo, defeating a force of 6,000 Spanish militia at El Cristo del Cardal on 20 January 1807. Auchmuty then fruitlessly demanded Governor Ruiz Huidobro surrender the well-defended Montevideo before a British four gun battery began pounding the city walls. Auchmuty's position was nevertheless now becoming increasingly dangerous since De Liniers and a 2,500 strong relief force had set out from Buenos Aires to relieve Huidobro. Desperate for success before De Liniers' arrival, Auchmuty assaulted Montevideo at 03.00 on 3 February 1807 through the smallest of breaches between the citadel and the south gate forced by a forlorn hope under Lieutenant Harry Smith (later of Aliwal, India 1849 fame). Several British infantry regiments and dragoons followed for a fight against spirited resistance within the town whilst the 95th Regiment of Foot scaled the north wall adjacent to the San Pedro Gate for a push toward the citadel, the Ciudadela. His city overrun, Huidobro surrendered at 05.00, Auchmuty having lost 600 men in the attack.

Lieutenant General John Whitelocke then attempted to retake Buenos Aires that July but was so decisively defeated by De Liniers that he lost Montevideo in the process and was cashiered. In 1810, while the mother country Spain was occupied by France, patriotism in Buenos Aires stirred by the British invasion and fanned by Manuel Belgrano led to the May Revolution, bringing independence from Spanish rule to much of South America.

4 February 1884

Mahdist Wars
First Battle of El Teb

GREAT BRITAIN BECAME involved in Egyptian financial affairs in 1879 when Ismael 'the Magnificent' Pasha, Khedive of Egypt on behalf of the Ottoman Sultans in Constantinople (Istanbul) (Abdulazziz I and Murad V) was no longer able to pay the interest accrued on the vast debts he had incurred in the development of his country. The 1869 opening of the Suez Canal had not only increased Ismael's debts but had also increased foreign political interest in Egypt especially in Britain since shipping to British India no longer needed to sail via the Cape of Good Hope. Whilst financial interests had forced the intervention of the more imperialist British Prime Minister Benjamin Disraeli (whose entire life in government and opposition had been spent with the shadow of Russian expansion threatening British global interests) it was left to his anti-imperialist successor, William Gladstone, to secure Egypt by force.

Gladstone sanctioned an 1882 military expedition to Egypt under General Garnet Wolseley which successfully crushed a nationalist Egyptian military uprising to bring Egypt and by extension the Sudan under British suzerainty. It was quite enough for Gladstone, he had no further interest in bringing to heel the vast deserts of the Sudan where an Islamic uprising was developing under Muhammad Ahmad, the self-proclaimed Mahdi (the guided one), but he was very much interested in maintaining the security of Egypt and the Red Sea. The Mahdi's cause, however, was not to be confined to the Sudan, already spreading the word throughout the Middle East he aimed for nothing less than the creation of an Islamic State to replace the vast but decaying Ottoman Empire. To that end his dramatically increasing following, the *Ansar* (dervishes), had also crushed an Egyptian Army, this one under British Colonel William Hicks at El Obeid in November 1883 leaving the whole of the Sudan likely to fall under Mahdist control. Under pressure from the British press and public, Gladstone appointed the unquestionably brave Major General Charles 'Chinese' Gordon, a veteran of the Crimean War, the

Taiping Rebellion and a former Governor General of the Sudan in the employ of the Ottomans but a man who had already publicly advocated standing against the Mahdi rather than performing the evacuation of Egyptian and loyal Sudanese garrisons so desired by his government. As Gordon journeyed to Khartoum, orders were issued from Cairo for south Sudanese garrisons to fall back to Khartoum leaving the Mahdi in control of western, central and southern Sudan whilst in the east the Mahdist Hadendoa tribesman of Sheikh Osman Digna besieged the inland garrisons at Sinkat and Tokar.

Later nicknamed Fuzzy Wuzzys by British soldiers, the Hadendoa were initially defeated in August 1883 at Sinkat, Digna seriously wounded, before again returning to besiege and isolate both Sinkat and Tokar. With 20–30,000 men at his disposal, Digna could also now contemplate attacks on the Red Sea port towns of Trinkitat and Suakin, a move preempted by the British authorities in Cairo who sent an army frighteningly similar in quality to that commanded by Hicks at El Obeid, 3,500 Egyptians under another long time Ottoman servant Valentine Baker, head of the Egyptian Police. Indeed most of the Egyptians were gendarmes themselves who had signed up for civil service in Egypt but who, after spending a night on the beach at Trinkitat, now found themselves on 4 February 1884 marching inland through the Sudanese desert toward Tokar looking for a fight with thousands of fearsome Hadendoa. They did not have to wait long, Baker halting the disorderly column at El Teb where it was suddenly attacked by 1,000 tribesmen, both mounted and on foot. After firing a single volley at the oncoming charge, Baker gave the order to form square, a risky tactic for unpractised soldiers who lacked the discipline of regular British troops. As the Hadendoa charged, the rear of Baker's square was still forming and was duly broken with disastrous consequences when the gunfire turned inward. Eventually nearly three-quarters of the Egyptian gendarmes would be ruthlessly slaughtered.

Baker, who narrowly avoided a Court Martial, and his officers fought their way back to Trinkitat. They would return to El Teb with British troops returning from India later that month. The bravery of the Hadendoa is commemorated in the Rudyard Kipling poem, *Fuzzy Wuzzy*.

5 February 1900

Second Boer War
Battle of Vaal Krantz

THE SECOND BOER War had dragged on for four painful months during which even the early British victories of November had ended in retreats. Mafeking, Kimberley and Ladysmith were still besieged as all British attempts to force Boer defences in central South Africa (North Cape Colony and the Orange Free State) and Natal had ended with heavy casualties, outright defeat or the mobile Boer commandos escaping to fight another day. Faith in General Sir Redvers Buller, who had left Southampton just months before to the tune of *For He's a Jolly Good Fellow*, had dropped so low in Britain that he was replaced as Commander-in-Chief in South Africa by Field Marshal Lord Frederick Roberts who was now about to move up from Cape Town to the Modder River, reinforce General Lord Paul Methuen and resume the British advance on Kimberley. Further east Buller had been retained as Commander-in-Chief of the Natal Field Force but his latest attempt at finding a key to unlock the door through the Drakensberg Mountains and Ladysmith had ended in abject disaster on 24 January at Spion Kop. That nadir of the whole campaign, with accompanying heavy losses, had not been without enlightenment when Lieutenant Colonel Robert Riddell successfully led two infantry battalions up the neighbouring Twin Peaks to force a general retreat of Boer forces in and around the Kop. That no one blamed the man on the spot, on the plateau of Spion Kop, Brigadier General Alec Thorneycroft for his own ill-timed retreat said much for his own performance that day but the same could not be said for his immediate superior Lieutenant General Sir Charles Warren or indeed Colonel Charles Long at Colenso or indeed Lieutenant General Sir George White at Ladysmith for creating the whole mess in the first place. Buller, now nicknamed 'Reverse Buller' by his men, did not rebuke his officers in public however, rather only in letters home to his wife. After retreating back across the Tugela River to Spearman's Camp he assured his war-weary troops that they had provided him with the key to victory, the one day set piece battle now replaced by an extended battle both in geography and timescale based on the Boer principles of fire and movement. If then Buller had found the key, he needed to find a door.

On 5 February 1900 the Natal Field Force began the search by again crossing the Tugela at Potgieters Drift where Major General Arthur Wynne's Lancashires, under cover of both field and naval artillery, made a feint attack on Boer defences at Brakfontein. A mile to the right at Munger's Drift the 4th Infantry Brigade under Major General Neville Lyttelton also crossed the river but deliberately slowly for the 'main effort' on Vaal Krantz (kopje). That Boer Generals Louis Botha and Benjamin Viljoen were therefore well aware of an impending attack meant both Brakfontein and Vaal Krantz were fully manned when the British artillery bombardment began. Boer artillery replied as Lyttelton moved forward to further pin down the enemy whilst behind him the 2nd Infantry Brigade under Major General Henry Hildyard moved right to assault Green Hill on the Boer left flank. This flank attack was designed to allow the Irish Brigade with supporting cavalry to move up between Lyttelton and Hildyard for a push down the valley to Ladysmith but critically Buller lost his nerve and held them back, Lyttelton asking for reinforcements to press the attack rather than obeying orders to retreat. The following day Buller sent Hildyard's brigade to relieve Lyttelton, both British and Boer counter-attacking in turn with rifle and bayonet as the artillery duel raged on. By the morning of 7 February, however, Buller had had enough, he simply did not have the room at Vaal Krantz in which to outflank the Boer defences and with over 300 casualties yet again retreated back across the Tugela earning himself another nickname 'the Ferryman of the Tugela'.

Whilst many at home had now also lost faith in Buller as Commander of the Natal Field Force, Roberts had not and nor had his men. Indeed they were more anxious than ever to finish the campaign. Buller, however, still had to find a door, he would look again, this time further north beyond Colenso at Hlangwane and the Tugela Heights where Boer defences were temptingly extended.

6 February 1806

Napoleonic Wars
Battle of Santo Domingo

NAPOLEON BONAPARTE, EMPEROR of the First French Empire had planned for the invasion of the United Kingdom of Great Britain and Ireland both during and after an interlude in hostilities created by the 1802 Treaty of Amiens. By 1805, however, his immediate plans were in some disarray – dashed by the formation of the Third Coalition by Britain, Russia and Austria. Out of necessity the Corsican General had marched his *Armée d'Angleterre* in the opposite direction to its intended destination from Boulogne to Ulm where he destroyed the entire Austrian Army of Karl Freiherr Mack von Leiberich before marching to Austerlitz to deal likewise with a mainly Russian Army under Tsar Alexander I and Michail Kutusov. Austria withdrew from the Third Coalition despite the Russians not yet having brought their full force to bear but whilst Napoleon felt more secure within his huge European empire, now stretching from the Low Countries through West Germany, Switzerland and soon Italy, any further expansion west to the British Isles was comprehensively dashed in October 1805 when Vice Admiral Horatio, Lord Nelson and the Royal Navy shattered a combined French and Spanish fleet at Trafalgar. Whilst Britons celebrated Trafalgar and mourned Nelson, First Lord of the Admiralty Charles Middleton, Lord Barham took the opportunity to save a few crowns by lifting the British blockade of the French coast mistakenly believing that what was left of the French fleet would not be able to embark on any winter operations.

On 13 December 1805 eleven French ships of the line, four frigates, two brigs and a corvette of the Brest Fleet under Vice Admiral Corentin-Urbain Leissègues that had not been involved at Trafalgar sailed out into the Atlantic completely unmolested. When Barham became aware of his error eleven days later two Royal Navy squadrons, thirteen ships of the line, were ordered to sea under Vice Admiral Sir John Borlase Warren and Rear Admiral Richard Strachan to search the mid Atlantic for the French who were already attacking British convoys. The French had, however, split into two squadrons themselves, one under Rear Admiral Jean

Baptiste Willaumez bound for the South Atlantic whilst the other under Leissègues sailed for the Caribbean with reinforcements for Santo Domingo, Hispaniola (Haiti, Dominican Republic). Strachan sailed after Willaumez while Warren sailed after Leissègues joining Rear Admiral Alexander Cochrane, Commander of the Leeward Islands Station at St Kitts. In the meantime, Vice Admiral Sir Thomas Duckworth, Commander of the Jamaica Station blockading Cadiz, abandoned his post to search for a French squadron off Madeira only to become involved in Strachan's pursuit of Willaumez before also putting in at St Kitts.

Both Duckworth and Cochrane were resupplying in St Kitts when HMS *Kingfisher* captained by Cochrane's nephew, Nathaniel Day Cochrane, reported that Leissègues was at Santo Domingo. Both Cochrane and Duckworth departed with seven ships of the line, two brigs and two frigates, arriving early on 6 February 1806 with Leissègues instantly in disarray. Duckworth aboard the 74-gun HMS *Superb* closed as Leissègues hurried his eight ships out to sea, battle commencing after a four hour chase when *Superb* fired on Alexandre and Cochrane's 74-gun flagship HMS *Northumberland* fired on Leissègues' 120-gun *Impérial*, Cochrane losing his hat but not his head to a returning cannonball. As the British ships behind caught up *Alexandre* was wrecked by successive broadsides before a general mêlée raged around *Impérial*. The superiority of the British gunnery was again brought to bear, the French *Brave* and *Jupiter* surrendering as several ships collided in the thick smoke of battle, masts crashing across decks. In the confusion *Impérial* and *Diomede* disengaged to make a run for shore rather than surrender, Leissègues crashing both onto the reefs a mile out. Both ships were badly holed but to prevent further French use they were boarded and burnt by Duckworth once most of their crews had been lifted off.

Duckworth received no award but escaped a Court Martial for deserting Cadiz. Willaumez returned north to the Caribbean before a hurricane forced him into American harbours. Santo Domingo was the last fleet engagement of the Napoleonic Wars, the British would henceforth fight on land.

7 February 1857
Anglo-Persian War
Battle of Khushab

 MAJOR GENERAL ARTHUR Wellesley's (future Duke of Wellington) 1803 defeat of the Maratha Army at Assaye had left the whole of India south of the River Sutlej under the influence of the British East India Company. The wealth created by India's huge resources and markets did not go unnoticed in Revolutionary France but Napoleon Bonaparte's efforts to destabilise British India had been thwarted by his own failings in the Middle East and by Tsar Alexander I reversing Russian policy to join a Third Coalition against France. Alexander was also at war with Persia (Iran) over territories in the Caucasus to which he would commit greater Russian resources once Napoleon had met final defeat – Persia lost out heavily at the 1813 Treaty of Gulistan. In 1826, Persian attempts to win back territory then badly backfired leading to a 'Great Game' of imperial ambition between Russia and Great Britain, the British anxious to maintain buffer states around India whilst the Russians wanted to prevent any further British expansion in South Asia. In 1838 a nervous Britain invaded Afghanistan concerned at both Persian and Afghan neutrality fueled by Persia's unsuccessful attack on the western Afghan city of Herat. Though a disaster, the British did then increase their influence up to the eastern Afghan border in 1849, a Sikh power vacuum following the death of Maharaja Ranjit Singh giving Governor General of India, Henry Hardinge, the opportunity to occupy the Punjab. As British India expanded, the Russian threat came physically and psychologically closer, both Britain and France also fighting a war in the Crimean Peninsular (1853–56) to prevent Russian expansion into the Mediterranean. When Persia's Shah Nasser-e-Din, a perceived Russian ally, then bettered his father by capturing Herat in 1856, adding to an incident concerning the British Ambassador and the Shah's sister-in-law, the now Governor General of India, Charles, Lord Canning declared war on Persia.

Perhaps scarred by history in Afghanistan and conscious of previous success by naval threat, 5,700 men of the British East India Company's Bombay Army under

Major General Foster Stalker looked to liberate Herat by sailing for the Persian Gulf. Two months after successfully capturing the port city of Bushehr, Stalker was reinforced by Lieutenant General James Outram who was now able to both secure the port and advance 4,600 men inland for a confrontation with the main Persian Army under Khanlar Mirza at Shiraz. After a halt at Khushab, Outram continued the advance in appalling weather but, unwilling to be drawn into the mountains by the Persians, then retreated back to Khushab. On 7 February 1857, Mirza and 8,000 Persians then suddenly appeared outside the British camp which formed square to fend off attacks throughout the night. As dawn broke the following day the Persians retired before drawing up for battle, Outram's infantry doing likewise while four troopers of the 3rd Bombay Light Cavalry under Brigadier John Jacob scouted the Persian lines seemingly oblivious to the many muskets aimed in their direction. Once Jacob had rejoined his colleagues the Bombay Lights advanced with the Poona Irregular Horse in close order to ride down Persian skirmishers but in so doing came under ineffective Persian artillery fire and musket volleys from the 1st Kushkai Regiment of Fars, the Shah's Guard, firing from a 500-strong infantry square. Captain John Forbes leading the Bombays then gave the order to draw swords before charging, Forbes receiving a ball in the thigh, Lieutenant Arthur Moore jumping the hedge of Kushkai bayonets and his brother, Captain Ross Moore, charging straight into them, both their horses instantly killed. Lieutenant John Malcolmson rode in to rescue Arthur whilst the huge Ross cut his own way out as the remainder of the Bombays flooded into the square to wreak havoc, exacting a terrible slaughter on the Kushkais who suffered almost complete annihilation. At the defeat of their finest the rest of the Persian Army fled before Outram could bring his infantry into action.

The charge of the Bombays is perhaps the only occasion when a predominantly native cavalry has defeated an infantry square, Malcolmson and Arthur Moore both awarded the Victoria Cross. Shortly after, Shah Nasser-e-Din signed the Treaty of Paris and withdrew from Herat. It would be not a moment too soon, Outram and his subordinate Henry Havelock were both required to quell an Indian uprising that had come sixty years too late for Napoleon.

8 February 1881
First Boer War
Battle of Ingogo

BRITISH FEARS OF a potential future German annexation of the Dutch-speaking mineral-rich Boer Republics of the Transvaal and the Orange Free State had led to an 1877 British annexation of the former with the latter likely to follow, the previously fiercely independent Boers reluctantly accepting in exchange for military protection against their historical foes, the Pedi and particularly the Zulu. Two years later, however, the Boers were already complaining that British rule had brought little, so that when the British defeated the Zulu, ironically removing a pillar of logic behind the annexation, Boer sentiment for a regaining of their independence surged. Though the new anti-imperialist British Prime Minister William Gladstone sympathised with Boer aims he could not, however, advise Queen Victoria to forego her suzerainty, the Boers therefore only able to achieve independence by force of arms once their delegations had failed. British complacency and the consequent delay in reinforcing their Transvaal garrisons then meant that just a two-company-strong relief column was en route from Natal to Pretoria in December 1880, the First Boer War ignited when this column was intercepted at Bronkhorstspruit on the Highveld, east of its destination. The news soon reached London by cable where Gladstone's attention was on troubles in Ireland and Afghanistan but as the British Isles were gripped by one of the coldest winters of all time, temperatures on the Highveld continued to rise as the Boer rebellion spread, thousands of Free Staters now rallying to the cause of their Transvaal cousins.

In Durban High Commissioner of South Eastern Africa Major General George Pomeroy Colley acted without waiting for the single infantry regiment he had requested as reinforcement. Marching north-west to Newcastle with just 1,200 men of the 58th Regiment of Foot and the 60th Rifles he prepared to advance through the Drakensberg Mountains by forcing the pass at Laing's Nek defended by double that number of Boers under Commandant General Piet Joubert. On the morning of 28 January 1881 Colley began the assault of Laing's Nek with an artillery barrage before his infantry advanced carrying the regiment's and the Queen's Colours into battle for the last ever time. Entrenched Boers put down heavy rifle fire before counter-attacking, effectively finishing the contest before lunch when Colley retreated to Mount Prospect with 200 casualties, his only success saving the Colours.

Boers now harassed British communications between Mount Prospect and Newcastle so that Colley, again failing to wait for the 92nd Highlanders that were now off Durban, resolved to clear the road through Schuinshoogte on the Ingogo Heights. On 8 February 1881 two companies of the 60th Rifles, thirty-eight cavalry and two guns left Mount Prospect, the guns remaining on the banks of the Ingogo River while Colley and his infantry advanced up the Heights to the crest of the ridge where they took up a defensive position against 300 mounted Boers under General Nicolaas Smit. The battle started in earnest at noon and soon became a shooting competition in which the British were at a serious disadvantage, the Boers wearing highly-camouflaged clothing were adept at using ground cover after years of hunting on the Highveld and also possessed the latest in rifle technology, some even Winchester repeaters, expert marksmen virtually to a man. The British on the other hand were wearing red or dark green uniforms with white pith helmets, some stained with tea but though possessing up-to-date weaponry were short of shooting practice having until very recently relied on concentrated volley fire. The gun battle continued with the Boers in the ascendancy until 17.00 when in the character of today's contests between the two sides, rain stopped play. So heavy was the deluge that the River Ingogo was now believed impassable, the Boers merely waiting for play to resume the next day in the belief that Colley was hopelessly trapped. The British position was indeed desperate, desperate enough for Colley to call in the 58th Foot to cover a river crossing in which several men drowned but what remained of the 60th Rifles was saved, half of them casualties.

Colley's agonies would seemingly soon be over since Gladstone was about to upset Queen Victoria by conceding to the demands of Transvaal President Paul Kruger. Colley was, however, in no mood to concede defeat, he would seek redemption by turning the Boer flank at Majuba Hill.

9 February 1586

Anglo-Spanish Wars
Battle of Cartagena

QUEEN OF ENGLAND Elizabeth I owed her very existence to the Protestant faith and the refusal of Pope Clement VII to grant her father, King Henry VIII, a divorce from Catherine of Aragon. Smitten with Elizabeth's mother Anne Boleyn, Henry had embraced the Protestant faith by the 1534 Act of Supremacy which saw the English monarch and not the Pope become the Supreme Head of the Church of England. The disinherited Catholic daughter of Henry's marriage to Catherine nevertheless became Queen Mary I of England in 1553 earning the sobriquet 'Bloody Mary' as she brutally attempted to restore Catholicism but on her death in 1558 a lack of issue with her Habsburg husband, King Philip II of Spain, left the English throne in the hands of her Protestant half-sister, Elizabeth. The new queen not only restored Protestantism but declined the disinherited (of the English throne but not the Spanish) Catholic Philip's hand in marriage who then mirrored the ways of his former wife by suppressing Protestant uprisings in the Spanish ruled Seventeen Provinces of the Netherlands.

Elizabeth's support for the Dutch vacillated, unwilling to risk outright war with Philip's Spain and the enormous Habsburg Empire, she did, however, at the very least turn a blind eye and at the most, anonymously sponsor piratical raids on Spanish possessions conducted by her foremost Sea Captain Sir Francis Drake, a man whose entire life was bent on bitter revenge for Spanish treachery at San Juan de Ulua, Mexico in 1568. Relations with Spain deteriorated, so that by 1585 Drake's raids were spearheading a more concerted effort to damage Spain prior to an inevitable war with England. Having recently ravaged Santiago, Cape Verde and Santo Domingo, Hispaniola (Haiti, Dominican Republic) the feared sea dog now aimed for a bigger prize, the principal city on the Spanish Main, Cartagena, Colombia.

Drake believed Cartagena to be well-defended and indeed the informed Governor Don Pedro Fernandez de Busto was already moving non combatants and valuables out of the town as well as improve the previously neglected defences and weaponry. De Busto, however, had no idea where Drake's attack might fall and had to guard against possible landings east of Cartagena, the town itself and the harbours a mile to the west. At the harbours a Spanish force was drawn up in two galleys, 2,000 men in the *Santiago* and the *Ocasion*, both moored in the inner harbour protected from the outer harbour by a chain across the Boqueron Channel whilst another 1,000 men with additional civilian militia were behind onshore defences.

While De Busto watched on from the beach, Drake, his thirty ships and 2,300 sailor/soldiers boldly sailed past the town making for the outer harbour where only a well-defended Fort at the Boqueron Channel was of any concern. In the dead of night, 9 February 1586, Christopher Carleill landed with 1,000 men to attack the Caleta, a narrow neck of land between the harbours and the town. Drake covered Carleill's advance by cannonading the harbour defences with De Busto's artillery replying from the galleys and from behind an old wall on the Caleta just as soon as Carleill's threat had been realised. After a solitary volley from the Spanish arquebuses, Carleill charged the Caleta wall through a gap on the seaward side to engage with sword and pike, the fighting short lived before De Busto and his men made a run for the town whilst his more resolute military advisor, Captain Alonso Bravo, was wounded and taken prisoner. As both sides ran into the town the English were hit by poison arrows from natives but nevertheless quickly overwhelmed the disorganised defenders. Back at the harbours, meanwhile, the chain across the Boqueron now served to trap the Spanish galleys, the crew of the *Santiago* fleeing after grounding their ship in an attempt to support the town whilst the *Ocasion* tried to make a run for the open sea. To reach the open sea, however, the Ocasion needed the key to the chain across the Boqueron Channel which was in the *Santiago*, the panicking crew on the verge of mutiny when a gunpowder barrel exploded causing the majority of the Spanish casualties.

Drake took the Boqueron Fort two days later and held the city to ransom. After burning 248 houses a sum of 107,000 ducats was agreed with more to come from private land and ship owners. On 27 April Drake left Cartagena just two days before the arrival of a revenge-seeking Spanish fleet. He headed for Roanoke Colony before returning to England with possibly the first ever cargo of tobacco and potatoes. A furious Philip sent engineers to fortify the Caribbean, an effort that would detract from his immediate ambition to overrun England.

10 February 1846

Sikh Wars
Battle of Sobraon

THE KHALSA, THE powerful army of the Sikh Empire, had been been defeated by the British East India Company's Bengal Army in all three major engagements of the First Anglo-Sikh War, Mudki, Ferozeshah and Aliwal. The performance of the Khalsa's two Sirdars Tej and Lal Singh had been so bad that accusations of treachery have abounded ever since but the regular Sikh troops had without doubt fought with resolute determination in the defence of their homeland, the Punjab. At Ferozeshah and Aliwal in particular both sides had taken heavy casualties, the former leaving the British unable to pursue, whilst the latter had left the Khalsa with just a bridgehead on the south bank of the River Sutlej at Sobraon as the only Sikh foothold on British Indian soil, this tenuously connected to the Punjabi north bank by just a makeshift pontoon bridge.

Commanded again by Tej Singh, the Sikh bridgehead was defended by 20,000 men and sixty-five guns; as at Aliwal arching with a perimeter of 4,000 yards with both its flanks on the Sutlej. Lal Singh additionally commanded the Sikh cavalry further east, up river with further reserves held back across the river. British Commander-in-Chief Sir Hugh Gough was anxious to attack as soon as Lieutenant General Sir Harry Smith, the 58-year-old architect of victory at Aliwal joined him but Governor General of India Sir Henry Hardinge urged Gough to delay further for the arrival of a large supply train from Delhi, replenishing ammunition and morale. During the delay, Sikh morale suffered at the gruesome sight of their dead comrades from Aliwal floating downstream but was bolstered by the arrival of the talismanic Sham Singh Attariwala.

At daybreak on 10 February 1846 Gough's British Bengal Army moved forward toward Sobraon but could not open proceedings due to a heavy mist shrouding the battlefield. The mist concealed the British approach but when it lifted the 20,000 Redcoats became clearly visible and were immediately fired upon by the well-drilled Sikh gunners. Gough's guns and howitzers returned fire but had little effect against the well constructed fortified Sikh positions and soon began running short of ammunition. Gough was not unhappy as this meant his favoured *modus operandi* of an assault with musket and bayonet would now be required though he had already run foul of Hardinge over these tactics at both Mudki and Ferozeshah. With little choice, however, he duly ordered the 7th and 8th Infantry Brigades under Major General Robert Dick supported by the Bengal Horse Artillery to attack the Sikh right. The Sikh gunners resisted strongly with Gough then ordering Smith's and Major General Sir Walter Raleigh Gilbert's infantry divisions to attack the Sikh left where a fierce hand-to-hand fight developed – bayonet against sword. Fighting all along the perimeter soon raged with Gurkhas, Bengalis and British gradually gaining footholds amongst the Sikh positions. Sappers then blew a breach in the entrenchments allowing the British cavalry under Lieutenant General Joseph Thackwell to ride into the centre of the Sikh position, rallying the British Indian infantry before charging the Sikh guns in the face of short range grapeshot. As they had before, the Sikhs fought doggedly on but slowly began to give way under pressure from the three-sided British assault. Disastrously, the pontoon bridge then gave way (allegedly through more of Tej Singh's treachery) trapping those Sikhs still on the south bank, many trying to swim to the north bank cut down by fire raining in from the Bengal Horse Artillery. The battle was over in two hours, the defeated Khalsa losing possibly 10,000 men including Sham Singh as well as all their guns. The British lost 320 dead with over 2,000 wounded.

Pursued by Gough, the Khalsa fled back to Lahore where on 15 February 1846 Raja Gulab Singh asked for terms of surrender, three days later the seven-year-old Maharaja Duleep Singh submitted. The Treaty of Lahore limited the Khalsa to 20,000 men and effectively meant the Punjab was now ruled by the British East India Company through Sikh Sirdars. The Sikhs were also to pay war reparations which included the 105 Carat Koh-i-Noor diamond which now rests in the Crown of Queen Elizabeth, The Queen Mother. Peace in the Punjab would last not much more than two years.

11 February 1942

Second World War
The Channel Dash

THE SECOND WORLD War had seemed a lost cause for Great Britain at the onset of the 1940 summer but Fighter Command's Battle of Britain victory had successfully thwarted a German invasion of the British Isles. As the British fought on alone there had, however, been no let up in *Luftwaffe* attacks on British cities or U-boat attacks on merchant shipping heading for the beleaguered but defiant islands. In early 1941 the powerful German surface fleet of Grand Admiral Erich Raeder had also sailed into the Atlantic adding to the misery of the British population as food imports halved, but a captured Enigma machine, rotors and code books soon enabled brilliant minds at Bletchley Park to break the Kriegsmarine Enigma Code. By June British Prime Minister Winston Churchill was party to conversations between Grand Admiral Karl Donitz and his U-boats whilst also gaining a new ally when Russia entered the war, albeit on the receiving end of history's greatest ever invasion, German Chancellor Adolf Hitler's Operation Barbarossa. Until victory had been achieved on his Eastern Front, Hitler was anxious to avoid war with the United States, urging Donitz to avoid US shipping but in December 1941 his and Italian Dictator Benito Mussolini's Tripartite Pact Ally, Hideki Tojo of Japan, attacked the US Pacific Fleet at Pearl Harbor, Hawaii simultaneous to attacks throughout South East Asia. To Churchill's delight Hitler and Mussolini then also declared war on the United States.

Initially US President Franklin D. Roosevelt opted for a holding strategy in the Pacific until Germany and Italy had been defeated in Europe (the US war machine would soon allow for an offensive in both) which for Donitz and Raeder meant more prey in the western Atlantic and Barents Sea. As Allied convoys also supplied Russia and the threat of a significant Allied landing in Norway increased, Hitler looked to support Raeder and Donitz by moving to Wilhelmshaven, North West Germany, the battleships Scharnhorst, Gneisenau and the heavy cruiser Prinz Eugen which at the time were under almost constant Royal Air Force attack in Brest Harbour, France.

On 11 February 1942, four months after Bletchley Park had been temporarily confounded by an extra rotor being added to the Kriegsmarine Enigma codes and a few days after British radar had been jammed, a German fleet of over sixty ships under Admiral Otto Ciliax slipped out of Brest to run the gauntlet of the Royal Navy in a dash up the English Channel, Operation Cerberus. The British Admiralty had nevertheless been aware of the 'Dash' and had positioned the submarine HMS *Sea Lion* off Brest but critically Lieutenant George Colvin had withdrawn just minutes earlier to recharge his batteries. Overnight and through early morning fog, Ciliax sailed around the coast of France, Vice Admiral Bertram Ramsay at Dover still unaware of his movements. At 11.00 on 12 February Ramsay was at last alerted when two Spitfires spotted the German fleet off Le Touquet, the coastal battery at South Foreland opening fire but into the mist. Ramsay began the British counter, Operation Fuller, by launching five motor torpedo boats which were met by a line of German *Schnellboot* and continuous relays from over 250 Messerschmidt and Focke Wulfe fighters and fighter-bombers. Against this formidable array of weaponry six Fairey Swordfish biplane torpedo bombers led by Irishman Lieutenant Commander Eugene Esmonde took off from RAF Manston with scant fighter protection, sighting Ciliax' fleet off the Hook of Holland. All six Swordfish were shot down, just five of the eighteen crew surviving but not Esmonde who was posthumously awarded the Victoria Cross. Following the Swordfish were three waves totaling 242 Handley Halifax, Avro Manchester and Short Stirling bombers accompanied by over 400 Spitfires, Hurricanes, Whirlwinds, Hudsons and Beauforts many of which, in deteriorating visibility, failed to locate their targets. On the surface Ramsay also sent out six destroyers but it was too late, only a solitary salvo of torpedos was fired as the German fleet sailed over the horizon.

Already damaged by mines, Scharnhorst, Gneisenau and Prinz Eugen would come under further aerial attack in Wilhelmshaven. Following the Dash *The Times* newspaper reported that Ciliax had succeeded where the Duke of Medina Sidonia (1588 Spanish Armada) had failed.

12 February 1429

Hundred Years' War
Battle of Rouvray (Herrings)

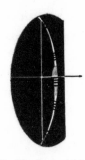

IN SUMMER 1428 John, Duke of Bedford, England's regent of France allowed his most able field commander Thomas Montagu, Earl of Salisbury to march south into central France looking to force a collapse of French forces fighting for the cause of the dispossessed French heir, the Dauphin Charles. Decisive defeats for the Dauphin at Cravant in 1423, Verneuil in 1424 and St James in 1426 had already left him vulnerable and worse, many of his commanders were now in open conflict. Bedford would have preferred Salisbury to attack Angers lower down the valley of the River Loire but if Salisbury could take Orléans the whole of southern France would lie open to further English conquest. On the Dauphin's defeat the kingdoms of England and France would then be undisputedly united under one crown, that of Henry VI, King of England.

While Bedford set out to reduce the defiant Mont St Michel off the French Atlantic coast, Salisbury invested Orléans in October 1428 with 5,500 men having first isolated his objective by capturing Chartres, Janville, Beaugency, Meung-Sur-Loire and Jargeau. The formidable Orléans was, however, prepared for a defence under Raoul, Sire de Gaucourt and later John, Count of Dunois, the Bastard of Orléans. Salisbury's initial assaults of the St Augustin's Friary and *Les Tourelles* barbican proved successful but the English commander then met an agonising death when an isolated cannon shot removed half his face. The more cautious William de la Pole, Earl of Suffolk took command but rather than assaulting the city settled for a winter siege despite his perimeter being too long for his army to police. To intercept supplies heading into the city from the north and east (a southern approach could not cross the Loire), Suffolk instead relied on patrols and a series of forts built by the more proactive John Talbot. By February 1429, the siege had become an artillery duel punctuated by the odd garrison sortie before the Dauphin at last began efforts to relieve Orléans by sending a 4,000 strong force under Charles de Bourbon, Count of Clermont, amongst them 3–400 Scots (all that was left in France after Verneuil) under John Stewart of Darnley whose ransom (he had been captured at Cravant) had been paid by the Dauphin. On receiving news of a large supply convoy heading for the besieging English Army, Clermont moved north-east from Blois to intercept.

The convoy, three miles of 300 carts carrying military hardware, tools and food, specifically hundreds of barrels of herrings for Lent, rumbled out of Rouvray for Janville on 12 February 1429, the protecting vanguard of mounted archers soon sighting their French equivalent on high ground to the south-west. The highly experienced commander of the 1,000 archers and Parisian militia escorting the convoy, Sir John Fastolf, immediately realised he could not make the relative safety of Janville, instead drawing in all his carts to form *a leaguer* – a defensive circle. The archers then dug in sharpened stakes, forming a hedgehog to protect the leaguer entrances from any mounted charge of French knights. When confronted with this makeshift fort Clermont had little interest in wasting his knights in a frontal assault against English longbows and instead began a steady bombardment with his field cannon. Bereft of artillery, Fastolf was unable to reply, his crumbling wagons spilling their cargoes and his men suffering under the weight of shot whilst the French, all still mounted in accordance with Clermont's orders, confidently watched on. The Scots, however, were less patient, Darnley completely failing to learn the lessons of Cravant and Verneuil now ignoring Clermont's order, dismounting with his countryfolk to charge the hated English archers head on. The brave but foolhardy Scots were then sent reeling backwards by volleys of arrows and crossbow bolts, a fate also received by the reluctant French cavalry who went to their assistance. The repulse of these two uncoordinated attacks handed Fastolf his chance and he grabbed it, the English immediately counter-attacking with a mounted charge of their own to send the remaining Dauphinists to flight, Clermont included.

Fastolf delivered his herrings. Orléans would have to wait for a saviour but that very day in Vaucouleurs a peasant girl was beseeching the town-Captain Robert de Baudricourt to provide her with an escort to address the Dauphin at his court in Chinon. Claiming divine powers the peasant girl foretold of the disaster at Rouvray, Baudricourt acquiescing on confirmation of the event. Six weeks later the Maid of Orléans, Joan of Arc, would ride into the town and change the course of the Hundred Years' War.

13 February 1945

Second World War Bombing of Dresden

IN THE BITTER weather of January 1945 the last major German offensive of the Second World War had been held in the Ardennes. Supreme Headquarters Allied Expeditionary Force commander Dwight D. Eisenhower had then immediately wanted to trap retreating Germans with a pincer movement by the United States 9th Army, (part of British Field Marshal Bernard Montgomery's 21st Army Group) and the US 3rd Army under General George Patton but the troublesome Montgomery was reluctant to send forces into a 'snowstorm'. As Allied Forces waited to assault the Siegried Line and cross the River Rhine, British Prime Minister Winston Churchill requested Soviet Secretary General Josef Stalin maintain pressure on the Eastern Front, Stalin obliging with a massive Red Army Vistula-Oder offensive which in turn Churchill looked to support with bombing raids into East Germany – now possible since Oboe and GEE navigation had improved their range with the advance of the Western Front.

Air Officer Commanding-in-Chief RAF Bomber Command Arthur Harris believed the strategic Autumn 1944 bombing of Germany had already been decisive and that by the year end 80 per cent of all German cities with populations of over 100,000 had been devastated. Nevertheless Churchill, fulfilling obligations to Stalin, turned to Harris to bomb the East German 'Jewel Box' city of Dresden, the baroque home of the kings of Saxony since 1485, a centre of modern art, architecture consisting of the Zwinger Palace, the Augustus Bridge, the Semper Oper Opera House, the Frauenkirche and the Katholische Hofkirche. The city also contained the Albertstadt military barracks, 127 factories supporting the German war effort and a rail marshalling yard for German troops and hardware moving to the Eastern Front. Germany's seventh largest city, Dresden's anti-aircraft defences had been moved to the front but the 640,000 population were confident they would never be targeted, a confidence that would be shattered by a bombing that would also serve warning to Stalin to honour agreements made the previous week at the Yalta Conference.

At 17.20 on 13 February 1945 Pathfinder Lancasters took off from RAF Coningsby to drop red magnesium flares on the Ostagehege Sports Stadium in the centre of Dresden. Eight De Havilland Mosquitos with Oboe navigation followed, dropping target indicators before 244 Lancasters arrived overhead at 10.15pm dropping 500 tons of high explosive, including blockbusters, and 350 tons of incendiary bombs. The depleted *Luftwaffe*, distracted by diversionary raids, could put up little resistance whilst, below, civilians cowered in air raid shelters as fires raged and buildings collapsed around them. The scene was clearly visible hundreds of miles away to the second wave of 529 Lancasters that arrived three hours later dropping another 1,800 tons of high explosive and incendiaries that caught rescue services on the ground and widened the devastation. As fires spread an eleven square mile firestorm developed around the Altstadt, air temperatures soared and hurricane force winds dragged victims into the flames. Those that stayed in the shelters were suffocated or roasted alive. The following morning 316 B-17 Flying Fortresses of the United States Army Air Force then dropped another 771 tons of ordnance on the beleaguered city, any precision lost in the cloud and smoke.

Dresden lay in ruins, 12,000 houses, 39 schools, 19 hospitals, 16 churches and chapels destroyed. At least 25,000 were dead but with refugees flooding into the city from the east probably considerably more. A furious Reichsminister of Propoganda, Joseph Goebbels demanded Reichsminister of Aviation Hermann Goring face a Court Martial and threatened to execute all Allied air prisoners of war. Goebbels' claim that 200,000 had perished shocked neutral countries as well as provoking a reaction in Britain, Churchill now distancing himself from the bombing campaign. The bombing has often been condemned as a war crime since the war was almost over and many of the military targets in Dresden's suburbs were left intact. Dresden has been gradually rebuilt, the Frauenkirche consecrated in 2005. The city is twinned with its British equivalent, Coventry. Bomber Command's undeniably brave airmen suffered a 50 per cent casualty rate during the Second World War, the highest of any service, but have never been awarded a campaign medal.

14 February 1900

Second Boer War
Battle of Tugela Heights

COMMANDER OF THE Natal Field Force General Sir Redvers Buller had been trying to prize open Boer defences on the Tugela River, Natal, since before Christmas 1899 after Lieutenant General Sir George White had ignored his orders not to go north of the river. Despite initial victories, White and 13,000 British troops had fallen back to Ladysmith where they were besieged by Transvaal and Free State Boers now under the command of General Louis Botha. With White trapped and before large British reinforcements could arrive Boer General Piet Joubert had spurned the opportunity to advance further into Natal, perhaps even as far as Durban, his attitude followed by other Boer generals who preferred to maintain the moral high ground rather than seek a chance of outright victory. Since there was still little appetite for an offensive strategy beyond Transvaal President Paul Kruger, Botha reconciled himself with a defensive strategy that made the most of favourable terrain and the marksmanship of his burghers, comfortably parrying all three of Buller's blows at Colenso, Spion Kop and Vaal Krantz whilst similarly in central South Africa General Koos De La Rey had halted General Lord Paul Methuen at Magersfontein. The newly appointed British Commander-in-Chief in South Africa, Field Marshal Lord Frederick Roberts had, however, reinforced Methuen and was now approaching Kimberley and Paardeberg in overwhelming strength.

In Natal, Buller had learnt through his three defeats that the key to victory was not by the traditional single day set piece battle, an artillery barrage followed by an infantry attack, but by fighting over an extended area on an extended timescale with decision making at a lower level, soldiers using movement and ground to maintain the offensive supported by artillery moving wherever required. Buller again turned his attention north beyond Colenso where 5,000 Boers were well entrenched on the Tugela Heights north of the river and on a line of hills and ridges to the east where the river turned north.

On 14 February 1900, Hussar Hill, the most southerly Boer outpost, was taken by Colonel Douglas Dundonald's Irregular Horse with thirty-four guns immediately hauled up to support an advance further north on Green Hill and north-east on Cingolo Hill by Major General Neville Lyttelton's 4th Infantry Brigade. The heavily outgunned Boers could only surrender or fall back but the pressure of Buller's plan was unrelenting, Major General Henry Hildyard's 2nd Infantry Brigade then capturing the 2,500-foot-high Monte Cristo in the face of stiffer resistance. The capture of Monte Cristo compromised the Boer defences to the south-west on Hlangwane Hill which was also overrun, Buller now moving more than fifty guns up south and east of the Tugela for a push across the river north through the hills and gorges before Ladysmith. Crossing the Tugela west of Hlangwane, Major General Arthur Wynne's Lancashire Brigade pushed on to capture Horseshoe Hill and Wynne's Hill while Major General Arthur Hart's Irish Brigade attacked Hart's Hill to the north, Hart suffering heavy losses largely due to repeating the time-honoured mistakes of the past. Intelligence now informed Buller of strong Boer defences at Pieters Hill, tantalisingly the last obstacle before Ladysmith. On 27 February (the anniversary of Majuba Hill 1881) Major General Geoffrey Barton's 6th Infantry Brigade attacked from the east through boulders and spiky scrub just 100 yards behind a creeping artillery barrage, the surprised Boers recovering to put down a heavy fire as their comrades to the west on Railway Hill also came under attack from Lieutenant General Walter Kitchener's 5th Infantry Brigade. Kitchener's 5th then also stormed the saddle connecting Railway Hill to Hart's Hill with a bayonet charge of immense ferocity before Hart's Hill itself was stormed by Major General Charles Norcott's 4th Infantry Brigade, another bayonet charge behind a devastating artillery barrage.

Boer resistance disintegrated. Buller had at last found the door to Ladysmith and turned the key, the town was relieved the same day. The Second Boer War was suddenly looking very different since, during the battle, 300 miles to the west at Paardeberg, the commando of Boer General Piet Cronje had been trapped by Roberts' Chief of Staff, Lieutenant General Lord Horatio Kitchener of Khartoum (brother of Walter).

15 February 1942

Second World War
Battle of Singapore

THE DECEMBER 1941 simultaneous Japanese invasions of the Dutch East Indies (Indonesia), Borneo, Philippines, Thailand, Malaya, Hong Kong and the infamous attack on the United States Pacific Fleet at Pearl Harbor, Hawaii had been designed to create a new economic order across South East Asia. Out of necessity, since Britain was still beleaguered at home and engaged in North Africa against Japan's Tripartite Pact partners, Germany and Italy, the British defence of Malaya had been left to the III Indian Corps and Australian 8th Division under Lieutenant General Arthur Percival, General Officer Commanding Malaya. British Prime Minister Winston Churchill was intent that the 'Gibraltar in the East', Singapore, should not fall and to that extent was rushing reinforcements to hold the city – Percival's task to delay the advance through Malaya of Lieutenant General Tomoyuki Yamashita's Japanese 25th Army until they could arrive but with planes smashed on the ground, the battleships HMS *Prince of Wales* and *Repulse* sunk, Japanese air and naval superiority had been total. On the ground Yamashita's tactics using armoured spearheads (the British had none) with support from bicycled infantry and flank attacks through 'impenetrable' jungle, had soon forced the Indian Corps back into southern Malaya before reinforcing Japanese Guards Divisions and the Japanese 18th Infantry Division forced both the Indians and Australians back across the Johore-Singapore Causeway onto Singapore Island itself.

Percival now had 85,000 British and Colonial troops to defend Singapore although many of them had only just arrived but he was deceived by Yamashita into believing the main Japanese attack would come in the north-east. Percival positioned there the fresh troops of the British 18th Infantry Division and 8th Indian Brigade with the battle weary remains of the 11th Indian Division whilst in the north-west he posted the Indian 44th Brigade and the Australian 8th Division. On 3 February 1942 British positions came under Japanese artillery and air attacks assisted by spotters from across the Johore Strait including several in the Sultan's

Palace. As the attacks intensified over the next few days, Lieutenant General Gordon Bennett refused to shell the Sultan's Palace whilst limited quantities of high explosive meant British and Australian artillery could only respond sporadically. Following a massive Japanese bombardment on 8 February a 13,000-man Japanese Infantry assault began across the western Straits of Johore against 6,000 Australians and 1,000 poorly armed Chinese in poorly-constructed defences around tidal mangrove swamps. In fierce night fighting the Japanese gained a foothold on Singapore Island before pushing inland for the Tengah Airfield using the many creeks and lush vegetation for cover. As Percival failed to reinforce the Australians, Brigadiers Harold Taylor and Duncan Maxwell prematurely retreated from the blown Johore-Singapore Causeway and Kranji River allowing the high casualty suffering Japanese to reinforce. When Percival then sent his heavily outnumbered aircraft to Sumatra he not only left his troops badly exposed but allowed Yamashita to begin ferrying over tanks. Churchill urged Percival to fight on for the reputation of the British race whilst Archibald Wavell, Commander in Chief ABDA (American, British, Dutch, Australian) advised there would be no surrender. By 13 February the causeway had been repaired, Yamashita bringing over yet more armour to force Percival back into a perimeter around Singapore City's one million citizens. As the last British evacuation ships left, order began to disintegrate, water, food and fuel fast disappearing. Yamashita's boast of capturing Singapore in a hundred days was achieved in just sixty-nine when despite Wavell's claim, Percival did indeed surrender on 15 February 1942. A shocked Churchill described the capitulation as 'the worst disaster... in British history'.

A new hell awaited the 80,000 captured Allied troops in Japanese labour camps. Up to 50,000 thousand Singaporean-Chinese were also executed as Yamashita purged Singapore (Sook Ching massacre) – he was hanged for war crimes in 1946. Twelve thousand Indians captured during the Malayan Campaign were recruited into the First Indian National Army of Mohan Singh and Rash Behari Bose to fight against the British who, in Burma, were now about to suffer the longest retreat in British military history. British imperialism in South East Asia was at an end.

16 February 1646

English Civil Wars
Battle of Torrington

KING CHARLES I of England had enjoyed a year of success until the summer of 1643 but ever since his fortunes had deteriorated in the face of a resurgent and now all conquering Parliamentary military arm, the New Model Army and its commander, Sir Thomas Fairfax. England had been in the grip of a deep freeze since 8 December 1645 but the English Civil War continued to its now inevitable conclusion. After defeat at Naseby in July 1645 and the subsequent capture of his personal papers, support for Charles had crumbled. Royalist garrisons at Carlisle, Scarborough, Bristol, Basing House and Hereford amongst others had fallen and in Scotland where the king had placed so much faith in the hitherto successes of James Graham, Earl of Montrose, a decisive reverse had been struck at Philiphaugh. In the Midlands, Oxford, where Charles held his court, held out, so too Newark in the North, Raglan in South Wales and Exeter on the south coast whilst at Chester John, Lord Byron was also holding out though once again in dire straits. When Sir William Vaughan's Royalist relief force from North Wales was intercepted and defeated by Parliament's Sir William Brereton, Byron was left with no option, his 3 February 1646 capitulation leaving the king nowhere to land his speculative army of last resort, his Irish Confederates.

Meanwhile in the South West, the Royalist Army was feared not so much by Parliament but by the civilian population. As the Royalist's cause collapsed, unemployed, disillusioned troops took to theft and plunder (beginning the golden age of the Footpads and Highwaymen) but were opposed by local 'clubmen' who exacted indiscriminate revenge before Fairfax and his Puritan soldiery moved in to grimly finish off what even the fifteen-year-old Prince of Wales, future King Charles II, labelled a 'dissolute, undisciplined, wicked, beaten army'. Nevertheless shortly before sailing for the Scilly Isles from Pendennis Castle, Falmouth the prince ordered Sir Ralph Hopton, the king's 1643 victor of Braddock Down, Roundway Down, and Lansdowne Hill, to take the fight to Fairfax, a forlorn hope if ever there was.

Hopton understood his predicament but with just 2,000 Cornish infantry and 800 cavalry under Thomas, Lord Wentworth decided on a march from Launceston to relieve Exeter. On departing, however, Hopton learnt of the fall of Dartmouth, the garrison of which Fairfax bribed with three shillings each to enlist in the ranks of the New Model Army leaving any Royalist relief of Exeter out of the question. Hopton therefore retreated to North Devon and a defence of Torrington upon which, on the evening of 16 February 1646 and in heavy rain, Fairfax advanced with 10,000 Parliament Roundheads, running into Hopton's dragoons short of the town. Fighting broke out as the dragoons retreated to the support of their heavier cavalry, infantry, cannon and defensive earthworks behind but Fairfax broke off the Parliament attack, preferring to wait for dawn while Oliver Cromwell moved up to reconnoitre the Royalist defences. Fearful Hopton was withdrawing, however, Cromwell sent forward his 'Ironside' cavalry, the fighting erupting again with Fairfax throwing more cavalry and infantry into the fray as a two hour push of pike developed. Eventually the Royalist Cornish infantry broke with the fighting continuing in the narrow streets of Torrington back towards the Church of Saint Michael and All Angels in which Hopton had stored eighty barrels of gunpowder and in which Fairfax now held 200 Royalist prisoners. As the battle raged outside a spark, possibly deliberately, caused a terrific explosion that lifted the roof off the building showering everyone in the vicinity, including Hopton and Fairfax who were in the thick of the fighting outside, with red hot timbers and lead. The explosion effectively ended the battle with Hopton and his Royalist survivors, short of all their guns and baggage, retreating west to Cornwall.

Hopton was pursued by Fairfax, surrendering at Truro on 14 March 1646 before eventually going into exile. King Charles had lost South West England and he would lose again a month later at Stow-on-the-Wold, the final battle of the First English Civil War. As Parliament forces closed on Oxford, the king escaped for Newark where he delivered himself to besieging Scottish Covenanters under David Leslie.

17 February 1461

Wars of the Roses
Second Battle of St Albans

IN 1455 THE Wars of the Roses had erupted in violence at St Albans where Richard Plantagenet, Duke of York had trapped the King of England Henry VI and his chief court advisor Edmund Beaufort, Duke of Somerset. The feud between York and Somerset had been ignited by the declining military situation in France at the conclusion of the Hundred Years' War where Somerset had replaced York as Henry's Lieutenant, Somerset then confirming his inability as a soldier with the loss of almost all English possessions. King Henry had done little to help, more comfortable with art and architecture than military conquest he had diverted funds for the building of, in particular, Kings College Chapel, Cambridge rather than sponsoring a more aggressive prosecution of the war. Nevertheless, the king had a mental breakdown on losing Gascony which preceded a final breakdown in relations between the feuding dukes.

At St Albans Somerset had been killed with a poleaxe but Henry had been spared. Indeed York had then protested his allegiance to the king until the 1460 Battle of Northampton after which he surprised all by proclaiming himself king. York's supporters were deeply uneasy at the thought of any usurpation of the Crown but Richard Neville, Earl of Warwick brokered a deal where York would instead inherit the throne upon the now imprisoned Henry's death. Henry's French Queen, Margaret of Anjou, however, was never going to allow her son Edward to be disinherited and assembled a Lancastrian Army of Northerners which defeated and killed York at Wakefield before marching south in freezing winter weather on Yorkist London for a potential reunion with her husband. In Wales, however, Lancastrians under Owen Tudor and his son Jasper Tudor, Earl of Pembroke had been defeated at Mortimer's Cross by Edward Plantagenet, Duke of March (now the Duke of York following his father's recent death) who, despite victory, would now be too late to assist Warwick's defence of London upon which Margaret's Lancastrians were about to fall.

On 12 February 1461 Warwick and an inexperienced 10,000 Yorkists marched out of London with their prisoner King Henry to St Albans where extensive defences were built north of the town across the old Roman road, Watling Street. Warwick's three battles were not unusual but rather than adjacent they were aligned diagonally from south-west to north-east over a wide front, each two miles apart, the rear under John Neville, Lord Montagu (Warwick's brother), the centre under Warwick and the vanguard under John de Mowbray, Duke of Norfolk, all of them in theory able to support each other if attacked. Warwick had no idea where the Lancastrian attack might fall, and remained unaware when John, Lord Clifford led the Lancastrian vanguard in a night march around his left flank into St Albans.

In poor visibility Clifford approached St Albans in the early hours of 17 February 1461, heading for the Abbey before he was hit with a hail of arrows from Yorkist archers stationed in the town. Clifford, however, out-flanked the archers by moving into St Peter's Street before annihilating them in a prolonged fight, hand-to-hand, house-by-house. Leading the Yorkist rear battle Montagu could hear the fighting behind him but was not convinced that it was the main Lancastrian attack until too late to save his colleagues. Sending word ahead to his brother both he and Warwick turned to face Clifford who had now been reinforced by Henry Beaufort, Duke of Somerset (son of Edmund). Somerset now attacked Montagu from the south, a vicious fight raging on Bernard's Heath with concentrated arrow fire and a hand-to-hand struggle with sword, mace, poleaxe and billhook, Montagu holding Somerset whilst waiting for Warwick's support. As indecisive as his brother, Warwick now held the same fears as had Montagu, failing to move until too late, Montagu's men eventually breaking and fleeing leaving Warwick to advance on Somerset and Clifford alone. Realising he was now heavily outnumbered, Warwick quickly disengaged to march north with Norfolk, finally joining York to fight another day; he had lost 4,000 men.

King Henry was left under a tree and reunited with his wife and son who promptly executed the two knights guarding him. The Lancastrian Army marched south on London but the gates remained firmly shut. Not wanting to alienate Londoners from their cause the king and queen began a grueling retreat back north through the freezing English winter. The Yorkists would follow them to Towton for the bloodiest ever battle on British soil.

18 February 1900

Second Boer War
Battle of Paardeberg

THE SECOND BOER War had become a bitter four-month struggle against Afrikaner Boers of the Transvaal and Orange Free State fiercely intent on preserving independence from British rule. Masters of the Highveld, the horse, and the German Mauser magazine-loading rifle they had frustrated British aggression from the Tugela River, Natal to the Modder River, Cape Colony inflicting heavy losses on successive commanders-in-chief of British forces in South Africa, General Sir Redvers Buller and his replacement Field Marshal Lord Frederick Roberts. Buller had, however, been retained as Commander of the Natal Field Force and by mid-February 1900, having grasped the tactical nettle, was inching his way through the Drakensberg Mountains to relieve Ladysmith. Simultaneously Roberts and his Chief of Staff, Lieutenant General Horatio Herbert Kitchener of Khartoum, had moved up with massive reinforcements from Cape Town to the Modder River where General Lord Paul Methuen had been nursing his bruises following an abject defeat at Magersfontein the previous December.

Roberts' first task was to relieve Kimberley, the garrison of which, under Colonel Robert Kekewich, had been besieged since the very beginning of the war. Boer General Piet Cronje and the 5,000 Boers still at Magersfontein believed that a British general would never march out into the veld and so continued to block Roberts' obvious route up the Cape Town/Bulawayo Railway. It was not often the Boers were wrong-footed but that is exactly what happened when Kitchener did just that, 5,000 cavalry under Major General John French circumventing the block with a ride across the veld that floored most of the horses but relieved Kimberley on 15 February 1900. Kimberley's liberation left Cronje's position at Magersfontein untenable and so he retreated east between French and the British 6th Infantry Division of Lieutenant Thomas Kelly-Kenny for Paardeberg Drift on the Modder River where he was 'caught' by the remaining 1,500 mounts of French's cavalry. Instead of attacking the weak British force, Cronje instead formed a defensive laager on the north bank, Kitchener reinforcing French to trap him. Cronje's only possible assistance was now from just a 300-strong commando under Christiaan De Wet thirty miles south at Koffyfontein.

At Paardeberg 15,000 British troops were soon present but Kelly-Kenny and Kitchener were at complete odds on how to proceed. Kelly-Kenny realised casualties could be minimised by allowing the British guns to do most of the work but unfortunately the hard hearted Kitchener, whose previous battle experience was against Mahdist spears at Omdurman, over-ruled to order an unimaginative full frontal attack. On 18 February 1900 Kelly-Kenny's 6th Infantry Division, Lieutenant General Henry Colville's 9th Infantry Division and two battalions of mounted infantry attacked Cronje's laager across 4,000 yards of difficult ground, none of them getting to within 200 yards of the objective before being mowed down by a wall of flying metal. Whilst Kelly-Kenny fumed at soaring casualties of 1,270, Kitchener impassively asked for a more determined assault. There was little time to argue, however, as another problem surfaced, De Wet arriving almost unnoticed to take the unguarded 'Kitcheners Kopje' threatening British units south of the Modder and offering a potential escape route to Cronje on the north bank. The following day Cronje asked for a ceasefire which the newly arrived Roberts declined, instead the Commander-in-Chief looked to renew Kitchener's *modus operandi* before his nerve failed. Incredibly, Roberts now began planning his own retreat but in a war of British blunders and a battle of British blunders it was the Boers who blundered last, De Wet sparing Roberts a humiliation by abandoning the kopje when Cronje failed to join him. Now pounded by British artillery, Cronje and his 4,000 Boers then finally surrendered.

The Orange Free State and the Transvaal were now open to Roberts who marched into Bloemfontein on 13 March, Mafeking on 17 May and Pretoria on 5 June. In Natal, Buller would soon relieve Ladysmith. The Boer War at last seemed to be over but there were still thousands of Boers on the veld under De Wet, Koos De La Rey, Jan Smuts and Louis Botha, *bitter-einders* who harboured no thoughts of surrender, a new type of war was about to begin.

19 February 1915

The Great War
The Dardanelles

THE GERMAN AND Austro-Hungarian (Central Powers) Schlieffen Plan to defeat Russia, France and Great Britain (Triple Entente) had instead been defeated by the French Army and the British Expeditionary Force in the Autumn of 1914 both on the River Marne and in a subsequent 'Race to the Sea'. Operative failings on the Western Front apart, the defeat was also attributable to German Field Marshal Helmuth von Moltke strengthening his Eastern Front against a Russia that had begun mobilising since even before the outbreak of war. Although Russian transportation and communication deficiencies had then been exploited by Field Marshal Paul von Hindenburg and Chief of Staff Erich Ludendorff to gain crushing German victories at Tannenberg and the Masurian Lakes, the transfer of forces required meant diminished German offensives in the west. Here, by Christmas 1914, lines of trenches now ran 400 miles from the Belgian coast to the mountains of Switzerland, German High Command effectively reversing the policy of the Schlieffen Plan (a quick victory in the west before defeating Russia) by now fighting on the defensive in the west and the offensive in the east. Moltke, however, believed he had already lost the war, admitting as much to Kaiser Wilhelm II before suffering a mental breakdown.

As the Central Powers faced the prospect of a continuous fight on two fronts they were at least bolstered by the November 1914 declaration, in their favour, of Turkey. Turkey (Ottoman Empire) had been a long time ally of Britain throughout the nineteenth century but recent German diplomacy and Turkish ambition to recover territory previously lost to Russia meant British interests in the Middle East, including the Suez Canal and Royal Navy oil, were now suddenly under threat. Since finding a flank on the Western Front was now impossible, First Lord of the Admiralty Winston Churchill proposed to knock Turkey out of the war and simultaneously open naval communications with Russia via the Mediterranean and Black Sea by forcing the Dardanelles Straits and the Sea of Marmara, Constantinople

(Istanbul), a move that if successful would encourage fence-sitting Italy, Greece and Bulgaria to open another front against Austria Hungary. Despite being the world's most powerful naval force and having French assistance, the task facing the Royal Navy was, however, far from straight forward, forty miles long, five miles wide, narrowing to a mile before Marmara, the Dardanelles Straits were defended by cliff top forts, mobile artillery, ten lines of minefields and submarine nets. Not only that but the Turkish Army had been fully alerted to any potential attack thanks to the straits being attacked by the Royal Navy in October 1914, an attack which had produced encouraging results though reappointed First Sea Lord Admiral John 'Jackie 'Fisher remained deeply unconvinced.

On 19 February 1915 Vice Admiral Sackville Carden, commanding the combined Anglo-French fleet of a battleship, three battlecruisers, sixteen pre dreadnoughts, four cruisers, eighteen destroyers, an aircraft carrier, six submarines and twenty-one trawlers, began the assault of the Dardanelles at long range, pounding the Cape Helles and Kumkale Forts at the entrance to the straits with little success before resuming at close range after a week-long weather delay. Largely due to the Turks retreating, Carden's fleet then entered the straits whilst his marines, the only British troops present, seized the outer forts but not the mobile Turkish gun batteries. Another week and Carden began pounding the intermediate Turkish defences while his trawlers attempted to clear the minefields under heavy fire from neighbouring cliff tops. The Anglo-French fleet could not proceed until the minefields had been cleared but the trawlermen refused to work under such a heavy fire leaving Carden no choice but to again employ his marines, this time repulsed by much tougher Turkish resistance. HMS *Elizabeth* then started firing on Turkish positions from the other side of the Gallipoli Peninsular before Carden fell ill leaving Rear Admiral John de Robeck to launch another attack with the entire fleet on 18 March. A ferocious artillery duel raged as the trawlers again attempted to clear the minefields but Robeck was unaware of newly-laid Turkish minefields in Eren Koy Bay which struck as the Entente ships turned. First the French *Bouvet* followed by HMS *Inflexible*, *Irresistible* and *Ocean*, all sunk, abandoned or heavily damaged with over 700 casualties. Robeck withdrew.

Despite the setback, Secretary for War Horatio Kitchener agreed to commit further ground troops for a clearance of the Gallipoli Peninsular. By the time further British, Australians and New Zealanders arrived in April the Turkish defenders would be even better prepared.

20 February 1653 o.s

Anglo-Dutch Wars
Battle of Portland

DUTCH DEVELOPMENT OF world trade while the English, Scots and Irish had been busy killing themselves during the English Civil Wars had sparked deep envy within the Rump Parliament of the Commonwealth of England. The two Protestant allies for decades against Catholic Spain had then fallen out completely after the Dutch spurned a somewhat opportunist offer of unification from Oliver Cromwell. Parliament reacted by prohibiting Dutch shipping from English harbours globally and by insisting that a Dutch ship encountering an English ship must pay tribute by lowering her colours. Off Dover in May 1652 Dutch Admiral Maarten Tromp had failed to do so resulting in the opening battle of the First Anglo-Dutch War. The English, under General-at-Sea Robert Blake, then believed that victory later that autumn at the Kentish Knock had been decisive but misjudged Dutch morale when Tromp, who had been replaced in the summer, returned to his former command. In late November the Dutch Admiral returned to defeat Blake off Dungeness exposing frailties within the English command structure and administration. Worse, the Dutch now controlled the English Channel, gateway to world trade for both countries.

Over the winter of 1652/53 Blake wrote a manual on naval tactics and Sir Henry Vane, former Governor of Massachusetts, Founder of Harvard University and the New Model Army, restructured naval administration so that English morale aboard the eighty ships that put to sea on 11 February 1653 was very different to that at Dungeness. Blake now sailed for the Channel Island of Alderney to intercept Tromp's seventy-five warships escorting a large Dutch merchant fleet back to the Dutch Republic but the width of the English Channel there increased the elusive Tromp's chances of passing undetected and sure enough, on 18 February 1653, an outmanouvred Blake required a race north to Portland for an intercept.

Aboard the 54-gun flagship *Brederode*, Tromp sailed south-east, attacking Blake aboard the 44-gun English flagship *Triumph* (the most decorated of ten British warships to sail under that name) who was sailing behind his vanguard squadron under William Penn. Both joined by their compatriots, the *Triumph* and *Brederode* began furiously exchanging broadsides, Penn bringing the English vanguard about to give further support but intercepted by a Dutch squadron under Michiel de Ruyter. Three of Penn's ships including the 48-gun *Assistance* under Nehemiah Bourne were boarded, fighting raging across the decks and up in the rigging. Blake's Red Squadron under Rear Admiral John Lawson in the 64-gun *Fairfax* then approached with a flanking move from the south-west in an attack that completely broke up that of the Dutch, restored Penn's boarded ships, relieved Blake and gained Lawson a promotion to Vice Admiral. Tromp now withdrew to protect his merchantmen and attempted to escape east. The following day the Dutch formed a defensive crescent formation as had the Spanish Armada sixty-five years before but were caught by the faster English who, as had Francis Drake and Martin Frobisher in exactly the same water, furiously assaulted the wings. As the light failed so too did Dutch discipline, several merchants breaking for French ports in desperation only to be picked off by swarming Englishmen.

On 20 February 1653, the two fleets passed Beachy Head, still furiously exchanging broadsides down the English Channel as Blake tried to block the Straights of Dover. All day fighting continued with the Dutch now down to half their original strength, low on ammunition and seemingly trapped to leeward of Cape Gris Nez. Blake anchored his fleet just three miles offshore waiting for morning to finish the job but again he reckoned without Tromp. The Dutchman, with staggering seamanship, tacked with little room off the French coast through the shallows, evading his pursuers and the cape to deliver his convoy the next morning. He had, however, lost perhaps 3,000 men.

Blake was wounded but his victory restored English control of the English Channel. The North Sea was now the only route open for Dutch trade and in June it would be the scene of the First Anglo-Dutch War's decisive encounter at the Gabbard.

21 February 1849
Sikh Wars
Battle of Gujrat

THE FIRST ANGLO-Sikh War of 1845–46 was concluded by the 1846 Treaty of Lahore signed by the seven-year-old Maharaja Duleep Singh and seven members of the Lahore Durbar (Court). The British East India Company now effectively ruled the Punjab through local Sirdars and, as they had in Bengal for the past ninety years, with their own man, Sir Henry Lawrence, as Resident in Lahore to oversee Sikh politics. War reparations were also exacted from the Sikhs to the tune of fifteen million rupees which included the Koh-i-Noor diamond and the enforced sale of territory, most notably Kashmir. The British then used former soldiers of the Khalsa (Sikh Army) to maintain order, sparing the expense of stationing Bengal or Bombay Regiments but consequently with no British soldier ever advancing beyond the River Ravi, most of the Punjab and much of the Khalsa remained untouched by the war or its consequences. Whilst all remained quiet for a year it was not long before Khalsa soldiers and their officers began talk of an anti-British uprising, convinced with some justification that defeat in the First Anglo-Sikh War had been entirely due to the treachery of their own commanders, Tej and Lal Singh.

The catalyst for the Second Anglo-Sikh War occurred at Multan 220 miles south-west of Lahore where, in April 1848, Diwan Mulraj, on receiving a tax demand, had murdered two British officials whilst their British Gurkha escort defected. Lieutenant Herbert Edwardes, later reinforced by Major General William Whish, reacted by marching from Dera Fateh Khan to besiege Multan but Mulraj's spirited resistance and a lack of decisive British action encouraged the Governor of Hazara (250 miles north-east of Multan) Sirdar Chattar Singh to revolt as well. Not only did Chattar Singh revolt but also somewhat unsurprisingly his son, Sirdar Sher Singh, who was commanding a large part of Edwardes' force at Multan.

Sher Singh marched north to join his father who was offering Peshawar back to the Emir of Afghanistan, Dost Mohammed Khan (from whom it had been captured in 1823), should he too join the anti-British uprising. Governor General of India James Broun-Ramsay, Lord Dalhousie quickly realised he would now have to prosecute the war with greater vigour and with his own troops, sending Commander-in-Chief Sir Hugh Gough with 17,000 reinforcements of the Bengal Army to Lahore and onward, crossing the River Chenab at Wazirabad to confront Sher Singh's rebel army of 30,000 at Chillianwala on 13 January 1849.

Despite 6,000 British and Sikh casualties there was no decisive outcome at Chillianwala, the suspect tactician Gough now sacked but remaining in command until his replacement, the sixty-six-year-old General Charles Napier arrived. Just nine days later, however, Mulraj surrendered at Multan after a nine-month siege, freeing Whish and his large artillery train for a move north in support of Gough. Sher Singh retreated to Gujrat but received reinforcements when his father joined him from Attock and from Dost Mohammad's Afghans approaching from the River Indus. At 07.30 on 21 February 1849 the 20,000-strong British East India Company's Bengal Army with ninety-six guns approached Sher Singh's 60,000-strong Sikh-Afghan Army with fifty-nine guns across a four mile front, the Sikh artillery opening fire at extended range but in the process giving away their position. Gough halted and retreated his infantry back out of range whilst moving his artillery forward, under the protection of skirmishers, to return fire with considerable interest. The highly disciplined Sikh gunners held their ground for three hours until the sheer weight of incoming metal inevitably forced them back. Gough's artillery again advanced and now so too did his infantry, Major General Sir Walter Raleigh Gilbert taking the village of Bara Kalra and Brigadier Hervey taking Chota Kalra in close quarter house-to-house fighting. The heavy British guns continued forward supported by the lighter guns of the Horse Artillery which also repulsed flanking attacks from Sikh cavalry. Finally the Sikhs broke before a twelve mile rout developed. Gough's reputation had been saved.

Chattar and Sher Singh surrendered three weeks later and Dost Mohammad was driven out of Peshawar bringing the Punjab back under British control. The Sikhs would support the British during the Indian Sepoy uprising of 1857 and, crucially so, on the Western Front in 1914.

22 February 1744

War of the Austrian Succession
Battle of Toulon

BRITAIN HAD BEEN at war with Spain since 1739 when in the House of Commons, Westminster, Captain Robert Jenkins reputedly produced an ear which had been severed eight years before off Florida by a Spanish customs boarding party. The War of Jenkins' Ear then became consumed by the War of the Austrian Succession when Charles VI, Holy Roman Emperor, Archduke of Austria and King of Bohemia, Hungary, Croatia and Serbia died, leaving the huge Habsburg Empire to his daughter Maria Theresa. Under Salic Law, however, Maria, being a woman, was not entitled to the inheritance and was challenged by King Frederick 'the Great' of Prussia who invaded Silesia. A series of alliances saw Britain again at war with Spain and France somewhat fortuitously defeating the latter at the June 1743 Battle of Dettingen although King George II's Pragmatic Army had failed to pursue.

The French then sought to destabilise Britain by initiating a Catholic Jacobite uprising in Scotland led by Italian-speaking Bonnie Prince Charlie, the 'Young Pretender', son of James Stuart, 'the Old Pretender', who had attempted Jacobite risings in 1715 and 1719. Charlie was the grandson of Catholic King James II of England, Scotland(VI) and Ireland who had been deposed by Protestant William of Orange and the Glorious Revolution of 1688. Not only that but in 1714 all of Charlie's Catholic ancestors had been overlooked for the British succession by the 1701 Act of Settlement leaving King George's German-speaking Protestant father to ascend the English throne as King George I. By 1744 Catholic-fearing Britain, with the bulk of its army on the European continent, was in near panic at the prospect of invasion, their fears only partially eased by a significant part of the Franco-Spanish fleet being blockaded in Toulon Harbour by thirty Royal Navy ships of the line and three frigates under Admiral Thomas Mathews.

Mathews had retired in 1724, returned to a desk job in 1736 before being promoted to Admiral of the Red in 1741, his Mediterranean Fleet ensuring that in Italy, Charles, Duke of Parma, son of Philip V of Spain, for now at least should remain relatively neutral (he would become King of Spain in 1759). Since 1742 Mathews had had the French and Spanish bottled up but on 21 February 1744 they put to sea, the Spanish commanded by Admiral Dom Jose Navarro with twelve ships of the line and the French under the 83-year-old Admiral Claude Élisée, Count of Bruyère, with fifteen ships of the line and three frigates. Standing off at Hyères, Mathews closed to challenge but the Spanish had little interest in battle. With the fleets scattered in light wind Mathews, aboard HMS *Namur*, signaled the Mediterranean Fleet form line of battle before signalling to come to (stop) as darkness fell. His rear under Rear Admiral Richard Lestock, a man whom Mathews had previously requested be returned to England, had not initially formed line, however, and was consequently out of position some distance from the van and centre. Royal Navy policy was to attack at any opportunity but Mathews was reluctant whilst disorganised, Lestock then failing to make more sail when requested. At 13.00 on 22 February 1744, Mathews attacked regardless but HMS *Namur* was accompanied only by HMS *Marlborough* with the remainder now confused by Mathews' signals. Both ships suffered considerable damage in the exchange of broadsides with *Marlborough* close to sinking. As more British ships at last joined battle the Spanish flagship, *Real Felipe* with *Hercules* and *Constantine* fired determined broadsides in a three-hour duel before the French joined the fray looking to double (surround) the British line. Mathews broke off north whilst the Franco-Spanish fleet continued south-west.

The failure to defeat an inferior foe was met with fury in England. Mathews and Lestock, who both faced a Court Martial, had given Navarro and Bruyère the chance to join the French Jacobite invasion building on the French Atlantic coast (in the event it was miraculously destroyed by another 'protestant storm') and supply French forces for an April attack on Villafranca, South East France. The well-connected Lestock would be exonerated whilst Mathews was seemingly unfairly dismissed.

23 February 1779

American War of Independence Battle of Vincennes

THE TREATY OF Paris that ended the Seven Years War (1756–63) gave Britain possession of North America east of the Mississippi River and Canada. The Treaty also protected Catholic French living under British rule but by the 1775 outbreak of the American War of Independence areas west of the Appalachian Mountains (West Virginia, Ohio, Indiana, Illinois and Kentucky) were still only inhabited by native American Indians, fur hunters and just a few thousand settlers of European descent. Based in Detroit, the British garrisoned several outposts with French Canadiens including the Fort at Vincennes, Indiana and further west at Fort Kaskaskia on the Mississippi River in Illinois Country (a territory running the length of and either side of the Mississippi). Although the main theatres of the war of independence were on the eastern seaboard, the British had been encouraging loyalists and indigenous allies in the Mid-West to raid American colonists in Kentucky but during the winter of 1777–78 American Lieutenant Colonel George Rogers Clark resolved to launch a raid of his own against British outposts north of the Ohio River. Approved by Governor Patrick Henry in Williamsburg, Clark with 175 Virginia volunteers and sixty settlers set out on an epic three-month voyage down the Monungahela River to Fort Pitt (Pittsburg) before continuing on down the mighty 980-mile Ohio River, covering the last 120 miles to Kaskaskia on foot. Achieving complete surprise Clark captured Philippe de Rocheblave, commanding at Fort Gage, in bed before securing the allegiance of locals there and at other outposts with the news that their mother country, France, had joined the American cause. Additionally Father Pierre Gibault travelled east from Kaskaskia to Vincennes where he too turned the population against the British.

On 7 October 1778 Lieutenant Governor and Superintendent of Indian Affairs Henry Hamilton reacted by departing from Fort Detroit, Quebec (now Michigan) with 175 troops to successfully recapture Vincennes, Captain Leonard Helm and his three men left at Fort Sackville, Vincennes by Clark having little choice but to surrender. Hamilton then planned a British spring offensive further west but first allowed the majority of his men to return home in the belief that Clark could and would not mount a counter-attack over the winter. Hamilton was, however, betrayed by Spaniard Francis Vigo who reported British intentions to Clark in Kaskaskia. Clark then responded by sending his brother Lieutenant John Clark down the Mississippi and back up the Ohio with a forward supply ship while he and 172 Americans and French set off across 180 miles of waterlogged floodplains, building boats to cross the flooding Rivers Wabash and Embarrass.

On the evening of 23 February 1779, after warning the Vincennes population to stay indoors, Clark's American militia opened fire at short range on Fort Sackville, interrupting Hamilton's game of cards. Immediately the British suffered casualties but a British patrol heard the firing and rushed back to the fort, Clark happy to let them do so rather than allowing them to raise local American Indians against him. Hamilton returned fire from the fort, blasting down several town houses but Clark's men in front of the main gate and those under Captain Joseph Bowman to the north-east were already so closely entrenched that they could fire through the gun ports, suppressing British cannon fire. A fierce exchange of musket fire then continued throughout the night, Clark deceiving Hamilton into believing he was under attack from a far larger force before, at 09.00 the following morning, Clark requested Hamilton surrender. The gun fight continued for another two hours just as soon as Hamilton declined only for Clark to repeated the request, this time declaring he was about to storm the fort. Hamilton met Clark in the local church to agree terms but in the meantime a loyalist American Indian and Canadien war party entered the town to be instantly captured. Clark released the Canadiens at the request of his own but unrepentently tomahawked the Indians to death as a warning to others.

Hamilton surrendered the following day surprised at the size of Clark's small force. In celebration of victory Clark's militia fired a British cannon which exploded mortally mortally wounding Bowman. Whilst Clark continued to raid British supply columns, Patriot settlers encouraged by his success began to move into Kentucky from Virginia, claiming the whole of Illinois Country for the American cause.

24 February 1303

Anglo-Scottish Wars
Battle of Roslin

KING EDWARD I of England had struggled to persuade the Scots to recognise him as their Lord Paramount but received a huge boost in 1298 at Falkirk when his English and Welsh archers annihilated the defensive schiltroms of William Wallace. Wallace's largely peasant Scottish Army had been stricken by the desertion of their cavalry and by two claimants of the Scottish throne, John 'Red' Comyn, Lord Badenoch and, on behalf of his father, Robert the Bruce VII, Earl of Carrick who reputedly had fought for the English. Both Comyn and Bruce were playing a game amidst a tangled web of Scottish politics and now benefited from Wallace's demise by becoming joint Guardians of Scotland. Bruce, however, soon resigned the position as his rivalry with Comyn intensified and also because a restoration of the previously impotent John Balliol as King of Scots had become a distinct possibility following Scottish diplomatic efforts in Paris.

Following Falkirk, Edward appointed Sir John Segrave as Governor of Scotland and Commander of Edinburgh Castle but it was not the rush of putting down Scottish revolts that stirred Segrave's blood but the love of a woman, Lady Margaret Ramsey of Dalhousie. Margaret had been the subject of Segrave's attention for several years but in 1302 he was astonished to learn that she had instead become betrothed to Sir Henry St Clair of Rosslyn. Since St Clair (who's father had recently died in the Tower of London) had previously sworn fealty to Edward but now backed reemerging Scottish independence through John Comyn and since most Scottish strongholds and abbeys had already been destroyed by earlier English raids, Edward granted the furious Segrave's request to head up another English invasion.

Crossing into Scotland in mid February 1303, Segrave made the catastrophic decision to split his force (30,000 but numbers are unreliable) into three with the intention of attacking three Scottish castles, Dalhousie, Rosslyn and Borthwick – the English moving so fast that the Scots were unaware until the alarm was raised by Prior Abernethy of Mount Lothian, a former Knight Templar. Wallace may have been present but the 8,000 Scots were led by Comyn who hid himself with 3,000 men in woods west of the River Esk, whilst the other 5,000 under Abernethy crossed east of the river to envelope Segrave who was about to besiege Rosslyn Castle, once his demands that Lady Margaret and her lover be handed over had been derisively rejected.

With complete knowledge of the local geography and achieving complete surprise, Abernethy and his 5,000 attacked early on 24 February 1303 catching most of Segrave's Englismen in bed rather than in armour. In a fierce but one-sided battle, the English began taking terrible losses, those that escaped running straight into Comyn who emerged from the woods to add to the rout before Segrave surrendered. In the meantime word of the battle had reached Dalhousie Castle where Sir Ralph Confrey commanding the English immediately abandoned the siege to ride to Segrave's assistance. On sighting the Scots in a prepared position, Confrey attacked, riding into a storm of arrows and advancing spearmen who drove him back over a precipice into a ravine. At the same time Segrave and his fellow prisoners attempted to escape but although Segrave was initially successful many of the others were caught and slaughtered. In the early afternoon the third English Army under Sir Robert Neville then approached from Borthwick Castle toward Mountmarle where the near exhausted Scots had been stirred into a final effort by Abernethy and reinforced by Sir Edward Ramsay (Margaret's brother) and Sir Gilbert Hay of Borthwick. Unaware of Confrey's fate Neville followed suit, riding straight into another trap, hit by another arrow storm from high ground above and in a desperate fight driven into a precipitous ravine at Roslin Glen.

The magnitude of the Scottish victory is debatable. The battle has been largely written out of the history books in that the Scottish victory was attributable to John Comyn, the bitter rival of Robert the Bruce. The English defeat, however, is certainly attributable to the reckless Segrave who was recaptured and ransomed. Edward would come north in person the following year to besiege Stirling Castle, gateway to the Highlands.

25 February 1921

Anglo-Irish War
Coolavokig Ambush

 FAILURE TO DELIVER Irish Home Rule after a final successful passage through Westminster led to nationalist Irish Volunteers declaring independence from British Rule on the steps of the Dublin General Post Office in 1916. The repression of the German-sponsored Easter Rising by 16,000 British troops destroyed the centre of Dublin just as 50,000 Irishmen – Catholics and Protestants, Nationalists and Unionists – were preparing to fight for 'King and Country' on the River Somme. The Irish public were hardly enthusiastic about the Rising at the time and though the majority of those found guilty of treason were treated leniently, Irish politics became polarised, the pro independence party Sinn Fein going on to win 73 of the 105 Irish seats in the 1918 British General Election. Sinn Fein did not take their seats at Westminster but instead formed the Dail Eireann, an independent Irish Parliament which suffered a very low turn out at its inaugural meeting since many of its elected members were in hiding or in custody.

The same day, at Soloheadbeg, two Royal Irish Constabulary (RIC) constables were shot dead by nationalist Irish Volunteers starting a subversive war of terror against continued British rule by the paramilitary arm of Sinn Fein, the Irish Republican Army (IRA) led by Michael Collins. To oppose the IRA, and to maintain order, the largely Irish-manned RIC was boosted by the Auxiliary Division (ADRIC) and Temporary Constables (Black and Tans) recruited from former British Army officers and servicemen of the Great War under the command of former artillery genius Lieutenant General Henry Tudor.

When Collins and the IRA then began a war on soft targets in rural Munster and Connacht, 'Tudors Toughs' sallied from their barracks to hand out brutal reprisals of their own. Meanwhile pro union, mainly Protestant Ulster remained quiet whilst assassinations, ambushes, robberies and arson became rife in the lawless south, most citizens, especially Protestants, living in fear of a midnight visit from paramilitary gunmen. A week after Bloody Sunday, November 1920, seventeen Auxiliaries were ambushed by IRA gunmen at Kilmichael and a fortnight later another thirteen were ambushed at Dillon's Cross, Cork precipitating a reprisal from 'Tudor's Toughs' who set ablaze the centre of Cork, destroying over 300 commercial and domestic properties. Violence intensified before another big IRA ambush was planned by the Cork No1 Brigade under Sean O'Hegarty at Ballyvourney, Cork.

O'Hegarty, who had already been captured and released by the security forces, had become aware that Auxiliaries based in Macroom habitually patrolled the road through Ballyvourney. Deciding on an ambush at Coolavokig where the road was dominated by rocky ground with good fields of fire O'Hegarty placed Lewis guns at the eastern and western ends of his position and a lookout post on Rahoonagh Hill which dominated the immediate area. He and his sixty-four men then waited a week, moving into position before dawn and leaving after dusk each day before at 08.00 on 25 February 1921, sighting nine lorries in the east. However, as the lorries approached O'Hegarty's position was given away by one of his own men rushing for position having been caught out by the sudden early arrival. The IRA gunmen still hoped to lure the Auxiliaries into the trap but opened fire with the eastern Lewis gun and several rifles when Major Seafield Grant and 111 heavily armed men jumped down a hundred yards short of the ambush killing zone. Grant was soon dead but other Auxiliaries advanced, some taking cover within two adjacent cottages whilst others tried to outflank the IRA gunmen. One of the lorries then departed hastily back to Macroom for reinforcements as an intense gun battle developed, the flanking Auxiliaries driven back to the cottages which then became the focus of a three-hour gun battle. Short of ammunition the Auxiliaries were about to be overrun but were saved by the arrival of several hundred reinforcements, O'Hegarty fighting a withdrawal north-west.

The security forces had lost another sixteen men dead and wounded and had failed to inflict any damage on O'Hegarty's flying column. As the British now withdrew from South West Ireland the killings and beatings continued, many Protestant civilians leaving for Ulster or England. Collins would soon take the war back to the heart of British Government in Ireland, braving 10,000 British troops to attack the Dublin Custom House.

26 February 1991
Gulf War
Battle of 7 Easting

 DURING THE 1980–88 Iran-Iraq War, Iraq had benefited from financial 'loans' from Saudi Arabia and Kuwait, the demand for repayment of which, on the war's conclusion, left Iraqi President Saddam Hussein struggling to rebuild his economy (Hussein claimed the loans had been free aid against Iranian aggression). The consequent difficulty in Iraq obtaining further loans, an excessively low oil price blamed on Kuwaiti over production and Kuwaiti slant drilling into Iraqi oilfields then led to a 1990 Iraqi invasion of Kuwait. The Iraqi Army, capable of fielding over a million men with several thousand T-72 and T-55 Soviet-built tanks, caught the Kuwaitis remarkably unprepared and within hours had taken the objective which Hussein then claimed as the 19th Province of Iraq (before the Great War British defeat of the Ottoman Empire, Kuwait had been ruled from Basra, Iraq but was created an autonomous state in 1922 to prevent her absorption into Saudi Arabia).

The Iraqi invasion was immediately condemned by the United Nations Security Council and the Arab League of Nations which pressed for a solution excluding non Arab military intervention before King Faud of Saudi Arabia, fearful for his own oil fields, requested military support from the United States of America. US President George H.W. Bush began reinforcing the US fleet in the Persian Gulf and patrolling Saudi airspace with Kuwait and Iraq as an international military coalition including several Arab nations assembled under US General Norman Schwarzkopf. On 15 January 1991 a massive aerial bombardment, Operation Desert Storm, began when Iraq not only failed to withdraw from Kuwait but advanced into Saudi Arabia, an advance defeated at Khafji by Arab troops and coalition air power. Hussein then also failed to derail the Arab coalition against him by launching Scud missile attacks on Israel. UN reconnaissance in force and Special Forces began crossing the Saudi/Iraq border with artillery barrages adding to the destruction of Iraqi infrastructure and front line units. On 24 February 1991, against a backdrop of armageddon, hundreds of oil wells fired by Iraqi troops, coalition armoured and infantry units crossed into Kuwait and further west into Iraq – Operation Desert Sabre.

On 26 February 1991 the US VII Corps, 1,500 tanks and 300,000 infantry including the US Task Force 1-41 Infantry, the 1st, 2nd and 3rd US Armored Divisions, the US 1st and 2nd Cavalry (Armored) Divisions (ACR) and British 1st Armoured Division (on the right flank) turned east to complete a huge left hook on demoralised Iraqi forces already retreating from southern Kuwait and on the elite of the Iraqi Army, the Republican Guard. Challenger Main battle tanks of the British 1st Armoured Division fought sharp engagements against the Iraqi Medina Division whilst to their left the 70-ton M1A1 Abrams tanks and Bradley fighting vehicles of the US 3rd Armored Division drove east across open desert through a sandstorm, their progress over the featureless terrain marked by a series of 'eastings'. The Americans, however, benefited from thermal imaging systems to identify their opponents, the 2nd ACR encountering the Tawakalna Division of the Republican Guard dug in on reverse slopes at the 73 Easting. Firing on the move at high speed through minefields surprise was complete, Iraqi armour destroyed before returning fire. The Tawakalna tried to counter-attack but they were no match for American firepower, their refusal to surrender leading to heavy casualties. 73 Easting was over in ninety minutes but that night the British began their biggest artillery barrage since the Second World War preparatory to a push by US 1st Infantry, 2nd Armored and British 1st Armoured Divisions to prevent surviving Iraqi units from retreating back into Iraq. The Tawakalna were among eleven Iraqi Divisions destroyed over two days of fighting, additional casualties mounting along 50 miles of the heavily bombed 'Highway of Death' to Basra.

On 28 February, after 100 hours of ground fighting, US President George Bush declared a ceasefire, Iraq had conceded the twelve resolutions of the UN Security Council. The coalition had suffered only 1,185 casualties many to 'friendly fire', the Iraqis over 50,000. The failure to push on into Iraq, a known sponsor of terrorist organisations, could have prevented a second conflict a decade later when coalition forces would have to do exactly that.

27 February 1881
First Boer War
Battle of Majuba Hill

THE 1879 BRITISH defeat of the Zulu had given Dutch Boers in the neighbouring Transvaal the confidence to declare independence from Great Britain and back it up with a force of arms. For two months the British High Commissioner of South Eastern Africa Major General George Colley had lurched from one disaster to another, Bronkhorstspruit, Laings Nek and Ingogo leaving British garrisons in the Transvaal besieged with scant chance of relief. In London the anti-imperialist Prime Minister William Gladstone was also under pressure dealing with the coldest winter on record as well as trouble in Ireland and Afghanistan from where he had recently ordered a British withdrawal. Gladstone was never enthusiastic expending finances on overseas ventures and he now offered Transvaal President Paul Kruger Boer independence under British suzerainty, Britain maintaining control of Transvaal foreign policy against any potential future Portuguese or worse, German annexation. Queen Victoria was not amused, her distrust of Gladstone, who she claimed addressed her as though she were a public meeting, reaching new highs but though she voiced her discontent privately there was little she could do.

In Natal meanwhile, Colley was bristling with indignation at his successive defeats but he had been reinforced by the 92nd (Gordon Highlanders) Regiment of Foot returning from Afghanistan and India. He now received a cable from London ordering him to offer the Boers terms and to give a 'reasonable' time for Kruger (believed to be in Heidelberg but in fact twelve days away in Rustenburg) to comply. Even less amused than Victoria, Colley took full advantage of the word 'reasonable' by insisting on forty-eight hours, the British commander instantly planning what would be a futile but daring expedition to turn the Boer right flank at Laing's Nek just as soon as this deadline expired. On the night of 26 February African guides led 405 men of the 92nd and 58th (Rutlandshire) Regiments of Foot forward with all their equipment for a scaling of the steep, rocky-faced, table-topped, Majuba Hill under the nose of Boer positions just a mile away. Thinking the war to be practically over, the complacent Boers, did not think it possible and had posted only weak pickets who with some good fortune at last for Colley had gotten themselves lost just as the British ascent began.

At 04.00 on 27 February 1881 Colley and his exhausted men reached the Majuba plateau with the Boers 2,000 feet below still unaware. By sunrise many of his men were asleep but Colley saw no need to raise them or further fortify the natural defences in the belief the British position was impregnable, indeed he claimed 'we could stay here forever'. On waking and realising they had been duped, the Boer Commandants Nicolaas Smit, Stephanus Roos and Joachim Ferreira restored initial panic to begin climbing Majuba with 500 men ranging from old men to teenagers, all expert marksmen with plenty of previous experience doing just this against the Zulu. Employing revolutionary fire and move tactics under covering fire from below the Boers gradually inched their way up the rocky slopes whilst the British fired harmlessly overhead. Watching from above, Lieutenant Ian Hamilton reported the gathering threat to Colley who, with supreme arrogance, did nothing except thank him. By the time an increasingly concerned Hamilton made his fourth report Colley was asleep in his tent.

The British lining the crest of the plateau continued to return fire but after several hours Ferreira and 200 Boers had successfully scaled a small Kopje (knoll) at one end of the plateau from where they fired on the charge into the Highlanders. The Highlanders fled back into the centre desperate for some cover, all cohesion lost as further British units retreated from the plateau rim. The superior Boer marksmanship now picked off retreating British infantry mercilessly with just a few holding their ground to engage in bitter hand-to-hand combat. Colley at last emerged from his tent and attempted to rally but it was too late, Boers now swarming over the plateau rim looking to exact a terrible price for his duplicity. As over half the Rutlandshires and Highlanders became casualties or were taken prisoner, only one man stood his ground, a bullet to the forehead ending his resistance, Colley.

Kruger had gained Boer independence but eighteen years later the British would 'Remember Majuba' when the issue resurfaced with interest.

28 February 1799

French Revolutionary War
Battle of the Hooghly River

IN 1789 NATIONAL fervour had swept through France after years of struggle against poor harvests and debts incurred from eighteenth-century wars that had not been borne by the nobility to anything like the extent of the general populace. As the 'Rights of Man and of the Citizen' were declared, overthrowing the *Ancien Regime*, neighbouring monarchies watched with alarm, expressing concern for the well-being of the French King Louis XVI and his family. As the revolutionaries became more radical, these monarchies led by Britain, Austria and Prussia began the War of the First Coalition against the Legislative Assembly of the French First Republic. Their concern did poor Louis no good, guillotined in La Place de la Révolution (Concorde) four months after the French had fought back at Valmy as belief in their cause of *liberté, egalité and fraternité* only increased. The French desire to spread their philosophies to the rest of Europe was then successful in the Dutch Republic and by extension Dutch territories globally, notably at the Cape of Good Hope and the Dutch East Indies which consequently came under French control. A disastrous expedition to Flanders apart the British role in containing France had been at sea, the Royal Navy blockading the French coast and overrunning the Dutch Cape Colony (Cape Town).

In 1796, France, now governed by the Directory, then nobly looked to spread the 'Rights of Man' by abolishing slavery in their only remaining Indian Ocean territory, Ile de France (Mauritius). Four frigates and two corvettes under Rear Admiral Pierre de Sercey ran the British blockade at Rochefort but only the frigates arrived in Port Louis which itself was also blockaded by the Royal Navy, albeit loosely. Those sent to abolish slavery, however, were given short shrift by the locals (it would have decimated the economy) and headed back to France but not Sercey who, with two extra ships from Port Louis headed for Batavia (Dutch East Indies) to raid British East Indiamen in the Bali Strait. Largely unsuccessful, Sercey returned to Port Louis only for his fleet to be broken up over the next two years leaving him with just his flagship, the world's most powerful frigate, the 52-gun *Forte* captained by Hubert de Beaulieu.

Meanwhile throughout 1798 the main threat to British India had been from a military expedition to Egypt by the 29-year-old French General Napoleon Bonaparte. By conquering Egypt, Napoleon was looking to support an uprising further east in Mysore, southern India by the fervently anti British Tipu Sultan, hopefully then also expelling the British from Bengal. At the beginning of 1799 the threat of Napoleon, marooned in Egypt after his fleet had been destroyed in Aboukir Bay by Rear Admiral Horatio Nelson, meant almost the entire British East India Station had left the Bay of Bengal for the Red Sea.

Since Sercey was now back in Batavia, Beaulieu acted independently, sailing into the Bay of Bengal where Forte devastated British traders exiting Calcutta on the River Hooghly. To oppose Beaulieu, Captain Edward Cooke sailed north from Madras (Chennai) on 19 February in the 48-gun HMS *Sybille*, a far less powerful frigate captured from the French in 1794. Searching for *Forte* off Balasore on the night of 28 February 1799, Cooke was attracted by flashes to the north-east, turning to investigate he found *Forte* and two captured East Indiamen at 21.30. Initially sailing west to catch the weather gauge *Sybille* then closed on *Forte* with a seemingly unconcerned Beaulieu returning only sporadic fire. Cooke approached to within twenty-five yards of the Frenchman's stern to deliver two catastrophic broadsides, immediately killing Beaulieu before a three-hour exchange of musketry and broadsides raged, the accuracy of the British gunners firing both balls and grape far superior to that of their French counterparts. *Forte's* hull was eventually shattered, bringing down her masts with 145 French sailors killed or wounded.

Cooke could not take the French surrender, among the twenty-two British casualties the captain died in Calcutta three months later, he is remembered in Westminster Abbey. Forte entered the Royal Navy under Cooke's Lieutenant, Lucius Hardyman. With the danger to British India from Egypt and the Bay of Bengal now averted, that from Mysore was left to one of Britain's greatest future Generals, Arthur Wellesley.

29 February 1884

Mahdist Wars
Second Battle of El Teb

 BY MID FEBRUARY 1884 the Islamic uprising of Muhammad Ahmad, the Mahdi (the guided one) and his *Ansar* (following) was threatening to overrun the Sudan completely. The British Government of William Gladstone had shored up financial and strategic liabilities in Egypt with an overwhelming show of force in 1882 at Tel El-Kebir but so far had shown little interest in subjugating the vast Sudanese deserts they had consequently inherited. After British Colonel William Hicks had been killed in a fateful 1883 Egyptian expedition to El Obeid and Valentine Baker had been defeated at El Teb in early February 1884 pressure increased from imperialists to stem the Mahdi's revolt but the reluctant anti-imperialist Gladstone resolved only to reinforce the borders of Egypt, protect the Suez Canal, the Red Sea Ports and by extension the route to India. With reservations Gladstone sent his 'best man', Major General Charles 'Chinese' Gordon, a former Governor General of the Sudan in Ottoman employ, to evacuate Egyptian garrisons and civilians before effectively leaving the country to its fate. A veteran of the Crimean War, Opium Wars and Taiping Rebellion the undeniably brave Gordon was much loved by the British people – Queen Victoria included – but evacuating the Sudan would be no easy task, he himself stating in the Pall Mall Gazette that to stand and fight would be his action of choice, questioning an evacuation with the words 'the moment it is known we have given up the game every man will go over to the Mahdi'. The man to provide that moment, however, was Gordon himself, announcing just that whilst en route to Khartoum to a dismayed garrison and officialdom at Berber, yet on arriving in Khartoum on 18 February 1884 Gordon immediately began to do the opposite by planning a defence of the city.

Gordon also opened a dialogue with the Mahdi, offering him the Governorship of Kordofan that though genuine showed a complete failure to understand the enemy cause especially since it was accompanied by a red cloak and a tarboosh, symbols of the hated Ottoman regime the Mahdi was looking to replace not just in the Sudan but across the whole Middle East. The Mahdi already controlled west, south and central Sudan anyway whilst in the north-east his ally, Osman Digna of the Hadendoa, had been victorious at El Teb. Not only were the *Ansar* growing in confidence but potentially so too also British Mohammedan subjects further east where the British were still mindful of the 1857 Muslim led, Indian Mutiny. Strong military action was called for by Lord Garnet Wolseley, victor of Tel El-Kebir, not least to aid Gordon's evacuations down the Nile but also to deter would be rebellions further east and provide security to the Red Sea ports. Fail now and a far larger war would be in the offing – having sent Gordon, Gladstone had no choice but to comply.

On 21 February Lieutenant General Gerald Graham marched out of the Red Sea port of Suakin with 4,500 regular British Army troops diverted en route home from India, twenty-two guns and six machine-guns for a second confrontation with Digna at El Teb. After an eight-day march guided by Baker himself across ground covered with the gruesome remains of his Egyptians from three weeks previous, Graham came across the Hadendoa on 29 February 1844 in well defended positions outside El Teb complete with six pieces of artillery (formerly Baker's) and reinforcements from other tribes including Tokar garrison defectors. A short artillery duel saw the British silence the Mahdist guns before the British infantry formed square and advanced. The Hadendoa did not charge en masse as per their usual *modus operandi* but remained in their trenches or attacked in pockets, the British devastating the charges with concerted volley fire before clearing the trenches with the bayonet. Fierce fighting raged for several hours until Abdallah Hasid commanding the Mahdists withdrew leaving over 4,000 casualties on the field.

As a favoured Mahdist tactic was to fake death and attack from the rear many of the wounded were shot causing uproar back in Britain, but Graham had achieved a temporary security of the Red Sea coast with only minor casualties. Digna was far from finished however, Graham would again fight the Hadendoa just two weeks later at Tamai.

March

"By God, we're still alive!"

LIEUTENANT TOM BOYD,
ST NAZAIRE, 1942

1 March 1579

Anglo-Spanish Wars
Capture of the Nuestra Señora
de la Concepción

ON 15 NOVEMBER 1577 five small ships sailed out of Plymouth to begin the greatest journey man had ever undertaken. A voyage so dangerous that only one of the previous dozen ships to have gone before had returned and even then without its Captain, Ferdinand Magellan. Captaining this expedition was the greatest sailor of his day, Francis Drake, a man feared by the Spanish from a piratical voyage to the Spanish Main five years before but who now had unwritten backing and sponsorship from Elizabeth I, Queen of England. Drake sailed in his flagship the 150-ton *Pelican*, accompanied by John Winter in the 80-ton *Elizabeth*, John Thomas in the 30-ton *Marigold*, John Chester in the 50-ton *Swan* and Tom Moone in the impossibly small 15-ton *Benedict*, together with 160 crewmen (80 of them in the *Pelican*) they were on their way to the very edge of the world, the South Pacific coasts of Chile and Peru by way of the Strait of Magellan. Drake's target was the vast riches being transported home across both the Atlantic and the Pacific oceans by the dominant colonial power in South America, Spain, and the treasury of their King, Philip II who was busy suppressing Protestantism in the Spanish Netherlands. Although Protestant England was not officially at war with Spain, Elizabeth, who owed her very existence to the demise of Catholicism, had little moral dilemma in relieving Philip of treasure just so long as her name could not be directly associated. Noblemen such as Thomas Doughty, however, were more than happy to seize the chance for enormous profit, joining the expedition in person.

A terrific Atlantic storm forced the English fleet home before setting sail again on 13 December. Sailing down the coast of West Africa to Cape Verde, Drake captured the Portuguese *Santa Maria*, renaming her the Mary and placing Doughty in command. It was not long, though, before Doughty and Drake were openly at odds, Drake trying to restore harmony by giving Doughty command of the *Pelican*. Doughty, however, continued to provoke discontent, scaring sailors with stories of witchcraft (a dangerous game in Elizabethan times) and was transferred from ship to ship by an increasingly irate Drake. Doughty's mutinous ways continued even when tied to a mizzen mast until Drake's patience finally snapped at Port St Julian, Argentina, where Doughty was tried, found guilty of treason and beheaded. Drake then renamed the *Pelican* the *Golden Hind* and for a fortnight fought his way through the ferocious storms and seas of the Strait of Magellan, losing his two accompanying ships, the *Marigold* to shipwreck and the *Elizabeth* which turned back (the open sea passage further south around Cape Horn was unknown at the time). The *Golden Hind* was now alone in the Pacific but began raiding the Chilean coast and Spanish shipping. The booty was disappointing but Drake soon learnt of a large treasure ship, the *Nuestra Señora de la Concepción*, sailing fully laden from Callao (Lima, Peru) to Panama. In pursuit, Drake raided Callao to gather further information and learnt he was now just three days behind. On 1 March 1579, just north of the equator off Ecuador, John Drake (cousin) spotted sails to seaward, it was the *Nuestra Señora* which had stopped several times en route and was still completely ignorant of any English presence in the Pacific. The *Golden Hind* gave chase but only slowly, towing barrels behind to give the pretence of a slow-moving merchantman but with a small pinnace hidden behind which after a ten hour pursuit swung to port as Drake called for the Spanish Captain, San Juan de Anton, to surrender. Despite a lack of artillery, Anton ignored the request only to receive a broadside of cannonballs and arquebuses which brought down his mizzen mast and sent his crew racing for cover. Drake's pinnace then moved alongside with her boarding party. Anton surrendered.

The *Nuestra Señora's* cargo did not disappoint, eighty pounds of gold, twenty-six tons of silver and fourteen chests of reals, £126,000 in Tudor money to add to previous gains, half the Crown's annual revenue. Drake now had every Spaniard in the Pacific looking for him and was a long, long way from home, he graciously gave his prisoners a souvenir as he freed them before heading north to what is now San Francisco Bay. After repairing the *Golden Hind* Drake crossed the Pacific, the Indian and the Atlantic oceans, arriving in Plymouth in September 1580 to receive a knighthood from a delighted queen. King Philip would fruitlessly argue for the return of his treasure but for Spain the scourge of Drake would only get worse, he would be back in the Caribbean in 1586. A replica of the Golden Hind exists in St Mary Overie Dock, Southwark, London.

2 March 1743

War of Jenkins' Ear
Battle of La Guaira

THE AFTERMATH OF the War of the Spanish Succession was highlighted by large numbers of unemployed soldiers and sailors making their way to the Caribbean for a living outside the law. Joining previously state-licensed privateers and log cutters from the swamps and jungles of Panama and Honduras there was still the temptingly lucrative targets of Spanish treasure ships heading across the Atlantic financing a decaying superpower while slave ships sailed in the opposite direction supplying the sugar plantations of the Caribbean and the indigo and rice plantations of the Carolinas and Georgia. The Asiento won by the British in 1713 to trade legally but in limited quantities with the Spanish New World was almost impossible to regulate, Spanish accusations of over-trading leading to Britain signing the Treaty of Seville in 1729 which allowed Spanish customs to board and inspect their merchantmen. In 1731, however, a British Captain, Robert Jenkins, reputedly had his ear severed by a Spanish coastguard who accused him of smuggling. When Jenkins reproduced the ear seven years later in the House of Commons, Westminster it was enough to ignite a more aggressive British policy in the Caribbean.

In 1739 Vice Admiral Edward Vernon sacked Portobello but was then catastrophically defeated in 1741 at Cartagena, losing fifty ships and possibly as many as 18,000 men largely to yellow fever. The War of Jenkins' Ear then became a sideshow as Europe was again consumed by a War of Succession, this time Austrian, caused by the death of Habsburg Holy Roman Emperor Charles VI and predominantly Prussian, Bavarian, Spanish and French opposition to his daughter Maria Theresa as the first and only Empress of the Holy Roman Empire. To maintain the European balance of power for which she had fought four decades earlier, Britain maintained her allegiance with the Habsburgs who were also backed by the Dutch Republic, Hanover, Saxony, Sardinia and Russia. Exposed to a French and/or a Spanish invasion of Britain the Royal Navy was kept on the eastern side of the Atlantic ocean which meant the prosecution of the War of Jenkins' Ear on the other side was less resolute, a 1741 Royal Navy blockade of Spanish St Augustine, Florida failing as well as a 1742 invasion of Cuba. Spain, for her part, that same year also failed with an invasion of Georgia.

Following the debacle at Cartagena, Sir Chaloner Ogle, knighted in 1722 for defeating the pirate Bartholomew Roberts (Black Bart), replaced Vice Admiral Edward Vernon as Commander in Chief Jamaica Station and resolved to assault the Spanish ports of La Guaira and Puerto Cabello, Venezuela. Ogle ordered Sir Charles Knowles to sail from Antigua with ten ships of the line and nine others to attack La Guaira, both men mistakenly believing the town to be poorly-defended despite Thomas Waterhouse suffering a heavy defeat there four years before. Knowles arrived off La Guaira early on 2 March 1743 sending a reconnaissance into the harbour as the town's well-informed Governor Gabriel de Zuloaga reinforced defences with local militia while the garrison of Captain Jose Iturriaga manned the guns. At midday HMS *Assistance, Advice, Burford, Eltham, Norwich* and *Suffolk* then sailed in closer to anchor in double line under a ferocious bombardment from six Spanish shore batteries. Once in position the British ships began a reply but in rough water were unable to land any troops. After three hours, three of Knowles' ships weighed anchor to move out of range whilst the other three continued firing for another five hours. The Spanish certainly had the better of the exchange but Knowles returned the following morning and again, on the 5 March, before throwing in the towel having suffered 400 casualties for no gain. He now sailed west for Puerto Cabello via Curacao.

On 26 April at Puerto Cabello, Knowles began another bombardment and successfully landed 1,200 troops who advanced only to be cut down by grapeshot. On 2 May Zuloaga then arrived with reinforcements from La Guaira as an artillery exchange developed under Fort San Felipe. By 5 May Knowles had had enough but could not retreat due to a lack of wind, suffering another 100 casualties whilst becalmed. Hostilities now concentrated in Europe but Knowles would manage more debacles off Cuba in 1748, the final actions of both the Austrian and War of Jenkins' Ear. After a Court Martial the beleaguered captain would emerge unscathed from a duel, one of several between his subordinates.

3 March 1942

Second World War Battle of Pegu

DURING THE 1633–1866 Sakoku Japan had been a 'closed' country but the Japanese were well aware of the growing domination of South East Asian trade and resources throughout the eighteenth and nineteenth centuries by the western imperial powers, specifically Great Britain, Holland and the United States. Initially hurt during the Great Depression of 1929–30 Japan's rapid recovery under Finance Minister Korekiyo Takahashi then led to fiscal tightening at the expense of the Japanese military which failed to usurp complete power but at least succeeded in becoming the main force in Japanese politics. The opportunity for the military to create a new order in South East Asia then came in 1940 with the demise of France, Holland and Great Britain at the hands of Nazi Germany, a surprise Japanese attack on the United States Pacific Fleet at Pearl Harbor coinciding with attacks on the Dutch East Indies, Borneo, the Philippines, Malaya and Thailand. By mid-February 1942 virtually all South East Asia was now controlled by Japan – Hong Kong and Singapore having fallen with the surrender of 130,000 British and Commonwealth troops. Japan had never envisaged a full invasion of British Burma despite widespread Burmese discontent at British rule but had planned to invade Tenasserim, an area bordering Thailand inland as far as Rangoon (Yangon), to prevent British counter-attacks on Malaya and to disrupt supplies reaching the Chinese Nationalist Army of Chiang Kai Shek via the Burma Road.

After strategic attacks on Victoria Point and the British airfields at Tavoy and Mergui, the Japanese 15th Army of Lieutenant General Shojiro Iida invaded Tenasserim through the jungles of the Kawkareik Pass on 22 January 1942. The efficient Japanese 55th Infantry Division was strongly resisted by Major General John Smyth's 17th Indian Infantry Division and three battalions of the Burma Rifles at Kawkareik and Moulmein, Smyth anxious to retreat but ordered to stand firm by General Officer Commanding Burma Thomas Hutton and Commander-in-Chief ABDACOM (American, British, Dutch, Australia Command) Archibald

Wavell. As Japanese forces began to infiltrate British positions, however, Smyth took it upon himself to withdraw across the Salween River before two days of hand-to-hand jungle fighting raged at the Bilin River. Hutton then allowed a further British retreat to the Sittang River and more specifically the Sittang Bridge. Under air attack and close Japanese contact on the ground Smyth desperately tried to get his division back across the bridge before blowing it; Rangoon certain to fall if the bridge fell into Japanese hands in tact. Faced with a terrible dilemma Smyth blew the bridge trapping half of his 8,000 men on the wrong side but at least forced Iida's 15th Army north to Pegu (Bago). With the 17th Indian Division now virtually destroyed Wavell sacked Smyth and demoted Hutton, replacing him with General Harold Alexander.

On 3 March 1942, confused fighting broke out at Pegu fifty miles north of Rangoon, a defence mounted by the 48th Indian Infantry Brigade containing Gurkhas, Dogras, Burma Rifles, Sikhs and British with support from light tanks of the British 7th Armoured Brigade under Brigadier John Anstice. Four days of heavy fighting raged with Japanese troops infiltrating British positions whilst further south in Rangoon the arriving Alexander was immediately under aerial bombardment. Japanese forward units to Alexander's west and the Imperial Japanese Navy in the Bay of Bengal now threatened British lines of retreat to India. Alexander ordered Anstice south-west to join with the 16th Indian Brigade at Hlegu but on arrival Anstice ran into a determined Japanese block initially preventing his linking up with Alexander who was about to abandon Rangoon for a concentration of British forces in the Irrawaddy Valley. Another Japanese block at Taukkyan then left Alexander unable to breakout from Rangoon for over twenty-four hours, his fortune turning when confused Japanese orders led to the removal of the block overnight, Iida transfixed with taking Rangoon rather than defeating Alexander.

Anstice too succeeded in breaking out to join Alexander's retreat up the Irrawaddy Valley. Meanwhile the First Burma Division also retreated from East Burma up the Sittang Valley to be relieved by Chiang Kai Shek's 5th Chinese Army before transferring west to form part of Burma Corps under Major General William Slim. Iida had presumed the British would stand and fight for Rangoon but now he would have to fight them across Burma to the borders of British India.

4 March 1941

Second World War
Raid on the Lofoten Islands

NORWAY HAD MAINTAINED neutrality during the Great War and was anxious to continue so doing at the outbreak of the Second World War but both Germany and Great Britain were sensitive to the country's strategic importance. In February 1940 the supply ship to the German heavy cruiser *Admiral Graf Spee* (now on the seabed off Montevideo), the *Altmark*, took a detour through safe Norwegian waters, a clear infringement of neutrality. Norwegian escort ships gave assurances that no British prisoners of war were onboard the *Altmark* only for British sailors from the destroyer HMS *Cossack* to board (again infringing Norwegian neutrality) the ship and release 299 British prisoners, killing seven Germans in the process.

Anxious to protect supplies of iron ore from Sweden and secure ice free ports for access to the Atlantic, German Chancellor Adolf Hitler then invaded Norway with 10,000 troops as far north as Narvik. The Royal Navy Home Fleet based at Scapa Flow, Orkney then contested Norwegian waters with the German Kriegsmarine, both sides suffering heavy losses as British, French and Polish troops joined Norwegian resistance on land. Narvik was recaptured but on 24 April 1940, with troops required in western Europe, the Allies began pulling out of Norway altogether, destroying the port at Narvik as they did so. The failure to defend Norway meant German warships and U-boats now had a multitude of ports and fjords from which to attack Allied shipping in the North Atlantic, the consequent 'Norway Debate' leading to the resignation of British Prime Minister Neville Chamberlain. After the June 1940 fall of France and the British evacuation from Dunkirk the incoming British Prime Minister Winston Churchill, anxious to maintain an offence that would bolster morale, formed the Special Operations Executive and Combined Operations Headquarters to conduct damaging raids on German military installations. The first commando raid, Operation Collar, an attack on Hardelot and Le Touquet, France, achieved nothing but by 1941 with more than 2,000 men now fully trained, a larger attack was planned off the Norwegian coast on the Lofoten Islands, Operation Claymore.

On 4 March 1941, a British fleet of five destroyers and two converted ex Dutch passenger liners arrived at Vestfjorden in the Lofoten Islands carrying 500 men of No.3 and 4 Commando under Major John Durnford-Slater and former British amateur heavyweight boxer Lieutenant Colonel Dudley Lister. Their mission, supported by engineers and fifty-two Norwegians, was to destroy all shipping under German control and the local industry of fish oil and glycerine used by the German Wehrmacht for the manufacture of explosives. The 06.50 landings at Stamsund, Svolvaer, Henningsvaer and Brettesnes achieved complete surprise with only an armed trawler *Krebs* offering any real resistance before being sunk. Once ashore, the commandos much to their disappointment also met minimal resistance, quickly going about their business in the snowbound streets to destroy eleven merchant ships, 800,000 gallons of fish oil and their eighteen factories. After sending a message to Hitler from the German radio station, the commandos reembarked at 13.00 with 225 German prisoners, sixty *Quislings* (Norwegian collaborators), over 300 Norwegians volunteering for Free Norwegian Forces and an English chemist working for Messrs Allen & Hanbury. The greatest prize, however, was recovered from *Krebs*, known to have an Enigma cipher machine onboard by British intelligence. Although the trawler captain had thrown the Enigma overboard into the icy depths before being killed, two rotors, code books and bigram tables were captured. German naval transmissions had been tougher to break than those of the *Luftwaffe* but now Bletchley Park would soon be discovering the locations of German warships and U-boat wolf packs so successfully that German Admiral Karl Donitz was soon questioning whether his codes had been broken.

Operation Claymore has been considered the first Allied victory of the Second World War. Churchill would go on to order a further thirty-seven commando raids over the next four years. Germany reinforced Norway to the extent that 300,000 troops were tied up there for the duration of the war.

5 March 1811

Napoleonic Wars
Battle of Barrosa

THROUGHOUT 1810 THE Napoleonic Wars had been confined to the Iberian Peninsular with the remainder of Continental Europe once again either allied to France or under French control. The short lived Fifth Coalition had effectively ended the year before when after just three months the French *Grande Armée* decisively defeated Austria at Wagram leaving the Emperor of the French, Napoleon Bonaparte facing active organised opposition once again from just Great Britain but also from rebellions and growing armies in Spain and Portugal, the latter under British tutelage. Austria's defeat, however, allowed Napoleon to bring his forces in Spain up to 325,000, opening the door to Portugal with Marshal André Masséna's victories at Ciudad Rodrigo and Almeida before being temporarily halted at Busaco by an Anglo-Portuguese Army under Lieutenant General Arthur Wellesley, Viscount Wellington. Wellington then retreated in considerable discomfort to his fortifications outside Lisbon, the lines of Torres Vedras the strength of which the pursuing Masséna immediately recognised, withdrawing to Santarem after a month of misery due to Wellington's additional scorched earth policy throughout the surrounding countryside. Further south, in early 1810, the King of Spain and catalyst for the Spanish uprising, Napoleon's brother Joseph Bonaparte, had advanced south into Andalusia with the army of Marshal Jean de Dieu Soult, capturing Seville before Soult and Marshal Claude Victor with 25,000 troops continued on to Cadiz. Only a few days before Cadiz had been completely undefended but now contained 12,000 Spanish troops under Jose Maria de la Cueva, Duke of Alburquerque who, combined with the geography and fortifications of Cadiz, meant Soult's chances of taking the city were now slim, even more so when more allied troops, including Anglo-Portuguese from Lisbon (Wellington now more than comfortable) arrived to bring defence strength up to 26,000. In January 1811 Soult gave up and marched back north with 10,000 troops to besiege Badajoz, potentially supporting Masséna's struggle in Portugal but now leaving Victor outside Cadiz vulnerable to a British, Spanish, Portuguese counter-attack.

On 23 February 1811 5,000 Anglo-Portuguese under Lieutenant General Thomas Graham landed at Algeciras, sixty miles east of Cadiz to be joined three days later by 10,000 Spaniards under General Manuel la Peña. La Peña and Graham then marched toward Cadiz to attack Victor from behind while General Jose de Zayas y Chacon would sortie from Cadiz itself. Delays and an errant message meant Zayas' premature sortie on 3 March was ruthlessly thrown back by Victor who, now aware of the allied coastal approach, prepared a trap. On 5 March 1811 la Peña advanced his Spanish vanguard from the Barrosa Ridge toward the block of General Eugene Villatte's French division at the Sancti Petri Creek. Aided by another Zayas sortie, Villatte was ousted but la Peña had left Graham in his rear dangerously exposed to two French divisions under General's Francois Ruffin and Jean Leval hidden in the Chiclana Forest. Graham reluctantly moved off the Barrosa Ridge to follow la Pena leaving five Spanish and one British battalion under Colonel John Browne to hold the position whilst Spaniards and the King's German Legion (cavalry) under Colonel Samuel Whittingham covered his flank. When Ruffin emerged from the forest, however, the Spaniards fled forcing Browne to leave the ridge under the protection of the KGL sent back by Whittingham. Now appraised of the danger in his rear, Graham ignored la Peña and ordered Brigadier General William Dilkes to retake the Barrosa Ridge while Colonel William Wheatley blocked Leval. Browne also turned back up the ridge but was halted by Ruffin's artillery. Dilkes, however, now arrived on the Browne's right, climbing the ridge to halt the descending French in an exchange of musket volleys before renewing his advance to break them. To their left Wheatley's skirmishers hounded Leval in the forest who then fled under fire from British field artillery.

Graham eventually marched into Cadiz having lost 1,200 men furious that la Peña had not moved to support his attack. The siege of Cadiz would continue until August 1812. The same day as Barrosa, Masséna's wretched army retreated from Lisbon. There would be many more French retreats ahead.

6 March 1426

Hundred Years' War
Battle of St James

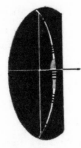

IN 1422 THE English regent of France John, Duke of Bedford had taken over where his brother King Henry V had left off. To both he and his younger brother Humphrey, Duke of Gloucester the Kingdoms of England and France were entrusted (and to a council of bishops and knights) during the minority of King Henry VI, the longest in English history. Henry had become King of France as well as England by the 1420 Treaty of Troyes and on the recent deaths of both his father and maternal grandfather but was opposed in France by his uncle, the Dauphin Charles, who now proclaimed himself King charles VII of France despite being disinherited by Troyes. Taking advantage of the death of Henry V, the Dauphin increased his offensives against English held Normandy and English allied Burgundy with an army based on the *Auld Alliance* with Scotland but Bedford and Thomas Montagu, Earl of Salisbury had been more than equal, handing defeats to the Dauphinists at Cravant and Verneuil (the 'Second Agincourt') of such magnitude that a Scottish Army would never again take the field during the Hundred Years' War. Following these English victories, an advance on the Dauphin's stronghold at Bourges seemed likely but as had King Edward III after Crécy and Henry V after Agincourt, Bedford now chose to consolidate with a series of sieges in Maine and Anjou before considering any advance to the River Loire and Dauphin territory.

The war now stagnated somewhat due to a faltering of the Anglo-Burgundian alliance caused by Jacqueline, Countess of Hainault and Holland who had dubiously left her husband John, Duke of Brabant, the cousin of Philip, Duke of Burgundy. Jacqueline had fled to England where she fell in love with and married Humphrey, Duke of Gloucester. Jacqueline's divorce from John, however, was not recognised outside England and whilst she sought a papal dispensation to validate her marriage to Gloucester she also required allies to maintain her lands (she was Countess in her own right), the losing of which prompted her gallant but hot headed new husband to regain them with an army of mercenaries who for good measure went on to ravage the lands of her former husband. In support of his cousin, Burgundy then challenged Gloucester to a duel which required all Bedford's skills of diplomacy to avoid, the situation dissipating when Brabant regained the upper hand against Gloucester's mercenaries. Bedford then returned to England to diffuse yet another Gloucester row, this time with his uncle Henry Beaufort, the Chancellor, over the guardianship of the four-year-old King.

Military operations in France only restarted in 1425 when Salisbury began operations in Champagne and Maine. The lull had tempted the fickle John, Duke of Brittany to change sides, now declaring for the Dauphin. The defection prompted an English invasion of Brittany by Sir Thomas Rempston who based himself at St James de Beuvron on the Brittany/Normandy border. Arthur de Richemont, who had fought against the English at Agincourt, defected to them afterward to be made Duke of Touraine, only to then defect back to the Dauphin, then arrived at St James in February 1426 as the Constable of France with 16,000 Dauphinists and siege artillery to assist his brother, Duke John. Pounding the walls for several days, Richemont made two breaches which on 6 March 1426 his men assaulted in an effort to take the town from Rempston's garrison of just 600 men, mainly archers. A desperate struggle raged all day as the defenders fought for their lives against impossible odds until the ingenious Rempston decided on a last desperate throw of the dice. Leaving a bare minimum force to hold the breaches Rempston sallied out through a side gate with the remainder, creeping around behind the French to attack them in the rear with cries of 'Salisbury and St George!'. The French believed they were now being attacked by the main English Army in Brittany, panicked and fled, many drowning in the nearby lake. With nerves frayed, panic again erupted that night in the French camp without an English arrow being launched, most of the stores and artillery abandoned as they fled back to Fougères.

The incredible English victory was then complimented by William de la Pole, Earl of Suffolk who arrived with 1,500 men and advanced on Rennes. It was too much for Duke John, he requested a truce and by 1427 once again recognised King Henry VI as the rightful King of France. Bedford returned to France in 1427, whilst he would seek to reduce Mont St Michel the following year, Salisbury would advance against the Dauphin at Orléans on the River Loire, the pivotal siege of the Hundred Years' War.

7 March 1902

Second Boer War
Battle of Tweebosch

THE MAIN CAMPAIGNS of the Second Boer War had ended in British victory two years before but the failings of Field Marshal Lord Frederick Roberts had allowed thousands of Boers to maintain the cause of independence against British rule by roaming the South African Veld, attacking British interests whenever the opportunity arose. Lieutenant General Horatio Herbert Kitchener had responded by conducting large sweeps of the country with mounted infantry and by burning the farms off which the Boers lived, the women and children of the Veld paying the price, forcibly removed from their homes for a desperate existence in concentration camps where they died of starvation and typhoid in their thousands. Emily Hobhouse and Millicent Fawcett (President of the National Union of Women's Suffrage Societies) brought the plight of these people back to Britain but Kitchener, a man of steel resolve, merely blamed the continued Boer tactics. Indeed, peace talks with General Louis Botha had been pursued but intermediaries had often been treated as traitors by the Boers and shot. Kitchener had even turned to the wives of the Boer generals for help but with so many hard liners (Kitchener not one of them) on both sides any compromise had so far proved impossible.

Kitchener's method of trapping the Boer commandos had developed across the veld with the use of 8,000 manned blockhouses connected by the new invention of barbed wire. In the eastern Transvaal the system had worked well but less so in the greater expanses of the western Transvaal and the Orange Free State where a lack of water meant fewer blockhouses. In early February 1902, in an effort to trap Christiaan de Wet and Martinus Steyn, President of the Orange Free State, Kitchener formed a giant sweep involving 9,000 troops, mostly mounted, marching west across a fifty-mile front, flanked by lines of blockhouses and supported by seven armoured trains complete with search lights. The results were again disappointing and so the sweep turned back east with Kitchener, for the first time in what had been considered a white man's war (although the vast majority of casualties were black) arming native Africans to assist the British. Lang Riet apart the eastward sweep was another disappointment and again it turned back west but already De Wet and Steyn had fled north toward Mafeking, Cape Colony looking to join the arch bitter-einder General Koos De La Rey. Always armed with a pocket Bible, De La Rey from the beginning had always claimed war to be avoidable to the point of being accused of cowardice by Paul Kruger, President of the Transvaal. De la Rey had prophetically answered Kruger that he, Kruger, would still find him, De la Rey, in the field long after he, Kruger, had departed the country. Kruger, an original Voortrekker of 1835, had fled the Transvaal in tears in September 1900 and would only return posthumously in 1904.

In the western Transvaal, Kitchener had nine columns under separate commands specifically looking to trap the elusive De La Rey and his 3,000 strong commando but the British manoeuvres had so far produced no results whatsoever. After a February attack on a British wagon convoy at Yzer Spruit, General Lord Paul Methuen led a column of 1,250 men and four field guns out from Vryburg in yet another effort to hunt down De la Rey but on 7 March 1902, it was De la Rey who attacked Methuen at Klip Drift on the Great Hart's River, Tweebosch. As Methuen's vanguard reached the drift, De la Rey's commando opened a furious fire on his rear, the British gun battery commanded by Lieutenant Thomas Nesham then returning fire spiritedly for an hour before the Boers charged. Methuen, with the infantry in the centre, extended his line to continue a furious fire supported with further artillery from the battery of Lieutenant Gordon Venning. Whilst the regulars of the British column stubbornly held their ground, however, the irregular horse and yeomanry fled leaving Methuen's predicament desperate. With the crews under their command dead, Nesham and Venning both now manned their own guns, refusing calls to surrender before suffering the same fate. Shot in the thigh as his column was finally overwhelmed, Methuen surrendered to become the only British general to be captured during the Second Boer War.

A shocked Kitchener retired to his room unable to speak or eat for two days but the war was almost at an end. Methuen was released to a British hospital as De la Rey returned a favour Methuen had performed for his wife earlier in the war. For his compassion the undeniably brave De la Rey faced a Boer Court Martial.

8 March 1944

Second World War
Battle of Imphal

IN DECEMBER 1941 the Imperial Japanese Army invaded Burma (Myanmar) to protect their western flank in Malaya and to cut supplies heading to Chinese forces via Rangoon and the Burma Road. After a shambolic retreat from the Thai border, incoming British General Officer Commanding Burma Harold Alexander had been left with little option but to vacate Rangoon for a concentration in force in the Irrawaddy Valley. With all British counter-attacks failing, the newly-formed British Burma Corps under Lieutenant General William Slim then completed the longest retreat in British history, plagued by poor supplies (Bengal was in the midst of a severe famine), poor roads, refugees, thick jungle, Burmese insurgents and pursuing Japanese up the Irrawaddy Valley, across the Chindwin River all the way to British India. On realising the British had retreated, Chinese forces in East Burma then did likewise back to their own border leaving virtually the whole country in Japanese hands. The five-month Burmese monsoon then intervened before Commander-in-Chief India Archibald Wavell made a failed counter-attack back into Arakan, South West Burma whilst in February 1943 Brigadier Orde Wingate led 3,000 'Chindits' on a four-month, 1,000 mile jungle trek to attack Japanese supply lines, just five per cent of them returned fit. Again in October 1943, Lord Louis Mountbatten, Commander-in-Chief South East Asia Command sent the Indian XV Corps (part of Slim's British 14th 'Forgotten' Army) back into Arakan under Lieutenant General Philip Christison. Christison's advance was, however, stopped by heavy counter-attacks from the Japanese 55th Division of Major General Tokutaro Sakurai although Brigadier Geoffrey Evans, commanding a surrounded back room staff of Gurkhas, Indians and Yorkshiremen, at least gained a morale boosting British tactical victory in the Battle of the Admin Box.

Lieutenant General Renya Mutaguchi commanding the Japanese 15th Army and Subhas Chandra Bose of the anti-British Indian National Army (INA) now pressed Tokyo for an attack on India to which Japanese Prime Minister Hideki Tojo approved. Operation U-GO, the Japanese 'Drive to Delhi', began across mountain jungle toward British bases at Imphal and Kohima, Mutaguchi's advance coinciding with Wingate's second Chindit Expedition, six times the size and better supplied than the first, capable of fighting for as long as malaria and dengue fever would allow.

On 8 March 1944 Mutaguchi's three divisions crossed the Chindwin River to engage weak forward units of the British 17th Division under Major General David Cowan south of Imphal at Tiddim. Lieutenant General Geoffrey Scoones commanding IV Corps was slow to react, Cowan narrowly escaping encirclement by the Japanese 33rd Division of Lieutenant General Motoso Yanagida by retreating to Imphal across the Manipur Bridge courtesy of the 23rd Indian Division's armour and RAF airstrikes. Meanwhile, to the east of Imphal at Tamu, the 20th Indian Division under Major General David Gracey was forced back by Yamamoto Force whilst to the north-east at Sangshak the 50th Indian Parachute Brigade under Brigadier Maxwell Hope-Thomson stood firm against part of the Japanese 31st Division heading for Kohima. After six days commanding 1,850 men in a 1/8-square-mile position trading bayonet charges, grenades, mortars, machine guns and artillery fire with the Japanese, Hope-Thomson suffered a nervous breakdown. Fighting around Imphal then continued to rage on into April as the separate battle of Kohima began eighty miles to the north. Meanwhile south of Imphal at Bishenpur the Japanese 33rd began to surround what was left of the town, attacking the 32nd Indian Brigade who countered with equal ferocity, a despairing Yanagida now sacked. To the east, Yamamoto Force then assaulted the 20th Indian Division on the Shenam Saddle determined to force an armoured advance on the British airfields but in furious fighting the pro Japanese INA were decimated by their pro British compatriots. To the north the Japanese 15th Division then cut the Kohima-Imphal road fighting to Nungshigum hill, four miles above Imphal. Jats retook the hill after an RAF strike but were forced off before a repeat RAF strike and artillery bombardment preceded Carabiniers and Dogras with armoured support making a triumphant climb back up. On 19 April Kohima was relieved but the heavy fighting was ongoing at Imphal, Scoones counter-attacking north where the now starving Japanese eventually lifted the siege. To the south the Japanese 33rd (reinforced by the 53rd) now under Lieutenant General Nubuo Tanaka still fought on fanatically under orders from Tokyo but by the July monsoon the exhausted Japanese Army began a retreat back across Burma.

Mutaguchi lost 55,000 men at Imphal, Scoones 12,000. Imphal-Kohima has been recognised as Britain's greatest battle and Japan's worst defeat. The last Japanese to surrender in Burma would do so only in September 1945.

9 March 1416

Hundred Years' War
Battle of Valmont

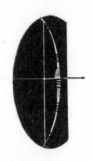

IN 1415, KING Henry V of England had reignited the Hundred Years' War against France with an ultimately successful siege of Harfleur at the mouth of the River Seine and a battlefield victory over the cream of French nobility at Agincourt that staggered the whole of Europe. The whole of France now seemingly lay before Henry but instead of marching on Paris to claim the French Crown the English king retreated to Calais and then London where he was received with a magnificent pageant and Te Deums sung at St Paul's Cathedral. Meanwhile, at the French court in Rouen, King Charles VI wept, his main commanders Charles Duke of Orléans (the king's nephew), John Duke of Bourbon, Jean le Maingre Marshal Boucicaut and Arthur Richemont had all been captured and Charles D'Albret, the Constable of France, was among the dead which also included over 1,500 knights.

Charles not only now had an English invasion to worry about but also the loyalty of Duke John 'the Fearless' of Burgundy who had been bitterly at odds with the House of Orléans since 1407 when he had murdered the king's brother, Louis, Duke of Orléans – John even boasted of the crime and had been conspicuous by his absence at Agincourt. Bernard VII, Count of Armagnac now became de facto head of the House of Orléans during his son-in-law, Charles, Duke of Orléans imprisonment (the Orléanists becoming known by his title, Armagnac) and arrived in Paris with an army of 6,000 French Gascons, half of whom he marched toward Rouen and Harfleur. In Harfleur Thomas Beaufort, Earl of Dorset returned from England to command a new garrison of 900 English men-at-arms and 1,500 archers under John Fastolf which had begun a series of chevauchées into the surrounding countryside designed to discredit the power of the French king. Not being able to sustain any losses that would impede the defence of the isolated Harfleur, Fastolf was mindful of the proximity of Rouen, France's second city just fifty miles away.

On 9 March 1416 Dorset and Fastolf set out with 1,000 mounted men-at-arms and archers for a three-day chevauchée north-east burning and looting villages as far as Cany-Barville. As the column began the return journey, however, they were spotted by a French patrol which allowed them to continue as far as Valmont where Armagnac's Gascons and 1,000 reinforcements from Rouen blocked their path. Dorset dismounted his small army to form up in a thin line, avoiding being outflanked but consequently dangerously weak. The French knights then charged, breaking through the line but rather than finishing Dorset's battered but spirited force carried on to plunder the English baggage train. A badly-wounded Dorset saw his chance and led his 850 survivors into a typically hedged Norman garden, forming a hedgehog (in 1944 the Allied Armies would struggle through 'le bocage' of Normandy). Armagnac hesitated to attack the new English position and offered terms which were firmly declined before Dorset realised much of the French Army had headed into Valmont for the night. In the darkness the English then crept out of the garden toward Fécamp and on to Les Loges where they hid in a wood. By nightfall the following day Armagnac's patrols had had no luck in finding their quarry before Dorset slipped out of the wood. Correctly guessing that Armagnac's patrols would cover the countryside, Dorset headed for the beach and a brutal thirty mile march across sand and shingle for Harfleur, himself transported by boat. As dawn broke over Cap de la Hève, however, just a few miles from Harfleur, the English troops ran into a French mounted column under Marshal Louis de Loigny. Loigny was under orders not to attack without the main column but disobeyed at the sight of such a tempting target, his men dismounting to charge in disorder down the steep cliffs only to be met by a hastily formed line of English men-at-arms who cut them to pieces. As the bodies of the French were tossed into the sea, Armagnac's main column arrived to be put to flight by a determined English attack back up the cliff face. French discomfort was still not over, the fighting had been heard in Harfleur from where the garrison now sallied, Armagnac only narrowly escaping.

A French fleet soon blockaded Harfleur whilst raids into the countryside were now too dangerous. Dorset recovered from his wounds but Harfleur was soon in dire straits, Henry would need to break the French fleet in the English Channel and in the Seine Estuary if he was to conquer Normandy.

10 March 1915

The Great War
Battle of Neuve Chapelle

 THE BELIEF THAT the Great War with Germany, Austria Hungary and more recently Turkey would be over by Christmas 1914 had been shattered on the Western Front in just four months of largely fluid fighting that had resulted in staggering casualties. The 80,000 professional soldiers of the British Expeditionary Force (BEF) that had left Britain in August 1914 under Field Marshal Sir John French had all but been wiped out despite orders not to over commit from Secretary of State for War, Lord Horatio Kitchener. All combatants were at the bottom of a steep learning curve as to the power of modern weaponry. Whilst many had planned for a short war, Kitchener fortunately had not, on the outbreak immediately asking for 100,000 men for a Volunteer Army (the Pals Battalions) whilst shipping tens of thousands of colonial troops, Indians, Australians, New Zealanders and Canadians to strengthen the British Territorials and those of the BEF that remained alive. By 1915 the 100,000 volunteers of Kitchener's Army had already become over one million (by the war's end they would become over five-and-a-half million) but they were not yet ready to fight.

The Indian Expeditionary Force (IEF) 'A' under Lieutenant General James Willcocks had already fought at Ypres whilst 'B' and 'C' had fought in East Africa. The ANZACs (Australians and New Zealanders) also were en route via Suez to Gallipoli where, since movement on the Western Front had seemingly been lost at the end of 1914, the British War Council had ordered Vice Admiral Sackville Carden and the Royal Navy to attempt a forcing of the Dardanelles Straits and the Gallipoli Peninsular. Carden's initial defeat had only prompted another more concerted attempt by the Mediterranean Expeditionary Force which was in composition and would be put into effect in April. In the meantime, French General Joseph Joffre urged French and the BEF to maintain pressure on the Western Front whilst the German Army was also at full stretch against the Russians on the more viscous Eastern Front, the French Army would attack in Champagne whilst the

BEF would attack in Artois. French agreed and planned a detailed attack on Neuve Chapelle, Aubers and Lille aided by reconnaissance from eighty-five planes of the Royal Flying Corps who would also direct artillery fire once the attack had begun.

At 07.30 on 10 March 1915, 50,000 men of the newly-formed British First Army waited in the trenches as 340 guns and howitzers rained over 3,000 shells (more than were fired during the entire Boer War just fifteen years previous) onto the German defences across a front of a mile-and-a-half, destroying German barbed wire and front line trenches. Thirty-five minutes later the barrage lifted onto further targets as Garwhals and Leicesters of the Meerut Infantry Division (IEF) under Brigadier General Charles Blackader made a successful assault on the centre of what was left of the German front line before pressing on toward Neuve Chapelle in the teeth of machine-gun and rifle fire. To the north the British IV Army Corps of Lieutenant General Sir Henry Rawlinson faced tougher resistance as the barrage had been ineffective, whilst further south the rest of the Indian advance had veered wildly right. Haig requested French send in the cavalry, still the fastest means of transport in 1915, to exploit the Garhwal breakthrough but against growing resistance, poor communications and the lack of flank support, the attack stalled. Overnight, Crown Prince Rupprecht of Bavaria commanding the German 6th Army then strengthened his second line before, in thick fog on 12 March, launching a massive 16,000 man counter-attack. In bitter hand-to-hand fighting, Rupprecht's attack was held by the British and Indians who maintained their two-mile gains with the loss of over 11,000 men, Rupprecht losing similar numbers.

French reported that a shortage of shells had caused the failure of the offensive, the resulting scandal along with imminent failures in Gallipoli contributing to the downfall of Herbert Asquith's Government. Though the attack at Neuve Chapelle had collapsed on the first day an insight had been gained on how to defeat an organised defensive trench system. The problems of communication and rapid movement required to exploit the breakthrough would, however, plague the French and British for the rest of the war. A second attempt on Aubers Ridge would be made in May.

11 March 1916

The Great War
Battle of the Latema – Reata Nek

AT THE OUTBREAK of the Great War German ambition was to unite her existing colonies of South West Africa (Namibia), East Africa (Tanzania, Rwanda) and West Africa (Cameroon) by annexing the Belgian Congo, Portuguese East Africa (Mozambique), Angola and Zanzibar to create a vast German Mittelafrika. Lieutenant Colonel Paul von Lettow-Vorbeck commanding German-African forces, however, simply did not have the *Shutztruppe* to achieve it, instead settling on a defence of German East Africa that would ultimately tie down over 400,000 British, Belgian and Portuguese troops.

German West Africa had been quickly overrun but South West Africa initially resisted, even invading British South Africa until defeated by the first Prime Minister of the Union of South Africa, Louis Botha and fellow Afrikaner Second Boer War hero, Jan Smuts. Reconciling Transvaalers and Orange Free Staters to support Britain against an imperial Germany that had been sympathetic to their own cause just a few years before had not been straight forward and since Transvaal elections were imminent, the British Secretary of State for War, Horatio Kitchener appointed the recently sacked Western Front General Horace Smith-Dorrien to command British forces in East Africa rather than Botha or Smuts. Smith-Dorrien, however, then fell ill en route to Cape Town and could not continue but by then the political situation in South Africa had fortunately stabilised and it was Smuts, predominantly a politician but now promoted to Lieutenant General, who was appointed to command the British, South African, East African and Indian troops in British East Africa.

Shortly before Smuts' arrival British Generals Wilfred Malleson and Mickey Tighe resolved to make a reconnaissance in force on Salaitia Hill, south-east of Mount Kilimanjaro, with 6,000 South African, British and Indian troops as a precursor to a full invasion of German East Africa. After shelling the upper slopes, Malleson's inexperienced troops were initially pinned down on open ground by

German rifle and artillery fire from the lower slopes but eventually succeeded in crossing into the bush only to be counter-attacked by German reinforcements on their flanks. In just a few hours Malleson and Tighe lost a third as many South Africans as had Smuts in the entire South West Africa Campaign. A furious Smuts then arrived a week later to continue the advance, Malleson and the British 2nd East African Division advancing west directly past Salaitia for Taveta whilst the Mounted and 3rd South African Infantry Brigades under Brigadier General Japie van Deventer marched on their northern flank. Simultaneously on the far side of Mount Kilimanjaro General Jimmie Stewart led the 1st British East African Division south from Longido across the west face of the mountain. Approached on three sides, Lettow-Vorbeck retreated further west but posted a block of 2,000 Shutztruppe under Major Georg Kraut on the Latema-Reata Nek which left Stewart dangerously isolated to the north where he was facing strengthening resistance in the Kilimanjaro foothills. Since Kilimanjaro to their north and swamps to their south prevented a flank march, Malleson and Deventer could only relieve Stewart by making a full frontal assault on the Latema-Reata Nek.

At 12.00 on 11 March 1916 1,000 British Baluchis and King's African Rifles advanced but were again pinned down on open ground by heavy German fire. The sick Malleson was replaced by Tighe who after five sunburnt hours sent forward 500 Rhodesians to resume the assault but casualties continued to mount against continued heavy fire and a determined German counter-attack. Tighe pressed again at 21.00, the 5th and 7th South African Divisions attacking with the bayonet with such ferocity that a handful of troops led by Lieutenant Colonels Joseph Freeth and William Thompson reached the summit to force a German withdrawal. Tighe and Smuts meanwhile had ordered a retreat themselves, realising only in the morning that they had been victorious.

Lettow-Vorbeck retreated down the Usambara Railway into German and eventually Portuguese East Africa, a guerilla war developing in which ninety per cent of casualties were native African. Surrendering a fortnight after the Armistice in Europe, Lettow-Vorbeck returned to a hero's welcome in Berlin. Under the Treaty of Versailles, German East Africa was broken up between Britain, Belgium and Portugal.

On signing the 1947 Treaty of Paris, Jan Smuts became the only man to have his signature on the peace treaties of both the First and Second World Wars.

12 March 1879

Zulu War
Battle of Intombe River

BRITISH IMPERIALISM IN South Africa had not been satisfied by the 1877 annexation of the Boer Republic of the Transvaal. High Commissioner Henry Bartle Frere and Transvaal Administrator Theophilius Shepstone expected the Boer Republic of the Orange Free State to follow suit whilst they also made a series of impossible demands on the previously British-friendly King Cetshwayo of the Zulu. Cetshwayo's proud defiance had then led to a three-pronged British invasion of Zululand under Lieutenant General Frederick Thesiger, Lord Chelmsford, the central column of which had met disaster at Isandlwana within days of crossing the border. The news of Isandlwana sent Victorian England, including her Prime Minister Benjamin Disraeli, into shock whilst the same day heroism of Rorke's Drift with Victoria Crosses to match was desperately promoted in a bid for credit but the truth was undeniable. With memories of the Indian Mutiny still fresh and a Russian threat in Afghanistan again apparent, Disraeli sent Field Marshal Garnet Wolseley to replace Chelmsford with a mandate to decisively restore British military prestige.

In South Africa, Natal was near panic in expectation of a Zulu invasion but Cetshwayo had forbade any Zulu crossing of the border still in hope of negotiating a peace. As for the other two British columns that had crossed into Zululand, the easternmost was now trapped at Eshowe awaiting relief whilst the other, in the north-west, retreated to Khambula. North West Zululand contained several groups outside Cetshwayo's influence; Mbilini waMswati, a Swazi commanded one such band near Luneberg, pillaging homesteads and butchering native farm hands including women and children. From Derby, further north still, Colonel Hugh Rowlands marched with five companies to reinforce Luneberg, skirmishing on his approach but then leaving Major Charles Tucker in command as he himself returned to Pretoria to deal with a Boer uprising. To resupply Tucker's new Luneberg garrison, a convoy of eighteen wagons then set out in late February from Lydenburg, a perilous one-hundred-mile journey across lawless country, several rivers and with no escort. On 1 March, Tucker sent out a company from Luneberg to find the convoy and at least provide an escort for the final few miles across the Intombe River but four days later, after torrential rain had turned the roads to mud, the convoy had still not crossed the Intombe. Tucker ordered his company to return but sent out another two days later under Captain David Moriarty who found seven wagons on the north bank with the others strung out back down the road. The lack of escort had encouraged minor Zulu attacks but apart from a few oxen nothing had been lost. With the river in near flood, Moriarty wasted no time in building a raft whilst also bringing the stragglers into a defensive laager on the river bank. The Intombe was now too dangerous to cross and the continuous rain quickly turned the laager into a sea of mud, Tucker visiting Moriarty to urge haste.

At 04.30 on 12 March 1879 a rifle shot awoke Lieutenant Henry Harward commanding thirty-five men on the southern bank. Asking Moriarty across the river for orders Harward was instructed to remain under arms but just minutes later with most of the seventy-one men on the northern bank still asleep Harward saw through the morning mist 1,000 of Mbilini's Zulu just yards from Moriarty's laager. Stopping to fire a volley the Zulu then rushed the wagons and tents from which the British were desperately trying to escape; Moriarty assegaied as he tried to shoot his way to the river bank. Others too fled for the river realising that any constructive defence was now impossible. From the southern bank Harward's troops poured fire into the Zulu for a full ten minutes in an attempt to cover the escape of their desperate colleagues but the Zulu were also crossing the Intombe, pursuing Moriarty's survivors and attacking those on the south bank. Harward mounted his horse and bolted for Luneburg leaving Sergeant Anthony Booth to organise a defence, winning a Victoria Cross in conducting a fighting retreat for two miles to Raby's Farm before the Zulu broke off. The British column on the north bank had been wiped out.

Harward and Tucker returned to the Intombe to find all ammunition, supplies and oxen had been looted. Harward faced a Court Martial but was acquitted, an acquittal later dissented by Wolseley. Within days Chelmsford would relaunch the British invasion of Zululand but would face grueling tests at Hlobane and Khambula.

13 March 1884

Mahdist Wars
Battle of Tamai

MAJOR GENERAL CHARLES Gordon had arrived in Khartoum on 18 February 1884 accompanied by Lieutenant Colonel John Stewart, the man whose report on the Sudan in conjunction with public and media support, had done so much to secure Gordon's appointment. Egyptian and loyal Sudanese garrisons had already begun to fall back on Khartoum in the face of the growing threat of the *Ansar*, the Islamic following of Muhammad Ahmad, the Mahdi, Gordon's orders being to oversee the continuation of this evacuation along with any European citizens who wished to leave. Gordon, however, began administering the city, reintroducing slave trading (he himself had banned it years before) to cheer up the populace who had previously made a good living from it. He also reinforced the garrison at Omdurman across the White Nile, organised a defence of the city and opened a dialogue with the Mahdi in which he offered him the Governorship of Kordofan (an area along with much else he already ruled) – hardly the actions of a man looking to run. The unimpressed Mahdi and his *Ansar* were just days away from tightening the noose around Khartoum but to the north-east, along a potential escape route for Gordon's garrisons, Lieutenant General Gerald Graham, a veteran of the Opium Wars and the Egyptian expedition of two years previous, was about to make a second effort to deliver a knockout blow to the Mahdist Sheikh Osman Digna and his Hadendoa (Fuzzy Wuzzy) tribesmen.

Digna's menace had to be removed in order to protect both the Red Sea ports and keep open the overland route from Berber, 200 miles down the River Nile from Khartoum, a considerably shorter, easier journey than through the great cataracts of the Nile between Berber and Wadi Halfa on the Egyptian border. Theoretically Graham's success would facilitate Gordon's evacuation out or any British relief army's march in to the Sudan.

After avenging Valentine Baker's defeat at the first battle El Teb by the second battle of El Teb on 29 February 1884, Graham replaced the Egyptian garrison at Suakin with a British one before again turning his mind to the destruction of Digna. Marching out of Suakin on 10 March with virtually the same force that had fought at the Second El Teb he headed fifty miles west for the Hadendoa camp at Tamai. The British vanguard advanced forward to occupy a thornbush defensive Zeriba left by Baker's hapless Egyptians a few weeks earlier before the main force caught up on 12 March for an extremely uncomfortable night lying face down in the sand under fire from Hadendoa riflemen.

The following morning 13 March 1884, the same day as the Mahdi's main *Ansar* appeared outside Khartoum, Graham formed his two infantry brigades into two separate squares for an advance behind cavalry towards 10,000 Hadendoa under Digna's cousin Mahsud Musa. On arrival the cavalry dropped back behind the 2nd Brigade in the forward square commanded by Major General John Davis with the 1st Brigade behind on the right in their own square commanded by Colonel Redvers Buller. The British were subjected to incoming rifle fire but it was the difficult ground that made the task of maintaining the squares difficult, especially in the forward square which was suddenly charged. British disorder was completed by the rising dust from the desert and the smoke of the British Martini Henry rifles, so much so that after the forward square had been temporarily breached (the Hadendoa earning eternal British respect for their feats – they had already broken a British-led Egyptian square at El Teb just a month before and would do so again at Abu Klea the following year) the 2nd Brigade was forced to retreat, abandoning their artillery. Buller, however, sensed the imminent danger and promptly advanced his square alongside the 2nd Brigade to begin pouring a heavy, suppressing fire into the Hadendoa. Graham and Davis now reformed, resupplied and recommenced their advance, recapturing their guns to pursue the Hadendoa across a ravine back into their own camp. The fierce fighting continued with the brave Hadendoa suffering 4,000 casualties against British machine-guns and artillery.

Graham was committed to destroying Digna (who had again escaped) and those Mahdists north of Khartoum but when about to send a force across the desert to Berber his Prime Minister, William Gladstone, would have none of it. The besieged Gordon would have to manage on his own.

14 March 1811

Napoleonic Wars
Battle of Casal Novo

IN 1807, THE Emperor of the First French Empire Napoleon Bonaparte invaded neutral Portugal to prosecute the Continental System – a Europe-wide trade embargo against his perennial foe Great Britain. General Jean-Andoche Junot had marched into Lisbon with no difficulty but Napoleon's subsequent deposition of Spain's King Charles IV and his son Prince Ferdinand for his own brother Joseph, left Junot dangerously isolated when the Spanish populace revolted. The following year British Major General Sir Arthur Wellesley then took full advantage of French difficulties by defeating Junot at Vimiero only for his superior Sir Hew Dalrymple to generously sail the French general and his men back to France fully armed. Having been ordered home as part of an inquiry into Dalrymple's actions, Wellesley returned to Lisbon in September 1809 after Lieutenant General Sir John Moore's expedition had been chased out of Spain by Marshal Jean de Dieu Soult. Soult was then surprised by Wellesley outside Oporto and retreated back to northern Spain allowing Wellesley to attempt what Moore had failed – a galvanising of the Spanish against the French forces of occupation. However, despite defeating Joseph Bonaparte at Talavera, a disillusioned Wellesley retreated back to Portugal refusing to cooperate in any way with Spain and instead, with the help of the people of Lisbon, built the defensive Lines of Torres Vedras.

A year later, massive French reinforcements, free after the defeat of Austria, poured into Spain and also for a third time into Portugal under Marshal André Masséna to take Ciudad Rodrigo, Spain and Almeida, Portugal. Wellesley, now Viscount Wellington, stalled Masséna at Busaco before retreating to the security of Torres Vedras where he was now so comfortable that he could even spare troops to assist in the defence of Cadiz. Outside Lisbon, in freezing winter weather and suffering from Wellington's scorched earth policy, Masséna and his 60,000 troops were soon in extremis, retreating to Santarem but ordered to hold until Soult's *Armée d'Andalusie* had taken Badajoz. By 5 March 1811, his resourcefulness over the previous five months having already astonished Wellington, Masséna could wait no longer and began the French retreat back to Spain, unaware when Soult took Badajoz just five days later.

Under cover of fog and using straw dummies as sentries, Masséna slipped away from Santarem with Wellington pursuing within hours looking to destroy the now highly vulnerable French Army. To do so Wellington would have to reckon with the covering French rear guard of 10,000 men under Marshal Michel Ney, fighting a sharp skirmish on 11 March at Pombal and a more violent action the following day at Redhinha where just 7,000 French held off 25,000 Anglo-Portuguese. Wellington, however, could not be careless, knowing that Masséna's main force was always close by he continued the pursuit to the River Mondego where the Portuguese Militia of Coimbra prevented a French crossing.

Masséna turned east leaving Ney and his rear guard at Condeixa but on spotting a flanking move by Major General Thomas Picton, Ney burnt the town and retreated to a new, stronger position around Miranda de Corvo and Casal Novo, the latter attacked by Major General William Erskine and five battalions of British light infantry on 14 March 1811. Doubtful of the whereabouts of the French, Erskine advanced through fog without a reconnaissance to be subjected to intense cannon fire for several hours from General Claude Ferey before entering the town, Ferey falling back to a defensive line held by General Jean Marchand on the heights behind. Erskine's lights consequently surged through Casal Novo to continue the attack but were cut down by French Hussars before being hit by more cannon fire and musket volleys. The flanking Picton then forced Ney to withdraw both Marchand and Ferey back to the Miranda de Corvo Heights where they joined the remainder of the French rear guard. The success of Ney's delaying tactics allowed Masséna to hasten his retreat from Portugal with much of his army in tact.

Erskine had lost 155 men and repeated the fiasco at Sabugal three weeks later but, Almeida apart, the French had now been forced from Portugal never to return. Throughout his campaign, Masséna had lost 25,000 of his original 65,000 men, most of them to starvation and disease. He would, nevertheless, attempt to relieve Almeida, a move strongly contested by Wellington in May 1811 at Fuentes de Oñoro.

15 March 1781

American War of Independence
Battle of Guildford Court House

THE BRITISH ARMY in North America had been staring at defeat following the surrender of Major General John Burgoyne at Saratoga in 1777 and the declaration of France and Spain for the cause of American independence. The decision therefore to change the offensive to the southern states of Georgia and the Carolinas, was, by early 1781, beginning to look like a master stroke. British victories from Savannah to Charleston to Camden had sent the Southern Continental Army and its attached militias under General Horatio Gates retreating back into North Carolina, General George Washington replacing the disgraced Gates with the hardline Major General Nathanael Greene. In the belief that the regular British regiments and loyalist militias of Lieutenant General Charles, Lord Cornwallis would soon advance into North Carolina and Virginia, Greene immediately set about rebuilding his army.

Cornwallis' army, however, was in no fit state itself, sickness spared no one, neither Cornwallis nor his aggressive subordinate Colonel Banastre Tarleton whilst their lengthy supply lines were harried by bands of Patriot partisans including a column under Daniel Morgan which roamed throughout South Carolina attacking British bases. In January 1781 Morgan had been caught by Tarleton at Cowpens but the impetuous Englishman's flying column of 1,000 cavalry had been virtually wiped out. Tarleton had escaped and though Cornwallis now received 1,200 reinforcements under Brigadier General Alexander Leslie he had just lost the ability to trap his highly-mobile enemy for a much desired decisive battle. Cornwallis nevertheless, resolved to chase Morgan and Greene knowing they would fight a retreat back to the River Dan on the border of Virginia. Fighting their way across the Catawba River the British followed but with the threat of Patriot Virginian reinforcements close by, Cornwallis called a halt short of the border and retreated to Hillsborough. Greene now returned south with nearly 5,000 Americans – regulars and militia – to confront Cornwallis and just 2,000 British Redcoats and Hessians who had survived the 300-mile march from Charleston. On hearing that Greene was at Guilford Court House half a day's march to his west, Cornwallis advanced at dawn on 15 March 1781, Tarleton again to the fore running into an ambush of cavalry under 'Light Horse' Harry Lee four miles short of the Court House but saved by the following Light Company of the British Guards.

Greene had drawn up the Continental Army in three lines with the doubtful North Carolina Militia to the front, the Virginia Militia a few hundred yards behind and, on higher ground further back, the American regulars, Virginians and Marylanders supported by artillery. Initially Cornwallis advanced down the left side of the Guildford Road where there was more cover, the 33rd Regiment of Foot led by Lieutenant Colonel James Webster approaching to within fifty yards of the North Carolinians who delivered a musket volley. Webster's men replied with a volley of their own before confirming Greene's reservations by immediately putting the Carolinians to flight with a bayonet charge. Webster pressed on to attack the right of the more resolute Virginia Militia behind whilst more British Redcoats and Hessians under Leslie and Lieutenant General Carl Von Bose moved against the Virginian left which gave way. Cornwallis also moved up in the centre with the Guards bringing extra pressure on the Virginian centre and right which also began to disintegrate. Amongst the chaos Webster held some of his light infantry together for an attack on the right flank of the Continental third line, trying to avoid open ground to his front but nevertheless on the receiving end of heavy fire from more disciplined American regulars. After moving through the Virginians, the Guards then charged the Marylanders on the left of the American third line who immediately fell back, losing their artillery and exposing their fellow Marylanders in the centre who volleyed desperately. A terrific hand-to-hand fight with sabre and bayonet then raged with American cavalry counter-attacks driving the Guards back only for the British regiments to regroup. Eventually defeated, Greene ordered a general American retreat but was pursued for just a couple of miles.

The cost of the British victory was too high, over 500 casualties including the brave Webster. Cornwallis could not go on. The British Army retreated south-east to Wilmington on the North Carolina coast leaving Greene to overrun the Carolinas and Georgia.

16 March 1781

American War of Independence
Battle of Cape Henry

THE AMERICAN WAR of Independence had taken a turn for the worse in 1777 when Major General John Burgoyne surrendered at Saratoga, a defeat that prompted France and Spain to enter the war against Great Britain. Surrounded in New York City for much of 1779 the British had then switched operations south to Georgia, the Carolinas and Virginia with quite some success under Lieutenant Generals Henry Clinton and Charles, Lord Cornwallis. After Clinton had taken Charleston, South Carolina in May 1780, Cornwallis had pushed north, defeating the Southern Continental Army under General Horatio Gates at Camden before pushing further north still in the spring of 1781 chasing that same army now under Nathanael Greene through North Carolina toward the Virginia border. Cornwallis' position was, however, precarious, his sickness-struck 2,000-strong force was operating in largely hostile country 200 miles from any naval support. In December 1780, in support of Cornwallis' advance, Clinton ordered 1,600 troops to Virginia under Brigadier General Benedict Arnold who had just recently defected from the American cause to that of King George III. As Arnold set about burning and looting much of Virginia, General George Washington ordered several Frenchmen to assist the Virginia Militia in bringing the defector to the gallows, Gilbert du Motier, Marquis de Lafayette with 1,200 men marching directly into Virginia whilst Admiral Charles Réne Dominique Sochet, Chevalier Destouches sailed from Newport, Rhode Island to Chesapeake Bay with Charles du Houx, Comte de Viomenil and another 1,200 men on board.

Concerned by the presence of the Royal Navy at anchor off Long Island, New York, Destouches was hardly enthusiastic, but when a February storm damaged the British he sailed for the Chesapeake with three ships of the line only to return when the small British fleet there retreated into the bay rather than give battle. Relations between the Americans and French had been strained since a French failure at Rhode Island in 1778, but Washington who was in Newport, realised that final victory could be his and America's if only he could persuade the Frenchman to try again with his entire fleet. Destouches duly sailed again on 8 March 1781, gaining a thirty-six hour lead over the British Rhode Island Fleet of Vice Admiral Mariot Arbuthnot. Brilliant seamanship, however, meant Arbuthnot was already off Cape Henry, the entrance of Chesapeake Bay, on the morning of 16 March 1781 when Destouches' seven ships came into view.

Also with seven ships of the line but with superior firepower, Arbuthnot turned north-east into the wind to immediately engage as was Royal Navy practice. As both fleets manoeuvred to gain the weather gage Arbuthnot's superior skills meant the British fleet was gaining on the French, both now heading south-east before Destouches turned his line across that of Arbuthnot. As Arbuthnot's vanguard of HMS *Robust*, HMS *Europe* and HMS *Prudent* turned with the French they were hit by the first broadsides of the battle and suffered significant damage but Arbuthnot continued the manoeuvre bringing up his four ships behind, including the massive triple-decker, 90-gun HMS *London*, which began broadsiding. The two fleets traded cannonballs for two hours before Destouches broke off having already taken nearly 200 casualties. Arbuthnot with half the casualties but with badly-damaged vessels limped back into Chesapeake Bay to prevent any possibility of a French landing. Destouches, however, was already on his way back to Rhode Island and an unhappy George Washington.

The British were able to reinforce Arnold in Virginia but 200 miles to the south-west Cornwallis had just won the Battle of Guildford Courthouse at such cost that he was unable to maintain an offensive and was retreating to Wilmington on the North Carolina coast. Cornwallis would soon march north to build a port at Yorktown, facilitating Clinton's ambition to take the Delaware Peninsular, but a French fleet under Admiral Francois Joseph Paul, Comte de Grasse would return to Chesapeake Bay from the Caribbean six months later. The subsequent battle would effectively trap Cornwallis in Yorktown and finish the war.

17 March 1776
American War of Independence
Siege of Boston

SINCE THE END of the French and Indian War (1754–63) Paul Revere and Samuel Adams had done much to undermine British authority in North America, provoking the Boston Massacre of 1770 and a punitive response to British taxes with the Boston Tea Party of 1773. As further violence seemed certain, two columns under Lieutenant Colonel Francis Smith and Brigadier General Hugh Percy marched out of Boston in April 1775 to capture American military supplies at the towns of Lexington and Concord but had sustained heavy casualties when running into considerable American Patriot resistance. By the time the British had returned to Boston from their harrowing experience, the countryside all around the town and the Charlestown Peninsular was in open revolt. The Patriot Massachusetts Militia under William Heath and General Artemas Ward sealed off land access to Charlestown and Boston leaving the 3,500-strong British Army under Commander-in-Chief in North America, General Thomas Gage effectively corked in a bottle, a position from which the only relief could come from the British-controlled Atlantic Ocean beyond.

Over the next few days Gage began to appreciate the level of grievance felt by the colonists as thousands more rebels from neighbouring states joined those surrounding King George III's forces. Gage abandoned the Charlestown Peninsular, building defensive positions at Roxbury to the south whilst loyalists moved from the country into Boston and Patriots moved in the opposite direction. The American militias were not just busy around Boston, short of heavy weaponry Benedict Arnold and Ethan Allen also launched a raid north in the Hudson Valley on Fort Ticonderoga, Lake Champlain capturing British cannon and ammunition without firing a shot.

Fighting was now continuously breaking out around Boston as the rebels tried to deny the British livestock and fodder for their horses and cattle. Worse, at the Battle of Chelsea Creek in late May 1775 HMS *Diana* was lost with all her gunnery and ammunition. With very little going his way, Gage now desperately offered a pardon to all those bar Adams and John Hancock (another long time antagonist partially responsible for the Boston Tea Party) who had taken up arms against the king. The offer merely increased tension further but Gage was now receiving reinforcements including Generals William Howe, John Burgoyne and Henry Clinton and planned to break the American stranglehold by retaking Charlestown. In the bloody June 1775 Battle of Bunker Hill, Gage succeeded but at such a heavy price that he could not press on. He also had another problem to contend with just days later when the formidable General George Washington, a former colonel in the British Army, arrived to take command of the Patriot militias, drilling them into the new Continental Army.

Washington strengthened the American grip on Boston and seized local shipping to threaten Royal Navy and British supply ships within the surrounding waters. He also ordered an American assault on British Quebec which, after a victory at Montreal, was eventually defeated at Quebec City. Washington then lobbied strongly for an all out assault on Boston to which his more cautious fellow commanders would not agree. As the winter snows fell, Washington was afraid his men would desert leaving his army vulnerable to British counter-attacks but since Boston was gripped by epidemics of smallpox and consumption, Howe, who had replaced Gage as Commander-in-Chief, remained inactive. Washington now resolved, by way of a remarkable feat of engineering by Henry Knox, to move the heavy cannon captured by Arnold at Ticonderoga 300 miles across the Berkshire Mountains and the frozen River Hudson into positions around Boston where they began a bombardment on 2 March 1776. The British returned fire but Washington moved more men and heavy cannon up to the Dorchester Heights overlooking Boston and the Royal Navy within the harbour. Howe was now in an untenable position, despite a furious counter-bombardment of the Dorchester Heights he had little option but to evacuate. On 17 March 1776 the British Army of 10,000 troops together with 1,200 women and children left Boston on 120 ships destined for Halifax, Nova Scotia where they would regroup for a renewed offensive further south on New York.

18 March 1643

English Civil Wars
Battle of New Ross

THE TUDOR CONQUEST of Ireland and its attempted imposition of Protestantism had often met with Spanish interventions aiding the Gaelic Irish observance of Catholicism. Under King Henry VIII and his daughter Queen Elizabeth I, England had sought to protect her vulnerable western flank against Catholic French and Spanish invasions, in 1583 finally crushing the Desmond Rebellions to plant Munster with English Anglicans and in 1603 the Tyrone Rebellion to plant Ulster with mainly Scottish Presbyterians but also some English Anglicans. James I, King of England and Scotland, then ruled Ireland through his Privy Council in Dublin with the Spanish reluctant to intervene after several damaging armada experiences and the death of their self-proclaimed defender of the Catholic faith, King Philip II. Viewing the exercise as civilising, James intended to convert Catholic Irish by resettling them around Protestant towns and churches at which their attendance, contrary to the exclusion of Gaelic Irish under the 1367 Statutes of Kilkenny, was now compulsory. Largely due to language difficulties, however, Catholicism remained deeply rooted so that when a feud escalated forty years later between James' son King Charles I and his Parliament at Westminster, a fear of the growing power of Puritan Protestants and the continued frustration at their lack of civil rights led Irish Catholics in Ulster to rebel. With violence on a terrifying scale the movement spread, its leader, Phelim O'Neill forming the Irish Catholic Confederation, all members of which swore allegiance to Parliament's enemy, King Charles. Uneasy at being identified with his new Catholic friends in the face of Parliament propaganda, Charles reacted by sending an army of Englishmen to Dublin and Scottish Covenanters to Ulster. Irish prospects appeared grim against the albeit barely professional king's forces but brief salvation arrived when Charles recalled most of his troops on the outbreak of the Civil War in England.

O'Neill and his Confederates looked to take advantage of the divided loyalties which hampered the English. By early 1643 relations in Ireland had become severely strained between the Parliament Privy Council and the Royalist Governor of Dublin James Butler, Earl of Ormonde, the former wanting a show of aggression toward the Irish Confederates who were potential recruits for the so far victorious Royalist War effort. A naturally reluctant Ormonde resolved to clear Leinster of Confederates by attacking south toward Kilkenny and Wexford, the latter used by Irish and Dunkirk privateers to prey on English Parliament shipping. Ormonde's army of 3,000 arrived on 11 March 1643 to besiege New Ross which held out despite several assaults and an artillery barrage enhanced by two English warships sailing up the River Barrow. The English besiegers were then threatened by the approach of the main Confederate Army under Thomas Preston looking to catch Ormonde between themselves and the New Ross garrison. Ormonde began a retreat to Dublin but on 18 March 1643 Preston and 6,500 Confederates blocked his path near the village of Ballinvegga.

Immediately Ormonde's musketeers under Sir Francis Willoughby moved forward to seize a hill between the two armies which were also separated by a stream. Ormonde then moved his cannon up to Willoughby's Hill as more English infantry advanced with cavalry to the flanks. The Confederates advanced themselves, crossing the stream under artillery fire before Preston ordered his cavalry to charge the English cannon. The Confederate cavalry were, however, intercepted by that of the English, a furious mounted mêlée of swordsmen developing while the infantry watched on. Unwilling to wait for the result of the cavalry battle, Willoughby took the opportunity to advance his guns and infantry downhill toward the Confederates, firing all the while. Preston's men across the stream retreated followed by their cavalry whilst Willoughby fought briefly with any that remained.

Ormonde was unable to pursue and returned to Dublin where, for three years he was urged by King Charles to negotiate Royalist assistance from the Confederates. At the end of the Civil War and with Charles in custody, the Confederates would again state their allegiance to the Crown, a stance that in 1649 would earn them a bloody visit from the New Model Army and its commander, Oliver Cromwell.

19 March 1643

English Civil Wars
Battle of Hopton Heath

KING CHARLES I of England's marriage to Catholic Henrietta Maria of France, his refusal to be accountable to Parliament, his peace policy with Spain and above all his attempts as Supreme Head of the Church of England to control not only the Protestant religion in Anglican England but also in Presbyterian Scotland had led to widespread civil discontent. Parliament's refusal to raise taxes for an invasion of Scotland, the bringing of the Trained Bands (militia) under Parliament control and the refusal to allow bishops a vote in the House of Commons then led to seething Royal discontent, Charles fleeing London after his failed attempt to arrest John Pym and four other Members of Parliament had sent the civil population into a rage. He was not without support in other areas of the country, however, particularly in the North of England and Wales. Having raised the Royal Standard at Nottingham, Charles and his nephew, Prince Rupert of the Rhine, fought the inconclusive Battle of Edgehill against Parliamentarian Robert Devereux, Earl of Essex before both sides spent the winter recruiting largely with the promise of profit and pay. To this purpose Charles' Queen Henrietta, rose to the occasion, travelling to the Spanish Netherlands and the Protestant Dutch Republic to raise money and arms for her husband's war effort. Despite the protection of a Dutch fleet under Admiral Maarten Tromp, a man who had finished Spain as a dominant seapower in 1639, the queen's convoy could not recross the English Channel in the face of a biblical six-day storm. Tromp eventually delivered his precious cargo at Bridlington Bay at the end of February, the queen travelling to York, consolidating Royalist Yorkshire and, by James Stanley, Earl of Derby's rough tactics, Lancashire. Scottish Royalists also pledged their allegiance and Cornwall had been secured by Sir Ralph Hopton at the Battle of Braddock Down whilst Wales, Pembroke apart, was Royalist. Elsewhere it was very different, South England and East Anglia were for Parliament as was most of the Midlands, the notable exceptions being King Charles' Court at Oxford, Stratford-upon-Avon, Lichfield and Stafford.

Queen Henrietta's new supply of ammunitions meant a Royalist advance from Lancashire to join King Charles at Oxford was now possible. The revered Parliamentarian Robert Grenville, Lord Brooke sought to prevent any such advance, successfully attacking Stratford-upon-Avon before moving on to Lichfield where Royalists made a last ditch stand in the cathedral. Brooke was killed in the fray but the Parliamentarians pressed on into the North Midlands seeking to link Brooke's force, now under Sir John Gell, with the Cheshire force of Sir William Brereton, the two Parliamentary armies moving toward a rendez-vous on Hopton Heath with the intention of attacking Royalist Stafford. Meanwhile, Charles had ordered Spencer Compton, Earl of Northampton to oppose Gell and Brereton and recover Lichfield. At midday on 19 March 1643 Gell marched onto Hopton Heath, taking up a defensive position with Brereton a short distance away to his north-west before Northampton's Cavaliers, who had arrived at Stafford the previous day, marched out to give battle, both sides about 1200 strong. On arrival and with Brereton's Parliament infantry still forming, Northampton began pounding the Parliamentary centre with 'Roaring Meg' (a massive cannon) before leading a cavalry charge which routed the Parliamentary horse. Northampton then charged a second time, overrunning eight guns but was halted by stubborn Parliament musketeers. In the mêlée, the unhorsed Northampton refused to surrender to the 'base rogues' who offered him quarter and was consequently despatched with a halberd to the head. Thomas Byron and Henry, Lord Hastings continued launching Royalist attacks but unable to break the Parliament infantry retired to Stafford whilst Gell and Brereton retired to Derby and Cheshire respectively.

Royalists were infuriated by Gell's refusal to return Northampton's body, the earl was buried in All Hallows Church, Derby though only after having been first paraded through the streets. The small-scale battles of early 1643 had been fought against the backdrop of peace negotiations which collapsed in April. The fighting would now escalate, starting in June on Adwalton Moor.

20 March 1799

French Revolutionary War
Siege of Acre

FROM THE REVOLUTION, France had emerged as an aggressive nationalist power intent on spreading the ideology of the Rights of Man and the Citizen across all of Europe. By 1797 the First Coalition of Austria, Prussia, Great Britain, Sardinia, Spain and the Dutch Republic had all but been defeated, not for the last time in history, just the British fighting on alone. To defeat this 'nation of shopkeepers'[1] and its tiny army would, however, be no easy task, not even for the brilliant young General Napoleon Bonaparte and the enormous one-million-man-plus French Revolutionary Army since France, even with the fleet of turncoat Spain, could not match the world's greatest sea power, the 'wooden walls' of Great Britain, the Royal Navy. Instead Napoleon, perhaps seeking to emulate Alexander the Great, persuaded the French Directory and Foreign Minister Charles Talleyrand to launch an offensive in the Eastern Mediterranean against the Ottoman Empire preemptive to a march overland and an instigation of uprisings against growing British interests in India. British Rear Admiral Horatio Nelson had chased Napoleon across the Mediterranean to Egypt, where he failed to prevent a French landing but emphatically destroyed the French fleet of Vice Admiral Francois Brueys D'Aigalliers at the August 1798 Battle of the Nile. With no transport home Napoleon and half his *Armée d'Orient* of 40,000 men had then marched inland decisively defeating 25,000 Mamluks at the Battle of the Pyramids before advancing on Cairo where a French administration claimed to liberate Egyptians from Ottoman (Turkish) oppression.

The liberation message failing, Arabs, Mamluks and peasants revolted in Cairo and the surrounding desert before Napoleon restored order with a show of force that culminated in a storming of the Great Mosque of Muhammad Ali Pasha and the execution of all suspects. Egypt was back under French control but in Constantinople (Istanbul, Turkey) the pro British Sultan Selim III looked to restore Ottoman rule in Egypt with a pincer movement on Cairo, sending an army of 8,000 Turks with 40,000 Greek and Albanian reinforcements under Mustafa Pasha directly from Rhodes whilst another of 30,000 marched via Damascus and Jerusalem under Jezzar Pasha. Napoleon had been surveying Suez as to the potential of building a canal but quickly reacted to the new Ottoman threat by marching north-east with 13,000 men across the Sinai Peninsular while sixteen siege guns moved at sea by gunboat. Napoleon then captured Arish before besieging Jaffa on 3 March, his envoy beheaded by the Ottoman defenders sparking a rage that ensured a massacre four days later when the French successfully stormed the city. As plague now began to spread through the French ranks, Napoleon moved on to Acre (now Akko, Israel) where still 42,000 Ottomans under Jezzar supported by HMS *Tigre* and HMS *Theseus* under Commodore Sidney Smith, prepared a defence.

On 20 March 1799 Napoleon attacked on arrival but now without his seaborne siege artillery which had been intercepted en route by Smith. The captured guns were then entrusted to French Royalist, anti-revolutionary and exile, Antoine le Picard de Phelippeaux, an ex-classmate of Napoleon from l'École Militaire, Paris who duly turned the guns on his own anti-Royalist, revolutionary countrymen. Napoleon then countered the broadsides from Acre's artillery, the two British warships and several captured gunboats offshore by bringing up his own field guns across the Sinai to support repeated infantry assaults against the city walls. After a month of bitter fighting and mounting casualties, the French forced a breach in the outer wall only to find another beyond behind for which thousands of Turks were still more than willing to fight. After three more ferocious assaults, exposure and continuing plague (which had also claimed Phelippeaux) adding to battle casualties, Napoleon and the *Armée d'Orient* retreated back to Egypt and Cairo.

Napoleon's predicament in Cairo was perilous, he marched north to Alexandria destroying Mustafa's Ottoman Army at Aboukir before deserting his army to return to France and the War of the Second Coalition (Britain, Austria and Russia). The day of reckoning for the *Armée d'Orient* would come at Alexandria in March 1801 against men sent specifically to destroy it, Lieutenant General Ralph Abercromby and the British Expeditionary Corps.

---

[1] Bertrand de Vieuzac

21 March 1918

The Great War
The Kaiserschlacht

FOLLOWING THE 1916 Battle of the Somme, German Chief-of-Staff Paul von Hindenburg and Quarter Master General Erich Luddendorff could see no possibility of winning the Great War. Unable to match the numerical and material advantages of the Triple Entente and in response to the Royal Navy blockade of Germany, Kaiser Wilhelm II had given the go ahead for unrestricted submarine warfare in an effort to starve Britain but the misery of acute food and fuel shortages in Britain and France was more than matched by that in Germany where food rationing dropped to a third of pre war levels. Whilst militarily the Kaiser's tactics caused the Royal and Merchant Navies considerable discomfort it not only failed in its objective but backfired spectacularly when the United States of America responded with their own declaration of war on Germany.

Field Marshal Douglas Haig commanding the British Expeditionary Force and his French counterpart General Joseph Joffre had been intent on maintaining pressure on the Western Front but Joffre had been sacked after the Somme to be finally replaced by the more defensive minded General Phillippe Pétain. Haig and the BEF had then maintained pressure almost single handed through the latter half of 1917 with Haig believing intelligence that Germany was close to collapse, intelligence questioned following Third Ypres (Passchendaele) with the result that Brigadier General John Charteris, Director of Military Intelligence, was sacked. Germany may well have been close to collapse but as the fighting died down over the coldest winter for a century it would be Russia that collapsed first. Under pressure from a Bolshevik Revolution, the Tsar had abdicated a year earlier and now Russia fully withdrew from the Triple Entente (Britain, France, Russia), negotiating their own armistice with the Central Powers by signing the Treaty of Brest-Litovsk.

In the knowledge that the first of a million Americans were arriving in Europe with the majority soon to follow but now free to transfer their eastern divisions (giving Germany 192 on the Western Front against 156 of the Entente) the Kaiser, Ludendorff and Hindenburg suddenly had a window of opportunity to win the war... or at least the peace with a Spring Offensive, the Kaiserschlacht.

Ludendorff believed the BEF to now be his main threat and planned a one million man attack from General Otto von Below's 17th Army, Georg von der Marwitz' 2nd Army and Oskar Hutier's 18th Army, breaking through between the British and French before wheeling north to roll up the British right flank. On 21st March 1918 Marwitz' 2nd Army attacked through dense fog around St Quentin against the blighted British Fifth Army of General Hubert Gough, battered in 1917 at Passchendaele and now under the heaviest bombardment of the entire war, 2,508 German guns firing one million shells at targets over 150 square miles for five hours. Hutier advanced on Marwitz' left to block any French reinforcements leaving Gough's twelve divisions to defend a forty-two mile front against forty-three German. Gough immediately gave ground since Haig had deliberately left his southern defences weak rather than his northern where, with his back to the English Channel, he could not afford any retreat. North of Gough, General Julian Byng's Third Army fared better defending twenty-eight miles of front with fourteen divisions against Von Below's nineteen but as Gough fell back Byng became outflanked on his right. Ludendorff then ordered Hutier to join Marwitz' main assault driving south-west while Von Below maintained pressure on Byng, German gains amounting to fifteen miles in a week. Fifth Army's predicament now became critical but crucially the line held, Gough's skill now rewarded with the sack. Luddendorf's battle plan, however, was not developing as intended, with difficulties mounting in advancing heavy guns over the old battlefields of the Somme and Cambrai he switched the attack north toward stronger British defences around Arras and Vimy Ridge but was repulsed by Byng. On 4 April Luddendorf again gambled at Amiens, using his own tanks against those of the British for the first armoured battle in history. The British Third Army again stood firm.

Luddendorf had by Great War standards made substantial gains of forty miles but at the cost of 250,000 casualties (similar British) and had merely created a salient vulnerable to a British counter-attack that would arrive decisively in August. Before then, the Kaiserschlacht would be continued at Lys, Flanders.

21 March 1801
French Revolutionary War
Battle of Alexandria

THE ENORMOUS FRENCH Army generated by the Revolution had by 1797 systematically defeated all her adversaries of the First Coalition with the exception of Great Britain. The brilliant young Corsican General Napoleon Bonaparte, however, would not be content with his gains until he had defeated Britain but his concern at the power of the Royal Navy prevented any French movement across the English Channel despite France having added the Spanish fleet to her own. Instead Napoleon persuaded the French Foreign Minister Charles Talleyrand to expand French ideology and rule into the Eastern Mediterranean against the Ottoman Empire before an advance on what was growing British power in India where France possessed an ally in Tipu Sultan, the Tiger of Mysore.

Rear Admiral Horatio Nelson's 1798 destruction of the French fleet at the Battle of the Nile then prevented the French *Armée d'Orient* from returning home but not from campaigning throughout Egypt and Syria for the next three years. The French Army, however, suffered a repulse at Acre before retreating first to Cairo and then Alexandria where Napoleon deserted to return to Paris, leading a coup against the ruling French Directory and installing himself as First Consul. In the meantime, the former partners of the First Coalition had taken advantage of Napoleon's absence to form a Second Coalition without a complacent Prussia but with an angry Russia upset at Napoleon's 1798 invasion of neutral Malta and overthrow of the Order of the Knights of St John (Hospitaller), Tsar Paul I being the Grand Master.

In 1799 Russia then joined Austria for an advance into Switzerland that was ultimately repulsed at Zurich, and also supported Great Britain's Prince Frederick, Duke of York for an advance into Holland that was ultimately defeated at Castricum, possibly contributing to the rewriting of an old nursery rhyme relating to the futility of the Duke's campaign but certainly leading to Russia withdrawing from the war. When Napoleon and General Jean Moreau then defeated the Austrians at Marengo and Hohenlinden respectively, the newly formed United Kingdom of

Great Britain and Ireland (1 January 1801) was again left to fight France alone. With no hope of defeating France in Continental Europe, 14,000 men and forty-six cannon under Lieutenant General Ralph Abercromby sailed for Alexandria, Egypt under Captain Alexander Cochrane to finish off a French *Armée d'Orient* still enraged at Napoleon's betrayal.

On 8 March 1801 at Aboukir Bay, 5,000 of Abercromby's marines successfully landed against 2,000 French largely, since it was impossible to keep their powder dry, at the point of the bayonet. Unloading the remainder of his force, Abercromby advanced south-west to Mandara defeating another 4,000 French under General Francois Lanusse on 13 March before continuing onto the outskirts of Alexandria where he formed a three-mile front from the sea to the Alexandria Canal. At 03.30 on 21st March 1801 the so far almost inactive General Jacques-Francois 'Abdullah' Menou commanding the *Armée d'Orient* advanced to attack Abercromby with 20,000 men in column, the main weight falling on the British right. Outflanked, 'Glosters' under Major General Sir John Moore came under severe pressure to front and rear, fighting back to back with continuous volleys holding off the French who then launched cavalry and infantry attacks on Highlanders and Guards in the British centre. Disciplined British musket volleys again repulsed the French attacks on the centre and now on the left, the sixty-six-year-old Abercromby in the thick of the fighting with a mortal leg wound before Menou again launched heavy cavalry and infantry assaults on the British right, the fighting raging in the Roman ruins of Nicopolis. After five hours of conflict and over 4,000 French casualties, Menou withdrew back into Alexandria where, on Abercromby's death a week later, he was besieged by General John Hely-Hutchinson and Major General Eyre Coote for the next five months.

Menou surrendered in September, the *Armée d'Orient* allowed to return home under arms in the erroneous belief that it would turn against Napoleon. The Rosetta Stone, key to Egyptian hieroglyphics, came into British possession during Abercromby's campaign.

22 March 1421

Hundred Years' War
Battle of Baugé

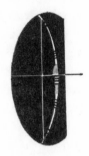

AT TROYES IN May 1420 it seemed that the King of England Henry V had at last achieved his 'just rights and inheritances' by becoming regent and heir to the Kingdom of France. The great English warlord also became betrothed to Catherine of Valois, daughter of King Charles VI of France, a marriage that would hopefully unite the Kingdoms of England and France indefinitely. There was just one problem, the dispossessed fifth son of Charles and Queen Isabelle, the Dauphin Charles. Just fifteen-years-old the Dauphin had escaped capture in Paris by John 'the fearless', Duke of Burgundy with whom his father's family had been at war for over a decade. Whilst John held the king and queen he sought not to usurp the throne but rather to restore his favour with the Royal Family. Now in a position of almost absolute power, Duke John was also expected to oppose his former ally Henry's invasion of Normandy but any chance of a Burgundian alliance with the Dauphinists was lost at Montereau when John was murdered by the Dauphin. For his part, the Dauphin already had an ally, duly calling upon the 'Auld Alliance' with Scotland.

Since King Charles was in poor health (often mad), Queen Isabelle, who preferred her daughter rather than her son to sit on the French throne, had sent for Henry who became her son-in-law, marrying Catherine in June 1420. After a one day honeymoon, Henry then set off to reduce Dauphinist strongholds at Sens, Montereau and Melun, the latter for a painful four months whilst English frontier garrisons in Normandy came under attack from Dauphinists and Scots led by John Stewart, Earl of Buchan. After Melun, Henry and his queen entered Paris to joyous scenes but when they then left the city for London so too did their ally Philip, the new Duke of Burgundy, who left for his own homelands. The power vacuum in France allowed Dauphinists and Scots reinforced by the defection of Jacques D'Harcourt, Sire of Tancarville to sever Burgundy's lands in Flanders and Burgundy from Henry's in Normandy, in retaliation of which the English king's brother, Thomas, Duke of Clarence set out on a punitive raid south toward Orléans.

The Dauphin sent for Buchan, whose men he already regarded as wine guzzlers, to join with Constable Gilbert Lafayette, 5,000 men moving south to cut Clarence's line of retreat. Clarence was at Beaufort with 1,500 men-at-arms but his archers were widely dispersed foraging throughout the countryside. Buchan arrived with most of his army at Vieil Baugé on Good Friday 21 March only to suffer the capture of one of his patrols the following morning Saturday 22 March 1421. On the news of Buchan and Lafayette's proximity, Clarence was annoyed at the prospect of of fighting over the Easter weekend but not only had he been largely excluded from Henry's inner court, he had also missed the 1415 glory of Agincourt – in the words of William Shakespeare (*Henry V*, Act IV, Scene III) believing himself 'accursed' he had not been there and 'holding his manhood cheap' ever since. Ignoring the advice of both John Holland, Earl of Huntingdon and Gilbert Umfraville who urged restraint, Clarence instead decided to attack there and then despite the absence of his archers and his dinner being unfinished. Thomas Montagu, Earl of Salisbury was left to follow on with the archers while Clarence advanced, approaching the bridge over the River Couosnon at Vieil Baugé at the same time as a French patrol under Lafayette who rallied the French defenders to prevent an English crossing. Under a hail of Scottish arrows and unable to reply, Clarence's cavalry charges could make no headway until the river was at last forded upstream, a move which turned the Scottish flank to face another charge, this time one that successfully cleared the bridge. Clarence, however, now found himself wading through heavy mud in the valley beyond, whilst much of his force was fighting in the streets of Vieil Baugé. Unknown to him, however, on the other side of the ridge to his front, Buchan had held back his main force for a surprise attack; Clarence, Umfraville, Huntingdon and Thomas Beaufort, Duke of Somerset (Clarence's cousin) now directly in their path. On seeing this overwhelming force crest the ridge Clarence turned his horse and charged, his loyal knights and men-at-arms following. A fearful mêlée raged but not for long before the English force was virtually wiped out, Clarence, Umfraville and John Welles, Lord Roos killed, Huntingdon and Somerset captured. Salisbury and the archers later recovered Clarence's body.

Baugé became the first occasion since the 1415 resumption of the Hundred Years' War that the English had been defeated in open battle. King Henry returned to France two months later, he would never see England again whilst Salisbury would catch up with Buchan two years later at Cravant.

23 March 1757

Seven Years' War (India)
Battle of Chandannagar

 IN DECEMBER 1600 England's Queen Elizabeth I granted a charter to the 'Governor and Company of Merchants of London trading into the East Indies' (the East India Company) effectively awarding a monopoly on all trade with countries east of the Cape of Good Hope and west of the Straits of Magellan. James Lancaster then set sail with five ships for a one-and-a-half year voyage to Sumatra where he was invited to trade along with the Dutch by the local Sultan. At the time, both England and the United Provinces (Netherlands) were allies against Spain and Portugal and coexisted well but as competition for trade increased, particularly spices, a series of clashes occurred including the 'Massacre of Amboyna' which amongst other disputes contributed to three Anglo-Dutch Wars during the second half of the seventeenth century.

By 1700, with Britain no longer at war with the Dutch, the British East India Company had left the East Indies looking to further trade in India where they had been granted a factory at Surat by the Mughal Emperor Jahangir. The Company then built another, Fort St George at Madras (Chennai), before acquiring Bombay (Mumbai) in 1662 by virtue of King Charles II's marriage to Portugal's Catherine of Braganza. The Company also had a presence in the Ganges Delta at Fort St William, Calcutta (Kolkota), West Bengal but here faced strong competition further up the River Hooghly not so much from the old Portuguese traders but from the French at Chandannagar and the Dutch at Chinsurah.

In 1715 Joseph Dupleix arrived in India, becoming French Governor of Chandannagar in 1730 as French commercial rivalry increased with the British East India Company, reaching a head in 1744 when the War of the Austrian Succession spilled over into India, the Second Carnatic War. The status quo ante bellum was achieved by the 1748 Treaty of Aix-la-Chapelle which effectively resolved very little but left a strong Royal Navy presence in the Bay of Bengal. The frailties of Aix-la-Chapelle were soon exposed, Dupleix recalled to France in 1754 as war again threatened, this time the Seven Years' War (1756–63) as France aimed to limit Prussian power in Europe and British power globally, particularly in North America, the Caribbean and India.

British Prime Minister William Pitt 'the Elder' financially subsidised his European allies, Prussia, Hanover and Portugal, to tie down French forces in Europe whilst he forced them out of North America, several Caribbean Islands, West Africa and their old trading posts in India, the third and final Carnatic War. Apart from the usual skirmishes the fighting was initiated by neither the French nor British but by the Nawab of Bengal, Siraj ud-Daulah who resented the British East India Company further fortifying Fort St William, Calcutta. The Nawab attacked and captured the fort on 20 June 1756, in the stifling summer heat his troops imprisoning 146 English and Indians in the fort's prison of just 250 square feet, the Black Hole of Calcutta – 123 died from suffocation and heat exhaustion. Siraj then moved the survivors north to Murshidabad and failed to reply to the letters of Lieutenant Colonel Robert Clive, victor over the French at Arcot, Arnee and Trichinopoly in 1751–52, and to Vice Admiral Charles Watson, Commander-in-Chief of the Royal Navy East Indies Station who sailed north where the Company's private army of 2,000 men and fourteen cannon ran the 'Calcutta Gauntlet' through an estimated 100,000 Bengalis to relieve Fort St William. After signing the Treaty of Alinagar, Siraj retreated to Murshidabad only for French Marquis Charles de Bussy to threaten Bengal. Clive and Watson now sailed on up the River Hooghly in the 64-gun HMS *Kent*, the 60-gun HMS *Tiger* and the 50-gun HMS *Salisbury*, on 23 March 1757 avoiding the French blockade to begin a bombardment of the French settlement at Chandannagar completely destroying Fort d'Orléans and all the town's housing.

Siraj was outraged by the British attack on Chandannagar but could do little whilst in fear of Maratha and Afghan threats on his borders. Clive resolved to remove the unreliable Nawab for a British puppet but first awaited reinforcements from Calcutta under Major James Kilpatrick before advancing upriver to Murshidabad. The Nawab would intercept him at Plassey in June for a battle that would shape the next two centuries of Indian history.

24 March 1944

Second World War
The Great Escape

THE SECOND WORLD War strategic bombing of Germany gave hope to millions of Europeans under German occupation but Royal Air Force Bomber Command casualty rates were terrifying. Of 125,000 airmen to serve in Bomber Command, almost half were killed in perilous night raids against belts of anti-aircraft defences and enemy night fighters whilst of the many 'lucky survivors' to be shot down 10,000 became prisoners of war. To house the increasing numbers of downed aircrew a new prisoner of war (POW) camp was built outside Sagan, Lower Silesia (now Poland), Stalag Luft III. Being far from neutral territory the site further discouraged escape since the earth beneath the thin grey top soil was a soft yellow sand which made tunneling both hazardous and obvious. Initially six huts were erected two feet above ground surrounded by two nine-foot barbed wire fences. Inside the fences any crossing of the warning wire was met with machine-gun fire from 'goon boxes' (German guards) spaced 100 yards apart which overlooked both the compound and the open ground beyond to the woods. Any POW misconduct was rewarded with a period in solitary confinement. Kommandant Colonel Friedrich von Lindeiner, a holder of the Iron Cross First and Second Class from the Great War, however, in an effort to discourage escape, attempted to make life pleasant, a life some POW's reluctantly accepted whilst many saw it as their duty to escape, hopefully tying up large enemy numbers in their recapture. In spring 1943 as a new north compound was being built at Stalag Luft III, Spitfire pilot Squadron Leader Roger Bushell, 'Big X' leading the X escape organisation, visited Group Captain Herbert Massey with a plan for three tunnels, Tom, Dick and Harry, to be constructed once inside this new compound. Bushell envisaged a mass escape comfortably bigger than previous British attempts at Kirchain, Warburg, Schubin, Eichstatt, Stalag Luft VI, Colditz and his own imminent effort at Stalag Luft III where two British POWs in 'German uniform' would march twenty-four others out of the main gate. They were all soon recaptured.

Despite a scarcity of resources, Bushell demanded 200 forged passes, 200 sets of civilian clothes, 200 compasses and 1,000 maps whilst Rhodesian genius Johnny Travis made air pipes, pumps, cables and a railway for the tunnels as well as the tools to dig them with. Goons were bribed and anything of use stolen. The tunnel entrances were well hidden, Massey visiting 'Tom' under the Chimney in hut 123 asking Bushell how he intended to conceal the evidence only to be informed he was already studying the finished article. The tunnels were then dug thirty feet down beyond prying German microphone range and to avoid a collapse under the weight of vehicles deliberately driven around the compound. A workshop, a sand collection area and staging posts were built along the two foot square, bed board bolstered tunnels which were lit by the tapping of the camp's electricity supply. As the sand was brought out 'Penguins' carried it outside in long woolen underpants where it was covered by top soil from an increasing number of vegetable gardens. Suspicious German guards, 'ferrets', watched on but were countered by an elaborate system of lookouts, 'stooges'. Nevertheless Tom was discovered in a sudden raid by chief ferret Sergeant Major Herman Glemnitz whilst Dick was then used to hide the vast quantities of sand from the 336 foot long Harry.

On 24 March 1944, after a nerve wracking visit from the Gestapo, Bushell decided to move despite snow and freezing temperatures, so cold that Harry's exit door had frozen solid. Another nerve wracking ninety minutes then passed before news broke that Harry was also short of the tree line. Bushell would still press ahead but was delayed further by an air raid warning cutting the camp's electricity. All luck finally ran out when the 77th escapee was spotted by a nearby guard, ferrets with dogs storming the huts but still unable to find Harry's entrance until Charlie Pfelz crawled back through to the stove in hut 104.

A national alert was issued as German Chancellor Adolf Hitler fumed. Wings Day and Pawel Tobolski were arrested in Stettin after a stay in Berlin, Alex Neely was arrested in Munich whilst Johnnie Dodge was caught, sent to Sachsenhausen concentration camp, escaped and was caught again. Just two Norwegians and a Dutchman reached England. Of the other seventy-three, fifty, including Bushell, were shot by the Gestapo. Several of the German High Command and eighteen suspects were later tried for the crime. The escape is celebrated somewhat incorrectly in the 1963 MGM film *The Great Escape*.

25 March 1595

Irish Wars
Battles of Crossdall and Clontibret

TWO CENTURIES AFTER the 1169 Norman Conquest of Ireland the Anglo-Irish community had become so intertwined with the native Irish that English culture, customs and law had to be reasserted by the Statutes of Kilkenny. Whilst Englishness had been maintained in 'the Pale' around Dublin it had not in the provinces where Anglo-Irish nobles generally acted outside the feudal system. These Gaelic speaking 'English' lords were now to learn English and ride a horse in English fashion (a leg either side) whilst the Irish were forbidden to attend English Churches or their minstrels and storytellers perform in English places. Inter marriage was also forbidden and for the defence of Ireland, England's vulnerable western flank, 'the use of plays, horling and coiting' were banned in favour of archery and 'lance throwing', any person practising otherwise to suffer attainder.

The Hundred Years' War and the Wars of the Roses, however, distracted a succession of English kings from Ireland until the sixteenth century when the Irish Parliament in Dublin urged Henry VIII, King of England and now Ireland, to force the issue. Henry began the Tudor Conquest in which the Irish nobility retained their lands and attended Parliament upon fealty to Henry. English law and customs were then implemented across Ireland as well as the religion of Henry's new Church of England, Anglicanism. As English relations then deteriorated with Catholic Spain, the need to secure Ireland became more acute but the intrusion into Gaelic life was contested, first in Munster and Connaught where the Fitzgeralds of Desmond rebelled twice before Fiach O'Byrne followed suit in Leinster. By 1583 the English Lord Deputy of Ireland, Baron Grey de Wilton had ruthlessly put down the rebellions with a scorched earth policy, a massacre of Papal troops at Smerwick and a man hunt for Gerald Fitzgerald, the Earl of Desmond. Munster then underwent a plantation of English settlers. In more isolated Ulster progress was slower but in 1594 produced the same result, a rebellion from Catholic Irish clans ultimately headed by Hugh O'Neill, Earl of Tyrone. O'Neill had previously been looking to gain the Presidency of Ulster until he realised that it was his brother-in-law, Henry Bagenal, who was favoured by Queen Elizabeth I.

O'Neill resolved to add to the eviction of English sheriffs begun by Hugh Roe O'Donnell by attacking the English fort at Monaghan. Bagenal reacted promptly by marching from Dundalk with 1,750 men – mainly infantry – to relieve the garrison but on approaching Monaghan from Newry on Lady Day, 25th March 1595,* the English column came under attack from 800 of O'Neill's men waiting in ambush at Crossdall. Still four miles from his destination Bagenal was fired upon from both sides by O'Neills surprisingly well-drilled musketeers, both the battle-hardened English veterans and green recruits holding off the Irish in what developed into a running battle to Monaghan. Bagenal had suffered only light casualties and having resupplied the garrison contemplated the return trip, setting off on 27 March via a more southerly route but desperately short of ammunition. O'Neill was hardly wrong-footed, attacking Bagenal from the outset on ground that promised and duly delivered an ambush in the pass at Clontibret. Again fired upon from both sides, Bagenal began taking much heavier casualties when the column came to a three hour standstill, desperately holding off O'Neill's now 4,000 Irishmen with a series of limited cavalry charges. Bagenal's pikemen were then forced into attacking when ammunition became critical before another cavalry charge narrowly failed to kill O'Neill but provided the English with a chance to force their way out of the pass. Exhausted after eight hours of fighting and with one hundred men dead, Bagenal led his survivors onto Ballymacowen Hill to form a defensive position for the night. Short of ammunition himself, however, O'Neill retired back north. Bagenal's column was relieved the following morning by reinforcements from Newry.

O'Neill was further encouraged by King Philip II of Spain who supported the Irish until a second Armada in 1596 met the same fate as the first, destroyed by Protestant storms in the Atlantic. The rebellion spread to Munster as the English poured in reinforcements under Robert Devereux, Earl of Essex making the Nine Years War in Ireland the Tudor dynasty's biggest conflict. Matters would come to a head at Kinsale in December 1601.

---

* Also, in medieval times, the beginning of the legal year.

26 March 1351

Hundred Years' War
Combat of the Thirty

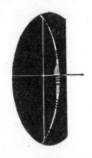

TO REINVIGORATE HIS claim to the French throne, King Edward III of England had invaded Brittany in 1342, taking sides in the Breton War of Succession. The war dragged on through 1347 despite the English-backed John de Montford having died and the French Bloisian candidate, Charles of Blois now residing in the Tower of London following his defeat at La Roche Derrien. Edward, meanwhile, was now campaigning in Normandy and the Calais Pale. As the Black Death then ravaged Western Europe a territorial stalemate persisted in Brittany with occasional sieges and vengeful sorties into each other's territory in the names of the two aforementioned protagonist's wives, De Montford's Joanna of Flanders, who had reputedly gone mad whilst in residence in England (possibly confined), and Blois' Jeanne de Penthièvre.

In Brittany the English were largely considered as unwelcome guests by the local inhabitants, none more so than Sir Robert Bemborough, possibly a German but more likely an English knight who was later 'celebrated' in ballads as a highly unpleasant, pitiless individual. Two possible chains of event are likely: that locals had tired of Bemborough's excesses and appealed for him to be brought to account by a knight of their own, Jehan de Beaumanoir or that Beaumanoir challenged Bemborough merely as a chivalric gesture to honour his duchess against that of Bemborough. The French chronicler Jean Froissart states that Beaumanoir challenged Bemborough to single combat but perhaps eager to avenge the death of Sir Thomas Dagworth (killed in an ambush six months previous), Bemborough favoured a wider contest involving thirty knights and squires on each side. Beaumanoir accepted and the contest was arranged as a Pas d'armes at the Chene de Mi Voie (the halfway oak) between Ploermel and Josselin, where the knights would either fight or be disgraced, Bemborough himself reputedly saying 'let us right there try ourselves... that people will speak of it in future times'. As so often in medieval times, honour was the prize.

Beaumanoir commanded thirty Bloisian Bretons whilst Bemborough commanded twenty English, six German and four Bretons sympathetic to the De Montford cause, all adhering to strict rules of combat which included not running when wounded or facing capture. The English included both Robert Knolles and Hugh Calveley who would go on to gain further renown, both knighted at later dates. The battle started in front of a large crowd of spectators and was fought on foot with swords, spears, axes and daggers to finish off the wounded. According to Froissart both sides fought with great bravery for several hours with just two English and four French fatalities before, more in the tradition of a cricket match, both sides agreed to break for refreshments. After also attending wounds, the contest was resumed with equal ferocity before a French squire, Alain de Keranrais, who had been angered by Bemborough's taunting of Beaumanoir, attacked and felled Bemborough with a thrust of his spear to the head, the Englishman regaining his feet only to be killed outright by an axe blow to the chest from the French knight, Geoffroy du Bois. This set back induced the English to close ranks, now fighting in a tight defensive wall with a German named Croquart to the fore. Eventually a Frenchman, Guillaume de Montauban, possibly against the rules of the engagement charged the English on his horse, devastating the English line. With a total of nine dead and many seriously wounded the English surrendered. The French for their part had suffered six dead with just as many seriously wounded. The English survivors were taken prisoner before being ransomed under the chivalric code albeit for token amounts. The battle had no effect on the Breton War or the Hundred Years' War but it was celebrated in French ballads, a statue of Beaumanoir also stands in Dinan to this day.

In some English literary works it is claimed that the contest was to be on foot and that by a mounted charge Montauban had cheated. In 1352, following the 1350 death of King Philip VI of France, his son and successor King John II would send Guy De Nestlé and the formidable Bertrand du Guesclin to Brittany where they would meet the freed Knollys and William Bentley in battle at Mauron.

27 March 1756
French and Indian War
Battle of Fort Bull

THE FRENCH AND Indian War had broken out in 1754 when, from across Lake Erie, French colonists and their American Indian allies had evicted British colonists from the Western Frontier at the confluence of the rivers Monongahela, Allegheny and Ohio. The French had then built Fort Duquesne (now Pittsburg), defending it from British attack before launching an attack of their own on Fort Edward on the shores of Lake George in the Hudson Valley. The British under Major General William Johnson had held the French attack but could not now achieve their ultimate objective – the taking of the French Fort of Saint Frédéric further north on Lake Champlain. Instead, Johnson built Fort William Henry at the southern end of Lake George forming part of a line of British forts stretching from the River Hudson west down the Mohawk Valley to Lake Ontario. Now looking to maintain a British presence in the disputed territories these forts were garrisoned over the 1755–56 winter, all them linked by waterways apart from the one to four mile 'Oneida Carry' where boats and supplies had to be carried overland between Rome and Wood Creek – indeed the forts were built to protect the route as a whole to Lake Ontario. The Oneida Carry was itself protected by Fort William on the River Mohawk and further west by Fort Bull at Wood Creek which was consequently the supply depot for the more isolated Fort Oswego and the Fort of the Six Nations further west still, on Lake Ontario.

The French determined to remove the threat of the two British forts on Lake Ontario by disrupting the British supply chain with an initial destruction of Fort Bull, Lieutenant Gaspard Joseph Chaussegros de Léry with a force of 360 French regulars, Canadian militia, Iroquois and Huron American Indians setting out from Ogdensburg on the St Lawrence River for a two-week winter march across thickly forested, mountainous country. Devoid of field artillery, Léry was heavily reliant on a surprise attack once he arrived in the vicinity of Fort Bull on 24 March and was fortunate enough to take a dozen prisoners the following day, learning from them that somewhat surprisingly Fort Bull, which was little more than a palisade, was also defended by only one hundred hungry men.

With many of his Indians refusing to make a front on assault, Léry attacked regardless on 27 March 1755 achieving complete surprise but for the Indian war cries of those that did take part. The defenders rushed back inside the fort where a firefight began, the French firing through the palisade with the British garrison Commander William Bull declining calls to surrender. When Léry's men forced the gates with axes the fight raged on with considerable ferocity within the walls to the detriment of the heavily outnumbered British garrison which was eventually overwhelmed, thirty-five of them taken alive, the others killed and scalped by Léry's Indians. The French then set fire to any ammunition, gunpowder and supplies that could not be carried and burnt Fort Bull to the ground.

Léry had successfully disrupted British offensive plans against the French Fort Niagara that same year and had weakened the British defence of Fort Oswego against French attacks that would begin in May. Fort Oswego would fall to the newly-arrived French Lieutenant General Louis Joseph de Montcalm in August 1756. Oswego was a bad loss for the British, losing over 1,000 men, but the French and Indian War in North America would soon take a different turn due to events that same month in Europe where Prussia had invaded Saxony to initiate the world's first truly global conflict, the Seven Years' War. In a reversal of the War of the Austrian Succession eight years before but still in an effort to maintain the European balance of power, Britain formed an alliance with Prussia against the weakening Habsburg monarchy of Austria (Holy Roman Empire) and, as always, France. Whilst Prussia would do most of the fighting in Europe, the British Whig Government led by William Pitt 'the Elder' would reinforce British armies overseas. In 1757, while the new British Commander, General John Campbell, Earl of Loudoun awaited instructions, the French would attack Fort William Henry from their own Fort Carillon (Ticonderoga), just the length of Lake George apart.

28 March 1942

Second World War
Raid on St Nazaire

THOUGH THE UNITED States of America had entered the Second World War in response to Japanese aggression in Asia and the Pacific, US President Franklin Roosevelt had deemed victory in Europe to be his priority. British Prime Minister Winston Churchill was much relieved but it would still be almost a year before American troops began to land across the Atlantic. Despite losing her European Allies, Great Britain had held the initial 1940 German onslaught but within eighteen months British armies around the nation's global Empire were retreating if indeed they fought on at all. Hong Kong, Malaya, Singapore and Rangoon had all fallen to the Japanese whilst the position in Borneo was desperate. In North Africa, German and Italian forces were pushing into British Egypt and Malta was being mercilessly pounded by a German *Luftwaffe* and Italian *Regia Aeronautica* enjoying complete air superiority. At least fears of an invasion of Britain passed when German Chancellor Adolf Hitler attacked the Soviet Union in June 1941 but the Battle of the Atlantic was very much on going with a resurgent German U-boat arm and, briefly, surface fleet keeping the British populace on strict rationing. The Royal Navy sinking of the pride of the Kriegsmarine, the *Bismarck*, and the dashing back to Wilhelmshaven and Kiel by the remainder of the German fleet had then lessened the surface threat, but Churchill was still anxious to contain *Bismarck's* more powerful sister ship, *Tirpitz*. In order to keep *Tirpitz* in the North Atlantic and Baltic, the British High Command looked to destroy the only dry dock capable of holding her on the Atlantic coast at St Nazaire, France, with a Combined Operations raid led by Commander Robert Ryder, Operation Chariot.

At 01.20 on 28th March 1942, having been directed in by the submarine HMS *Sturgeon*, the obsolete destroyer HMS *Campbeltown* captained by Lieutenant Commander Stephen Beattie entered the difficult estuary of the River Loire flying the German Ensign. Led by a motor gun boat and two wooden torpedo motor launches with astern another fourteen motor launches and a motor torpedo boat, *Campbeltown* was packed with explosive, intent on ramming the gates of the giant Normandie dock. On board the small fleet were 611 sailors and commandos under Lieutenant Colonel Charles Newman who, once ashore, would wreak further havoc against the German harbour defences of seventy plus guns, 5,000 troops, two U-boat flotillas and other ships which were on full alert following an earlier desultory British bombing raid. Two miles from the dock gates German searchlights lit up Ryder's fleet, a signal station to port and a minesweeper requesting identification. Leading seaman Seymour Pike in the lead MGB responded in German code temporarily satisfying Harbour Command but not the minesweeper which again challenged before opening fire. Pike and Beattie desperately signaled 'friendly forces' temporarily halting German fire as the small British fleet continued. Still a mile from the objective their bluff was finally called at 01.28 when the harbour erupted in gunfire, Beattie now running up the White Ensign of the Royal Navy and ringing his bell to signal a return of fire. As tracer flooded the harbour the British surprised the defenders with the ferocity of their reply, Able Seaman William Savage raking the minesweeper as Beattie swung in for the final run on the Normandie gates at twenty knots. Avoiding the south entrance and harbour mole, *Campbeltown* rammed the dock gates at 1.34am, Beattie casually remarking that he was four minutes late.

Behind *Campbeltown,* however, the motor launches had suffered, many did not reach their objectives but, nevertheless, enough commandos moved ashore in seven demolition and assault teams to destroy pumping stations and gun emplacements whilst Newman organised a defence of the perimeter and bridge into the docks against rapidly responding German resistance. After completing all objectives the survivors then retreated to scenes of desolation in the harbour before making an about turn to fight their way out of the dockyard into the town against impossible odds. Incredibly five men reached Spain.

Unaware of the danger within *Campeltown*, 300 Germans were killed later that morning when the ship exploded. The Normandie dock was put out of service for the duration of the war. The British lost 169 men dead with 215 taken prisoner. Ryder, Newman, Beattie and Savage were among five Victoria Cross winners, with another 135 men decorated or mentioned in despatches. The *Tirpitz* never sailed into the Atlantic.

29 March 1461

Wars of the Roses
Battle of Towton

THERE HAD BEEN four bloody battles in the past nine months alone as the internecine fighting of the Wars of the Roses continued to leave many a peer dead on a battlefield or kneeling over an axe man's block. The resolve of both sides to exact revenge only seemed to be deepening despite the two protagonists, whose feud had been responsible for starting the conflict, both now lying dead – Edmund Beaufort, Duke of Somerset killed at the May 1455 First Battle of St Albans and Richard Plantagenet, Duke of York killed or executed immediately after the December 1460 Battle of Wakefield.

The news of his father's death soon reached his son Edward, now Duke of York who, in February 1461, defeated Owen and Jasper Tudor at Mortimer's Cross, but Edward could not return in time to prevent his Yorkist ally Richard Neville, Earl of Warwick from suffering a heavy defeat at the Second Battle of St Albans to the Queen of England, Margaret of Anjou, the devoted wife of King Henry VI. Margaret's victorious army of Northerners had then advanced on London only to find the gates had been firmly shut by the petrified Yorkist inhabitants. Since the queen and her husband, who had been left under a tree at St Albans, had no wish to alienate Londoners further they began a grueling retreat through the bitter cold of winter to York. Edward and Warwick reentered London on 27 February, crowds cheering in relief whilst Edward contentiously proclaimed himself King Edward IV but across the country still two-thirds of the English peerage supported the cause of King Henry, that of the House of Lancaster. To possess any credibility Edward required a decisive victory and quickly, he promptly headed north to Yorkshire with Warwick, William Neville Lord Fauconberg and John De Mowbray Duke of Norfolk all gathering support for what would be the greatest ever battle on British soil... at least since Roman times.

On 28 March Edward skirmished with archers under the formidable John, Lord Clifford contesting the crossing of the River Aire at Ferrybridge before Fauconberg crossed upstream at Castleford to trap and kill Clifford with an arrow through the throat. After a short march the Lancastrian position came into view on a plateau between Towton and Saxton with its right on the Dintingdale Valley of the Cock Beck River. Edward, however, was not yet at full strength and delayed any attack until the following day with both armies, each about 30,000 strong, sleeping out in the snow and rain.

On the morning of the 29 March 1461 Edward advanced to just outside bowshot range of the Lancastrians whose King Henry had remained in York leaving Henry Beaufort (son of Edmund), Duke of Somerset to do his bidding. Both sides then remained stationary for several hours trading insults. Outnumbered, Edward was still awaiting the arrival of Norfolk whilst opposite, Somerset, Henry Percy, Earl of Northumberland and Henry Holland, Duke of Exeter were reluctant to forsake what was a favourable Lancastrian position. At about 11.00 though snow began to fall, blowing into the faces of the Lancastrians so that Fauconberg ordered the Yorkist archers forward to fire before retreating back out of range. Their blinded Lancastrian counterparts replied spiritedly but exhausted their quivers hitting no one. Fauconberg then launched another goose-feathered attack using the additional Lancastrian arrows to gain yet more deadly results that stung the Lancastrians into an advance. Additionally attacked by mounted Lancastrian knights hidden in Castle Hill Wood above the Cock Beck, the Yorkist left soon fell back before Edward himself restored order. Edward's right then held the advance of Northumberland as the entire half-mile front swung anti-clockwise in a mêlée of terrifying violence, no quarter given as the chivalry of the previous century was consigned to history. Slowly Lancastrian numbers forced Edward back up the ridge but Norfolk then arrived on the London Road to attack the Lancastrian left and decisively change the course of the battle. Fighting raged throughout the afternoon and after dark as late as 22.00, a bloodbath of sword, axe, bills and maces until the Lancastrians broke and fled. Pursued for up to six miles over the course of the next twenty-four hours they either drowned in the Cock Beck or were cut down. Twenty thousand men may have died at Towton, almost 1 per cent of England's population.

Edward was crowned at Westminster Abbey on 28 June 1461, he would need to deal with a Lancastrian uprising three years later but otherwise enjoyed five years of peace before his reign began to falter. Turmoil would begin again in 1470, the bloody murder in 1471 at Barnet.

29 March 1879

Zulu War
Battle of Khambula

THE BRITISH ANNEXATION of Zululand had been expected to be a formality by the instigators, High Commissioner Henry Bartle Frere and Transvaal Administrator Theophilius Shepstone but that arrogance had been shattered in January 1879 at Isandlwana. The defeat and loss of life on both sides had shocked the British nation including Queen Victoria and her Prime Minister Benjamin Disraeli. That the situation should be restored quickly was paramount to British military prestige and power globally at a time when the Russian threat to British India through Afghanistan had again become a grave concern.

Lieutenant General Frederick Thesiger, Lord Chelmsford had initially launched a three-pronged invasion of Zululand on exterior lines from Natal hoping the Zulu King Cetshwayo would divide his forces. It had been Chelmsford, however, who had done the dividing, the catastrophe at Isandlwana and the withdrawal of what remained of the centre column back across the Buffalo River resulting. This left the eastern British column under Colonel Charles Pearson isolated at Eshowe whilst the weaker north-west column under Lieutenant General Evelyn Wood could do little more than harass Zulu forces around Khambula.

Anxious to atone for Isandlwana before his replacement Field Marshal Garnet Wolseley arrived, Chelmsford reinforced his centre column and resolved to relieve Eshowe, requesting Wood create diversionary attacks to prevent Cetshwayo launching the full Zulu Army in the south. Wood therefore decided to capture the large herd of Zulu cattle on the mountain plateau at Hlobane, a feat that would draw the 2-3,000 Zulu believed to be in the area into a favourable set piece battle and economically ruin them.

On 28 March 1879, the British advanced up the eastern approach of Hlobane with 700 mounted men under Lieutenant Colonel Redvers Buller and up the western approach with a similar number, including Zulu defectors, under Lieutenant Colonel John Russell. After light skirmishing over the difficult rocky approaches the situation on the plateau suddenly began to deteriorate rapidly. The Zulu, a well trained force capable of covering fifty miles a day since the reign of Shaka Zulu (1816–28), had been alerted to the threat at Hlobane by the presence of British scouts and had set a trap. Large numbers of Zulu now began ascending the slopes themselves to trap the British who also became aware, in the valley below, of the approach of a 20,000-strong Zulu Impi already in Buffalo chest and horns attack formation. In a desperate rush down the ravines leading from the plateau and an escape back to Khambula, Buller and Russell abandoned the cattle, fighting their way out with the loss of over 200 men and officers, Buller winning a VC amidst the debacle.

The fright at Hlobane following that of Isandlwana meant a nervous night for Wood's 2,000 men in the defensive laager at Khambula. Acknowledging the superiority of British firepower, Cetshwayo had forbade attacks on defensive positions but for younger, headstrong Zulu not to attack a prone enemy that only a day before was in such disarray, was too much-especially as they were commanded by Buthelezi Chief Mnyamana, a hero of Isandlwana. On 29 March 1879, 20,000 Zulu on a six-mile-wide front crossed the White Mfolozi River to approach Khambula again in Buffalo formation, the chest from the east while the horns moved around the north and south. At 13.30 Buller rode out with a mounted force to successfully provoke the Zulu right horn into an attack before the chest and left arrived from across a marsh. The Zulu charge across the open ground was met with terrific British volleys of rifle and cannon fire, the fearless Zulu soon unable to sustain the attack which was then taken up when the left horn approached over a ridge. In turn the Zulu left horn was also rocked by volley fire but with grim determination held its ground, returning fire from the protection of rocks and vegetation with weapons captured at Isandlwana and Hlobane. Major Robert Hackett then led a spirited British bayonet charge which halted the Zulu advance but left him blinded by a bullet through both temples. The Zulu centre now launched a series of attacks to within yards of the British lines where they were met with canister. At 17.30 the Zulu began a dispirited retreat, Buller pursuing to turn the victory into a rout, perhaps 2,000 Zulu were dead for the loss of 80 British.

The Zulu War had suddenly taken a very different turn. Three days later Chelmsford achieved a similar victory at Gingindlovu to relieve his eastern column at Eshowe. The fate of the Zulu and King Cetshwayo would be finally decided in July at Ulundi.

30 March 1296

Anglo-Scottish Wars
The Sack of Berwick

KING EDWARD I of England had played a prominent role for his father King Henry III in putting down the 1265 Baron's Rebellion of Simon De Montford before, in 1271, going on the Ninth Crusade to the Holy Land. The news of his father's death reached Edward a year later in Acre, the 35-year-old king returning home in 1274 to be crowned at Westminster with a military reputation second to none and an ambition to bring all parts of the British Isles under his influence; a goal achieved in Wales by 1284 after a military effort that included the construction of Caernafon, Conwy and Harlech Castles. In Scotland, Edward already had influence since his sister Margaret had been married to Alexander III of Scotland before her death in 1275. Margaret's granddaughter, also Margaret, Maid of Norway then became Queen of Scots in 1286 on Alexander's death. However, in 1290 aged just seven, having never set foot in Scotland (she made it as far as Orkney), Margaret died prompting no less than thirteen claimants to step forward for the Scottish throne. Edward's arbitration in the matter was sought and confirmed at a June 1291 ceremony which also recognised him as the direct Lord of Scotland. Edward's decision realistically lay between John Balliol and Robert the Bruce, 5th Lord of Annandale (grandfather of the future King of Scots), both of whom had supported Edward on his Welsh campaigns. Ultimately the English king awarded in favour of Balliol whose line of descent was marginally better, the decision backed by the votes of 104 English and Scottish picked judiciaries. Edward, however, continued to remember the June ceremony, insisting Scotland remain an English vassal state and that as his overlord Balliol must pay him homage, including the provision of military support against France.

Edward's stance severely compromised Balliol, he was King of Scots courtesy of the English king but any thought of homage or allegiance to the English Crown was anathema to almost all Scots. The beleaguered Balliol was then insulted in person at Westminster until he eventually recognised Edward as his overlord, an admission that snapped Scottish patience. In 1295, as an anti-English rebellion rose in Wales, Balliol was replaced by the Scots, a council of twelve meeting at Stirling which also promptly renewed the 'Auld Alliance' with France. An enraged Edward, who had also just been duped out of his own French possessions, immediately began strengthening his defences along the Anglo-Scottish border and ordered the powerless Balliol to evacuate the castles of Jedburgh, Berwick and Roxburgh, all of which were then in Scotland.

Edward first marched on Berwick, a large army on foot and a fleet of twenty-four warships sailing up the east coast of England to the mouth of the Tweed Estuary. That Edward could afford to do so at all after his previous expenditure in Wales was due to two pogroms against the Jewish community whose moneylenders had facilitated the conquest. Anti-Semitic propaganda, the enforced wearing of yellow badges and eventually their expulsion from England, usually with atrocities, had brought Edward's treasury much needed profits including medieval England's greatest ever tax revenue raised from his delighted subjects, particularly the Church. On 28 March 1296, Edward crossed the River Tweed at Coldstream Priory to summon Berwick's surrender. William the Hardy, Lord Douglas commanding the Berwick garrison already had a history with Edward after his 1388 abduction of Eleanor De Ferrers (an Essex estate owner by Edward's benevolence) from Fa'side Castle before marrying her (Eleanor regarded her abduction as a compliment). Edward's orders to arrest Douglas had been ignored then by Scotland's Guardians and his summons regarding Berwick's surrender was ignored now by Douglas himself. On Good Friday 30 March 1296, having received no reply, Edward's ships entered the harbour for a sharp engagement before the English Army led by Robert, Baron Clifford attacked from the north. The town's poorly maintained, mainly wooden pallisade defences gave Clifford's rampaging men little difficulty in entering the town where the cowardly Douglas and his 2,000-strong garrison had retreated to the castle leaving the wretched inhabitants at the mercy of the unwelcome arrivals. Of mercy there was none. The town, the most prosperous Scottish trading port of the day was ruthlessly sacked with virtually its entire population murdered over a two-day orgy of violence which even by medieval standards has few equals. Over 7,000 lives were lost before Douglas and his garrison negotiated a surrender, saving their own lives.

Edward defeated a small Scottish Army at Dunbar a month later and symbolically removed the Stone of Scone to Westminster Abbey (it was returned in 1996). Scottish Lords initially submitted but resistance would again increase the following year when Douglas was joined by William Wallace and Andrew Moray.

31 March 1944

Second World War Bombing of Nuremberg

GERMAN CHANCELLOR ADOLF Hitler had once called the city of Nuremberg 'the most German of German cities'. Built around the medieval *Altstadt* (old town) Nuremberg had become, since the early 1930s, the iconic heart of Hitler's National Socialist (Nazi) Party, the city where the Fuhrer had held his greatest rallies. By 1939 Nuremberg was under development, architect Albert Speer designing stadia for sport, political rallies, military rallies and the Grosse Strasse for military parades that were to celebrate the power of the Third Reich for the next 1,000 years. Even Royal Air Force Bomber Command had declared Nuremberg 'one of the Holy cities of the Nazi creed' but it was also an industrial city containing nearly one hundred factories and plants, twenty-eight military targets including an SS barracks and sixteen Nazi Party offices for administration and communication.

Since the August 1943 bombing of Hamburg, the area bombing tactics of Air Officer Commanding-in-Chief RAF Bomber Command Arthur Harris had been viewed with considerable discomfort by much of the British population and political establishment even though they themselves had been put through a similar ordeal three years before by the German *Luftwaffe*. Harris believed he could end the war without the need for large scale landings in Italy and northern France, sparing the lives of many Allied soldiers but though navigation had improved with the development of GEE and Oboe, area bombing was still wildly inaccurate – hundreds of bombers often missing targets entirely, especially those beyond Oboe range. Losses in Bomber Command remained painfully high since German cities were now better defended whilst Hitler had responded to Harris' 'Battle of Berlin' (five months of bombing during the long winter nights of 1943–44) with a sudden two-month long 'Baby Blitz' of Britain in the spring of 1944. The end of the war once again seemed as far away as ever.

Harris' opportunities to strike deep into Germany were now becoming limited, the approaching short, clear summer nights would be unfriendly to bomber crews and the needs of the British, Canadian and United States armies would soon be paramount. On 30 March 1944 with time for just one more major bombing raid Harris had just to decide where. The weather was a risk, clear skies were likely over North Germany and the moon would set only at near 02.00 the next morning. A cold front to the south indicating possible cloud, however, may have influenced Harris' decision, it would be distant Nuremberg. Up and down the length of England, RAF briefing rooms then filled with cigarette smoke and unparalleled terror, every airman understanding just how long and dangerous this mission would be.

At 21.16 782 Lancasters and Halifaxes began taking off to form into five waves led by a hundred Pathfinder Mosquitos, the weather was clear and many aircrew had believed up until the last moment that the raid would be cancelled. Raids into North Germany flew much of their route over the North Sea but not into South Germany where much of the seven to eight hour flight would be contested by Messerschmidt 110, Focke Wulf 190 and Junkers 88 night fighters, two hundred of them scrambling as soon as the bomber stream was picked up by radar even before exiting Belgium. Over the next hour fifty-nine British aircraft were shot down, picked out by their vapour trails at just 16,000 feet many by German fighters playing Schragemusik, upward firing guns that could bring down an enemy bomber from underneath. Despite adverse winds and still under continuous attack the bomber stream continued on, arriving in the area of Nuremberg behind their allotted Pathfinders at 01.10 on 31 March 1944 for a twelve-minute bombing spree, the weather once again eluding them as cloud now obscured the targets all of which were missed bar three ball-bearing factories. The bombers then turned for home on a more southerly route across northern France but into a westerly wind, several badly damaged Lancasters and Halifaxes barely staying aloft.

Nuremberg was the worst night of the Second World War for RAF Bomber Command, ninety-five aircraft were lost with 670 aircrew. Much criticised for allowing the raid to go ahead, the resolute Harris validly claimed 'we were very lucky there weren't half-a-dozen Nurembergs'. Bomber Command now prepared for D-Day but the bombing of British and German cities was far from over.

April

*"You know Foley, I have only one eye
and I have a right to be blind sometimes.
I really do not see the signal."*

VICE ADMIRAL HORATIO, LORD NELSON,
COPENHAGEN, 1801

1 April 1955
Colonial Uprising
Cyprus Emergency

THE BRITISH EMPIRE was the largest in world history, governing almost 25 per cent of the world's population and land surface at its peak just after the Great War. After the Second World War, however, a bankrupt Britain had ceased to be the world's major superpower, replaced by the communist Soviet Union and the anti-imperialist, anti-communist United States of America. Whilst maintaining colonies had become a financial problem for the British; Canada, Australia, New Zealand, Rhodesia and South Africa had already become self-governed before, in 1947, India gained independence, partitioning with Pakistan (in a union with Bangladesh). Ceylon (Sri Lanka) and Burma (Myanmar) followed in 1948. The British then fought to retain Malaya against a communist insurgency and Kenya against a 1952 Mau-Mau uprising. Also in 1952, a coup d'etat against British rule left Egypt a republic and Britain to grimly defend the Suez Canal for the next four years. Whilst in all these territories the British generally knew their enemy, a very different struggle was about to erupt in the Eastern Mediterranean on the island of the Goddess of Love, Aphrodite.

Cyprus had been under British administration after 1878 Turkish (Ottoman) defeats left Anatolia and the Eastern Mediterranean vulnerable to Russian expansion. When Turkey joined the Central Powers in 1914 Britain offered Greece enosis (union) with mainly Greek-speaking Cyprus in return for military support but to the shock of many Cypriots, the Greeks did not accept. Cyprus then became a full Crown Colony in 1925. Following the Second World War, the Cypriot call for enosis was then taken up by the Greek Orthodox Church under Archbishop Makarios III who contacted Cypriot Nationalist and Greek Colonel Georgios Grivas (*Dighenis* – the leader) to initiate a military arm EOKA (Ethniki Organisos Kuprion Agoniston – National Organisation of Cypriot Fighters) for the liberation of Cyprus. Though known to British Intelligence, Grivas was successfully smuggled back into Cyprus in 1954 to intensify recruitment for a violent insurgency.

On 1 April 1955 sixteen bombs exploded: in Nicosia at the Government Radio Station, the Education Office and the Wolseley Barracks; in Larnaca at the Police Station, the Courts, the Police Superintendent's and Governor Robert Armitage's houses; in Limassol at two police stations and at the Dhekelia British Army barracks. The attacks, committed by EOKA fighters under oaths administered by priests of the Orthodox Church, were immediately followed by a propaganda war, EOKA leaflets justifying their cause and warning any pro-British opposition would pay a heavy price. This included soldiers, policemen, administrators, shopkeepers, workers and their families. The Agios Nicolaos barracks, the Nicosia cinema, the Nicosia, Amiandos and Kyrenia Police stations were all attacked and individuals murdered in broad daylight whilst terrified Cypriots saw nothing. As the violence escalated, Armitage was replaced by Field Marshal John Harding, a veteran of Malaya and Kenya, who declared a state of emergency, imposed curfews, detention without trial and death penalties for the possession of arms. Despite the presence of 25,000 British troops the situation deteriorated, gun battles in Famagusta and in the Troodos Mountains nearly catching Grivas on whose head Harding placed a bounty but who in turn reciprocated with several assassination attempts on Harding. In March 1956 Harding then exiled Makarios to the Seychelles creating further animosity. The bombings, assassinations, executions and street beatings continued, even the Nicosia hospital came under fire in an EOKA rescue attempt. Grivas remained at large but Harding killed his number two, Grigoris Afxentiou in a firefight outside Machairas Monastery. British standing in the Eastern Mediterranean was by now at a low, humiliated at Suez and unable to contain the Cyprus Emergency. Harding resigned. The violence, however, continued through 1958 before the United Nations appealed for a resolution, Makarios triumphantly returning the following year, Grivas and EOKA laying down their arms that same month.

Cyprus did not and never has achieved enosis with Greece but she did gain full independence. President Makarios' alterations to the constitution would then spark events leading to a 1974 partition of the island with Turkey. Aphrodite lives on, more than one million Britons now visit Cyprus every year, double any other nation.

2 April 1801
French Revolutionary War
Battle of Copenhagen

IN 1797 BRITAIN had fought on alone against Revolutionary France after her partners of the First Coalition, Prussia, Austria and the Dutch Republic had been defeated and Spain had changed sides. Again, in 1801, Britain fought on alone during the War of the Second Coalition after Russo-Austrian advances into Switzerland had been repulsed, an Anglo-Russian invasion of Holland under King George III's second son, Prince Frederick Duke of York had failed and the Austrians had been defeated by Napoleon Bonaparte at Marengo and by Jean Moreau at Hohenlinden. The small British Army could not match the French in Continental Europe by itself and instead Lieutenant General Ralph Abercromby departed for Egypt to finish the *Armée d'Orient*, abandoned in 1799 by Napoleon. The consequent March 1801 Battle of Alexandria had been a decisive victory for Abercromby with the French now besieged, destined to surrender. Any remaining French threat to British India had therefore been fully extinguished but back in Europe the newly-formed United Kingdom of Great Britain and Ireland was becoming increasingly isolated.

On his early return from Egypt, Napoleon had led a coup against the ruling French Directory installing himself as First Consul, consolidating power after an attempt on his life by purging France of all revolutionary enemies largely by guillotine or, almost as bad, the penal colonies of French Guiana. As the only power now actively opposing an all powerful Napoleonic France, Britain defended herself with a Royal Navy blockade of the French and Spanish coasts, searched all neutral shipping and confiscated any cargo thought bound for France. On Russia's withdrawal from the war and in direct conflict with the interests of his recent ally, Tsar Paul I renewed the League of Armed Neutrality, Russia, Prussia, Sweden, Denmark and Norway now promoting free trade with France, enraging their former allies, the British Government of Prime Minister Henry Addington.

To crush the League, Admiral Sir Hyde Parker and Vice Admiral Horatio Nelson sailed with a fleet of thirty ships to the entrance of the Baltic Sea whilst final diplomatic efforts were pursued with Denmark. Crown Prince Frederik of Denmark, however, refused to resign from the League prompting the British fleet to sail through the Danish Straits anxious to attack the large Danish fleet before melting ice freed the Russian fleet in Tallin. With time to prepare, the Danes had formed a north-south defensive line in the Royal Passage off Copenhagen consisting of near forty warships with support behind from land batteries. At 08.00 on 2 April 1801, after Captain Thomas Hardy had taken depth soundings of the shoals under the noses of the Danish ships, Nelson's plan went into operation with HMS *Edgar* leading into the southern end of the Royal Passage. *Edgar* engaged at nearly a cable (200 yards) range but despite Hardy's efforts HMS *Agamemnon* behind ran aground on the middle shoal as did HMS *Bellona* and HMS *Russell*. The remainder, including Nelson's HMS *Elephant*, all moved up into line beyond each other to engage. At both the southern and northern ends of the passage Nelson positioned more ships to rake the Danish line while his bomb ships fired mortars over the British line into the Danish. The battle raged broadside for broadside from 10.00 until 13.00 as the Danes put up unexpected resistance. Unable to ascertain proceedings through the heavy smoke, Parker signaled Nelson to withdraw in the knowledge that his Vice Admiral would ignore the order if he was fit to continue. Holding a telescope with his one arm to his blind eye, Nelson claimed he could not see the signal and duly continued. An hour later only a few Danish ships were still firing supported by the land batteries, the seafront a mass of burning ships. Nelson sought a ceasefire from Prince Frederik who sent his Adjutant General to negotiate. The battle was at an end but not before the Danish flagship *Dannebroge* exploded, increasing to nearly 3,000 the men of both sides who lay dead or wounded.

The following day Nelson negotiated an indefinite armistice with Prince Frederik under threat of renewing the British bombardment on Copenhagen itself. Shortly news would arrive of the assassination of Tsar Paul and the accession of his anti-French son Alexander I – the League of Armed Neutrality collapsed. Britain and France signed the Peace of Amiens in October 1802 ending the War of the Second Coalition but the peace would last just a year.

2 April 1982

Falklands War
Battle for Port Stanley

GREAT BRITAIN'S CLAIM to the South Atlantic Falkland Islands originates from their first sighting in 1592 by Captain John Davis, but it was almost a century later that Captain John Strong set foot on the islands – only in 1765 did Commodore John Byron name a point, Port Egmont reaffirming Britain's claim. However, unbeknown to the British, the French had just sold a 150-strong settlement at Port St Louis to Spain whose claim to the islands rested on a 1493 Papal Bull *Inter Caetera* issued by Pope Alexander VI. The Protestant British were hardly likely to adhere to a Papal directive and were forcibly evicted from the islands by Spain in 1770, returning a year later by an unrecorded 'Secret Understanding' before again departing in 1774, leaving a lead plaque recording their claim but the islands now ruled by the Viceroyalty of the River Plate in Buenos Aires. The Spanish then left a plaque of their own in 1811 when their South American Colonies revolted during the Napoleonic Wars, the windswept islands now used by British and American whalers before German (possibly French) Louis Vernet attempted to colonise East Falkland, the Argentine Government appointing him Governor of the Falkland Islands (an appointment challenged by the British). When Vernet then arrested Americans for illegal seal hunting, his colony, now Puerto Luis inhabited by Spaniards, was destroyed by the United States warship USS *Lexington*. British Captain John James Onslow then sailed from Rio de Janeiro, Brazil to inform the remaining Spanish under Commander Jose Maria Pinedo that he was putting into effect Britain's sovereign rights over the Falklands. Between 1849 and 1941, exceeding the generally accepted fifty years in international law, Argentina failed to protest against British sovereignty thereby forfeiting their claim. Only in 1976 did the dispute again flare up but now with far greater intensity, Argentina landing on Southern Thule before cutting fuel supplies and refusing to fly the Red Ensign of the Royal Navy in British waters. In 1982 a military junta ruling Argentina, led by Lieutenant General Leopoldo Galtieri, facing civil disobedience at economic collapse and human rights abuses, then sought to restore their waning popularity by launching Operation Rosario, an Argentine invasion of the Falkland Islands.

At 04.30 on 2 April 1982 fourteen elite Argentine troops under Captain Alfredo Cufré were landed by the submarine ARA *Santa Fe* at Yorke Bay, north of the capital Port Stanley facilitating the main Argentine attack by taking the island's airfield and lighthouse. Further south at 05.30 a group of Argentine marines made their way from Mullet Creek to the west of Port Stanley where they attacked the vacated British Moody Brook Barracks. Both Governor of the Falklands Rex Hunt and Major Mike Norman of the Royal Marines, however, had prior warning of a possible attack, Norman now ordering all his troops, fifty-seven Royal Marines, eleven sailors and twenty-five to forty Defence Force Volunteers to concentrate around Government House which was attacked at 06.30 by sixteen Argentine commandos in an exchange of rifle fire and stun grenades. British snipers, however, believed they were under attack from a much larger force despite Argentines obeying orders to avoid British casualties. The fighting escalated, Argentine Lieutenant Commander Pedro Giachino and four of his comrades entering Government House before being fought back (Giachino mortally wounded) whilst to the east twenty Argentinian amphibious armoured personnel carriers that had followed Cufré into Yorke Bay rumbled into Port Stanley encountering machine-gun fire and anti-tank rockets from British marines still retreating. With reports of Argentine naval vessels in the vicinity, including an aircraft carrier, the town now occupied by Argentine troops and with further reinforcements arriving by air, Hunt finally asked local Argentines to negotiate a ceasefire, Rear Admiral Carlos Busser assuring him that further resistance was hopeless. Hunt duly surrendered but 6,000 rounds had already been fired in the British defence of Port Stanley.

In Buenos Aires huge Argentine crowds celebrated whilst 8,000 miles away in London, Foreign Secretary Lord Carrington resigned from a British Government in shock. Secretary of State for Defence Sir John Nott and the Americans doubted the islands could be recovered but not First Sea Lord and Chief of Naval Staff Sir Henry Leach who had little difficulty in persuading his formidable Prime Minister Margaret Thatcher, that it could and had to be done.

3 April 1367

Hundred Years' War
Battle of Nájera

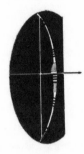

EXHAUSTED AFTER TWENTY-THREE years of war but from a position of strength, King Edward III of England signed the Treaty of Bretigny in 1360. The treaty recognised the English Crown as the lawful owner of nearly a third of French soil mainly in Aquitaine, southern France, on which fealty to the French Crown was no longer payable. The King of France John II, captured at Poitiers in 1356, was also released to raise his colossal ransom whilst his son Louis, Duke of Anjou alongside forty nobles replaced him as guarantors. Louis, however, then escaped much to the disgrace of his father who voluntarily returned to England, dying in captivity in 1364. Following Poitiers, France had been ruled by John's other son, the eighteen-year-old Dauphin Charles, but chaos reigned as armed thieves and vagabonds roamed the countryside, a situation that worsened following Bretigny as thousands of unemployed soldiers formed Free Companies. Neither were the unemployment statistics helped in 1364 at Auray when the English backed John de Montford finally defeated and killed his longterm family rival in Brittany, Charles of Blois, De Montford retaining English forces to guard his Duchy whilst both France and England also maintained garrisons in their respective territories, all, however, greatly reduced. Work and the opportunity for plunder largely eluded many professional soldiers until the Castilian Civil War (Succession), which had been ongoing intermittently for fourteen years, erupted again in 1365.

Pedro the Cruel had been King of Castile for sixteen years, a man of dubious moral fibre who advanced his own causes before those of his subjects particularly in wars against Aragon. In 1365, many of Pedro's own nobles along with the Aragonese, French and even Pope Urban V lent support to his bastard half brother Enrique of Trastamara by hiring the services of the Free Companies, including Hugh Calveley and Bertrand du Guesclin, who just a year earlier, had been fighting each other at Auray. Invading Castile from France, Enrique soon had Pedro departing in the opposite direction to Bayonne where he asked the Duke of Aquitaine, Edward's son Edward, the Prince of Wales, the Black Prince for assistance in return for cash and territory. Since any opportunity to fight the French was not to be missed by the prince he reemployed the services of Calveley, who by necessity changed sides, joining an Anglo-Gascon Army at least 10,000-strong that in April 1367 marched from Bordeaux into Spain.

Harassed by guerilla tactics, the Anglo-Gascons crossed the Pyrenees to reach the plain of Nájera on 3 April 1367 where the Castilian Army of 4,500 was quickly reorganised by Du Guesclin to face the Black Prince's flanking manoeuvre, both armies similarly arranged in three battles. From bitter experience, Du Guesclin tried to dissuade his employer from attacking head on but Enrique, as had Blois at Auray three years earlier, overruled and ordered forward Du Guesclin's vanguard to meet Henry of Lancaster, the two fighting each other for the entire battle. The Castilian Light Cavalry of Tello Alfonso, Lord of Aguilar de Campoo then charged the English flanks to get their first taste of the power of the English longbow, shot down in droves they were replaced by the heavy cavalry. Learning little from the attack of their colleagues, Enrique's heavies, who refused to fight on foot, also charged and were also shot down in droves. The English flanks under Sir Thomas Percy and the Gascon Jean de Grailly, Captal de Buch had moved forward to meet these cavalry charges and now closed up on the beleaguered Du Guesclin and the flanks of the oncoming main Castilian Army. As the Anglo-Gascon Army slowly advanced and despite Enrique's pleas, the Castilians broke and fled only to be trapped by the swollen River Najarilla. Whilst they were brutally cut down Du Guesclin's isolated vanguard fought on, Du Guesclin himself captured for a second time in just a few years (the first at Auray). Almost half the Castilian Army had been killed.

Another crushing English longbow victory, Nájera returned Pedro to the Castilian throne but, true to form, the king reneged on his financial commitments, paying a high price two years later when Enrique returned from France to murder him. Seriously out of pocket, the Black Prince returned to Aquitaine to raise taxes, incurring the wrath of the population who sought address from the now King of France, Charles V.

4 April 1944

Second World War
Battle of Kohima

THE JAPANESE CONQUEST of British Burma (Myanmar) had been accomplished in just five months after the January 1942 attack on Victoria Point (Kawthaung). The first task of the newly-formed Burma Corps of Lieutenant General William Slim had been a traversing of heavy jungle, the Irrawaddy & Chindwin Rivers and the mountainous country of West Burma back to British India, far out-distancing the 1809 retreat of Sir John Moore's British Army to Corunna. Following the five-month Burmese monsoon, a British counter-attack into Arakan, south-west Burma failed before Brigadier Orde Wingate led the first 'Chindit' expedition on a four-month, 1,000 mile jungle trek behind enemy lines, losing fifty per cent of his 3,000 men to disease and battle, the wounded left behind with a revolver in preference to captivity. Throughout 1943, with the Japanese existing on extended supply lines, the British consolidated, overcoming their own supply difficulties from famine struck Bengal (but increasing the suffering of the population) whilst reorganising forces under Lord Louis Mountbatten, South East Asia Command, Slim now commanding the British 14th 'Forgotten' Army and American Joseph Stillwell the Northern Combat Area Command (American trained Chinese and Merrill's Marauders similar to Chindits).

The railhead from Calcutta at Dimapur now served as the main supply base for 14th Army whose XV Indian Corps advanced into Arakan once again to be halted by Japanese 55th Division though holding off furious onslaughts themselves at the Battle of the Admin Box. Meanwhile to their north at Imphal and Kohima the British IV Corps under Lieutenant General Geoffrey Scoones was about to be attacked by the Japanese 15th Army under the ambitious Lieutenant General Renya Mutaguchi. Supported by Subhas Chandra Bose commanding the anti-British Indian National Army, Mutaguchi had been granted permission by Japanese Prime Minister Hideki Tojo for a 'March on Delhi'. First looking to capture the strategically important Dimapur, Mutaguchi's three divisions crossed the Chindwin to first assault Imphal, the 33rd Division from the south, the 15th Division from the north whilst the 15,000-strong 31st Division under Lieutenant General Kotoku Sato, after a bloody encounter with 50th Indian Parachute Brigade at Sangshak, headed further north to cut the Dimapur-Imphal Road at Kohima.

Following Sangshak, the Japanese 31st Division climbed up to the heavily wooded pass at Kohima early on 4 April 1944. Lieutenant General Montagu Stopford had rushed troops to contest the town but just 1,500 West Kents, Rajputs, Assams and 1,000 non-combatants commanded by Colonel Hugh Richards were on hand to defend the ridge above the road when the Japanese 1st Battalion, 58th Regiment attacked that night. Within twenty-four hours Sato had surrounded Kohima, beginning evening rounds of mortar fire followed by infantry inching forward along the ridge for fierce close quarter night fighting. On 6 April, Richards' difficulties were compounded when his water supply was lost, British artillery firing in support from Jotsoma three miles away to maintain his position but unable to hit Japanese on the reverse slopes. Richards' perimeter then shrank when the Japanese 138th Infantry Regiment moved behind him to block British reinforcements from Dimapur before, on 8 April the Japanese 58th attacked the north-east corner of the Kohima Ridge where the road turns west to Dimapur. Inside the corner, at the District Commissioners Bungalow, British, Indians and Gurkhas were forced back before a company of West Kents arrived on the commissioner's tennis court for a battle that would rage for over a month with unrelenting hand-to-hand fighting, men buried where they died. Eventually Punjabis of 161st Brigade from Jotsoma pushed through the Japanese block to enter the maelstrom, lifting the siege around the desolate wasteland of body parts and rats that was now Kohima. The British 2nd Division then arrived from Arakan, so too the Indian 7th Division, eighty-eight guns, howitzers and air strikes hammering Japanese positions whilst infantry moved to outflank to north and south. Sato counter-attacked, retaking Kohima Hill but now in despair at casualties and non-existent supplies requesting a withdrawal. Mutaguchi ordered him to stay but astonishingly for a Japanese General, Sato disobeyed, retreating on 6 June 1944 allowing the British 2nd Division to link with the Indian 5th Division from Imphal and reopen the Kohima-Imphal Road.

Sato was spared a Court Martial whilst Mutaguchi was sacked. The Japanese lost 7,000 men at Kohima, the British 4,000. The Imphal-Kohima battles decisively turned the war in South East Asia. The very same day that Japan began her retreat in Burma so too did her Axis partner, Germany, begin her own in France.

5 April 1799

French Revolutionary War (India) Siege of Seringapatam

 BY 1765 THE British East India Company had defeated the French at Chandannagar, the Dutch at Chinsurah and two Nawabs of Bengal at Plassey and Buxar, the highly unreliable Mir Jafar Khan, previously defeated at Plassey, then restored as Nawab but under British suzerainty. Threatened by Maratha ambition to the north and west, the British East India Company were keeping Mir Jafar in office largely for their own benefit since the Nawab was prepared to levy high taxes on his fellow Bengalis to pay for their military services. As well as Bengal, the Marathas were also looking to expand south to Hyderabad (where the Nizam of Hyderabad paid them protection money) and Mysore where the Sultan of Mysore, Hyder Ali Khan, had expanded north from central southern India along the west coast.

The pro French Hyder Ali had been prominent against the British in the Carnatic Wars and against other Indian kingdoms before joining with the Nizam of Hyderabad, Asaf Jah II in a dispute with the British over territories on the Indian east coast – the inconclusive First Anglo-Mysore War. Conscious of events in Bengal and suspicious of British intentions in southern India Hyder Ali made an ally of France during the American War of Independence (1775–1783) but died in 1782 during this, the Second Anglo-Mysore War. His son Tipu Sultan, the Tiger of Mysore, then continued his father's legacy, signing the 1784 Treaty of Mangalore with the East India Company only to resume hostilities in 1789, the Third Anglo-Mysore War in which he was defeated by British, Marathas and Hyderabadis in his capital, Seringapatam (Srirangapatna). Having lost half his kingdom and two sons hostage in the consequent 1792 Peace Treaty of Seringapatam, Tipu unsuccessfully looked west for support from Ottomans and Afghans before Revolutionary France's young General Napoleon Bonaparte headed east to Egypt with the intention of eventually combining with Tipu to throw the British out of India. Rear Admiral

Horatio Nelson's destruction of the French fleet at the Nile and Napoleon's failure at the siege of Acre, however, meant Tipu lost his ally just as the well-informed British Governor-General of India Richard Wellesley, Lord Mornington was about to start the Fourth Anglo-Mysore War with an invasion of Mysore and another siege of Seringapatam.

The British invasion was two-pronged, the Bombay Army of 6,500 (1,600 European, 4,900 Indian sepoys) under General James Stuart would march east through heavy jungle from Cannanore on the Indian west coast and link with the Madras Army of 40,000 (4,000 Europeans, 36,000 Indian sepoys) under General George Harris and Colonel Arthur Wellesley (the Governor's younger brother) marching 200 miles from the east coast. On 6 March 1799. the Bombay Army held off an attack from a superior Mysorean force at Seedaseer whilst on 27 March the Madras Army repulsed a Mysorean attack at Mallavelly. On 5 April 1799, the British began arriving outside Seringapatam (built on an island in the River Kaveri) to immediately launch a disastrous attack on Sultanpet Tope against a new weapon, Mysorean rockets. Wellesley was nearly captured in the attack but Sultanpet Tope was taken two days later. A classic siege then endured for nearly a month with both sides bombarding each other with cannon and rockets to which were added spirited sorties across the Kaveri by Tipu's 20,000 plus defenders. At 13.00 on 4 May, having at last breached the formidable walls in the north-west, the British stormed Seringapatam. Two forlorn hopes under Major General David Baird led the assault, moving along the north and east ramparts against heavy musket fire enabling the main army following to crush all Mysorean resistance within two hours. The cornered Tipu Sultan fought to the bitter end firing muskets handed to him by servants but lost his life with another 6,000 Mysoreans.

From Tipu's Palace, Wellesley brought southern India under the control of the British East India Company. The Maratha Empire would now fall into civil war, defeated at Poona the Peshwa (prime minister) Baji Rao II appealed to the British East India Company for assistance. In 1803 Wellesley would represent him at Assaye. The Mysorean use of rockets inspired William Congreve to develop his own, first used in 1806 against Napoleon at Boulogne. Tipu's favourite toy of a tiger mauling a British soldier resides in the Victoria and Albert Museum and two of his cannon front the Royal Military Academy, Sandhurst

6 April 1812

Napoleonic Wars
Siege of Badajoz

IN 1808 GENERAL Sir Arthur Wellesley had landed at Mondego Bay, Portugal with just 15,000 men, the first British campaign on the European Continent against the *Grande Armée* of Napoleon Bonaparte, Emperor of the French, since a Flanders disaster thirteen years before. Since Flanders, Britain had fought almost exclusively at sea leaving land operations in Europe to Prussia, Russia and Austria with whom they had formed, by 1812, five coalitions, all of which had collapsed in the face of French Revolutionary and Napoleonic might. Wellesley, Viscount Wellington since the 1809 Battle of Talavera, and his government initially of William Cavendish-Bentinck, Duke of Portland but now of Spencer Perceval wished to support Spanish partisan uprisings in the Iberian Peninsular the catalyst of which had been Napoleon's deposition of Spain's King Charles IV and son Ferdinand for his own brother Joseph Bonaparte. Allied with a poor but improving Portuguese Army and an indisciplined, poorly commanded Spanish Army against overwhelming French troop numbers (near 400,000 in 1810), Wellington had been hard pressed just to stay in the war, returning to his impressive Portuguese-built siege lines at Torres Vedras, Lisbon when required in 1810/11.

The July 1809, French defeat of Austria at Wagram meant Napoleon controlled all of northern Europe but relations between he and his temporary ally, Russia's Tsar Alexander I, became strained largely over Alexander's duplicity in applying the Continental System (Napoleon's trade embargo aimed at starving Britain) and Napoleon's lack of support for Russia's war with Turkey. Learning nothing from the hornet's nest of discontent stirred up in Portugal and Spain which he had invaded for similar reasons, Napoleon prepared to punish Russia with a French army of 600,000, half of them Prussian and Austrian, whilst continuing the fight against the British in Spain. It would not be the last time a resurgent European nationalist power would become embroiled in major conflicts on two fronts and Wellington was not to miss such an opportunity to increase his enemy's discomfort. In January

1812 he successfully besieged the French held fortress town of Ciudad Rodrigo, key to access in and out of northern Spain from Portugal before marching to Badajoz, key to the south.

A 35,000-strong Anglo-Portuguese-Spanish Army had fought the bloody Battle of Albuera outside Badajoz a year previous, before, on 16th March 1812, another of 27,000 arrived directly outside the city walls to begin building siege works in rain so torrential that any movement of siege guns was near impossible. Watching from the impressive ramparts and bastions, the French garrison of 4,700 under General Armand Philippon immediately launched a sortie of 1,500 infantry and cavalry that inflicted 150 British casualties but was ultimately repulsed. Over the next two weeks the British began firing on the walls as infantry under Lieutenant General Thomas Picton stormed Fort Picurina to the south-east. The French defenders, however, continued to sortie, desperate to distance the British guns but by the end of March heavy howitzers of up to 24-pounds were hammering away at the town walls. A few more days of intense bombardment produced three breaches, at the bastions of Santa Maria, Trinidad and in the connecting wall between, Wellington choosing to storm the breaches on the night of 6 April 1812 on receiving news of the approach of Marshal Jean de Dieu Soult's *Armée d'Andalusie*. At 22.00 a Forlorn Hope led by Major Peter O'Hare, who would have been promoted had he survived, and the 95th Regiment of Foot stormed the first two breaches whilst light infantry stormed the third, all accompanied by diversionary attacks north of the town from across the River Guardiana. On full alert, the defenders repeatedly shattered the assaults with intense musket fire, grapeshot, grenades, exploding barrels of gunpowder and masonry before Lieutenant Generals Thomas Picton and James Leith's 3rd and 5th Infantry Divisions scaled the north wall and San Vicente bastion respectively. Over forty assaults had already been launched and repulsed but now the town fell as the French defenders were assailed from all sides. Furious at losses of 5,000 at which even Wellington, the 'Iron Duke', wept, the British troops then turned a great British military achievement into one of shame with a three-day sack of Badajoz that inflicted 4,000 casualties on their allies, the Spanish inhabitants.

With Central Spain now open, Wellington marched north to Salamanca for a battle with 40,000 French under Marshal Auguste Marmont.

7 April 1918

The Great War
Battle of Lys

SUCCESSIVE GERMAN CHIEFS-of-staff had considered their strategic position hopeless, in 1914 Helmuth von Moltke, in early 1916 Erich von Falkenhayn and in early 1917 Paul von Hindenburg as well as his Quarter Master General Erich Luddendorf. But in early 1918, a year after Tsar Nicholas II had abdicated amidst a developing Bolshevik revolution, Russia withdrew from the Great War on signing the Treaty of Brest-Litovsk. German divisions on the Eastern Front were now free to give Kaiser Wilhelm II and the German High Command an opportunity to defeat the British and French Entente on the Western Front before the arrival of one million Americans. It was not the first or last time Russian diplomacy left her wartime allies in a predicament, a century previous the Treaty of Tilsit (albeit under duress) freed Napoleon Bonaparte to concentrate on defeating Britain whilst twenty-one years later the Molotov-Ribbentrop Pact would free Adolf Hitler to attack Poland, Belgium, Netherlands, France and Great Britain.

Field Marshal Douglas Haig and his French counterpart General Phillippe Pétain now suddenly faced 192 German divisions against their own 156 as Luddendorf launched Operation Michael on 21 March 1918, part of the German Spring Offensive (Kaiserschlacht). Attempting to break through between the British and French lines across the Somme and Cambrai battlefields, German forces made gains of up to 1,200 square miles but crucially General Julian Byng's British Third Army and Hubert Gough's battered British Fifth Army had held the line denying Luddendorf an exposed flank. As the German advance then ran into ever tougher British defences around Arras and Amiens their gains petered out when they experienced the same mobility difficulties encountered by numerous previous British offensives. Luddendorf had suffered 250,000 casualties in sixteen days, many of them irreplaceable, highly-trained shock troops, and had merely created a fifty-mile-wide, forty-mile-deep salient vulnerable to counter-attack. Frustrated at the lack of further progress, Luddendorff then switched the German attack north to Flanders. On 7 April 1918, north of the River Lys, the German 4th Army of General Sixt von Armin began an artillery bombardment upon the British Second Army of General Herbert Plumer whilst south of the river the German 6th Army of General Ferdinand von Quast did likewise upon the British First Army of General Henry Horne, 470 guns in total.

The two British armies were badly outgunned by high explosive, shrapnel and gas shells for over a day before on 9 April, Quast's 6th Army devastated the 2nd Portuguese Division at Neuve Chappelle. Such was the gap created in his line that Horne was forced to pull British divisions back but still managed to hold the German advance in the south, conceding between three and five miles across the front. Luddendorf, however, increased German pressure with Armin's 4th Army now attacking toward Messines north of the Lys, breaking into the right flank of Plumer's Second Army. Desperately short of reserves with the British position crumbling, Haig was incredibly staring at total defeat, issuing the famous order 'there is no course open to us but to fight it out. Every position must be held to the last man...believing in the justice of our cause each one us must fight on to the end'. With the BEF fully stretched, Quast now made a drive to capture the vital railway junction at Hazebrouck eight miles away but was stopped by the cork in the British bottle that was the 1st Australian Division. Meanwhile Second Army's right flank was under increasing pressure, forced out of Bailleul, Plumer then made the agonising decision to give up all the ground won in such despair the previous year at the Third Battle of Ypres, retreating from the Passchendaele Ridge back to Ypres. The decision, however, saved the BEF as the line consolidated, fighting on for another fortnight as Quast was repulsed at Bethune and, after capturing Mount Kemmel, Armin again at Hazebrouck.

The men of the BEF, British, Australians, New Zealanders, Canadians, South Africans, Portuguese and American had followed Haig's order to the letter. Luddendorf halted his Lys offensive before unsuccessfully attacking again on the Aisne and Marne. Between 21 March and mid-July 1918 the German Army lost almost a million men, a figure matched by the Entente who would counter-attack at Amiens in August. One of Germany's most notable casualties had been Manfred von Richthofen, the Red Baron, shot down and killed over Morlancourt Ridge on 21 April.

8 April 1898

Mahdist Wars
Battle of Atbara

IN 1896 GREAT Britain looked to reassert her authority in the Sudan and avenge the 1885 murder of Major General Charles Gordon by the Mahdi, Mohammad Ahmad. Following the Mahdi's death that same year the Khalifa Abdallahi had ruled the Sudan with an iron fist, crushing internal revolts before terrorising Egyptian border towns and spreading Mahdism to Abyssinia (Ethiopia). Since the French were also pushing east from the Congo into Equatorial Sudan on the Upper River Nile and were seen as a possible ally of the Khalifa (France had armed the Ethiopians against the Italians a few years before) an Anglo-Egyptian Army, also consisting of loyal Sudanese, headed by Sirdar Horatio Herbert Kitchener was charged with a reconquest of the Sudan, Kitchener in the service of the Khedive of Egypt but effectively reporting directly to the British Prime Minister in London Robert Gascoyne-Cecil, Lord Salisbury.

Kitchener advanced with all the subtlety of a steam roller, assembling his forces at Wadi Halfa with time largely on his side. To assist the movement of troops and materials the construction of the Sudan Military Railway began which by the end of 1896 was stretching south from Kosheh to Kerma and the Third Cataract of the River Nile. Further upriver the Nile is navigable by steamer so that having secured Dongola Province Egyptian forces could now push further ahead to Merawi, the decision made to begin building a second railway line from Wadi Halfa through the Nubian Desert across the Great Bend of the Nile to Abu Hamed which, when finished, would speed up reinforcements and supplies without relying on river levels. First Abu Hamed was taken in August 1897 by loyal Sudanese under Major General Archibald Hunter with the head of the railway following three months later. Mahdist forces around Abu Hamed were unsure of support from Khartoum and now evacuated Berber further south, Kitchener taking the dangerous gamble to capture and hold Berber as well with the railway again following closely behind. Only now did the Khalifa in Omdurman resolve to stop Kitchener's inexorable advance, sending to the western Sudan for Emir Mahmud Ahmed but then halting him whilst mobilising the entire Mahdist *Ansar* (following).

Alert to the danger, Kitchener began reinforcing Berber and Fort Atbara at the confluence of the Rivers Atbara and Nile, now bringing in British brigades under Major General William Forbes Gatacre but the *Ansar* failed to appear. After several weeks of inexplicable delays, the Khalifa at last ordered Mahmud along with the old eastern warlord, Osman Digna of the Handendoa, to retake Berber. With 14,000 men the two proceeded north-east intent on outflanking the Anglo-Egyptian left flank but Kitchener was equal to it, marching south to force the Mahdists further out into the Sudanese desert. At Nakheila, Mahmud and Digna were stuck, a lack of water between there and Berber leaving them unable to continue. A confident Kitchener with four infantry brigades and four artillery batteries advanced to finish them.

In the early hours of 8 April 1898, the Anglo-Egyptian Army closed to within half a mile and began raking the Mahdist zeriba (thorn bush protected camp) from back to front and back again. After an hour of shelling the infantry brigades formed in column ready for an assault which was signaled by bugle, the pipes and drums of the British regiments accompanying a continuous rifle fusillade on the entrenched Mahdist positions within the Zeriba. At 250 yards the Mahdists returned fire, inflicting heavy casualties but before the battle Kitchener had asked his men to 'Remember Gordon' and now they did just that. The impetus of the attack was too much, British, Egyptians and Sudanese all breaking into the zeriba to engage 12,000 Mahdists either standing their ground against the bayonet or fighting a retreat back to the Atbara where many were gunned down. After forty minutes the battle was over; just 4,000 Mahdists escaping, including the elusive Digna but not Mahmud who was taken prisoner.

Kitchener would now wait at Berber over the hot summer before advancing on Khartoum, new gunboats from Britain were on their way and from Cairo two 40-pounders, four Maxim guns, a howitzer battery, another British infantry brigade and the 21st Lancers.

9 April 1917

The Great War
Battle of Arras

FRENCH AND BRITISH casualties suffered in 1916 at Verdun and the Somme had been horrific but the campaigns had not been disasters militarily. Germany had also suffered, in fact so much so that incoming German Quarter Master General Erich Ludendorff was left to comment that 'if the war lasted, defeat seemed inevitable'. The German High Seas Fleet had also been confined to port following the 1916 Battle of Jutland with the task of stemming growing reinforcements joining the British Expeditionary Force (BEF) now resting on a policy of unrestricted submarine warfare, damaging British global trade but directly resulting in the United States of America entering the Great War.

The Entente's problems were largely political, French General Joseph Joffre ultimately paid for his failure to break the deadlock in France and was replaced by the half-English General Robert Nivelle whilst British Prime Minister Herbert Asquith fell to be replaced by his Secretary for War, David Lloyd George. Lloyd George wanted something to cheer the British nation, eyeing Palestine and the capture of Jerusalem whilst on the Western Front he was anxious to avoid a repeat of what he considered the 'ghastly failure' of the Somme. Still wishing to deliver a 'knockout blow', however, and impressed by Nivelle, Lloyd George subordinated his own generals, including the promoted Field Marshal Douglas Haig who since the beginning of 1916 had argued for an offensive in Flanders where gains would improve British positions around Ypres and threaten German naval operations, including their troublesome submarines operating from the Belgian coast. Further south on the Somme, offensive plans were complicated by a forty-mile German winter withdrawal to the impressive defences of the Hindenburg Line, but it was here on the southern end, the Chemin Des Dames, that Nivelle proposed a French offensive supported on the northern end by a British diversionary offensive at Arras and Vimy Ridge. Haig agreed but nevertheless continued planning his Ypres offensive despite Nivelle confidently predicting a crushing war-winning victory.

The preliminary British bombardment across the twenty mile Arras front lasted five days (three weeks at Vimy) achieving a density of fire five times that of the Somme with flash spotters and sound rangers eliminating the majority of German guns. Increasing in the last few hours and including gas shells, the bombardment became a creeping barrage behind which fourteen divisions of Canadian, British and Colonial infantry advanced through a snowstorm, machine-gunners firing above them whilst forty MK II tanks rumbled alongside them. At Vimy Ridge, Canadians under Lieutenant General Julian Byng and Major General Arthur Currie moved up through underground tunnels, successfully assaulting the position using highly-practised plans to overrun large concentrations of Germans caught in the front lines. Further south the British Third Army of Lieutenant General Edmund Allenby was also successful east of Arras on the River Scarpe, XVII Corps advancing over three miles whilst VII Corps advanced over a mile capturing a part of the Hindenburg line. The following day the British 62nd and Australian 4th Infantry Divisions attacked Bullecourt but in a return to previous mistakes the attack was poorly planned and executed. German reserves, previously held too far back by 6th Army General Ludwig von Falkenhausen, now arrived to stall the British advance which was also hampered by the difficulty in moving heavy artillery over the shattered ground.

Haig dutifully supported his French allies with further major offensives on 23 April at the Scarpe and 3 May again, this time successfully at Bullecourt. The first day gains were, however, soon a distant memory and worse, Nivelle had failed dismally, General Philippe Pétain now taking command of a French Army partially in mutiny. Arras had been a comparative success for the British but at the price of the highest daily casualty rate of the war, 4,076. In the air, the Royal Flying Corps had also suffered, losing 245 aircraft in 'Bloody April' to the superior machines of the Luftstreitkrafte and in particular Jasta 11 – the Flying Circus of the Red Baron, Manfred von Richthofen.

French mutiny, Russian Revolution, the British Expeditionary Force would have to win the war. Haig would now attempt it on ground of his choosing, Flanders Fields.

10 April 1868

Abbyssinian Expedition
Battle of Magdala

ABYSSINIA, NOW ETHIOPIA, has long been considered the birth place of mankind but in the eighteenth and nineteenth centuries, rather than a single Garden of Eden, had been a series of competing fiefdoms with any emperor in the capital, Gondar, little more than a figurehead with little control outside his immediate realm. An eighty-six year 'Era of Princes' which saw no less than twenty-three emperors came to end in 1853 when the Emperor Yohannes III and more importantly his wife Menen Liben Amede were defeated at Ayshal by their grandson-in-law Dejazmach Kassa Hailu. Kassa Hailu then went on to defeat Wube Haile Maryam at the 1855 Battle of Derasge, crowning himself Emperor Tewodros II (Theodore) whilst moving the capital of Abyssinia to Magdala, an idyllic Zion in the mountain region of Amhara, home to the source of the Blue Nile.

The Christian Abyssinia had been through a century of relative isolation but this period ended in 1862 when Tewodros, fearing Islamic powers to his north, wrote to various European rulers for military assistance including Queen Victoria of Great Britain and Ireland who had several missionaries in the country and a Consul, Charles Cameron. Cameron, however, failed to deliver Tewodros' plea to Victoria in person, instead touring the Sudan (an Islamic enemy of the Abyssinia) much to the fury of Tewodros. On returning without a reply, Cameron was promptly imprisoned along with his staff and missionaries, including Henry Stern who had compounded ill-feeling by writing a demeaning biography of the emperor. When Hormuzd Rassam, an archaeologist turned diplomat, then arrived in Magdala in 1865 with a letter from Victoria, Cameron, his staff, Stern and his fellow missionaries were temporarily released only for the Tewodros to have a change of heart and return them to irons along with Rassam.

Instead of a letter, this time Victoria sent 13,000 British and Indian troops of the Bombay Army, 26,000 support staff and 36,000 transport animals, including elephants, under the command of Lieutenant General Robert Napier, a veteran of the Sikh Wars and the Indian Mutiny. The task facing Napier was eye watering, 400 miles of mountainous, road free tribal territories traditionally hostile to Europeans lay before him but with Victorian engineering and brilliant diplomacy Napier overcame both, arriving at the Plateau of Arogi outside Magdala on 9 April 1868.

On Good Friday, 10 April 1868, Napier moved his army onto the plateau in full view of 7,000 Abyssinian warriors fully prepared to defend their emperor. Knowing that Tewodros possessed heavy artillery and mortars, Napier was not expecting to be attacked but attacked he was just as a huge thunderstorm broke, Tewodros' prize mortar exploding at the first ask before his warriors, mainly armed with spears rather than muskets, ran across open ground into British rockets and cannon. Briefly checked, the Abyssinian charge then resumed into disciplined British and Indian rifle fire, the battle over in ninety minutes with 2,000 dead and wounded Abyssinians lying on the field. Napier immediately pressed on to Magdala itself, a now desperate Tewodros releasing his prisoners but Napier insisting on an unconditional surrender having found hundreds of corpses at the bottom of a nearby cliff. Tewodros refused and on 13 April Napier began bombarding Magdala whilst engineers and infantry climbed the slopes under covering rifle fire only to find the explosives required to force an entry had been left far below. Without waiting, soldiers of the 33rd Regiment of Foot then won two Victoria Crosses by fighting their way into the fortress. Abyssinian resistance then collapsed completely when Tewodros shot himself with a revolver previously gifted by Victoria.

Napier raised Magdala to the ground before returning to the coast with Tewodros' son Ala Mayu. Abyssinia was left to three feuding rivals, Dejazmach Kassa of Tigre, Wagshum Gobeze of Lasta and King Menelik of Shoa, the former becoming Emperor Yohannes IV three years later but the latter becoming emperor in 1889 on Yohannes' death at the hands of the Mahdists. Claiming a direct descent through the male line from King Solomon and the Queen of Sheba, Menelik's daughter Zewditu became empress in 1916 but governed under a regent, Menelik's cousin Ras Tafari Makonnen, who himself as an heir through the female line became Emperor Haile Selassie in 1930, the living God of the Ethiopianist Rastafarian Movement.

11 April 1902

Second Boer War
Battle of Rooiwal

THE MAIN THEATRES of Natal and the Orange Free State had been left behind two years before after overwhelming British reinforcements had broken Boer defences in the Drakensberg Mountains and on the Modder River putting an apparent end to the Second Boer War. Field Marshal Lord Frederick Roberts, however, had allowed thousands of Boers to escape to the South African Veld where they maintained the Afrikaner cause of independence from British rule, attacking British interests whenever and wherever they found opportunity. Though Roberts returned home to an earldom and a £100,000 bonus his predecessor as Commander-in-Chief in South Africa General Sir Redvers Buller returned home to a small hero's welcome from the British public but a sacking from the British Government (prompted by Roberts). British forces still in South Africa then also suffered several bloody noses, including a small Boer invasion of Cape Colony and more recently the capture of General Lord Paul Methuen and his column at Tweebosch.

The new Commander-in-Chief in South Africa Lieutenant General Horatio Herbert Kitchener of Khartoum had responded to the Boer guerrilla tactics by burning their farms and 'rehousing' their women and children in concentration camps but he more than anyone had endeavoured to bring both sides to the negotiating table. His usual fortitude had been shaken by the recent calamity at Tweebosch but were then suddenly reinvigorated by the news of a Boer delegation heading for peace talks at Klerksdorp. Suspecting the steel resolve of the Boer *bitter-einders* was waning just as he rediscovered his own, Kitchener decided to prosecute the war with ever more vigour toward a final conclusion. Looking to take advantage of General Koos De La Rey's presence at the peace talks, he ordered Colonel Ian Hamilton with thirteen columns of mounted infantry to launch new drives on the remainder of De La Rey's 3,000-strong commando which had so far evaded him.

Hamilton merged his columns into four, three of them under Colonel Robert

Kekewich, Lieutenant Colonel Henry Rawlinson and Lieutenant General Walter Kitchener (brother), to pursue De La Rey's commando which he assumed was somewhere in the valley formed by the Brakspruit and Little Harts Rivers. Hamilton feinted south-west before doubling back hoping the Boers would look to side step him to the east. It worked magnificently and, all the better, when Kekewich moved his column to a farm at Rooiwal having become entangled with Rawlinson. De La Rey's commando, now just 1,700-strong under the command of Ferdinandus Potgieter who was aware of the impending British trap and had scouted the previously poorly-defended block at Rooiwal the day before. By the morning of 11 April 1902, the block was, however, no longer poorly defended – 3,000 British infantry with six field guns and two pom-poms, were now in position waiting for him.

Potgieter approached at 07.15, first encountering a British outpost under Major Roy who thought he was Rawlinson. Roy was quickly overrun by Potgieter's horsemen firing from the saddle who continued on, cresting a rise a mile and a half from Rooiwal which fully exposed the gravity of the task now in front of them. Some of Kekewich's men were inexperienced yeomanry who, as had Methuen's at Tweebosch, now fled at the sight of the oncoming tide whilst of those that did stand firm, many shot too high. Kekewich's field guns and pom-poms, however, began to rip holes in Potgieter's massed ranks who in conducting their own 'Charge of the Light Brigade' continued on hoping the rest of the British would turn and run. None of them reached the British lines, Potgieter killed thirty yards short with another 230 dead, wounded or captured. As surviving Boers turned to escape now was Hamilton's chance to crush them with Walter Kitchener's 5,000 men to the east and another 7,000 under Kekewich and Rawlinson close by but he fatally hesitated fearing a counter-attack, capturing only another fifty when he did eventually send his columns forward.

Rooiwal was the last set piece battle of the Second Boer War. After nearly two months of negotiation the Treaty of Vereeniging was signed on 31 May 1902 forming the Union of South Africa. In lives lost and financial cost it had come at a shocking price with the British Army given 'no end of a lesson'. A complete reorganisation of the British Army would follow over the next decade and not a moment too soon, in Europe the lights were about to go out.

12 April 1782

American War of Independence
Battle of Providien

THE SURRENDER OF General John Burgoyne at Saratoga in 1777 had been a disaster for the British prevention of American Independence. The loss of the upper Hudson Valley, Lake George and Lake Champlain were just minor considerations compared to the declaration of France and Spain, the former in particular with huge military and naval capability, in favour of the American cause. A cause they now believed might just be worth fighting for especially if it reversed British influence in North America gained at their expense during the 1754–63 French and Indian War and in India during the 1756–63 Third Carnatic War, both subsidiary theatres of the 1756–63 Seven Years' War in Europe.

The consequences of France's declaration were therefore not confined to just North America but rippled across the globe to the Indian subcontinent where France, Britain and the Dutch Republic (who were also now at war with Britain) had been competing for trade for nearly two centuries. During the Seven Years' War, the British East India Company under Colonel Robert Clive had defeated both the French and Dutch in Bengal before General Hector Munro defeated the Nawab of Bengal Mir Qasim, the Mughal Emperor Shah Alam II and the Mughal Grand Vizier Shuja ud Daula in 1764 at Buxar. In southern India, however, it was French trade that was still paramount with the Kingdom of Mysore and its ruler Hyder Ali Khan. Hyder Ali had defeated the British in the First Anglo-Mysore War (1767–69) after the Nizam of Hyderabad Asaf Jah II had changed sides. The British had then been content to watch over the next ten years while Hyder Ali fought his northern neighbours, the Marathas, before in 1780 uniting with them, Asaf Jah II, the French and the Dutch against the British (the Second Anglo-Mysore War), the two traditional European adversaries having resumed hostilities in India just as soon as news arrived of France's allegiance with the American Patriot rebels. The British East India Company Madras Army under Munro, assisted by the Royal

Navy Fleet of Admiral Edward Vernon successfully besieged the Capital of French India, Pondicherry, between August and October 1778 before seizing all other French Indian assets. The Second Anglo-Mysore War was therefore, by extension, part of the American War of Independence, Britain in danger of losing colonies in the west and east as a joint effort from the southern and central Indian kingdoms alongside the French and Dutch was launched to drive the British out of India.

In an effort to support the French colonies and their Indian allies, King Louis XVI of France sent Admiral Pierre André de Suffren, Comte de Saint Tropez with five ships of the line south around the Cape of Good Hope. En route Suffren was up against a similar sized Royal Navy Fleet under Commodore George Johnstone who was on his way to seize the Cape from the Dutch. Suffren, however, won a strategic victory at Porto Praya to beat Johnstone to the Cape and reinforce it against any British attack. Suffren then joined Admiral Destienne D'Orves to increase his fleet to eleven before sailing across the Indian Ocean to attack the British at Madras. Finding Admiral Sir Edward Hughes and nine British ships of the line at anchor, Suffren benefited from an inconclusive encounter before breaking south to unload troops at Porto Novo who, under Hyder Ali, recaptured Cuddalore on 4 April 1782. Suffren then sailed back out to renew his battle with Hughes, sighting him on 8 April heading for Trincomalee, Ceylon (Sri Lanka) before catching him at 00.30 on 12 April 1782 near Providien Rock. As the two lines closed, the vans first came into contact with the British opening fire, the French returning. Aboard *Heros*, Suffren then ordered his van away as he closed in the centre with Hughes' flagship HMS *Superb*, exchanging furious broadsides that left both ships badly damaged. Unable to cut sail *Heros* then sailed past *Superb* to deliver more broadsides on the outgunned HMS *Monmouth* which lost her mizzen and main mast and dropped out of the line. *Heros* was followed by *L'Orient* and *Brilliant*, both of whom continued the battle with *Superb* before, at 16.00, Hughes turned his line to temporarily gain ascendancy. The battle finished when a storm broke at 18.00 with both fleets in danger of grounding.

Suffren had suffered over 200 casualties, Hughes over 500, the latter continuing on to Trincomlee. The pair would fight another three times over the next year, all inconclusive, all in the Bay of Bengal; the final battles of the American War of Independence.

12 April 1782

American War of Independence
Battle of the Saintes

ON 19 OCTOBER 1781 at Yorktown, Virginia British Brigadier General Charles O'Hara had presented the sword of his commanding officer General Charles, Lord Cornwallis to American General George Washington and Major General Benjamin Lincoln. The British surrender had arrived after a six year struggle defending the Thirteen Colonies of North America, strategic mistakes both in London and across the Atlantic compounded by the entry into the war of France and Spain on the side of the American 'Sons of Liberty' (the original organisation formed to defend American rights against British rule) and Washington's Continental Army. That France was barely a free country itself, ruled by an absolute monarchist King Louis XVI, and was still several years from declaring her own *liberté, equalité et fraternité* meant their decision had little to do with freedom especially since Britain was already a developing democracy. Louis would come to regret lifting the lid off liberty and the rights of man but for now France was delighted to significantly reduce British influence won across the Atlantic two decades earlier, enshrined in the 1763 Treaty of Paris.

While the British had just lost in terms of future prosperity, its greatest ever colony, the French were not satisfied, the antagonism between the two nations ongoing in India via the Second Anglo-Mysore War and in Europe where, with their ally Spain, they were still struggling to take British Gibraltar by siege. Additionally the French were also aided by the Dutch whose covert assistance of the Americans had been uncovered in 1780, sparking a Fourth Anglo-Dutch War. With maritime foes all around, British colonies looked vulnerable, Canada in particular – though now receiving an influx of loyalists from the Thirteen Colonies of the Americas – but at the time it did nor produce great wealth. Instead the French wished to extend the sweet taste of victory to the sugar-rich islands of the Caribbean. They had already taken seven of Britain's ten largest but now they wanted the biggest and richest of them all, taken from the Spanish in 1655 by the Western Design of Oliver Cromwell, Jamaica.

Whilst the British Army had suffered a bruising ordeal in North America the Royal Navy was, however, very much in good shape. In fact due to the coppering of ships' hulls by First Sea Lord John Montague, Lord Sandwich and the Controller of the Navy Charles Middleton in better shape than ever, their ships now vastly more resistant to corrosion, faster and possessing a new, faster firing deck gun, the Carronade – advantages that had already seen results in the acquisition of Dutch Caribbean prizes.

In January 1782 fresh from his efforts in Chesapeake Bay, French Admiral Francois Joseph, Comte de Grasse had landed on St Kitts. Rear Admiral Samuel Hood had so far been unable to oust him but both he and Admiral George Rodney covered French movements when they sailed to join a Spanish fleet carrying 15,000 troops for the protection of a merchant convoy off Saint Domingue (Haiti). Rodney with thirty-seven ships of the line now moved in to intercept the thirty-three of De Grasse, making contact with the Frenchman on 9 April in which both sides suffered light damage. The two fleets then remained in proximity until 12 April 1782 when at 08.00 they began passing each other on opposite tacks off the small islands of the Saintes near Dominica, the British sailing north, the French south, both sides broadsiding ferociously. Perhaps in the confused smoke of battle, Rodney aboard HMS *Formidable* then led a change of tack toward the French line which was subsequently broken, five French ships shattered by the weight of British shot striking their colours including de Grasse's *Ville de Paris*, the French Admiral the only one of his officers aboard to emerge unscathed..

Rodney's manouvre was much criticised since it allowed the majority of French to escape west. De Grasse, however, had been decisively defeated and would spend the next two years in a British jail. After the catastrophe of Yorktown and the resignation of Prime Minister Frederick, Lord North just three weeks earlier the Saintes was much celebrated by the British populace. Attempting to inflict catastrophic damage, Vice Admiral Horatio Nelson would adopt Rodney's 'unusual' tactic more successfully twenty-three years later at Trafalgar. Charles O'Hara made a habit of surrendering to big names, at the 1793 Siege of Toulon he would repeat the act with the twenty-four-year-old French Brigadier General Napoleon Bonaparte.

13 April 1919

India
The Amritsar Massacre

IN 1915 AN Indian barrister of the London Inner Temple, Mohandas Gandhi, returned to his homeland from South Africa to spend the next two years travelling the country. At the same time more than a million Indians were fighting for the British in different theatres of the Great War. Anxious to maintain this support the British crushed any signs of nationalist uprisings (notably in Bengal and the Punjab) and passed the Defence of India Act which deliberately limited civil liberties. After the war various Indian nationalist parties then unified under Gandhi and his Congress Party who rattled the Raj (British Crown rule in India) with a policy of *Satyagraha*, a non violent protest in the form of prayer, fasting and a refusal to work. As support for Gandhi increased so too did concern within the Raj, passing the Rowlatt Acts further restricting the right to free speech and assembly but merely serving to inflame Indian rage further. Unrest spread none more so than in the Punjab, ironically the province which had provided critical support to Britain during the Great War on the Western Front. On 10 April 1919 Lieutenant Governor of the Punjab Sir Michael O'Dwyer arrested two Indian nationalist Doctors, Saiffudin Kitchlew and Satyapal, in Amritsar sparking protests in which four Englishmen were murdered and an English school teacher, Marcella Sherwood, was brutally attacked. As violence spread with many government buildings, banks and railways set ablaze, many British considered a repeat of the 1857 Indian Mutiny a very real possibility.

Since O'Dwyer had been warned on his 1913 appointment by the then Viceroy of India Sir Henry Lord Hardinge of Penshurst that the Punjab was the province over which the British Government was most concerned he declared martial law on 13 April 1919, including a ban on public assemblies of more than four persons. The proclamation was read that morning in English, Urdu, Hindi and Punjabi at various points in Amritsar but the organisers of a meeting protesting at the arrest of the two doctors to be held that afternoon in the Jallianwala Bagh (a walled garden of six acres popular for recreation and socialising) decided to proceed as planned.

News of this protest reached Brigadier General Reginald Dyer, acting British commander for Amritsar, but neither he nor Deputy Commissioner Miles Irving sought to prevent it. Instead Dyer, furious at the treatment of a white female, made his way to the Jallianwala Bagh to find a crowd of 10–20,000 Sikhs, Muslims and Hindus many of them farmers who that day had been attending the annual horse and cattle fair, part of the Baisakhi Festival and who were perhaps unaware that martial law had been declared. Arriving one hour after the start of the meeting, Dyer mercifully could not enter the walled garden with his two accompanying armoured cars but his sixty-five Gurkhas and twenty-five Balochis & Pathans did enter to block the main entrance. The other exits were small and many of them were locked, effectively trapping the crowd inside. Without warning and without provocation, Dyer opened fire and continued for ten minutes killing nearly 400 men, women and children and wounding over 1,000 more (the figures were disputed by the Indian National Congress and could easily have been considerably higher) later claiming he was punishing the Indians for disobedience. Neither did he offer medical assistance, insisting the wounded were 'free to apply' to him for help.

Dyer's actions were of course widely condemned – former British Prime Minister Herbert Asquith described the massacre as 'one of the worst outrages in the whole of our history' – but incredibly Dyer also received considerable support including a fund set up on his behalf by the *Morning Post* and was made an honorary Sikh by the Guardians of the Golden Temple on the basis he had maintained order. No legal proceedings were brought against Dyer following an official inquiry and despite Winston Churchill's calls to Parliament he was only relieved of command and put on half pay. The episode is portrayed in the 1982 Columbia Pictures film *Gandhi*. In 1940 Michael O'Dwyer was assassinated by Udam Singh. In 1947 after 2.5 million Indians had volunteered for service in World War II, India (and Pakistan, Bangladesh) finally gained independence.

14 April 1471

Wars of the Roses
Battle of Barnet

A BITTER FEUD between Richard Plantagenet, Duke of York and Edmund Beaufort, Duke of Somerset had erupted in violence at St Albans in 1455 and within five years had cost the lives of both men. York's quest for redress from King Henry VI had developed into a quest for the English Crown itself which was continued after his death by his son Edward, Duke of York. Edward then became King Edward IV after victory in 1461 at Towton where Lancastrian casualties made the battle the bloodiest ever on British soil. Both Henry and his redoubtable Queen Margaret of Anjou had, however, escaped along with several other nobles including Somerset's son, Henry Beaufort, Duke of Somerset. Whilst Margaret desperately tried to gain armed support from France and Scotland, Somerset defected to the Yorkist cause only to defect back again to lead a Lancastrian rising in Northumbria in which he was defeated and executed after the 1464 Battle of Hexham. This time Henry was captured and watched on from the Tower of London as Edward enjoyed another five years of almost uncontested rule. Though admired as a soldier Edward was, however, disappointing domestically and economically, vagabonds and thieves roamed the country and prosperity stagnated. Politically too, Edward alienated several of his closest courtiers, in particular Richard Neville, Earl of Warwick, by secretly marrying Elizabeth Woodville upon whose family Edward's favours now fell often at Warwick's expense.

Warwick won over his own brother John, Lord Montagu and more importantly Edward's brother George, Duke of Clarence whom he now backed for the throne before realising his only chance of maintaining his own wealth and power was to go over to the Lancastrian cause. Warwick therefore fled to France to make his peace with Queen Margaret before returning to England on 13 September 1470. In just eleven days, with the assistance of Clarence, Montagu, John De Vere, Earl of Oxford and Jasper Tudor the Earl of Pembroke, Warwick hounded Edward out of the country. Henry was once again king but Yorkist London was in turmoil, drunken rioting, looting, rape and murder rife until Warwick 'the Kingmaker' could restore order. No one doubted the bloodshed would begin again and Edward duly landed near Ravenspur on 14 March 1471. Due to the efforts of his loyal servant William, Lord Hastings, Edward's paltry force was soon built into an impressive army, investing Coventry where Warwick declined to give battle, before triumphantly marching into London to yet again capture the hapless Henry. Whilst Clarence now defected back to his brother, Warwick finally resolved to fight, marching south with 10–25,000 men as Edward with 10–15,000 men, marched north out of London for a confrontation near Chipping Barnet (Barnet).

Warwick's Lancastrians took up a position across the Great North Road, Oxford commanding the right, Montagu the centre and Henry Holland, Duke of Exeter the left with Warwick in reserve. Edward approached the battlefield on the evening of 13 April with Hastings on the left, Clarence and himself the centre and his other brother Richard, Duke of Gloucester the right – incredibly all the major commanders of both sides inter-related. Looking for a dawn assault, Edward had silently moved up in the dark of night to within yards of the Lancastrians who consequently cannonaded all night high over the Yorkist ranks. In the thick early morning fog of 14 April 1471, both sides engaged in a mêlée of bloody fighting with all the tools of medieval warfare. The fog meant, however, that the two armies were not aligned, both outflanking the other on the right. Hastings on the Yorkist left broke first with Oxford pursuing but concealed by fog Edward's centre carried on fighting unaware and undeterred. Conversely Gloucester on the Yorkist right then began to overwhelm Exeter with the battle line consequently turning through ninety degrees. Oxford soon returned but wearing similar jupons to Edward's his battle was mistakenly attacked by Montagu. Suspecting treason, Lancastrian mayhem then doubled when Edward recognised their distress, sending in the Yorkist reserve to decisively settle the contest.

Warwick and Montagu were amongst 1,500 dead, both their corpses soon to be displayed outside St Paul's Cathedral. Edward had little time to rest, at that very moment his father's old foe Queen Margaret was landing at Weymouth, he would meet her at Tewkesbury in just twenty days time.

15 April 1450

Hundred Years' War
Battle of Formigny

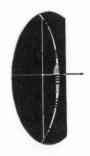

THOMAS, DUKE OF Bedford the English regent of France had invaded southern France in 1428 but the English Army of William de la Pole, Earl of Suffolk had been defeated at the siege of Orléans once the collapsing cause of the Dauphin Charles had found a heroine in 'La Pucelle' Joan of Arc, the Maid of Orléans. Inspired by Joan and compounding English losses at Orléans, the French then completed a reconquest of the Loire Valley with victory at Patay in June 1429, capturing the 'English Achilles' John Talbot. The Dauphin was crowned King Charles VII of France at Rheims just weeks later but Joan's subsequent capture and burning at the stake by the English coincided with Talbot's return after Richard Beauchamp, Earl of Warwick had captured Jean Poton de Xaintrailles, the pair exchanged. King Henry VI of England was then also crowned King of France at Notre Dame Cathedral, Paris backed by pro Burgundy Parisians whose Duke Philip was still an English ally. This allegiance, critical to the English hold on the North of France, then critically lost a binding in 1432 on the death of Bedford's wife Anne, Philip's sister, before, three years later, collapsing completely when Burgundy and Charles signed the Treaty of Arras leaving the English to fight alone. Worse still, Bedford, the great soldier, administrator and diplomat, died that same year.

The English cause now seemed lost but any thought of quitting France was dismissed as Talbot and Richard Plantagenet, Duke of York took the offensive in the defence of English held Normandy. The 1444 Treaty of Tours and Henry's 1445 marriage to fifteen-year-old Margaret of Anjou offered a tentative truce whilst in an attempt to extend the peace further the English king, a lover of art and architecture rather than war, ceded Maine back to France in 1448. On Henry's weakness, however, Charles' confidence grew, orchestrating a series of treaty violations including an opportunist capture of Rouen and an advance into Lower Normandy. Henry and his chief advisor, Suffolk, at last reacted but Henry's massive debts incurred not least by his new venture, King's College Chapel, Cambridge, meant only a small army of 2,500 men under Thomas Kyriell landed at Cherbourg in 1450. Reinforced by another 1,800 men under Matthew Gough, Kyriell suffered heavy casualties at Valognes before continuing toward the safety of English Bayeaux. By now the English Army was being shadowed by two French, one from Carentan under the twenty-four-year-old Jean de Clermont and one from Coutances under the Constable of France, Arthur de Richemont.

Aware of Richemont's proximity Clermont caught up with Kyriell at Formigny on 15 April 1450, the Englishman happy to engage since he was likely not aware of Richemont. Kyriell drew up his army in the time-honoured English fashion with dismounted men-at-arms in the centre and archers on the flanks protected against the charges of the French mounted knights by stakes and pot holes dug to their front. To buy Richemont time and learning from his father, Charles, the Count of Clermont's 1429 defeat to John Fastolf at Rouvray (Herrings), Clermont remained motionless but, as at Rouvray, impetuosity soon got the better of the French who advanced only to be comfortably beaten off by the fury of the English archers. The French mounted knights then advanced on the flanks where they ran into a similar devastating arrow storm. Clermont senior had sought to let his cannon do the job at Rouvray and now his son did likewise at Formigny, the English remaining in position but suffering until their patience cracked for a successful charge on Clermont's offending guns. The disconcerted French troops began to quit the field but Kyriell critically failed to press the attack, allowing Richemont, who was now approaching from the south, and Clermont to rally. Kyriell began manoeuvring his line to face the double threat but short of time and outnumbered by the combined 5,000 Frenchmen was attacked to his front and left flank simultaneously, he began to give ground. The last English Army of the Hundred Years' War in Normandy bravely fought back to the bridge on the Carentan-Bayeaux Road but were given no quarter.

Normandy was lost leaving just Calais and Gascony as English possessions in France, the latter since 1152. A furious nation blamed Suffolk, a suspect traitor whose demise since Orléans was now complete, he was beheaded on the deck of the boat carrying him into exile. If anyone could now defend Gascony it was Talbot, the test would come in 1453 at Castillon.

16 April 1746
Jacobite Rebellion
Battle of Culloden

IN SEPTEMBER 1745 the Italian speaking Bonnie Prince Charlie, Charles Edward Stuart, had ignited the Jacobite (Latin: James) cause by defeating a British Army led by Lieutenant General Sir John Cope at Prestonpans. Charlie had partially succeeded where his father, James Francis Stuart, had failed so dismally between 1715–19 attempting to right the wrongs done to his father – the Catholic King James II (VII of Scotland) of England, Scotland and Ireland – by the 1688 Glorious Revolution of Protestant William III of Orange. Charlie had lost much of his ammunition on the voyage to Scotland when one of his two ships, the *Elizabeth*, which was also carrying 700 Irish mercenaries was intercepted by HMS *Lion* off Cornwall but his stunning victory, the work of Lord George Murray on the back of a farmer's knowledge of the local topography, had rectified this shortfall with the capture of Cope's baggage train. Fully armed and with new adherents the 'Young Pretender' resolved to march into England to claim the Crown of Great Britain, a quest similar to that of Charles Stuart (later King Charles II) a century before which had ended in abject defeat at Worcester at the hands of Oliver Cromwell and the New Model Army.

Despite the War of the Austrian Succession demanding the presence of the current king, George II's main British Army in Continental Europe, the Scottish clansmen were nervous at campaigning away from the Highlands but acquiesced with the intention of drawing any English Army north once a Jacobite rising was in effect, a rising that in turn would encourage King Louis XV of France to support them with a French invasion.

The 6,000-strong Jacobite Army set off in November 1745 on a westerly route successfully avoiding the army of Lieutenant General Henry Hawley in Newcastle but of an English Jacobite uprising there was no sign. A French invasion, however, did occur only behind the Jacobites back in Scotland and with only 700 Irishmen, *Elizabeth's* cargo. Nevertheless London was close to panic, there was a run on the fifty-two-year-old Bank of England and a new version of the national anthem was sung, 'God Save the King'. Charlie's Highlanders had, however, grown even more nervous with many deserting in fear of the army of George's youngest son Prince William Augustus, Duke of Cumberland. At Derby, Highlander nerve then failed completely and so they turned back north chased by Hawley who they comfortably defeated on home ground at Falkirk Muir. Now Cumberland did arrive and with naval support, marching his 9,000 Hanoverian (George I, II, III and IV were of the House of Hanover as was William IV and Queen Victoria) troops to Aberdeen for six weeks intensive training. By 8 April Hessian reinforcements had moved to block any Jacobite retreat south from Inverness leaving Cumberland to march around the coast to Nairn. Trapped, Charlie and his 5,000 men marched east to Culloden House before attempting to spoil Cumberland's 15 April birthday celebrations. The Jacobite night march was, however, a fiasco so that when they returned to form up on Drummossie Moor the following day, 16 April 1746, they were tired and hungry with absentees aplenty.

The Jacobite infantry were in two lines, cavalry behind, artillery in front. Cumberland strengthened his front, also of two lines extending left to the wall of Culloden Park whilst dragoons moved further left of the wall and to the right ready to strike the Jacobite flanks, all forming up with impressive efficiency. The scene did nothing for Jacobite morale which was then lowered further when rain swept in from the east blowing into their faces. At 13.00 Murray, again commanding the Jacobites, started the battle with an ineffective artillery barrage which was answered with interest by Cumberland's artillery silencing the Jacobite guns. The Jacobites then advanced across the soft ground of the moor to be met with disciplined volleys of musket and canister which devastated their left. The better ground on the Jacobite right allowed the two armies to close for a savage contest of broadsword and bayonet, Cumberland's support line picking off Highlanders with their muskets. However, on the Jacobite left the struggling Highlanders were finally routed by Cumberland's dragoons leaving their centre exposed, they broke and ran, headed by Bonnie Prince Charlie himself who continued on back to France never to return.

Two thousand five hundred Jacobites lay dead, the wounded shown no quarter with many executed for treason. Culloden was the last pitched battle ever to be fought on British soil.

17 April 1780

American War of Independence
Battle of Martinique

AFTER THE 1777 surrender of British General John Burgoyne at Saratoga, France became ever more confident that American independence was a cause worth pursuing with a realistic opportunity of reversing British influence won in North America twenty years before during the French and Indian War. The prospect of King George III regaining control of his colonies indeed now looked very bleak especially since the arrival of a powerful French fleet under Admiral Charles Hector, Comte D'Estaing off the American Atlantic seaboard negated the presence of the Royal Navy and also threatened British possessions in the Caribbean. D'Estaing, however, was worsted by a storm off Rhode Island when about to do battle with his opposite Richard Howe, Admiral of the British fleet, and repaired to Boston amidst accusations of treachery from his new American allies who subsequently retreated under British fire from Rhode Island in August 1778.

In November D'Estaing then sailed for the Caribbean where hostilities between Britain, France and Spain had never been far from the surface over the past two centuries and were now firmly back on the agenda after Francois Amour, Marquis de Bouillé had seized Dominica (a British possession since the French and Indian War) in September 1778. D'Estaing was, however, defeated in December by Admiral Samuel Barrington who was attempting to redeem himself having remained impassive in Barbados when Dominica had been under Bouillé's attack. Barrington's victory also meant St Lucia fell into British hands.

The remainder of 1778 and 1779 in the West Indies was then spent in more minor engagements except at Granada in July 1779 which D'Estaing captured before giving a bloody nose to a British relief effort led by Admiral John Byron. D'Estaing then returned to the southern states of North America where the British had launched a new offensive in an effort to realise loyalist support in Georgia and the Carolinas. Major General Sir Archibald Campbell with 3,000 men had captured Savannah, Georgia at the end of 1778 giving the Royal Navy a base to attack American interests up and down the coast for the next four years but not before a combined American-French force attempted to take it back by siege. In October 1779 D'Estaing was wounded storming Savannah and returned to France, his replacement Vice Admiral Luc de Bouexic, Comte de Guichen sent to Martinique from where he planned to attack the British in Barbados or St Lucia which, since the French were in possession of Guadeloupe, Dominica, Martinique and St Vincent, were both a direct threat to French shipping. Guichen was aware that a strong British fleet under Admiral Sir George Rodney was in St Lucia but he sailed from Martinique in mid-April attempting to lure Rodney out to sea and consequently leave St Lucia or Barbados open to attack.

Rodney's intelligence was good, however, and he left St Lucia as soon as he received word that Guichen had put to sea, sighting twenty-two French ships of the line loaded with 3,000 soldiers on 16 April 1780. Rodney's twenty ships of the line gave chase throughout the night on into the morning of 17 April 1780, both commanders going through a series of manoeuvres to gain the weather gauge. Rodney's intention was to attack in force the rear and centre of Guichen's line to exact maximum damage but Robert Carkett commanding the lead British ship HMS *Stirling Castle* misunderstood his Admiral's innovative signals and moved up alongside the French lead ship with those behind engaging ship for ship. The exchange of broadsides that followed was therefore on a par rather than in overwhelming force and although both Rodney's flagship, HMS *Sandwich*, and Guichen's *Couronne* were involved in heavy fighting the French managed to sheer off with no loss of shipping and just a few hundred casualties.

Accusations were rife in the wake of Rodney's failure to exact a damaging defeat on Guichen, a task which would be completed six months later by the Great Hurricane of 1780. Britain and France continued hostilities in the West Indies but the American War of Independence would follow the Great Hurricane north-west back to the main theatre now in Georgia and the Carolinas.

18 April 1945

Second World War
Battle of Hamburg

THE BLOODIEST CONFLICT in world history was drawing to its conclusion in early 1945. German Chancellor Adolf Hitler's gamble to split the Allied Armies with an assault through the Ardennes had left his forces on the Western Front catastrophically weak but with the Soviet Red Army approaching Berlin on the Eastern Front he had little choice but to weaken them further. After crossing the Siegfried Line, the formidable obstacle of the River Rhine faced the Allies, the British 21st Army Group under Field Marshal Bernard Montgomery to the north, United States 12th Army Group under General Omar Bradley in the centre and U.S 6th Army Group under General Jacob Devers to the south. All bridges across the river were believed to have been destroyed by the retreating Germans until Lieutenant Karl Timmerman and the US 9th Armoured Division opportunistically captured the Ludendorff Railway Bridge at Remagen whilst further north, the British 2nd Army under General Miles Dempsey and US 9th Army under General William Simpson crossed the Rhine between Rheinberg and Rees courtesy of a 1,900 gun barrage supported by Lancasters dropping 1,000 tons of high explosive. Paratroops of the British 6th and US 17th Airborne Divisions then dropped ahead of the main assault to seize key objectives including further bridges over the River Issel, within four days Montgomery ferrying seventeen infantry divisions across the Rhine into a thirty-mile-wide, eight-mile-deep bridgehead. The British 21st Army Group now drove north-east whilst Simpson's 9th Army reverted to Bradley's US 12th Army Group to encircle the Ruhr Industrial area with General Courtney Hodges' US 1st Army. Trapped German Army Group B Commander Field Marshal Walter Model shot himself.

Meanwhile Montgomery's 21st Army Group pushed on toward the River Elbe intent on racing across the plains of North Germany but Supreme Allied Commander Dwight D. Eisenhower was content to leave the symbolic prize of Berlin to the Soviets (it would cost them 300,000 casualties). Instead he directed

Montgomery and the British north to Hamburg and Lubeck to protect the Jutland Peninsular (Denmark) from the Red Army for, though the post war division of Europe had already been agreed at Yalta, there was little trust in Soviet Secretary General Josef Stalin.

On 18 April 1945 the 7th Armoured Division of Dempsey's British 2nd Army spearheaded the push for Hamburg, capturing Welle and Tostedt to the south-west and Luneberg to the south before taking Hollenstedt with flame throwers in fierce house-to-house fighting. The defence stiffened as Dempsey approached the suburb of Harburg, the defenders, a mix of General Kurt Student's 1st Parachute Division, Volkssturm (German Home Guard), sailors, police and fanatical Hitler Youth even counter-attacking at Vahrendorf. In another sharp fight, British Armour drove them back as the 5th Royal Tank Regiment, Durham Light Infantry and 1st Rifle Brigade advanced up the autobahn from the south to enter Hamburg on 28 April. The German defenders tried to force their way out across the Elbe but were cut off by the British 11th Armoured Division which had already mopped up pockets of resistance to the south. The battle raged until 1 May 1945 when two representatives of General Alwin Woltz commanding the Hamburg garrison arrived to surrender the city. Hours later news broke that German Chancellor Adolf Hitler had committed suicide the day before.

British troops entering Hamburg after the battle were appalled at the devastation and stench of rotting corpses buried under rubble since the bombing of Hamburg two years before. On 4 May, at Montgomery's Headquarters on Luneberg Heath, Commander-in-Chief of the Kriegsmarine Hans-Georg von Friedeburg, acting as representative for the new German President Grand Admiral Karl von Donitz, surrendered all German forces in North-West Germany, Holland and Denmark. The 7th Armoured Division moved to Lubeck preventing any Russian advance to the Jutland Peninsular. Their 'glorious pilgrimage of war'* had started with Montgomery at Alamein, Egypt two and a half years before.

General Alfred Jodl representing the German High Command signed the Instrument of Surrender on all fronts at Rheims on 7 May 1945. The definitive version was signed in Berlin the following day with the Supreme High Command of the Red Army. 8 May is therefore Victory in Europe Day.

---

*Winston Churchill, Berlin 1945

19 April 1587 o.s

Anglo-Spanish Wars
Raid on Cadiz

FOR OVER TWO decades relations between England and Spain had been deteriorating. King Philip II of Spain had been Jure Uxoris of England whilst his Catholic wife Queen Mary I of England had been alive but had then been turned down in marriage by Mary's successor, the Protestant Queen Elizabeth I, before embarking on what would become an Eighty Year War against Dutch protestants revolting against his Habsburg Catholic rule in the Spanish Netherlands. Philip's Spanish and Habsburg empires not only covered the Iberian Peninsular, southern Italy, Milan and much of South America but was even more powerful, thanks to treasure flotas from the Spanish Main, than that of his Uncle Ferdinand I, Holy Roman Emperor ruling from Vienna lands in Austria, Hungary, Bohemia and Croatia. It was therefore perhaps understandable that Elizabeth did not want to risk war with the Habsburgs but when Philip joined the French Catholic League in 1576 – unleashing the Spanish Inquisition against Protestant heresy – the prospect of a Protestant defeat in the Netherlands now became a distinct possibility, potentially isolating Protestant England. Still Elizabeth vacillated, attempting to anglicise Ireland, her vulnerable western flank, whilst sponsoring privateering raids around the globe, particularly in the Caribbean by the scourge of Spaniards everywhere, Francis 'El Draque (the Dragon)' Drake. By 1585 Elizabeth could no longer stand by while the Dutch faced defeat, she signed the Treaty of Nonsuch with them and sent Drake to raid the Caribbean once again.

Philip had once supported Elizabeth against Papal excommunication but now it was war. That his Catholic candidate for England's throne, Mary, Queen of Scots was then executed by Elizabeth further deepened Philip's resolve but on virtually the same wind that brought news of Drake's anti-Spanish, Caribbean enterprises sailed the man himself. As a huge Spanish Armada designed to conquer heretic England began gathering at Cadiz, Drake was at sea once again intent on increasing Spanish pain acutely.

Sailing out of Plymouth on 12 April 1587, Drake had left early, fearing his queen would change her mind, indeed her reconsidered directives arrived too late. Drake had dedicated his life to repaying Spanish treachery at San Juan de Ulua, Mexico and was determined to strike another blow on the ambitions of the Spanish 'anti-Christ and all its members'. His fleet dispersed by a storm en route, Drake arrived off Cadiz on 19 April 1587 aboard his flagship the 600-ton *Elizabeth Bonaventure*. Wasting no time reconnoitring or waiting for stragglers he immediately sailed into the massive outer harbour. The port was packed with Spanish warships and transports revictualing and refitting, perhaps near one hundred in all, but initially only a couple of inquisitive oared galleys approached. On realising their worst fears, and being no match for Drake's carracks and galleons, the Spanish galleys beat a hasty retreat, receiving a volley of cannon for their troubles. Drake now raised the Queen's Colours as the whole port became aware of the danger. More Spanish galleys approached to receive volleys of English cannon, an art at which the English gunners were far superior, whilst many other Spaniards ran for cover. A massive Genoese warship then put up a spirited defence but was inevitably sent to the bottom as Drake took control of the whole outer harbour, panic now spreading ashore as the citizens of Cadiz, fearing an English sack, sent distress calls inland for reinforcements. As darkness fell, Drake, his gunners and boarding parties got down to work removing anything of value and setting ablaze the almost undefended Spanish shipping, the Spanish gun batteries ashore proving ineffective. Fully consumed by the task, Drake ignored pleas of caution from his Vice Admiral William Borough and advanced into the inner harbour for a repeat dosage. Here he found the pride of the Spanish Navy, the 1,500 ton *La Loba* of Alvaro de Bazan, Marquis of Santa Cruz which, shorn of her guns, was soon ablaze along with many others. Arriving Spanish reinforcements included Alonso Perez de Guzman, Duke of Medina-Sidonia, Admiral of the following year's Spanish Armada, but he could only watch while Cadiz harbour became an inferno.

As many as thirty-nine ships (Drake's estimate) were captured or destroyed over two days of destruction before the English fleet burnt every ship they came across along the Portuguese coast. Drake then sailed for the Azores, paying for the entire venture by capturing the heavily-laden East India treasure ship *San Felipe*, King Philip's very own. As he put it himself Drake had 'singed the King of Spain's beard' but though a great victory he had merely bought time before the main event the following year.

19 April 1775

American War of Independence
Lexington and Concord

THE 1763 TREATY of Paris signaled the end of the Seven Years' War in Europe and the French and Indian War in North America, leaving almost all of North America east of the River Mississippi, a population diverse in culture and religion from Catholic Quebecois French to Anglican English to American Indian, under British Government. The cost of maintaining the British Army in these 'thirteen colonies', however, was to be paid by an imposition of tax on American colonists but without offering them any representation in Parliament far away across the Atlantic Ocean in London. Resentment against 'taxation without representation' reached a tipping point in Boston in 1773 when a consignment of cheap tea was delivered by the British East India Company only to be destroyed by the Sons of Liberty (American rights protestors) who saw the shipment as a cynical ploy to sweeten British tax policy – the Boston Tea Party. The British Government reacted by ending local government in Massachusetts and closing the Port of Boston, further enraging colonists all the way down the east coast of North America. By 1775 twelve of the colonies had responded by organising a Congress in Philadelphia, empowering much of the population to rebel against British rule.

On 18 April 1775, in a surprise operation to seize rebel military supplies, 700 British troops under Lieutenant Colonel Francis Smith began a fifteen-mile march from Boston to Concord to be followed the following morning 19 April 1775 by another of 1,200 men under Brigadier General Henry Percy. However, Percy was late, leaving Smith isolated on Lexington Green where he was confronted by 130 American Patriot militia under Captain John Parker who was fully aware of British objectives having been alerted by Paul Revere's alarm system. Up against the numerically superior professional 'Redcoats' of the British Army the resolve of Parker's Patriots soon wavered but as they dispersed certain British elements lost discipline and charged with the bayonet, initiating gunfire and casualties on both sides. As Parker's militia scattered into the trees, Smith restored order in his own ranks for the march on Concord a further two miles away where he divided his force, grenadiers searching the town whilst the remainder covered bridges south and north and a detachment under Captain Lawrence Parsons investigated a mile further north.

The Patriots had already removed much of their ammunition but their immovable cannon were destroyed as well as the Liberty pole and flag in the town centre. As Smith and Parsons searched, thousands of Patriots gathered around Concord fearing their homes were being torched and now approached the north bridge in force. Again British discipline failed, ignoring strict orders not to fire first they did just that, the Patriots returning with interest instantly killing three Redcoats. Alerted by the gunfire Parsons returned to Concord, the Patriots curiously allowing him to cross back unmolested before Smith ordered a retreat to Lexington. The route was, however, now lined by 1,000 Patriots, Smith sending out light infantry to protect his front and flanks, engaging rebels whenever they revealed themselves. Under fire with ammunition running low and still no sign of Percy, panic began to induce all out flight. At Lexington British officers turned, leveling their bayonets at their own men in an effort to again restore order before salvation at last appeared in the form of Percy. The brigadier immediately appreciated the gravity of the situation, sending several musket and cannon volleys crashing into the undergrowth at the invisible enemy which bought the British columns time to regroup. At 15.30 the single column of now 1,700 men marched for Boston encircled by an angry swarm of Patriot militia exchanging gunfire every yard. British light infantry again patrolled to front and flank surprising awaiting Patriot sharpshooters with cold steel as well as flushing out all farms and houses along the route in bitter hand-to-hand fighting. Percy was, however, marching directly into an organised ambush at Cambridge but mercifully he had the good sense to alter his return route through Charlestown. At 19.00 the shaken British column marched onto the Charlestown Peninsular for a lengthy operation by boat back into Boston. They had lost 300 men.

The American War of Independence had begun and the British were trapped in Boston, they would try to get out two months later with an attack on Bunker Hill.

20 April 1744

War of the Austrian Succession
Battle of Villafranca

BRITAIN HAD BEEN at War with Spain since 1739 after a customs dispute off Florida in 1731 involving the loss of Captain Robert Jenkins' ear but this dispute paled into insignificance when Charles VI, Holy Roman Emperor, Archduke of Austria and King of Bohemia, Hungary, Croatia and Serbia, died in 1740. Because Charles left his inheritance to a woman, his daughter, the Prussian King Frederick II 'the Great' threw down a challenge by invading Silesia, triggering a series of alliances that not for the last time plunged the whole of Europe into a bloody, economy-sapping contest for the next eight years, the War of the Austrian Succession.

Naturally, the gentlemen of Britain sided with the unfortunate lady in question, Maria Theresa, along with Russia, the Dutch Republic, Hanover and Savoy against Prussia, France and Spain. The small British Army, led by King George II, with Austrian and Hanoverian assistance (together the Pragmatic Army), had notably defeated the French in 1743 at Dettingen while the virtually all-powerful Royal Navy aided the war effort by blockading French and Spanish ports. Following Dettingen, the Catholic French were looking to invade Protestant England and ignite a Jacobite uprising which would place the Catholic Bonnie Prince Charlie, grandson of the deposed King James II (1685–1688), on the throne of Great Britain. The blockade of the French coast was therefore vital to the defence of Britain and this included the port of Toulon on the French Mediterranean coast. On 21 February 1744, a French and Spanish fleet of thirty-three ships had, however, sailed out of Toulon to strategically defeat the more powerful Royal Navy fleet of Admiral Thomas Mathews. Mathews would later face a Court Martial and be dismissed for a failure that was not entirely of his own doing but in the meantime, whilst his fleet was nursing its wounds repairing in Minorca, the Spanish and French fleet had the option of joining the imminent Jacobite invasion of Britain or, with the freedom of the Mediterranean, supply their armies fighting in Italy.

In Italy, the Austrians had forced the Spanish Army under Jean Bonaventure

Thierry du Mont, Comte de Gages back to Rimini whilst the Infante Philip, Duke of Parma, son of King Philip V of Spain, after a march through France, had only achieved minor success against the Sardinians (Savoy) – the Kingdom of Savoy being not just Sardinia but also the area directly north between France, Italy and Switzerland. Philip now received reinforcements and supplies, including Frenchmen under Louis Francois, Prince of Conti, 30,000 men in total for an attempt to force his way through to northern Italy and his countrymen further south. The first task would be to attack Sardinians under Vittorio Francesco of Savoy who were defending the heights above Villafranca (Villefranche sur mer) with 8,000 men and eighty British naval guns courtesy of Mathews who had arrived with 1,000 reinforcements to clear up a mess for which he was at least partially responsible.

Conti attacked the heights on the night of 19/20 April 1744 beginning with a diversionary attack at midnight on the west side of the defences before delivering the main assault at 03.00 from the north. The diversion worked perfectly, Conti capturing the ridge between Nice and Villefranca and also Vittorio Francesco himself. The attacks from the north and east, however, lost impetus in the darkness under heavy fire from the British guns. The Sardinian second-in-command, Alessio della Chiesa the Knight of Cinzano, then led a counter-attack to retake the ridge, by evening Conti back where he had started despite having inflicted over 1,000 casualties and taken 1,500 prisoners. Conti resigned himself to defeat but Cinzano and Mathews, believing they were no longer able to hold Villafranca with just 5,000 men, then conducted a night evacuation by ship.

A surprised Conti found his route now open but command disagreements meant the Austrians would eventually be victorious in northern Italy with just the Duchy of Parma remaining Spanish by the 1748 Treaty of Aix-la-Chapelle – the Spanish Queen, Elisabeth of Farnese, was after all, the heiress to Parma. In 1760, Conti retired to make what are now eye-wateringly expensive wines, buying a vineyard, Romanée-Conti in Burgundy, France.

21 April 1918

The Great War
The Red Baron

JUST ELEVEN YEARS after the Wright Brothers had achieved powered flight, sixty-three unarmed aircraft of the Royal Flying Corps (RFC) arrived in France at the outbreak of the Great War. The value of aerial reconnaissance was soon realised when French Corporal Louis Breguet reported the left turn north of Paris of General Alexander von Kluck's German 1st Army which allowed the British and French to counter-attack on the Marne. Initially reconnaissance was the main task for airmen, both sides also using balloons and, in the case of the Germans, Zeppelin airships. Reconnaissance developed with cameras, pilots armed only with basic weapons, hand-held bombs and pistols until major aircraft manufacturers Morane-Saulnier and Fokker began work on synchronising machine-gun fire with the blades of a propellor. The French and their chief pilot Roland Garros initially led the technological race with deflector wedges but when Garros was downed behind German lines in April 1915, Fokker perfected the system with a Parabellum MG14 machine-gun on their Eindeckers instantly eclipsing the B.E.2s, Morane-Saulniers, Farmans and Nieuports of the French and British Entente. The British and French, however, soon successfully matched the Eindecker with the Airco DH2 and the Nieuport 11, ending the 'Fokker Scourge' but as pilots became 'Knights of the Air', rising to national hero status their average lifespan plummeted to just a few hours. Battle casualty rates were matched by those in training; if a pilot made it into combat he did so with little flying experience and no parachute; 14,000 British airmen dying during the Great War.

Britain's greatest pilot Edward Mannock was killed in a dreaded 'Flamerino' with sixty-one confirmed kills, Canadian William Bishop recorded seventy-two and Frenchman René Fonck seventy-five on an Allied list that also included James McCudden fifty-seven, Irishman George McElroy forty-seven, and Albert Ball fourty-four. It proved to be a German however who became the 'Ace of all Aces', Manfred, Freiherr (Baron) von Richthofen with eighty kills.

Richthofen transferred from the cavalry to the luftstreitkrafte in May 1915, initially an observer in August 1916 he was invited by 'Ace' Hauptmann Oswald Boelcke to join fighter squadron Jagdstaffel II, flying the Albatros DI. Boelcke was killed shortly after but Richthofen adhered to the *Dicta Boelcke* when flying combat, sun behind, attacking from above with several wingmen unlike the lone hunters Ball, Mannock, his brother Lothar von Richthofen and Werner Voss. He collected souvenirs from his victims and ordered himself a silver cup for each kill. Awarded the Blue Max in January 1917, he became commander of Squadron Jasta 11, painting red his Albatros DV and DIII before in summer 1917 taking command of the Fighter Wing *Jagdgeschwader* 1, Richthofen's Flying Circus. A leading 'Ace' alongside Lothar and Werner Voss, Richthofen downed four aircraft in a single day during the RFC's 'Bloody April' of 1917. In August 1917 *Jagdgeschwader* 1 received the famous Fokker Dr1 Triplane in which Voss led with ten kills while a wounded Richthofen recuperated. Though the British and French were gaining ascendancy in the sky with thousands of Sopwith Camels, SE5as and SPAD SXIIIs, in early 1918 Germany had an opportunity to win the war on the ground.

Supporting the German Spring Offensive on 21 April 1918 six Fokker Dr1s of Jasta 11 led by Richthofen, his cousin Wolfram and the future Commander-in-Chief of the *Luftwaffe* Hermann Goring intercepted British RE8s of 3 Squadron and Sopwith Camels of 209 Squadron over Mourlancourt Ridge. Richthofen ignored the *Dicta Boelcke* to chase Canadian newcomer Lieutenant Wilfrid May down across the River Somme within range of Australian ground fire whilst from above Canadian Arthur 'Roy' Brown, flying a Sopwith Camel, saw May's difficulty and dived to attack the red Fokker. Targeted from behind and below Richthofen was fatally hit in the chest by a Vickers .303 bullet, landing at Vaux-sur-Somme, reputedly only uttering 'kaputt' as Australian infantrymen reached him.

Brown was credited with the kill but Australian anti-aircraft gunner Cedric Popkin, firing the same ammunition, is also a likely candidate. Manfred von Richthofen was buried in Bertangles Cemetery with full military honours. A wreath read 'to our gallant and worthy foe', he was twenty-five.

22 April 1951

Korean War
Battle of Imjin River

THE SECOND WORLD War concluded in the Far East with two American atomic bombs on the Japanese mainland and an opportunistic but overwhelming Soviet invasion of Japanese held Manchuria, North East China. The Korean Peninsular, annexed by Japan thirty-five years earlier, was left exposed to further Soviet advances but Secretary General Josef Stalin and United States President Harry Truman agreed to split the country across the 38th parallel. South Korea was then governed by the US backed Nationalist Syngman Rhee and North Korea by the Soviet-backed Communist Kim Il-Sung. By June 1949 the Soviets and the U.S had both departed, the US unhappy with Rhee's leadership leaving the South's Republic of Korea Army (ROK) badly ill-equipped to deal with any threat from the Soviet-trained and equipped North Korean People's Army (NKPA). Kim recognised just that, and with Stalin's approval invaded South Korea on 25 June 1950.

With the United Nations' backing, General Douglas MacArthur and US reinforcements arrived from Japan but, inferior in every facet, were forced back into a 130-mile perimeter around the south-east port of Pusan. As NKPA losses mounted, however, the 1st US Marine Division arrived amongst further United Nations reinforcements allowing MacArthur to outflank the North Koreans with an amphibious landing in the north west at Inchon. Now the NKPA reeled back across the 38th parallel, Pyongyang falling on 19 October as MacArthur pressed on to the Yalu River, the border with China. With victory in sight the warnings of Indian Prime Minister Jawarhalal Nehru were then brutally realised when the Chinese People's Volunteer Army (CPVA) of Chairman Mao Zedong violently appeared. On 25 November, a second CPVA attack in overwhelming strength then smashed through ROK units to force the US 8th Army into the longest and coldest (-35°C) retreat in American history back across the parallel. Truman replaced MacArthur with Lieutenant General Matthew Ridgeway who stopped the rout with limited offensives backed by massive air and artillery strikes, recapturing Seoul and returning to the parallel. Marshal Peng Dehuai of the CPVA then planned a 270,000 man 'Spring Offensive' over the Imjin River and down the Pukhan Valley back to Seoul.

On the evening of 22 April 1951, the British 29th Infantry Brigade under Brigadier Thomas Brodie were holding seven miles of hills south of the Imjin River, the three dispersed British and one Belgian battalion unable to support each other despite any defeat here likely to precipitate a collapse of the entire United Nations front. Two Chinese divisions attacked after nightfall, the Belgians falling back across the river under heavy fire but pursued by the Chinese who were halted by Gloucesters across the Imjin, the Chinese attacking the Gloucesters' positions with suicidal bayonet charges, machine-gun fire and hand-to-hand fighting. To the right, however, Northumberland Fusiliers were outflanked by the Chinese in fierce fighting and fell back, Ulstermen moving forward to block Chinese infiltrations. Royal Artillery and UN air strikes, including napalm, hammered the Chinese throughout St George's Day allowing the Fusiliers to counter-attack while the Gloucester's Lieutenant Colonel James Carne continued to hold 'Gloster Hill', 400 men holding off 10,000 Chinese. Again the following morning United Nations artillery and aircraft hammered the Chinese but British armour failed to get through. To the right of the British 29th the Americans retreated when the ROK units collapsed before the British 27th Commonwealth Brigade partially stabilised the situation. By the night of 24 April, the whole British 29th were almost out of ammunition but still they held, Carne calling artillery strikes on his own position and counter-attacking with the bayonet. Brodie then retreated the brigade on the morning of the 25 April, each company providing covering fire in turn while tanks machine-gunned the hillsides. The Gloucesters on the flank, however, were left behind, Chinese now swarming around and behind them with Carne attempting to breakout in groups. Only sixty-three men made the UN lines, 530 including Carne captured.

James Carne was awarded the Victoria Cross, his battalion's efforts allowed the US 8th Army to retreat to a defensive position outside Seoul. The UN had lost 25,000 men but Chinese losses were so great Mao was already looking to negotiate. The fighting would, however, continue.

23 April 1918

The Great War
Battle of Zeebrugge

THE GREAT WAR had been preceded by a colossal arms race as Kaiser Wilhelm II had looked to advance the ambitions of his relatively young Germany across Continental Europe, the Middle East, Far East and Africa. The vast expenditure had been evident nowhere more so than in Germany's naval dockyards, particularly Kiel and Wilhelmshaven, but the world's premier naval superpower Great Britain had been in no mood to relinquish control of the seas and had more than matched the Kaiser's spending, building a fleet that in wartime was powerful enough to maintain an economically crippling blockade of the German coast and encourage the German High Seas Fleet to remain in port.

After the 1916 attritional battles of Verdun and the Somme, German High Command could see little hope of defeating the Triple Entente of Great Britain, France and Russia in the field and instead determined to knock their main threat, Great Britain, out of the war with a strategy of unrestricted submarine (U-boat) warfare directed against both the Royal Navy and particularly the British Merchant Navy. So effective was this strategy (25 per cent of all British bound shipping was sunk in March 1917) that First Sea Lord Admiral John Jellicoe claimed the Royal Navy could not continue the war on into 1918. Though both Prime Minister David Lloyd George and Field Marshal Douglas Haig believed him to be exaggerating, the revelation won Haig the argument for a major 1917 offensive in Flanders that if reasonably successful would force a German withdrawal from Belgium and her submarine ports. Operation Hush, an amphibious attack around Middelkirke, Belgium was planned to coincide with such an eventuality but the Third Battle of Ypres did not come anywhere close to expectation. Despite Third Ypres' failings, Hush was then revisited by incoming Dover Patrol commander Rear Admiral Roger Keyes who was intent on decisively limiting the German submarine menace. As Germany launched their 1918 Spring Offensive (Kaiserschlacht) on the Western Front in an effort to defeat the Entente before the arrival of one million Americans directly responding to German submarine policy, Keyes sought to trap the offending German U-boats by blocking the Bruges Canal at Zeebrugge and Ostend.

After several cancellations, German defences at Zeebrugge and Ostend were subject to a short bombardment from monitors and an air attack before British coastal patrol boats laid down a smokescreen that was blown into port. At one minute past midnight on St George's Day, 23 April 1918, Keyes' fleet of seventy-five ships arrived with HMS *Vindictive, Daffodil* and *Iris* moving through the dispersing smoke toward the outside of the mile long Zeebrugge mole. Greeted by a furious fire from German troops, shore batteries and a destroyer moored on the inside, *Vindictive* captained by Alfred Carpenter struggled in the heavy swell and had to be pushed into the mole by *Daffodil*, the Royal Marines cramming her decks then clambering up just two surviving ramps onto the mole parapet to engage German defenders at close quarters. Meanwhile toward the landward end of the mole the British submarine C3 sailed under the viaduct, her crew disembarking before the cargo of high explosive was detonated severing the mole from the mainland to prevent the Germans from reinforcing. The concrete-filled cruisers HMS *Intrepid* and *Iphigenia* then sailed in behind the mole making for the canal entrance under heavy fire from German shore batteries. On reaching their objective and still under a furious fusillade the crews were picked up by launches before *Intrepid* and *Iphigenia* were scuttled, successfully blocking the canal. Miraculously HMS *Vindictive* also managed to sail away from the mole but of her original 1,300 Royal Marines 600 had become casualties.

The assault at Ostend had failed but *Vindictive* returned there in May to complete the task. Zeebrugge was the biggest special forces operation of the Great War (eight Victoria Crosses) but only succeeded in blocking the Bruges Canal for a few days. In 1918 King Albert I of Belgium presented the Zeebrugge Bell to the town of Dover and in 1943 Keyes became Baron Keyes of Zeebrugge and Dover.

24 April 1916
Anglo-Irish Wars
The Easter Rising

FOLLOWING THE 1798 defeat of the nationalist Society of United Irishmen, the 1800 Act of Union formed the United Kingdom of Great Britain and Ireland. In defeat the United Irishmen, Protestants and Catholics now lived under the new Union Flag, incorporating the cross of Saint Patrick, and were ruled from Westminster. Catholic Emancipation came with the 1829 Roman Catholic Relief Act backed by Prime Minister Arthur Wellesley, Duke of Wellington under whom many Irishmen had fought against Napoleonic France (some had fought for Napoleon) but following the Great Famine of 1845–52 which depopulated Ireland by a quarter, the drive for Irish Home Rule was reborn. The 1858 formation of the Irish Republican Brotherhood (IRB) was followed by the more conservative Irish Home Government Association which, by 1874, had become the Irish Parliamentary Party (IPP) under Charles Stewart Parnell. The IPP then held the balance of power at Westminster in 1885 for William Gladstone's Liberals against Robert Cecil, Lord Salisbury's Conservatives. Gladstone's subsequent 1886 Irish Home Rule Bill, however, failed to pass the House of Commons but eight years later, after a fist fight on the benches, a second attempt did pass the Commons only to fail in the House of Lords. In 1910 the IPP again held the balance of power for Herbert Asquith's Liberals against Arthur Balfour's Conservatives, the price another Home Rule Bill. In 1914 the Bill at last passed to the Statute Books with strong arguments for the exclusion of predominantly Protestant, Unionist Ulster. Sectarian violence looked certain as 100,000 signed for the pro union Ulster Volunteer Force and 200,000 signed for the nationalist Irish Volunteers which included the IRB. But for Great Britain there was a more pressing enemy, Kaiser Wilhelm II and the German Empire which led to a suspension of the Bill. In frustration, Roger Casement of the Irish Volunteers visited the Kaiser who declined to provide troops but did send a shipment of arms specifically for a 1916 Easter Rising. The cargo and Casement were intercepted, leaving Ivor Guest, Lord Wimborne, the Lord Lieutenant of Ireland to arrest the other nationalist leaders but he was too late, the Rising was already beginning.

On Easter Monday 24 April 1916, 1,200 Citizen Army and Irish Volunteers under the Military Council of the IRB gathered in central Dublin occupying several strategic buildings including the General Post Office and Liberty Hall. Thoroughfares into the city centre were barricaded particularly those before British Army barracks. Patrick Pearse then read a proclamation declaring an Irish Republic while just a few hundred more joined the uprising. With the British slow to react, the IRB took Dublin City Hall but not Dublin Castle where a fierce firefight erupted. Fighting began elsewhere when British cavalry arrived to investigate, new recruits stumbled into an Irish Volunteers' outpost at Beggars Bush and the Royal Irish Regiment assaulted the Volunteers at the South Dublin Union. Looting then broke out when the Police were withdrawn. The following morning fighting erupted around St Stephen's Green and in the afternoon a British armoured train was strongly repulsed at Annersley Bridge. As the situation deteriorated, Wimborne declared martial law and British artillery began to shell IRB positions in the city centre. Pearse called for Dublin citizens to support the rising against the swelling numbers of British reinforcements (16,000 by the week's end), Brigadier General William Lowe now attacking rebel positions in strength albeit with little imagination. Bitter fighting raged from house-to-house, street-to-street, civilians caught in the cross fire and the intense shelling forcing Pearse to move his headquarters from the Post Office to Moore Street. On Saturday 29 April, with his position hopeless, Pearse ordered all units to surrender. Nearly 3,000 people lay dead or wounded, most of them Irish civilians.

Elsewhere in Ireland limited uprisings were put down, in Galway with naval bombardments. Fifteen IRB leaders including Pearse were executed whilst others were only interned as the British Government looked to pacify the country. Casement was hanged in Pentonville Prison. In 1919 Sinn Fein, representing all republicans, formed an independent government again declaring independence from Britain. The fighting would restart.

25 April 1915

The Great War
Gallipoli

 THE BRITISH AND French defeat of the German Schlieffen Plan in the Autumn of 1914 had resulted in a stalemate of trench warfare on the Western Front stretching from the Channel coast to Switzerland. The huge casualty rates already incurred in stopping the German advance and the magnitude of the problems involved in assaulting their now heavily-prepared defensive positions (the taste of which the British had experienced in South Africa fifteen years before) prompted the British War Cabinet to seek an offensive opportunity elsewhere.

Turkey had declared for the Central Powers in Autumn 1914 in order to regain territory from Russia but it was now the ambition of First Lord of the Admiralty Winston Churchill to knock them back out of the war with an attack through the Dardanelles Straits to the Sea of Marmara, Constantinople (Istanbul) and the Black Sea. If successful an opportunity would be created for the so far uncommitted Italy, Greece and Bulgaria, to open another front against the two main protagonists of the Central Powers, Germany and Austria Hungary. Churchill optimistically believed the Dardanelles could be forced purely with the combined power of the Royal and French navies but Vice Admiral Sackville Carden's Mediterranean Fleet and a limited number of troops had been comprehensively defeated in the Dardanelles Straits in March 1915. Undeterred, the British Secretary for War Horatio Kitchener now supported an amphibious attack, the Navy used this time to land 75,000 troops (familiar with the topography, Greece suggested 150,000 would be required) of the Mediterranean Expeditionary Force (MEF) for a clearance of the Gallipoli Peninsular which would allow the Royal Navy and French fleets passage through the Dardanelles. Commanding the MEF General Ian Hamilton, a veteran of Majuba Hill 1880, was surprised at his own appointment since he knew nothing of the land or the enemy whilst ominously First Sea Lord, Admiral John Fisher gave his disapproval, claiming the Dardenelles 'will be our grave!'.

After the Dardanelles Campaign the Turks knew very well that a further British attack was likely and had four weeks to prepare 85,000 men of the Turkish 5th Army under Prussian General, Otto von Sanders. On 25 April 1915, Sanders began receiving reports of British and French landings around Kumkale on the Asiatic shore, Sedd-el-Bahr on the southern end of the Gallipoli Peninsular (Helles) and at Gaba Tepe (Anzac Cove) twenty miles up the west coast whilst the Royal Navy was shelling the Peninsular Heights and the Bolayir Neck further north. Sanders realised that the Allied forces were too small for all the landings to be genuine and held his main force back on the Heights advised correctly by Lieutenant Colonel Mustafa Kemal Ataturk of the Turkish 19th Division that Helles and Anzac Cove would be the main British targets.

At Helles on S, X and Y beach the British landings went well but at W many men became trapped on barbed wire defences and were mown down by Turkish machine-gunners. At V the troop ship River Clyde came under heavy Turkish artillery fire whilst her open boats, loaded with Munstermen, Hampshires and Dubliners, were swept by machine-gun fire, just forty men reaching the cliffs. Despite the bloodbath, Major General Aylmer Hunter Weston commanding the British 29th Infantry Division sent 1,000 Lancashire reinforcements in to the beach suffering another 600 casualties but successfully taking the front Turkish trench with the bayonet.

At Anzac Cove 8,000 Australians were slowly towed in by steam pinnaces which gave the Turk defenders plenty of warning. Casualties mounted in the boats and on landing, troops running toward the sandbanks but many landing too far north where their planned advance on Gun Ridge was obstructed by high cliffs. As Turkish reinforcements began arriving, New Zealanders joined the battle developing over ravines of bare rock and thorny scrub with so many wounded returning that Lieutenant General William Birdwood was soon considering calling off the attack. By 21.00 Ataturk had moved to the high ground above Anzac Cove, launching a counter-attack two days later in an attempt to force the Anzacs back to the beach. The Turkish attack was checked only by Royal Navy artillery.

In extreme heat the bitter fighting of the next three months would leave British positions largely unchanged with casualty rates equal to those on the Western Front. In August, Hamilton would look to breakout from Anzac Cove with a support landing at Suvla Bay, both converging at Sari Bair.

25 April 1707 n.s

War of the Spanish Succession
Battle of Almansa

AFTER THE 1706 Battle of Ramillies, John Churchill, Duke of Marlborough continued to press the advantageous military position of the Grand Alliance (England, Dutch Republic, Austria, Portugal) to force the Bourbon Franco-Bavarian Army from the Spanish Netherlands but he could not force a decisive victory. In Italy, Austrians under Prince Eugene of Savoy had also been successful but in March 1707 Joseph I, Holy Roman Emperor, who had succeeded his father Leopold in 1705, granted King Louis XIV of France terms for the Duchy of Milan which not only allowed Joseph to secure the whole of Italy for Austria but also allowed Louis to move the army of Jacques Rouxel de Grancey, Count of Medavy back to France in opposition to the soon to become British (the Act of Union between England and Scotland was passed on 1 May 1707), Dutch and German Armies.

Meanwhile in Spain, the dispute over whose succession had begun the conflict (a choice between Bourbon Philip, Duke of Anjou and Habsburg Archduke Charles of Austria, the former having been indicated in the previous monarch's will but the latter preferred by the Grand Alliance to maintain the European balance of power), military activity dramatically increased when Portugal declared for the Habsburg cause after recognising the power of the Royal Navy at Vigo in 1702. Led by an English citizen of France, James Fitzjames, Duke of Berwick, Spain had initially invaded Portugal in 1704 with 19,000 troops but the naval attack and capture of Gibraltar by the Alliance that same year and subsequent Bourbon attempts to regain it meant Berwick could not sustain his efforts against Portugal. In 1705 an army of the Alliance commanded by Henri de Massue, Earl of Galway, a French exile who had served King William III of England in 1690, then invaded Spain from Portugal but was easily repelled. The following year the Portuguese Antonio Luis de Souza, Marquis of Minas then took advantage of a vacuum of opposition to repeat the exercise, marching into Madrid where he triumphantly proclaimed

Archduke Charles, King Charles III of Spain. Such was Madrid's lack of enthusiasm for Charles, however, that it soon became clear Minas was dangerously isolated. He departed for Valencia where he joined Galway but Berwick, now Marshal of France, and his Bourbon Army were following.

On 25 April 1707, the two armies, 25,000 Franco-Spanish Bourbons led by an Englishman and 22,000 British-Dutch-Portuguese Habsburgs of the Grand Alliance led by a Frenchman met at Almansa, south-west of Valencia. The Bourbons were drawn up on a slope, infantry in the centre and cavalry on the flanks. The Alliance similarly, British and Dutch left and left centre, Portuguese on the right centre and right with Galway placing additional infantry on his flanks in support of the cavalry. After an initial artillery bombardment, Galway led the Alliance left flank and centre forward, his tactic of infantry supporting the cavalry charge paying off when the Bourbon front right began to give way. Berwick reacted by pushing the Bourbon second line forward which successfully halted the Alliance advance. The Portuguese on the right of centre then also moved forward to hold the Bourbon centre as fierce fighting with musket and bayonet continued on the Alliance left. Realising the Portuguese cavalry and infantry on the Alliance right were merely spectating and had not moved forward to cover the consequently exposed flank of their compatriots in the Alliance centre, Berwick then delivered the decisive blow, ordering his cavalry forward to charge them. The Portuguese cavalry fled immediately but their infantry stood firm for some time before eventually being overwhelmed by the sheer weight of the Berwick's attack, their defeat now further exposing Galway's centre. Galway himself was completely unaware of these events as he had retired to treat wounds but returned in time to witness the impending disaster. Galvanising his cavalry, he managed to orchestrate something of a retreat but not before the Alliance had lost 17,000 men.

The catastrophic defeat of the Grand Alliance at Almansa left the cause of Archduke Charles in Spain desperate. Berwick would bring much of eastern Spain, Catalonia excepted, under the Bourbon flag before marching north to the Low Countries. He would, however, miss the 1708 Battle of Oudenaarde against his uncle, Marlborough.

26 April 1797
French Revolutionary War
Battle of Cadiz

THE FRENCH REVOLUTION of 1789 had given rise to an aggressive Republican France intent on spreading the ideologies of Montesquieu, Rousseau and Voltaire and the Declaration of the Rights of Man and the Citizen to all other countries in Europe – by force if necessary. Fearful of French inspired revolutionary unrest in their own lands Austria, Prussia, Great Britain, the Dutch Republic, Spain and Sardinia formed the First Coalition in response but, swelled by revolutionary nationalism and a levée en masse (one million men in 1794 alone) the French had by early 1797 conquered the Low Countries to form the Batavian Republic which included, by extension, the Cape of Good Hope and the routes to the East Indies and India; defeated Sardinia; forced the mighty Prussian Army out of the war; Spain to change sides and was now about to force Austria into a favourable peace. Not for the last time would just one European country remain alone actively fighting an expansionist, nationalist, militarised nation, Great Britain.

For the past four years Prime Minister William Pitt and Secretary for War, Henry Dundas had offered the coalition little in the way of an army but instead used the power of the Royal Navy to blockade the French coast, menace French global possessions from India to the West Indies and prevent French invasions of Wales and particularly Ireland, Britain's traditional back door. The signing of the Second Treaty of San Ildefonso by Spain and France and, more recently, the attempted French landing in Bantry Bay, Ireland had left the Royal Navy Mediterranean Fleet isolated, necessitating a move west through the Straits of Gibraltar to the coast of Portugal. On 1 February 1797, Spanish Admiral Don Jose de Cordoba y Ramos followed the Royal Navy by sailing from Cartagena, South East Spain on the *Santisima Trinidad* with another twenty-seven ships of the line to Cadiz intending to join with the French fleet at Brest. While Cordoba was blown off course by strong winds Admiral John Jervis commanding the ten-strong Mediterranean Fleet aboard perhaps the most famous ship in the history of maritime warfare, the impressive

112-gun HMS *Victory*, was reinforced by five ships of the Channel Fleet under Rear Admiral William Parker, by the frigate HMS *Minerve* under Commodore Horatio Nelson and six others. Off Cape St Vincent, Jervis then sailed in line astern through the middle of the surprised Spaniards firing in both directions during a five hour battle for a famous victory after which he was honoured with an earldom, Nelson with a promotion and a knighthood. In contrast, Cordoba was dismissed having lost four ships and over 3,000 men, the rest limping into Cadiz.

The Royal Navy was now attempting to blockade the European Atlantic coast from Holland to Gibraltar but with Spanish strength now in Cadiz, Jervis kept his proximity, investing the harbour entrance with two ships, an inshore squadron and his main fleet fifteen miles out to sea. The Spanish countered with shallow gunboats and shore batteries backed up by broadsides from their trapped warships to aggressively force back the British whose crews were suffering from the continuous ardour of life at sea, mutiny as ever never far away. British hardship would of course be eased should any treasure laden ships from the New World be captured and two such 34-gun frigates, *Santa Elena* and *Ninfa*, loaded with silver bullion at Havana, Cuba unwittingly now sailed straight into the Royal Navy blockade. Warned of the danger, however, by a Spanish fisherman upon whom they unloaded their cargo they then made the run for Cadiz but were spotted at 06.00 on 26 April 1797 by Captain Velterers Berkeley in the 36-gun HMS *Emerald* and Captain George Martin in the 74-gun HMS *Irresistible*. The two Spaniards took refuge in Conil Bay behind the Laja de Capa Rocha around which the British navigated to begin a two-hour battle at anchor, broadside for broadside. Having taken nearly fifty casualties the Spanish surrendered but escaped after drifting the *Santa Elena* onto the rocks.

The Spanish fisherman safely landed his lucrative catch. The Royal Navy blockade of Cadiz lasted five years until the 1802 Treaty of Amiens before resuming again a year later. Meanwhile Rear Admiral Horatio Nelson lost an arm in a July 1797 attack on Santa Cruz de Tenerife but recovered to command the Mediterranean Fleet the following year when Napoleon Bonaparte would look to conquer the Ottoman Empire and British India.

27 April 1669 o.s

Anglo-Spanish Wars
Raid on Maracaibo

TENSION IN THE Caribbean between England and Spain continued to simmer after the Spanish Armada of 1588 well into the seventeenth century. Sixty years later, following civil war in the three kingdoms of England, Scotland and Ireland, Oliver Cromwell resumed attacks on Spain as part of his 'Western Design'; an attempt to damage Spanish domination of the western Atlantic which included a failure to take Hispaniola (Haiti, Dominican Rep) but succeeded in taking Jamaica. Following Cromwell's death and the 1660 Restoration of the monarchy, King Charles II rescinded privateering licences in the Caribbean until war broke out for the second time in just over a decade between England and the Dutch Republic. Once again the Caribbean became an opportunistic hunting ground for state licensed buccaneers to loot treasure, shipping and land which did not stop when the Anglo-Dutch War ended in 1667. Although not officially at war with Spain, Robert Searle saw fit to sack St Augustine (Florida) in March 1668 before Henry Morgan sacked and ransomed Portobello, Panama four months later, the fate of the latter leading to several reprisals from the Spanish including the sacking of several small towns in Jamaica. An enraged Morgan called out for buccaneers of all nationalities to join him for another attack on the Spanish Main.

Morgan collected 1,000 men in eleven ships off Isla Vaca (Haiti) where it was decided to attack Cartagena, Colombia. Not only was Cartagena wealthy but any attack would likely provoke yet further Spanish reprisals assuring further privateering licences from the Governor of Jamaica Sir Thomas Modyford that would keep the Morgan and his buccaneers in business for some time to come. A pre-emptive celebration, however, resulted in a drunkard blowing up Morgan's powerful flagship, *Oxford*. Morgan escaped with his life but many did not and with the omen causing desertions the buccaneering fleet was soon down to ten ships and 800 men. Undeterred, Morgan made for Cartagena but with the wind against and crews suffering (now just 500) he was persuaded by a French corsair to instead target Maracaibo, Venezuela.

Maracaibo had been sacked by the brutal French pirate Francois L'Ollonais just two years previous which prompted the Spanish to constructed Fort La Barra on the narrows between the Gulf of Venezuela and Lake Maracaibo. On March 9 1669, on Morgan's approach, the defenders at La Barra, having unsuccessfully booby trapped the fort, fled to Maracaibo to warn the inhabitants who in turn fled into the surrounding countryside. The buccaneers therefore arrived to find Maracaibo deserted necessitating several weeks spent hunting down the residents who were robbed and tortured (including the rack) to reveal their hidden valuables and the whereabouts of their fellow citizens. After exhausting Maracaibo Morgan then sailed across the lake to administer a repeat dosage to the town of Gibraltar.

Meanwhile the Spanish Admiral Don Alonzo de Campos y Espinoza had learnt of Morgan's intentions and with two powerful frigates and an armed French merchantman headed to Maracaibo where he remanned Fort La Barra and parked his three ships across the lake, blocking Morgan's exit. Morgan was called to surrender and return his ill-gotten gains or face the consequences, any one of Don Alonzo's ships being more than a match for any of his own. The buccaneers, however, were not the sort of men to meekly throw in the towel and on 27 April 1669 they sailed directly at Don Alonzo's small fleet led by a merchantman disguised as Morgan's flagship. As the ship pulled up against the huge *Magdalena*, Don Alonzo's flagship, the Spanish jumped down for a fight only to find no one onboard and the buccaneering crew hurriedly paddling away in a canoe. A few moments later both ships disappeared in a huge explosion with the remains of the *Magdalena* going to the bottom. The *Soledad* was then captured by the buccaneers and the *San Luis* was torched underneath Fort La Barra which was then reinforced by the shipless Spanish crews including a shaken Don Alonzo. Morgan still had to get past the fort's cannon and again using deception staged a fake landing in preparation for a land attack on the fort. The outwitted Spanish moved their cannon accordingly before, under cover of darkness, Morgan sailed silently past and out to sea.

Morgan returned to a hero's welcome in Jamaica while Don Alonzo returned to Madrid in chains. Morgan initially retired to his plantation but would come out of retirement in just two years time for his greatest venture, another assault on Panama, this time its capital, Panama City.

28 April 1760

French and Indian War
Battle of Sainte Foy

THE ANNUS MIRABILIS of 1759 had seen a Seven Years' War Anglo-Prussian-Hanoverian defeat of the French at Minden; British Royal Navy victories at Lagos and Quiberon Bay off the European Atlantic coast; the capture of sugar-rich Guadeloupe in the Caribbean; a Third Carnatic War repulse of the French at Madras, India; and in North America, French and Indian War British victories at Fort Carillon (now Ticonderoga) on Lake Champlain, Fort Niagara on Lake Ontario and Quebec on the St Lawrence River. If ever there was a year that saw Great Britain rise above France and the Dutch Republic as the dominant global colonial power it will be remembered as 1759. However, the French in India, North America and Europe alongside their Austro-Russian allies were not finished, indeed just eleven days after Minden, Russia and Austria defeated Prussia at Kunersdorf though with huge losses on both sides. The Anglo-Prusso-Hanoverian military situation in Europe therefore remained precarious whilst in North America it was still far from secure despite the Royal Navy blockade of France which effectively isolated French colonies from their motherland.

Following Major General James Wolfe's 1759 victory a British garrison of 6,000 had been left in Quebec City under Major General James Murray whilst the French retreated west to Montreal. The Royal Navy under Admiral Charles Saunders was neither able to follow nor remain outside Quebec due to winter pack ice forming on the St Lawrence River, the fleet returning to New York or crossing the Atlantic to further tighten the British blockade of France.

Alone in Quebec, Murray had a difficult winter subsisting on meagre supplies in a freezing city that had largely been destroyed by his own artillery earlier in the year. By the spring of 1760, Murray's garrison was down to just 4,000 actives mainly due to scurvy and was desperately in need of the returning fleet. The French were also expecting the arrival of the British fleet just as soon as the ice melted and with that in mind Francis de Gaston, Chevalier de Lévis, a future Marshal of France but now

Commander-in-Chief of French Forces in New France, led 7,000 men, regulars, militia and American Indians from Montreal down the St Lawrence River in an attempt to retake Quebec. Rather than staying within the walls of Quebec, Murray ventured out just as had Lévis' predecessor, Louis Joseph de Montcalm, against Wolfe the previous autumn with such disastrous results.

On 28 April 1760, in the snow west of Quebec City at Sainte Foy, Murray's 4,000 men, virtually all regulars but in poor physical condition, were drawn up in two lines across a front of one mile supported by a reserve and twenty-two field guns. Lévis' army had also shrunk to just 5,000 men and three guns by the time he arrived on the battlefield, Murray beginning an artillery bombardment as the French deployed before advancing to attack the French left in an attempt to turn their entire position and trap their right against the St Lawrence River. The British infantry were indeed successful in driving back the French left but Lévis recognised the danger and pulled back his right before counter-attacking with his left. Bitter fighting raged around the Sainte Foy windmill with Lévis, having restored the situation on his left, now attacking the British left with his right. Murray was soon forced to send in his reserve and centre just to hold the French attack only for the superiority of the British guns to then dramatically decline when ammunition became exhausted. The British left then soon collapsed gifting Lévis an opportunity to block a British retreat to Quebec. The French right, however, crucially misunderstood the order and headed over to assist the French left allowing Murray and his survivors to escape. Nevertheless, the British had already suffered over 1,000 casualties.

Lévis besieged Quebec for two weeks before retreating to Montreal. The Royal Navy shortly relieved Murray and in July defeated a French fleet on the River Restigouche. In September 1760 the French Governor of New France Pierre de Riguaud, Marquis de Vaudreuil surrendered to Major General James Amherst, the 1763 Treaty of Paris leaving Britain as masters of all North America east of the River Mississippi, Florida and New Orleans excepted. Though Canada would remain loyal the British would have to fight for their prize once again in just over a decade.

29 April 1781

American War of Independence
Fort Royal, Martinique

THE SMALL BRITISH Army in North America had been caught unawares by the strength of resentment against British rule in 1775, suffering a humiliating siege of Boston where they were trapped for eleven months before reasserting authority further south in New York. The 1776 campaigns into New Jersey had then been largely successful but General George Washington had commanded the American Continental Army with such dexterity that he had avoided all British attempts to force a decisive battle. The Americans had not only grown in strength but had also progressed professionally, their dogged resistance rewarded by their own successful advances from the River Delaware back to the outskirts of New York City and in the Hudson Valley where British failures in command led to the surrender at Saratoga of General John Burgoyne to Major General Horatio Gates. These successes then encouraged both France and Spain to enter the war on the side of the Americans, not so much because they believed in the rights of man and democracy, not yet anyway, but because they sensed an ideal opportunity to deal a blow to British imperial ambitions not only in North America but also globally.

The British, now commanded by the temperamental General Henry Clinton following the resignation of General William Howe, resorted to a 'Southern Strategy', transferring the offensive further south, first to Savannah, Georgia in 1779 before repeating the exercise at Charleston, South Carolina a year later. Whilst Clinton's subordinate, Lieutenant General Charles, Lord Cornwallis was making surprising headway through the hinterland of the Carolinas, rallying loyalist support, he was at the end of exhausting supply lines from Charleston, itself supplied by the Royal Navy on an Atlantic seaboard no longer their exclusive domain but also that of the French Navy. Not only that but Britain's ally of the eighteenth century Wars of Succession, the Dutch Republic, was also covertly supplying the Americans via France, the outrage sparking a Fourth Anglo-Dutch

War which left British, Dutch, French and Spanish possessions in the lucrative sugar and coffee rich Caribbean islands fair game as all contenders sought to wreck the economies of the other.

In the British Leeward Islands, Admiral George Rodney had reacted to news of the Dutch intervention by attacking and sacking the island of St Eustatius, both he and General John Vaughan keeping much of the proceeds for themselves. Rodney now divided his fleet to escort his new found wealth home, leaving Rear Admiral Samuel Hood blockading Fort Royal, Martinique with seventeen ships of the line. Almost simultaneously, however, two French fleets were leaving Brest, France one under Admiral Pierre, Comte de Suffren heading for the Bay of Bengal to support the efforts of Sultan of Mysore Hyder Ali Khan (Second Anglo Mysore War) and one under Admiral Francois Joseph, Compte de Grasse, twenty ships of the line protecting a 150-strong merchant convoy destined for the very same Fort Royal.

On 29 April 1781, De Grasse arrived off Martinique to find Hood in an unfavourable position to leeward. Though he had vigorously protested, Hood was under orders from Rodney and now had little option to pull away allowing four blockaded French ships of the line to sail out whilst the merchant convoy sailed serenely in. A two-day exchange of long range gunfire, the first hour intense, now exploded into action, De Grasse failing to engage more closely but, nevertheless, Hood was hopelessly outgunned. Having suffered slight damage the British Admiral finally withdrew to St Eustatius.

Hood then sailed north to join Rodney allowing De Grasse to capture Tobago but the failures of the two British Admirals to inflict any meaningful damage on De Grasse would only bear significant consequences four months later. In the main theatre, Cornwallis' imminent but costly victory at the Battle of Guildford Courthouse would result in a British retreat ultimately to Yorktown, Virginia. As American and French troops marched hundreds of miles to trap the British by land, De Grasse sailed his entire fleet (the Spanish Representative in the West Indies Don Francisco Saavedre de Sangronis agreed to protect French possessions in the meantime) two thousand miles north to Chesapeake Bay completing the siege. The days of British rule in the Thirteen Colonies of North America were numbered.

30 April 1690

Williamite Wars
Battle of Cromdale

THE 1685 DEATH of King Charles II of England, Scotland and Ireland had spread fear around the Protestant communities of the Three Kingdoms. In 1680 the Exclusion Bill had been presented in Parliament which would have prevented a Catholic, more specifically Charles' brother James, Duke of York, from the succession but since the Bill failed James was duly crowned King James II of England, VII of Scotland in February 1685. That James was crowned amidst a European background of monarchic absolutism and the Catholic persecution of Protestant Huguenots in France did little for the peace of mind of his own Protestant subjects. Additionally James had first married Anne Hyde, a Catholic convert and secondly Mary of Modena, a devout Catholic. He did have two legitimate surviving daughters, both Protestant, but he also had an eighteen-month-old Catholic son, James Stuart who stood to inherit the throne on James' death (absolute primogeniture only replaced male primogeniture in 2015). That James was a similar threat to Protestants as had been the previous Catholic monarch, Mary I, was perhaps unlikely but nevertheless he had opened formal English relations with the Pope for the first time since 1530 and had looked to reinstate and advance his brother Charles' 1672 Royal Declaration of Indulgence with the 1687 Declaration of Indulgence, promoting religious freedom particularly to Roman Catholics, many of whom he appointed to positions of favour and influence. By 1688 Protestant England was already at the end of its tether, a letter signed by six leading Parliamentarians and Churchmen was delivered by former Admiral Arthur Herbert to Prince William III of Orange, Stadtholder of the wealthy Dutch Republic, Protestant nephew to James by virtue of his mother Mary, Princess Royal and son-in-law by virtue of his marriage to James' daughter Mary. The letter requested William invade England and depose James. Backed by the Dutch States General (Parliament) and despite a menacing

French Army on his own border William achieved both without firing a shot by the 'Glorious Revolution' of 1688, James fleeing to France.

Whilst Protestant England rejoiced there was considerable unrest in William's other two new kingdoms, Scotland and Ireland. William sent a 35,000-strong Anglo-Dutch Army under Prince Goerg of Waldeck and John Churchill, Earl of Marlborough to counter the French threat to the Dutch Republic while he looked to confront French troops who had landed in Ireland with the returning James.

Just a month after James' Irish landing, John Graham, Viscount Dundee raised James' standard on the Dundee Law even though Scots were divided on James' restoration – generally Catholic Highlanders supporting whereas Presbyterian Lowlanders were against. Dundee was among the exceptions, being a Lowlander who had gained the confidence of the Highland clans to lead the Jacobites (Latin, Jacobus-James). As an exception so too was Dundee's enemy General Hugh Mackay, a Highlander of the Scots Brigade who led the Government/Williamite forces. Initially a Government force of 4,000 was defeated at Killiecrankie in July 1689, a ferocious Highlander charge killing 2,000 Williamites but the Jacobites also suffered losses which included Dundee. Now with Colonel Alexander Cannon commanding, the Jacobites advanced on Edinburgh whilst for William Lieutenant Colonel William Cleland moved north to hold Dunkeld. Though heavily outnumbered Cleland defeated Cannon inflicting heavy losses that forced the Highlanders to return to the Glens. James then responded to the pleas of his remaining loyal Scots by sending supplies and a few officers including Major General Thomas Buchan who decided to wait for summer 1690 before conducting another major campaign. In the meantime Buchan intended for 1,200 men to harass William's forces in the Lowlands and advanced down Speyside attempting to recruit but instead suffered desertion. Undeterred, Buchan marched on before, on 30 April 1690, his now 800 Jacobites were confronted on the opposite bank of the River Spey by Sir Thomas Livingston and the Inverness Government garrison. The Jacobites retreated in the face of this much larger force but were cut off by Government cavalry. Forced back to the Haughs of Cromdale Buchan made a desperate last stand losing perhaps half his men before fog spared him total annihilation.

Cromdale temporarily ended Jacobite resistance in Scotland. The Highlanders would suffer a massacre at Glencoe in 1692 before James instructed them to accept William's pardon. Jacobite uprisings in Scotland would, however, continue for over fifty years in the names of James' son and grandson.

May

"Wallis, I didn't believe a word you said when you came to see me, but now you could sell me a pink elephant."

AIR OFFICER COMMANDING-IN-CHIEF,
RAF BOMBER COMMAND
ARTHUR HARRIS TO BARNES WALLIS,
GRANTHAM, 1943

1 May 1982
Falklands War
Black Buck One

BRITISH, FRENCH, SPANISH and by extension Argentine sovereignty of the Falkland Islands had been disputed for nearly 250 years, but in 1976 tension escalated with an Argentine invasion of neighbouring Southern Thule and in 1977 with a disconnection of fuel supplies from the South American mainland. In 1982 Lieutenant General Leopoldo Galtieri, leading an unpopular military junta governing Argentina, then sought to distract attention from his poor economic record and human rights abuses by stoking national fervour with an invasion of *Las Malvinas* (the Falklands), populated by 1,800 souls loyal to the British Crown. On 2 April 1982, the Governor of the Falklands Sir Rex Hunt and Major Mike Norman of the Royal Marines had surrendered to Argentine commandos after a short but fierce defence of the capital, Port Stanley and in particular Government House. In London the Government of Prime Minister Margaret Thatcher had been caught by surprise even though the news had been partly preempted, Foreign Secretary Peter Carington, Lord Carrington resigning. The news was then decisively acted upon once Chief of Naval Staff Admiral Sir Henry Leach had persuaded Thatcher that Britain could and must recapture the islands. Diplomatic negotiations continued but within just three days of the Argentine invasion a Royal Navy Task Force of 127 vessels headed by aircraft carriers HMS *Hermes* and *Invincible* under Admiral John Fieldhouse began to sail from Portsmouth, joining the nuclear submarines HMS *Splendid, Spartan* and *Conqueror* already en route.

As the main Naval Task Force steamed south, fears remained over the imminent vulnerability of the Royal Navy to Argentine Air Force fast jets using the islands only paved runway outside Port Stanley. Chief of the Air Staff Sir Michael Beetham therefore looked to destroy the 120-yard-wide runway with an ambitious bombing raid, at the time the longest in history, involving a round trip of 8,000 miles from Ascension Island by a lone, near obsolete Avro Vulcan which contained no electronics and no accurate maps. Resources were available for only one Vulcan and a reserve from 101 Squadron Strike Command which would need to refuel four times in mid air from a complex series of eleven Victor tankers (and two reserves) which would additionally have to refuel each other until just one Victor saw the Vulcan into her target. On 29 April, two Vulcan crews left RAF Waddington for Ascension Island, the following morning receiving the order that Operation Black Buck was to be launched at 23.00 that night.

Both Vulcans took off, the lead XM598 failing to pressurise leaving the reserve of XM607 under Flight Lieutenant Martin Withers to fly on through the night unaware that returning Victor pilots realised his Vulcan was burning more fuel than provisioned. Concern then intensified further when refueling between the last two Victors had to be conducted through a violent thunderstorm, Squadron Leader Bob Tuxford unable to break radio silence to inform the Vulcan crew that both he and they lacked the fuel to complete their respective missions. Withers realised his predicament soon enough, however, but pressed on regardless, lowering to 300 feet before navigational difficulties necessitated a climb that caught his Vulcan on Argentinian radar. Two minutes out and Argentine anti-aircraft defence batteries locked on to the British flight which jammed the signal and opened the bomb doors to approach a beautifully lit up Port Stanley airfield. At 04.00 1 May 1982, Vulcan XM607 released twenty-one 1,000 pound bombs at 10,000 feet, before turning away with her characteristic howl, chased by anti-aircraft fire as her bombs struck below. Flying for home back past the Task Force, Electronics Officer Hugh Prior signaled 'Superfuse' indicating a successful mission but the crew still faced a 3,000 mile flight over the freezing South Atlantic Ocean with a fast emptying fuel tank. Just as XM607 seemed certain to ditch, however, a Victor mercifully appeared out of the side window.

The first bomb dropped hit the Port Stanley runway, putting it out of action for Argentine fast jets. Now in fear of the Royal Air Force, Argentina withdrew her fighters back to the mainland, lessening the threat to British shipping and her troops. Operation Black Buck was repeated six times throughout the Falklands War, the Vulcan's first and last action. Wither's Vulcan XM607 now resides by the runway at RAF Waddington.

2 May 1982

Falklands War
Sinking of ARA General Belgrano

ARGENTINE GENERAL LEOPOLDO Galtieri had ignited the more than 200-year-old historical dispute over sovereignty of the Falkland Islands, a British Crown Colony since 1840, with a full invasion of the islands on 2 April 1982. Whilst the attack was condemned by the United Nations, Galtieri and his military junta ruling Argentina, previously heavily criticised on human rights abuses and economic grounds, had immediately achieved one of their goals by gaining the support of euphoric Argentines. In London, however, despite doubts from within the British military and the United States, the Chief-of-Naval-Staff Sir Henry Leach had persuaded his resolute Prime Minister Margaret Thatcher that Britain could and should recover the Falklands not just for the sake of the 1,800 loyal British inhabitants but also for the country's world standing.

The Royal Navy already had HMS *Endurance* in the South Atlantic and had already preemptively sent two nuclear-powered submarines, now they sent another, HMS *Conqueror* commanded by Captain Christopher Wreford-Brown. On 5 April a Naval Task Force of 127 vessels including forty-three warships followed from Portsmouth for the 8,000 mile voyage south to the Falklands under the commands of Admiral Sir John Fieldhouse and Rear Admiral Sandy Woodward. A week after their departure, amidst intensifying diplomatic negotiations, the British Government announced a 200-mile Maritime Exclusion Zone (MEZ) around the Falklands indicating any Argentine vessel or plane within the MEZ would be deemed hostile. On 23 April, Britain then advised Argentina via the Swiss Government that 'any approach on the part of Argentine warships, including submarines, naval auxiliaries or military aircraft, which could amount to a threat to interfere with the mission of British forces in the South Atlantic will encounter the appropriate response'. The message that the whole of the South Atlantic was now a war-zone was not lost on Argentine Vice Admiral Juan Lombardo or Captain Hector Bonzo aboard the ARA *General Belgrano*, a Second World War, former United States light cruiser which had survived the 1941 Japanese attack on Pearl Harbor, Hawaii and which had been renamed after the Argentine War of Independence hero Manuel Belgrano. What Bonzo did not know, however, was that as from 30 April 1982 his ship was being stalked by HMS *Conqueror*.

The main British Task Force was now within 200 miles of the Falklands with Woodward anxious to avoid a pincer movement from the north by at least six Argentine warships including the aircraft carrier *Veinticinco de Mayo* and from the south-west by the *Belgrano* and her two accompanying destroyers. Woodward sent an order to Wreford-Brown to engage *Belgrano* but, routed via London, the order landed in front of Thatcher's War Cabinet. On 1 May Lombardo then gave an order for all Argentine naval units to assemble within the MEZ the following day for a massive attack on the British Task Force, an order also intercepted by British intelligence. Thatcher thus confirmed the order for Wreford-Brown and *Conqueror* to engage the *Belgrano*.

At 4pm on 2 May 1982 at 2,000 yards HMS *Conqueror* fired three 21-inch MK8 mod 4 torpedoes each with an 805-pound warhead, the first blowing off the ships bow whilst the second catastrophically hit three-quarters back exploding in the aft machine room, blasting everything above it to leave a 70-foot hole in the deck. Water flooding in could not be pumped back out through a complete loss of power which also prevented Bonzo from making a distress call to his two accompanying destroyers separated in the gloomy weather. Worse, the water tight doors, though closed in the bow were not closed in the rear. As the ship listed and began to sink, Bonzo ordered the abandon ship but adrift in the dark many of the survivors would face an icy three days drifting in the South Atlantic. Over 300 men from the ship's company of 1,093 were killed in the attack.

The sinking of the *Belgrano* has been criticised as a war crime since at the time she was outside, sailing away from the MEZ but in the light of Lombardo's order she clearly represented a threat. The loss prompted the Argentine fleet to return to port for the duration of the conflict. Port Stanley airfield bombed the previous day by an RAF Vulcan and the absence of an aircraft carrier in the vicinity meant Argentine aircraft would now have to operate at full range from the mainland.

3 May 1811

Napoleonic Wars
Battle of Fuentes de Oñoro

IN APRIL 1811 Lieutenant General Sir Arthur Wellesley, Viscount Wellington had forced the French out of Portugal for a third time after Marshal Andre Masséna and his army of 65,000 had spent a winter of misery starving outside Lisbon. Masséna had been ordered by Napoleon Bonaparte, Emperor of the French to hold his position at Santarem until Marshal Jean de Dieu Soult and the *Armée d'Andalusie* had taken the Fortress of Badajoz governing the southern pass from Spain into Portugal. Masséna's fortitude, however, which had astonished even Wellington, gave out on 6 March 1811 just four days before the fall of Badajoz but once he had begun his long retreat back to the French-held fortress town of Ciudad Rodrigo he could not turn back. Harried by Wellington's well supplied pursuing Anglo-Portuguese Army, Masséna's rear guard commanded by Marshal Michel Ney was fighting almost continuous actions to protect the main French column. Under extreme pressure the relationship between the two French Marshals was disintegrating, resulting finally in Masséna sacking Ney. On 8 April 1811, the French Army marched out of Portugal, leaving behind a garrison at Almeida under General Antoine Brennier which was now besieged. The Portugal expedition had already cost France 25,000 troops mostly to starvation and disease but still Masséna harboured the belief he could relieve Brennier.

In Masséna's favour, Ciudad Rodrigo and Badajoz were both still in French hands controlling the northern and southern accesses to Portugal whilst Wellington, with his own supply difficulties 200 miles from Lisbon, needed to split his forces to cover both towns and maintain the siege of Almeida. General William Beresford marched south with 20,000 men to Albuera covering any potential advance from Badajoz by Soult whilst Wellington remained north with 38,000 men watching Masséna who had requested reinforcements from General Jean Baptiste Bessières and the *Armée du Nord*. Bessières arrived with just 1,500 men but regardless Masséna's 48,000 still comfortably outnumbered Wellington and he resolutely advanced to relieve

Almeida by attempting to break through well prepared Anglo-Portuguese positions on the Spanish border at the village of Fuentes de Oñoro.

On 3 May 1811, Masséna opened the battle with an artillery bombardment and frontal assault across the Don Casas stream. General's Claude Ferey and Jean Marchand, the French heroes of Casal Novo fought their way into the village where a bitter house-to-house struggle raged throughout the entire day before the British infantry of Major General Brent Spencer and Lieutenant General Thomas Picton evicted the intruders with a bayonet charge. The next day there was no fighting but Wellington observed Masséna moving columns south clearly with the intention of turning his right flank. Wellington duly responded by moving the British 7th Infantry Division across the plains to Poco Velha, until then defended only by Spanish *guerilleros*, but it was not enough. The following day the Spanish *guerilleros* were quickly overrun by cavalry and infantry under Bessières who then threatened to move on and destroy the 7th Division. Wellington sent the Light Division of Major General Robert Crauford beyond Poco Velha onto the right flank of the 7th to facilitate a withdrawal but once the 7th had extricated themselves Crauford's Lights were in turn isolated. Forming square, however, they marched back across the plain volleying at Bessière's circling cavalry. The French attack on Wellington's right now stalled, Masséna again launching massed columns of infantry against Fuentes de Oñoro almost forcing the British back out of the village in bitter hand-to-hand fighting before Wellington counter-attacked with British and Portuguese infantry to drive the French back over the Don Casas. Masséna now resorted to an artillery duel but broke off the battle three days later and retreated to Ciudad Rodrigo with 3,000 casualties, he was replaced by Marshal Auguste Marmont. Wellington had lost 2,000 men.

Two days later Brennier's garrison at Almeida made a run through the British lines to complete the disgrace of Major General William Erskine who had previously blundered at Casal Novo. Two weeks later Beresford would have problems with Soult at Albuera outside Badajoz.

4 May 1471

Wars of the Roses
Battle of Tewkesbury

THE FEUD BETWEEN Richard Plantagenet, Duke of York and Edmund Beaufort, Duke of Somerset had evolved into a struggle for the Crown of England between the Houses of York (Plantagenet) and Lancaster (King Henry VI). Somerset and York had long since been killed amidst battlefield violence and executions that had claimed much of the English nobility since 1455 and by mid April 1471 Somerset's son, Henry Beaufort, Duke of Somerset was also dead. King Henry was again languishing in the Tower of London whilst King Edward IV, the son of Richard Plantagenet, was back on the throne following a decisive Yorkist victory at Barnet over his ally turned traitor, Richard Neville, Earl of Warwick. While the bodies of Warwick and his brother John Neville, Lord Montagu were retrieved from Barnet for display outside St Paul's Cathedral in Yorkist London, King Henry's devoted French Queen, Margaret of Anjou was landing at Weymouth with her seventeen-year-old son Edward of Lancaster, Prince of Wales after a period of exile in France. Lancastrian support soon joined her from Devon and Cornwall bringing Lancastrian strength up to 5–6,000 men, the queen then looking to join with Welsh Lancastrians under Jasper Tudor, Earl of Pembroke (half brother of King Henry by his mother Catherine of Valois). If Margaret and Tudor could unite, King Edward would face another serious challenge; to prevent it, he marched out of Windsor Castle on 24 April.

Meanwhile Margaret's Lancastrians commanded by Edmund Beaufort, Duke of Somerset (Henry Beaufort's brother), John Courtenay Earl of Devon and John, Lord Wenlock had gained supplies in Bristol before marching to Gloucester but here the gates were not opened to them. Fatigued and with morale no doubt suffering they were also now pursued by Edward. Somerset marched for Tewkesbury where, in the grounds of the Abbey, exhausted, threatened to the rear and with no sign of Pembroke, the Lancastrian Army reluctantly turned to give battle.

Edward's 5,000 Yorkists (but with more men-at-arms than Margaret) were no less tired so that when his scouts reported the halt of the Lancastrian Army he gave his men a brief rest before marching at dusk on 3 May to within three miles of Tewkesbury Abbey. The following morning 4 May 1471 Edward organised his army into the usual medieval formation of three battles with his eighteen-year-old brother Richard, Duke of Gloucester commanding the left, himself the centre and his loyal servant William, Lord Hastings the right. Additionally Edward put 200 mounted infantry in a thick wood to his left to cover his flank before advancing with banners and trumpets to 'commit his cause and quarrel to Almighty God'.

Margaret's Lancastrians were in a strong natural position with dykes, hedges, trees, bushes and 'evil lanes' protecting them from the Yorkist advance. Devon led the left, Wenlock the centre and Somerset the right intending to fight in the preferred English way on the defensive but Edward opened the battle with cannon and archers to such effect that Somerset's men were soon so distressed that they charged through the hedges to engage Gloucester on the Yorkist left. Edward's mounted infantry in the wood counter-attacked, routing Somerset who then accused Wenlock of treachery, settling the argument by cleaving his head with a battle axe. The event did little for Lancastrian morale which came under further duress when Edward pressed the Yorkist attack across the whole front, the Prince of Wales unable to restore the situation before the whole Lancastrian Army broke and fled. The aftermath of many Wars of the Roses battles had been merciless and Tewkesbury was no different, 2,000 Lancastrians dying in the fight or by drowning. The Prince of Wales was executed whilst pleading for his life, Devon died on the field and Somerset, after hiding in the Abbey, was executed.

King Henry VI died shortly after Tewkesbury, probably murdered by Gloucester. Just Pembroke and his nephew Henry Tudor remained of the House of Lancaster and they duly fled to France. Edward defeated an attack on London by Thomas Neville, the Bastard of Fauconberg (cousin of Warwick) but then enjoyed twelve years of rule. On Edward's death in 1483, Gloucester usurped the throne but any ambition of a long reign would depend on him defeating a returning Henry Tudor at Bosworth Field.

5 May 1942

Second World War
Battle for Madagascar

LIKE JAPAN, MADAGASCAR in 1833 became a closed country. Ruled for thirty three years by the harsh Queen Ranavalona I the population halved, Christian missionaries were restricted and a friendship treaty with Great Britain was terminated. Madagascar reopened when King Radama II succeeded Ranavalona but it would be France that benefitted under the Lambert Charter until 1863 when Radama was murdered. Shortly after the 1883 succession to the throne of Ranavalona III tension between Madagascar and France escalated over the Charter, France invading in 1894 to send Ranavalona into exile. Madagascar then remained a French colony until the outbreak of the Second World War, coming under Vichy France in 1940 and briefly considered by the Nazi German Foreign Ministry, Jewish Department, as a possible destination for the deportation of European Jews.

In September 1940 the Tripartite Act between Germany, Italy and Japan consolidated the military aims of the Axis Powers which by early 1942 were at their zenith. Germany had pushed deep into Russia having conquered western Europe save Great Britain whilst Italy, with German assistance, controlled the Balkans where several states joined the Axis. In North Africa, Germans and Italians were pushing the British 8th Army back toward the Libyan/Egyptian border and in South East Asia, Japan was seemingly unstoppable having advanced as far as Singapore and Rangoon, their attacks based from Vichy French Indo-China (Vietnam, Cambodia). As the Imperial Japanese Navy (IJN) advanced west into the Indian Ocean, Germans and Italians advanced east across North Africa and the anti-British Indian National Army came into being under Mohan Singh, British Prime Minister Winston Churchill and Free French leader General Charles de Gaulle became convinced that Madagascar and her main port of Diego Suarez (Antsiranana) should be captured to prevent its use as a submarine base by the IJN against the Cape of Good Hope sea routes from Britain to naval bases in North and East Africa, India, Ceylon (Sri Lanka), Burma (Myanmar) and Australia.

Operation Ironclad commenced on 5 May 1942 when Force 121 from the Clyde, Scotland commanded by Major General Robert Sturges arrived off Diego Suarez in conjunction with Naval Force H from Gibraltar commanded by Rear Admiral Edward Syfret. Force H, consisting of the battleship HMS *Ramillies*, two aircraft carriers, two cruisers, eleven destroyers, six minesweepers and six corvettes carried three infantry brigades and No. 5 Commando (12,000 men). The commandos and the 29th Independent Infantry Brigade under Brigadier Francis Festing then successfully negotiated coral reefs and fifty-foot-high cliffs to overcome Vichy French shore batteries at Courrier and Ambararata Bay west of Diego Suarez while HMS *Hermione* created a diversion to the east in Ambode Vahibe Bay. Moving inland under massive air cover from the Fleet Air Arm and land based aircraft of the South African Air Force, the main British invasion (now including two brigades of the British 5th Infantry Division supported by light tanks) followed but ran into determined resistance from around 3,000 Malagasy and Senegalese *Tirailleurs* led by Governor General Armand Annet. Meanwhile, having sailed around the northern tip of Madagascar, HMS *Anthony* steamed into French Bay Harbour, Diego Suarez under heavy fire to deliver her cargo of fifty Royal Marines under Captain Martin Price. The marines according to the official report 'created a disturbance in the town out of all proportion to their numbers' and broke the Vichy defence. Diego Suarez surrendered the following day.

Annet and the majority of Vichy forces escaped south into heavy jungle with Sturges unwilling to immediately follow. Three weeks later three Japanese submarines arrived off Diego Suarez, launching two midget submarines that seriously damaged Ramillies and sank an oil tanker before, in November, Operation Streamline Jane, conducted by mainly African troops, completed the British conquest of Madagascar. Any threat from the IJN was additionally diminished by the US Pacific Fleet simultaneous to the invasion of Madagascar at the Battle of Coral Sea and a month later at the Battle of Midway. A build up of military hardware for an October British desert counter-offensive at El Alamein, Egypt could now commence.

6 May 878

Viking
Battle of Edington

IN APRIL 871 Alfred had become King of Wessex on the death of his brother Aethelred. The previous months had seen several indecisive battles fought by Aethelred and Alfred's Saxon *fyrd* (militia) against the 'Great Heathen Army' of Danish Vikings led by Halfdan Ragnarsson and the now dead Bagsecg. Violent Viking raids on Britain had started before the turn of the ninth century but since 839 the Norse and Danish armies had not always returned to their homelands suggesting their dangerous open boat forays across the North Sea were driven as much by economics as pure plunder. The Great Heathen Army had been in England since 865, initially landing in East Anglia before moving north to York and then back again. After six years of violence during which no one was safe, particularly the clergy, the pagan Vikings had gained control of Northumbria, East Anglia and Mercia, Wessex being the only Anglo-Saxon Kingdom holding out and only by way of determined armed resistance. The battles of early 871 had largely been Viking victories but only marginally and certainly indecisively, each time the Saxons able to fight another day. When Alfred lost again at Wilton in May 871 however, the fyrd were close to exhaustion, unable to resist much longer, Alfred agreed a truce with Ragnarsson which probably included a cash payment (Danegeld).

The Great Heathen Army retreated to London in Mercia, still uncomfortably close but with Ragnarsson for the time being concentrating on consolidating Viking authority in Mercia and Northumbria. By 876 the Danes were fully back in control of all England bar Wessex, the wealth of which was again eyed by the new and ambitious Viking commander, Guthrum. Breaking the truce with Alfred, Guthrum attacked far to the south capturing Wareham and Exeter before Alfred again raised the *fyrd* to besiege him in Wareham. After a Viking supply fleet was wrecked off the south coast, Guthrum agreed another truce which saw the Heathen Army retreat to Gloucester. Two years later on 6 January 878, however, the treacherous Guthrum almost certainly in conjunction with a Saxon coup, broke the truce with a cynical attack on Chippenham in the knowledge that the Christian Alfred would be celebrating the Epiphany. Alfred only narrowly escaped.

According to the ninth century Welsh monk Asser, Alfred fled to the marshlands of Athelney where he began a guerilla war against the Danes using the inaccessible bogs as a defence. Asser relates a life of misery, Alfred reduced to foraging raids, begging local peasants for food and reputedly being severely admonished for burning the cakes of a pig farmer's wife. On this low, Alfred received a spiritual visitation from St Cuthbert, the former Bishop of Lindisfarne whose own monastery had been mercilessly sacked by a Viking raid in 793, Cuthbert urging the king to keep calm and carry on.

By early May 878 Alfred had regained enough control of Wessex to again confront Guthrum, summoning the *fyrd* at Egbert's Stone before moving on to Ethandun (Edington). On 6 May 878, Alfred's Anglo-Saxons fought the whole Heathen Army in a bloody shield wall battle lasting all day with great slaughter on both sides, the Danes in particular suffering before eventually breaking and fleeing back into Chippenham where they were besieged for two weeks. On the point of starvation, Guthrum surrendered, agreeing under the Treaty of Wedmore to leave Wessex and convert to Christianity, the former pagan Viking christened Aethelstan with Alfred as his Godfather.

Guthrum/Aethelstan moved back north into what was now the Danelaw, an area north of the Thames including East Mercia (the East Midlands) and East Anglia where his own kingdom developed. In Wessex and English Mercia (West Midlands), which he came to inherit by marrying his daughter to the Ealdorman Aethelred, Alfred began building a system of Burhs (forts or fortified towns including Lundenburh-London) manned by civilians in rotating shifts that successfully defeated a renewed 892 Viking offensive under Haesten. By 918 Alfred's son, Edward the Elder, had reconquered East Mercia and East Anglia before his grandson, Aethelstan, conquered Northumbria in 927. From the marshes of Athelney, Alfred and his lads had united England into one Saxon Kingdom. The Danes, however, were not finished, they would return a century later under their King, Cnut (Canute).

7 May 1709 n.s

War of the Spanish Succession
Battle of La Gudina

EIGHT YEARS HAD passed since the death of Habsburg King Charles II of Spain but the War of the Spanish Succession rumbled on to decide who would rule Spain, Bourbon Philip, Duke of Anjou or Habsburg Archduke Charles of Austria. The Grand Alliance of Britain, the Dutch Republic, Portugal and the Holy Roman Empire commanded by Captain General John Churchill, Duke of Marlborough had already enjoyed stunning victories at Blenheim 1704, Ramillies 1706 and Oudenaarde 1708 but were no nearer preventing a potential future Bourbon unification of France and Spain by getting their man, Archduke Charles, on the Spanish throne. Grand Alliance military gains in the Spanish Netherlands (Belgium, Luxembourg), diplomacy in the Duchy of Milan, Austrian advances in Italy and continued domination of the sea, both Atlantic and Mediterranean, had not been negated by losses in Spain (particularly Almansa 1707) but neither had they been enough to force the Bourbon French, Spanish and Bavarians to the negotiating table.

It was in Italy that the tide turned decisively against the Bourbon cause when the Austrians under Joseph I, Holy Roman Emperor (brother of Archduke Charles) fighting the anti-imperialist Vatican Army forced Pope Clement XI into a favourable peace and recognition of Archduke Charles as King Charles III of Spain. Austrian troops were now free to transfer from Italy for a renewed Grand Alliance effort in both the Low Countries and Spain whilst a particularly harsh winter crippled the French economy. It was too much for Bourbon King Louis XIV of France who sent for terms with the Dutch at Moerdijk. The talks collapsed in April 1709 due to British and Holy Roman insistence that France, by military action if necessary, remove Philip (grandson of Louis) from the Spanish throne. Not only was Louis reluctant but he had little influence over Philip, who regardless of his grandfather's difficulties, was enjoying a relatively easier life in his own kingdom. Louis may have been looking for a way out but Philip certainly was not.

The British had already begun to reinforce Henri de Massue, Earl of Galway in the Iberian Peninsular who joined forces with the Portuguese Joao Mascarenhas, Marquis de Fronteira. Galway had split Grand Alliance reinforcements for a defence of Portugal and Catalonia leaving a combined Anglo-Portuguese Army totaling over 20,000 men now sitting on the Portuguese side of the River Caya short of Badajoz. On the other side of the Caya was the Bourbon Army of Alexandre Maître, Marquis of Bay, 18,000-strong who were pillaging the surrounding countryside in order to hinder any potential Grand Alliance advance into Spain. On 7 May 1709, having been provoked by several Spanish attacks, the Portuguese cavalry accompanied by a significant part of their infantry and against the advice of Galway crossed the Caya onto the plain of La Gudina to begin cannonading Bay's Bourbons.

Realising immediately that the Alliance force before him was isolated, Bay charged unsuccessfully three times before personally leading a fourth to force what was now becoming a nasty habit, the desertion of the Portuguese cavalry along with the loss of several cannon. Galway reacted by advancing three Portuguese infantry battalions to recover the cannon but was soon overwhelmed, himself escaping after having his horse shot from under him but not several of his commanders. The bulk of the British and Portuguese infantry behind, however, stood firm under increasing pressure from Bay's horsemen until Galway brought up British infantry and horse to launch a diversionary counter-attack. This assault was so successful in engaging Bay's forces that the Portuguese infantry managed to disengage for a retreat back across the Caya to Elvas. The British followed but had already suffered losses of 4,000 dead, wounded and captured,

In London, news of the battle did not go down well. Parliament deigned to send the Portuguese no further assistance and instead ordered General James Stanhope in Catalonia and a Naval Squadron under Rear Admiral John Baker to launch speculative attacks on Cadiz and Gibraltar. The attacks did not happen but their threat at least prevented a Bourbon invasion of Portugal. Instead, the quarrel would return to North France and a day that would shock Europe, the bloodiest of the eighteenth century, at Malplaquet.

8 May 1648

English Civil Wars
Battle of St Fagan's

 THE ENGLISH CIVIL War had supposedly ended on 5 May 1646 when King Charles I appeared in the camp of the Scottish Covenanters besieging Newark. The king had given himself up to the Scots because he believed they were more likely to retain the monarchy than Independents who were beginning to gain ascendancy over Presbyterians in the Westminster Parliament. The Civil War had always been fought to limit the power of the king rather than depose him but the Covenanters were happy to take the king from his prison cell in Newcastle back to Scotland only on the condition that he became one of them. With few, if any, cards left to play Charles need only sign the Covenant to save himself but, ever obdurate, he would not.

Further, the English Parliament and the commanders of the New Model Army (NMA) owed the Scottish Covenanter Army payment in arrears for their services during the Civil War, a payment that was duly paid since the Independents now saw the Covenanters as their only possible threat and the Presbyterians saw continued Covenanter presence on English soil as damaging to their own cause. Although the Scots had been conscious to keep separate the payment and negotiations regarding the king, once they accepted the money and refused to maintain Charles it looked very much like the beleaguered king had been sold.

The money paid to the Scottish Covenanters compounded the problems of the Treasury, the war had left the country all the poorer and Parliament could now only pay the Puritan soldiers of the Independent-dominated New Model Army and their many garrisons with increased difficulty. These soldiers, including many officers, were low born, poorly paid and now faced being disbanded short of their arrears. Civilians, particularly in Canterbury had revolted against the 1647 Parliament suppression of Christmas Day and now, in 1648, unpaid garrisons of dubious loyalty followed suit.

Sir Thomas Fairfax and the New Model Army had crushed the 1647 civilian revolts but animosity over religious freedom and the future of the monarchy developed further in early 1648, Parliament's Presbyterians allying themselves with the Scottish Covenanters whilst diehard Royalists again aligned themselves against the hardline Parliament Independents. The Second English Civil War began in Pembroke, Wales, the garrison of which commanded by former Parliamentarian John Poyer was in a former Royalist enclave. Initially campaigning for pay, Poyer soon declared for the king with disgruntled soldiers, enlisted and disbanded, joining him across South Wales. Fairfax sent 1,700 horse and 1,000 infantry under Thomas Horton with Oliver Cromwell following on to check the rebellion which had grown quickly to 7,500 infantry and 500 cavalry, Poyer having been joined by two former Parliament commanders in Rowland Laugharne and Rice Powell. In the knowledge Horton was soon to be supported by Cromwell, the Royalists marched toward Cardiff anxious to do battle with Horton at the earliest opportunity, but they also knew that their huge numerical superiority would count for little against the professionalism of the New Model Army.

At 07.00 on 8 May 1648, Laugharne launched an attack with 500 infantry across the Nant Dowlais stream into the village of St Fagan's where he hoped to catch Horton off guard. The Royalist effort failed dismally as Horton broke up their attack before breaking out of the village into the open fields where Parliament cavalry and dragoons attacked both wings of the Royalists across hedges, ditches and lanes whilst the infantry advanced in the centre. Skirmishing ensued over the broken ground for nearly two hours before the superior arms and discipline of the New Model Army overcame the Royalists who broke and fled leaving 300 dead and 3,000 captured. Laugharne and Poyer fled back to Pembroke Castle where they later surrendered to Cromwell, Poyer to be executed in Covent Garden.

The Second English Civil War spread to Maidstone, Colchester and Preston, the Royalists winning not a single battle. The renewal of fighting and the ultimate Royalist/ Presbyterian defeat only served to strengthen the Independents in their hard line policy against King Charles. After refusing to defend himself at trial, Charles was executed at Whitehall on 30 January 1649. England became a Republic for the next eleven years.

9 May 1915

The Great War
Battle of Aubers Ridge

 IN EARLY 1915 the Central Powers of Germany and Austria Hungary reversed the essential policy of the Schlieffen Plan by now pressing for a decisive victory against Russia on the Eastern Front before any return to the offensive on the Western Front where they were building an impressive, four-hundred-mile-long system of defences from the Channel coast to Switzerland. French General Joseph Joffre wanted to maintain pressure on Germany in the west and together with Field Marshal Sir John French commanding the British Expeditionary Force (BEF) had launched attacks in Champagne and Artois (Neuve Chapelle) with limited success before the Germans counter-attacked with chlorine gas at the Second Battle of Ypres, an attack which failed only due to a lack of men already transferred to the east. Despite offensives against Central Power declaring Turkey on the Gallipoli Peninsular and a shortage of shells, Joffre and French then planned a Second Battle of Artois, another offensive northward designed to cut German rail communications. Joffre would attack with the French 10th Army at Notre Dame de Lorette and Vimy Ridge while to his north, the British First Army under General Douglas Haig would attack Aubers Ridge over the same flat, heavy ground as the attack on Neuve Chapelle two months before.

Haig planned the same intense bombardment as at Neuve Chapelle but was attacking over a wider front and had not been in receipt of any extra guns from the British Second Army of General Horace Smith-Dorrien, a man who was actually seeking a withdrawal from the Ypres Salient altogether. Surprise would also be forfeit since Joffre planned a lengthy French bombardment and worse, the reconnoitering Royal Flying Corps had failed to appreciate the recent huge overhaul of the German defences. The British First Army would now face German trenches protected by twenty-foot-wide breastworks front and back, additional barbed wire, machine-guns firing obliquely across no-man's-land (interlocking fire), support trenches preventing flank attacks and break-ins, a second trench 200 yards back with dug outs, a line of concrete machine-gun posts a further 800 yards back with field artillery on Aubers Ridge supported by heavy artillery further back still, all manned by the German 6th Army of Crown Prince Rupprecht of Bavaria.

At 05.00 on 9 May 1915, the British bombardment from 625 field and heavy guns plus howitzers opened with a mix of shrapnel and high explosive to smash the breastworks but was not accompanied by a planned mine explosion under the German lines because the tunnels had flooded. After half an hour, IV Army Corps under Lieutenant General Henry Rawlinson began the northern part of a two pincer subsidiary attack, initially 8th Division followed by 7th Division who even when forming up suffered casualties from rifle fire coming from German trenches still under bombardment. As Lancashires, Northamptonshires, Sherwood Foresters, Irish and Londoners moved from their cover they then became bogged down in fields of uncut barbed wire where German machine-gunners dramatically increased their misery. Small parties did, however, make it to the German front line only to struggle against ever more determined counter-attacks and were eventually cut off when German artillery fire prevented their retreat back across no-man's-land. Rawlinson was ordered to press the attack but continuing, intense German artillery meant his second wave of troops could not make it even to their own support trenches. To Rawlinson's south, I Corps and the Indian Corps fared even worse, Sussexmen, Northamptonshires, Munsters, Highlanders, Welsh, Meerutis and Gurkhas shelled in their own trenches with those that did make it out into no-man's-land cut down by German machine-gunners, the advance stalling after just half an hour. On news of French successes at Vimy and unaware of the scale of his losses, Haig then ordered a renewed attack, German shelling again inflicting heavy losses in the formation areas. As Guards, Highlanders, Gloucesters, Welsh and Indians advanced into no-man's-land they were again cut down within yards, Haig taking over 11,000 casualties for no gain, most lying dead just yards from their own trenches.

Today's view of the Great War, futile losses caused by incompetent generals, is endorsed by Aubers Ridge and 1915 as a whole but 1915 was not over, French and Haig would push again in September at Loos.

10 May 1307

Anglo-Scottish Wars
Battle of Loudoun Hill

KING EDWARD I at last seemed to have Scotland firmly under control after a ten year struggle. In 1291 the English king had been asked to arbitrate on a dispute for the Scottish throne but had since insisted on remaining Lord Paramount of Scotland and that his choice, John Balliol, pay him homage as his liege Lord, an intolerable state of affairs for almost all Scots. In 1296, having been replaced by a council of twelve compatriots, Balliol abdicated, spending a period languishing in the Tower of London before exile and custody in France at a residence belonging to Pope Boniface VIII. Since 1301, as the struggle for Scotland raged on, the former Scottish king lived in Picardy playing no further part in the cause for Scottish independence while two other strong claimants for the Scottish throne remained prominent, John 'Red 'Comyn, Lord Badenoch who was related to King Edward by marriage and Robert the Bruce, 7th Earl of Annandale and of Carrick who inherited his father's claim in 1304. Having played politics for a decade but now finding himself directly in line for the Scottish throne, Bruce was once again intent on promoting Scotland's independence from England and in the knowledge that his rival Comyn would never agree, murdered him at GreyFriars Church, Dumfries in 1306. Bruce was then quickly crowned King of the Scots at Scone before that same year an English retaliatory army led by Comyn's brother-in-law, Aymer de Valence, routed Bruce at Methven. Bruce was outlawed by Edward, excommunicated by the Pope, his captured accomplices (who included his brother Niall) executed, and his wife and daughters imprisoned as a reign of terror swept Scotland. When he was given a further beating at Dalrigh by the Macdougalls, Bruce fled Scotland for the Hebrides, Ireland and possibly Orkney where he was reputedly inspired by a spider before beginning a Scottish tale equivalent to that of England's Alfred the Great (though Alfred was only ever King of the West Saxons, never of all England).

In spring 1307 Bruce returned to his own Earldom of Carrick, Ayrshire where every stronghold was held by the English. He immediately suffered yet another setback when his surviving brothers Thomas and Alexander and their small army of Irishmen were annihilated at Loch Ryan, Galloway by Dungal Macdouall on behalf of Edward, both brothers executed at Carlisle. Realising his only advantage over the English was his knowledge of the terrain and that the local population was at least sympathetic to his cause, Bruce then began a guerilla war similar to that of William Wallace a decade before, raiding English supply columns, burning crops and hiding livestock. After ambushing Valence's cavalry force at Glen Trool, Bruce moved north gathering further support before Valence again caught up with him at Loudoun Hill, east of Kilmarnock.

Valence (now the Earl of Pembroke) and his 3,000 men heavily outnumbered Bruce's 600, an advantage which Bruce sought to negate by the terrain of the battlefield. Pembroke could only approach Bruce's army over a bog and a narrow meadow bound on both sides by a wide marsh, a hazardous approach the danger of which Bruce further increased by digging ditches to his front. On 10 May 1307 an undeterred Valence began the Battle of Loudoun Hill with a full frontal attack up the steep slopes towards the Scottish spearmen who, seeing the English struggling in the heavy ground, ran down to meet them with a charge of their own. A fearsome mêlée of lance, sword, spear, axe and dagger raged, the more heavily armoured English knights struggling in the mud. As the Scots began to prevail it was the rear ranks of Pembroke's force that departed the field first leaving their immobile forward ranks isolated to face a rout. Valence escaped to Bothwell Castle but had lost several hundred men whilst Bruce's losses were light.

The Battle of Loudoun Hill is recorded in a rhyming chronicle by John Barbour (1320–1395). The Scottish victory won Bruce new adherents but a greater boost he would receive just two months later when King Edward I of England, 'Hammer of the Scots', died at Burgh by Sands, Cumbria on his way to Scotland. The new King of England Edward II was no coward but he was not his father. Bruce would spend seven years waging a guerrilla war on both sides of the border before meeting Edward at Bannockburn.

11 May 1745

War of the Austrian Succession
Battle of Fontenoy

THE WAR OF the Austrian Succession arose when Charles VI, Holy Roman Emperor, (Austria, Bohemia, Hungary, Croatia, Serbia) died leaving the throne to his daughter Maria Theresa. Maria's inheritance was, however, challenged under Salic Law by Prussian King Frederick II who invaded Silesia. A series of alliances then meant Austria, Britain, Hanover, the Dutch Republic and Russia stood against France, Prussia, Spain and Bavaria with the conflict spreading across the globe from North America to India. In Europe, British involvement had been notable at the 1743 Battle of Dettingen when King of Great Britain George II's Pragmatic Army fought its way out of a French 'mousetrap'. The French then planned an invasion of England led by the Italian speaking Catholic Jacobite, Bonnie Prince Charlie 'the Young Pretender' whose chances of success were relatively slim. To prevent it the French coasts, both Atlantic and Mediterranean, were blockaded by the Royal Navy but a strategic defeat off Toulon in February 1744 left the defences weakened, indeed just two days later the English coast was only spared a Catholic invasion when yet another 'protestant wind' wrecked Charlie's fleet. The Jacobites would try again but their threat paled into insignificance compared to that threatening Austrian interests on the Continent – by 1745 Prussia had 80,000 troops in Bohemia whilst France had 90,000 in the Austrian Netherlands (previously the Spanish Netherlands, now Belgium and Luxembourg). In response Prince Charles of Lorraine, commanding the Austrians, retreated from the Netherlands to defend Austria, defeating a Franco-Bavarian Army at Pfaffenhofen but in doing so allowing the Marshal of France, Maurice de Saxe, Count of Saxony to resume the French conquest of the Netherlands with a siege of Tournai protected by his main force at Fontenoy.

The Allies of the new Quadruple Alliance (Britain, Austria, Hanover and the Dutch Republic), led by George II's twenty-four-year-old youngest son Prince William, Duke of Cumberland, marched from Brussels through dismal weather to arrive near Tournai on 9 May 1745. Saxe left the besieging force to contain

Tournai's garrison whilst he arranged his main force of 50,000 men with 100 guns on a concentrated front at Fontenoy, his left protected by the Wood of Barré and his right by the River Scheldt.

In similar strength (mainly Dutch and British), Cumberland began the Battle of Fontenoy on 11 May 1745 with an ineffective long-range artillery barrage against well entrenched French positions before assaulting both flanks. On the British right Brigadier General Richard Ingoldsby had specific orders to take the Redoubt of Eu whatever the cost, whilst on the left the Dutch would tie down the French around Fontenoy allowing Cumberland's infantry in the centre to finally overwhelm them. Ingoldsby, however, hesitated despite intensified artillery support whilst the Dutch, having been devastated by musket volleys, retired to spectate. Undeterred, Cumberland continued with his main infantry advance but the narrow front put him at the mercy of French guns to his front and the unscathed Redoubt of Eu to his right. Cumberland brought up his own guns, both sides now firing at close range, the British advancing in perfect close order, arms shouldered, until they reached the top of a ridge facing the French Guards just thirty yards distant. Charles, Lord Hay politely doffed his hat as he introduced both sides to each other before the French volleyed weakly. The British reply was the first volley of their advance and it devastated the French front line, the British volleys then continuing as each rank stepped through the one in front to fire. Saxe reacted by sending forward his cavalry to restore the French position but they were repulsed, Saxe attacking again with the elite *Maison du Roi* (cavalry) and with cannon from the flanks. The continued French counter-attacks, however, eventually forced the British into a defensive semicircle in which Cumberland's men bravely stood firm but, increasingly exposed to French artillery and musket fire, were forced to withdraw around their colours before make a fighting retreat protected by their own cavalry, they had lost over 10,000 men.

The French took the Austrian Netherlands and Cumberland returned to face Bonnie Prince Charlie at Culloden. Ingoldsby faced a Court Martial. After all the bloodshed, Maria Theresa remained Holy Roman Empress by the 1748 Treaty of Aix-La-Chapelle but Austrian power would diminish to the benefit of Prussia. It would be they with whom Britain would side in the next war – the Seven Years' War – in just nine years' time.

12 May 1780

American War of Independence
Siege of Charleston

THE AMERICAN WAR of Independence had swung heavily against the British in 1777 and 1778 but they had themselves largely to blame. Indecisive orders from the very top in London had contributed to a disastrous surrender at Saratoga, a retreat from Philadelphia back to New York as well as prompting the entry of France and Spain into the war on the side of the American Patriots. General George Washington's Continental Army had also spent the 1777–78 winter at Valley Forge under Prussian tuition to become a far more formidable opponent and with morale soaring had then bottled up most of the British Redcoats in New York and Rhode Island. King George III, however, was not about to relinquish his thirteen colonies; at the end of 1778 British command changed the point of attack further south where Major General Sir Archibald Campbell took Savannah, Georgia before fighting off several American and French attempts to retake it.

In December 1779 Commander-in-Chief North America Henry Clinton with a force of nearly 14,000 soldiers and sailors in over one hundred vessels commanded by Vice Admiral Marriott Arbuthnot then left New York bound for Charleston, South Carolina to open another front in an area where there was believed to be significant loyalist support, especially on the indigo, rice and tobacco plantations. The Americans, however, had no small garrison in Charleston and could also call on support from ten heavily armed warships and forty cannon from Fort Moultrie at the northern entrance to the harbour. After a thirty-eight-day sea voyage, racked by storms which blew the British fleet to all parts, including Ireland, Clinton did not initially attack Charleston harbour, instead landing his army under Lieutenant General Charles, Lord Cornwallis on James Island across the Ashley River to the south of the town. Cornwallis then made his way inland across mosquito and snake infested swamps, skirmishing with American defenders until he crossed the Ashley onto the Charleston neck, the Americans retreating back into Charleston itself whilst outside and under heavy artillery fire the British began digging in 800 yards from their defences but soon moved up to a mere thirty yards.

To the seaward side of Charleston, the stubborn American defence did not materialise since Commodore Abraham Whipple retreated to the Cooper River at first sight of the Royal Navy before scuttling almost his entire fleet. Just Fort Moultrie was left to resist but before Arbuthnot sailed into Charleston harbour, Cornwallis began completing a fifty-mile-radius encirclement of the city to the north. The American commander Brigadier General Benjamin Lincoln, under pressure from the Charleston's locals, now made the tactical error of pulling more men into an impossible defence rather than getting them out but he did have defended positions at Monck's Corner and Lenuds Ferry to keep his communications open. Not for long though, both positions soon attacked and overrun by British flying columns under Colonel Banastre Tarleton which allowed Cornwallis to complete his encirclement. Lincoln was now in a desperate position, he had been under artillery bombardment from the south and west for several weeks and whilst he had replied with spirit – harassing his besiegers with several sorties – he had little hope of relief. Fighting along the defences now intensified until on 11 May the Americans repulsed a determined effort by Hessians under Captain Johann von Ewald. To gain victory Clinton had not flinched at upsetting the inhabitants of New York State and neither did he flinch now at upsetting those of Charleston, forcing the issue that night, 12 May 1780, by firing red hot shot into the wooden town. Lincoln quickly asked for terms of surrender.

Initially the British were unaware of the scale of their victory and were wholly unprepared for the 6,500 American troops that marched out of Charleston. The majority were released upon their word that they would not take up arms again against the king but Clinton denied Lincoln the honours of war. Charleston was worth a fortune in goods, shipping, firearms and cannon but whilst an initiative had been gained in the southern states, it was a huge area for an army to control that had previously not ventured more than fifteen miles from the Royal Navy. A good deal richer, Clinton sailed back to New York leaving the task to Cornwallis.

13 May 1568

Marian Civil War
Battle of Langside

KING HENRY VIII of England's attempts to unite the two Crowns of Scotland and England had failed by the time of his death in 1547. Scottish Catholics emboldened by the 'Auld Alliance' with Henry's enemy King Francis I of France had repudiated the Treaty of Greenwich that would have ensured a marriage between Henry's son Edward, the Prince of Wales and Mary I, Queen of Scots. The marriage would have hopefully ended centuries of Anglo-Scottish aggression but Henry, furious at Scottish duplicity, was not to throw in the towel, embarking on a 'Rough Wooing' which included a burning of Edinburgh in an attempt to bully the Scots back into the treaty. Henry's ally against France, Charles V, Holy Roman Emperor, then weakened Henry's position by suddenly negotiating his own peace with Francis leaving the English alone but successful in a defence of Boulogne and in defeating a French invasion fleet in the Solent. Following Henry's death, Edward Seymour, Lord Protector of England took up the cause of Anglo-Scottish unification to decisively defeat the Scottish regent James Hamilton, Earl of Arran at Pinkie Cleugh but the late Henry's worst fears were soon realised in 1548 when Arran agreed Mary's betrothal to the Dauphin of France, also Francis. Mary then spent the next eleven years at the French court, becoming Queen Consort of France in 1558, King Francis II of France also becoming King Consort of Scotland.

In 1553 King Edward VI of England then died prematurely leaving Lady Jane Grey to be convicted of high treason before Queen Mary I of England embarked upon a five-year-reign of terror, burning nearly 300 Protestants during a Catholic Restoration. Following Mary's premature death in 1558, her husband Philip, the King of Spain, proposed marrying the incoming Protestant Queen Elizabeth I. At a time of unparalleled religious intolerance both Protestants and Catholics disapproved – the latter because they believed Elizabeth, born to Henry VIII's second wife, Anne Boleyn, was illegitimate and that the Catholic Mary, Queen of Scots, as a legitimate grand-daughter of Henry's sister Margaret Tudor, held a stronger claim to the English Crown. Following the death of her French husband Mary, Queen of Scots returned to Scotland in 1561, itself a powder keg of religious intolerance, but on failing to secure a marriage with Don Carlos of Spain and declined by Elizabeth's favourite Robert Dudley, Earl of Leicester, married her first cousin, the Catholic Henry Stuart, Lord Darnley. The decision infuriated Protestants and Catholics alike since no Papal dispensation had been given. The marriage, however, did not survive Darnley's murder of Mary's Private Secretary David Rizzio before Darnley himself was murdered, possibly by James Hepburn, Lord Bothwell who Mary then married. The scandal was too much, denounced a murderer and an adulteress, Mary was forced to abdicate in favour of her infant son King James VI (likely born to Darnley), whilst James Stewart, Earl of Moray became regent. Imprisoned in Loch Leven Castle, Mary's sympathetic gaoler helped her escape, and with the support of a multitude of bishops, lords and 6,000 men she made for Dumbarton.

On 13 May 1568, Moray was waiting to intercept Mary at Langside, South Glasgow, just yards from what is now Hampden Park Football Stadium. Predicting Mary's route through a narrow lane, Moray lined the hedges and houses of the village with musketeers under Sir William Kirkaldy of Grange while the rest of his 4,000 strong army formed a line around the village. Archibald Campbell, Earl of Argyll, commanded the Queen's forces but the impatient Claude Hamilton, son of Arran, immediately tried to force his way through. Initially staggered by intense fire from Kirkaldy's musketeers, Hamilton advanced to the top of the hill only to meet 600 of Moray's pikemen. An epic struggle of 'push of pike' then raged with Moray's right flank under pressure before the alert Kirkaldy called in his reserve led by Sir William Douglas. Hamilton continued fighting but Argyll's Highlanders behind him not only failed to support but instead made good their escape. The battle lasted barely forty-five minutes but though losses were light Mary had been routed, she escaped by fishing boat across the Solway Firth to Carlisle Castle.

Mary was held in luxurious custody for the next eighteen years until convicted of treason, the death warrant signed by Elizabeth herself. On 8 February 1587 Mary was beheaded at Fotheringhay Castle, an execution that would further ignite Anglo-Spanish animosity. In 1603 Mary's son James would at last unite the crowns of Scotland and England.

14 May 1264

Baron's War
Battle of Lewes

WHEN ENGLAND'S KING John signed Magna Carta in 1215 the King's Council gained powers to check the extravagances of the Crown as they saw fit, in particular taxation. Henry III ascended the throne just a year after his father had reluctantly signed the document, confirming his own recognition in 1225 and again on every occasion that he requested a tax raise. Although Henry had designs on recovering lands in France by military conquest it was architecture and the building of castles and palaces at home that were the extravagances his Council would eventually check. Not only that but Henry increasingly employed 'foreigners' at his court, something that would have been unremarkable a few years before but, since England was now beginning to define herself as a distinct nation following 200 years of Norman conquest, the policy aroused suspicion and envy amongst Henry's 'English' Barons.

One such foreigner, Simon de Montford (whose father had been instrumental in the mass genocide of Albigensian heretics and Jews in southern France) had inherited the Earldom of Leicester in 1229 increasing baronial suspicions even before he secretly wed Henry's sister Eleanor in 1238. Henry, however, was also furious since Eleanor's marriage should have been a matter of state. De Montford evaded arrest by fleeing to France, returning in the 1240s only once his and Henry's relationship had improved. By the 1250s, Henry was again demanding money to pay for the Kingdom of Sicily for his second son Edmund, his relationship with De Montford again deteriorating when the earl introduced the Provisions of Oxford further limiting the king's powers. With baronial support the pious De Montford was now so convinced of his own self-righteousness against Henry's extravagances that he led a coup d'état in 1263, Henry retreating to the Tower of London whilst his unpopular Queen Eleanor of Provence was pelted with stones from London Bridge as she attempted to escape to her son Prince Edward, 'Longshanks' (on account of his height). The queen was eventually forced to seek sanctity in St Paul's Cathedral.

England now degenerated into the Second Barons War, both sides campaigning for support throughout the country before facing each other on 14 May 1264 on the South Downs outside Lewes. King Henry's Royalist Army was approximately 10,000-strong including 1,500 cavalry and at least twice the size of De Montford's baronials but the latter held the high ground overlooking the town. De Montford, commanding from a cart with a broken leg, split his force into four divisions, three in front commanded by his son Henry de Montford, William of Montchensy and Nicholas Seagrave with himself commanding the reserve behind. Henry split into just three, himself and Prince Edward commanding the centre, William de Valence, Earl of Pembroke and John de Warenne, Earl of Surrey the right and Richard of Cornwall the left.

Hostilities began when De Monford's Baronial forces attacked royalist foragers at dawn prompting Prince Edward to lead a cavalry charge against Seagrave's fragile Londoners on the left of the baronial line. The Londoners duly broke and fled but as so often in medieval battles Edward did not turn to attack the exposed Baronial flank but instead continued the pursuit and rout of the Londoners for a full four miles. Meanwhile De Montford's main body of knights, men-at-arms and archers advanced downhill to engage the Royalists in a bloody mêlée of hand to hand fighting. On the king's left, Cornwall faltered almost immediately but the king's centre held firm until De Montford sent in the Baronial reserve. By the time Prince Edward returned to the battlefield he was horrified to see that the Royalist Army had not completed the expected rout but were themselves being routed. It was too late to counter-attack, the battle was beyond recovery with King Henry hiding in a local priory.

Henry had no option but to sue for terms, agreeing the imprisonment of Prince Edward as a guarantee for his own conduct. For a year England became more or less a republic but Edward would not stay captive for long. After a daring escape in May 1265 the prince would lead another Royalist Army against De Montford whose own popularity had waned disastrously. In August 1265 the struggle would be resolved at Evesham.

15 May 1464

Wars of the Roses
Battle of Hexham

IN THE FIFTEENTH century the character of the English was not viewed as it is today but rather as a nation of hotheads capable of delivering both highly-organised society and extreme violence, the latter typified by a century of warfare with France which had not even come close to exhausting the English nobility's propensity for a fight. Indeed failures in France at the end of the Hundred Years' War led to an internecine feud between Richard Plantagenet, Duke of York and Edmund Beaufort, Duke of Somerset which, by 1460, had left both men dead; the Wars of the Roses. If the rest of Europe then expected the scale of English violence to relent they were to be further astonished in March 1461 when the death toll reached an all time British high at Towton, up to 20,000 men, almost one per cent of England's population, lying dead on the battlefield or in a twenty square mile area covered by the pursuit. Towton had, however, been the decisive victory sought by Edward, Duke of York (son of Richard) who was subsequently crowned King Edward IV at Westminster. Correspondingly the defeat had come as a crushing blow for King Henry VI of the House of Lancaster, especially since his wife Queen Margaret of Anjou had scored a significant victory at St Alban's only weeks earlier over Edward's chief ally Richard Neville, Earl of Warwick. Several of the king's loyal nobles, however, had escaped Towton including Henry Beaufort, Duke of Somerset (son of Edmund) and Henry Holland, Duke of Exeter as well as the king and queen who headed for Scotland.

Margaret then made her way to France and the court of King Louis XI of France, promising to return the English town of Calais, of which Warwick was the Captain, in return for armed support. She returned to Scotland with 1,000 Frenchmen before sailing for Bamburgh but whilst half of Northumbria quickly came under Lancastrian control it was felt Scottish reinforcements were needed to maintain momentum. The indefatigable queen sailed back north to find them only for disaster to strike when her fleet was hit by a storm marooning many of the French on Lindisfarne Island where they were annihilated by Yorkists. In 1463, with assistance from King James III of Scotland, Margaret yet again marched into Northumbria seizing several castles only to again be repulsed this time by Warwick and his brother John Neville, Lord Montagu. Henry's prospects looked bleak and they became bleaker still when Somerset defected to be not only pardoned by Edward but taken into his inner Court. Everyone was stunned but such was Yorkist resentment for his previous depredations that on narrowly being spared a lynching from locals in Northampton, Somerset realised he had little alternative but to return to Henry's and the Lancastrian cause. Somerset made his way to Bamburgh where he attempted once again to lead a Northumbrian Lancastrian uprising and sabotage peace talks between Edward and the Scots.

Montagu's Yorkists also headed north to York before successfully holding off Somerset at Hedgeley Moor in April 1464. Somerset's Lancastrians then regrouped at Alnwick before moving up the River Tyne to Hexham, any hope of a Lancastrian uprising depending on a decisive victory over Montagu before Edward's main army could arrive. Somerset was again given his chance when Montagu marched his 4,000 Yorkists out of Newcastle in pursuit but such was the latters speed he took by surprise Somerset's perhaps only 500-strong force at Linnel's Bridge over the Devils Water (a tributary of the Tyne) on the morning of 15 May 1464. Appreciating Lancastrian discomfort, Montagu ordered an immediate Yorkist attack from high ground above the river valley at the sight of which the Lancastrian right under Thomas, Lord Roos turned and ran into the Devil's Water behind leaving Somerset's predicament desperate. A brief fight raged before the Lancastrians were overwhelmed and thrown back into the river, Somerset attempting to fight his way out on horseback before being knocked down and running with the rest of his men. He was soon found hiding in a cottage, taken to Hexham gaol and, along with Roos, was beheaded in the town square the following day.

The hapless King Henry VI was again captured and returned to the Tower of London. Lancastrian resistance collapsed allowing Edward to enjoy a few years of peace before he alienated his right-hand man, Warwick. The latter would become the 'kingmaker' when he too defected to the House of Lancaster in 1470.

16 May 1811

Napoleonic Wars
Battle of Albuera

IN A DIRECT reference to the Royal Standard of the United Kingdom of Great Britain and Ireland, Napoleon Bonaparte, Emperor of the French and ruler of virtually all Europe had declared 'the hideous leopard contaminates by its very presence the Peninsula of Spain, let us carry our victorious eagles to the Pillars of Hercules (Gibraltar)'. That was in 1809 after France had overcome Prussia, Russia and Austria allowing Napoleon to bring his forces in the Iberian Peninsular up to 325,000 men, battle-hardened veterans of Ulm, Austerlitz, Jena-Auerstadt, Friedland and Wagram. The Anglo-Portuguese Army of 50,000 men under Lieutenant General Sir Arthur Wellesley, Viscount Wellington and unlimited numbers of Spaniards rebelling against the French occupation and imposition of a French king (Napoleon's brother Joseph) had held on but only by their fingertips. Wellington had retreated first in 1809 from Talavera, Spain and again in 1810 from Busaco, Portugal to the defensive Lines of Torres Vedras, Lisbon whilst in Spain partisans desperately held out at Badajoz and Cadiz, the British at Gibraltar.

The French advance into Portugal had, however, run into serious difficulty outside Lisbon and with no navy to supply him Marshal André Masséna had been forced to retreat north after a miserable five month siege. In an effort to support Masséna, Napoleon had ordered Marshal Jean de Dieu Soult, besieging Cadiz to march north into Extremadura but although Soult knew the task to be perilous he advanced his *Armée d'Andalusie* to take Spanish-held Badajoz opening the southern route into Portugal between the Sierra Morena and the mountains of Toledo. He was, however, four days too late for Masséna who was now on the run back to Ciudad Rodrigo, vigorously pursued by Wellington who, for good measure, despatched General William Beresford south with 20,000 men to cover the new threat from Soult. Soult had a threat of his own, his departure from Cadiz left Marshal Claude Victor understrength and consequently defeated at Barrosa by Lieutenant General Thomas Graham. To restore the situation south, Soult garrisoned Badajoz before beginning a round trip to Andalusia, arriving back in the vicinity of Badajoz with 25,000 men only to find his path to the town now blocked by the Anglo-Spanish-Portuguese Army under Beresford and the Irish Spaniard, Lieutenant General Joaquin Blake, 30,000 troops in a defensive position facing east in the hills from Santa Marta to Albuera.

On 16 May 1811 Soult launched a feint attack north on Albuera with infantry under General Nicolas Godinot supported by cavalry and an artillery barrage. The feint worked perfectly as Beresford and Blake moved units to support the King's German Legion in the village. Meanwhile Soult swung two divisions of infantry and a cavalry brigade to his left for the main attack through olive groves against Spaniards on the allied right. Beresford ordered Blake to turn his line to face the new flank threat on his right but Blake moved only four battalions under Jose de Zayas y Chacon to face the two French infantry divisions advancing in column. Unsurprisingly De Zayas quickly gave ground as all but Godinot now joined the massed French attack but crucially the Spaniard held long enough for Beresford, who decided to act himself rather than continuing to plead with Blake, to bring up British, Portuguese and Spanish reinforcements for devastating exchanges of musket volleys that rocked both sides. A hail storm then rendered the use of muskets impossible but the battle raged on as both sides charged with the bayonet. Out of the storm then appeared French and Polish cavalry charging British infantry under Lieutenant Colonel John Colborne and Beresford's HQ but, in conjunction with De Zayas, the attack was held before being driven off by dragoons under Major General William Lumley. Casualties were mounting on both sides but Soult advanced yet another infantry division in column supported by artillery to attack Major General Daniel Hoghton's battalion standing in line, the resulting exchanges of musket again devastating both sides, Hoghton killed with two thirds of his men casualties, the battle totaling possibly 17,000 casualties, most of them French .

The two armies held their ground the following day, Soult then retreating to combine forces with Marshal Auguste Marmont before returning to relieve Badajoz a month later. The following year, 1812, would be the pivotal year of the Napoleonic Wars, Badajoz would not be spared another bloodbath.

17 May 1943

Second World War
The Great Dams of Germany

SINCE THE SUMMER of 1942 Soviet Secretary General Josef Stalin had urged British Prime Minister Winston Churchill to open a new front against the Axis Powers in the west. Since then the British 8th Army had counter-attacked in Egypt, Anglo-American forces had landed in Morocco and Algeria and on the Eastern Front the Russians had counter-attacked at Stalingrad. By May 1943 the Allies were planning to invade Italy but in the meantime there was to be no let up in pressure on Axis forces or their supporting industries. Over 1,000 British and American bombers now raided Germany but with minimal accuracy and at a high cost.

Of specific targets the British Air Ministry had identified Germany's great hydro-electric dams in the Ruhr Valley as far back as 1937 but, with no bomber capable of carrying a load that could compensate for the lack of accuracy, any attack was deemed futile. That was until British engineer Barnes Wallis developed an idea skipping marbles with his daughter across the garden pond into a spinning 9,250 pound explosive mine 'Upkeep'. Nineteen modified Avro Lancaster bombers of 617 Squadron commanded by the twenty-four year old Wing Commander Guy Gibson were to take off from RAF Scampton, fly at sixty feet over the North Sea, Holland and Germany, avoid electricity pylons, concentrations of flak and enemy night fighters to release their Upkeeps at exactly 232 mph, still at an altitude of sixty feet, 450 yards from the face of the Mohne Dam and, if successful, the Eder and Sorpe Dams. Upkeep would bounce over the torpedo nets, hit the dam wall, sink and detonate via hydrostatic pistols, breaching the dam to cause catastrophic flooding – Operation Chastise.

Flight Lieutenant Bill Astell hit electric cables over Germany leaving Gibson to arrive over the Mohne Dam shortly after midnight on 17 May 1943 with the first wave of now eight Lancasters. Though coming under fire from twelve anti-aircraft guns Gibson 'liked the look of it', coming round a second time to drop his Upkeep which exploded fifty yards from the wall but failed to breach. Flight Lieutenant

John Hopwood was then hit on his approach, dropping his Upkeep late to destroy the power station below the Dam before climbing sharply, giving his crew a chance to escape before his Lancaster exploded (two survived). Flight Lieutenant Micky Martin then approached with Gibson to starboard drawing German fire but Martin's Upkeep bounced left. With Gibson again to starboard Squadron Leader Dinghy Young followed to deliver perfectly, the mine exploding against the dam wall but seemingly still not breaching (Young was shot down returning). Gibson and Martin then drew fire to either side as the Lancaster of Flight Lieutenant David Maltby flew in, his mine hitting left but the Mohne was already disintegrating, releasing 8,800 cubic metres of water per second to produce record floods fifty miles distant, farmland, bridges, roads, houses, factories and fish stocks all swept away. Gibson radioed Wallis and Air Officer Commanding-in-Chief RAF Bomber Command Arthur Harris as the remainder of the first wave continued to the Eder Dam, the second wave of five Lancasters now flying directly to the Sorpe Dam.

At the Eder, Flight Lieutenant David Shannon unsuccessfully delivered after several dummy runs before Squadron Leader Henry Maudslay dropped his Upkeep too late and was brought down by his own explosion. Flight Officer Les Knight then made a precise approach breaching the Eder to send a thirty foot wall of water down the valley, flooding 300 miles distant. Just one Lancaster of the second wave (Flight Lieutenant Les Munro, Pilot Officer Geoff Rice both damaged whilst Pilot Officer Vernon Byers, Flight Lieutenant Bob Barlow had been shot down) now arrived at the Sorpe Dam, Flight Lieutenant Joe McCarthy flying parallel to the dam dropping his Upkeep at the tenth attempt from thirty feet smashing the top but failing to breach. The third wave of five Lancasters was now airborne, Pilot Officer Warner Ottley and Lewis Burpee shot down but Flight Sergeant Ken Brown located the Sorpe in heavy mist to increase the damage done by McCarthy. Flight Sergeant Bill Townsend then unsuccessfully attacked the Ennepe Dam, whilst Flight Lieutenant Cyril Anderson failed to find a target.

The Dambusters Raid caused short-term damage to Germany. Even Stalin sent his congratulations but for Wallis, inconsolable at the loss of fifty-three airmen, a telegram from his daughter Mary meant more, 'Hooray Wonderful Daddy'. Gibson received the Victoria Cross but he did not survive the war.

18 May 1944

Second World War
Battle of Monte Cassino

AS FIRST LORD of the Admiralty, Winston Churchill had been the chief proponent of the 1915 Dardanelles Campaign; an attempt to knock Turkey out of the Great War, which had ultimately resulted in a bloodbath on the Gallipoli Peninsular and achieved only Churchill's resignation. In 1944, now as British Prime Minister, Churchill was intent on a similar tactic, an Allied invasion of Italy, whereas United States President Franklin D. Roosevelt preferred an invasion of France. The two settled for a compromise, Italy followed by France. Credence was then given to Churchill's belief that Italy was the Axis' 'soft underbelly of Europe' as soon as the British 8th Army crossed the Straits of Messina from Sicily and the US 5th Army landed at Salerno, the Italians surrendering immediately. German Field Marshal Albert Kesselring, however, followed his brilliant evacuation of Sicily by securing Rome and retreating the German 10th Army of Heinrich von Vietinghoff to a naturally strong defensive position stretching across Italy north of Naples, the Winter Line. Winter was in fact three lines, Bernhardt, Gustav and Adolf Hitler (later Senger) which hinged on the town and monastery of Monte Cassino. In a taste of what was to come the Bernhardt Line held up the US 5th Army for six weeks before they were joined by the British X Corps of Lieutenant General Richard McCreery for an attack on the Gustav Line, Lieutenant General Mark Clark commanding the Americans with no time to rest since the Landing Craft required for a flank attack at Anzio were also needed for the invasion of France.

The first British attack on 17 January 1944 failed but conveniently prompted Kesselring to reinforce his front lines from Rome. Three days later the US 36th Division attacked on the British right but were unable to move armour across the Rapido River and consequently suffered heavy casualties. Further right still the US 34th Division and Free French moved across the upper Rapido for a three week battle of endurance until stopped outside the sixth century Benedictine Monastery of Cassino which towered 1,700 feet above San Angelo, gateway to the Liri Valley and Rome. Clark's Anzio landing was now put into effect by the US 6th Corps but Major General John Lucas, with no comprehension of urgency, critically halted the operation to consolidate his bridgehead which allowed Kesselring to contain him.

At Cassino, New Zealanders and Indians of the British 8th Army replaced the Americans for a second effort. Commander-in-Chief of the Allied 15th Army Group Harold Alexander, believed the defenders to be using the Monastery and controversially ordered it to be destroyed by 229 USAAF bombers but succeeding only in killing 230 civilians, no Germans and enraging the Vatican. Royal Sussex, Gurkhas and Rajputs of 4th Indian Division then advanced up Snakeshead Ridge against the German 1st Parachute Division who did now move into the monastery remains whilst Maoris assaulted the town of Cassino. All were repulsed.

A third Allied effort began in March with an impressive artillery barrage and aerial bombing of Cassino town which allowed New Zealanders and Gurkhas some gains. Meanwhile Gurkhas below the monastery on Hangman's Hill awaited reinforcements from the Essex Regiment before advancing up Castle Hill. Determined German counter-attacks ended the effort with both sides again suffering heavy casualties.

Alexander now waited for British 8th Army reinforcements and better weather. On 11 May, 1,700 Allied guns hammered German positions across a twenty-mile front before twenty-eight infantry divisions of the US 5th and British 8th Armies attacked for a fourth time. British engineers forded the Rapido River to give the British 4th and Indian 8th Divisions armoured support against intense machine-gun fire. In bitter fighting the British bridgeheads across the Rapido withstood furious German counter-attacks while to the north Poles took Snakeshead Ridge despite fearful losses. Alexander now brought up the British 78th Infantry Division which broke into the Liri Valley aided by flanking Free French in the mountains. With the road to Rome open the German position now became untenable forcing Kesselring and Vietinghoff to retreat. At 09.00 on 18 May 1944, the Poles covered the last few yards up to the ruins of the once great monastery.

One of the bloodiest battles of the Second World War, Monte Cassino cost the Allies over 50,000 men. On 4 June 1944, Clark liberated Rome but in so doing allowed Kesselring to retreat to the Gothic Line. Two days later an Allied assault in Normandy, France would decisively alter the course of the twentieth century.

19 May 1652 o.s

Anglo-Dutch Wars
Battle of Goodwin Sands

THE ENGLISH NAVY had developed in the late sixteenth century under cousins John Hawkins and Sir Francis Drake principally as a weapon against Catholic Spain, but by 1605 the two bitter adversaries were at peace. In 1625 war with Spain again broke out when Maria Anna of Spain refused to marry the about to be King Charles I, the three Kingdoms of England, Scotland and Ireland joining with the fellow Protestant Dutch Republic who were in the midst of their own Eighty Year War against Spain. The next five years exposed the shortcomings of the now somewhat neglected English Navy and yet left the Dutch so powerful, particularly in the Baltic and East Indies, that Charles sought to curb their power with Spanish assistance. At home Charles' relations with Catholic Spain did him no favours with his increasingly antagonistic Protestant Parliament, the joint Anglo-Spanish exercise however left in tatters in 1639 when Dutch Admiral Maarten Tromp defeated the Spanish at the Battle of the Downs, finishing Spain as a major naval power.

The Dutch then passed a decade developing huge merchant fleets to trade in the Atlantic and Indian oceans, the South China Sea and the Pacific while the English, Scots and Irish fought themselves in a series of three bitter civil wars. In 1650 civil war then threatened the Dutch as William II, Prince of Orange, son-in-law of King Charles I of England, fought with the Dutch States General (Parliament) for control of the Dutch Army. In the now Commonwealth of England, Oliver Cromwell's Parliament, aware of obvious Orange sympathy toward the displaced English monarchy (the future King Charles II) and dispossessed English Royalists, sought to unify the Dutch with the English as a single Protestant state that could dominate world trade (Parliament had rebuilt the Navy during the Civil War). The Dutch refusal went down badly with English Parliament which, with an 'either with us or against us' attitude, reacted by passing the Navigation Acts preventing Dutch shipping from using English ports, allowing English pirates to harass Dutch shipping, continuing to claim sovereignty of the sea up to the Dutch coast and, as 'Lords of the Sea', insisting that, when in the presence of an English ship, all foreign shipping pay tribute by lowering their colours.

On 19 May 1652, off Dover, Tromp failed to pay tribute with due haste to English General-at-Sea Robert Blake (the acknowledged founder of British naval power over and above Hawkins and Drake). The previous day Nehemiah Bourne and nine English ships mainly ranging between thirty and forty guns had been lying in the shelter of the Downs when Tromp's forty-two strong fleet came into view heading for the Goodwin Sands, many ships on both sides carrying guns cast at the Horsmonden Ironworks, Kent. Tromp sent two ships to Bourne, duly saluting his flag and explaining that he too was merely seeking shelter. Bourne acquiesced insisting that Tromp depart as soon as the opportunity arose but sent warning of a potential Dutch attack to Blake in his flagship, the 60-gun *James*, and his thirteen-strong fleet in Rye Bay. Blake began to sail north-east toward Dover requesting Bourne join him. The following morning Tromp was as good as his word and departed toward Calais before, perhaps to protect a Dutch convoy, turning about and heading back toward Dover. Also now approaching Dover, was Blake who caught sight of Tromp's return and fired a warning shot for the Dutchman to lower his colours, Tromp declined. At 16.00 Blake's third warning shot hit Tromp's flagship, the 54-gun *Brederode*, the Dutchman replying with a broadside before the respective vanguards engaged in ragged line astern. The Dutch vastly outnumbered the English but were inferior in fire power and additionally had to contend with Bourne's approach from the north-east attacking their rear. A fierce battle of broadsides raged for several hours on into the night with Kentish fishermen sailing to assist. By morning the English had captured two Dutch ships but the *James* had taken seventy shots to the hull and rigging, losing her mizzen mast with forty men dead or wounded.

Tension increased, Blake sailed north to intercept a Dutch East Indies convoy whilst Sir George Ayscue attacked a Dutch convoy off Calais before Tromp and an eighty-two strong Dutch fleet intervened. Tromp then sailed north after Blake but was scattered by a storm. On 10 July 1652, the English Parliament officially declared war on the Dutch Republic, the first of three wars fought entirely at sea in a race for world trade.

20 May 1941

Second World War
Battle for Crete

BRITISH PRIME MINISTERS William Cavendish-Bentinck, Duke of Portland and Spencer Perceval had supported the 1809 deployment of the British Army to Portugal from a position of desperate isolation but had gone on to eventually defeat Napoleon Bonaparte's France.

In 1941, from a similar position, British Prime Minister Winston Churchill now looked to support Greece against an ominous build up of German forces in the Balkans coming to the rescue of Chancellor Adolf Hitler's ally, the Italian Dictator Benito Mussolini. In October 1940, Greek dictator Ioannis Metaxas had declined Mussolini's invitation to surrender with a firm 'Oxi! (No)' before forcing half a million Italians back to Albania. In North Africa also, Mussolini had been forced out of Egypt by Major General Richard O'Connor and the Western Desert Force but with Tripoli and an end to the Desert War in sight, O'Connor and his superior General Archibald Wavell were ordered by Churchill to transfer Australians, New Zealanders and British for the dubious defence of Greece after a March 1941 coup d'état in Belgrade, where the German ambassador was abused, had given Hitler an excuse to invade the Balkans.

The Greeks continued to fight tenaciously, defending on the Metaxas Line in Thrace and Macedonia whilst most of their troops were still in Albania but the collapse of the one million strong Yugoslav Army exposed the route into Greece via the Monastir Gap. The deficiencies of the position were then brutally exploited by the crack German SS Leibstandarte Adolf Hitler Division, the Greeks unable to retreat to the Aliakmon Line as expected by the British with consequences that led to the defence of Greece collapsing completely.

British orders to evacuate from Athens and the Peleponnese to the island of Crete were given on 22 April with troops still fighting a chaotic retreat southward. The German High Command however continued to pursue with the added incentive that a further invasion of Crete would consolidate southern Europe and put German oil fields at Ploesti, Romania beyond the reach of the Royal Air Force.

Initially concerned at the presence of the British Mediterranean Fleet, Hitler was initially doubtful that it could be done but was won over by the sheer audacity of a planned airborne attack by the paratroops of General Kurt Student.

On 20 May 1941, two waves of Messerschmidt 109 fighters strafed British positions around Xania and the Maleme airfield, the second accompanied by Junkers 88 and Dornier 17 bombers on whose tail arrived fifty gliders full of German assault troops who were greeted by a hail of British anti-Aircraft and small arms fire. As the battle erupted the clear blue Mediterranean sky was then blackened with hundreds of Junkers 52 transports which began dropping the first of 7,000 Paratroops. East of the Maleme airfield New Zealanders took a terrible toll on the hapless descenders but enough survived in the west to begin forming an attack on Hill 107 from the dry Tavronitis river bed. Fierce fighting developed in Xania and Suda Bay with civilians joining the bloodlust on stricken Germans before another flight of 2,000 Paratroops arrived in the late afternoon further east over Rethymno and Heraklion. Lieutenant Colonel Ian Campbell led Australian and Cretans at Rethymno and Brigadier Brian Chappell the British 14th Brigade and Greeks at Heraklion in counter-attacks that, by the following morning, had overwhelmed the German paratroops. Back at Maleme however Major General Bernard Freyberg VC commanding allied forces was convinced that an imminent German seaborne invasion was about to occur and hesitated to counter-attack. Worse, a misunderstanding between Brigadier James Hargest of the 2nd New Zealand Brigade and Colonel Leslie Andrew commanding his 21st Battalion, led to a withdrawal from Hill 107. The German Storm Regiment now under Major Edgar Stentzler took full advantage so that a forlorn Student back in Athens was suddenly delighted to hear his Junkers could now land, albeit under a galling fire, on the extreme western edge of the Maleme airfield. Too late Freyberg ordered his counter attack. The build up of German troops with overwhelming air support then continued remorselessly, eventually forcing the British and Commonwealth troops south for another evacuation on 28 May, this time to Egypt. The 12,000 British troops left on Crete were taken prisoner.

The four-year German occupation of Crete saw spirited local resistance met with brutal atrocities. The Germans suffered heavy casualties in the battle itself, 6–8,000 but more critically their Greek campaign had delayed Operation Barbarossa, the German invasion of Russia, by thirty-eight days.

21 May 1940

Second World War
Battle of Arras

FRENCH DEFENCE STRATEGY following the Great War began disintegrating as soon as they failed to react to German Chancellor Adolf Hitler's 1936 reoccupation of the Rhineland. The inaction frightened Belgium into declaring neutrality leaving the French Army trapped in North East France behind their own magnificently expensive but purely defensive Maginot Line, whilst in the North West the French could not now advance through Belgium. Worse, France's predicament was realised by Russian Secretary General Josef Stalin who served his own short-term interest by signing the 1939 Molotov-Ribbentrop Non-aggression Pact with Hitler, despite the pair being ideological enemies. Stalin and Hitler agreed to divide Poland; Germany invading on 1 September 1939 with 2,750 Tanks, 2,315 aircraft, 9,000 guns and sixty infantry divisions combining in lightning attacks on Polish military and civilian targets, Blitzkrieg. In 1938 Britain and France had shamelessly abandoned Czechoslovakia but they now honoured obligations to Poland by declaring war on Germany.

While Poland was being ransacked French Commander-in-Chief Maurice Gamelin remained inactive despite facing negligible opposition in Germany's south, preferring instead to wait for the British Expeditionary Force (BEF) whilst he touched up the Maginot Line. Crucially Gamelin also failed to coordinate with Belgium whose neutrality he refused to violate. On the German defeat of Poland a 'Phoney War' then continued over the freezing winter of 1939–40, Hitler anxious to attack in western Europe but informed by Commander-in-Chief Walter von Brauchitsch that the Wehrmacht (German Armed Forces) had not recovered from their Polish exploits. The delay was used, however, by General Erich von Manstein to plan a radical assault, a copy of which fell into Allied hands only for a disbelieving Gamelin to remain convinced that Germany would copy the 1914 Schlieffen Plan – a right hook through Belgium.

On 10 May 1940, Gamelin appeared justified when German General Fedor von Bock's twenty-nine-division-strong Army Group B including 4,500 Paratroops under General Kurt Student attacked the Netherlands and General Gerd von Rundstedt's thirty-five-division-strong Army Group A attacked Belgium, taking the massive Fortress of Eben Emael by glider attack in a single day. Only now did Gamelin move troops north into Belgium according to the Dyle Plan, including the nine-division-strong BEF under General John Standish Surtees Prendergast Vereker, Lord 'Tiger' Gort VC, GCB, CBE, DSO & Two Bars, MVO, MC but Gamelin had been hopelessly outmanoeuvred. As the Allies moved north a forty-five mile wide left hook from Von Rundstedt's seven Panzer (1,500 tanks) and three motorised divisions crashed through the supposedly impenetrable Ardennes Forest, breaking through weak French defences at Sedan on the River Meuse as German execution matched planning; the Wehrmacht reaching the English Channel on 20 May 1940.

Coordinated Allied resistance under French General Gaston Bilotte disintegrated, indeed Gort received no orders for eight days. Winston Churchill visited Paris to instill some fight, Gamelin was sacked for General Maxime Weygand and a service was held in Notre Dame Cathedral, Paris – in centuries bygone so often for French deliverance from the English but now from the Germans. Gort was not a man inclined to retreat, indeed he had been mentioned in dispatches no less than eight times during the Great War, but even he was considering withdrawing the BEF when Chief of the Imperial Staff General Edmund Ironside suddenly ordered a counter-attack north of Arras on the exposed right flank of German General Erwin Rommel's 7th Panzer Division, the French 1st Army to also attack from the south. On 21 May 1940, the BEF attacked in two columns but, instead of the originally planned two divisions, with just two battalions of Durham Light Infantry plus 74 Mark I and Matilda tanks under Major General Giffard Martel. As Gort suspected, the French failed to attack at all. Strafed by the *Luftwaffe*, the right hand column of Durhams advanced in fierce fighting through to Berneville and Wailly before being halted by the crack German SS Totenkopf Division. The left column meanwhile advanced ten miles through Dainville destroying a German motorised column and anti-tank batteries as well as inflicting heavy casualties as far as Wancourt, the shaken Rommel personally involved in directing every German gun available in the belief he faced five British divisions. Short of Infantry and soon in danger of encirclement Martel however was forced to withdraw.

The British counter-attack at Arras shocked the German High Command sufficiently to induce unnecessary caution. Gort, however, realised the French were beaten, outflanked on his right and with Belgium collapsing on his left he ignored orders, withdrawing the BEF to Dunkirk but in need of a miracle.

22 May 1455

Wars of the Roses
Battle of St Albans

THE HUNDRED YEARS' War between England and France had ended in 1453 with the loss of all English possessions in France save Calais. England's King Henry VI of the House of Lancaster had at nine years of age become the only English king to be crowned King of France due to the efforts of his father, King Henry V, and his Uncle John, Duke of Bedford but military conquest had not been Henry's forté, rather art and architecture, his weak rule on coming of age overseeing a complete English collapse. Bitter recriminations over the losses in France abounded in England, none more so than between Richard Plantagenet, Duke of York and Edmund Beaufort, Duke of Somerset. The rivalry between the feuding pair was also fuelled by York possessing a claim to the throne of England perhaps stronger than that of King Henry – by King Edward III's second surviving son, Lionel, Duke of Clarence rather than Henry's claim through the third son, John of Gaunt, Duke of Lancaster (in 1399 Henry's grandfather Henry IV had usurped the throne from Richard II). York was also sidelined to Lord Lieutenant of Ireland whilst Somerset, closer to Henry's court, profited handsomely from the offices lavished upon him.

While the relationship between York and Somerset disintegrated so too did law and order as thousands of soldiers returned from defeats in France to find employment scarce. As had Wat Tyler in 1381 so had Jack Cade led a revolt in 1450, demanding the dismissal of Henry's profligate courtiers and a return to prominence of York but, much to Somerset's advantage Cade was hunted down following a day of rioting on London Bridge. Owed huge sums by the Crown, York was facing ruin but on the final 1453 English defeat in France (Castillon) King Henry suffered a complete mental breakdown, leaving the House of Lords to appoint York as Lord Protector rather than have England in the hands of Henry's French Queen, Margaret of Anjou, an aghast Somerset sent to the Tower albeit largely for his own protection. A degree of order returned to England for sixteen months until January 1455 when Henry's sanity also returned. Shortly after his release Somerset persuaded the King to hold a Great Council of the Realm at Leicester. York had every reason to believe he would fare very poorly.

The Wars of the Roses began not just as a personal feud between Somerset and York but also between the powerful northern families of the Percys, headed by Henry Percy, Earl of Northumberland (son of Harry Hotspur) and the Nevilles, headed by Richard Neville, Earl of Salisbury and his son Richard Neville, Earl of Warwick. Somerset and Northumberland joined the king heading for Leicester whilst York, Salisbury and Warwick wrote to him of their displeasure at being excluded. Complete with armed retinues, the King continued regardless to St Albans for a rendez-vous with John De Mowbray, Duke of Norfolk and John De Vere, Earl of Oxford before continuing to Leicester. York, Salisbury and Warwick, however, were aware that there would be at least a day between the arrival of the king's separate parties and planned a *coup de main*.

King Henry with 2,000 Lancastrians approached St Albans in the early morning of 22 May 1455 to receive reports of Yorkist forces in the area. Replacing Somerset, a notoriously poor soldier, with Humphrey Stafford, Duke of Buckingham, Henry pressed on into St Peter Street at 09.00 only for York to spring the trap, barricading both ends of the street before sending a herald to the king for Somerset to be handed over. York, however, received the response 'to void the field' or face a hang, draw and quartering, Buckingham and the king believing him to be bluffing but barricading themselves in the town centre nevertheless. At 10.00 York then dispelled all thoughts of a bluff by attacking from the north whilst Warwick attacked from the south-east through gardens between the Keys and Chequers Inns in Holywell Street. The King's Lancastrians scrambled for their armour as they were hit by arrows before engaging in a vicious hand-to-hand mêlée of sword, axe and dagger. Henry was wounded in the neck by an arrow and retreated to a tanners cottage whilst Buckingham fled to the Abbey. Somerset then became surrounded in the Castle Inn but defiantly came out fighting when York's troops began to batter down the doors, he was killed by a poleaxe but not before taking down four Yorkists with him.

York, Salisbury and Warwick swore loyalty to King Henry and an uneasy truce would last four years. It would break at Blore Heath and Ludlow with York, Salisbury and Warwick defeated at the latter and fleeing. Warwick would return to England in 1460 to face a Lancastrian Army at Northampton.

23 May 1706 n.s

War of the Spanish Succession
Battle of Ramillies

THE WAR OF the Spanish Succession had been caused by the death of the childless King Charles II of Spain bequeathing his inheritance to Philip, Duke of Anjou. That a Habsburg should do such a favour for a Bourbon upset the balance of power in Europe since Philip was the grandson of Bourbon King Louis XIV of France and could now potentially inherit both the kingdoms of France and Spain. The ruling House of Habsburg in Vienna headed by Leopold I, Holy Roman Emperor was naturally most upset that Spain had not come the way of Archduke Charles of Austria (Leopold's son) and formed a Grand Alliance to right the wrong principally with England and the Dutch Republic against France, Spain and Bavaria. Leopold's diplomacy soon paid as France and Bavaria looked likely to overrun Austria following victories at Friedlingen in 1702 and Hochstadt in 1703 only for John Churchill, Duke of Marlborough to record a stunning Grand Alliance victory at Blenheim in 1704. The Grand Alliance, however, failed to press home the advantage gained largely due to the reluctance of the Dutch who would not denude their defences and Germans who instead sent troops to aid Prince Eugene of Savoy in Italy. The hesitation allowed the resourceful King Louis to consolidate French possessions in the Spanish Netherlands (Belgium, Luxembourg) and in 1706 successfully take the offensive in both Alsace, north-east France and Italy. Since Blenheim, Marlborough had been unable to bring Louis to a decisive battle, Louis unwilling to risk another defeat but now desiring a significant French Bourbon victory to at the very least conclude a favourable peace settlement. He pressed his generals accordingly.

On 23 May 1706, Marlborough's Scouts and the Hussars of Francois de Neufville, Duke de Villeroi, at the head of armies both 60,000 strong, ran into each other near Ramillies in the Spanish Netherlands. Riding forward to observe the French drawing up impressively in a semicircle on a ridge across a four mile front, Marlborough immediately recognised the weakness of their position. The French right was anchored by the village of Taviers and the River Mehaigne and the left by the village of Autre-Eglise behind the Petite Geete stream, not only was it too long but with the baggage train immediately behind, units could not easily be moved.

At 13.00 Grand Alliance artillery began firing as Dutch Guards advanced toward Taviers, driving Bourbon Swiss before them before initiating a bloody battle in the village. Simultaneously, Field Marshal George Hamilton, Earl of Orkney and English Redcoats advanced across the Petite Geete towards Autre-Eglise taking heavy casualties from concentrated volley fire but forcing back opposing Walloons. Now exposed to a counter-attack from Maximilian Emanuel, the Elector of Bavaria, Marlborough ordered a protesting Orkney to withdraw. In the centre the alliance infantry of Dutch, Saxons and Scots then attacked the village of Ramillies itself but met strong resistance from French, Bavarian and Irish defenders. Marlborough reinforced the effort on Ramillies with Orkney's so far unused British and Danes but Villeroi had not noticed and was continuing to move troops to his left flank. As additional support for the Alliance attack on Ramillies, the Dutchman Henry de Nassau, Lord Overkirk advanced his cavalry south where they were met by the Maison du Roi, elite French horsemen who broke up the attack. Marlborough himself now rode forward to rally the Dutch only to be unhorsed but was saved by Major General Robert Murray and his Protestant Swiss (the same could not be done for Marlborough's equerry who lost his head to a cannonball). The centre was now a vast cavalry battle with Marlborough's numbers gaining the advantage, Villeroi only now moving more cavalry from Autre-Eglise. It was too difficult and too late, the Dutch and Danes broke through the French lines to the north of Taviers and began to roll up the French right flank. In Ramillies too the Alliance broke through sending the French Bourbon Army into a retreat that became a rout, Villeroi and the Elector narrowly escaping, they had lost near 20,000 men. The Grand Alliance just 3,500.

The Grand Alliance took territorial advantage in the Spanish Netherlands but again could not force a decisive victory against stubborn French defences. The British would use an alliance with King Pedro II of Portugal to launch an assault in Spain that would culminate at Almansa the following year.

24 May 1941

Second World War
Battle of the Denmark Strait

THROUGH THE SUMMER of 1940 the Royal Air Force had succeeded in preventing the German *Luftwaffe* from gaining air superiority over the British Isles, eradicating the chances of an imminent German cross Channel invasion. *Luftwaffe* attacks on RAF airfields had reduced but British cities and areas of industrial production had come under increasingly intense bombardment as German Chancellor Adolf Hitler sought to bring about the collapse of the British economy. Whilst the people of Britain suffered attack from above so too did they from attacks on their diet as German U-boat 'wolfpacks' replicated the submarine warfare of the Great War to take a terrible toll of merchant shipping heading to and from British ports, the ports themselves of course also bombed. Before the outbreak of the Second World War Britain had imported 22 million tons of food per year but by late 1940 the tonnage was down to 12 million, the Government of Prime Minister Winston Churchill urging Britons to 'Dig for Victory'. Churchill fretted, later claiming 'the only thing to really frighten me was the U-boat peril' and that 'It is terrifying, if it goes on it will be the end of us'. In early 1941, however, the British predicament looked even worse, with virtually every Royal Navy capital ship already engaged in convoy protection an additional menace began appearing in the Atlantic, the German battlecruisers *Scharnhorst* and *Gneisenau*, the heavy cruiser *Admiral Hipper* and the pocket battleship *Admiral Scheer*, the two former sinking sixteen British ships in just two days. It would, however, prove to be the high point for the Kriegsmarine since their previously unbreakable cyphers were soon penetrated following the capture of two Enigma rotors and codebooks in a raid on the Lofoten Islands, a breakthrough capitalised upon when HMS *Aubretia, Bulldog* and *Broadway* forced U-110 to the surface capturing a prized Enigma machine in tact. German Admiral Karl Donitz would soon be questioning his security when U-boat successes plummeted but before then, two more German surface vessels powered out into the North Atlantic, the heavy cruiser *Prinz Eugen* and Germany's greatest battleship, the *Bismarck*.

Despite poor weather the two German warships were spotted by heavy British cruisers HMS *Norfolk* and *Suffolk* which allowed the battleship *Prince of Wales*, the pride of the Royal Navy but flawed battlecruiser HMS *Hood* and six British destroyers to form an intercepting cordon in the Denmark Strait, north-west of Iceland. At just past 00.00 on 24 May 1941, the shadowing *Suffolk* lost contact with the German pair, Vice Admiral Lancelot Holland on HMS *Hood* turning south-west with the *Prince of Wales* while the destroyers searched north. At 03.00 Suffolk regained contact with both *Bismarck* and *Prinz Eugen* thirty-five miles to the north of *Hood*. Holland closed on an unfavourable line, firing from his forward guns at the lead German ship which he incorrectly believed to be the *Bismarck*. On realising his error Holland then changed target, recording two hits with minimal damage whilst a third struck *Bismarck* below the waterline causing mechanical damage, flooding and a consequent list. On board Admiral Gunther Lutjens held fire until Kapitan zur See Ernst Lindemann exclaimed, 'Im not letting my ship get shot out from under me. Open fire!'. *Hood* was soon hit on the boat deck starting a fire before being struck near the bridge and on the radar. Holland turned *Hood* to port bringing his aft guns to bear as she was straddled by two 15-inch shells, a third crashing into the main mast and X turret striking the magazine. A huge flame erupted from the ship's centre followed by a huge explosion that ripped her in two, just three of the 1421 crew surviving as Britain's greatest warship sank in minutes. *Prince of Wales* was having problems of her own, her guns had jammed and she had received seven hits. Better protected than *Hood* she remained in tact though disengaged. The battle of the Denmark Strait had lasted just seventeen minutes.

Lutjens now shocked the German Admiralty by sailing for St Nazaire, France rather than Bergen, Norway. A row also erupted in the British Admiralty between Admiral John Tovey of the Home Fleet and Admiral of the Fleet Sir Dudley Pound, Tovey offering to appear at a Court Martial. The British public were aghast at the loss of *Hood* but already a Royal Navy reception party was being organised for the *Bismarck* as she headed for France.

25 May 1595

Tudor Conquest of Ireland Battles of Crossdall and Clontibret

TWO CENTURIES AFTER the 1169 Norman conquest of Ireland the Anglo-Irish community had become so intertwined with the native Irish that English culture, customs and law had to be reasserted by the Statutes of Kilkenny. Gaelic speaking 'English' Lords were to learn English and ride a horse in the English fashion whilst the Irish were forbidden to attend English churches or their minstrels and storytellers perform in English places. Intermarriage was also forbidden and for the defence of Ireland, England's vulnerable western flank, 'the use of plays, horling and coiting' were banned in favour of archery and 'lance throwing'. Any person practising otherwise would suffer attainder. Whilst Englishness had been maintained in 'the Pale' around Dublin it had not in the provinces where Anglo-Irish nobles acted outside the feudal system. The Hundred Years' War and the Wars of the Roses then distracted a succession of English kings from Ireland until the sixteenth century when the Irish Parliament in Dublin urged Henry VIII, King of England and now Ireland, to show a stronger hand.

Henry began a Tudor Conquest in which the Irish nobility retained their lands and attended Parliament upon fealty to Henry. English law and customs were then implemented across Ireland as well as the religion of Henry's new Church of England, Anglicanism. As England's relations deteriorated with Catholic Spain during the second half of the sixteenth century the need to secure Ireland became more acute but the consequent intrusion into Catholic Gaelic life was contested, first in Munster and Connaught where the Fitzgeralds of Desmond rebelled twice before Fiach O'Byrne followed suit in Leinster. By 1583 the English Lord Deputy of Ireland, Baron Grey de Wilton, had ruthlessly put down the rebellions with a scorched earth policy, a massacre of Papal troops at Smerwick and a man hunt for Gerald Fitzgerald, Earl of Desmond. Munster then underwent a plantation of English Protestant settlers. In more isolated Ulster anglicisation was slower but in 1594 produced the same result, a rebellion by Catholic-Irish clans ultimately headed by Hugh O'Neill, Earl of Tyrone. O'Neill had been looking to gain the Presidency of Ulster before realising that it was his angry brother-in-law Henry Bagenal who was favoured by Queen Elizabeth I.

O'Neill decided to add to an eviction of English sheriffs begun by Hugh Roe O'Donnell by attacking the English Fort at Monaghan. Bagenal however reacted promptly by marching with 1,750 men, mainly infantry, from Dundalk to the garrisons relief. Having left Newry on 25 May 1595 Bagenal's column approached Monaghan coming under attack from 800 of O'Neill's men waiting in ambush at Crossdall, four miles from the destination. Fired upon from both sides by O'Neills surprisingly well-drilled musketeers, Bagenal's combination of battle-hardened veterans and green recruits held off the Irish in a running battle to reach Monaghan with light casualties. Having resupplied the garrison, however, Bagenal faced the return trip short of ammunition, setting off on 27 March via a more southerly route. O'Neill was hardly wrong-footed, attacking Bagenal from the outset on ground that promised and duly delivered an ambush in the pass at Clontibret. Again fired upon from both sides Bagenal began taking much heavier casualties as his column came to a three hour standstill, desperately holding off the now 4,000 Irishmen with a series of limited cavalry charges. Bagenal's pikemen were then forced into attacking when ammunition became critical before another cavalry charge narrowly failed to kill O'Neill but did at least give the English a chance to force their way out of the pass. Exhausted after eight hours of fighting Bagenal, with one hundred men dead, led his survivors onto Ballymacowen Hill and a defensive position for the night. O'Neill, however, short of ammunition himself, failed to attack and retired back north. Bagenal's column was relieved the following morning by reinforcements from Newry.

O'Neill was encouraged by King Philip II of Spain who sent a Second Armada in 1596 that met the same fate as the first, destroyed by protestant storms in the Atlantic. The Irish rebellion spread to Munster as the English poured in reinforcements under Robert Devereux, Earl of Essex making the Nine Years' War in Ireland the Tudor dynasty's biggest conflict. Matters would come to a head at Kinsale in December 1601.

25 May 1921

Anglo-Irish War
Battle of the Dublin Custom House

NO SOONER HAD the Great War finished than Great Britain faced armed insurrections in Mesopotamia (Iraq) and Ireland. In the former, fatwas and mass demonstrations against recently imposed British rule turned violent whilst closer to home Ireland's centuries old struggle against British rule did likewise. Frustration at Home Rule for Ireland, delayed for decades by the Houses of Commons and Lords at Westminster and for four years by Germany's Kaiser Wilhelm II, had prompted a misjudged 1916 Easter Rising in Dublin but a landslide 1918 Sinn Fein General Election victory across Ireland. Sinn Fein leader Eamon De Valera, spared execution after the Rising, believed this mandate gave his party the right to go beyond Home Rule for full Irish Independence and by what ever means necessary. Indeed violence broke out the day of the inaugural meeting of Sinn Fein's, at the time, illegal independent parliament, the Dail Eireann, and quickly spread across Ireland to Connacht and Munster. With no hope of defeating the British Army, the Royal Irish Constabulary (RIC), its Auxiliaries (ADRIC) and the Temporary Constables (Black and Tans) in set piece battles the Irish Republican Army (IRA) led by Michael Collins attacked soft targets, opponents of independence, the security services and anyone who served them, including tradesmen and shopkeepers.

Ambushes, assassinations, robberies and arson were met with brutal reprisals from the ADRICs and Black and Tans (named Tudor's Toughs after their commander Henry Tudor), bodies regularly found on the roadside as rural southern Ireland became lawless. Though Collins had made significant breakthroughs in intelligence and was winning the propaganda war neither side was winning on the ground, Protestant Ulster was pro Union with Britain and the IRA simply could not match the resources of the British Government. De Valera needed a show of force to strengthen his hand in negotiations that were only now in an embryo stage, and so looked to Dublin where the IRA had so far deliberately avoided confrontations with the 10,000 strong British Armed Forces. De Valera, opposed by Collins, now decided to attack the Dublin Custom House, a building originally for the collection of tax on imports entering Ireland via the River Liffey but now the centre of Local Government.

Around midday on 25 May 1921, 120 men of the 1st and 2nd Battalions IRA Dublin Brigade under Tom Ennis armed with just revolvers began gathering in small groups outside the Custom House. At 13.00 the Custom House was rushed, the small police presence quickly overwhelmed as a lorry load of inflammables, straw, cotton, paraffin pulled up outside. The staff, many of them women, were herded into stone passages but violence erupted when the caretaker tried to telephone the authorities and was shot dead. Then, within minutes of a tip off, three lorries and an armoured car full of Auxiliaries arrived to begin a fierce firefight with IRA pickets around the Custom House. As the gun fight raged along the Liffey another lorry load of Auxiliaries arrived directly in front of the Custom House to be hit immediately with grenades and gun fire starting another fierce firefight outside the building which on the inside was now ablaze. The Fire brigade was en route but ran into yet more IRA groups deliberately delaying their arrival. Meanwhile, outside the Custom House, Auxiliaries and the supporting Royal Wiltshire Regiment poured a relentless fire into the building, the IRA soon running short of ammunition. After half an hour the Custom House was stormed trapping eighty IRA gunmen, five of them dead.

The Old Custom House was destroyed in a five day inferno but the attack was not greeted as a success by the IRA or pro Independence supporters, an historic building had been destroyed for no gain. A truce was called six weeks later, British Prime Minister David Lloyd George offering a self governing Irish Free State under the British Crown with Ulster remaining part of the United Kingdom. The Treaty was agreeable to Collins but not De Valera. Though Collins and former Sinn Fein leader Arthur Griffith won a close vote a divided Sinn Fein and IRA descended into a bitter civil war, Collins killed by Irishmen in 1922. Lloyd George's belief that Northern Ireland would become unviable and be consumed by the Free State has never been realised. The Irish Free State became the Republic of Ireland in 1949, Ulster's determination to resist joining bringing more violence twenty years later.

26 May 1940

Second World War
Evacuation from Dunkirk

IN AUGUST 1939 the defence strategy of western Europe disintegrated when Russian Bolshevik Josef Stalin agreed a somewhat short-sighted Pact of Non-aggression (Molotov-Ribbentrop) with his ideological enemy, Nazi Germany's Adolf Hitler. Sceptical of French assistance in the event of a German attack, Stalin had been bought with half of Poland whilst Hitler was satisfied Germany could now avoid fighting a war simultaneously on two fronts. After overrunning Poland Hitler turned back west, General Erich von Manstein planning a daring May 1940 attack on Holland, Belgium and France. In the meantime French Commander-in-Chief (CIC) Maurice Gamelin had done little to upset the Germans on their southern borders, unwilling to violate Belgian neutrality but confident the German attack would come there in the form of a right hook as per the 1914 Schlieffen Plan. When on 10 May 1940 the German Wehrmacht, the Heer (land forces) and *Luftwaffe* (air force) pounded Dutch and Belgian targets Gamelin at last duly moved Allied forces north including the British Expeditionary Force (BEF) under CIC General John Vereker, Lord 'Tiger' Gort, only to be badly caught out by a left hook, Sichelschnitt (sickle cut), from 1,500 German Panzer tanks crashing through the Ardennes Forest to cross the River Meuse at Sedan.

French defences crumbled as the German Panzers raced across northern France, reaching the English Channel on 20 May but in doing so left themselves exposed to a flank attack by just two British infantry battalions and seventy-four tanks at Arras. Major General Giffard Martel was repulsed but the German command had been sufficiently shaken for Hitler to order a twenty-four-hour halt for a consolidation. New British Prime Minister Winston Churchill and Chief of Imperial General Staff Edmund Ironside continued to press the French for clarity of action but Gort believed them beaten and retreated to the Channel coast. Here Boulogne was already under attack from the 2nd Panzer Division and two days later Calais from the 10th Panzer Division before Hitler issued another halt order, one that arguably changed the outcome of the entire war. Alerted to the German halt by codebreakers at Bletchley Park who had broken the *Luftwaffe* Red Enigma code, Gort entered Dunkirk, building a strong defensive perimeter but nevertheless still in a desperate position. Ironside predicted an escape of just 30,000 troops but Hitler now made yet another mistake, trusting the destruction of the BEF on the Dunkirk beaches to the *Luftwaffe* of Reichsminister of Aviation Hermann Goring.

On 26 May 1940, a day of prayer was held across Britain and the Commonwealth, King George VI attending Westminster Abbey with thousands more listening outside in the rain. Meanwhile, across the English Channel, Operation Dynamo, the evacuation of Dunkirk, began with the Royal Air Force throwing every available plane against the *Luftwaffe* and German positions around the town. At sea a Royal Navy fleet left the Thames Estuary and nearby ports to fetch troops from Dunkirk's harbour and beaches but it was not enough. The Navy now called out for any craft, 800 'little ships', motor boats, yachts, sloops and fishing boats manned by their own crews answering the call. Hitler lifted the halt order but still did not order a full scale attack, Gort's position then eased by strong French resistance at Lille but again dangerously exposed when Belgium surrendered with much of the BEF still struggling to gain the Dunkirk perimeter. Churchill prepared the House of Commons for the worst. Only now did General Georges Blanchard commanding the French 1st Army realise Gort was evacuating, refusing cooperation but by 29 May most of the BEF and French 1st Army had reached the beachhead as the 'little ships', aided by Dutch Shuyts, increased the pace of evacuation despite intense harassment from the *Luftwaffe*. Men were lifted mainly from the harbour mole but also formed long queues out into the cold sea desperate for a boat. The evacuation rate rose to 68,000 on 31 May, Royal Navy losses mounting but mercifully the weather deserting Goring. The last British troops departed on 3 June with another 53,000 French over the following twenty-four hours while their comrades gallantly held off German attacks just a mile away.

Despite 68,000 casualties and the loss of 445 tanks in just three weeks Lord Gort had saved the BEF, 338,000 British and French troops had escaped to fight another day, a 'miracle of deliverance'. Two weeks later Churchill would announce 'the Battle of France is over… the Battle of Britain is about to begin'.

27 May 1941

Second World War
Sinking of the *Bismarck*

ALTHOUGH THE ROYAL Air Force had won the Battle of Britain on 15 September 1940 Prime Minister Winston Churchill's woes were far from over as Britain's major cities and ports then endured night after night of bombing raids that would claim 40,000 lives and leave millions homeless. Hardships multiplied with increased rationing as German U-boats aided by long range Focke-Wulf Condor aircraft savaged merchant convoys heading to Britain, cutting food supplies almost in half. Leading up to New Year 1941 there had at least been some good news from the Mediterranean where Admiral Andrew Cunningham and the Mediterranean Fleet had badly bruised the Italian *Regia Marina* at Taranto and Major General Richard O'Connor commanding the Western Desert Force was driving the Italian Regio Esercito (Army) out of Egypt back toward Tripoli, Libya. British optimism would prove to be short-lived, however, when German Chancellor Adolf Hitler came to the rescue his Italian ally and fellow dictator Benito Mussolini, sending General Leutnant Erwin Rommel and the Afrika Korps to force the British from North Africa whilst Field Marshal Wilhelm List and the German 12th Army attempted likewise in Greece. By May 1941 Rommel had crossed into Egypt, capturing O'Connor in the process and List had taken Athens, the British performing their third major evacuation in a year of war, this time to Crete. It would get worse, command failures on Crete allowed the *Fallshirmjager* (paratroops) of General Kurt Student to gain a foothold at Maleme whilst Cunningham's subsequent desperate attempts to supply the beleaguered British, Anzac and Greek troops was resulting in catastrophic Royal Navy losses.

In the Atlantic too the German U-boats had been joined by their surface fleet, the *Scharnhorst, Gneisenau, Admiral Hipper, Admiral Scheer* and now the *Prinz Eugen* accompanying the world's most powerful battleship the 50,000 ton *Bismarck*. On 24 May, at the Battle of Denmark Strait, Churchill's policy of hunting the Kriegsmarine at every opportunity had then met abject failure when

Bismarck sank the pride of the Royal Navy, the battlecruiser HMS *Hood* with the loss of 1418 men. Accustomed to centuries of naval victories, the British public were in shock but the *Bismarck* had been damaged in the brief exchange and was now making a run for the port of St Nazaire, France. Though the German battleship had evaded HMS *Norfolk* the following day, the very recent Bletchley Park breaking of the Kriegsmarine Enigma Code meant Admiral John Tovey, Commander-in-Chief of the Home Fleet, aboard the battleship HMS *King George V* was aware of her exact position and was bringing every available ship to bear, including Force H from Gibraltar.

To disguise the Enigma breakthrough a Catalina Flying Boat was sent out from Northern Ireland and with remarkable 'luck' spotted the *Bismarck* in the vast expanses of the Atlantic Ocean. Later that evening 26 May fifteen Fairey Swordfish biplanes from HMS *Ark Royal*, flying at just 100 mph into strong winds and a hail of fire launched their torpedoes, critically one fired by Lieutenant John Moffat crippling *Bismarck's* port rudder. As *Bismarck* circled, all attempts to free the rudder failed, Admiral Gunther Lutjens signalling to Berlin he would fight to the last shell. Throughout the early morning of 27 May 1941 *Bismarck* came under torpedo attack from the Tribal Class Destroyers *Zulu, Maori, Sikh* and *Cossack* as well as a Polish Destroyer but was not further damaged. HMS *Rodney* and HMS *King George V* then approached from the west opening fire at 08.47 on the now slow moving and listing German. Struck several times by 14 and 16 inch shells yet only able to return a paltry fire the decisive blow fell when the bridge and forward guns were struck by a 16 inch shell from Rodney. HMS *Norfolk* and *Dorsetshire* added their weight of fire but the fate of the *Bismarck* had already been sealed with 400 hits from 2,800 shells. Scuttled by her own crew she sank with her battle ensign still flying.

More than 2,000 sailors had crewed the *Bismarck*, hundreds of them now in icy Atlantic water. *Dorsetshire* and *Maori* picked up 114 survivors before a U-boat warning (U-74) and the presence of Heinkel and Focke Wulf bombers forced them to abandon the remainder. Churchill and Hitler had both now lost the prides of their navies.

28 May 1982

Falklands War
Battle of Goose Green

ARGENTINA HAD INHERITED a claim to the Falkland Islands on defeating her mother nation Spain in the 1810–18 Argentine War of Independence but the islands had been inhabited for most of the next 160 years by settlers loyal to the British Crown. Lieutenant General Leopold Galtieri then exploded the sovereignty dispute in April 1982 with a full-scale invasion of the islands, temporarily winning support from Argentines previously critical of his ruling military junta but seriously underestimating British resolve.

A hastily convened British Naval Task Force sent to the South Atlantic in response began arriving in a 200 mile Maritime Exclusion Zone around the Falklands on 1 May 1982. Meanwhile Royal Navy vessels already in the area had been reinforced by arriving nuclear submarines and had already recaptured South Georgia and sunk the Argentine submarine ARA *Santa Fe*. Whilst preparing to attack the arriving British task force the Argentine light cruiser ARA *General Belgrano* (named after the hero of that War of Independence) had also been sunk by the submarine HMS *Conqueror* causing Argentina's navy, including aircraft carrier *Vienticinco de Mayo* to return to port, isolating Argentine troops on the islands. All Argentinian air attacks would now be at long range since a Royal Air Force Vulcan had put out of action the only runway capable of accomodating fast jets on the islands, at the capital Port Stanley. Argentine air attacks intensified over the next few weeks, however, as Skyhawks, Daggers, Canberras, Mirages and Super Étendards inflicted serious reverses on the British fleet, notably HMS *Sheffield, Ardent, Antelope, Coventry* and the *Atlantic Conveyor* carrying six Wessex and five Chinook helicopters. The loss of these helicopters would hamper the troops of 3 Commando Brigade who, on 21 May had landed in the area of San Carlos Bay on the west coast of East Falkland. 3 Commando had met little resistance, consolidating a bridgehead, initially advancing no further but as British Naval losses increased, pressure was building for a ground offensive across East Falkland toward Port Stanley, fifty miles away.

On the right of the British advance the Argentines had moved the 12th Infantry Regiment (1,083 men) to garrison the airfield at Goose Green on the two-mile-wide isthmus separating the north from the south of East Falkland. Originally only intending to raid and withdraw, Brigadier Julian Thompson of 3 Commando was now ordered to capture the position, a far tougher prospect for the 2nd Battalion, Parachute Regiment (part of 3 Commando) led by Lieutenant Colonel Herbert 'H' Jones. Jones and 690 paratroops, lacking the helicopters that went down with the *Atlantic Conveyor* now 'yomped' fifteen miles across the desolate, windswept landscape without most of their heavy weaponry and toward an enemy advised of their approach by the BBC World Service.

Once in position at Camilla Creek House, Jones called in Harrier air strikes on Argentine positions in the hills above Goose Green but one Harrier was shot down and reconnaissance units withdrew in the face of heavy Argentine machine gun fire. At 03.30 28 May 1982, A, B, C and D Companies were in position across the isthmus and began the attack with an assault to their left at Burntside House supported by artillery from HMS *Arrow* in Falkland Sound. Argentines fought a delaying action back to Darwin Ridge across the centre of the isthmus as a general British assault developed in fierce hand-to-hand fighting. In poor weather, unable to outflank the Argentine position and bogged down under artillery, machine-gun and sniper fire Jones took the initiative himself with a brave but reckless charge on the Argentine trench – killed by a sniper, he was awarded the Victoria Cross. Now led by Major Chris Keeble, 2 Para continued launching assaults throughout the day against additional Argentine reinforcements as air strikes from both sides added to the chaos until Major Dair Farrar-Hockley and A Company cleared the eastern end of Darwin Ridge, opening the route to Goose Green. Exhausted and short of ammunition but with reinforcements and airstrikes planned for the morning, Keeble speculatively called on Argentine Colonel Italo Piaggi to surrender. Also short of ammunition and concerned that British forces would devastate his position, Piaggi capitulated, a decision that would see him cashiered on his return to Argentina.

2 Para had lost eighty-two dead and wounded but the British right flank had been secured for the main advance against Argentine defensive positions in the mountains before Port Stanley.

29 May 1668

Anglo-Spanish Wars
Sack of St Augustine

HOWARD, HAWKINS, DRAKE and Frobisher had decisively defeated the 1588 Spanish Armada but conflict between Spain and England continued until 1604. King James VI of Scotland and now I of England saw himself as a European peacemaker but, in support of the Dutch Republic, went to war again with Spain in 1624 shortly before his death. His son, King Charles I, then launched an attack on Cadiz resulting in an unmitigated disaster which Charles was happy to sweep under the carpet but his Parliament, when eventually called in 1640, were not. Charles then dissolved Parliament rather than suffer impeachment, initiating a series of disagreements that would end in 1649 with the king losing his head in Whitehall. Oliver Cromwell would then go on to vigorously wage war in Ireland, crushing Catholic Royalist rebellions, before fighting the Dutch for world trade and resuming the English offensive against Spain – Cromwell's 'Western Design'. Targeting Spanish treasure ships and territory for the lucrative sugar trade, Cromwell ordered an expedition to the Caribbean with specifics left to the commanders on the spot. After Hispaniola (Domincan Republic, Haiti) had held out, Jamaica became English in 1655 for the reinforcement of which the governor granted letters of marque to both English sailors and French boucaniers from Tortuga (collectively known as buccaneers) to attack Spanish interests.

The buccaneers profited from their organised attacks and a ready market in Port Royal, Jamaica but, on Cromwell's death and the 1660 Restoration of King Charles II, licensed buccaneering seemed to be at an end. Jamaica, however, remained in English hands despite royal promises to hand it back to Spain, the Governor Edward D'Oyley, asserting English naval power by issuing privateering licenses to the likes of Henry Morgan, Christopher Myngs and Robert Searle. As English state sponsored aggression in the Caribbean again increased, the Spanish ambassador protested in London as Spain still failed to recognise England's claim to Jamaica. King Charles, however, ordered the new Governor of Jamaica Sir Thomas Modyford to cease operations and punish offenders as pirates but the letter only arrived in September 1664 just after Searle and 1,300 Buccaneers had raided Santiago de Cuba, indeed two of Searle's prizes were in Port Royal waiting to be unloaded. Modyford had no option but to comply, returning the ships and booty whilst rescinding Searle's privateering licence. Searle's understandable rage was complete when he also had his rudder and sails confiscated to ensure that he could not put to sea.

In 1665 a resumption of war with the Dutch Republic brought Searle out of unemployment, attacks on Dutch islands included the 1666 sack of Tobago but when this, the Second Anglo Dutch War, concluded the following year Searle's privateering licence was again in doubt. Regarding Spain, there was no official war but nevertheless both sides raided each other given an opportunity. Searle was sailing off Cuba with another vessel when he captured two Spanish ships from whom he likely ascertained the vulnerability of St Augustine, a Spanish settlement on what is now Florida, previously sacked in 1586 by Sir Francis Drake. Taking the Spanish ships with him the English privateer arrived off St Augustine on 28 May 1668, sailing the two Spanish ships closer to identify themselves as merchants, Searle and his men well hidden below decks. Just after midnight on 29 May 1668 Searle's privateers sailed silently into the harbour and were rowing ashore when Corporal Miguel de Monzon, who was out fishing, realised an attack was developing. Despite being shot twice he reached the shore to alert the defenders but it was too late, Searle beginning a twenty hour orgy of violence, killing and looting indiscriminately as the inhabitants ran for their lives to the forest or fort. The English robbed every building in St Augustine, including the church and monastery, before taking seventy women and children hostage in exchange for supplies.

When Searle returned to Jamaica a year later he was arrested by Modyford but had to wait on London as to his fate. While Searle fretted, the Spanish launched several reprisal raids on English possessions which required a punitive counter-attack. Captain Henry Morgan would lead it but Searle and his undoubted qualities were back in demand, their target being at the very heart of the Spanish Main – Panama.

30 May 1942

Second World War
Bombing of Cologne

THE BATTLE OF Britain began in the summer of 1940 with German *Luftwaffe* raids on British airfields, ports and shipping in preparation for a seaborne invasion of the British Isles. The Royal Air Force had however stunned German intelligence by inflicting such heavy losses on 15th September 1940 that German Chancellor Adolf Hitler changed tactics in an attempt to smash British morale with the large scale night bombing of British cities, the Blitz. British Prime Minister Winston Churchill and the RAF however had their own plans. As early as August 1940 Berlin had been attacked by eighty-nine British bombers in retaliation for an 'accidental' German bombing of London and in December 1940 Mannheim had been attacked by 134 British bombers in retaliation for the German bombing of Coventry. The Blitz continued until May 1941 before German attention turned east for an invasion of the Soviet Union but British bombers continued to fly over Germany – for millions of oppressed Belgians and Dutch their Bristol and Rolls Royce engines a source of hope.

As under pressure Soviet Secretary General Josef Stalin began to agitate for the opening of a second front in the west beyond a British bombing campaign, civil servant David Bensusan-Butt produced a report which amongst other statistical horrors reported that only one in ten British aircraft attacking the Ruhr Industrial Area got within five miles of the target they claimed to have bombed. Any notion of precision bombing was then completely forgotten in February 1942 when the British Air Ministry issued Area Bombing Directive No. 5 instructing attacks on German industry by bombing German cities and their working populations. Arthur 'Bomber' Harris, a former bugler of the 1st Rhodesian Regiment, was appointed Commander-in-Chief RAF Bomber Command claiming he could win the war in just months by replacing scattered raids with massive concentrations of bombers in a tight stream. Harris believed he could overwhelm the German aerial defences of the Kammhuber Line and with the use of improved GEE navigation obliterate a single target, preferably the port city of Hamburg but since Hamburg was beyond

GEE range and the weather was poor Harris settled for Cologne, Germany's third largest city, Operation Millenium.

At 10.30pm on 30 May 1942, 1,047 Wellingtons, Stirlings, Halifaxes, Manchesters, Hampdens, Whitleys and new Lancasters began taking off from fifty-three RAF bases. Many of the aircraft were, however, crewed by novices as Harris strained every sinew to make the thousand. Flying conveniently above low cloud over Holland the lead aircraft largely escaped the heavy concentrations of 500 German anti-aircraft guns and searchlights to target Neumarkt in Cologne's city centre on the west bank of the River Rhine. Incendiaries immediately caused a multitude of fires which directed in the streams of British bombers following to attack north and south of the city centre causing 2,500 fires to spread. High explosive then shattered the old medieval city leaving just the cathedral standing tall. In all 868 aircraft flew over Cologne in a ninety-minute period dropping 1,500 tons of ordnance, just the wide streets sparing the population a firestorm. Nevertheless, the fires could be seen over one hundred miles distant. Three hundred acres of the city centre were totally destroyed with bridges, hospitals, gas mains, water mains, electricity cables, tram lines and sewers shattered. Five thousand Germans became casualties, 45,000 were rendered homeless and 150,000 fled the city after the raid. For his part Harris had lost forty-one aircraft to flak, night fighters and collisions

Though hampered by thick smoke from still burning fires reconnaissance following Operation Millenium dramatically demonstrated the increased devastation caused by the concentrated attack. Churchill immediately promised United States President Franklin D. Roosevelt more of the same as the unwritten agreements to avoid bombing civilians proffered by Roosevelt himself in 1940 were well and truly consigned to the dustbin of history. Harris delivered another attack just two days later on Essen and a month later on Bremen but both lacked the destructive power of Cologne. As the USAAF soon began arriving in Britain Harris' scope for more heavy raids would increase further, his first choice target of Hamburg subject to previously unparalleled violence the following year.

31 May 1916

The Great War
Battle of Jutland

GERMANY'S KAISER WILHELM II's attempts to replicate the Naval power of his British cousin King George V had not come to fruition by the 1914 outbreak of the Great War. British First Sea Lord John Fisher had more than matched the development of the Kaiserliche Marine but such was the threat presented by both German arms, the High Seas Fleet and the U-boat Fleet that Fisher suggested it be 'Copenhagenized' in Kiel harbour even before any declaration of war (in 1807 the Danish Navy at Copenhagen had been destroyed by the Royal Navy). Now at war, Britain countered the German threat to the North Sea from Kiel and Wilhelmshaven by stationing the Grand Fleet under Admiral Sir John Jellicoe at Scapa Flow, Rosyth and on the Forth whilst in the English Channel just a line of submarines and mines protected British troop transports heading to France. Any German movement south would, however, be countered by the Grand Fleet sailing to prevent their return.

Once the Kaiser had been defeated off Heligoland in August 1914, however, he had been content with a naval stalemate, maintaining a fleet in being by restricting German naval operations to raids on the English coast in an attempt to draw out and destroy isolated Grand Fleet shipping. The British blockade of Germany was also answered with a minefield and U-boat blockade of the Kaiser's own which in May 1915 resulted in the sinking of the passenger liner RMS *Lusitania*. In early 1916 the Kaiser then intensified German naval policy, allowing the new, more aggressive Commander of the German High Seas Fleet, Admiral Reinhard Sheer, to increase the activity of Vice Admiral Franz von Hipper's battlecruisers. Hipper now sought to draw out larger parts of the British Grand Fleet before attacking them with the remainder of the German High Seas Fleet, U-boats and even Zeppelins, a policy fully endorsed by the Chief of the German General Staff Erich von Falkenhayn who had just initiated the greatest battle of the Great War on the Western Front at Verdun.

On the morning of 31 May 1916, the entire German High Seas Fleet of ninety-nine ships including sixteen dreadnoughts and sixty-one destroyers sailed from Wilhelmshaven, Hipper confident that only the battlecruiser squadron of Vice Admiral David Beatty stationed in the Forth would offer any resistance. British intelligence had, however, already decoded German radio communications so that Jellicoe and Beatty similarly sailed with one hundred and fifty one ships including twenty-eight dreadnoughts, seventy-nine destroyers and a search aircraft carrier. Beatty's sixty-one ships headed Jellicoe with whom he was to combine ninety miles west of Jutland to counter German moves with a concentration in force. At 14.20 Beatty sighted Hipper and in Royal Navy tradition turned south-east to attack immediately but stringing out his force in the process. Hipper turned to lead Beatty onto Scheer's main fleet further to the south-east, both sides exchanging fire, Beatty's HMS *Lion* badly damaged whilst HMS *Indefatigable* and HMS *Mary's* magazines exploded. On sighting Scheer, Beattie then turned for a 'Run to the North' taking on fire from Hipper to his east and Scheer to his south-east but now leading the Germans back onto Jellicoe's Grand Fleet. The battle was hardly going to plan however as HMS *Defence's* magazine then also exploded, HMS *Warrior* was so badly damaged that she later sank before HMS *Invincible's* magazine exploded, the ship going down with Rear Admiral Horace Hood. At 18.30, however, it was German fortunes that turned for the worse, astonished to see Jellicoe's Grand Fleet to his front Scheer immediately disengaged when ten British dreadnoughts opened fire. Jellicoe continued south keeping Scheer to his west blocking the German's return to Wilhelmshaven but under a concentrated fire the German High Seas Fleet began a series of turns amidst a smokescreen, launching torpedoes and a near suicidal battlecruiser attack.

Overnight Scheer doubled back to cross the rear of the Grand Fleet, sightings went unreported and the Admiralty failed to pass on intercepted German radio messages. To the British public's dismay Jellicoe had missed what would turn out to be his only opportunity of the Great War to destroy the German High Seas Fleet. The Royal Navy lost fourteen major ships and 6,000 men at Jutland (twice the tonnage of German losses) but the kaiser could not afford another such encounter and reverted to unrestricted submarine warfare, a decision that would precipitate the entry into the war of the United States of America.

June

"When I saw the enemy draw up and march in gallant order towards us, and we a company of poor ignorant men... I could not but smile out to God in praises, in assurance of victory because God would by things that are not, bring to naught things that are... and God did it."

OLIVER CROMWELL, NASEBY, 1645

1 June 1794

French Revolutionary War
Glorious First of June

IN 1789 FRANCE was ruled by a feudal system and an absolute monarch, King Louis XVI, the last in a long line of absolute monarchs. Despite lacking their own liberty the French had recently incurred huge debts fighting for American liberty against British rule which had brought the country to near bankruptcy. Louis resolved to tackle these debts with new taxes on the upper classes but the upper classes resisted, insisting Louis call, for the first time since 1614, the Estates General, an assembly of clergy, nobility and commoners. However, just as King Charles I of England had been reluctant to call Parliament over a century before so now hesitated Louis, causing unrest to spread through the non aristocratic 98 per cent of society, the Third Estate, who had already suffered more than their fair share of poor harvests and high taxes. Louis relented but dissent within the Estates General led to an evermore confident Third Estate forming their own National Assembly. Louis moved troops to Paris intent on crushing the Assembly but merely added to existing commoners fears of lawlessness – the 'Great Fear' of 1789 – as violence now spiralled dangerously out of control. On 14 July Commoners, rioting in Paris, then stormed the state prison 'La Bastille' but again Louis reacted only weakly.

Influenced by the American Independence declarations of 1776 the National Assembly then issued 'the Declaration of the Rights of Man and of the Citizen', ending the feudal system and arresting a non-cooperative Louis as he fled France. The Assembly then went further, spreading the philosophy of 'the Rights of Man' in International Law before, in 1792, declaring war on all Europe, beginning with monarchist Austria and Prussia. The French Revolution itself and the French Revolutionary War, now backed by a popularity-seeking Louis, sent nationalism soaring in France but reverses on the battlefield pointed to a conspiracy, Louis' Queen Marie Antoinette being an Austrian. The Royal Family were again arrested, both Louis and Marie guillotined in 1793 as a 'Reign of Terror' against suspected anti revolutionaries gripped France.

Across the English Channel, Great Britain was a more developed democracy and the attitude to monarchy was very different. King George III, recovering from insanity and an attempt on his life, enjoyed the support of his Prime Minister William Pitt (the Younger) and from a more liberated populace horrified at the barbarity next door. On 1 February 1793 France's now ruling Committee of Public Safety then declared war on Great Britain who joined the First Coalition (still mainly Prussia and Austria) with a small army but with a Royal Navy, largely press ganged, that could defend British shores and potentially strangle French overseas trade. This included a huge American supply convoy sailing to relieve the economic extremities of their old revolutionary ally from the scene of the great Franco-American victory over the British of thirteen years previous, Chesapeake Bay. To protect this convoy, Rear Admiral Louis Villaret-Joyeuse and a thirty-nine-strong French fleet sailed from Brest, initially evading the British Channel Fleet of Admiral Lord Richard Howe who gave chase picking off stragglers.

On 1 June 1794, in the mid Atlantic, twenty-five Royal Navy ships of the line sailing line ahead on an identical course to Villaret's now twenty-six ships began exchanging ineffective broadsides at long range before Howe, aboard HMS *Queen Charlotte*, signaled the fleet turn simultaneously, attempting to slice the French line at every point rather than as usual maintaining line ahead. Some captains failed to understand the order, however, and those that did sailed at various speeds so that the attack was piecemeal rather than concerted with only HMS *Queen Charlotte*, *Defence, Marlborough, Royal George* and *Glory* breaking the French line whilst others failed to close for an effective engagement. Three separate engagements of close range artillery developed over several hours with the British gaining the upper hand by virtue of their more experienced Commanders. At 11.30 Villaret broke off but reformed his line to give battle once again, Howe responding likewise, both sides now down to a dozen ships capable of fighting whilst shattered ships drifted and sank amongst them. In late afternoon, after a bitter fight, Villaret broke off again, this time his fleet returning to France.

Villaret had lost seven ships and 7,000 men dead, wounded or captured. Howe, with 1,200 casualties, could not maintain the offensive but claimed victory and received the congratulations of King George. The American supply convoy was never detected and sailed into France.

2 June 1653 o.s

Anglo-Dutch Wars
Battle of the Gabbard

A YEAR HAD passed since the first shots had been fired in a war entirely fought at sea between the Dutch Republic and the Commonwealth of England. The old Protestant allies against Catholic Spain had failed to unify once an Oliver Cromwell offer had been declined by the Dutch and were now fighting for ascendancy over world trade, the routes of which outside the English Channel were very much the possession of the Dutch, the envy of the English. Within the Channel, however, quite the reverse was now the case. The first three major engagements to be fought following the outbreak of war in May 1652, off Dover (Goodwin Sands), the Thames Estuary (Kentish Knock) and Dungeness had failed to provide decisive outcomes and had left the enormous Dutch fleets, merchant and naval, still dominant, a position of strength that suddenly collapsed in February 1653 during a running three day battle from Portland Bill to Cap Gris-Nez between the adversaries principal commanders, England's General-at-Sea Robert Blake and the Dutch Admiral Maarten Tromp. The English Navy's improved performance off Portland had been due to a major overhaul, administratively by Sir Henry Vane and tactically by the production of 'Fighting Instructions' written by Blake, George Monck and Richard Deane (commander of the New Model Army artillery at Naseby, 1645). The Dutch were now well aware of their shortcomings against the faster, larger and more heavily gunned English warships but these were deficiencies that would require more than a book to correct. With the English Channel firmly back under English control, the Dutch were left to maintain their global trade routes in the only direction possible, the North Sea.

On 5 May 1653, Tromp and eighty Dutch warships sailed from Texel escorting a large merchant fleet north around the Shetland Isles before returning to the North Sea. Reinforced by a further sixteen warships they then began a search for the English fleet thought to be in the Downs and the Dover Roads. The only greeting the Dutch received, however, was from Dover Castle since Blake, Monck and Deane, after a fruitless search themselves for the Dutch off Zeeland, were now off Yarmouth and south of Harwich. On 1 June 1653 the Dutch fleet was at last sighted sailing north near the Gabbard Shoal off Suffolk and were immediately approached by the main English fleet of 105 warships under Monck and Deane aboard the massive 88-gun, 1,200 ton *Resolution*. In light winds, darkness fell with both fleets still several miles apart.

On 2 June 1653, the English advanced in three squadrons with Rear Admiral John Lawson, promoted after his feats off Portland, leading the vanguard in the 58-gun *George* but, still in light wind, it was not until 11.00 that the two fleets engaged, the English now in line as dictated by Blake's Fighting Instructions. 'Commodore' Michiel de Ruyter leading the Dutch vanguard in the 40-gun *Witte Lam* attempted to head off Lawson by crossing his bows and broadsiding but Lawson turned with De Ruyter with first Tromp in the 54-gun *Brederode* coming up behind and the whole of each line eventually joining battle, two hundred ships broadsiding each other with balls and canister at close range for over six hours with Dutch attempts to close and board brutally met by the numerically superior and more powerful English guns. Eventually the Dutch disengaged, attempting to run in the still light winds pursued by the English south to the Weilings Anchorage where they were trapped by Monck and the arrival of Blake from Harwich. The following morning the Dutch Fleet was further battered by English artillery, escaping by running into shallow water, nineteen ships lost with unknown but undoubtably high casualties. The English lost no ships but 126 crew perished including General-at-Sea Richard Deane who had been struck by a cannon ball. Another 236 were wounded.

The Gabbard was the decisive battle of the First Anglo-Dutch War, leaving the Dutch fleet in near ruin and blockaded in port by Monck. As the Dutch economy consequently collapsed, mediators were sent to London to negotiate but Tromp would try one last time to break Monck's blockade at Sheveningen.

3 June 1665 o.s

Anglo-Dutch Wars
Battle of Lowestoft

THE FIRST ANGLO Dutch War of 1652–53 ended with the signing of the 1654 Treaty of Westminster but many issues, largely concerning trade, were left unresolved. Although the Commonwealth of England and its Lord Protector, Oliver Cromwell, had been victorious the Dutch economy, which had come under severe pressure during the conflict, recovered faster as its developed trade routes resumed business as normal. Meanwhile, the English became embroiled once again in war with Spain, Cromwell's 'Western design', principally attacking Spanish possessions in the Caribbean (Jamaica was captured in 1655) but economically damaging both nations to Dutch advantage. Fearful of Dutch support for the restoration of the English monarchy, Cromwell had insisted by the Treaty of Westminster that Prince William of Orange, the nephew of Charles, Prince of Wales (future Charles II), could never become Stadtholder (head of state) of the Dutch Republic but following Cromwell's death and the 1660 Restoration, the now King Charles II of England, Scotland and Ireland immediately began promoting Prince William's cause, antagonising the prospering States General (Dutch Parliament). Diplomacy and the Dutch Gift of 1660 brought some calm but, in 1663, King Louis XIV of France rivalled Dutch claims to parts of the Spanish Netherlands (now Belgium, Luxembourg). Advised by his Catholic brother James, Duke of York, Lord High Admiral, Charles decided more was to be gained politically and economically by siding with the Catholic French rather than the Protestant Dutch, hostilities breaking out both in the colonies where outposts could not be protected and in home waters where the new Royal Navy now faced a much more formidable Dutch Navy than a decade previous. Worse, the port of London was about to be gripped by the Great Plague of 1665.

The Dutch Navy had learnt lessons from the First Anglo-Dutch War and had been building better ships ever since but, with Admirals Maarten Tromp and Witte de With both dead and Michiel De Ruyter in the Americas, confidence was lacking. The Dutch Lieutenant Admiral Jacob van Wassenaer Obdam (De Ruyter had declined the post) had initially claimed any Dutch attack on the English whilst De Ruyter was elsewhere was completely out of the question but acquiesced following an accusation of cowardice from the Head of the States General, Johan de Witt.

Wassanaer's fleet of 107 ships, in seven squadrons reflecting their provinces, delayed off the Dutch coast incurring De Witt's displeasure once again before sighting the English fleet of 109 ships forty miles east of Lowestoft on 1 June 1665. York, commanding the English vanguard, was outgunned and to leeward but Wassenaer continued delaying until 3 June 1665. The wind had most likely changed to a north-westerly (records are unclear) so that Wassenaer sailed due west attempting to attack from the south-west with the wind behind for a clear run home should there be any mishap. As the Dutch approached from the south-west the English approached them from the north-east, both fleets passing each other before coming about, the lengthy manoeuvre then repeated a second time with Dutch inexperience and the variation of their shipping coming under added pressure from a few English broadsides that caused a loss of order. By the time the two fleets came about for a third time Dutch order had been completely lost and, worse, the wind had changed to a south-westerly, pushing them into the oncoming English whose Edward Montagu, Earl of Sandwich seized the opportunity to cut their line initiating a general mêlée. Wassenaer now paid for his earlier hesitation as the English rear sailed south, blocking his route home, battle raging for several hours in the centre with the Dutch flagship *Eendracht* fighting bitterly with York's HMS *Royal Charles* before the *Eendracht* blew up, killing almost all her crew including Wassenaer. The heavy English guns then began taking a terrible toll of the smaller Dutch ships before Dutch command was assumed by Cornelis Tromp and Johan Evertsen who covered a retreat. The Dutch had lost sixteen ships with 4,500 men lost, casualties or taken prisoner, against just one English ship and 500 dead.

The Duke of York did not pursue, having narrowly escaped death when a chain shot decapitated several of his close courtiers it is possible his nerve failed. A year later off North Foreland the Dutch Navy, now back under De Ruyter, would prove equal to that of the Royal Navy.

4 June 1673 o.s

Anglo-Dutch Wars
Battle of Schooneveld

THE 1667 DUTCH Raid on the Medway had left the King of England Charles II (restored to the English throne only seven years earlier) in a state of fury at Dutch treachery whilst peace negotiations had been ongoing. The raid finished the Second Anglo-Dutch War with nothing settled at all. In 1668 Charles then signed an alliance with the Dutch protecting the Spanish Netherlands (Belgium, Luxembourg) from French aggression but in 1670, determined to avenge Medway, he secretly signed the Treaty of Dover with France against the Dutch. Additionally the king continued to promote his nephew Prince William of Orange as Stadtholder (head of state) of the Dutch Republic much to the irritation of the Grand Pensionary (prime minister) of the Dutch States General, Johan de Witt. England could not provide the French with a strong army but they could provide the Royal Navy; Charles also needing an excuse for war but successfully creating one when in Brielle, Holland Dutch shipping struck their colours but failed to salute an English yacht, the Merlin – a seemingly minor incident which had similarly started the 1652 First Anglo-Dutch War. The Dutch were assured no war was imminent but they could not help but notice French diplomats appearing in neighbouring German states and increasing activity in English dockyards.

When French and German armies then invaded the Dutch Republic Prince William was forced back behind the Hollandic Water Line which turned the Province of Holland into a defensible island. Lieutenant Admiral Michiel de Ruyter was ordered by De Witt to take the war to the Royal Navy and did so at Solebay in May 1672 with both sides heavily damaged. The customary English tactic of blockading the Dutch coast was therefore postponed but the proximity of a large French Army quickly frayed the nerves of the Dutch populace who rebelled against De Witt. In July 1672, in direct conflict with Oliver Cromwell's 1654 Treaty of Westminster (considered null and void), William then became Stadtholder of the

Dutch Republic (William III of Orange) and was immediately offered, by Charles, the title of Sovereign Prince of Holland and a peace deal with England upon the payment of a large gratuity and an annual pension for herring rights. William however, even more secure as Stadtholder once De Witt had been murdered, furiously declined. Charles protested he had only been anti the De Witt regime but he was now set against his ungrateful nephew.

The French had failed to cross the Water Line during the winter frosts of 1673 and now planned a Royal Navy assisted amphibious landing in the Sheldt River estuary defended by De Ruyter and Lieutenant Admiral Cornelis Tromp. At Schooneveld on 28 May 1673 General and Vice Admiral of England Prince Rupert of the Rhine attacked De Ruyter but was given a lesson in seamanship when the Dutchman suddenly went on the offensive himself, carving up the Anglo French Fleet which escaped only when the Dutchman opted to rescue Tromp rather than press his attack.

De Ruyter returned to the Schooneveld basin as Rupert's fleet of eighty-six ships cruised off the coast reluctant to negotiate the shoals in any attack but optimistically hoping to lure De Ruyter back out to sea. On 4 June 1673, De Ruyter and sixty-four Dutch ships, having been completely resupplied, then suddenly obliged, attacking the English line just as Rupert was meeting with his Vice Admiral Edward Spragge. The Anglo-French fleet was not in the best of order after a week at sea since the previous battle and became further disorganised when Rupert decided to take to the vanguard without advising the French who were ahead of him and who were desperately trying to stay there. Even De Ruyter was confused by Rupert's manoeuvres, broadsiding him at long range with the advantage that, being to leeward, he could open his lower gun ports in the heavy sea whereas Rupert could not. The same applied when Rear Admiral Adriaen Bankert, behind De Ruyter, engaged the French who immediately departed leaving the two bitter enemies Spragge and Tromp to fight out a personal duel until 22.00. By the following morning both fleets had retreated to home ports, Rupert with a considerable repair bill.

Prince Rupert sailed again two months later, again seeking to draw De Ruyter out from the Schooneveld. With the Dutch Admiral having little choice but to protect a valuable East India convoy approaching the besieged civilians of Holland, they would meet again in August 1673 off Texel.

5 June 1944
Second World War
Capture of Pegasus Bridge

TWO YEARS AFTER the 1939 outbreak of the Second World War, Germany and Axis partner Italy had been on the verge of conquering the whole of Europe, the Mediterranean, North Africa and Russia but, by 1944, the picture had changed dramatically. Germany had been abandoned by Italy and though minor allies Bulgaria, Hungary and Romania fought on they were about to be overrun by a two million man Soviet attack on the central Eastern Front. In Italy, German Field Marshal Albert Kesselring was now in retreat whilst the United States 5th Army was liberating Rome, they and the British 8th Army having broken the Winter Line at Monte Cassino. US President Franklin D. Roosevelt's earlier compromise with British Prime Minister Winston Churchill meant the Allied invasion of Italy would now be followed by another in France.

German Chancellor Adolf Hitler, aware of a likely Allied landing, had belatedly given Field Marshal Erwin Rommel responsibility for improving the defences of the 2,400 mile, north Norway to the South of France Atlantic Wall but opinion was split in the German High Command over defensive strategy behind the wall – keep the Panzers back for a counter-attack in strength or keep them closer, more widely dispersed but exposed to Allied aerial bombing? Hitler, who had maintained direct command of the German Panzer divisions, opted largely for a fatal compromise that would achieve neither.

Meanwhile in southern England the greatest concentration of men and military hardware in the history of warfare was taking place in preparation for Allied landings on the beaches of Normandy. Despite an extensive aerial and naval artillery bombardment the troops landing on these beaches would face concrete gun emplacements, interlocking machine-gun and suppressing artillery fire, much of which would be targeted in turn by 20,000 British and American paratroops landing just hours beforehand. Before even then, to protect the British 6th Airborne Division from potential German armoured counter-attacks and to allow a breakout from Sword Beach by the British 3rd Infantry Division, a coup de main was required north of Caen to seize the bridges over the River Orne, the Caen Canal Bridge (Pegasus) and the Ranville Bridge (Horsa), Operation Deadstick.

At 23.00 on 5 June 1944, Halifax bombers took off from RAF Tarrant Rushton towing six Horsa gliders loaded with 181 men of D Company, Oxford and Buckinghamshire Light Infantry and Royal Engineers led by Major John Howard. An hour later the gliders were released, 1–3 flying to Pegasus Bridge, 4–6 to Horsa Bridge. In an incredible piece of night flying Staff Sergeant Jim Wallwork landed glider 1 at sixteen minutes past midnight just 47 yards from Pegasus, Lieutenant Den Brotheridge then leading an attack which had been practiced forty-two times back in England. Firing at surprised sentries and throwing grenades into machine-gun boxes Brotheridge stormed across the bridge only to be killed by a machine-gunner. His platoon's charge however, supported by those from the following two gliders succeeded in overwhelming the fifty defenders of the German 736th Grenadier Regiment. In just five minutes Howard's men had completed their mission and awaited news from Horsa Bridge 400 yards to their east. Here glider 5 landed at nineteen minutes past midnight 330 yards distant, the platoon of Lieutenant Dennis Fox eliminating a machine-gun position with mortar fire before crossing Horsa with the platoon of glider 6 following up. Within half an hour the British 6th Airborne Division then began to drop from above but were short of the heavy weapons (part relieved when sixty-nine gliders flew in at 03.00) required to contain Colonel Hans von Luck's 21st Panzer Division nearby. Von Luck, however, was out of luck since he could not move without Hitler's permission and Hitler was asleep. Rommel too was away visiting his wife. The 192nd Panzergrenadier Regiment could move, however, and attacked through Benouville, a fierce battle developing after the lead Panzer had been destroyed with a PIAT gun before German mortars, machine guns, snipers and gunboats pinned down Howard's platoons. After the dawn British landings on Sword Beach, Luck at last advanced but now via a detour through Caen, it was too late, his Panzers now badly strafed by Allied aircraft and artillery. At 13.30 on 6 June, British armour from Sword Beach passed across the Pegasus and Horsa bridges as the Oxford and Bucks were relieved by Royal Warwickshires.

Howard was awarded the Distinguised Service Order and the Croix de Guerre. The road connecting the two bridges is now the 'Esplanade Major John Howard'.

6 June 1944

Second World War Normandy Landings

IN HIS AUTOBIOGRAPHY *Mein Kampf* German Chancellor Adolf Hitler had criticised Kaiser Wilhelm II for fighting the Great War on two fronts but by early 1944 he himself faced at least as many. British and American aircraft bombed German cities; in Italy, the Balkans and Greece forty-seven German divisions were tied down; in the Soviet Union 200 German, Bulgarian, Hungarian and Romanian divisions fought across a 1,200 mile front whilst on the 2,400 mile Atlantic Wall forty German divisions awaited an expected Allied invasion. In 1943 defeat at Kursk to the Soviet Red Army had doomed Nazi Germany to defeat in the East but Hitler still had 1,000 miles of territory there to trade while he transferred divisions to France and the Low Countries to defend against Americans, Canadians and British. Here, just a short distance from Germany's industrial Ruhr, Hitler had little room for error but he did have the incentive that a costly Allied failure on the beaches would deter a repeat effort that in turn could potentially persuade the Soviets to sign an armistice. Should Hitler fail to prevent a successful Allied landing, however, the full combined military might of the United States as well as that of Russia would be brought to bear, D-Day, the battle for the beaches of Normandy, France would therefore be the decisive battle of the Second World War.

Hitler and his Atlantic Wall commander Field Marshal Erwin Rommel well understood the doctrine of eighteenth century Frederick the Great of Prussia who stated 'he who defends everywhere, defends nowhere' but they disagreed on strategy. Now with sixty-one mostly depleted divisions to resist a maximum first day Allied five, Rommel wanted his Panzer tanks close to the coast but was compromised by Hitler and Field Marshal Gerd von Rundstedt who wanted them held further back for massed counter-attacks. German High Command also wrongly surmised that Supreme Headquarters Allied Expeditionary Force commander General Dwight D. Eisenhower would need to capture the ports of the Pas de Calais, not realising that the Allies possessed their own portable Mulberry harbours. Two million

Allied soldiers and near 7,000 vessels now readied for Operation Overlord, 'the most difficult and complicated operation ever to take place',* a small window of opportunity now emerging with the moon, tides and weather all satisfactorily aligned and additional good news that Rommel was away visiting his wife.

In the early hours of D-Day, 6 June 1944, 20,400 paratroops jumped from 1,000 C47 Dakotas north of Caen on the Allied left flank and north of Carentan on the right. As 2,200 Allied aircraft bombed areas behind the beaches, 255 Minesweepers cleared lanes for over 2,200 landing craft carrying heavy armour and over 1,000 carrying the first of 57,000 American, 55,000 British and 21,500 Canadians toward the beaches of Normandy – west to east, Utah (US), Omaha (US), Gold (British), Juno (Canadian) and Sword (British). Behind them six battleships, twenty cruisers and sixty-eight destroyers engaged the German coastal defences. Despite meticulous preparation however twenty-seven of the twenty-nine tanks in flotation screens foundered in the six foot swells and many of the landing craft drifted off course but determined leadership on the beaches proved decisive. After fierce fighting at Utah US troops moved four miles inland but at Omaha strong defences at Pointe du Hoc, the exit points through 140-foot cliffs and the German 352nd Infantry Division had the US 1st and 29th Infantry Divisions pinned down on the narrow beach for almost the entire day. At Gold the British took advantage of shattered German defences to make six mile gains whilst to their left at Juno the Canadians fought hard before advancing several miles to join them. At Sword the British 3rd Division benefited from the British 6th Airborne destroying the Merville Battery, by the Le Havre Battery's duel with HMS *Warspite* and by tanks coming ashore to clear paths through the German minefields. German 88mm guns delayed the British advance but the nearby 21st Panzer Division remained motionless while Hitler slept. In bitter hand-to-hand fighting the British took Ouistreham and pushed inland, commandos linking up with the Oxford and Bucks whose successful coup de main at Pegasus and Horsa Bridge forced the now active 21st Panzer into a six hour detour and failed counter-attack between Juno and Sword. By nightfall Allied gains had not matched objectives but a decisive victory had certainly been won. The American military would now flex its might through France.

Adolf Hitler had lost the war but it would be Andrew Higgins, the amphibious landing craft designer, who Eisenhower would celebrate as the man who won it.

---

* Winston Churchill

7 June 1917

The Great War
Battle of Messines

IN LATE 1916 David Lloyd George had become British Prime Minister determined to reduce the casualties suffered by the British Expeditionary Force (BEF) on the Western Front. An arch 'easterner' Lloyd George was looking to advance from Egypt into Ottoman Palestine whilst transferring the main Great War effort to Italy, a suggestion declined by the Italians before French General Robert Nivelle proposed a French offensive south of the Hindenburg Line (to which the Germans had retreated in March 1917) supported 'only' by a British diversionary attack north at Arras and Vimy Ridge. Impressed by Nivelle Lloyd George subordinated BEF command incurring the wrath of Field Marshal Douglas Haig who favoured an offensive in Flanders where British gains would force the withdrawal of the German Navy, particularly their troublesome submarines, from Belgian ports. Nevertheless, with the French leading the offensive both Lloyd George and Haig agreed to let Nivelle have his day but, whilst the largely British and Canadian attacks had been a qualified success at Arras and Vimy (despite the highest daily casualty rates of the war), Nivelle's offensive had been a disaster. Some French divisions were now in mutiny and Nivelle had been replaced by General Phillipe Pétain, a man happy for France to sit on the defensive awaiting the arrival, at least a year away, of the United States of America (responding to German submarine warfare). With France exhausted and Russia increasingly consumed by a Bolshevik Revolution, Haig's BEF would now attempt to win the war in the exposed Ypres Salient, the southern flank of which, the Messines Ridge, required clearing before the main assault could proceed further north. A 'bite and hold' attack that suited the meticulous planning of British Second Army General Herbert Plumer began with an artillery bombardment on 8 May, 2,266 guns firing over 3.5 million shells, including gas, across a 17,000 yard front, increasing in intensity on 23 May as the Royal Flying Corps observed and strafed enemy defences with 500 Bristol F.2s, S.E 5s and Sopwith Triplanes that were now capable of competing with the 300

Albatros DIII's and Halberstadt DII's of the Luftstreitkrafte, including those of Manfred von Richthofen's Jasta 11.

At 03.10 on 7 June 1917, nineteen mines each containing over 20 tons of explosive erupted underneath the German front lines signalling the start of the main British assault. Audible in England, this man made earthquake rocked the entire front, instantly killing 10,000 Germans in the front lines over which then swept nine British and Anzac infantry divisions, 80,000 men supported by machine-gunners, 72 MK IV tanks and an artillery bombardment that included creeping and standing barrages with aircraft continuing to strafe targets beyond. The German artillery struggled to recover as British flash spotters and sounders directed precise counter battery fire so that by 05.00 IX Corps in the centre, X Corps to the north and the Anzac Corps to the south had taken their initial objective, the crest of Messines Ridge. The standing barrage now moved forward as reinforcements moved up 'leap-frogging' the first wave. At 07.00 the creeping barrage was then repeated on the reverse slopes of Messines Ridge, now aided by the artillery's own observers overlooking German positions for the first time in nearly three years. The infantry again advanced, eliminating German resistance at Messines village, Wytshaete and Grand Woods, Dammstrasse and on the Comines Canal but exposed on the reverse slopes and with their own artillery now firing at long range, the British and Anzacs began to suffer as German artillery conversely recovered. Having achieved his second objective, Plumer again consolidated, moving up artillery as far as the ground would allow before launching another attack at 15.10 in an attempt to capture the German defences of the Oostraverne Line. Again the assault began with a creeping barrage behind which troops advanced with those tanks that remained up against German pill boxes manned by machine-gunners who began exacting a heavy toll. In bitter fighting and with their own artillery shells falling amongst them, Second Army took the line the following day.

Haig wanted to push on but difficulties in moving artillery meant a three day delay. Arriving German reinforcements then meant further advances would have to wait for Haig's main effort at the Third Battle of Ypres on 31 July. In 1919 Plumer was created Baron Plumer of Messines.

7 June 1896

Mahdist Wars
Battle of Ferkeh

IN 1885 THE British had been unceremoniously kicked out of the Sudan after the fall of Khartoum and the murder of Major General Charles Gordon. The episode had been an embarrassment not only for Queen Victoria and the British Army but also contributed to the downfall of William Gladstone's Liberal Government. Meanwhile, in the Sudan, just months after his victory, Mohammad Ahmed, the Mahdi, had fallen fatally ill, (likely to typhus) leaving his loyal servant the Khalifa Abdullahi to continue the Mahdist cause without anything like the authority of his former master. During the temporary power vacuum the Khalifa brutally suppressed several revolts to regain total power before attempting to expand the Mahdist State into both Egypt, where he was defeated in 1889 by Major General Francis Grenfell at Toski, and Abbyssinia (Ethiopia) where he enjoyed more success. As British and Egyptian spies in Khartoum reported barbarous governance, European interest in the Sudan and Abbyssinia again began to increase, the Italians invading Abbyssinia in 1894 (only to be defeated at Adowa in 1896) before a long term Austrian prisoner of the Mahdists, Rudolf Slatin, escaped in 1895, fully briefing the British in Cairo and publishing a successful book 'Fire and Sword in the Sudan'. Since the French were also about to launch a two year expedition under General Jean Baptiste Marchand across the northern Congo (Zaire) to Fashoda in Equatorial Sudan, the imperialist British Prime Minister Robert Gascoyne Cecil, Lord Salisbury gave himself a free reign in the region by buying the French out of their Egyptian debts before ordering Sirdar Horatio Herbert Kitchener to lead an Anglo-Egyptian expedition into Dongola Province, North Sudan.

In June 1896 a British reconquest of the Sudan began that would use loyal Sudanese troops wherever possible whilst Egyptians, British (a minimum) and Indians would garrison the Red Sea ports, particularly Suakin which had been held for eleven long years against the Mahdist threat. From Egypt, Kitchener ordered Colonel Archibald Hunter forward to capture Akasha whilst a further build up of troops and supplies occurred at Wadi Halfa on the Egypt/Sudan border. Hunter was exposed at Akasha but remained remarkably free from Mahdist attack due to the inactivity the local Emir Hammuda Idris but that situation would certainly change once the Mahdist Governor of Dongola, Wad Bishara, had replaced him with Osman Azrak, a man already infamous for his aggressive raids across the Egyptian border. Since Kitchener needed to secure the area before beginning the construction of the Sudan Military Railroad he decided to lead a pre emptive attack on the Mahdist camp at Ferkeh.

Marching out of Akasha on the afternoon of 6 June with a mixed force of 9,000 Egyptians and Sudanese Kitchener split his force in two, the River Column of infantry marching along the difficult Nile Road to attack from the north whilst a Mounted Camel Desert Column under Major John Burn-Murdoch rode across the desert to attack from the south-east. Progress was treacherous through the narrow defiles of the mountain passes but no Mahdist attacks transpired before, at 05.00 on 7 July 1896, the River Column, urged on by Kitchener, began to deploy on the plain before Ferkeh. Sporadic gunfire opened up from in and around Ferkeh but so too did the artillery of Burn-Murdoch's Desert Column which had arrived with perfect timing. Taken completely by surprise having just finished morning prayer 3,000 Mahdists ran for their defences with Hammuda now springing into action to lead a cavalry charge against the loyal Sudanese left. The Sudanese stopped the Mahdist charge in its tracks with a devastating volley, killing all including Hammuda, before countering with a bayonet charge over the defensive breastworks. As Egyptians and Sudanese pressed forward on all sides desperate hand-to-hand fighting raged street by street, house-by-house with those Mahdists that refused to surrender whilst others, including Azrak, attempted to escape up the Nile. After a two and a half hour fight Azrak had lost nearly two thirds of his force with British losses minimal.

Kitchener now began constructing the Military Railroad to Abu Hamed, facilitating the movement of reinforcements and supplies including gunboats and steamers above the Second Cataract of the Nile. It would, however, be two years of attention to detail and hard labour before he could advance upon Khartoum.

8 June 793

Viking
Sack of Lindisfarne

DESPITE ROMAN ATTEMPTS to spread Christianity throughout the British Isles Anglo-Saxon paganism was still the dominant religion in early seventh century England. In the North of England, Oswald had become King of Northumbria (Bernicia and Deira) after defeating Cadwallon ap Cadfan, King of Gwynedd, at Heavenfield in 633 and, having enjoyed a Christian upbringing in Dal Riata (West Scotland/ Ulster), now wished to spread the Christian gospel amongst the heathen peoples of his realm. Oswald's request to his Irish Christians for a bishop initially met with failure but the following year, 635, Aidan arrived from the Monastery of Iona to be given the Island of Lindisfarne, off the coast of Northumbria, as his ecclesiastical seat. Aidan and Oswald there founded a monastic cathedral with Oswald working as Aidan's Celtic-speaking interpreter until he was killed at the 642 Battle of Maserfield. Aidan continued Oswald's work with support from King Oswine of Deira (who assumed control of half Oswald's kingdom), building more monasteries, churches and schools before following Oswald to the grave in 651 shortly after a pagan uprising. No formal act of canonization existed at the time but all three men were venerated as Saints by the general populace.

Aidan's body was buried in the monastery at Lindisfarne but his mission lived on through Cuthbert, a man who had reputedly taken up the monastic life after seeing a vision on the night of Aidan's death. After becoming Prior at Melrose, Cuthbert became Prior of Lindisfarne in 665, extending Aidan's missionary work across the British Isles and Ireland before, in 676, retiring to lead a hermitic lifestyle on Inner Farne. Talked out of retirement in 684 by King Ecgfrith of Northumbria, Cuthbert became Bishop of Lindisfarne before his death in 687. He was buried in the monastery at Lindisfarne and was also venerated as a Saint.

On top of the missionary work of Oswald, Aidan and Cuthbert a monk named Eadfrith, who became Bishop of Lindisfarne in 698, is believed responsible for the Lindisfarne Gospels, a highly ornate manuscript, binded by Ethelwald, Bishop of the Islanders, and decorated with ornate jewelry by Billfrith the Anchorite – the book no doubt an object that made a deep impression on the peasant population who were turning from paganism to Christianity in ever increasing numbers. Through its missionaries and scriptures, Lindisfarne played a huge part in the birth of Christian Britain, becoming a seat of learning, knowledge and wealth as God-fearing inhabitants and regular pilgrims donated generously on visiting the graves of Saint Aidan and Cuthbert. In early 793, however, the Anglo-Saxon Chronicle reports 'foreboding omens came over the land of Northumbria and the wretched people shook; there were excessive whirlwinds, lightening and fiery dragons seen in the sky'.

On 8 June 793 ships were seen out at sea that turned towards the Holy Island. They contained not pilgrims but heathen men from the north who would signify the beginning of a new age with a show of violence on Northumbria's Holy Island that would shock the whole of Europe. Most likely Norwegian Vikings who had come from Orkney and Shetland they, according to the monk Simeon of Durham, 'miserably ravaged and pillaged everything; they trod holy things under their polluted feet, they dug down the altars and plundered all the treasures of the Church. Some of the brethren they slew, some they carried off in chains, the greater number they stripped naked, insulted, and cast out of doors, and some they drowned in the sea.'

The Monastery was looted and burnt but the Lindisfarne Gospels and Cuthbert's grave, containing his own Gospel – the St Cuthbert Gospel – were miraculously spared. The monks then fled Lindisfarne with the Gospels and Cuthbert's remains when Danish Vikings moved into Northumbria from York in 875, Vikings now looking beyond mere raiding to instead conquer the whole of Anglo-Saxon Britain.

The Lindisfarne Priory was rebuilt in 1093 following the 1066 Viking defeat at Stamford Bridge. It would be an English King, Henry VIII, that would finally end its days in 1536. The 1,300-year-old Gospels of Lindisfarne and Cuthbert now reside in the British Library whilst Cuthbert's remains reside in Durham Cathedral.

9 June 1667 o.s

Anglo-Dutch Wars
Raid on the Medway

KING CHARLES II had benefited from Dutch support whilst in exile from England between 1646 and 1660 but once 'restored' to the English throne he demanded that his nephew, Prince William of Orange, should succeed as Stadtholder of the Dutch Republic. Charles' persistence, however, fell on the deaf ears of Dutch officials who had profited from Oliver Cromwell's insistence by the 1654 Treaty of Westminster that William, the grandson of the executed King Charles I, could never do so. Charles' demands were then compromised when France rivalled Dutch claims over the Spanish Netherlands (Belgium, Luxembourg), Charles advised by his brother James, Duke of York that more was to be gained fighting against the Dutch Republic whose trade routes were the envy of the English. For two decades already England had sought to compete with Dutch global trade, particularly in the Far East where the British East India Company was building trade in China and India, indeed Charles' Queen Catherine of Braganza had come with Bombay as part of her dowry. England's defeat of the Dutch in the First Anglo-Dutch War had ultimately accomplished little, the Dutch quickly resurrected their economy whilst this, the Second Anglo Dutch War, had so far witnessed three hard-won English victories in the English Channel and North Sea, as well as a raid on the Dutch mainland (Holmes' Bonfire) for all of which Charles and James had little to show. The Dutch fleet remained intact and, as the world's greatest trading nation, the States General (Dutch Parliament) had plenty of money to continue the struggle. An English blockade might bring about a Dutch submission as had occurred in the first war but Charles and the Royal Navy, administered by Clerk of the Acts, Samuel Pepys, were broke. The finances of England's inferior trade had been exacerbated by the 1665 Great Plague and the 1666 Great Fire of London, whilst Charles, noting his father's misfortunes, refused absolutely to go cap in hand to his Parliament.

Since the June 1666 Dutch victory at the Four Days Battle, the Grand Pensionary of the Dutch States General, Johan de Witt, had urged Lieutenant Admiral Michiel De Ruyter to launch a combined raid now in alliance with the French on the Royal Navy dockyard at Chatham on the River Medway but the unwelcome defeat off North Foreland in July that year delayed De Ruyter by nearly a year. It mattered not for in Chatham, the only fighting likely to be conducted by sailors of the Royal Navy was in the Greenwich office of Pepys who, judging by his diaries, was not suffering the same privations as everyone else.

On 6 June 1667, De Ruyter's eighty-nine ships at last sailed into the Thames Estuary where Cornelis de Witt (brother) read out the orders to the astonishment of senior Dutch commanders who objected for the record but who were really more than enthusiastic. On 9 June 1667, thirty Dutch ships then approached Sheerness and Canvey Island, landing 1,000 Marines under Willem Joseph Baron van Ghent who met stiff resistance from local militias mobilised in the Home Counties only the day before. On 10 June, the Dutch fleet attacked Garrison Point Fort in an artillery exchange with the only English ship capable of putting up a defence, *Unity*, running up the Medway after delivering a single broadside. The fort was then evacuated when Dutch marines again landed on Sheerness leaving their fleet to proceed up river where General-at-Sea George Monck arrived to organise the English defence, blockships were sunk whilst gun batteries were hastily erected to defend the boom chain with gun ships moored on either side. On 12 June, however, the defences around the chain disintegrated under attack once again from Dutch marines and several fireships which sailed straight over the chain to send the defending English ships up in flames. The *Royal Charles*, the very ship that had brought Charles back from the Dutch Republic for the Restoration, pride of the Royal Navy but now abandoned by her crew, was then captured and towed back to Amsterdam to become a tourist attraction. On 13 June, the Dutch continued toward the docks spearheaded by more fireships causing Monck to withdraw ever further up river, the *Loyal London*, *Royal James* and the *Royal Oak* all sunk to avoid capture. On 14 June, Dutch engineers rowed out to further destroy any reachable English ships before De Ruyter ordered a withdrawal. Dutch attacks now continued in the Thames Estuary, panic breaking out along the south bank and in London from where civilians fled believing a full scale Franco Dutch invasion to be taking place.

The Dutch attack on the Medway still stands as the Royal Navy's greatest ever defeat. A furious Charles would secretly sign the 1670 Treaty of Dover with France ensuring another Anglo-Dutch War which would clear Prince William's path to become Dutch Stadtholder and, as it would turn out, King of England. Charles' brother James, Duke of York would pay the price.

10 June 1719

Jacobite Rebellion
Battle of Glenshiel

THE FAILURE TO pass the House of Commons, of the 1679 Bill of Exclusion preventing a Roman Catholic, from inheriting the throne meant James Stuart became King James II of England (VII of Scotland) and Ireland in February 1685. James' reign, the last by a Catholic in the British Isles, was, however, cut short when discontented Englishmen engineered a 'Glorious Revolution' in 1688 in favour of his nephew, the Protestant Prince William III of Orange. William initially ruled England, Scotland and Ireland jointly with his wife and cousin, Queen Mary II who was James' daughter by his first wife, Anne Hyde. Whilst family acrimony was no doubt high, Mary was crucially an Anglican as indeed was her sister Anne who inherited the throne in 1702 on William's death (Mary died in 1694).

The experience of James' reign did not pass from memory, the 1701 Act of Settlement passing the House of Commons to achieve the same end as the failed 1679 Bill of Exclusion. The acid test for the Act then arrived in 1714 when Anne died with no issue, the nearest fifty-six claimants being Catholic, including James Francis Edward Stuart, the son of James II by his second wife, the devoutly Catholic, Mary of Modena. The nearest Protestant relative was always likely to be Sophia, Electress of Hanover, granddaughter of King James I (1603–1625) but Sophia died just weeks before Anne, leaving her fifty-four-year-old son, His Most Serene Highness George Louis, Archbannerbearer of the Holy Roman Empire and Elector of Hanover to become King of England. Amidst widespread rioting across what was now Great Britain (by the 1707 Act of Union) George, who spoke no English, was crowned in October 1714, a full scale civil war in the offing just as soon as the 'Old Pretender' James Stuart arrived in force from exile in France. Indeed John Erskine, Earl of Mar led a premature Jacobite Rising in 1715 ('the Fifteen' which did not get out of Scotland) only for James' ambitions to suffer an almost terminal blow when his chief benefactor, King Louis XIV of France died that same year. Since Louis' son and grandson had predeceased him the Kingdom of France passed to his five-year-old great-grandson Louis XV – Phillippe, Duke of Orléans ruling as regent in Louis' minority over a country economically ruined by the War of the Spanish Succession (1701–14) and who, consequently, was in no position to lend James support– financial or military– for any speculative invasion of Britain.

By the 1713 Treaty of Utrecht, ending the Spanish War, King Philip of Spain, uncle of Louis XV, had retained his Spanish Crown but renounced that of France. Married to Elisabeth Farnese of Parma, however, he now attempted to regain his Italian possessions, including Sicily, only to be opposed by a Quadruple Alliance of Britain, France, the Dutch Republic and, after they had extricated themselves from war with Turkey, Austria. Following a heavy defeat at Cape Passero in 1718 at the hands of the Royal Navy, it would be Philip who gave Spanish support to James in his next attempt to wrest the Crown of Great Britain.

The Jacobite Rising of 1719 (the Nineteen) planned a two-pronged Spanishinvasion launched from Cadiz by twenty-seven ships of the line loaded with 5,000 troops for South West England and just two with 300 troops for West Scotland. Once in Scotland the 300 were to raise the Catholic Highland Clans, march south into England, gather support from disaffected Catholics and join with the main force to overthrow King George. Unfortunately for James, however, the main Spanish Armada did not get as far as the one, much larger, over a century previous, but it did suffer the same fate – wrecked by storms– this time before leaving Spanish waters. The Jacobite cause was now left with a hopelessly small force which landed at Eilean Donan Castle to begin recruiting Scots and still numbered only 1,000 when the Royal Navy arrived

to bombard the Castle, blowing up most of the Jacobite ammunition. On 10 June 1719, the Jacobites commanded by Lord George Murray had moved to a defensive position at Glenshiel as a Government Army of similar size under General Joseph Wightman approached from Inverness. Four Government mortars concentrated fire on Murray's Spaniards in the centre before Wightman sent in the Government infantry to attack the flanks. The Jacobite right gave way first, soon followed by the left despite support from Rob Roy MacGregor. The Spaniards were now left fighting the entirety of Wightman's Government force but offered stubborn resistance for over three hours until, in the absence of any allies, they began a fighting retreat to the 'Peak of the Spaniards' where they surrendered.

The 'Nineteen' was over but James Stuart's son, Bonnie Prince Charlie, 'the Young Pretender', would again try to regain his family's crown in 1745. Philip sued for peace in 1720 after the war of the Quadruple Alliance had spread to America. From now on European conflicts would resonate globally.

11 June 1982
Falklands War
Battle of Mount Longdon

ARGENTINA'S LONG STANDING claim to the British Overseas Territory of the Falkland Islands had violently exploded on 2 April 1982 when a military invasion overran the capital Port Stanley and Government House. The invasion was received joyfully in Argentina's capital Buenos Aires but since the arrival of a British Naval Task Force of 127 ships (including two aircraft carriers and 27,000 British service personnel) Argentina's grip on the islands had become increasingly tenuous. The runway at Port Stanley airfield had been bombed rendering it useless to Argentinian fast jets and the Argentine Navy now sat in port following the sinking of the light cruiser ARA *General Belgrano*. Argentine troops on the Falklands were therefore isolated, supported only by air attacks launched at long range from Argentina itself. Nevertheless, well-equipped Argentine aircraft had inflicted serious losses on Royal Navy and related British merchant shipping, denying counter-invasion ground forces much of their heavy lift helicopter support across the desolate, weather beaten landscape of East Falkland, fifty miles of which they now had to 'yomp' (a loaded march in Royal Marine slang) or 'tab' (Army slang) from San Carlos Bay toward Port Stanley.

On 28 May, the 2nd Battalion, Parachute Regiment captured Goose Green on the southern flank of 3 Commando's march across East Falkland whilst additional British troops from the 5th Infantry Brigade meant Major General Jeremy Moore could now contemplate an assault on what the Argentine command believed to be impregnable defensive positions in the mountains surrounding Port Stanley. After the capitulation of Argentine troops at Goose Green, 2 Para advanced north-east to be joined by Scots and Welsh Guards, all supplied by sea at Fitzroy and Bluff Cove on the east coast of East Falkland. Determined Argentine resistance in the air however resulted in the loss of RFA *Sir Galahad* and RFA *Sir Tristram* delaying the southern approach to Port Stanley while further north Argentine special forces began moving onto Mount Kent before strong patrols from British marines and commandos forced them into a retreat to Mounts Harriet, Two Sisters and Longdon.

Late on 11 June 1982 simultaneous attacks went in on all three, Mount Harriet and Two Sisters taken with a classic naval bombardment, mortar fire and a series of running battles between trenches and fox holes with grenades, machine-guns and bayonets, 42 Commando taking the former, 45 Commando the latter. At Mount Longdon, however, the going was even tougher. Here 450 men of the 3rd Battalion, Parachute Regiment under Lieutenant Colonel Hew Pike were up against a mixture of 280 well-entrenched Argentine conscripts, reservists and special forces under Carlos Carrizo-Salvadores. As British artillery rained down on Pike's objectives 'fly half, full back and wing forward', the advance of 4th, 5th and 6th Platoon, B Company, 3 Para went unnoticed until a mine exploded (most had frozen solid) alerting the Argentine defenders at 'fly half' to the danger on their western front. The Paras now rushed forward catching many defenders unprepared, taking the position bunker by foxhole with grenades and gunfire until Corporal Stewart Mclaughlin led a bayonet charge on the last. Argentine reinforcements then arrived on the ridge, putting down heavy fire from a well-fortified central bunker which was charged several times by men under Sergeant Ian Mackay who was posthumously awarded a VC. The Paras, however, were then temporarily forced back from 'fly half' when Salvadores ordered an Argentine counter-attack. Brigadier Julian Thompson was close to calling off the British attack before artillery from Mount Kent restored the immediate situation allowing 4th and 5th Platoons to regain 'fly half' and, reinforced by A Company, attack 'full back'. In vicious hand-to-hand fighting A Company began to get the upper hand over the resolute Argentine defenders, rock-by-rock, Salvadores evacuating his bunker only when it was almost completely destroyed by an anti-tank missile and retreating back to Wireless Ridge. Under increasing pressure Salvadores then retreated with his survivors into Port Stanley while the battle for Mount Longdon became a two day artillery contest.

The fighting on Mount Longdon had lasted twelve hours, 3 Para had taken seventy casualties in the fighting and subsequent shelling. Now fired upon from Wireless Ridge and Mount Tumbledown, the final, decisive British attack of the Falklands War would come the following day.

12 June 1798
French Revolutionary War (Ireland)
Battle of Ballynahinch

IRELAND HAD ALWAYS been England's vulnerable western flank and became more so as the science of sail developed. In 1367 King Edward III had instigated an anglicising of Ireland but the distractions of over a century of war for the crowns of France and England left King Henry VIII to complete the task of imposing English law, customs and religion (Anglicanism) on the Catholic Gaelic Irish communities. Queen Elizabeth I then continued the Tudor Conquest against a series of bloody Irish rebellions with the previously virtually independent Irish earls turning to Catholic Spain for support. Finally defeated in 1601 at Kinsale, the earls fled in 1607, King James I of England (VI of Scotland) then initiating a plantation of sparsely populated Ulster with English Anglicans and Scottish Presbyterians. Catholic Irish were excluded from the Irish Parliament in Dublin but, while the Spanish were occupied in the Low Countries, they could do little to rectify their predicament until tension created by the English Long Parliament's disputes with King Charles I led to another violent Catholic uprising in 1641. The uprisings in Ireland helped spark the English Civil War which saw the defeat of King Charles in 1646. Upon the Royalist defeat, Ireland, perceived to be Charles' friend, was then paid a visit by the victorious Oliver Cromwell and the New Model Army who repaid the atrocities of a decade before with their own. Ireland was then used by the deposed Catholic King James II as a base to resist the Protestant King William III (of Orange) following the 'Glorious Revolution' of 1688. James' subsequent defeat in 1690 at the River Boyne then condemned Irish Catholics to live under a 'Protestant Ascendancy' of landowners for a century until the world order seemed to be undergoing change.

American settlers across the Atlantic had gained independence from Britain, whilst in France a revolution was beginning based on the 'Rights of Man and of the Citizen' against the *Ancien Regime* of an absolutist monarchy and the landed gentry. The French had a man willing to spread this philosophy of religious and cultural freedom and there was no riper field to sow than Ireland but the Irish themselves were divided religiously and politically. A Protestant lawyer, Theobald Wolfe Tone now tried to unite them under the 'Society of United Irishmen' – initially looking for Parliamentary reform in Ireland but ultimately complete Independence from Great Britain.

After the 1793 French declaration of war on Great Britain the pro French United Irishmen went underground whilst the 'Orange Order' was formed in Armagh backing the Protestant Ascendancy. Ireland and consequently British security was hugely exposed to a French landing which looked hideously likely in 1796 when a French fleet carrying Tone and 15,000 troops sailed into Bantry Bay. As Spanish Armadas had experienced before, however, an adverse wind hit the French, changing history and leaving Tone distraught. By 1798 the patience of the more radical United Irishmen had run out, they rebelled regardless across Ireland with possibly 30,000 dying in vicious sectarian violence and predominantly small scale battles with the British Army. For the biggest battle of the rebellion, Henry Munro, leader of the County Down United Irishmen, marched to Ballynahinch with 7,000 men armed with pikes, pitchforks and muskets whilst Major General George Nugent commanding King George III's forces in the North of Ireland arrived from Belfast and Downpatrick with 2,000 loyalists, militia, orangemen and some regulars. Nugent warned Munro to disperse, burning several local villages before on 12 June 1798, Munro sent 500 men to Windmill Hill, successfully blocking Nugent's advance on Ballynahinch. Munro declined to press a full attack that night, costing him a number of deserters but he then withdrew his outpost the following morning hoping to draw Nugent into a close quarter street fight in Ballynahinch. At dawn the artillery duel recommenced before Nugent duly advanced into Ballynahinch for an all day fight in which United Irish casualties mounted alarmingly. By 19.00 the worsted Munro began a United Irish retreat which turned into a rout when Nugent's merciless forces pursued. Munro eventually escaped with 150 men only to be betrayed by a farmer and hanged in Lisburn.

In August limited French forces landed in Mayo but after victories at Castlebar and Collooney were defeated at Ballinamuck and Killala. In October Tone was captured aboard a French ship off Donegal before committing suicide in a Dublin jail. The rebellion over, the Irish Parliament was absorbed into that at Westminster, upsetting even the Protestant Ascendancy. In 1801 Great Britain became the United Kingdom of Great Britain and Ireland but Home Rule for Ireland would eventually return. Before then Napoleon and Kaiser Wilhelm II would have to be reckoned with.

13 June 1982

Falklands War
Battle of Mount Tumbledown

LIEUTENANT GENERAL LEOPOLDO Galtieri's ruling military junta in Buenos Aires, Argentina had launched a full scale invasion of the Falkland Islands in April 1982. Facing civil disobedience at home, Galtieri had made a cynical attempt to restore popularity by stoking nationalist fervour over a 250-year-old territorial claim derived from Argentina's mother country, Spain. Crowds had celebrated in Buenos Aires whilst British Prime Minister Margaret Thatcher's Cabinet reeled with shock in London, initially uncertain whether the islands could be recaptured. By June, however, Galtieri's forces on the Falklands had been isolated by Argentina's Navy that would not put to sea, by the Royal Navy and by 27,000 British service personnel intent on liberating the island's 1,800 loyal British inhabitants. Whilst Argentine aircraft, operating at long range, inflicted serious losses on British shipping and equipment, British troops had begun landing in San Carlos Bay on the west coast of East Falkland. The Argentine garrison at Goose Green had then been defeated by 2nd Battalion, Parachute Regiment, eliminating a flank threat to the fifty mile march across the island toward the capital, Port Stanley above which, in the rocky, desolate mountains, awaited strong Argentine defences manned by conscripts, regulars, trained reservists and special forces with supporting artillery. On 11 June, Mounts Harriet, Two Sisters and Longdon were all taken by 42 Commando, 45 Commando and 3rd Para respectively forcing the Argentine Governor of the Falklands and head of Malvinas Joint Command Mario Menendez to retreat on Wireless Ridge, Mount William and the formidable Mount Tumbledown for a final desperate defence of the capital Port Stanley, Galtieri expecting him to fight until he had suffered at least 50 per cent losses.

The British plan was for 2 Para to move around Mount Longdon onto Wireless Ridge and for Gurkhas to move east between Mounts Harriet and Two Sisters, swing south of Tumbledown and onto Mount William. First however, 641 Scots Guards, flown up from Fitzroy, would have to crack the main obstacle,

Tumbledown. On the evening of 13 June 1982 British aerial attacks including the first ever use of laser guided bombs were matched by Argentinian aircraft strafing British positions around Mounts Kent and Longdon. The artillery of both sides also added their weight before the Scots under Lieutenant Colonel Mike Scot moved beyond Goat Ridge ready to assault the western slope of Tumbledown. Shortly before their final advance a diversionary attack by the Blues and Royals with two Scimitar and two Scorpion Tanks advanced up the southern slope where they could give fire support to the main attack. Almost immediately the diversionary attack encountered heavy close range resistance but the tactic allowed the main offensive to work up the western slope unnoticed (the north slope is a sheer face). At 22.30 the Argentine defenders initiated a ferocious two-hour firefight amongst the crags of Tumbledown before they retreated to their main defences. Four more hours of hard fighting had the Scots pinned down under mortars, grenades and machine-gun fire from Argentina's best troops who were themselves pounded by artillery from HMS *Yarmouth* and HMS *Active*. At 02.30 13 Platoon on the far left of the Left Flank Company, then scaled the sheer north rock face, climbing above Argentine positions from where they fired rockets and machine-guns in support of a new offensive over nearly 1,000 yards of rock by their comrades on the western slope. The Right Flank Company now came up to continue the assault, grenading machine-gun nests as they cleared the ridge rock-by-rock often with the bayonet. Eventually the Argentine defence broke, the Scots Guards continuing on east of Tumbledown while the Gurkhas successfully assaulted Mount William and 2 Para took Wireless Ridge to the north.

As Pipe Major James Riddell played 'the Crags of Tumbledown Mountain' on the summit immediately after the battle, the British Army looked down into Port Stanley. British armed forces had achieved what even the United States thought impossible when Menendez surrendered all Argentine forces at 21.00 that day. Galtieri was deposed within days and later imprisoned before receiving a 1989 pardon from Carlos Menem. In London, Prime Minister Margaret Thatcher was never more popular. The sovereignty dispute, however, continues to this day.

14 June 1645
English Civil Wars
Battle of Naseby

BY JULY 1644 a resurgent Parliament had already recovered many towns, cities and territories previously lost to King Charles I before the combined forces of Ferdinand, Lord Fairfax, Edward Montagu, Earl of Manchester, Oliver Cromwell and Alexander Leslie, Earl of Leven inflicted a defeat of such magnitude at Marston Moor that the whole of North England came under Parliament control. Royalist command was then split asunder when William Cavendish, Duke of Newcastle, who had stubbornly held out for the king at York, sailed for Hamburg in disgust at the performance of the king's nephew and senior commander Prince Rupert of the Rhine. Further south, however, Parliament armies under Sir William Waller and Robert Devereux, Earl of Essex had once again failed to support each other allowing Charles to once again advance on London as far as Newbury. Even here the numerically superior Parliament Army was in a strong position to decisively defeat the king but errors in command allowed yet another escape.

Over the 1644–45 winter, bitter recriminations abounded in the House of Commons, Parliament again divided into a faction for a peace settlement and 'Independents' who favoured a more vigorous prosecution of the war by way of a professional New Model Army commanded by men of merit rather than mere gentlemen. The resultant Self Denying Ordinance meant the resignation of Lords Fairfax, Manchester and Essex and in theory also Cromwell who was a Member of Parliament but who, by resigning, maintained his command in the field – the others, as Lords, could not. The Navy too lost its Lord High Admiral, Robert Rich, Earl of Warwick who transferred his skills for an elimination of witchcraft in East Anglia, hanging no less than nineteen women the following summer alone in that hotbed of sorcery, Chelmsford.

Charles was aware of the rifts within Parliament but seriously misjudged his enemy's resolve. Serious rifts also existed within the remaining Royal command, in talks at Uxbridge Charles' line was as unyielding as ever whilst Prince Rupert, doubtful of victory, favoured a negotiated peace. Rupert also favoured a march north in support of a Royalist uprising by James Graham, Marquess of Montrose, whilst others favoured marching south. Rupert had his way, initially advancing to the Welsh Marches pursued by Cromwell whilst for Parliament Sir Thomas Fairfax marched south to relieve the Royalist siege of Taunton. Fairfax was then recalled to besiege Oxford when Rupert and Charles marched east to Market Harborough. Here they were joined by Marmaduke, Lord Langdale but kept on the move, now marching to Leicester which declined to surrender and paid the traditional price, sacked by the Royalist Welsh Infantry which additionally prompted Fairfax to quit Oxford, Cromwell following on. Whilst the king and his chief advisor George Digby, Earl of Bristol were, however, eager to fight Fairfax, Rupert was not, for even without Cromwell, Fairfax was at least as strong as the Royalists. Rupert was overruled.

At Clipston on the morning of the 14 June 1645 as he peered through the morning fog, Rupert could make out the grim sight of the newly arrived Cromwell and his 'Ironsides' (cavalry) on Fairfax' right wing, infantry under Philip Skippon stood in the centre with the cavalry of Henry Ireton on the left, 14,000 men of the New Model Army, twice as many as had the king. With no possibility of retreating and not wishing to repeat the mistakes of Marston Moor, Rupert attacked immediately, the Royalist cavalry advancing abreast of their infantry across a small ditch, unchecked by musket fire to their right from Parliament dragoons under John Okey. Rupert's cavaliers then charged Ireton whose ranks broke after their wounded commander had tried to rally them. In the centre the Royalist infantry closed with that of Skippon who fought with a musket ball in the ribs as a battle of pikemen and musketeers raged around him. On the Royalist left however Langdale and his opposite Cromwell, concerned that one would outflank the other, remained motionless for thirty minutes before Langdale charged. He was met by just half of Cromwell's Ironsides who routed him. Cromwell then committed the remainder of his Ironsides to attack the Royalist infantry on their left flank whilst Okey, in Rupert's undisciplined absence pursuing Ireton, attacked their right. The king's infantry, surrounded on three sides, fought a dogged retreat, Charles restrained when he personally moved to rally them. The massacre continued for over a mile, 1,000 Royalists dead and 5,000 captured with all artillery.

Naseby proved to be the decisive battle of the English Civil War whilst, just as bad for the king, his private papers were captured proving that he had intended to gain support from Irish and European Catholics. His cause was condemned to collapse.

15 June 1429

Hundred Years' War
Battles of Meung-Sur-Loire, Beaugency, Patay

IN AUTUMN 1428 it seemed John, Duke of Bedford was about to complete the work of his brother King Henry V by indisputably uniting the Kingdoms of France and England under his seven-year-old nephew King Henry VI of England. The English conquest and the territories of their Burgundian allies covered France as far south as the River Loire where Thomas Montagu, Earl of Salisbury sought to break the formidable defences of Orléans for a further advance that would likely end the resistance of the dispossessed Dauphin Charles. The English Army, however, was not the force it once was, Salisbury was soon dead and just 4,000 Englishmen besieged Orléans once their Burgundian allies had deserted. Now under the cautious William de la Pole, Earl of Suffolk and the 'English Achilles' John Talbot, the besieging army was then on the receiving end of perhaps the most astonishing story in global military history when collapsing French command was suddenly instilled with self-belief by a seventeen-year-old peasant girl from Domrémy calling herself 'La Pucelle' (the Maid), Joan of Arc. The resurgent French garrison under John, Count of Dunois, the Bastard of Orléans, then overwhelmed the main besieging fortifications forcing Suffolk to lift the siege. Suddenly, the isolated English Army had become highly vulnerable.

Suffolk dangerously dispersed his forces on retreating from Orléans, marching upstream himself to Jargeau whilst Talbot marched downstream to Meung-sur-Loire and Beaugency. The Bastard marched against Jargeau whilst the Maid visited the Dauphin at Tours urging an attack in force before John Fastolf could arrive with English reinforcements from Paris. John, Duke of Alencon, captured at Verneuil in 1424 and the 'poorest man in France' after paying his ransom, then reinforced the Bastard who had initially been repulsed by Suffolk, Alencon and Dunois now beginning a French reconquest of the Loire Valley.

A returning Maid again galvanised the French before Jargeau, storming the town after a bombardment, capturing Suffolk and executing all those English without worth. The Bastard and the Maid now looked to clear the Loire Valley below Orléans prior to an advance on Rheims for Charles' coronation. On 15 June 1429, the 8,000 strong French Army marched along the southern bank of the Loire to Meung-sur-Loire, successfully taking the bridge over the 350 yard wide river but leaving the town unharmed. The following day, five miles further on at Beaugency, the Dauphin's cannon targeted the bridge that still stands today forcing Matthew Gough, a veteran of Cravant and Verneuil, back into the castle. As Gough fought on, Talbot met with the arriving Fastolf two miles to the north, Fastolf reluctant to counter-attack but Talbot insistent. On approaching Beaugency, however, the pair were confronted by the Dauphinist Army drawn up for battle. Fastolf drew up his own smaller force and waited, sending heralds to offer a three man combat which was declined as was any invitation to attack. The stalemate continued until evening when Fastolf retired to cannonade the bridge at Meung-sur-Loire but after battering the defenders all night received news of Gough's capitulation at Beaugency. A retreat toward Patay was now Fastolf and Talbot's only option but, spurred on by the Maid, Alencon was soon in hot pursuit with 6,000 men including a mounted advance guard under Jean Poton de Xaintrailles and the highly unpleasant La Hire. On 18 June 1429, south of Patay, Fastolf and Talbot turned to give battle. Setting an ambush, Talbot's archers were covered by a series of hedges to their front whilst Fastolf's main army remained on a ridge behind. Unknown to both, however, Talbot's position had been exposed by a startled stag just as the French vanguard approached. This time the Maid was not required as Xaintrailles and La Hire's immediate attack caught the inexperienced English recruits badly unprepared. Assaulted from front and flank by the French vanguard and soon after by the following main Dauphinist Army, Fastolf's army collapsed, himself escaping with a few archers but not Talbot who was captured.

The Dauphin was crowned King Charles VII of France at Rheims on 17 July 1429 as was King Henry VI of England and France two years later in Paris. The Maid, Joan of Arc was captured at Compiègne by Burgundians, convicted of heresy by the French Church and, in 1431, burnt at the stake by the English, she was canonised in 1920. In 1435 Philip, Duke of Burgundy made his peace with Charles. His life's work consequently in ruins Bedford died shortly after. Talbot, however, was exchanged and would continue the English struggle for France.

16 June 1815

Napoleonic Wars
Battle of Quatre Bras

FRANCE HAD BEEN ruled by a succession of absolutist monarchs since time immemorial but even after a quarter of a century of hitherto unimaginable bloodshed since the 1789 Revolution she had moved only from governance by a king to that of an emperor, Napoleon Bonaparte, a man determined to enforce the ideologies of that revolution on the rest of Europe. By 1812, France had been opposed by no less than five coalitions drawn from old monarchic European states unconvinced at the sincerity of the *liberté, egalité* and *fraternité* offered by Napoleonic rule but the man himself had defeated them all, controlling territory by conquest, satellite state or ally from Cadiz to Moscow, Copenhagen to Otranto. Napoleon, however, had then overstretched even the might of the *Grande Armée* with a disastrous advance and retreat to and from Moscow that also sapped French strength in the troublesome Iberian Peninsular. All of his genius was required just to fight on against a sixth coalition; suffering defeat again against Russia, Prussia, Austria and Sweden in a titanic struggle at Leipzig in 1813. As those victorious armies then threatened northern France and an Anglo-Portuguese Army entered southern France, Napoleon's Marshals refused to continue, the resulting Treaty of Fontainebleau forcing their emperor's abdication and exile to the Island of Elba.

British Foreign Secretary Robert Stewart, Lord Castlereagh had refused to be a party to Fontainebleau on account of Elba's proximity to France and his cynicism was brutally realised in February 1815 when Napoleon escaped back to Paris, old adherents flocking to his cause after a few unhappy months under King Louis XVIII. Time was of the essence for Napoleon, concerned at the presence in the Low Countries of 90,000 British and Dutch troops under Field Marshal Sir Arthur Wellesley, Duke of Wellington and 120,000 Prussians under Marshal Gephard von Blucher, the Corsican General marched north with 125,000 of his French faithful intent on defeating each in turn before turning east yet again to confront Russia and Austria. Uncertain of Napoleon's advance, Wellington at Brussels and Blucher at Ligny resolved to stay in close mutual support, both relying on spies rather than light cavalry so that when the *Grande Armée* suddenly appeared at Charleroi on 15 June 1815 Wellington exclaimed 'Napoleon has humbugged me, by God!'.

The following day, 16 June 1815, Napoleon attacked Blucher at Ligny whilst Wellington advanced from Brussels to defend the strategic crossroads at Quatre Bras. Blucher was nearly killed as Napoleon showed he had not lost his touch but crucially the Prussians retreated north-east to Wavre where they remained in touch with the British for the main event two days later. While Napoleon was attacking Blucher at Ligny his left under Marshal Michel Ney, 18,000 infantry and 2,000 cavalry, was to have advanced to take Quatre Bras but Ney delayed, initially reconnoitring 8,000 Dutch under William, Prince of Orange defending the position before advancing his light infantry with artillery support only at 14.00. The Dutch immediately gave ground as additional French forces followed up but they held on for an hour of fighting before the British 5th Infantry Division under Lieutenant General Thomas Picton arrived with the Dutch 3rd Light Cavalry, the fight intensifying when Napoleon ordered Ney to press his attack more vigorously. As the French onslaught increased the French II Corps under General Honoré Reille was about to take the crossroads but the British 3rd Infantry Division under Major General Carl von Alten then arrived to force them back. Ney now pleaded with Napoleon to return I Corps under General Jean-Baptiste Drouet, Comte D'Erlon which had earlier been summoned to Ligny. Nevertheless French cuirassiers charged into British grapeshot and musket volleys before the British 1st Infantry Division under Major General George Cook counter-attacked through Bossu Wood only to be repulsed in turn by French musket volleys and cavalry charges from lancers and chasseurs. As the battle then petered out into skirmishing and Wellington learnt of the Prussian retreat, the Anglo Dutch Army withdrew to a ridge south of Mont St Jean, Waterloo covered by the cavalry of Lieutenant General Henry Paget, Marquis of Uxbridge.

Believing Blucher beaten, Napoleon for the first time now prepared to fight in person the one nation that had consistently thwarted his and French ambition for over two decades.

17 June 1775

American War of Independence
Battle of Bunker Hill

ADMINISTRATION AND TAXATION from across the Atlantic with no representation beyond local government led Patriot Americans to make a 1773 protest in Boston Harbour by casting into the depths of the River Charles, a consignment of tea. The British Government in London responded by introducing the Coercive Acts (in America, the Intolerable Acts) which included the closure of the Port of Boston, stirring up American discontent further. To restore order General Thomas Cage, a veteran of the French and Indian War, respected on both sides of the Atlantic, was appointed Military Governor of Massachusetts but over the previous decade the British Army had been cut from 200,000 men to 45,000, just 3,500 of them now at Gage's disposal to confront many times that number of American Patriots joining the insurgent 'Sons of Liberty'.

The discontent further turned violent in April 1775 when two British columns left Boston separately for an attack on American ammunition dumps at Lexington and Concord, an attack that saw many British veterans of Minden relieved to return alive. Gage was now hemmed in on the headland that is Boston whilst across the bay to the north of the River Charles, the British vacated positions on the Charlestown Heights fearing that any additional uprising in Charlestown would leave troops there isolated. With the arrival of reinforcements including General William Howe sentiment altered such as to reoccupy the heights and thus prevent the Americans from using artillery recently captured at Fort Ticonderoga against shipping in the harbour and Boston itself. Charlestown would also serve for any future British attack on the American block at the then more narrow Charlestown neck and their base at Cambridge. The evening before the sortie, however, Patriots of the Massachussets and Connecticut Regiments advanced, preempting Gage by taking Bunker and Breeds Hill above Charlestown. Under fire from HMS *Lively*, the Patriots then constructed a large redoubt on the front of Breeds Hill with attached lines of trenches across the Peninsular. Having spent two months trapped in Boston British soldiers were only too happy for an opportunity to counter-attack the American amateurs with what they expected to be a classic artillery bombardment, an infantry advance of disciplined musket volleys and finally, a pleasing victory at the point of the bayonet.

On the morning of the 17 June 1775, a massive British artillery bombardment commenced from both Boston and adjacent warships with Gage spectating from well back but Howe further forward moving men across to the Charlestown Peninsula in rowing boats. A shortage of boats meant two lifts were required just for the initial 1,500 men whilst Howe immediately sent for another 1,500 following a reconnaissance of the American positions. The impressive British display unsettled many of the American defenders but it was only at 15.00 that the main British attack got under way with Brigadier Robert Pigot feinting an attack on the Breed's Hill redoubt whilst Howe led grenadiers and light infantry along the north beach against the supposedly weaker American left flank. As Howe approached, discipline failed with the men crowding, firing too early and consequently ineffectively. Staggering forward over obstacles they were then met with a crashing volley from the Americans which sent them reeling backwards, in the confusion of battle the British now firing on each other. Howe struggled to regain order, sending orders to Pigot, who had already set Charlestown alight and was now moving closer to the Breeds Hill redoubt, to now attack in earnest from the south while he attacked again from the north. Initially the result was the same, indisciplined British musketry met by crashing volleys from the American amateurs. As ammunition ran low British officers then began leading men forward with the bayonet achieving greater success by reaching the very edges of the earthworks. After more hesitation in the face of heavy fire they finally scrambled over the ramparts with the now less resolute American defence disintegrating. A scene of slaughter then developed as Americans ran for their lives only for British Redcoats to cut them down with musket ball and bayonet. Fleeing across the Charlestown Peninsular the American defenders turned to fire on the pursuing British from behind walls and fences losing a total 450 men killed and wounded.

The British victory had been expensive, over 1,000 casualties, many of them officers, and yet they had failed to break the American grip on Boston, the siege would continue.

18 June 1815

Napoleonic Wars
Battle of Waterloo

BY THE 1814 Treaty of Fontainebleau Napoleon Bonaparte, Emperor of the French abdicated and was exiled to Elba. Napoleon's fall had been precipitated by his desperation to defeat the United Kingdom of Great Britain and Ireland with a trade embargo, the Continental System, the enforcing of which had necessitated disastrous French invasions in 1807 of the Iberian Peninsular and in 1812, of Russia. After a desperate winter retreat from Moscow Napoleon had again been catastrophically defeated at the epic two-day battle of Leipzig (the biggest of the entire French Revolutionary and Napoleonic Wars) by Russia, Prussia, Austria and Sweden who then subsequently advanced into northern France whilst an Anglo-Portuguese Army similarly advanced into the south.

Napoleon's stay on Elba was however not to last long, the Emperor escaping back to Paris in March 1815 for a final hundred days (111) with thousands of Frenchmen flocking to his cause already unhappy at the rule of King Louis XVIII. Surrounded by the armies of the Seventh Coalition but intent on defeating each in turn Napoleon immediately advanced north from Paris to Ligny where he defeated 85,000 Prussians under General Gephard von Blucher who received no significant support from the Anglo-Dutch Army of Field Marshal Sir Arthur Wellesley, Duke of Wellington. For his part Wellington had fought Napoleon's left that same day at Quatre Bras before retreating to a ridge south of Mont St Jean, Waterloo. Advised that Blucher had retreated east rather than north-east and was therefore thought to no longer pose a threat, Napoleon pursued Wellington with an army 73,000-strong for what would be the first and only open battle (he was at the 1793 Siege of Toulon) in which he was personally present against the one nation that had continuously thwarted his and French ambition over the past two decades.

On a three mile front Wellington characteristically concealed much of his 68,000 Anglo-Dutch Army behind the ridge. On the front left two villages, Papelotte and La Haye, were defended by Dutch and Belgians, whilst in the centre the farm of La Haye Sainte was defended by Hanoverians with supporting British light infantry. On the right, in the Chateau of Hougoumont, Wellington put 1,500 of his toughest men, Guards and Dutch Nassauer's under the reliable Scot, Lieutenant Colonel James Macdonnell. Critically, these isolated positions would break up the approach of the massed French columns.

At 11.30 on 18 June 1815 eighty French guns bombarded the British centre left whilst Hougoumont on the right was besieged by French infantry under Jerome Bonaparte (brother). Wellington, however, stood firm between La Haye Sainte and Papelotte to receive 16,000 French infantry in column under General Jean-Baptiste Drouet, Comte D'Erlon. Hit by British artillery and Dutch skirmishers over 1,300 yards of head high corn D'Erlon reached the ridge where he was hit by further musket volleys from Lieutenant General Thomas Picton's British 5th Infantry Division who for good measure followed up with the bayonet. The heavy cavalry of Lieutenant General Henry Paget, Marquis of Uxbridge then routed D'Erlon but continued on toward the French guns only to be routed in turn by French lancers. Skirmishing continued until 16.00 when Marshal Michel Ney led 7,000 French cavalry against the British and Dutch infantry squares on the centre right, gunners and officers taking cover within them but the squares suffering from continuous French artillery. Disaster then struck the Anglo-Dutch when La Haye Sainte fell to a combined French artillery, cavalry and infantry attack. Wellington, desperate to restore his centre, now ordered that 'I and every Englishman... must die on the spot we now occupy'. As the British line struggled to hold, Napoleon was suddenly obliged to strengthen his right flank when Blucher's Prussians began arriving but with Hougoumont still soaking up men on his left, he had now to break Wellington or retreat to Paris. Since there was no 'La Gloire' to be gained by the latter, the never before defeated in battle, 5,000-strong, Garde Impériale advanced unchecked by British artillery until they reached the ridge of Mont St Jean where the British Grenadier Guards under Major General Peregrine Maitland rose from a prone position, Wellington shouting 'now Maitland, now is your time!'. A musket volley at fifty yards staggered the Garde, they fell back, hit again on both flanks as they did so by light infantry under Colonel John Colborne. Still the French artillery checked the British, 'Go on Colborne! Go on! they won't stand!' Wellington waved his hat and ordered the whole Anglo-Dutch line to advance. Victory was theirs.

For Napoleon it was the end, ignominiously chased from the battlefield he was finally exiled to the Atlantic island of St Helena where he died of stomach cancer in 1821. In 1828 Wellington became Prime Minister of Great Britain, a country that would go on to dominate the globe for the next century.

19 June 1306

Anglo-Scottish Wars
Battle of Methven

 FOLLOWING DEFEAT TO the King of England Edward I at the 1298 Battle of Falkirk, William Wallace resigned as the Guardian of Scotland having received little help for his cause of Scottish Independence from the squabbling Scottish nobility. In his place as joint Guardians were Robert the Bruce VII, Earl of Carrick and John 'Red' Comyn, Lord of Badenoch both with Royal Scottish ancestry and both with designs on the Scottish Crown themselves. Unsurprisingly the pair found it impossible to work together and with a likely return of John Balliol as King of Scotland, Bruce resigned, for the time being 'returning to the King's (Edward's) peace'. Comyn was related to Edward by marriage and naturally believed he would prosper if Edward conquered Scotland, he therefore followed Bruce in submitting to Edward's suzerainty and, as had Bruce, received the king's pardon. There was to be no pardon for Wallace, however, not that he was ever likely to forego the cause of Independence but in 1305 he was shamefully betrayed at Robroyston, Glasgow by the Scottish Lords that had knelt before the English king. The Scottish rebel was taken to London to stand trial at Westminster Hall before being dragged through the city by horse to Smithfield Market where he was hung, drawn and quartered.

The straightforward anti-English stance of Wallace was in contrast to that of Comyn and Bruce. Once Bruce had inherited his father's claim to the Scottish throne in 1304 he then quietly sought to regain Scottish Independence but Comyn would never back an uprising that would see Bruce King of the Scots (Bruce's grandfather had lost out to Balliol in 1292) – according to Bruce, Comyn going as far as betraying him to Edward. In early 1306 the two rivals met in the Church of the Greyfriars, Dumfries where Bruce ruthlessly murdered Comyn at the high altar. After then defeating Comyn's supporters in a series of running battles Bruce declared himself King Robert I of Scotland and, before Pope Clement V could excommunicate him, hastily crowned himself at Scone on 25 March 1306.

Again, many Scottish factions rallied to support independence including former supporters of Wallace whilst any English still in Scotland fled for sanctuary.

Following the 1304 siege of Stirling Castle, Edward had believed Scotland to at last be pacified so that when news of Bruce's uprising reached him at Winchester thirteen days later he flew into a legendary rage vowing to avenge Comyn with no quarter given. Not in the best of health himself the old warlord then ordered north Comyn's brother-in-law Aymer de Valence, heir to the Earldom of Pembroke, with orders for the powerful Percy and Clifford families of the Northern Counties to join him. Pembroke was also joined by supporters of Comyn.

The English Army of about 6,000 crossed the River Forth and headed to Perth to confront the rebels. Outnumbered by 1,500 (numbers are not reliable), Bruce was urged to adopt a Wallace type scorched earth policy rather than risk all in a set piece battle but he disregarded the advice insisting that the English Army could adequately provision itself for quite some time and that he had cavalry to match Valence whereas Wallace had not. Bruce sent Valence a challenge to meet in battle immediately but the Englishman declined since it was late in the day and instead agreed to meet in battle the next morning. The Scots then retired to camp at Methven a few miles distant. Taking Valence at his word, Bruce failed to position pickets with his men removing their armour and relaxing for the night but whilst Valence would indeed meet Bruce the next morning, 19 June 1306, it was at a considerably earlier hour than a surprised Bruce and his army had expected. A desperate struggle raged with those Scots that stood to fight but most ran for their lives into the woods where, in a reversal of fortunes at Roslin, 1303, they were cut down by waiting English men-at-arms. Amidst the chaos the Bruce led a personal attack on Valence, unseating him from his horse before being unseated himself and rescued by his brother-in-law, Sir Christopher Seton.

Robert the Bruce's army was routed at Methven with many captured Scots, including Seton later hung, drawn and quartered. Bruce fled to the Highlands, the Hebrides and perhaps even Ireland where inspiration would be provided by a spider. He would fight Valence again at Loudoun Hill the following year.

20 June 1347
Hundred Years' War
Battle of La Roche Derrien

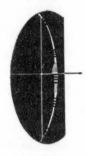

A SERIES OF disputes between King Edward III of England and King Philip VI of France had led to the 1337 outbreak of the Hundred Years' War. Then adding to the original disputes concerning territory and fealty was Edward's claim to the French throne for which he had been passed over nine years earlier under a technicality of Salic Law. Building allies in Flanders and the Holy Roman Empire Edward's initial forays into France had met with failure but he then devastated a French naval fleet at Sluys before taking the side of John and Joanna de Montford in the Breton (Brittany) War of Succession. Here Sir Walter Manny first caused De Montford's rival Charles, Count of Blois (backed by King Philip) considerable discomfort before in 1342 both he and William de Bohun, Earl of Northampton decisively defeated him at Morlaix.

The struggle for Brittany now became one of skirmish and siege, at one point all three major cities in the region, Nantes, Rennes and Vannes held by Blois but besieged by De Montford's Englishmen. In 1343, King Philip eventually came to Blois' support physically by marching on Vannes where Manny and Northampton had joined with King Edward himself. Just as the two armies seemed about to settle their difference, however, Pope Clement VI intervened with a truce – a truce that would be repeatedly broken by the French. Just two years later Northampton was back in the field, this time assisted by the resourceful Sir Thomas Dagworth as Edward continued the Breton War with renewed vigour as part of his greater struggle for France despite the recent death of John de Montford.

In June 1346, Blois, with a much larger force, caught up with Dagworth at St Pol de Léon and attacked him on three sides but the English archers exacted such a heavy toll that Blois suffered yet another defeat. Blois retreated when Edward then invaded Normandy and northern France, the English king delivering a crushing defeat on Philip's army at Crécy before beginning a siege of Calais. Only a year later with the siege of Calais still ongoing did Blois raise an army strong enough to resume the conflict in Brittany. In May 1347, the pious count arrived before the walls of the English held La Roche Derrien complete with nine massive siege engines capable of throwing 2–300 pound stones, terrifying the inhabitants both French and English, but not the Governor Richard Totsham who refused to submit in the hope that Dagworth or Northampton would come to his relief. Sure enough Dagworth would oblige Totsham but only after a delay and with what seemed a hopelessly small force.

Dagworth approached La Roche Derrien and the at least 4–5,000 French besiegers with just 300 mounted men-at-arms and 400 archers in darkness through wooded country on the east bank of the River Jaudi, a hazardous procedure in medieval times but successfully arriving before dawn on 20 June 1347. Resolving to attack Blois' eastern encampment immediately, Dagworth caught the French by surprise and, still in darkness, managed to create enough confusion to hide his own shortcomings. The confusion spread to Blois' three other camps but the count had issued strict instructions that no one was to move from his defensive position. The French Eastern Camp was therefore in some disarray before managing to mount a counter-attack which soon turned the tables against the small English force, temporarily capturing Dagworth. A prompt English counter-attack in turn then rescued Dagworth only for daylight to arrive, the French defenders immediately realising the English were present in vastly inferior numbers than thought but rather than attacking in overwhelming numbers they remained under orders in their own encampments. Watching from the walls of La Roche Derrien, Totsham did exactly the opposite, leaving a few men on garrison duty the Governor led a sortie out of the eastern gate into the backs of the French, before both he and Dagworth overcame each camp in turn. As French resistance crumbled, a wounded Blois was captured and sent to the Tower of London where he joined the Scottish King, David II.

The bloodbath of La Roche Derrien was not over, on Dagworth's departure King Philip himself attacked, forcing an entry to slaughter the disloyal French townsfolk. The English garrison however negotiated a passage free of arms before marching to Chateauneuf where they were attacked by the local population and slaughtered to a man. The Breton War became a stalemate, Dagworth killed in 1350. The Bloisian faction was now headed by Blois' wife Jeanne de Penthièvre and the Montford faction by John's wife, Joanna of Flanders. In 1351, sixty knights would fight a chivalric combat in their honour at Chêne de Mi-Voie.

21 June 1813

Napoleonic Wars
Battle of Vitoria

THE 'GRANDE ARMÉE' of Napoleon Bonaparte, Emperor of the French was in disarray following a disastrous 1812 advance into and retreat out of Russia. Despite victories at Smolensk and Borodino, Napoleon had been unable to fully defeat the Russian Army of Field Marshal Prince Michael Andreas Barclay de Tolly, arriving in Moscow only to find the city deserted. Through the snows of the Russian winter, Napoleon had then retreated, harassed by the vengeful Russians whose Cossacks mercilessly cut down French stragglers. Amidst scenes of appalling human suffering, particularly on crossing the River Beresina, French losses amounted to a staggering 90 per cent of the original 600,000 strong *Grande Armée* and forced a hurried recruitment campaign once back in France that incredibly, and only by Napoleon's genius, raised another army of 400,000. Enemies of France were, however, swarming on all sides, Russia and a defecting Prussia (a recent French ally) forming the Sixth Coalition with Sweden and as ever the United Kingdom of Great Britain and Ireland who were fighting with the Portuguese and Spanish in the Iberian Peninsular.

In May 1813, just when all seemed lost, Napoleon then suddenly defeated the Russo-Prussian Army at Lutzen and Bautzen albeit with casualties he could ill afford. Despite the victory, pressure therefore continued to mount on the French, General Arthur Wellesley, Marquess of Wellington, commanding the Anglo-Portuguese and now Spanish, again taking to the offensive in Spain after the previous year's victories at Ciudad Rodrigo, Badajoz and Salamanca. Wellington sought to drive the 200,000 French concentrating in northern Spain under 'King' Joseph Bonaparte, back over the Pyrenees but to do so required his supply base to move from Lisbon to Santander on Spain's northern shore. With diversionary attacks and heightened Spanish guerila activity, the 100,000-strong Anglo-Portuguese-Spanish Army marched north from Ciudad Rodrigo around the French flank at Valladolid toward Burgos, taking Salamanca on 26 May 1813 and Zamorra on 2 June. Joseph

Bonaparte now fled from Madrid to join Marshal Jean-Baptiste Jourdan, retreating to Burgos which Wellington, through bitter experience, bypassed forcing Jourdan and his 66,000-strong army to retreat further north to the River Ebro and a defensive position around Vitoria on the River Zadorra and the Heights of Puebla where they hoped to be reinforced by General Bertrand Clausel.

After a vigorous pursuit and aware of Clausel's proximity, Wellington rounded the Heights of Puebla to the west of Jourdan's position and attacked at 08.00 on 21 June 1813. Lieutenant General Rowland Hill's 2nd Infantry Division including Portuguese and Spaniards attacked the French left flank under General Honoré Gazan south of the Zadorra before the 1st and 5th Infantry Divisions under Lieutenant General Thomas Graham advanced on the French right under General Honoré Reille in an attempt to cut off their retreat to Bayonne, France. The Light Brigade of Major General James Kempt then captured bridges across the Zadorra at Villodas, Tres Puentes and Mendoza allowing the 4th Infantry Division of Lieutenant General Lowry Cole to join Hill's attack on the French left while the 3rd and 7th Infantry Divisions under Lieutenant Generals Thomas Picton and George Ramsay, Earl of Dalhousie advanced over the river to engage the French centre under General Jean Baptiste Drouet, Comte D'Erlon. The two-pronged British attacks on the French left flank and centre resulted in Gazan folding back into the village of Arinez and the hard pressed D'Erlon. A terrific eight-hour fight then developed as the French attempted to halt the British advance with ball, grapeshot, canister and musket but ultimately Gazan and D'Erlon were forced further back into their right flank under Reille. Joseph Bonaparte realised the danger only as the retreat became a rout, sending Reille's division north-east to oppose Graham's attempted block, he himself escaping from his coach when attacked by a British Hussar. The French disintegrated, abandoning all their artillery as a flight east commenced, Reille still desperately holding off Graham. The British pursued until the entire French baggage train was discovered in Vitoria, troops now fighting each other for profit rather than destroying the enemy. An enraged Wellington remarked 'We have in the service the scum of the earth'.

Wellington would advance into France soon enough but first he would have to deal with French garrisons at San Sebastian and Pamplona. Ludwig van Beethoven's Opus 91 is to Wellingtons victory at Vitoria as Pyotr Ilyich Tchaikovsky's 1812 Overture is to Russia's victory over Napoleon.

22 June 1402

Glyndwr Rebellion
Battle of Bryn Glas

ON THE 1377 death of King Edward III, the English crown passed to his ten-year-old grandson, Richard of Bordeaux, son of Edward of Woodstock, the Black Prince. Whilst a minor King Richard II's affairs were managed by a series of councils in which many Lords had a vested interest but when an increasingly autocratic Richard began to take personal charge, his court diminished to a privileged few. Amongst the discontented Lords, the Earls of Arundel, Gloucester and Warwick formed the 'Lords Appellant' calling the king's actions to account before defeating him at the 1387 Battle of Radcot Bridge. The 'Merciless Parliament' that followed then kept Richard as head of state but stripped him of virtually all power. Richard had no option but to bide his time, his power gradually restored over the next decade while his cousin Henry of Bolingbroke, who had opposed him throughout, delicately remained on terms until 1398. A row then resulted in Henry's banishment and, on the death of his father (John of Gaunt, Duke of Lancaster, third son of Edward III), the confiscation of his hereditary lands, the most extensive in England. Henry returned to England in June, landing at Ravenspur, Yorkshire, taking advantage of Richard's absence in Ireland to gain support from other disgruntled Lords before declaring himself King Henry IV of England. The returning Richard was imprisoned in the Tower of London before dying six months later in dubious circumstances, most likely dehydration.

For most of the previous century the Welsh had supported the English in both Scottish and French wars. One such, Owain Glyndwr (Owen Glendower), Squire of Sycharth and Glyndyfrwy in the Welsh Marches (England/ Wales borderlands), had served King Richard in a military capacity for three years. In 1400 Reginald, Baron Grey de Ruthyn, as he had done before but with no favour from Richard, claimed some of Glyndwr's lands. This time Ruthyn was not only supported by his King but Henry granted him further concessions. Ruthyn then added to the injustice by delaying a summons for service in Scotland of Glyndwr's levy leaving the Welshman unable to fulfill his duty; an act of treason which left his estates forfeit. Glyndwr, his brothers and other disaffected welshmen then retaliated by burning Ruthyn's property and pillaging the countryside around it. Though subsequently defeated at Welshpool, Glyndwr escaped, hiding in the Marches which at the time were heavily wooded, whilst his lands were passed to Henry's half-brother John Beaufort, Earl of Somerset, a decision that prompted a surge of support for Glyndwr and resulted in Rhys ap Tudur capturing Conwy Castle in 1401. In 1402 Glyndwr then captured Ruthyn before threatening English towns and garrisons in the Marches. King Henry ordered his Lieutenant in the Marches Henry Percy (Harry Hotspur) to crush the revolt but it was Henry's cousin Sir Edmund Mortimer who advanced with 2,000 men through the difficult country to confront Glyndwr.

Mortimer had a better claim to the throne than Henry since he was the grandson of Edward III's second son, (Lionel of Antwerp, Duke of Clarence), he was also the brother-in-law of Hotspur and owned significant lands in the Marches and Herefordshire giving him a strong incentive to end Glyndwr's rebellion. On 22 June 1402, Mortimer came across Glyndwr and his army of a similar size outside Bryn Glas. Glyndwr had split his force, the main army on a slope up which Mortimer now advanced whilst a smaller force waited in the valley to his left. An archery duel began proceedings with the highly proficient Welsh making full use of the extra range offered by the high ground. Badly stung, Mortimer's men-at-arms resolved to close and pushed forward in an unimaginative full-frontal attack upon which Glyndwr called in his hidden force, attacking Mortimer in the flank and rear. It seemed Mortimer's problems could hardly become any worse but they did when Welsh bowmen in his pay treacherously changed sides to begin firing on the English at point-blank range. The results were devastating, Mortimer's army was annihilated, the bodies of his men left to rot on the hillside though he himself was taken alive.

Believing in a conspiracy and no doubt aware of Mortimer's ancestry, King Henry refused to pay his ransom causing Mortimer to throw in his lot with Glyndwr who resolved to restore Richard 'if alive' to the throne. Furious that their brother-in-law had been forsaken the Percys then also rebelled, matters would come to a head at Shrewsbury.

23 June 1757

India
Battle of Plassey

IN 1682 THE British East India Company conceded defeat to the Dutch in the East Indies to concentrate on developing trade in India. Facing stiff competition here also, four major trade centres were developed at Surat, Bombay (Mumbai), Madras (Chennai) and Calcutta (Kolkata) all protected by forts and the company's own private army. As the Dutch concentrated on trade in the East Indies and the Portuguese satisfied themselves around Goa, Britain and France were left to court favour in North and Central India with Muslim Mughal Nizams and Nawabs in return for military support – both in local disputes and against Pashtun Afghan and Hindu Maratha (Mahratta) expansion. This delicate political game lasted until the Austrian War of Succession 1740–48 (Second Carnatic War in India, 1746–50) after which the Treaty of Aix-la-Chapelle settled little, particularly in India.

The efficiency of the French and British armies (which included many Indian sepoys) impressed the locals, their soldiers firing a musket several times a minute as opposed to a barely-trained Indian who fired once every ten minutes. Not only that but the British possessed a significant naval presence in the Bay of Bengal. A fact missed in 1756 at the start of the Seven Years' War in Europe (Third Carnatic in India) by the Nawab of Bengal Siraj-ud-Daulah who was uncomfortable with the increased British fortification of Fort William, Calcutta. Siraj attacked and captured Calcutta in August that year only for Lieutenant Colonel Robert Clive and Vice Admiral Charles Watson to relieve the city before a small force under Captain Eyre Coote and Major James Kilpatrick sacked Hooghly for good measure. Undeterred, Siraj attacked Calcutta again in early 1757, Clive again responding despite being heavily outnumbered, to run the 'Gauntlet of Calcutta' in a successful relief of Fort William. Also at war with the French and aware of the approach of Marquis Charles de Bussy, Watson's warships then levelled the French settlement at Chandannagar further infuriating Siraj who relied on French support to check British ambition.

Clive, however, had already decided to replace the unreliable Nawab with one more compliant, bribing Siraj' uncle Mir Jafar Khan (who commanded a part of Siraj' army) with the Nawabship of Bengal should he defect. Clive then marched his 3,000 British and Indian sepoys with ten light cannon through the Bengal monsoon up the River Hooghly to Plassey where 60,000 Bengalis and French with fifty-nine heavy cannon awaited him.

On 23 June 1757, Siraj' Bengal Army had taken up a position with its right on the River Hooghly, extending east in an arc outflanking the British right and threatening the rear. His left on the Hooghly, Clive marched the company army north out of their overnight mango grove camp to within 800 yards of the enemy, the Bengali gunners opening fire along the line at 08.00 with Clive's returning. The lighter more modern British guns fired quicker and more accurately but nonetheless, after half an hour, Clive moved his line back into defensive positions in the mango grove, Siraj responding by moving forward to continue his ineffective bombardment. When the British guns then resumed firing the effect was far more deadly, the artillery duel continuing until around midday when an hour long rainstorm broke over the battlefield. As both sets of gunners ceased firing the Bengali commander Mir Madan Khan believed the British cannon to be inoperable during the downpour and took the opportunity to lead a cavalry charge. Mir Madan was, however, met with short range blasts of British grapeshot since the more experienced British gunners had covered their guns with tarpaulins, quickly returning to action with predictably catastrophic results for the Bengali horsemen. Rightly suspicious of the loyalty of his other Generals, Siraj now returned with 2,000 horsemen to Mushidabad leaving Mahan Lal to withdraw to a more protected position but in doing so exposed the French cannon. Mir Jafar Khan meanwhile moved left and remained motionless conspicuously failing to support his fellow Bengalis. Major James Kilpatrick began a British advance which Clive halted, bringing up the entire army to continue the British bombardment before launching a three-pronged infantry attack. By 17.00 Siraj' Bengalis and French, battered by British cannon, musket volleys and bayonet charges, were in complete flight.

Plassey effectively ended French interest in North India. Siraj-ud-Daulah was murdered shortly after by relatives of the new Nawab Mir Jafar Khan who would not turn out to be as compliant as the British had hoped. The British would do battle with Mir Jafar and the Dutch at Chinsurah two years later.

24 June 1314

Anglo-Scottish Wars
Battle of Bannockburn

ROBERT THE BRUCE, 7th Earl of Annandale and Earl of Carrick inherited his claim as King of Scots in 1304 on the death of his father. Having played politics for a decade, often siding against Scottish Independence with the 'Hammer of the Scots' England's King Edward I, Bruce now pinned his true colours to the mast by leading the fight for independence himself. In 1306 Bruce ruthlessly murdered his rival John 'Red' Comyn, Earl of Badenoch at the high altar of the Greyfriars Church in Dumfries, enraging Edward who sent Comyn's brother-in-law Aymer de Valence, the future Earl of Pembroke, to defeat Bruce at Methven. Bruce fled Scotland, leaving his wife and daughters imprisoned and a brother to be hanged, drawn and quartered but returned the following year only to suffer another defeat at Loch Ryan and the beheading of another two brothers. Bruce then avenged Methven by defeating an impetuous Valence at Loudoun Hill before receiving the welcome news two months later that King Edward was dead.

Bruce then pursued several years of guerilla warfare against Comyn support and the English on both sides of the border in response to which Edward's son, King Edward II, struggled to coordinate a coherent defence. Regularly falling out with his barons over his friend and advisor in all matters, Piers Gaveston, Edward's enmity was further deepened when Gaveston was banished by the barons in 1311, returning in 1312 to be murdered by Guy de Beauchamp, Earl of Warwick. Meanwhile in Scotland, Bruce had eliminated most of his adversaries but continued to avoid a decisive battle against the more powerful English, successfully undermining Edward's suzerainty to gain control of all Scotland except Stirling Castle. Even here in 1314, the English stronghold was besieged by another brother, Edward Bruce, now Earl of Carrick. Edward Bruce, however, dubiously agreed with Philip Mowbray, the English garrison commander, that the castle was to be surrendered if a relieving army did not approach within three leagues by midsummers day. When a 16,000-strong English Army marched into Falkirk on 22 June, the Scots were therefore obliged to either raise the siege or fight a decisive battle.

On 23 June, Robert, Baron de Clifford and 300 English men-at-arms sought to relieve the Stirling garrison but strong Scottish resistance led by Thomas Randolph, Earl of Moray forced them back to Edward's main army crossing the Bannock burn in the vicinity of another 6–7,000 Scots under Robert the Bruce. As the two armies closed, Henry de Bohun in the English vanguard caught sight of Bruce in the open and charged but the Scot swerved, avoiding De Bohun's lance before cleaving the English knight's head with his battle axe. As Scottish morale soared it sank further in the English camp when the Constable of England, Humphrey de Bohun (cousin), Earl of Hereford and Gilbert de Clare, Earl of Gloucester argued with each other and Edward over command, tactics and bravery, Gloucester in particular slighted by the English king. Edward decided not to fight late in the day and instead fatefully camped between the Bannock burn and the Pelstream burn further north, a position Bruce attacked at first light 24 June 1314. Advancing in schiltroms of densely packed spearmen and pikemen toward the alarmed English, Bruce then received another morale boost when Gloucester demonstrated his mettle by suicidally charging the Scots single-handed. The massed English cavalry then followed, charging the schiltroms but only on a narrow front since they were confined by the two burns which negated their mobility and numerical superiority. As the English men-at-arms struggled in the resultant press their archers moved onto the right flank, achieving some success before being driven off by Scottish cavalry under Robert Keith. Falling back, the archers continued to fire, hitting not just Scots but many of their own men whose discomfort Bruce increased by further advancing the schiltroms and adding his lightly-armed 'small folk'. Believing more 'regular' Scots were joining the battle English resistance began to crumble as the schiltroms relentlessly advanced like a medieval combine harvester. As a disaster was clearly unfolding Edward departed on horseback for Dunbar leaving 10–12,000 Englishmen, including thirty-seven lords, to perish. The surrender of Stirling Castle followed shortly after.

After years of ravaging North England, Robert the Bruce was recognised as King of the Scots by the 1328 Treaty of Edinburgh-Northampton. King Edward II was brutally murdered at Berkeley Castle in 1327 but six years later his formidable son, Edward III, would march again on the then Scottish town of Berwick.

25 June 1658
Anglo-Spanish Wars
Siege of Rio Nuevo, Jamaica

IN 1653 OLIVER Cromwell had become Lord Protector of England, Ireland and Scotland following Parliament victories in three English Civil Wars which also included a bloody conquest of Ireland and a crushing of Charles Stuart's (later Charles II) Royalist Army at the Battle of Worcester. There was no let up in fighting, however, since Cromwell was now at war with England's former Protestant ally against Catholic Spain, the Dutch Republic who, the English believed, had cynically taken commercial advantage of the civil strife throughout the British Isles over the past decade. The First Anglo-Dutch War (of four) finished a year later with an English victory but whilst both nations had been distracted, Spain reemerged as a commercial threat. Cromwell once again proposed a union with the Dutch to fight Spain but was rejected by their Parliament, the States General, forcing England to go it alone. Cromwell's obvious targets were the old treasure routes of the Caribbean attacked the previous century by the likes of Sir Francis Drake, Sir John Hawkins and Sir Walter Raleigh but with sugar also now at stake, the acquisition of territory was paramount, Cromwell's 'Western Design'.

On Christmas Day 1654 General-at-Sea William Penn and Colonel Robert Venables sailed with thirty-eight ships from Plymouth to Barbados where their troop strength was increased to 6,000. The pair decided to repeat Drake's 1586 capture of Santo Domingo, Hispaniola (Dominican Republic) but two separate attacks both ended in ambushes from which Venables only escaped courtesy of his highly disciplined naval regiment. Following a rethink, Penn and Venables then headed for the lightly defended but, at the time, less valuable Spanish possession of Jamaica. Covered by a naval bombardment on Port Royal, Venables' troops landed to occupy Santiago de la Vega (now Spanish Town) without a fight but allowed the Spanish garrison to escape to Cuba once they had released their slaves, maroons, into the mountains of Jamaica's interior. Remarkably both Penn and Venables now considered their work to be done and abandoned their posts to return to England where they were both promptly imprisoned in the Tower of London.

In Jamaica both English and Spanish settlers were severely weakened by disease (the first two English governors each survived only a year) but Cromwell nevertheless actively promoted immigration from England, Scotland and Ireland as well as encouraging privateers and buccaneers (the Brethren of the Coast) to use Fort Cromwell (Port Royal) as their base, effectively to discourage Spanish counter-attacks.

In October 1657, however, an undeterred Spaniard, Cristobal Arnaldo de Issasi, attempted to retake the island with several hundred reinforcements from Cuba but was defeated on the north coast at Ocho Rios by the rapid reaction of the new English Governor of Jamaica, Edward D'Oyley. Eight months later Issasi was ready for a second attempt, this time with reinforcements from New Spain including a Regiment of Mexicans who also landed on the north coast, this time at Rio Nuevo. Again D'Oyley reacted quickly before further Spanish reinforcements could arrive, on 25 June 1568 mustering 700 men in ten ships that sailed around the island to capture the Spanish transport ships, isolating Issasi's men ashore. Behind a newly built stockade, however, Issasi refused to surrender and was consequently bombarded for two days by D'Oyley's cannon. The Spaniards returned fire but were taking heavy casualties behind their inadequate defences before on 27 June, after a circuitous march through thick forest and across difficult terrain, D'Oyley stormed the Spanish stockade from the rear. Issasi escaped but his force was routed, 300 of them dead with 150 captured. The Spanish guns were then added to the defences of Fort Cromwell.

Rio Nuevo is the biggest battle ever to be fought in Jamaica which was recognised as a British possession by the 1670 Treaty of Madrid. The treaty ended lawful state-sponsored privateering between Spain and England but turned many privateers to unlawful piracy. Settlers continued to arrive in Jamaica along with thousands of slaves who were shipped from Africa and later South East Asia to work the cane fields as the colony developed the world's largest sugar industry. In turn Jamaican sugar had a detrimental effect on English teeth but by 1666 the dental industry had progressed to such a degree that rotten teeth could be replaced with those of a deceased Great Plague victim.

26 June 1740

War of Jenkins' Ear
Battle of Fort Mose

BRITAIN AND SPAIN had waged war upon each other on and off for nearly two centuries famously over King Philip II of Spain's desire to restore Roman Catholicism to England but more recently over the succession of Spain's King Philip V and the European balance of power. The loss of Captain Robert Jenkins' ear during a legitimate Spanish boarding and customs search off Florida in 1731 seems an unlikely catalyst for yet another war but the subsequent War of Jenkin's Ear, which began a full eight years after the event itself, would come at a price of six hundred ships and over 25,000 casualties. It was not just public indignation at Jenkins' loss that angered the British but also concern that Spain was reneging on the 1713 Treaty of Utrecht and the 'Asiento' that permitted Britain's South Sea Company to supply the Spanish South American, Caribbean and Florida colonies with 4,800 slaves and 500 tons of goods annually. Trade with the Spanish Main had been fought for since the days of Hawkins and Drake and the British Public were in no mood to give it up, Sir Robert Walpole, the first and longest serving British Prime Minister in history, acting against his own better judgement to protect the Asiento by sending a British fleet to Gibraltar and the Caribbean to demand an end to Spanish boarding parties. Spain reacted by annulling the Asiento whilst Walpole reacted by recalling the British ambassador from Madrid. At war once again with Spain, Britain rejoiced, it had usually been a profitable business.

In the Caribbean Captain Thomas Waterhouse was repulsed at La Guaira, Venezuela before Vice Admiral Edward Vernon sacked Portobello, Panama – inspiring the Scottish poet James Thomson to write 'Rule Britannia'. In March 1740 the Vice Admiral then unsuccessfully attacked Cartagena, Colombia before destroying the Fort of San Lorenzo at Portobello. Meawhile, further north, Spanish Florida had been a haven for slaves escaping British plantations in South Carolina and Georgia since 1693, gaining their freedom following four years of service in the Spanish military and a conversion to Catholicism. To encourage escapees the

Spanish built the first 'Free Black' settlement in America at Fort Mose near St Augustine with the specific objective of damaging the mass labour reliant British Colonial economy further north. Indeed eighty slaves had made a run for Fort Mose in September 1739, the Stono Rebellion, burning plantations and killing forty-four whites before being killed or captured themselves.

As Vernon was cruising the Caribbean, British colonists from Georgia and South Carolina advanced into Spanish Florida to attack St Augustine with a force of 1,400 American Indians and black slaves supported by seven ships of the Royal Navy, 3100 men in total. The British advance into Spanish Florida was led by General James Oglethorpe, the founder of Georgia, who had been an opponent of slavery in that state not so much through philanthropic goodwill but due to the danger of Spain reinforcing her military with his escapees. Oglethorpe ordered a force of 170 Georgia Militia under Colonel John Palmer to attack Fort Mose but on arrival Palmer found the fort had been abandoned by the Royal Governor of La Florida, Manuel de Montiano y Luyando who had withdrawn three miles south to St Augustine. On 13 June 1740, Oglethorpe began a siege of St Augustine with an artillery bombardment that would last twenty-seven days, Montiano and 600 Spanish regulars leading a spirited resistance from the Castillo San Marcos whilst also recognising the strategic value of Fort Mose. In the early hours of 26 June 1740 Spanish regulars under Captain Antonio Salgado and a militia of former slaves under Francisco Menendez, himself a South Carolina escapee, 300 men in total, achieved complete surprise, attacking and routing Palmer in a bitter hand-to-hand fight of musket, bayonet, sword, knife and club. Palmer was killed in the struggle along with seventy men as Menendez and Salgado retook what was left of the fort.

The British loss of Fort Mose and the inability of the Royal Navy to blockade St Augustine saw Oglethorpe return to Georgia in July. In 1742 and 1743, he again unsuccessfully attacked St Augustine but did successfully maintain a defence of Georgia. In 1763, Florida became British in exchange for Havana, Cuba but in 1783, following the American War of Independence, returned to Spain, joining the United States of America only in 1845.

27 June 1743

War of the Austrian Succession
Battle of Dettingen

THE REIGNS OF King George I and George II oversaw the development of Parliament under the Whig Party and Britain's first Prime Minister Robert Walpole who governed without interval between 1715 and 1760. Walpole navigated Great Britain through the bursting of the South Sea Bubble, the Gin Epidemic (in 1743 an ongoing problem) and since 1719 had avoided further conflict with the Jacobite cause which, with Spanish assistance, had looked to restore the Catholic House of Stuart to the British throne. Having come to power immediately after the thirteen-year War of the Spanish Succession Walpole then managed to avoid any serious national altercation until 1731 when, in the face of growing Spanish animosity, he signed the Treaty of Vienna, effectively a British alliance with Austria against France, Spain and Prussia to maintain the European balance of power. Walpole's ability to avoid a major conflict then failed him in 1739 when a dispute with Spain in the West Indies led to the War of Jenkins Ear. In 1740, this dispute then became part of the War of the Austrian Succession when Charles VI, Holy Roman Emperor died leaving the thrones of Austria, Bohemia, Hungary, Croatia, Serbia for the first time to a female, his daughter Maria Theresa.

King Frederick II of Prussia (the Great) challenged Maria's claim under Salic Law and invaded Silesia (Eastern Germany, Czech Republic, Poland), defeating Maria's Austrians at Mollwitz. As had the War of the Spanish Succession forty years earlier, treaties then drew in all the main kingdoms of Europe, Britain again fighting the old enemy France though ironically, having started the conflict, Prussia withdrew. Frederick's ally France, however, still had three armies in the field, two near Prague and Vienna with another east of the River Rhine covering their line of retreat.

The British Army under seventy-year-old John Dalrymple, Earl of Stair with Hanoverians and Hessians (40,000 men, collectively the Pragmatic Army) marched east from Flanders toward Frankfurt and the French who were retreating from their Austro-Hungarian offensive. King George II, anxious to protect his family's ancestral homeland of Hanover, then arrived in June 1743 to take command of the Pragmatic Army, becoming the last British monarch to lead his army in the field, perhaps with good reason. Against Stair's advice the British king moved the Pragmatic Army north of the River Main but in so doing lost manouevrability, the Main hampering movement south whilst the Spessart Hills did likewise to the north. Recognising George's folly the French Marshal Adrian Maurice, Duc de Noailles duly blocked the Pragmatic Army's retreat west, cutting their supply lines. Five French brigades then moved south of the Main ready to enfilade the Pragmatics and attack their rear, Noailles boasting he had George *dans une souricière* (in a mousetrap).

The Pragmatic Army walked into the 45,000 strong French mousetrap at 09.00 on 27 June 1743 just short of Dettingen. French artillery began pounding the forward Pragmatic units which formed into battle lines as the rear units caught up. The inexperienced Pragmatic troops took three hours to complete the manoeuvre only to soon realise that they were about to be caught between two forces when the French moved around their rear south of the Main. King George acted to block this move whilst the French to his front, rather than fight on the defensive and allow their artillery do most of the work, advanced to meet him along the north bank of the Main. George too ordered his men forward, both sides in poor order with the British firing uneven volleys at too great a distance on the French elite troops, the infantry and cavalry of the Maison du Roi. When George's horse then somewhat fortuitously bolted taking his rider with him, Stair reformed the Pragmatic units to meet the Maison du Roi with more disciplined volleys of musket and a series of bayonet charges from infantry squares that succeeded in repulsing the entire French attack. The battle lasted until mid afternoon when having suffered 5,000 casualties Nouailles quit the field unmolested by the Pragmatics who continued their retreat back to Flanders leaving 2,500 dead and wounded.

Dettingen had been a narrow escape, Nouailles had missed a great opportunity to win the War of the Austrian Succession which would now go global, the ongoing conflicts in the West Indies, North America and Continental Europe soon joined by those in Scotland and India.

28 June 1778

American War of Independence
Battle of Monmouth

BRITISH FORTUNES IN America had deteriorated dramatically throughout 1777 and it had largely been of their own doing. General William Howe had taken Philadelphia, the seat of Congress, but his gains there were of little significance. In moving on Philadelphia Howe had forsaken the strategic 1777 plan by failing to support 8,000 men under General John Burgoyne who was attempting to isolate New England with an advance from Quebec down Lake Champlain to Albany in the Hudson Valley. Burgoyne's ultimate surrender at Saratoga was compounded further south by Major General George Washington's performance against Howe's main army. The Americans had evacuated Philadelphia before the British arrival, leaving a city of minimal strategic value which the British had taken following heavy casualties at the battles of Brandywine and Germantown. Spirited American resistance had also swept away further French and Spanish hesitation at joining a war to minimalise British influence in North America. The now imminent arrival of a French fleet off the American eastern seaboard would now not only nullify Royal Navy domination of American Atlantic waters but also threaten British territories in the Caribbean and indeed the British Isles themselves. King George III's grasp on his thirteen American colonies was suddenly therefore by his finger tips only.

Knighted for his 1776 successes Howe resigned to be replaced by General Sir Henry Clinton who was ordered to defend North Florida, the Caribbean, return the main army from Philadelphia to New York and if necessary reinforce Quebec – no one in London seemed particularly anxious to hold Philadelphia. A lack of shipping however meant that to return to New York Clinton faced a march of 100 miles across New Jersey, 11,000 regulars, 1,000 loyalists, men, women and children in a column twelve miles long with temperatures soaring over 100f and an enemy potentially on all fronts. Washington knew the British column was highly vulnerable and moved out of his winter camp at Valley Forge, where the

Continental Army had been significantly improved by Prussian Friedrich Wilhelm von Steuben, to give chase. Despite the caution of his fellow officers Washington then ordered an attack on the rear of Clinton's column as it left Monmouth Court House, just two days march out from New York.

On 28 June 1778, Washington's vanguard of 5,000 men under the reluctant Major General Charles Lee caught up with the British rearguard under Lieutenant General Charles, Lord Cornwallis. Clinton and Cornwallis were aware of Lee's proximity and turned in good order to receive the American attack which lacked conviction and was sent reeling backwards by the British Grenadiers. As Washington came up behind to join the assault he found Lee's men streaming back towards him and immediately began to rally them against an imminent British counter-attack. Clinton had indeed sensed the opportunity to counter-attack just as Washington's main army was passing out from a series of ravines. The British Redcoats, over 9,000-strong, moved quickly, many succumbing to heat stroke, to crash into the American front line which consisted largely of the remnants of Lee's force who, nevertheless, held together just long enough for the main Continental Army to deploy in the woods and hills behind. As the British moved through Lee's hapless men Clinton urged them to attack the American left under Major General William Stirling but they were halted by disciplined volley fire and grapeshot before Clinton brought up his own cannon. Cornwallis with British and Hessians then attacked the American right under Quartermaster General Nathaniel Greene but again met a resolute response as Von Steuben's drilling proved its worth. Clinton was not finished, however, and began a series of attacks on the American centre under Brigadier General Anthony Wayne which eventually gave way, falling back on the French reserve of Major General Motier, Marquis de Lafayette.

Both sides were exhausted, battle having raged for several bloody hours (500 casualties each) in terrific heat. An artillery duel then lasted until dusk with Washington unsuccessfully calling for an American counter-attack. Two days later the British were crossing back into Manhattan courtesy of the Royal Navy. The roles of fox and hounds were now very different to those of two years previous.

29 June 1644

English Civil Wars
Battle of Cropredy Bridge

CHARLES I, KING of England had achieved some notable early gains during the first year of the English Civil War, consolidating his strongholds of North England, Wales and Cornwall as well as advancing as close to London as Newbury by September 1643. The Parliament supporting inhabitants of England's capital city had been in a state of near panic at the prospect of a return of their no doubt angry king but had been spared by the bravery of Edward Massey, the Governor of Gloucester and his fellow citizens who had inspired a Parliament revival. Despite having being forced back from Newbury and Arundel, Charles, however, still held most of the South West but in the North his situation was starting to deteriorate.

Royalist Yorkshire and Lancashire were now threatened by the English Parliament enlisting support from Scottish Covenanters who marched across the Scottish Border to Durham. Additionally the Parliament Army of the Eastern Association under Edward Montagu, Earl of Manchester and Oliver Cromwell moved into North Lincolnshire while another, in Hull under Ferdinando, Lord Fairfax and his son Sir Thomas Fairfax, defeated a Royalist Army under John Belasyse at Selby. Charles' commander in the North, William Cavendish, Marquis of Newcastle, had consequently been forced back to the Royalist stronghold of York where he was soon besieged but with Charles' nephew and senior commander Prince Rupert, who had relieved Newark in March, on his way to repeat the feat. Rupert began his advance through Lancashire leaving Charles in Oxford strict instructions to stay on the defensive but instead the king withdrew his garrisons from Reading and Abingdon to increase the mobility of his army. The invitation to overrun Berkshire was immediately accepted by Parliament commanders Robert Devereux, Earl of Essex and Sir William Waller who put their differences aside to send Charles fleeing from Oxford into the surrounding countryside. Essex then dubiously decided to leave the King to Waller while he himself moved south to raise the siege of Lyme and attempt the capture, at Exeter, of the expecting Queen Henrietta Maria.

Charles, however, managed to throw Waller off his trail, returning to Oxford for reinforcements whilst Waller retired to Gloucester where Massey refused to help him. Waller complained bitterly of Massey and Essex but grudgingly resumed the search for the king who was now wandering Worcestershire ever more desperate for Rupert's return. On realising that he was now being pursued only by Waller, Charles decided to turn and fight, marching toward Banbury on 28 June 1644 with Waller closing in from the west. The following morning 29 June 1644, Charles and 9,000 Royalists moved up the east bank of the north/south flowing River Cherwell with the shadow of Waller and his force of a similar size and strength on the opposite bank. As both armies approached Cropredy Charles received news that Parliament reinforcements were approaching from the north and therefore promptly ordered forward his vanguard to intercept whilst placing a guard on Cropredy Bridge to block Waller from crossing. Recognising that the Royalists were now over extended, Waller ordered John Middleton to attack Cropredy Bridge with 1,200 horse and 2,000 infantry and, once successful, advance north to Hays Bridge (across a tributary further north) to prevent a return of Charles' vanguard. Simultaneously Waller himself led 1,000 cavalry south across a ford at Slat Mill to attack the Royalist rear but the Parliamentary plan to trap the Royalists failed immediately when his crossing was foiled by an aggressive attack by James Compton, Earl of Northumberland. Further north, Middleton successfully brushed aside the Royalist guard on Cropredy Bridge but was then attacked himself by Thomas Wentworth, Earl of Cleveland from the front of the Royalist rear. Cleveland's attack allowed the Royalist vanguard ahead to cross back over Hays bridge and join the fray, Middleton, now in a Royalist pincer, forced into a desperate fighting retreat back to Cropredy Bridge which included a series of cavalry charges with covering fire from cannon and musketeers.

The two armies watched each other across the Cherwell for another two days before Charles withdrew. The king had scored another small victory but further north he needed another one, much larger, for outside York on the moor at Long Marston his nephew was about to fight one of the greatest battles in British history.

30 June 1643

English Civil Wars
Battle of Adwalton Moor

A SERIES OF disputes between King Charles I of England, Scotland and Ireland (the Three Kingdoms) and his Parliament in London had led to the outbreak of the English Civil War in the Autumn of 1642. Often termed the Wars of the Three Kingdoms, violence had erupted in Scotland when Charles had imposed a new Book of Common Prayer and in Ireland by growing Catholic concern at the rise in power of the English Protestant Parliament. Following an inconclusive contest at Edgehill both sides had been busy recruiting over the winter while peace talks had been ongoing. The argument was not so much who but how the Three Kingdoms were to be governed – Parliament frustrated at Charles' failures to consult whilst the king firmly believed in his divine, god given, right to rule. Small-scale battles and skirmishes had continued over the early months of 1643 but after a short truce, negotiations finally broke down on 8 April. Within hours the civil war began again in earnest, many towns around the country declaring for one side or the other.

The cannon of Prince Rupert of the Rhine, the king's nephew and most experienced soldier, soon began pounding Parliament-held Lichfield. On 20 April, after exploding a mine under the walls, Royalists stormed the resultant breach for a ferocious but successful struggle. Having garrisoned Lichfield Rupert then rode south to relieve Royalist Reading which was taking its own pounding from the Parliament cannon of Robert Devereux, Earl of Essex. On Rupert's failure, Reading surrendered to Essex on 26 April but at a heavy price to the Parliament Army. Further north Charles received another blow when Wakefield and its vast store of supplies fell in another fierce fight to Parliamentarian Sir Thomas Fairfax. The successful Fairfax then retreated back to Leeds where he remained a serious threat to predominantly Royalist Yorkshire and Lancashire. Charles, however, received better news from South West England where Sir Ralph Hopton had advanced from Cornwall into Devon, defeating Henry Grey, Earl of Stamford at Stratton.

The Royalists now looked to join the two armies of William Seymour, Marquis of Hertford at Oxford with that of Hopton who was now advancing on Somerset. Prince Rupert too harried Essex' advance on Oxford so successfully that Essex retreated threatening to resign. Their main army seemingly in disarray Parliament London was near panic but there was a minor victory at Belton, Lincolnshire, the first for a forty-four-year-old Parliamentary cavalry commander, Oliver Cromwell.

As Royalist forces advanced in the South West and the Midlands, William Cavendish, Duke of Newcastle looked to consolidate Yorkshire for the king by attacking weakly defended Parliament Bradford. If Newcastle could secure Yorkshire, Royalist forces could then attack Parliament-held Lincolnshire in force but Newcastle had to reckon with the smaller, albeit better-armed Parliament Army in Leeds. This army, 4,000-strong, now under Ferdinando, Lord Fairfax (Thomas' father) marched to defend Bradford but, due to the town's poor defences, then made for Adwalton Moor and a pitched battle with Newcastle's 10,000 infantry and horse.

On 30 June 1643, Ferdinando, Lord Fairfax, with Sir Thomas commanding the Parliament horse, arrived to find Newcastle's Royalists already on the outer perimeter of the moor in defensive positions formed of hedges, small lanes, cottages and other buildings. Lord Fairfax attacked with muskets and cannon, driving the Royalists back from the hedges onto the higher ground of the moor but in doing so left himself vulnerable to a flank attack from Newcastle's cavalry which appeared behind him. Thinking they were fully surrounded the Parliament Roundheads panicked and fled, both Fairfaxs escaping the rout, Sir Thomas to Halifax and Lord Fairfax back to Leeds.

Thomas Fairfax immediately returned to Bradford to rescue his wife and daughter. Lady Fairfax had, however, been captured by the Royalists but was delivered to Sir Thomas in Hull courtesy of Newcastle's own personal coach. Thomas then escaped Newcastle's siege of Hull to join Cromwell in Lincolnshire. Further south on Lansdowne Hill, Bath, Hopton was about to advance the Royalist cause against his old friend fighting for Parliament, William Waller. Joined at last in Oxford by his Queen Henrietta Maria, King Charles could hardly have been in better heart.

July

"They need not pursue me for I will meet them this day."

KING EDWARD I OF ENGLAND,
FALKIRK, 1298

1 July 1916

The Great War
Battle of the Somme

THE SHOCKING CASUALTIES of 1914 and 1915 had no bearing on the irreconcilable differences that still existed in 1916 between the combatants on the Western Front. The success of the 1915 Galice-Tarnow offensive on the Eastern Front had, however, fulfilled the basic aims of the Central Powers (Germany, Austria Hungary) with huge territorial gains in Poland and Russia added to those in France and Belgium. The demise of the Russian Army, with discontent that would lead to a Bolshevik Revolution, allowed German Chief of Staff Erich von Falkenhayn to end his sixteen month purely defensive stance on the Western Front by threatening the historically important French town of Verdun, the aggressive defence of which he believed would result in catastrophic French losses in a battle of attrition, Germany posturing but fighting on the defensive. Backed by British Secretary for War Horatio Kitchener (who in June was lost at sea en route to Russia), the Commander-in-Chief of the British Expeditionary Force (BEF) General Sir Douglas Haig and French General Joseph Joffre had planned a joint offensive later in 1916, Haig in the knowledge that although the now five Armies of the BEF were up in strength from the original six divisions, almost all were constituted from Kitchener's Volunteers and were not yet fully trained for battle. As French losses mounted and morale plummeted to the point of mutiny at Verdun, however, Haig was forced by the moral obligations of the Entente to support France by attacking, as he had at Loos the year before, at a time and place not of his choosing. The consequent battle, fought astride the River Somme, would ultimately define the tragedy of the Great War and the Pals Battalions- the Accrington Pals, the Preston Pals, the Wool Textile Pioneers, the Tyneside Scottish, the Tyneside Irish, the London Welsh, the Leeds Pals, the Stockbrokers, the Grimsby Chums, the Church Lads, the Arts and Crafts, the Footballers and many, many more.

The German High Command were well aware of British preparations and any surprise was completely forfeit by a British six-day, 1.5 million-shell bombardment from 1,600 guns across a front 20,000 yards wide to a depth of 2,500 yards. Critically, however, Haig's bombardment would not match the intensity successful the year before at Neuve Chapelle and worse, most of the shells fired were shrapnel rather than high explosive, many of them dud which left banks of barbed wire and German defences largely untouched. At 07.20 on 1 July 1916, several mines were then exploded under the German front lines before the 07.30 whistles blew and the British Fourth Army, twenty-five infantry divisions under General Henry Rawlinson, climbed out into no-man's-land towards Beaumont Hamel, Thiepval, La Boiselle, Mametz and Montauban. To their north General Edmund Allenby made a diversionary attack with three divisions of the British Third Army toward Gommecourt and to the south, on both sides of the River Somme, the French 6th Army under General Emile Fayolle attacked with eight divisions. Defending were just ten divisions of the German 2nd Army under General Fritz von Below whose weakness to the south enabled Fayolle and the southernmost British to make impressive gains though missing opportunities through a lack of reserves. To their north, south of the Albert-Bapaume Road, the British XV Corps successfully captured Mametz but north of the road the situation differed dramatically as the Pals were machine-gunned crossing wide expanses of no-mans land, failing at Thiepval after capturing the Leipzig Redoubt and Allenby failing at Gommecourt. The 36th (Ulster) Division succeeded in capturing the Schwaben and Stuff Redoubts but with attacks failing on either side were forced back by determined German counter-attacks. The northern part of the battlefield now became a death trap as Haig, with communications failing but anxious not to repeat the mistakes of Loos, fed in reserves. Intensifying German artillery, however, prevented further British advances and trapped those already further forward against increasing German resistance on the ground. By the day's end all gains north had been lost with 57,470 casualties suffered.

1 July 1916, had been the bloodiest day in the history of the British Army but confined by coalition demands and initially unaware of the scale of his losses, Haig continued, taking another 25,000 casualties fighting piecemeal before renewing the offensive two weeks later on Bazentin Ridge.

2 July 1644

English Civil Wars
Battle of Marston Moor

IN MID 1643 King of England, Charles I had been contemplating an advance on Parliament held London but heavy casualties sustained throughout the year particularly at the siege of Bristol meant, just a year later, he was being hunted through the countryside of the Midlands. Meanwhile his nephew and Commander-in-Chief, Prince Rupert of the Rhine, moved to confront resurgent Parliament forces and their Presbyterian Scottish Covenanter allies in the North of England. Following his defeat at Selby in April 1644 the king's commander in the North, William Cavendish, Marquis of Newcastle had retreated to York but had been pursued by the Parliament Army of Ferdinando, Lord Fairfax and the Covenanters under Alexander Leslie, Lord Leven. In May, Parliament's Eastern Association under Edward Montagu, Earl of Manchester and Oliver Cromwell then stormed Lincoln before joining Leven and Fairfax outside York, the combined 25,000-strong Parliament forces now continuously attacking the 6,000 Royalists defending the city. In the knowledge that Rupert was moving to assist him Newcastle declined to surrender, his exhausted troops holding off Parliament assaults until 30 June when the Parliamentarians, now aware of Rupert's presence fourteen miles to their west, drew off to block him at Knaresborough. Rupert, however, audaciously sidestepped the block through the Forest of Galtres to relieve York but with no consideration for the condition of the garrison, messaged Newcastle to meet him on Marston Moor at 04.00 the following morning, 2 July 1644, ready to give battle.

At the given time Rupert was discovered alone on the moor by Parliament patrols. A shocked Manchester, Fairfax and Leven desperately recalled their infantry in expectation of an imminent attack but in the absence of Newcastle (his ranks had mutinied) and Royalist Scots under James King, Lord Eythin, Rupert did not move. At 09.00 the Parliament Army was still vulnerable when Newcastle arrived to join Rupert but not so at 16.00 when Eythin arrived, in fact it was now fully drawn up in battle order across a 1.5 mile front, the cavalry of Cromwell on the left, that of Thomas Fairfax on the right, Covenanter behind with the infantry under Lords Leven and Fairfax in the centre, 23,000 men. Personally anxious to fight Cromwell, Rupert's cavalry was on the Royalist right, George Goring on the left with the Lancashire, Yorkshire and Scottish infantry under Newcastle and Eythin in the centre, 17,000 men. Rupert deliberately closed with his adversaries in order to provoke a Parliament attack which he intended to counter aggressively as it crossed a ditch to his front.

Neither side, however, moved until 19.30 when Rupert, believing it too late in the day for battle, allowed his men to fall out for dinner, he himself also riding to the rear. Cromwell seized the opportunity and charged. John, Lord Byron, commanding Rupert's front line, hurriedly gathered his cavalry and countered but he was too late to prevent Cromwell from making a successful crossing of the ditch. The opposing cavalries now engaged in a mêlée of sword fighting with Rupert's musketeers line of fire now blocked by Byron's Horse. Parliament's Scottish Covenanter cavalry then entered the fray on Cromwell's left, attacking the flank of the Royalist right which began to give way until briefly rallied by the returning Rupert. In contrast, however, on the Royalist left Goring charged and routed the Parliament cavalry of Thomas Fairfax, spreading panic to Parliament infantry in the centre, some of whom fled, including Lords Fairfax and Leven. The Parliament infantry of the Eastern Association and the Covenanters, however, advanced against the Lancashire Royalists who threw down their weapons leaving the Yorkshires to fight on. Cromwell's cavalry, without their wounded commander, finished the rout of Rupert and Byron before swinging behind to surround the Yorkshire Royalist infantry. The fighting continued until midnight as the Yorkshires, minus Newcastle and Eythin who had fled, fought virtually to the bitter end, Thomas Fairfax leading calls to end the bloodbath.

Marston Moor had been a Royal disaster, 4,000 dead and wounded, 1,500 prisoners taken and all cannon lost. Newcastle left for Hamburg disgusted that in just a few hours Rupert had undone three months of effort. York surrendered on 16 July 1644. King Charles had lost the North of England and although his cause was still strong in the South, Cromwell and Manchester would soon be on their way to do it harm.

3 July 1940

Second World War
Battle of Mers El Kebir (Oran)

EVER SINCE THE 1919 Treaty of Versailles had been brought into force by the victorious powers of the Great War the limits imposed on the German Wehrmacht (Armed forces) had been flagrantly disregarded, initially by the Weimar Republic and particularly by the Nazi Third Reich under Chancellor and *Fuhrer* Adolf Hitler. The German Police and the border protecting Reichswehr had been covertly armed before Paramilitary groups including the Freikorps, Reichsbanner, Ruhr Red Army, Nazi Sturm Abteilung (SA) and Nazi Shutzstaffel (SS) followed. A German pacifist Carl von Ossietzky, exposed the deception as early as 1931, earning himself the 1935 Nobel Peace Prize but also arrest, torture and eventual death three years later at the hands of the Nazis. The Nazi rearming of the *Heer*, *Luftwaffe* and *Kriegsmarine* after 1935 then comfortably outstripped that of the Allies, France and Great Britain. Not only that but military doctine, as promoted by Generals Heinz Guderian, Erwin Rommel and Erich von Manstein who had benefited from British military theories, was revolutionary, all arms combined, concentrated through a Schwerpunkt (focal point) of heavy armour and motorised infantry with air support. The *Blitzkrieg* when it came consequently overwhelmed the barely prepared Allies in Holland, Belgium and France with a broad offensive and a devastating armoured 'Sichelschnitt' (sickle cut) through the Ardennes Forest. With the British Expeditionary Force and French 1st Army now trapped in Dunkirk on 26 May 1940, King George V attended a prayer service at Westminster Abbey where many thousands stood outside listening in the rain. Their prayers were not in vain, 338,000 troops including 110,000 French returned to Britain over the next few days.

An imminent German invasion was expected but Bletchley Park intelligence intercepts pointed to a German consolidation in France since no plans existed for a crossing of the English Channel. Germany still also had to reckon with the Royal Air Force and the Royal Navy, not as modern as the Kriegsmarine, any one German battleship outclassing its British counterpart, but collectively still the world's most powerful navy. On 10 June a new threat was then realised when Germany's Axis partner Italy, with her own modern fleet, declared war increasing the anxiety of British Prime Minister Winston Churchill that France should fight on and that the French Navy, second only in size to the Royal Navy, be safeguarded by Britain. French Prime Minister Paul Reynaud, however, resigned on 16 June to be replaced by Marshal Phillippe Pétain who showed none of the 1916 spirit of Verdun by immediately seeking an armistice. With Britain now resisting alone Churchill implored Pétain to hand over the French fleet but by July it had not moved.

In the early morning of 3 July 1940, fourteen French warships along with a further 200 smaller vessels and submarines were boarded by British troops in Plymouth and Portsmouth, just one resisting. In Alexandria, Egypt five French ships and escorts surrendered to Admiral Sir Andrew Cunningham but by far the largest concentration of French naval vessels was at Mers El Kebir (Oran), Algeria off which appeared seventeen British ships from Force H Gibraltar including the aircraft carrier HMS *Ark Royal*. Admiral James Somerville delivered an ultimatum to French Admiral Marcelo Grensoul with three options, further advising that unless Grensoul comply within six hours the French fleet would be sunk. Negotiations dragged on throughout the day, Grensoul not fully informing French Naval Minister Francois Darlan of his options while protesting that he would never hand his fleet over to the Germans. Back in London, however, Churchill's patience and trust had gone and he ordered Somerville to settle the matter quickly. *Ark Royal's* planes first blocked the port with mines before HMS *Resolution, Hood* and *Valiant* opened fire at 17,500 yards with 15-inch shells smashing into the nine French ships and the harbour. Within minutes the French battleship *Bretagne's* magazine exploded, severely damaging *Mogador* next door. The French ships returned fire as the nadir of coalition warfare was reached, *Strasbourg* making a run for the open sea with the five destroyers covered by gunfire fire from shore batteries which forced Somerville to alter course. The French escaped but they had lost a battleship and a destroyer with five other capital ships damaged and 1,300 men.

The British seamen had been horrified at having to attack the French, men they had played football with just a few years before. The French fleet at Toulon was scuttled by Vichy France in 1942 somewhat justifying Grensoul's protests.

4 July 1879
Zulu War
Battle of Ulundi

KING CETSHWAYO HAD believed the great Zulu victory won at Isandlwana in January 1879 would strengthen his negotiating hand with the British but it had merely strengthened Victorian resolve. The Zulu king had never wanted war, indeed his endless messengers continued to seek peace but the British were intent on nothing less than the annexation of Zululand and an ultimate confederation of tribal and Boer Republics within British controlled South Africa. Cetshwayo, however, was the king of a proud nation formed by his uncle Shaka Zulu and would not surrender without a fight to the impossible demands of High Commissioner Henry Bartle Frere and Transvaal Administrator Theophilius Shepstone.

The Zulu always intended to fight out in the open where their mobility could counter the overwhelming industrially produced firepower of the world's foremost equipped army. It had worked at Isandlwana, Intombe and Hlobane but their astonishing powers of movement had been counterbalanced by undisciplined (albeit with fearless bravery) attacks on British defensive positions at Rorke's Drift, Khambula and Gingindlovu with consequent losses that Cetshwayo could not afford. Despite the overwhelming advantage in firepower and successive victories following Isandlwana the British performance had hardly been impressive, Lieutenant General Frederick Thesiger, Lord Chelmsford had been widely criticised following Isandlwana and indeed his replacement Field Marshal Garnet Wolseley was now en route. Chelmsford, however, was anxious to restore his reputation before Wolseley's arrival, with reinforcements he relieved Colonel Charles Pearson's Eastern Column at Eshowe whilst in north-west Zululand Lieutenant Colonel Evelyn Wood had been victorious at Khambula.

Chelmsford had now been able to embark on a second invasion of Zululand but with many green recruits from England he was mindful not to cross the Buffalo River at Rorke's Drift since his line of march would have led through the Isandlwana battlefield where the bodies of both sides remained unburied. He did, however, send a detachment to bury the British dead and collect all the abandoned wagons but his main force marched north-west around the border to Koppie Alleen on the Blood River. Wood then moved south from Khambula as Chelmsford moved east from Koppie Alleen, both columns continuously skirmishing. By the 23 June Chelmsford reported to Wolseley in Cape Town that the two columns had met up and were now advancing on Ulundi, Cetshwayo's Royal Homestead, a mere seventeen miles away. Still Cetshwayo looked for peace but the British terms had not changed, Chelmsford giving the Zulu Chief until 3 July to comply. No reply was received and hostilities immediately resumed when an advanced British mounted column under Lieutenant Colonel Redvers Buller was nearly caught in a deadly trap before Ulundi.

At 06.45 the following day, 4 July 1879, the 5,600 strong British Column crossed the White Mfolozi River to move across the plain in a hollow square toward Ulundi, cavalry to the front and rear. Chelmsford manoeuvred the square on to a rise in the plain whilst to his front, on left and right and around his rear advanced 15,000 Zulu. Again, learning nothing from their previous attacks on British defensive positions, the Zulu were goaded into another by the British cavalry who then retreated back into the square. The Zulu were soon attacking on all sides, their heavy fire and the dense formation of the square giving rise to mounting British casualties but they were insignificant when compared to those inflicted by the concentrated volley fire of the British Martini Henry rifles and field guns that met the Zulu advance. After half an hour of fighting not a single Zulu had reached the square, Chelmsford sensing victory now ordering his lancers and dragoons to counter-attack, pursuing the now fleeing enemy.

The royal Zulu homesteads were burnt as surviving Zulu melted away beyond the hills. Cetshwayo had not watched the battle, instead he had sat with a blanket over his head unable to speak, everything he had sought to avoid had come to fruition. The proud king was captured and later imprisoned on Robben Island before meeting Queen Victoria at Osborne House in 1882, returning to his homeland a year later. Chelmsford never again commanded in the field. Zululand was annexed into Natal, now KwaZulu Natal, but an old threat to British power in South Africa would soon be on the rise now that their traditional enemy had been defeated – the Dutch Boers of the Transvaal wanted their independence back.

5 July 1643

English Civil Wars
Battle of Lansdown Hill

THE ENGLISH CIVIL War had begun over a series of disputes between King Charles I of England, Scotland and Ireland and his Parliament. Since 1629 Charles had ruled personally, failing to call a Parliament for eleven years but it was his involvement in the running of the church, particularly in Scotland, which had caused the initial outbreak of violence. A lack of trust then resulted in Parliament's systematic dismantling of almost all vestiges of the king's rule until Charles fatefully attempted and failed to arrest the men he held responsible, his folly making war inevitable. The inconclusive autumn 1642 Battle of Edgehill led to a winter where both Royalists and Parliamentarians were busy recruiting armies and garrisons, none more so than Charles' Queen Henrietta Maria in the Low Countries. Parliamentarians never intended for the Three Kingdoms to become a republic and peace talks had been ongoing but hardliners on both sides, including Charles who sincerely believed in his divine, God given right to rule, had caused the talks to collapse on 8 April 1643. The Civil War resumed with renewed vigour, Parliament dominating the Eastern Counties, the Midlands, the South and South East whilst Royalists held the North, the extreme South West and Wales. Each side also had pockets of resistance within each others territory, most notably the king at Oxford. The problems facing both sides were similar but were weighed in favour of Parliament since almost all of England's major ports and their respective import and export revenues were in their hands. Common men had been conscripted for pay or profit with both sides understanding that, tax wise, the population could not to be impoverished. Limited funds and men that fought out of personal loyalty rather than for a cause therefore meant Charles required a quick victory or likely he would not have one at all.

By the end of June 1643, however, that is exactly the outcome that looked the most likely. William Cavendish, Duke of Newcastle had consolidated the North of England for the king allowing Queen Henrietta to travel to the king's court at

Oxford. From here Prince Rupert, Charles' nephew, harried the roads into London to such effect that the capital was near panic. Additionally, Robert Devereux, Earl of Essex, commanding Parliament forces in the Midlands was threatening to resign. In the South West meanwhile Sir Ralph Hopton's Royalists had advanced from Cornwall and were approaching Bath to join the Midlands' Army of William Seymour, Marquis of Hertford and Rupert's brother, Prince Maurice, their ultimate objective the valuable but heavily defended port of Bristol. Charged with stopping Hopton was the Parliament Army of his friend Sir William Waller, both men distressed at having to fight each other but determined to do so with honour.

Aware of Waller's Parliamentarians to his north-west, Hopton swung his Royalists to the north of Bath for Lansdown Hill only to find Waller had beaten him to it. Hopton then continued further north to Marshfield harried by Waller's cavalry but now blocking the Parliament line of retreat to Bristol. On 5 July 1643, Hopton's 6,000-strong Royalist Army advanced down Marshfield and up Lansdown Hill towards Wallers 4,000 Parliament Roundheads. The Parliamentarians lined the lanes, walls, hedges and woods with musketeers who put down such a heavy fire that the Royalist advance stalled before partially retreating in the face of Waller's Parliament cavalry. Partially because the tough Royalist Cornish infantry under Sir Bevil Grenville had instead stood their ground, eventually repulsing the Parliament cavalry before advancing with their own back up Lansdown Hill. Now Waller's musketeers were forced back, though not without taking a heavy toll of the Royalist cavalry who again departed leaving the Cornish pikemen alone to attack Parliament defences on the ridge. Bitter fighting raged in clouds of smoke from volleys of musket and cannon fire, the Cornish fighting off repeated Parliament cavalry charges before their own musketeers began outflanking Waller's position. Falling back to a wall the Parliamentarians held out until dark before retreating to Bath where Waller called for reinforcements from Bristol.

Waller was again ready for battle just a week later when the two commanders would renew their 'friendship' on Roundway Down. A monument to the mortally wounded Sir Bevil Grenville and Waller's Wall stand on Lansdown Hill to this day.

6 July 1917

The Great War
Battle of Aqaba

PRIOR TO THE Great War German diplomats had promised Turkey the recovery of territories lost to Russia over thirty years previous and the development of infrastructure throughout the Ottoman (Turkish) Empire, especially railways to Baghdad, Mesopotamia (Iraq) and Medina, Arabia not just for a consolidation of Ottoman rule but to further German influence throughout the Middle East, Asia and East Africa at British expense. When in 1914, Turkey then openly declared for the Central Powers (Germany and Austria Hungary) Britain reacted by securing the oil fields of southern Mesopotamia (Iraq) for the Royal Navy whilst further west in Egypt holding a defence line along the Suez Canal. Initial Ottoman advances across the Sinai Peninsular to Suez would be added to by the 1916 defeat of 13,000 British and Indian troops under Major General Charles Townshend at Kut south of Baghdad but these achievements would prove to be the zenith of Turkish and by extension German ambition in the Middle East.

In 1916, following the British withdrawal from Gallipoli, Lieutenant General Archibald Murray had taken command of the new Egyptian Expeditionary Force (EEF) in Cairo, immediately losing 240,000 of his 300,000 strong force to the Western Front but successfully counter-attacking Turkish forces at Romani, Egypt in August. Murray then began an advance complete with railway, road and water pipelines across the northern Sinai under Lieutenant General Philip Chetwode whilst also sending a twenty-eight-year-old archaeologist from the Intelligence Staff, Colonel Thomas E Lawrence, competent in Arabic and with first hand knowledge of the Negev Desert to liaise with Hussein bin Ali, Sharif of Mecca who was leading a Hashemite Arab Revolt against Ottoman rule in the Arabian Hejaz (Western Saudi Arabia). In return for Arab support against the Germans/ Ottomans, their common enemy, the British High Commissioner in Cairo Sir Henry McMahon promised Hussein an independent Arab State covering what is now Syria, Lebanon, Israel, Palestine, Jordan and Saudi Arabia, a promise that would be shattered by the 1916 Sykes-Picot (Anglo-French) Agreement that would divide the Ottoman Empire at the end of the Great War into the Middle East that exists today.

Soon, in the knowledge of Sykes-Picot, an unhappy Lawrence found himself a trusting ally in Hussein's son Emir Faisal and began a guerilla war against Ottoman garrisons throughout the Hejaz and in particular their supply line, the Hejaz Railway. As Murray's EEF advanced east across the Sinai to attack Rafa and then Gaza in March 1917, the Arab Revolt moved north towards him, Lawrence and Faisal agreeing to attack the Ottoman garrison at Aqaba which threatened Murray's right flank. The capture of Aqaba would also provide a northern Red Sea supply port for Faisal's ultimate push north into Jordan, Palestine and Syria but it would be no easy task since Aqaba was protected on the seaward side by heavy Ottoman guns and to landward by the Nefud Desert. Lawrence opted for the latter, deceiving the Turks that his target was Damascus before he, Faisal's cousin Sharif Nasir and Auda ibu Tayi of the Huweitat Bedouin recruited for two months across hundreds of miles of burning rock and sand that even many of the Bedouin considered impassable. On 5 July 1917, Lawrence and 500 tribesmen bought with British pounds sterling emerged from the mountains before Aqaba to attack the fortified Ottoman blockhouse at Abu el Lissal. The lengthy exchange of fire was ineffectual until Auda led a flank charge from the hills to overwhelm the garrison, Lawrence shooting his own camel by accident. The following day 6 July 1917, Lawrence and Auda, now with possibly 2,500 Bedouin, moved past the outer defences onto Aqaba itself where the garrison, having been shelled by British warships, promptly surrendered.

Fearing strong Turkish counter-attacks and unsure that his Arab irregulars could hold Aqaba, Lawrence rode across the Sinai to advise an astonished General Edmund Allenby (replacing Murray) in Cairo that he had taken Aqaba and that his Arab forces required resupplying and reinforcing. Ottoman forces were now badly isolated in the Hejaz particularly at Medina. Allenby would invade southern Palestine at Beersheba in October 1917. The Battle of Aqaba is depicted in the historically imprecise 1962 Columbia Pictures film *Lawrence of Arabia* starring Peter O'Toole.

7 July 1777

American War of Independence
Battle of Hubbardton

THE BRITISH ARMY in North America had the Continental Army on the run throughout most of 1776 but crucially General George Washington had then delivered three reverses in quick succession on the British around the turn of the year. General William Howe pulled almost the entire British Army back into New York for the winter while back in London, General John Burgoyne put together a plan for 1777 with the Secretary of State for the Colonies (North America) Lord George Germain, Viscount Sackville. The strategic objective was nothing new in that it involved isolating the strong Patriot support in New England, believed to be the hot seat of the rebellion, from the rest of the colonies by controlling the Hudson Valley from New York to Lake Champlain and Quebec in British Canada. The military generally prefer a simple plan but Burgoyne's and Sackville's involved three armies advancing through the wildernesse to converge on a single spot more or less simultaneously, in the eighteenth century anything but simple – the Saratoga Campaign.

On 14 June 1777, Burgoyne left Quebec with 7,000 British Redcoats accompanied by about 1,000 American Indians for an advance down Lake Champlain, Lake George and the Hudson Valley to take Albany. A second column of 2,000 under Brigadier General Barrimore St Leger also moved on Albany but from Lake Ontario further west marching down the Mohawk Valley. At Albany these two columns would then in theory meet up with an army under Howe moving up the Hudson Valley from New York. Washington had little idea of British intentions and in trying to defend everywhere he ran the danger of actually defending nowhere but he did hold back four regiments around New York that could move whenever and wherever required.

The one place that was heavily fortified by the Americans was Fort Ticonderoga at the southern end of Lake Champlain which Burgoyne's column approached on 2 July 1777. Since capturing Ticonderoga at the start of the war the Americans had greatly extended its fortifications with redoubts and defences not just on the fort itself but also on the neighbouring hilltops. Burgoyne, however, was allowed to occupy Rattlesnake Hill (what is now Mount Defiance) without a fuss causing General Arthur St Clair (under orders from General Philip Shuyler to hold out as long as possible) and his 3,000 American defenders to vacate Fort Ticonderoga with barely a shot being fired. Shuyler was sacked and replaced by General Horatio Gates.

St Clair retreated south-east toward Castleton but he left behind a 1,200 strong rearguard commanded by Seth Warner which stopped at Hubbardton on the night of 6 July. On the morning of the 7 July 1777, General Simon Fraser with 1,000 British grenadiers, light infantry and American Indians who had set off in pursuit of St Clair approached Hubbardton, catching Warner's column marching out of the town directly to their front. On spotting Fraser, the American rear under Ebeneezer Francis wasted no time in taking cover, forming into line to begin firing disciplined volleys at the approaching Redcoats. Fraser attempted to outflank the Americans on their left which left him exposed on his own left but he knew that 1,500 German Brunswickers under Baron Friedrich Adolf Riedesel were coming up to support and hoped his left would hold long enough. After an hour of intense fighting Riedesel and his Brunswickers duly arrived, the baron immediately realising Fraser's left was under pressure, his men marching forward as required singing hymns whilst their band played. The increased pressure created by the Brunswickers on the American right was too much, they broke and fled forcing the whole line to give way, the brave Francis killed.

Fraser continued the pursuit of St Clair without Riedesel but he had taken over 200 casualties and could only mop up stragglers. St Clair, who had heard the fighting but failed to support Francis, marched on to Fort Edward to meet up with Shuyler. Burgoyne's advance appeared to be going well but a month later he received news that Howe was not now heading to Albany but in the opposite direction to Philadelphia. St Leger too had retreated from a siege of Fort Stanwix in the Mohawk Valley despite inflicting heavy casualties on the Americans at Oriskany. To triple the blow, on 16 August Burgoyne lost 1,000 men at Bennington. He would soldier on down the Hudson Valley toward Albany but he and his men were very much alone.

8 July 1758

French and Indian War
Battle of Fort Carillon

THE FIRST FEW years of the French and Indian War on the western frontier of North America had been poor for British interests, particularly 1756 and 1757. The French had consolidated gains over the disputed territories immediately east of Lake Erie, Lake Ontario, the St Lawrence River and up the Mohawk Valley with a victory at Fort Bull leading to another at Fort Oswego on the shores of Lake Ontario. Even worse for British interests, in August 1757, at the southern end of Lake George, Commander-in-Chief of French Forces Brigadier General Louis-Joseph de Montcalm had defeated British Lieutenant General George Monro at Fort William Henry to threaten the Hudson Valley and the route into New York. Montcalm, however, did not take advantage of British distress by immediately advancing on Fort Edward.

Meanwhile further north-east, British Commander-in-Chief General John Campbell, Earl of Loudoun had been repulsed at Louisbourg (now Cape Breton Island, Nova Scotia) and was replaced by Major General James Abercrombie who would benefit from the outbreak of the Seven Years' War back in Europe. Here at Westminster, William Pitt 'the Elder', Earl of Chatham, Leader of the House of Commons, preferred to financially subsidise his allies, the principal and most powerful being Prussia, rather than commit large numbers of British troops to European soil. A Royal Navy blockade of France would also prevent the reinforcement of French garrisons globally making them vulnerable to British attack. Accordingly in Bengal, India Major General Robert Clive soon defeated the French at Chandannagar and Plassey, feats that Abercrombie would now try to emulate in North America.

In Montreal, Canada Montcalm was over ruled by Governor Pierre de Rigaud, Marquis de Vaudreuil who favoured dividing his forces to meet three separate British offensives on Fort Duquesne in the Ohio Valley, again on Louisbourg and again north of the Hudson this time on Fort Carillon (later Ticonderoga) at the southern end of Lake Champlain. To Fort Carillon he sent Montcalm.

A British force of 16,000 men, enormous by eighteenth century American standards, led by Abercrombie sailed the length of Lake George, disembarking on 6 July at the River La Chute which connects Lake George to Lake Champlain. Skirmishers advanced, scouting the forests ahead to protect the landing but running into a retreating French patrol under Colonel Francois Charles de Bourlamaque who damaged British morale by killing second in Command, the highly respected Brigadier General George Howe. Further north, at Fort Carillon, Montcalm prepared French defences on the north-west land approach whilst the La Chute gave natural protection to the south, Lake Champlain to the east and north. Abercrombie relied on information from engineer Lieutenant Matthew Clerk and Captain James Abercrombie (a possible relation) who recognised Montcalm's rush to complete the defences but nevertheless recommended the attack should be supported with artillery from Rattlesnake Hill (Mount Defiance) south of the La Chute and from on the La Chute itself.

Ignoring all other possibilities Abercrombie ordered a full frontal assault which began at 12.30 on 8 July 1758. Initially piecemeal but developing soon enough along the whole front the British assault was met with devastating volleys from Montcalm's 3,500 defenders. After the failure of his first assault and from a position well to the rear, Abercrombie then ordered another as his artillery sailed into La Chute. The second assault received the same treatment as the first whilst the artillery barges, which had sailed within range of the fort, were sunk by cannon fire. Abercrombie's frontal assaults continued regardless, Montcalm in the thick of the action gallantly directing the fire of his men until nightfall when Abercrombie, having lost 2,500 dead and wounded, at last withdrew.

Abercrombie was sacked (but later promoted to Lieutenant General) and replaced by Major General Jeffrey Amherst who was about to finally take Louisbourg. British prospects improved further with a victory on Lake Ontario at Fort Frontenac and a French withdrawal from Fort Duquesne on the Ohio River. The immediate future of North America would be decided during the Annus Mirabilis of 1759, by Amherst at Carillon, by Major General James Wolfe on the Plains of Abraham outside Quebec and in Europe where Britons, Prussians and Hanoverians would make a massive effort against the French at Minden.

9 July 1755

French and Indian War
Battle of Monungahela

THE WAR OF the Austrian Succession (1740–48) which had involved all the major European powers ended with the Treaty of Aix-la-Chapelle which was effectively little more than a truce. Whilst the war had been fought ostensibly for the right of Maria Theresa to remain Empress of the vast Holy Roman Empire centered on Vienna, the British had predominantly been fighting to retain the balance of power in Europe, preventing the establishment of an all-powerful alliance between Prussia, Bavaria, France, Italy and Spain and, if these five had had their way, a Prussian dominated Austria. The war was arguably the first to spread across the globe, in particular subsuming the War of Jenkins' Ear fought in the Caribbean over disputed trading rights between Spain and Great Britain. Immediately following the Austrian War, Britain governed two million subjects on mainly the eastern seaboard of what is now the United States of America whilst France governed perhaps just 60,000 subjects in an area mainly north and west of the St Lawrence River, Canada, Lake Ontario and Lake Erie – the American Midwest. The territories in between were disputed, particularly at the confluence of the Rivers Allegheny and Monongahela which flow into the Ohio River and where in 1754 the French had destroyed the British Fort Prince George before building their own Fort Duquesne. Aware of French expansionist designs, the British sent the twenty-two-year-old Colonel George Washington with forty men of the Virginia Regiment to deal with the situation but though Washington was victorious ambushing French and American Indians at Jumonville Glen, he was subsequently forced into a conditional surrender at Fort Necessity. Meanwhile in Europe, since Austria now desired the recovery of Silesia (lost to Prussia at the start of the Austrian War), a conflict was begun with different alliances (Britain now siding with Prussia against Austria and France) that would again span the globe, in North America the French and Indian War, in Europe the Seven Years' War and in India the Third Carnatic War.

In early 1755 General Edward Braddock arrived in Hampton, Virginia as

Commander-in-Chief of the thirteen British American colonies to plan a four-pronged attack into the disputed territories, in late May himself leading the main column of 2,100 men including two regular infantry regiments with artillery toward Fort Duquesne. The progress of Braddock's five-mile-long column was so slow negotiating 180 miles of thick forest (largely through building a road with which to supply his expected new acquisition) that Braddock resolved to lead forward a flying column of 1,300 men. The French Commander at Duquesne, Claude-Pierre Pecaudy de Contrecour, knew that the disposition of his fort, overlooked on three sides by higher ground, would make it indefensible against British artillery and sent out his Field Commander Daniel de Beaujeu complete with war paint, Ottawa, Huron, Potawatomi and Ojibwa American Indians (850 in total) to ambush Braddock before he could reach the Monongahela eight miles away. The British flying column were soon losing inexperienced skirmishers to De Beaujeu's Indians, masters of the art, but Braddock nevertheless beat Beaujeu's main force to the Monongahela. The extended British column then executed a textbook river crossing, establishing a bridgehead on the opposite bank where the now supremely confident Braddock ignored Washington's warnings, pulled in his scouts and formed close order for a march on Fort Duquesne.

At 14.00 on 9 July 1755, the British column collided head on with Beaujeu's main French and Indian column, the French firing an ineffective volley at range only to be stunned by the reply from the British vanguard under Lieutenant Colonel Thomas Gage, Beaujeu amongst the dead. The Indians, however, knew little of close order volley fire and had taken cover in the trees, outflanking the British column to begin firing from hidden positions on the tightly packed British infantry still on the confines of the road. The battle raged for three hours, the British officers targeted including the defiant Braddock who took a bullet to his arm and chest as his column began to disintegrate. Washington now assumed command of a British retreat, firing a 6-pound cannon to hold off the Indian pursuers.

The British dead and wounded were scalped by the Indians or tortured to death back at Fort Duquesne. They had lost 456 dead with 422 wounded as well as a vast quantity of supplies and money. Braddock's expedition had been a disaster, he died three days later on the retreat back to Philadelphia. The British would attack again three months later 500 miles to the north-east at Lake George.

10 July 1460

Wars of the Roses
Battle of Northampton

DISSATISFACTION AT KING of England Henry VI's rule had led to a peasant's revolt led by Jack Cade in 1450 and a feud between Richard Plantagenet, Duke of York and Edmund Beaufort, Duke of Somerset both of whom had been Henry's Lieutenants in France over the previous decade. The feud was partly due to Somerset's military incompetence but also his close relationship with the king which, despite having overseen England's final collapse in France at the end of the Hundred Years' War, Somerset had maintained often at York's expense. The feud between the pair had exploded in violence in 1455 at St Albans where, caught in a planned coup, Somerset had been killed. York along with his allies Richard Neville, Earl of Salisbury and Salisbury's son Richard, Earl of Warwick, however, continued to pledge allegiance to Henry (House of Lancaster) during the uneasy four year truce that followed. All the while accusations and rumour dominated the Royal Court particularly concerning Henry's French Queen, Margaret of Anjou who effectively replaced Somerset as the king's primary advisor. Henry's weakness, his bouts of insanity and his inaccessibility whilst in confinement in Kenilworth Castle now merely served to further fuel the fires of suspicion and distrust between York and Margaret, the two becoming bitter enemies.

In 1459 York, Warwick and Salisbury, whose opposition to Margaret was widely known, were invited to Coventry for a Great Council of the Realm but recognised it as a trap set by the devious queen and failed to show. Salisbury then defeated a Lancastrian Army under James Tuchet, Lord Audley at Blore Heath in September 1459 before the three rebel lords combined forces only to retreat in disarray a month later before Henry's main Lancastrian Army at Ludford Bridge. York now departed for Ireland whilst Warwick, Salisbury and York's son Edward, Earl of March made the shorter journey across the English Channel to Calais, a still formidable English military base which remained loyal to Warwick, the town's captain, rather than Henry. Accused of treason by the subsequent 'Parliament of Devils' the four were duly served a bill of attainder but no one in England doubted the *Lords of Calais* would soon be back.

In June 1460, Warwick landed at Sandwich with 2,000 men before marching on London all the while recruiting 'the true commoners of Kent' and amongst others John De Mowbray, Duke of Norfolk, a former Lancastrian peer. The populace in London were welcoming to the rebels, a mercers riot against foreign business had taken place only four years before and discontent toward Henry still simmered strongly. The Tower of London, however, strongly garrisoned by Lancastrians under Thomas, Lord Scales refused to surrender under a blockade from Salisbury. Scales responded with a diplomatic disaster by directing cannon fire from the Tower's walls into the City which turned Londoner's discontent into outright rage. Meanwhile Warwick, William Neville, Lord Fauconberg (uncle) and March now with 10,000 men marched north seeking to destroy the Lancastrian Army whilst all the time still protesting loyalty to the King.

Henry was still awaiting various contingents but nevertheless 5,000 Lancastrians, mostly men-at-arms but with a few archers and cannon, had formed a strong defensive position north of Northampton with the River Nene to their rear and a fortified ditch to their front. On 10 July 1460, Warwick advanced through Northampton, burning the town en route toward the king's position but his requests to parley with Henry were denied by the Royal commander Humphrey Stafford, Earl of Buckingham. Diplomacy having failed, Warwick again advanced this time through rain (which negated the Lancastrian cannon) and a brief hail of arrows as if to engage Henry's left under Edmund, Baron Grey of Ruthyn. The Yorkists, however, had already bribed Grey with a promise to back him in a property dispute should his men lay down their arms. Once Grey had obliged, Warwick pressed on into the consequently exposed left of Buckingham's centre. The slaughter lasted just half an hour, Henry's loyal supporters, Buckingham, John Talbot Earl of Shrewsbury, Thomas Percy Lord Egremont, John Lord Beaumont all dying in his defence.

Henry was captured by an archer in his tent and returned to London a prisoner where Scales was apprehended in the act of escape, stabbed and hanged by the mob. York too arrived in London from exile in Dublin but rather than asking merely for redress from Henry claimed the throne for himself. Concerned at consequent ill feeling Warwick urged a compromise that Henry would disinherit his son Edward, Prince of Wales and instead recognise York as his heir. Queen Margaret, however, could be guaranteed to carry on the fight. In December York would march north to meet her at Wakefield.

11 July 1708 n.s

War of the Spanish Succession
Battle of Oudenaarde

THE WAR OF the Spanish Succession had been ongoing for six years with neither set of alliances able to gain a significant advantage, not for outright victory nor even for a favourable peace. A crushing victory at Blenheim in 1704 for the Grand Alliance of England, Scotland, the Dutch Republic and Holy Roman Empire had prevented the defeat of Austria and the collapse of the Romans whilst another at Ramillies in 1706 had forced the Bourbon French and Bavarians out of the Spanish Netherlands (Belgium, Luxembourg). In Spain itself, however, the Grand Alliance and consequently the cause of Habsburg Archduke Charles of Austria were in a pitiful state after Henri de Massue, Earl of Galway, a Frenchman commanding the Anglo-Dutch-Portuguese Army, had been defeated at Almansa in 1707. As no significant threat to Bourbon King Philip V of Spain (grandson of King Louis XIV of France) now existed in the Iberian Peninsular the Englishman James, Fitzjames, Duke of Berwick, commanding Bourbon-Franco-Spanish forces, moved north to join Maximilian Emmanuel, the Elector of Bavaria campaigning for the Bourbon cause on the River Rhine. A lack of action then saw Berwick move his forces west to join Louis Joseph, Duke of Vendome and Louis, Duke of Burgundy (brother of Philip V) who had moved into Flanders to capture Ghent and Bruges and who were now holding the whole of the River Sheldt north of France. If the Bourbon armies of Berwick and the two Louis' could take Oudenaarde, Berwick's uncle, John Churchill, Duke of Marlborough, Captain General of the Grand Alliance and the British Army, would be cut off from the English Channel.

Marlborough, Prince Eugene of Savoy and the Dutch Henry de Nassau, Lord Overkirk, however, correctly guessed Bourbon intentions and began a series of forced marches. On 11 July 1708, Prussian cavalry under Prince Eugene and British infantry under John Campbell, Duke of Argyle crossed to the west bank of the Scheldt just as the Bourbons were arriving. With just a few units across the predicament of the Grand Alliance was precarious but the French commander on the spot Charles-Armand de Gontaut, Duke de Biron crucially hesitated, allowing the Alliance to not only reinforce their bridgehead but go on the offensive with Hanoverian dragoons amongst whom was Prince George Augustus of Hanover, Marquess of Cambridge and future King George I of Great Britain (once the 1701 Act of Settlement had dispensed with over fifty Catholic claims, George was second in line for the British Crown behind his mother, Sophia of Hanover).

As more and more Grand Alliance units crossed the Sheldt they took up positions behind the Diepenbeck stream stretching north up to Huerne, Marlborough with just over 100,000 men at his disposal. The French in similar numbers were moving south from Ghent and should have attacked the weaker right flank of the Grand Alliance but Burgundy instead attacked the stronger defences on the left. Not for the last time on Belgian soil was there a fierce fight between Prussians, British and French as the Alliance held firm against the two Louis' onslaught. As more troops entered the battlefield on both sides the line began to stretch so that the French now threatened to outflank the Alliance left. Vendome, who was in the thick of the fighting, however, requested Burgundy attack the Alliance right which would in turn expose the centre. Marlborough reinforced Prince Eugene on the Alliance right with Prussians under Carl Phillipp, Reichsgraf von Wylich und Lottum and the left with newly arriving Hessians and Hanoverians. The Duke also brought up the Dutch Army of Marshal Count Hendrik Overkirk on his far left to outflank the French but initially they struggled to cross the Sheldt. As Marlborough and Eugene patiently waited for the Dutch to cross the bridges in Oudenaarde it was as much as they could do to hold off French attacks. At 20.30, an hour late, with the Dutch at last in position, Marlborough counter attacked along the whole line supported by Overkirk attacking the now exposed French right. The move devastated the French who, with many units having not made it into battle at all, broke off for a retreat back to Ghent.

The French had lost 15,000 men but again Marlborough could not press home his victory, it being too late in the day to make the difficult river crossings required. The French Bourbons had survived to fight another day, a day that would come at Malplaquet fourteen months later, the bloodiest of the entire eighteenth century.

12 July 1690 n.s (celebrated)/1691 o.s

Williamite Wars
Battles of the Boyne and Aughrim

IN 1688 SEVEN Members of Parliament, churchmen and a former Admiral invited the Protestant Prince William III of Orange, Stadtholder (Head of State) of the Dutch Republic, to depose his uncle and father-in-law, the Catholic King James II of England and Ireland, VII of Scotland. Following a *Glorious Revolution* in which not a shot was fired, William and his co-ruling Queen Mary II, James' daughter, were then crowned at Westminster Abbey in April 1689.

James had only himself to blame, a devout Catholic, he had initially been married to a Catholic convert, Anne Hyde, who had given him two surviving Protestant daughters before he secondly married a devout Catholic, Mary of Modena, who gave him a surviving Catholic son, also James, who by male preference primogeniture stood to inherit the throne of the Three Kingdoms of England, Scotland and Ireland. King James had also been friendly with the Catholic King Louis XIV of France (an absolute monarch who had driven thousands of Protestant Huguenots out of France), had reopened relations with the Vatican, raised many Catholics to offices of wealth and influence and had reinforced his brother King Charles II's leniency toward Catholics by the 1687 Declaration of Indulgence. Protestants had always been concerned, introducing a failed Bill of Exclusion in 1679 specifically aimed at preventing James' succession but now their patience finally expired. Whilst it was clear on William and Mary's landing in Torbay that Protestant England would not fight for James, the Catholics of Scotland and Ireland certainly would. James had been allowed to escape to the court of Louis XIV before, in March 1689, sailing with 20,000 French troops for Ireland where the Irish Patriot Parliament confirmed him as their king and began to increase the size of his army.

For his part William was already fighting a war against France in the Spanish Netherlands (Belgium, Luxembourg) but an Anglo-Dutch victory at Walcourt at least eased fears of an invasion of the Dutch Republic. In Scotland too, mainly

Highlander Jacobites (*Jacobus* – Latin James) were defeated at Dunkeld after an initial victory at Killiecrankie. The Dutch Republic, England and Scotland may have now been secure but the threat to William and Mary's rule in Ireland was increasing after James had acquiesced to Catholic demands that lands confiscated by Oliver Cromwell forty years earlier be reconfiscated from Protestant Williamites and that from here on Ireland would pass its own laws.

In Northern Ireland the Apprentice Boys of Derry had miraculously withstood a Jacobite siege but the Williamite Army under Marshal Frederick, Duke of Schomberg then began suffering winter losses to disease and malnutrition when the Jacobites retreated south with a scorched earth policy. In June 1690 William himself then arrived at Carrickfergus with 36,000 Dutch, English, German, Danish and French Huguenots, all remarkably supported by Pope Alexander VIII (who was anti-Louis XIV), before marching south to Drogheda where 29,000 Irish and French Jacobites formed a defence on the south bank of the River Boyne. On 11 July 1690 (ns),12 July celebrated, William's Army began crossing the Boyne at several points only to be pinned down in four hours of fierce fighting with Jacobites armed largely with tools of the farmyard and by charges from highly drilled French cavalry. William, who had been grazed by a cannon ball the previous day and who now suffered an asthma attack, had, however, wrong-footed James and now attacked with his main force downstream at Oldbridge, increasing the battle front to over a mile. Outflanked, the Jacobites retreated to Donore Hill where they were cut off by William's dragoons to their south before being left to their fate by their departing king, James earning himself the nickname 'the shit' as he fled to France never to return.

A year later, 12 July 1691(os) at Aughrim, Galway 18,000 Jacobites led by Charles Chalmont, Marquis de St Ruth had retreated to a defensive position behind the River Shannon pursued by 20,000 Williamites under Godert de Ginkell. After several costly assaults against well entrenched positions De Ginkell forced his way across a causeway against a Jacobite left hampered by English ammunition not fitting French muskets. De St Ruth tried to restore order but was decapitated by a cannon ball leaving the Jacobite effort to disintegrate. By the day's end 7,000 men lay dead.

The Battles of the Boyne and Aughrim gave King William (Billy) and Queen Mary ascendancy in Ireland where, in want of a lasting peace, the Treaty of Limerick was signed. The Crown of the Three Kingdoms would pass back from the House of Orange to the House of Stuart on William's death in 1702.

13 July 1643

English Civil Wars
Battle of Roundway Down

KING CHARLES I needed victory quickly if he was ever to regain full authority over his troublesome realms of England, Scotland and Ireland. Plunged into civil war in late 1642 the Three Kingdoms had been torn asunder with those loyal to the Crown in England consolidating control throughout the North, the South West and, by mid 1643, the Midlands whilst Parliamentary forces not only dominated the rest of England, including London, but also all the major ports, controlling trade and revenues to pay soldiers faithful to their cause. London, however, was in near panic at news of the activities of Charles' nephew and most able commander Prince Rupert of the Rhine operating from the King's Court at Oxford up to the approaches of the capital, at news from Adwalton Moor, Bradford where a Royalist Army under William Cavendish, Duke of Newcastle had defeated Ferdinando, Lord Fairfax and at news from Bath where Sir Ralph Hopton had added to his Royalist victory at Braddock Down by advancing into Somerset to defeat his old friend, Sir William Waller on Lansdown Hill.

The Royalist victory at Lansdown Hill had, however, come at the heavy price a full frontal assault against lanes, hedges and walls lined with musketeers always promised, Sir Bevil Grenville leading the tough Cornish infantry had been killed along with nearly 1,000 Royalist casualties. Worse still, the following day Hopton himself was nearly blinded in a gunpowder explosion that added to Royalist supply shortages and further demoralised his troops. Waller on the other hand had retreated in good order to Bath where he repaired his relatively minor losses with reinforcements from the Parliament garrison at Bristol. Returning to the field just two days after Lansdown Hill on 7 July Waller's cavalry caught up with Hopton three miles from Devizes but were held off by their Royalist counterparts under Prince Maurice of the Palatinate. Hopton retreated into Devizes to which Waller laid siege, his cannon firing into the town from the overlooking Roundway Down. On 9 July an increasingly uncomfortable Hopton then sent Maurice with

William Seymour, Marquis of Hertford on a desperate circuitous fifty-mile-ride to Oxford for reinforcements but since Prince Rupert was away escorting Queen Henrietta Maria across the North Midlands the only force available for a relief were 1,800 horse under Henry Wilmot, Earl of Rochester. Wilmot's Horse rode out of Oxford that same day with Maurice still in the saddle, arriving back in the vicinity of Devizes on 13 July 1643. Their haste had not been in vain, Hopton had been spared a barrage of artillery by heavy rain but was nevertheless barely holding on, melting guttering for musket balls in a near continuous three days of fighting around the outskirts of the town. The confident Waller had been seemingly unaware of Maurice's and Hertford's departure and only now became aware of theirs and Wilmot's return, angry that Robert Devereux, Earl of Essex and Parliament's Midlands Army had not prevented the Royalist sortie from Oxford.

Waller hastily withdrew his forces back to Roundway Down and, mindful of Hopton to his rear, prepared to meet Wilmot who despite having already ridden twenty-five miles attacked the Parliament left immediately. Here Wilmot caught the London Lobsters, cavalry of Arthur Haselrig (who had escaped arrest in Parliament by King Charles the year before) at a stand and threw them into a retreat. On the opposite flank Royalist cavalry under John Byron attacked and routed Waller's own cavalry which fled back over the chalk precipice at Olivers Castle. By now Hopton's Cornishmen were arriving from Devizes to join their horsemen for a battle on the remaining, isolated Parliament infantry. It was too much, having lost 1,400 men and all artillery, what remained of Waller's Parliament Army fled.

Following Roundway Down, Bristol fell to King Charles but at a terrible price. Poole, Portland, Weymouth and Dorchester also followed but iconically not Gloucester. The *Royalist Summer* would not last, in July Oliver Cromwell would defeat Charles Cavendish at Gainsborough to begin a series of Royalist reverses. London, however, still had cause for concern, the critical battle of 1643 would be just outside it, in September at Newbury.

14 July 1916

The Great War
Battle of Bazentin Ridge

BY THE END of 1915 huge territorial gains in Poland and Russia added to those in France and Belgium would almost certainly have satisfied German Chief-of-Staff Erich von Falkenhayn who was well aware that the greater resources of the Triple Entente (Russia, France and Great Britain) and the Royal Navy blockade of the German coast could and would eventually prove decisive. In early 1916 with the demise of the Russian Army on the Eastern Front, Falkenhayn resolved to break the Anglo-French Entente with an attack on the historically symbolic French town of Verdun, dragging French General Joseph Joffre into a war of attrition the catastrophic casualties of which he believed would force the Government of President Raymond Poincaré to the negotiating table. Relatively safe behind the now steel walls of the Royal Navy it was unlikely that Great Britain would have continued without France and anyway it was not their soil that millions of German troops now occupied.

As the battle of Verdun did indeed pull in ever greater reserves of the French Army morale did indeed begin to waver, Joffre requesting Commander-in-Chief of the British Expeditionary Force (BEF) General Douglas Haig relieve pressure on the French by bringing forward a planned joint but now mainly British offensive astride the River Somme rather than pursue Haig's preferred choice further north at Ypres, Flanders. Haig's attack on 1 July 1916 had met some success largely due to the concentrated firepower of French artillery and southern weaknesses of the German 2nd Army under General Fritz von Below but further north the BEF had met with much tougher German resistance behind banks of barbed wire which were still in tact after seven days of shelling as well as interlocking machine-gun fire across wide expanses of no-man's-land, precision artillery and aggressive German counter-attacks that eliminated all the initial gains whilst inflicting 57,470 casualties, the bloodiest day in the history of the British Army. Even if Haig had been fully aware of the scale of the disaster he would still have been duty bound by the Triple Entente to continue the offensive which he did with a series of piecemeal attacks that by 13 July had achieved little and resulted in yet another 25,000 casualties. To break the deadlock, Haig now employed a plan devised by British Fourth Army General Henry Rawlinson and XIII Corps Major General Walter Congreve, a renewed attack over just a 6,000-yard front on the Bazentin Ridge from Longueval to Bazentin le Petit Wood.

After a three day preliminary bombardment and capture of Trones Wood on the right flank, the British artillery launched a hurricane bombardment at 03.20 on 14 July 1916 lasting just just five minutes but with five times the intensity of shell fire as they had two weeks previous. Facing expanses of no-man's-land up to 1,200-yards-wide, six infantry brigades crept up behind the artillery barrage before rushing through destroyed wire to surprise the German defenders. Scots rolled up the German left flank at Longueval whilst to their left (north) Northumberlands passed through the 8th and 9th British Infantry Brigades to capture the village of Bazentin le Grand. Continuing left, Bazentin le Grand Wood was stormed as soon as the barrage lifted allowing Leicesters, Royal Warwicks and Irish to advance and take the village of Bazentin le Petit amidst fierce hand-to-hand fighting and determined German counter-attacks. Continuing left again, Bazentin le Petit Wood was also cleared apart from determined resistance in the north-west corner. German artillery then began shelling Longueval and the adjoining Delville Wood on the British right, South Africans moving forward to contest the position against growing German reinforcements for over two months of ferocious fighting. To their north the Deccan Horse of the Indian cavalry and the Dragoon Guards advanced to High Wood but could not hold the position unsupported, a failure that would cost dear over the coming weeks.

Bazentin Ridge had been a welcome success despite another 9,000 casualties. Fighting continued piecemeal over the wet 1916 summer turning the battlefield to mud and would claim Falkenhayn, sacked in August. The lessons of intense bombardment and limited objective attacks directed from the air would, however, not be fully appreciated until 1917. Before then, in September, Haig would press with a new weapon at Fleurs-Courcelette and Thiepval.

15 July 1761

Seven Years' War
Battle of Villinghausen

THE SEVEN YEARS' War in Europe had progressed uncomfortably for the British, Prussian and Hanoverian alliance since 1756. In Continental Europe the British had largely honoured the alliance with cash rather than military force preferring instead to blockade the French coast and press colonial interests globally, particularly in North America and India. In 1758 the Prussians and Hanoverians had struggled in the east against Austrian and Russian aggression but the latter's logistical problems along lengthy supply lines (so bad that the Austrians undertook to supply them) meant they were unable to exact a decisive victory. Against more resolute French aggression in the west the Prusso-Hanoverian Army had retreated east, back across the Rhine suffering several defeats before the following August 1759 a largely British and Hanoverian Army defeated the French at Minden. Minden could have been a decisive allied victory but for Lord George Sackville's refusal to send in his cavalry, the British commander cashiered after being found damningly guilty at a Court Martial called by himself.

Minden did not, however, stop the run of Prussian defeats which continued on into early 1760 before a July victory at Warburg. By this time the Royal Navy had prevented a French invasion of Britain with victories in Quiberon Bay and off Lagos, Portugal whilst British colonial ambitions had benefited nicely from significant victories over the French at Wandiwash in southern India, at Fort Carillon (renamed Ticonderoga) on Lake Champlain, North America and at Quebec, Canada.

By mid 1761 King Frederick 'the Great' of Prussia had fought the Russians to a virtual standstill in the east, both sides having suffered heavy losses whilst in North West Germany, the Prussian Army of Field Marshal Prince Ferdinand of Brunswick, now a Knight of the Order of the Garter, was once again threatened by a large French Army under the Marshal of France, Victor Francois, Duke de Broglie and Charles, Prince de Soubise, 90,000 men in total. French thinking mirrored that of the allies, tired of war they were anxious to force an emphatic victory for a favourable peace settlement but faced British and Hanoverians under the command of John Manners, Marquess of Granby who had restored the honour of the British cavalry at Warburg after being held back by Sackville at Minden. Reinforced by Hanoverians under Friedrich von Sporcken, Granby was 65,000-strong and took up a position on a series of hills near Villinghausen, North West Prussia from the River Lippe south to the River Ahse and further south still behind a tributary, the River Salzbach. The French approached from the east, Broglie agreeing to attack the allied left in between the Lippe and the Ahse whilst Soubise attacked further south over the Salzbach.

On the evening of 15 July 1761, Broglie approached south of the Lippe, achieving complete surprise against Hessians under General Wilhelm von Wutginau. As the Hessians began to give way Broglie extended his attack further south on Dunkerburg Hill which was defended by Granby's British and Hanoverian infantry and cavalry. Granby stood firm, fighting for several hours until nightfall when Broglie retreated. Overnight Prince Ferdinand moved allied troops from south of the Ahse (his right flank) over to the left flank in expectation of a renewed Broglie effort which duly arrived at dawn the following morning. Broglie expected Soubise to take advantage of the now weakened Allied right behind the Salzbach but Soubise, unwilling to take orders from Broglie, only made a weak effort and was easily held. So too was Broglie now held by Granby and Wutginau as further allied reinforcements arrived on the north bank of the Lippe to fire into Broglie's right flank. Having accumulated 5,000 casualties, Broglie broke off his attack at midday, retreating in some disorder but not pursued by the allies who had not yet realised they had won an important victory.

France attempted another advance in 1762 only to be defeated at Wilhelmsthal albeit with minimal losses. The victories at Villinghausen and Wilhelmstahl meant favourable terms for Britain by the 1763 Treaty of Paris, keeping all their gains in North America (the French insisting Catholicism be permitted) and India. Just fifteen years later, however, France would have an opportunity to reverse them.

16 July 1779

American War of Independence Battle of Stony Point

FOLLOWING THE CATASTROPHIC failure to adhere to the 1777 strategic objective in North America, Commander-in-Chief General William Howe offered his resignation to Secretary of State for the Colonies, George Germain, Viscount Sackville. Howe was replaced by his second in command General Sir Henry Clinton who with Lieutenant General Charles, Lord Cornwallis had marched back into New York City from Philadelphia after a sharp encounter with Major General George Washington and the Continental Army at Monmouth. The American War of Independence had once again taken a turn for the worse, the British Army now holed up in New York this time with a seaboard that was no longer the sole domain of the Royal Navy but also hostile French who, just fifteen years after being evicted from North America following the French and Indian War, had returned as the first ally of American Patriots in their bid for independence from British rule. Unperturbed back in London, however, King George III and Sackville still maintained the belief that Washington's now Prussian trained army could not stand in a set piece battle against British Redcoats despite recent conflicting evidence offered by the surrender of General John Burgoyne at Saratoga. To be fair the Franco-American alliance was hardly secure and even less so when the French Navy deserted Nathanael Greene at Rhode Island in August 1778, the Americans consequently suffering an unexpected defeat.

Whilst the king and Sackville favoured a vigorous prosecution of the war to exacerbate Franco-American relationship frailties Clinton was more inclined to fight an attritional war largely on the defensive. At the beginning of 1779 Clinton, as had been Howe in Boston three years before, was surrounded in New York City by the Continental Army to the south in New Jersey and to the north in the highlands of the Hudson Valley. To harass them Clinton resolved to march 8,000 Redcoats thirty miles up the Hudson River to cut Washington's supply lines by gaining control of the King's Ferry crossing. On 1 June 1779. Clinton took his objectives, including the adjacent Forts at Stony Point and Verplanck Point before sending Major General William Tryon with 2,600 men up the Connecticut coastline, burning settlements, stores, ships and even churches in an attempt to bring Washington out for a decisive battle. As Clinton's actions merely served to ostracise the local population, Washington patiently resisted the temptation, instead observing by telescope the British strengthening of Stony Point with earthworks and felled trees – abatis. Exasperated Clinton finally returned to New York leaving a garrison of 600 men under Lieutenant Colonel Henry Johnson protected by the Point's strong natural defences (on three steep sides by the Hudson River and to the west by a marshy stream) whilst the man made defences consisted of artillery and HMS *Vulture* on the Hudson. To test the defences of Stony Point Washington sent Major General 'Mad' Anthony Wayne with 1,350 hand picked light infantry on a fourteen-mile-march from Fort Montgomery, south through the mountains, arriving to the west on the evening of 15 July before setting off again before midnight in two columns, one each along the north and south shores of the Point, both headed by twenty-men of a forlorn hope.

On a dark 16 July 1779 night, buffeted by high winds whilst struggling through four feet of water the two columns reached their respective abatis. The two forlorn hopes then began cutting their way through with axes while North Carolinians under Major Hardy Murfree launched a feint attack on the western front of the fort. Johnson greeted Murfree and the northern forlorn hope with musket volleys and cannon fire taking a heavy toll of both but crucially allowed the southern forlorn hope, under Lieutenant George Knox, to cut through their abati. Once through Knox was joined by Wayne and the rest of the column to storm the summit with the bayonet. Unable to sufficiently depress their cannon, Johnson's gunners could only reply with musket shot and were consequently overwhelmed, surrendering within minutes. Nearly all 600 British were dead or taken into captivity.

Still unwilling to risk a pitched battle, Washington abandoned Stony Point. Johnson was released in a prisoner exchange only to face a Court Martial. In December 1779 Clinton would open a new front by taking the American War of Independence south to Virginia, Georgia and the Carolinas.

17 July 1453

Hundred Years' War
Battle of Castillon

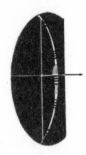

THE 1450 FRENCH victory at Formigny meant King Charles VII of France had defeated the last English Army to march in Normandy during the Hundred Years' War. The English conquest of France begun by King Henry V and continued by his brother John, Duke of Bedford on behalf of King Henry VI had now crumbled from its zenith at Orléans just twenty-two years before despite the tireless efforts of the 'English Achilles' John Talbot, now Earl of Shrewsbury. All remaining English strongholds quickly capitulated as Charles reclaimed all territory in northern France save Calais, Shrewsbury, who had been captured at Rouen, negotiating his freedom at Falaise (he had also been captured at Patay, 1429) on condition that he would never again don armour against France. Fury at the losses gripped England but Gascony, South West France had been an English possession since 1152 (when King Henry II married Eleanor of Aquitaine) and wished to remain so, particularly Bordeaux where the inhabitants benefited from copious wine exports to England. Devoid of English troops, however, and with Gascons powerless to resist, Charles entered Bordeaux in June 1451. No doubt consumed by the progress of his architectural masterpiece, King's College Chapel, Cambridge, Henry responded by doing nothing for an entire year before a representation of Bordeaux' burgesses requested an English 'liberating' Army. Mindful of recent fury, Henry appointed the now seventy-year-old Shrewsbury to lead this army just 3,000 strong which landed at Bordeaux in October 1452, taking the town after the citizens, who hailed him as 'Le Roi Talbot', had driven out the French garrison.

Shrewsbury was then strengthened by his son John Talbot, Lord de Lisle and Gascon recruits, 6,000 men in total who reclaimed Western Gascony while Charles remained passive over the winter. Assembling an army in the spring of 1453 the French king would attempt to finish the Hundred Years' War much as King Edward III had started it over a century previous, three armies consisting of impressive numbers converging on exterior lines with his own in reserve. Since each French

Army was similar in size to his own, Shrewsbury wisely chose to wait in Bordeaux, striking only when one of them came within striking distance.

In July 1453 the central French Army under master gunner Jean Bureau arrived at Castillon outside which pioneers built a thirty-acre entrenched camp and gun park to the south of the River Lidoire, a tributary of the River Dordogne which was 1,000 yards further south. Despite detailed explanation Shrewsbury's strategy, however, did not much appeal to the citizens of Castillon who were soon feeling the pinch of Bureau's 300 guns. Appeals for their relief were supported by the Burgesses of Bordeaux who went as far as to question Shrewsbury's integrity – the English Achilles, against his better judgement, fatefully agreeing to engage Bureau forthwith.

Leaving Bordeaux in the heat of summer on 16 July the Anglo-Gascon Army marched twenty miles to Libourne. Continuing again at midnight through thick woods high above the Dordogne Valley, the mounted vanguard then surprised and overwhelmed French archers in the Priory of St Lorent, north of Castillon, at first light on 17 July 1453. Since surprise was now forfeit Shrewsbury was content to wait for his infantry but on receiving reports that Bureau was retreating decided to attack immediately. Honouring his oath by not wearing armour, he swept south between Castillon itself and the French camp, crossing the Lidoire only to find ranks of French soldiers and lines of cannon waiting for him, it now becoming evident that just the camp followers had been leaving. The task facing Shrewsbury and the now dismounted vanguard was daunting but, unable to disengage and in the desperate hope that the Anglo-Gascon infantry was close behind, they advanced with the last 'St George' battle cry to be heard in France in over a hundred years of war. Blasted by cannon the Anglo-Gascons engaged Bureau's men-at-arms in a bloody mêlée across the defences with reinforcements arriving all the while and the result in the balance until 1,000 Bretons stationed north of the camp crossed the Lidoire to charge Shrewsbury's right flank. The Anglo-Gascon Army fell back toward the Dordogne where they were cut down or drowned, just a few escaping via a ford. Trapped when his white charger fell from under him, Shrewsbury was killed by a battle axe to the head, his son dying with him.

In the face of Bureau's guns Bordeaux surrendered ending the Hundred Years' War. King Henry VI now suffered a complete mental breakdown but his problems were only just beginning, dissension at his court was about to lead to internecine violence that would stagger Europe, the Wars of the Roses.

18 July 1545

Italian Wars
Battle of the Solent

THE DUCHY OF Milan had been the subject of dispute between Valois France and the Habsburg Holy Roman Empire (Holland, Belgium, Germany, Austria, North Italy, Switzerland, Czech Republic) since 1494. In 1511 Louis XII of France's control of the Duchy was then also opposed by the Holy League formed by Pope Julius II to which King Henry VIII of England opportunistically signed with a view to recovering English territories in France (lost during the Hundred Years' War). The dispute died down when both Julius and Louis died but flared up again in 1519 when Maximilian I, Holy Roman Emperor died. Charles V succeeded his grandfather as Holy Roman Emperor despite also being the King of Spain by virtue of his mother, Joanna of Castile, Queen of Spain. A now Habsburg surrounded Valois Francis I of France, who also had a Habsburg claim, started a personal feud with Charles that resulted in his own capture at the 1525 Battle of Pavia. The fighting was not over, however, Francis renounced his Italian claims by the Treaty of Madrid but once out of jail reneged to reignite the dispute when Charles personally took over Milan following the death of his son-in-law Francesco II Sforza. Francis also enlisted assistance from Suleiman the Magnificent, Sultan of the Ottoman Empire (Turkey) but after unsatisfactory gains at high expense opted to sign the 1538 Treaty of Nice with Charles.

Four years later and the dispute flared yet again, this time Francis suspicious of Habsburg involvement in the murder of his ambassador to Suleiman. Henry VIII again allied himself with the House of Habsburg since Francis was also sabotaging English efforts to bully the Scots into marrying Mary, Queen of Scots (Henry's niece) to his son Prince Edward. It was not love that was at stake so much as Henry's wish to deny France a renewing of the 'Auld Alliance' with Scotland, a romantic vision that began with a burning of Edinburgh and Lowland Scotland. The Scots were subdued just enough to precipitate a 40,000 man English invasion of France via Calais, still an English possession, and a successful English siege of Boulogne.

Charles also invaded France from the north-east but was soon at odds with Henry over tactics; the tables suddenly turning when Charles made his own peace with Francis which allowed the French King to not only counter-attack Boulogne but, with the added incentive of restoring Catholicism, prepare a French invasion of Protestant England.

On 18 July 1545, 200 French ships under Admiral Claude D'Annebault sailed into the St Helen's Roads off the Isle of Wight loaded with 30,000 troops. Four Mediterranean oared galleys commanded by Antoine des Aimars, Captain Polain then advanced to locate the eighty warship, 12,000 man English fleet which had formed a defence off Portsmouth Harbour. In light wind the English fleet weighed anchor to drive the French into the shallows but Polain retreated, exchanging cannon balls at long range, both he and D'Annebault also careful to avoid Southsea Castle's cannon. That night Henry dined with Admiral John Dudley, Viscount Lisle aboard the 1,000 ton *Henry Grace á Dieu* (Great Harry), a four deck, four mast, 151-gun, 800-man carrack built from 3,900 trees but the flat calm of the following morning served only Polain's returning oared galleys. Stung by French artillery the static English carracks were defended by rowing barges until an afternoon wind enabled the 500-ton English flagship *Mary Rose* under Vice Admiral George Carew to attack. As the King and Lady Carew watched on in horror from Southsea, however, the much modified warship heeled over to starboard taking on water through her open gun ports and sank with the loss of all but thirty-five of her 400 crew. The other English carracks then advanced with the row barges as the French galleys continued retreating in fear of being rammed. In more open water D'Annebault now considered engaging but could not outmanoeuvre Lisle who enjoyed the advantage of a westerly wind. To lure Lisle further out D'Annebault then landed several hundred troops on the Isle of Wight from Bembridge to Bonchurch (Ventnor) intent on attacking Sandown Castle but the local militia, including female archers, forced the French back. With little chance of defeating Lisle at sea and defeated at Sandown, D'Annebault withdrew to join the French attack on Boulogne.

Henry died in 1547 without uniting the Crowns of Scotland and England. After 211 years of English occupation Calais was lost to France in 1558, Boulogne having already been sold. In 1982 the *Mary Rose* was raised from the seabed. She now resides in her own Portsmouth museum.

19 July 1333

Anglo-Scottish Wars
Battle of Halidon Hill

AFTER DEFEATING THE English Army of King Edward II at Bannockburn in 1314 Robert the Bruce, King of Scots began consolidating control of Scotland against supporters of the murdered John 'Red' Comyn and launched raids into North England. In 1320 the Declaration of Arbroath was received by Pope John XXII, requesting recognition for Scotland as an independent nation and a lifting of Bruce's excommunication but only in 1328 was the peace treaty of Edinburgh-Northampton signed by the regents of England (on behalf of the fifteen-year-old King Edward III), the French born Queen Isabella and her lover Roger Mortimer, Earl of March. With Scotland recognised as an independent nation, Bruce was finally restored to christianity five months later but died the following year leaving his five-year-old son David II as King of Scots with Thomas Randolph, Earl of Moray and then Domhnall II, Earl of Mar serving consecutively as Guardians of a still deeply divided nation. Following Bruce's death Edward Balliol, son of John Balliol who had originally been awarded the Scottish Crown by Edward I of England in 1292, then stepped forward to claim his birthright supported by a now nineteen-year-old Edward III (even though Edward was already David's brother-in-law) and Scottish nobles determined to recover lands owned prior to Bruce's ascendancy – *the disinherited*.

In 1332 Balliol landed at Kinghorn, Fife with a numerically vastly inferior army commanded by Henry Beaumont that nevertheless defeated and killed Mar at the Battle of Dupplin Moor primarily with massed longbowmen. Balliol was then crowned a month later at Scone, acknowledging Edward as his liege Lord only to be defeated in December at Annan by the new Guardian of Scotland, Archibald Douglas, Balliol forced to flee Scotland in his night shirt. Edward needed little encouragement for a chance to avenge his father's Bannockburn defeat and in March 1333 came to Balliol's aid by marching on the then Scottish port of Berwick, a town which had been sacked by the English in 1296 and which Alexander Seton was now ordered to defend by Douglas. In June, with his garrison close to exhaustion, Seton agreed a truce with Edward on the condition that if the town was not relieved by 11 July he would surrender, as a guarantee handing over amongst others his son Thomas as a hostage. On the last day of the truce Douglas entered Northumberland with a large army of 13,000 that tried to draw Edward away from Berwick by sacking Tweedmouth. Edward resolutely maintained the siege however arguing that the town had not been relieved and that Seton should surrender, hanging the hapless Thomas when his father refused whilst also threatening to hang the remaining hostages two a day. Seton then negotiated another truce to expire on 20th July leaving Douglas no option but to confront Edward in a pitched battle to prevent the fall of Berwick.

On 19 July 1333, 9,000 English and *disinherited* Scots had taken up a position on Halidon Hill overlooking all approaches to Berwick whilst the Scots approached from Duns. Edward formed up in three battles all fighting on foot, Balliol commanding the left, himself the centre and Thomas of Brotherton, Earl of Norfolk the right, each battle flanked by longbowmen who could fire obliquely as well as forward. Douglas formed into four schiltroms led by John Randolph Earl of Moray, Robert Stewart the High Steward of Scotland, Hugh Earl of Ross and himself the rear. After a single combat curtain-raiser in which the English knight Robert Benhale killed Raoul Turnbull, the Scottish schiltroms began to move forward crossing a marsh where the first English arrows began to fall. Bravely but somewhat foolhardily the schiltroms continued up Halidon Hill as the white goose-feathered storm intensified, Scots unable to look forward and, in some cases, now only crawling toward their enemy. On the English left Moray joined battle with Balliol before the whole line became engaged in a brutal hand-to-hand mêlée. Moray was soon in disarray, his front suffering at the hands of Balliol's pikemen while his flanks were still under fire from the English longbows. Moray's men then broke leaving Stewart, Ross and Douglas assailed on three sides, just Ross' Highlanders standing firm for a fight to the bitter end which included a merciless English mounted pursuit. Douglas and five Scottish earls lay dead with perhaps 5,000 others.

Berwick surrendered and Balliol was restored as King of Scots but his reign would be brief. Edward's longbowmen would now be employed in a lengthy dispute with Scotland's ally France.

20 July 1304

Anglo-Scottish Wars
Siege of Stirling Castle

TOWERING ON VOLCANIC rock above the River Forth, Stirling Castle has been a symbol of Scottish Independence for centuries. Halfway between Glasgow and Edinburgh, guarding the uppermost crossing of the River Forth as it descends from the western Highlands toward the Lowlands of the Firth of Forth, in medieval times it was of enormous strategic importance.

King Edward I of England, self-proclaimed 'Lord Paramount' of Scotland after his arbitration of the *Great Cause* (the Scottish succession) had insisted that his choice, John Balliol, pay him fealty. Though Balliol himself eventually succumbed, his fellow Scots would not, allying themselves instead with France rather than become a vassal state of England. When Edward then tried to implement his will by force large numbers of Scots rebelled but any unity within their struggle was conspicuously absent – much of the land-owning nobility hesitating, anxious to maintain their personal wealth whilst the peasantry led by William Wallace fought on. A year after his heavy 1297 Stirling Bridge defeat to Wallace, Edward ruthlessly exploited this disunity at Falkirk; John 'Red' Comyn, Lord Badenoch deserting the Scots whilst Robert the Bruce VII, Earl of Carrick had reputedly fought for Edward. The Scottish peasantry had consequently been annihilated although Wallace himself had managed to escape the final rout.

Following Falkirk the English military conducted violent raids ever deeper into Scotland, campaigns of destruction rather than the castle building occupation of Wales of a decade previous but Edward knew that for any effective governance of northern Scotland he would need to hold Stirling Castle and control the crossing of the River Forth beneath it. Edward had held Stirling Castle after sacking Berwick in 1296 but subsequently lost it the following year when an English attempt to relieve a Scottish siege had ended in the aforementioned disaster at Stirling Bridge, the English garrison surrendering to Wallace. The castle came back under English occupation after Falkirk but changed hands yet again in 1299 when an English traitor betrayed the garrison. During the five years since, as English armies attempted to gain control of northern Scotland, Stirling Castle had stubbornly held out as a beacon for Scottish independence. Garrisoned by Sir William Oliphant, a veteran of the 1296 Battle of Dunbar, and just thirty men, the reduction of the great walls would be the supreme test for the engineers and carpenters of the English Army.

Edward and his besieging force moved up to the walls in April 1304 with virtually every device known to a medieval army. In an attempt to reduce the defences no less than twelve siege engines began a three month pulverising of the walls with lead and stone balls, Greek fire (an incendiary liquid) and even an early form of gunpowder (sulphur and saltpetre). Oliphant, however, resolutely stood firm despite scant chance of relief and with food and water running desperately low. A frustrated Edward ordered his engineer Master James of St George, who had designed Edward's impressive Welsh castles, to build a yet bigger siege engine. The new machine, perhaps the largest Trebuchet of all time, took five master carpenters and forty-nine labourers three months to build. Nicknamed *Warwolf* it was powerful enough to throw a 300-pound ball. Legend suggests that just the sight of it was enough to send Oliphant asking for terms but Edward, a man of considerable spirit, was now more interested in the performance of his new weapon than any Scottish surrender and he would not be disappointed. Warwolf destroyed an outer wall in quick time before Edward did eventually allow Oliphant and his garrison to surrender on 20 July 1304. All but one of the defenders, the traitor of 1299, were spared though Oliphant was sent to the Tower of London (he had already served time in Devizes Castle following Dunbar).

Edward had at last seemingly conquered Scotland but rebellion would erupt once again just two years later when Robert the Bruce, who had just inherited his father's claim to the Scottish throne, murdered his rival John Comyn and finally denounced his vacillating allegiance to Edward. Aylmer de Valence would renew Edward's efforts to conquer Scotland by attempting to destroy Bruce at Methven.

21 July 1403

Percy Rebellion
Battle of Shrewsbury

AFTER YEARS OF antagonism with many of his Lords, revolts by the English peasantry and the Scots, King Richard II of England paid the price for an ill-timed visit to Ireland when his cousin Henry of Bolingbroke, Earl of Derby returned from exile, forced him to abdicate and claimed the throne for himself. Richard died in dubious circumstances in the Tower of London shortly after but his problems were as alive as ever and were inherited by the new king, now Henry IV, who created another in the Welsh Marches in June 1402 at Bryn Glas. Here Owain Glyndwr, leading a rebellion against Henry, defeated an English Army containing many treacherous Welshmen who captured the English commander, Sir Edmund Mortimer – the ransom of whom Henry would not pay.

Just a few months later, Henry defeated a large troublesome Scottish Army at Homildon Hill with the help of Henry Percy, Earl of Northumberland and his son Henry Percy (Harry Hotspur) but then wasted his victory with abject diplomacy. Believing in a conspiracy, Henry not only refused to allow the Percys to pay Mortimer's ransom (Mortimer was Hotspur's brother-in-law and possessed a stronger claim to the English throne than Henry) but also refused them to ransom their own Scottish captives from Homildon Hill, including the valuable Archibald, Earl of Douglas. This restraint of trade was too much for a proud family who had previously supported Henry. Consequently Mortimer transferred his allegiance to Glyndwr, married his daughter Catrin and put forward his nephew, Edmund Mortimer, Earl of March for the English throne whilst the Percys accused the king of perjury in usurping the throne, taxing the clergy, murdering King Richard II and refusing a just ransom.

Joined by his uncle Thomas Percy, Earl of Worcester and Douglas, Hotspur led the rebel march south in July 1403, en route gaining large numbers of recruits particularly battle hardened Cheshire archers formerly loyal to King Richard.

Hotspur's father, Northumberland, was also following with his own army and no doubt they hoped to join with Glendywr and Mortimer. At the same time, however, King Henry, somewhat ironically, was marching north with a 14,000 strong Royalist Army to support the Percys against Scottish incursions in North England but when advised of the approaching threat the king immediately turned west to meet it.

The Royalist and Rebel Armies met outside Shrewsbury on 21 July 1403, Hotspur, whose nickname was well earned, not waiting for his father to join him. There was also no sign of Glendywr or Mortimer who were possibly unaware of recent developments but, nevertheless, Hotspur's army was formidable, similar in size to that of Henry but with superior bowmen. The morning was spent with Thomas Prestbury, the Abbot of Shrewsbury, trying to avoid bloodshed but negotiations broke down with Worcester and the king trading insults before the two armies closed. Initially an archery contest rained with Hotspur's Cheshire bowmen causing such a death toll that the king's right under Edmund, Earl of Stafford broke and fled. Hotspur had let his bowmen do his work at Homildon Hill but there was no restraining him now and with Douglas he charged to engage in a bloody mêlée of hand-to-hand fighting. Henry's men-at-arms however stood firm, amongst them leading the left his teenage son Henry, Prince of Wales (future King Henry V) who was hit in the face by an arrow. The battle raged on with Hotspur and Douglas charging the Royal Standard, killing the Standard Bearer Walter Blount and, it was initially thought, the king himself. Many northern knights now claimed Hotspur to be king but a very much alive Henry exclaimed that it was Hotspur who was in fact dead. Indeed there was no reply, Hotspur had fatally lifted his visor and had been struck by an arrow. On his death the Rebel Army fled.

Henry, Prince of Wales was saved when unanaesthetised surgery removed the arrow head from his skull before the tissue damage was treated with honey and alcohol – all his surviving portraits are from the opposite side. Worcester was hanged, drawn and quartered with three other knights two days later in Shrewsbury. To show the rebellion was dead a distraught King Henry had Hotspur quartered and sent to the four corners of England, his head on a spike on the north gate of York, before considerately returning the remains to his wife.

22 July 1298
Anglo-Scottish Wars
Battle of Falkirk

KING EDWARD I of England's argument with the Scots over their refusal to pay him homage as Lord Paramount of Scotland and their treaty of alliance with France against England had so far resulted in a bloody English sack of the Scottish port of Berwick, an English victory at the Battle of Dunbar and an English defeat at the Battle of Stirling Bridge. The Scots however remained divided in their determination to oppose the formidable English King, several nobles vacillating in their support for the cry of independence which was resolutely pursued by William Wallace and Andrew Moray, the victors of Stirling Bridge. Whilst Moray had been mortally wounded at Stirling, Wallace had gone on to attack English towns in Northumberland taking advantage of Edward's and the main English Army's absence in Flanders. By March 1298, however, Edward had agreed a truce with King Phillip IV of France and, according to the oldest English Roll of Arms (Falkirk), headed north with a paid army of 18,000 men, including Gascons and 10,900 Welsh longbowmen.

Edward sent Anthony Bek, Bishop of Durham to clear the coast south of the River Forth up which an English supply fleet would sail but although Bek was successful the fleet was delayed. Regardless, Edward's Army marched into central Scotland but soon began suffering from Wallace's scorched earth tactics and the lack of supplies. As morale dropped, discipline faltered, a drunken riot at Temple Liston in which eighty Welsh archers were killed by English men-at-arms persuaded the king to make a retreat to Edinburgh but just as he was about to move Edward received news that Wallace was just twenty miles away in Callendar Wood, Falkirk. Wallace had been shadowing Edward but, numerically inferior, had avoided battle, only now moving closer to harass the English Army as it retreated. Delighted at Wallace's approach having sought a set piece battle all along Edward claimed 'they need not pursue me, for I will meet them this day'.

On the morning of 22 July 1298, the English Army reached Callendar Wood to find Wallace's 6,000 Scots drawn up in four defensive Schiltroms of densely packed spearmen supported in between by archers. Behind, Wallace had just 1,000 mounted knights but his position was on high ground protected to the front by the Westquarter Burn and its marsh and behind by Callendar Wood itself. The English vanguard of mounted knights split left and right to attack Wallace immediately, Roger Bigod, Earl of Norfolk and Earl Marshall of England leading the left which struggled to cross the marsh making a wide detour to the west. Bek, commanding the right, tried to hold his knights back but failed with the result that the dual flank attack was disorganised. It was enough, however, for John 'Red' Comyn, Lord of Badenoch, himself a claimant for the Scottish throne and who had already spent time in the Tower of London, to desert Wallace along with his retainers. The Scottish archers were then immediately cut down by the English cavalry although no headway could be made against the twelve-foot-long spears of the schiltroms. Edward now arrived in person to order the withdrawal of his horsemen, the Scottish cavalry giving chase but having a sudden change of heart on sighting the approaching mass of English and Welsh longbowmen, a scene which prompted them to join Comyn in withdrawing. Edward could now take advantage of the unprotected, immobile and consequently fatally exposed schiltroms by continuing the attack with the longbow alone. Unable to retreat or advance, the Scots were hit by up to 40,000 arrows in the next minute, Edward continuing the storm until the Scottish ranks were so badly depleted that he could order his mounted knights back into the fray to finish them off. Scottish casualties were horrendous but Wallace escaped through Callendar Wood, albeit his military reputation in tatters.

Wallace resigned as the Guardian of Scotland to be replaced by a politically delicate triumvirate that included Comyn and, temporarily, Robert the Bruce who had reputedly sided with the English at Falkirk. For the next five years the English would launch raids against Scottish strongholds, perhaps the biggest in February 1303 led by the commander of Edinburgh Castle, Sir John Segrave, who would run into trouble at Roslin.

The Battles of Stirling Bridge and Falkirk are depicted, albeit woefully inaccurately, in the 1995 multi-award winning Icon Production and Ladd Company film *Braveheart* starring Mel Gibson.

22 July 1812

Napoleonic Wars
Battle of Salamanca

IN 1807 FIGHTING had erupted in the Iberian Peninsular after Napoleon Bonaparte, Emperor of the First French Republic had deposed King Charles IV of Spain and his son Ferdinand in favour of his own brother Joseph. The British had sought to assist Spanish partisans form organised resistance against French rule by sending an army to Portugal under the command of the now General Sir Arthur Wellesley, Earl of Wellington. The Anglo-Portuguese Army had then held its ground against determined French efforts to drive it from the Peninsular whilst the rest of Europe had remained under the French yoke. In late 1811, however, Napoleon began recalling French troops from Spain for an invasion of Russia where Tsar Alexander I had been failing to prosecute the Europe wide Continental System – a trade embargo aimed at destroying British commerce. Ironically the very nation Napoleon was ultimately trying to defeat, the United Kingdom of Great Britain and Ireland, now benefited as the overstretched French Armies provided Wellington with an opportunity to advance into Spain by first successfully attacking the Portuguese/ Spanish border fortress towns of Ciudad Rodrigo and Badajoz, both by bloody siege.

In June 1812 the United States of America, chafing at British restrictions on her trade with France and British support for American Indians, declared war on Great Britain but it mattered not a jot when compared to the seismic events in Europe. At almost the same time the *Grande Armée*, at the time the largest army in European history with an equally impressive yet insufficient supply train, crossed the River Niemen into Russia with 600,000 French, Prussians and Austrians to begin one of the greatest advances and catastrophic retreats in military history. Meanwhile, in Spain Wellington marched north from Badajoz to confront Marshal Auguste Marmont who retreated yet further north drawing in his 50,000 strong forces. With Joseph Bonaparte in Madrid urging Marmont to fight a decisive action, a series of counter marches found him south-east of Salamanca where on 22 July 1812 he sighted the British 7th Infantry Division on a right-angled ridge at Los

Arapiles with a cloud of dust in the distance that he believed to be Wellington's hastily retreating 52,000-strong main Anglo-Spanish-Portuguese Army.

Marmont continued south before turning west attempting to turn the British right flank unaware that the rest of the British Army was concealed behind the ridge, Wellington's favoured *modus operandi*. Advancing in column the French vanguard under Brigadier Jean Guillaume Thomières soon became dangerously over extended and was aggressively attacked by Adjutant General Edward Pakenham's 3rd British Infantry Division delivering musket volleys before routing Thomières with the bayonet. General Antoine Maucune, behind Thomiéres, formed square expecting a cavalry charge but instead was similarly devastated by musket volleys, this time from Lieutenant General James Leith's British 5th Infantry Division. In a fast pace battle 800 heavy dragoons under Major General John Le Marchant then charged from the British right flank, defeating eight French infantry brigades in succession with what Wellington claimed was 'the most beautiful thing he'd ever seen', Le Marchant, however, sadly killed by a musket ball. Wellington had defeated 40,000 Frenchmen in forty minutes but with Marmont wounded by shrapnel, General Bertrand Clausel assumed command of a French Army in a desperate predicament. Clausel, however, brilliantly counter-attacked with General Jacques Sarrut supporting the French vanguard while he and General Jean Pierre Bonnet attacked further north against the British 4th and 5th Divisions of Major Generals Lowry Cole and Leith before the British 6th Division under Major General Henry Clinton counter-attacked in turn. As battle raged Portuguese of the British 5th Division under Marshal William Beresford added to the British counter-attack on Bonnet and Clausel which, with support from the British 1st and 7th Infantry Divisions under Major Generals Henry Campbell and John Hope, sent the French into a headlong retreat for the bridge at Alba de Tormes. Covered by the divisions of General Claude Ferey and Maximilien Foy the French escaped since the Spanish General Carlos de España had inexplicably vacated the bridge. Nevertheless Marmont had lost 14,000 men.

The soon to be honoured Marquess of Wellington triumphantly entered Madrid but withdrew after a failed siege of Burgos. The decisive battle for the Iberian Peninsular would come at Vitoria the following year. Meanwhile 2,000 miles to the north-east Napoleon was about to defeat Prince Michael Andreas Barclay de Tolley and Prince Pyotr Bagration at Smolensk and Borodino only to find Moscow deserted. His subsequent retreat would shatter the *Grande Armée*.

23 July 1839

Afghan Wars
Battle of Ghazni

VICTORY AT ASSAYE in 1803 meant all of India south of the River Sutlej was now governed by the British East India Company but across the Sutlej, on the North West Frontier, lay the fiercely independent Sikh Empire and Afghanistan. The Sikh Army, the Khalsa, was European trained and equipped whilst the Afghans were expert in the mountainous terrain of their homeland. The two had been at war with each other since 1747 but in the early nineteenth century the Afghans were suffering internal strife – Dost Mohammad Khan becoming Emir of Afghanistan in 1834 after defeating Shuja Shah Durrani at Kandahar. Afghan difficulties were exploited by Sikh Maharaja Ranjit Singh who took advantage by capturing and annexing Peshawar at the eastern end of the Khyber Pass, now Pakistan.

Instability in the wider region had also been steadily increasing during and after the Napoleonic Wars through Russian expansion into Central Asia under Tsar Nicholas I, the consequent 1828 Treaty of Turkmenchay consolidating Russian gains in the Caucasus and extending Russian influence into Persia (Iran). Governor General of India (1836–1842) George Eden, Lord Auckland, believed any further Russian invasion of, or alliance with Afghanistan (which was effectively a buffer state between Russian Persia and British India) would be a direct threat to British interests and responded by sending Alexander Burnes to negotiate an alliance with Dost Mohammad in Kabul. Initially in favour until the British refused to support his retrieval of Peshawar, Dost Mohammed turned to Russia and their envoy Yan Vitkevich but when these talks also broke down, a Russo-Persian Army invaded western Afghanistan to besiege Herat. The 'Great Game' between Britain and Russia which had begun in 1830 now sparked the First Anglo-Afghan War when Auckland launched a British military campaign to replace the unreliable Dost Mohammed with his predecessor Shuja Shah Durrani.

As the British mobilised, the Russo-Persian Army withdrew from Herat making the British invasion effort largely redundant but Auckland merely reduced his invading force from three divisions to two, one each from the Bengal and Bombay Army. The obvious route to Kabul from Peshawar through the Khyber Pass was out of the question since Ranjit Singh would not allow any large army through the Punjab, especially a British one. The Bengal Army therefore marched from Ferozepur overland through the Bolan Pass to Quetta where it combined with the Bombay Army which had marched from the mouth of the River Indus after sailing up the west coast of India. The 14,500 British troops under the command of Lieutenant General John Keane were then joined by 6,000 Afghans loyal to Durrani before marching 150 miles over mountainous passes to reach Kandahar on 25 April 1839. To reach Kabul, Keane had still to assault the Afghan fortress at Ghazni, a further 200 mile distant, and since he had few horses he would have to accomplish it without siege equipment. At Ghazni Keane faced 3,500 men under Dost Mohammed's son Hyder Khan protected by a moat and towering seventy-five foot walls with a full frontal assault the only means of attack. Luck, however, was on Keane's side when Colonel George Thomson of the Bengal Engineers learnt that all the gates of Ghazni were reinforced with stone piles except the Kabul Gate in the north.

After Durrani's Afghans had blocked a Ghilzai relief attempt, the British attacked the Kabul Gate at Ghazni at 03.00 on 23 July 1839. An artillery barrage covered an advance of engineers and miners who were followed by a storming party of four light companies led by Colonel William Dennie. The engineers successfully blew up the gate with Dennie's men rushing into the breach for a bitter hand-to-hand fight with the defending Afghans. As more Afghans counter-attacked Dennie became surrounded but was relieved by Brevet Colonel Robert 'Fighting Bob' Sale who fought through with four infantry regiments to secure the town.

The British suffered 200 casualties in the assault with Sale amongst the wounded. The Afghans with over 2,000 casualties not only surrendered Ghazni but also Kabul from where Dost Mohammed fled into west Afghanistan. Shuja Shah Durrani became emir but he would not have time to make himself too comfortable.

24 July 1943
Second World War Bombing of Hamburg

THE FORTUNES OF the Second World War had dramatically changed in late 1942, early 1943. Japan had frustrated British counter-attacks in Burma but had been defeated at Guadalcanal, Solomon Islands by United States marines who now began an island hopping campaign toward the Japanese homeland. Meanwhile, in North Africa, Germans and Italians had surrendered in droves following British 8th Army advances from Egypt and Anglo-American landings in Morocco and Algeria, an Allied invasion of Sicily now imminent. On the Eastern Front, the Soviet Red Army had also counter-attacked at Stalingrad, Hitler's preoccupation with holding ground again costing dear but by July 1943 Fieldmarshal Erich von Manstein had recovered the situation to counter-attack aggressively at Kursk, the greatest armoured battle in history. Further west, British Prime Minister Winston Churchill more so than United States President Franklin D. Roosevelt was still not prepared to risk a major assault on the German Atlantic Wall but continued to bomb German industrial centres and cities. Differences in opinion resulted in American 'precision' bombing during daylight hours whilst the Royal Air Force, who through experience and statistics believed precision bombing to be a pipe dream, area bombed at night. Since February 1942 Commander-in-Chief RAF Bomber Command Arthur Harris, supported by Churchill and Air Chief Marshal Charles Portal, had attempted to smash German civilian morale by devastating the medieval port cities of Lubeck and Rostock and the Ruhr cities of Cologne, Essen and Bremen. It was Germany's second largest city, however, the port of Hamburg, her shipyards and oil refineries that had always been Harris' first choice target. With improved tactics he now planned another massive raid over several days to overwhelm the formidable air and anti-aircraft defences protecting the two million souls living in the city. Aptly named Operation Gomorrah, the scale of Hamburg's imminent destruction would surpass anything hitherto witnessed or imagined.

At 21.45 on 24 July 1942 from airfields in the East Midlands the first of 800 Mosquito, Halifax, Wellington, Lancaster and Stirling bombers began taking off to form a bomber stream over 200 miles long. In near perfect weather the attack was picked up by German radar at one hundred mile range giving Messerschmidt and Junkers night fighters time to intercept. As the two forces closed, however, the British bombers began dropping 'window' – strips of tin foil that blinded German radar and left each fighter pilot to find his own target. Only hours earlier Hamburg had been basking in warm summer weather but now Pathfinder Mosquitos arrived in the skies above to drop marker flares around the city centre over which the bomber stream flew for the next hour dropping 1,000 tons of incendiaries and 1,300 tons of high explosive, shattering buildings and setting the medieval city ablaze. The overwhelmed firefighters below could barely move through the shattered streets and called in thousands of reinforcements from neighbouring towns as Hamburg continued burning throughout the following day. But now the US Eighth Air Force arrived with near 300 B-17 Flying Fortresses fighting off Messerschmidt 109 fighter attacks to drop 190 tons of incendiaries and explosive over a far wider area than anticipated due to the heavy smoke. Mosquitos carried out a nuisance raid that night with the Americans returning the following day to deliver another 100 plus tons of Incendiaries and Explosive. On the night of 27/28 July the British then returned with near 750 aircraft dropping another 2,300 tons of incendiary and explosive in a fifty minute window that again set the city ablaze, a terrifying howl developing as air rushed through the streets. As the fires grew, temperatures raced up to 800C, 150 mph winds dragging in oxygen that created a tornado of fire 1,500 feet high, a firestorm. Eight square miles of the city were destroyed as roads melted and oil tanks exploded, even the canals burned. Almost all of Hamburg's railways, half the factories and half the housing was destroyed or damaged as 80,000 civilians were killed or injured by suffocation and burns whilst a million fled. Harris pummelled what remained of Hamburg again on 29 July and 3 August with another 700 aircraft.

To Harris' frustration Bomber Command was then directed to bomb strategic targets in Italy and France preparatory to forthcoming invasions. German Chancellor Adolf Hitler could never bring himself to visit Hamburg. The ruined spires of St Nicholas Church, Hamburg now stand as a monument against war.

25 July 1666 o.s

Anglo-Dutch Wars
Battle of North Foreland

THE SECOND ANGLO-Dutch War broke out over many of the same trade disputes that had started the first a decade before but whilst the Dutch had always supported the restoration of the English monarchy they were now not so happy when King Charles II, who had indeed been restored to the English throne, promoted his nephew Prince William of Orange as Stadtholder (head of state) to the Dutch Republic.

The fickle Dutch ruling class of the States General (parliament) had benefited from a period of regency following the death of William's father in 1651 and his ascendancy would now be to their detriment. England also supported France over disputed territories in the Spanish Netherlands (Belgium, Luxembourg) believing more was to be gained in defeating the Dutch rather than the French. Dutch prosperity had grown over the past decade with a system of free trade whilst the English, although far more numerous, struggled to compete with a system of tariffs. Indeed no one knew better than the Royal Navy's own Clerk of Acts, Samuel Pepys, that in any war against the Dutch Republic, England had not the finances for a conflict of any length. Although victorious at Lowestoft in June 1665 disappointingly an English fleet of thirty ships had then been defeated at Vagen, Norway whilst attempting to capture a valuable Dutch East India convoy.

As English finances worsened and London was gripped by the Great Plague (ironically likely started by a Dutch flea), King Charles and his Generals-at-Sea George Monck and Prince Rupert became alarmed at reports that the French were about to change sides and side with the Dutch, their treachery prompted by fears of an Anglo-Spanish coalition. Indeed, Louis XIV of France did declare war on England in January 1666 causing Charles to relax his promotion of Prince William but the Dutch, now with a powerful new naval fleet, were in no mood to listen. Monck and Rupert put to sea in late May, Rupert blocking the Straights of Dover from a French attack that did not materialise whilst Monck attacked the

Dutch fleet of famed Lieutenant Admiral Michiel De Ruyter in the Four Days Battle off Dunkirk. Despite being rejoined by Rupert the battle was a disaster for Monck who lost twenty-three ships and 5,000 men including Vice Admiral William Berkeley and former pirate, now Vice Admiral, Sir Christopher Myngs. De Ruyter briefly pursued but, himself heavily damaged, returned to prepare for a combined attack with the French on the Chatham Dockyards.

De Ruyter, however, returned without the French on 25 July 1666 sailing with 118 ships across a north-westerly wind to find a 106-strong English fleet in a six-mile line-of-battle off the North Foreland. As the Dutch came up parallel and to windward of the English, Sir Thomas Allen turned the English van to the east in an attempt to gain the weather gauge but Admiral Johan Evertsen countered by turning with him. The two centres closed behind but further back the Dutch rear under Lieutenant Admiral Cornelis Tromp made a break through the line of the English rear under Sir Jeremy Smyth. It was midday as the vans and centres headed east in continuous exchanges of cannon ball and canister, the heavy English guns in the van causing the deaths of Evertsen and fellow officers Tjerck Hiddes de Vries and Rudolf Coenders. In the centre De Ruyter, aboard the dismasted *Zeven Provincien*, was not alone in suffering, Rupert also having to leave the battered *Royal Charles* for the *Royal James*. In the rear the squadrons of Smyth and Tromp had disappeared south in a separate fight, Tromp bettering Smyth in a confused mêlée, destroying the 64-gun *Resolution* with a fireship but becoming dangerously isolated when De Ruyter and Evertsen's squadrons further east began to sail for the Dutch coast. Monck and Rupert looked to pursue De Ruyter but the Dutchman was saved by a westerly wind and by Vice Admiral Adriaen Banckert covering his rear.

The following morning, Tromp initially believed himself trapped but headed east to join a multitude of Dutch ships limping into port. De Ruyter meanwhile, believed the Dutch fleet to have been devastated but in fact, although he had suffered 5,000 casualties, most of his ships were recoverable. For King Charles the victory at North Foreland could have been decisive but as it was, with money scarce, he could not press the English offensive. Things would only get worse, five weeks later a baker in Pudding Lane, London, would exacerbate his financial problems by starting a fire of legendary proportions.

26 July 1346

Hundred Years' War
Sack of Caen

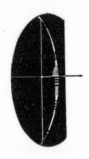

KING EDWARD III of England, like so many English Kings before had been unhappy paying homage for his French possessions to the King of France, in his case King Philip VI. His obvious reluctance to do so contributed to Philip confiscating the Duchy of Aquitaine in 1337, infuriating Edward who responded by seeking allies in the Low Countries and with Louis of Bavaria, Holy Roman Emperor. The English king then raised his own arguably better claim to the French throne by virtue of his mother Isabella (the she-wolf of France), daughter of King Philip IV of France. After an expensive military foray into northern France only to be deserted by his well paid but fickle allies, Edward reopened hostilities in 1342 by supporting John and Joanna de Montford in the War of the Breton (Brittany) Succession– the English Army reaching as far east as Nantes before Philip arrived at Rennes with a large French Army in support of the rival claimant, Charles, Count of Blois. Then, just as the dispute was about to be violently settled, Pope Clement VI intervened to negotiate a fragile truce.

When hostilities in Brittany reopened in 1345, the English campaigned under Thomas Dagworth and John de Montford himself but Edward had bigger plans, an ambitious English invasion of northern France on three exterior lines as part of a concerted effort to rule the entire country. Having taxed or fined his own population at eye-watering levels, the English king and an army of 12-15,000 (mainly archers) aboard over seven hundred cogs left England on 11 July 1346, initially leaving the destination shrouded in secrecy but with forces already in Brittany and longtime English possession of Gascony (Aquitaine) Edward was sailing for St Vaast La Hogue on the Cotentin Peninsular. On landing Edward knighted his son, the sixteen-year-old Edward of Woodstock, the Black Prince before, with the fleet shadowing at sea, marching the English Army south on a front several miles wide burning and pillaging everything in its path to send the

French inhabitants fleeing in terror, a tactic Edward believed would bring Philip to a decisive battle.

By 25 July the English were only ten miles from the ancient city of Caen, burial place of Edward's ancestor William I, 'the Conqueror', King of England. Edward sent an envoy into the city assuring those inhabitants who had not already fled, that their lives and property would be spared just as long as they peacefully submit to he, the English king, the rightful King of France. The offer was rejected by Wilhelm IV Bertrand, Bishop of Bayeux who imprisoned the envoy and retreated to the castle with 300 crossbowmen and men-at-arms. This left Raoul of Brienne, Count of Eu to defend Caen which was split into the Old Town beneath the castle and the poorly defended New Town across a branch of the River Orne on the Isle de St Jean.

The English Army arrived directly outside the walls of Caen on 26th July 1346, Edward, with no siege engines, looking to assault the Old Town immediately. No doubt under pressure from wealthy merchants, Eu had, however, decided to defend the New Town which was surrounded by water but in doing so separated his forces from those of the Bishop in the castle. Edward seized his opportunity, blockading the castle while the remainder of his men formed to attack the defended bridges into the New Town, north at St Pierre and south at La Boucherie. Men under Thomas de Beauchamp, Earl of Warwick and William de Bohun, Earl of Northampton began the assault with archers unleashing a terrific covering fire as men-at-arms surged forward to engage the defenders. In fierce fighting little headway was made at St Pierre but at La Boucherie resistance soon wavered when English longbowmen forded the river. With the Bishop and his garrison still watching on from the castle, the English soon forced their way into the New Town, turning the defenders at St Pierre which allowed Warwick, in fierce hand-to-hand fighting, to force his own entrance and capture Eu. A body of French made a desperate bid to reach the castle but most of them fled back through the New Town, the majority cut down in a frenzy of bloody murder that would lead to a five day sack, render Caen a smoking ruin and leave perhaps 2,500–5,000 Frenchmen dead.

Unable to reduce the castle, Edward resumed his march north to link up with an Anglo-Flemish Army marching south from Ypres. In response, an enraged King Philip collected the sacred Oriflamme from the Abbey of St Denys and marched out of Paris for a confrontation that is undoubtably one of medieval history's greatest battles, Crécy.

27 July 1880
Afghan Wars
Battle of Maiwand

 BRITISH FEARS OF Russian expansion had led to the 1838 First Afghan War, the 1854 Crimean War and more recently the 1878 Second Afghan War when the presence of Russian diplomats in Kabul and an Afghan refusal to admit a British envoy prompted another British invasion of Afghanistan. The British Indian Army had again initially been successful, replacing the ruling Afghan Emir Sher Ali Khan with his son Mohammad Yakoub Khan whilst British Representatives now administered Afghan Foreign affairs. Denounced as a puppet by his compatriots, Yakoub and the British Representative Sir Louis Napoleon Cavagnari, signed the 1879 Treaty of Gandamack and for a while all seemed well. Since no Russian threat had materialised, British forces then withdrew but just four months later Cavagnari and his staff were dead, having been murdered in the Kabul Residency.

This time a smaller British force under Major General Sir Frederick Roberts fought through to restore order in Kabul, Yakoub remaining emir and given refuge within the British Sherpur Military Cantonment north of the city despite considerable suspicion over his involvement in Cavagnari's death. Far from restoring order, however, Roberts stirred up a hornet's nest of discontent when his widespread execution of suspected Afghan mutineers caused another rebellion, this time by 50,000 Afghans under Mohammad Jan Khan Wardak. Roberts, however, successfully withstood an eight-day siege and a mass assault on the Cantonment before scattering Jan Khan's tribesmen. Nevertheless Yakoub now abdicated, in his place as emir Roberts appointing Yakoub's cousin Abdur Rahman Khan, the news of which sufficiently enraged Yakoub's younger brother Ayub Khan, the Governor of Herat, to march on Kandahar the following summer 1880. In Kandahar Major General James Primrose reacted by sending two infantry brigades under Brigadier General George Burrows to first join Afghans under the ruling Wali at Girishk before considering any interception of Ayub. Primrose's plan disintegrated immediately, however, since the Wali's troops had defected to Ayub. Regardless, an undeterred Burrows determined to intercept Ayub's now 25,000 Afghans with just one tenth that number at Maiwand.

On 27 July 1880, from a perfect defensive position behind a ravine the somewhat cavalier Burrows advanced out onto the open plain seemingly oblivious of Ayub's overwhelming strength. The British guns then advanced into a dangerously exposed position forcing the 66th (Berkshire) Regiment of Foot on the right, Jacobs Rifles in the centre and the Bombay Grenadiers on the left, to follow on into the maelstrom of a two-and-a-half-hour artillery duel in which the British were outgunned by a native army using superior weapons manufactured in the Royal Arsenal at Woolwich. Burrows then compounded his initial mistake by attacking with his grenadiers only to cancel the order as soon as casualties began to mount, exposing them further to Afghan horsemen. Worse, unknown to Burrows, the ravine from which he had originally departed continued on his right and was now being infiltrated by Afghans forcing the Berkshires to wheel right. When the British guns on the left then ran out of ammunition and withdrew thousands of Afghans charged, forcing the Grenadiers and Jacobs Rifles into the backs of the Berkshires who were themselves coming under attack from Afghan guns advancing down the ravine. Burrows desperately ordered a cavalry charge but could not halt the Afghan advance. The Royal Horse Artillery now pulled back over the ravine continuing to fire as the British infantry came under increasing pressure, the line eventually breaking. The Berkshires and Grenadiers fought a retreat back into Khig and a defensive position in a walled garden where just eleven men and their regimental dog 'Bobbie' remained for a final back to back stand whilst those that could fled for Kandahar.

Victorian Britain was dismayed at the defeat of Maiwand but the battle is celebrated by the Maiwand Lion in the Forbury Gardens, Reading, the poems *The Last Berkshire Eleven* by William McGonagall and *That Day* by Rudyard Kipling. The Berkshire's surgeon, Major Alexander Preston, was the inspiration behind Sherlock Holmes' Doctor Watson. Bobbie survived the battle to receive his campaign medal in person from Queen Victoria, he was killed by a Gosport taxi the following year but now resides in the regimental museum courtesy of taxidermist.

28 July 1809

Napoleonic Wars
Battle of Talavera

NOT SINCE 1795 and the War of the First Coalition (a siege of Toulon and a Flanders Campaign) had the British Army set foot on European soil for a concerted military effort against Revolutionary and Napoleonic France but by the end of January 1809 Lieutenant General John Moore's 30,000 strong British expeditionary force had been chased out of Spain initially by Napoleon himself and finally by Marshal Jean de Dieu Soult. Just months earlier Napoleon had deposed Spain's King Charles VI and his son Crown Prince Ferdinand for his own brother Joseph but had reckoned without Spanish patriotism and defiance, none more so than at Zaragoza where the Spanish had suffered more than 50,000 dead during a bloody two month siege. With virtually the entirety of Europe under Napoleon's yoke the British government of William Cavendish-Bentinck, Duke of Portland had looked to support the Spanish insurrection with their own military operation, Moore marching into northern Spain only to find British optimism at Spanish capabilities hopelessly misplaced. Moore paid with his life defending an evacuation from Corunna that 131 years later would be closely resembled by another from Dunkirk, France. The British, however, were undeterred, Major General Arthur Wellesley was about to return to Portugal from a court of enquiry (at which he was exonerated from any involvement in the decision by Lieutenant General Hew Dalrymple to allow the French Army defeated at Vimeiro to be shipped home fully armed) to command 20,000 British troops in Lisbon, organise the Portuguese Army and assist the Spanish whilst Napoleon's *Grande Armée* were distracted by the forming of the Fifth Coalition which included the return to war in Eastern Europe of a 340,000-strong Austrian Army.

Wellesley arrived back in Portugal in April 1809, attaching one Portuguese battalion to each of his British brigades in preparation for an attack on any one of three vulnerable French Armies, Soult at Porto, General Pierre Lapisse at Ciudad Rodrigo or Marshal Claude Victor at Talavera, ideally before they could unite.

Wellesley marched 19,000 men north to Porto while General William, Lord Beresford marched 6,000 further east to block Soult's retreat. Soult was surprised when the British crossed the River Douro on wine rafts but escaped Beresford's block by retreating through the mountains of North Portugal. Wellesley then marched up the Tagus River Valley to join 35,000 Spaniards under General Gregorio Garcia de la Cuesta near Talavera, agreeing to attack Victor's 22,000 strong French Army on 23 July 1809. On the said date, however, Wellesley was in position while Cuesta slept, the bleary-eyed Spaniard routed the following day when his pursuit of a withdrawing Victor stumbled into the path of Joseph Bonaparte arriving from Madrid.

Still with 20,000 men and the remnants of Cuesta's Spanish Army, Wellesley now faced 46,000 French, taking up his definitive defensive position on the Cerro de Medellin Heights, two lines of infantry behind a ridge that gave protection from enemy artillery. On the evening of 27 July French General Francois Ruffin surprised the British left by reaching the summit of the Cerro only to be driven off by the British reserve of General Rowland Hill. At 05.00 on 28 July 1809, a French artillery bombardment of the British left provided the alarm to begin proceedings in earnest, again Ruffin advancing, this time toward a fully expectant Hill who duly repulsed him with a close range musket volley followed by a bayonet charge. After a delay of several hours and no doubt indecision in the French HQ another attack was launched this time by General Jean Leval against the British right where Brigadier Henry Campbell linked with the Marquis de Portago's Spaniards. Again the attack was repulsed but with Campbell caught on lower ground suffering heavy losses to artillery fire and determined French counter-attacks. As Leval was attacking the British right, Major General Horace Sebastiani and General Pierre Lapisse assisted by an 80-gun bombardment launched another French effort on the Cerro de Medellin but were repulsed by Major General John Sherbrooke and Major General Alex Mckenzie before Wellesley delivered a cavalry attack on Ruffin's final assault. Badly bruised, the French withdrew with over 7,000 casualties.

British casualties of over 5,000 and the news that Soult was again advancing from Salamanca forced Wellesley to begin a retreat to Lisbon where the populace would begin building the defensive Lines of Torres Vedras. Talavera earnt Wellesley a peerage, becoming Viscount Wellington of Talavera and of Wellington.

29 July 1588 o.s

Anglo-Spanish Wars
Battle of Gravelines

PROTESTANTS HAD ENDURED a bloody five years under the Catholic rule of Queen Mary I (1553–58) but her successor Queen Elizabeth I immediately returned England to Protestantism before also covertly supporting the Dutch Protestant Revolt against Mary's husband, King Philip of Spain. A few years later Elizabeth's opposition to the Catholic League (France and Spain) was more open, exasperating Philip whose possessions had suffered at the hands of Sir Francis Drake for many years already. Now intent on restoring Catholicism to heretic England, Philip resolved to do it personally when Elizabeth executed the Catholic Mary, Queen of Scots in February 1587.

For the invasion of England, Philip planned to collect the 30,000-strong Army of Alexander Farnese, Duke of Parma from the Spanish Netherlands with an impressive Armada but preparations did not go well. First in April 1587 the feared Drake had set fire to much of it in Cadiz Harbour before in February 1588 his leading Admiral, Alvaro Bazan, Marquis of Santa Cruz, died to be replaced by Don Alonso Perez de Guzman, Duke of Medina Sidonia, a man so short of confidence that he protested against his own appointment.

Scattered by storms, the initial Armada foray returned to Corunna with Medina Sidonia already in despair but sailed again on 12 July 1588, the 130 Spanish warships spotted a week later off the Lizard, Cornwall prompting beacons to be lit from the coast inland so that within hours all England knew the hour had come. In Plymouth, Drake finished his legendary game of bowls and with Lord High Admiral Charles Howard, Rear Admiral John Hawkins and Martin Frobisher slipped out of the harbour in the *Revenge, Ark Royal, Victory and Triumph* respectively with over fifty others. Thanks to the foresight of Hawkins, the English were aboard more agile ships armed with rows of guns that could deliver devastating broadsides whilst the Spaniards, in bigger ships with 19,000 soldiers aboard, were looking for a medieval style battle across decks.

Medina Sidonia took up a wide defensive crescent formation from which the English behind looked to pick off stragglers, Juan Martinez de Recalde's *San Juan* in particular trying to tempt them closer. Though fighting intensified off Portland Bill neither side inflicted any serious damage until 26 July when south of the Isle of Wight, Drake to seaward took advantage of a strengthening wind to attack north-eastward, driving the Spaniards toward the Owers Banks. Any plans Medina Sidonia had for a respite in the Solent were now ditched as the Armada sailed south-east for the relative safety of the open sea and Calais. On 28 July, having barely arrived off Calais, Medina Sidonia was then attacked in darkness by eight fireships that caused little damage but succeeded in breaking up the Armada, many sailing north-east isolating the *San Martin*, the *San Juan* and three others. Off Gravelines the following morning, 29 July 1588, Drake's *Revenge* followed by four squadrons under Hawkins, Frobisher, Henry Lord Seymour and Thomas Fenner sailed downwind to join battle with the lone Spaniards before the wider Armada could reassemble, Medina Sidonia turning the *San Martin* to meet the attack whilst signalling to his distant fleet. The English now favoured a close quarter gun battle, avoiding Spanish boardings to deliver a series of broadsides at point-blank range before sailing on to similarly greet the remaining Spanish who suffered badly against bigger cannon fired at a greater rate. The battle raged for several hours before a shortage of ammunition and the north-westerly wind forced the English to break off, both fleets nearing shallows off Zeeland. Since the Spanish would likely receive little mercy ashore Medina Sidonia had little choice but to sail north.

Still England remained on high alert, even Elizabeth arrived at Tilbury to give her troops a rousing speech but Parma would not move without naval protection. Unseaworthy, full of sick and dying, the Spanish galleons were forced into the North Atlantic, many of them going down or smashed on Ireland's rocky west coast where fearful of Catholic Irish uprisings the English executed any survivors. A more relaxed Elizabeth now posed for her Armada painting while Medina Sidonia arrived back in Santander too ill to go ashore unaided. A half-century later religion would again be the catalyst for war, one purely of England's own making.

29 July 1653 o.s
Anglo-Dutch Wars
Battle of Sheveningen

THE FIRST ANGLO-Dutch War had broken out over the ascendancy of global trade gained by the Dutch Republic while their former Protestant allies against Catholic Spain, England, had been involved in a bitter Civil War. It did not help diplomatic efforts that during the conflict the Dutch had given support to King Charles I and that following it they maintained the cause for the restoration of the British monarchy through Charles, Prince of Wales (future King Charles II) who was the brother of Mary, Princess Consort to Prince William II of Orange, Stadtholder (Head of State) of the Dutch Republic.

Oliver Cromwell's offer of a unification between the two Protestant nations had been turned down by the Dutch States General leading to England imposing draconian laws against Dutch shipping, tension eventually snapping off Dover in May 1652 when the first broadsides were fired in a war that would be entirely fought at sea. Having gone through a period of decline two decades earlier, the English Navy had achieved two significant victories by the summer of 1653 off Portland and the Gabbard courtesy of General-at-Sea Robert Blake's production of 'Fighting Instructions' and an administrative overhaul by Sir Henry Vane. The bigger, faster, better armed English ships specifically designed for war by John Hawkins prior to the Spanish Armada meant the navy had become a formidable fighting machine in just a matter of months leaving English diplomats in a position of strength at on going peace talks during which they made ever stronger demands for Dutch reparations.

Following the Gabbard, Blake returned to dry land to nurse wounds incurred off Portland leaving George Monck to blockade the Dutch coast. The Dutch economy, reliant on global overseas trade, was soon in sufficient distress for Admiral Maarten Tromp to attempt a lifting of the blockade without waiting for Dutch commissioners to return from negotiations in London. Tromp sailed north from the River Maas in his 54-gun flagship *Brederode* with an eighty-strong fleet to join a thirty-strong fleet blockaded in the Frisian Islands under the command of his long time rival Vice Admiral Withe Corneliszoon de With. On his part De With moved to Helder where he could move from a defensive position to assist Tromp at the given moment.

Monck, in the 88-gun *Resolution*, identified Dutch intentions immediately and decided to attack Tromp before any possible rendez-vous with De With. Tromp turned back south, content to draw the English away from Helder to facilitate De With's escape but at 17.00 on 29 July 1653 his rear was caught by Monck's vanguard off Katwijk, a few miles north of Sheveningen where a fierce exchange of broadsides continued until dark. The following day both fleets contended with strong north-westerly winds blowing onshore and were unable to resume battle but the wind did assist De With sailing south to join Tromp. On the morning of the 31 July the wind lightened from the north-east behind the Dutch who, now in similar numbers to Monck, attacked at 07.00 breaking through the English line for a terrific gun battle. The great Dutch Admiral Tromp was killed by an English sniper in the rigging of the 66-gun *James* but his colours remained flying to preserve Dutch morale. The two lines of ships passed through each other on a number of occasions with the Dutch also using the wind to send in fireships, the floating infernos killing the English Admirals Thomas Graves aboard the 56-gun *Andrew* and James Peacock aboard the 60-gun *Triumph*. By the early afternoon, however, the wind had again changed to a north-westerly giving the advantage back to the English whose superior firepower was now beginning to take its toll. Losses mounting, perhaps thirty ships and 2,000 men, De With retreated back to Helder having inflicted enough damage on Monck (two ships sunk with many now unseaworthy and 1,000 casualties) to lift the blockade.

In April 1654 the Dutch signed the Treaty of Westminster by which Cromwell insisted that Prince William III of Orange, son of William II and Mary, could never become Dutch Stadtholder. Not only did William do so in 1672 but he also became King William III of England by the Glorious Revolution of 1688. Dutch trade continued to grow whilst England again quarrelled with Spain. To protect it they would build a more powerful navy, the force of which would be felt by the English in a Second Anglo-Dutch War just eleven years away.

30 July 1809
Napoleonic Wars
Battle of Walcheren Island

BY 1807 NAPOLEON Bonaparte, Emperor of the French had come to dominate Continental Europe having defeated two of the principal members of the Fourth Coalition, Prussia and Russia. The third, the United Kingdom of Great Britain and Ireland, had fought on at sea backed as ever by the world's most powerful navy, and now only more recently on land in the Iberian Peninsular in support of a Spanish insurrection against the French occupation. In 1805 a frustrated Napoleon had seen his plan to invade Britain dashed off Cape Trafalgar by Vice Admiral Horatio Nelson before in 1807 Major General Arthur Wellesley captured the then neutral Denmark's large shipping fleet at anchor off Copenhagen. Napoleon had then looked to enforce the 'Continental System', a Europe wide embargo on British trade whilst beginning a rebuilding of the French Navy. In 1809, after British spies had reported over twenty French ships either in or under construction in the Dutch Batavian ports of Antwerp and Flushing, British Secretary of State for War and the Colonies, Robert Stewart, Lord Castlereagh pushed for an invasion of Walcheren Island in the Scheldt Estuary. Castlereagh was, however, opposed by his Foreign Secretary, George Canning, who preferred a reinforcement of the Iberian Peninsular where Wellesley was struggling to advance from Lisbon.

British anxiety at French boat building, however, coincided with Austria resuming hostilities against France, forming the Fifth Coalition principally with Britain from whom they requested subsidies and increased British offensives. After a May 1809 Austrian victory at Aspern-Essling the many doubters of Castlereagh's proposed Walcheren expedition were swept aside, the British Government of William Cavendish-Bentinck, Duke of Portland selling the plan as the diversion for which Austria asked. Just two months later though the Austrians were heavily defeated at Wagram, catastrophically losing near 40,000 men in a battle fought by over 300,000. Despite being too late to save Austria's King Francis II, who now signed an armistice with Napoleon in the Schonbrunn Palace, Vienna, the British attack on Walcheren would go ahead regardless.

Master General of the Ordnance John Pitt, Lord Chatham commanded 40,000 British troops shipped by the Royal Navy under the command of Rear Admiral Sir Richard Strachan, landing on Walcheren Island from where both Flushing and Antwerp could be attacked. On 30 July 1809 the assault of Walcheren by 13,000 men under Lieutenant General Eyre Coote swept aside 1,200 Napoleonic troops of Irish, Prussian and French origin before two days later 5,000 men under Lieutenant General Sir John Hope landed on South Beveland to take an evacuated Fort Batz. Crucially, however, at Cadsand bad weather and confusion between George Gordon, Earl of Huntly and his commanders meant the landings were aborted allowing French troops in northern France and Belgium to march north over the next week for a reinforcement of Flushing and the Sheldt Estuary from where they could fire upon British shipping. Meanwhile, all French shipping in the estuary was withdrawn to Antwerp whilst in Flushing French General Louis Claude Monnet reluctantly opened the dykes, flooding the areas around. Only on 13 August did Flushing come under bombardment from British artillery which was increased by naval artillery two days later. Monnet soon surrendered the city in ruins having suffered losses of 7,500 men but Castlereagh's plan was already beginning to unravel. The delay in assaulting Antwerp had left the town well defended by Marshal Jean Baptiste Bernadotte and infinitely worse, the low lying ground of Walcheren, surrounded by dykes clogged with alluvial, animal and human waste had become a fetid malarial swamp in the heat of summer. On 20 August the first man died of 'Walcheren Fever', the sickness quickly becoming an epidemic with 100 men a day succumbing, the fortunate shipped back to England. In September Chatham returned with all but 17,000 troops to England but within a week only a half of those left were fit for duty, by October just 4,500. By December 4,000 men had died, just 100 of those in battle, whilst a further 12,000 were sick. Since all prospects of success were long gone the expedition was finally abandoned with bitter recriminations abounding.

Canning now sought Castlereagh's dismissal, the two Cabinet Ministers fighting a duel on Putney Heath in which Canning was shot in the thigh but survived. In Portugal the now Lieutenant General Arthur Wellesley, Viscount Wellington refused to admit Walcheren veterans to his ranks through fear of sickness.

31 July 1423

Hundred Years' War
Battle of Cravant

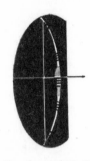

KING HENRY V of England had died at Bois de Vincennes, France on 31 August 1422, his body embalmed before a two month journey back to Westminster Abbey, London. Crowds lined the route and requiems were held for his pious soul at every stop. Henry had left only verbal instructions in his will for the governance of England and also France which, under the 1420 Treaty of Troyes, also became the Kingdom of his son King Henry VI when King Charles VI of France died on 21 October 1422. Henry VI, however, was just ten months old, his French mother, Catherine of Valois just twenty and who, as the daughter of Charles VI and sister of the dispossessed Dauphin Charles (who now proclaimed himself King Charles VII of France), was viewed with such suspicion in England that she could be trusted neither with matters of state nor her son's upbringing. These both fell to a compromise, which like most compromises would be flawed, Henry V's elder brother John, Duke of Bedford was appointed Protector, Defender and Chief Councillor of England when in the country and when not his younger brother Humphrey, Duke of Gloucester was to step up. Gloucester fumed believing the arrangement violated his right to become Regent of England having also been appointed Guardian to the young Henry. A council of bishops and knights was also appointed which further restricted Bedford's and Gloucester's powers in England but not in France where Bedford became regent over and above England's ally Philip, Duke of Burgundy. To be fair Philip probably did not particularly fancy the task on behalf of an English king but his sister Anne did marry Bedford in May 1423, further cementing the Anglo-Burgundian alliance formed by their recent ancestors.

The Dauphin remained somewhat inactive immediately after Henry V's death but began to accumulate a large army of French, Italians, Spanish and Scots after three further setbacks – the defeat of Jacques D'Harcourt at Le Crotoy by Richard Beauchamp, Earl of Warwick; the defection of John 'the wise', Duke of Brittany to the English and the advance into Dauphinist Champagne by Thomas Montagu, Earl of Salisbury who was now besieging Montaiguillon. The Dauphin reacted by sending a largely Scottish army under John Stewart of Darnley and John Stewart, Earl of Buchan to begin a siege of his own at Cravant in Philip's Burgundy. Spoiling for a decisive battle with the Dauphin, Bedford sent reinforcements to Salisbury who also received further assistance of dubious quality from the Dowager Duchess of Burgundy, his force now 4,000 men in total who relieved the beleaguered garrison at Cravant on 29 July.

The following morning, in the heat of French midsummer, Salisbury began a march north along the eastern bank of the River Yonne searching for and finding the Stewarts on Saturday 31 July 1423, their army at least twice the strength of his own, drawn up in an impregnable position. Salisbury declined to attack and instead withdrew to Vincelles where he crossed to the west bank of the River Yonne before cutting across the bend in the river for Cravant. On arrival before Cravant but on the wrong side of the Yonne, Salisbury was dismayed to find the Stewarts had outpaced him and were now clearly intent on contesting his crossing back into the town. Both armies spent three hours eyeballing each other across the river before Salisbury sounded an advance, English men-at-arms leading across the shallow Yonne for a fight with lance and axe protected by an overhead storm of arrows from their longbowmen behind. On the English right Robert, Lord Willoughby de Eresby, a veteran of Harfleur, Agincourt, Caen, Rouen and possibly Meaux attacked the Scots defending the bridge. A bloody fight raged (skeletons were still being excavated centuries later) until the Scots began to give ground. Seeing this retreat from a watch tower behind, the half starved, Burgundian garrison sallied out, trapping the Dauphinists on three sides with the Italians and Spanish first to flee south, the only possible line of escape. The Scots who had done most of the fighting so far suffered grievously, perhaps half the total of 6,000 perishing, Buchan and Darnley minus an eye captured.

The Dauphin's defeat at Cravant sparked a levy in southern France and a reinforcement of 6,500 Scots under Archibald, Earl of Douglas. Fifteen thousand Dauphinists would next gather at Le Mans determined to drive the English out of France. Salisbury meanwhile continued to reduce Dauphinist strongholds in the east while Bedford collected reinforcements, 10,000 Englishmen gathering in Rouen for a 'Second Agincourt' at Verneuil.

31 July 1917
The Great War
Third Battle of Ypres
(Passchendaele)

THE TRIPLE ENTENTE was not in good health in mid 1917, Tsar Nicholas II of Russia had abdicated amidst a developing Bolshevik Revolution and the French Army had been close to outright mutiny following huge butchers bills at Verdun, the Somme and on the Chemin des Dames (Second Aisne). Despite similar casualties the British Expeditionary Force, however, was beginning to find a way of breaking the deadlock on the Western Front, limited objective offensives combined with innovative artillery tactics at Arras and Messines had been encouraging. Wanting to extend British gains at Messines Field Marshal Douglas Haig had encouraged British Second Army General Herbert Plumer to advance east of Ypres onto the Gheluvelt Plateau but Plumer had demanded a three day preparation. An impatient Haig therefore turned to the more aggressive Fifth Army General Hubert Gough but even he hesitated, believing any gains would merely extend the deadly Ypres Salient that had already claimed many a British and Colonial life.

Based on intelligence that Germany was close to collapse after the attritional battles of the past year and also in the knowledge that German divisions were transferring from the Eastern Front, Haig was anxious to maintain pressure in the west but the new French Commander-in-Chief (the third in six months) General Phillipe Pétain was of the opposite view, happy to delay further offensives for nearly a year until the arrival of a mobilising United States of America. Haig felt Pétain would be emboldened should the BEF expose German frailty but his cautious Prime Minister David Lloyd George believed contrasting War Office reports that Germany's eastern divisions already on the Western Front gave them such a superiority in men and artillery that any British offensive would be doomed to failure without substantial French support – stating 'a mere gamble would be both a folly and a crime'. The dilemma was broken when First Sea Lord, Admiral

John Jellicoe sensationally claimed that the success of German submarine warfare meant the Royal Navy would be unable to continue on into 1918. Proceeding on the basis that the offensive would be halted if initial objectives were not met, Haig appointed Gough to lead what in terms of human endurance would be the greatest British battle of all time.

At 03.50 on 31 July 1917, following a ten-day artillery bombardment from 3,000 guns firing 4.25 million shells across a twelve mile front, fourteen British, Australian, New Zealand and Canadian infantry divisions supported by two French advanced across ground scarred by nearly three years of war against six lines of defences manned by the German 4th Army of Crown Prince Rupprecht of Bavaria. Gough had set ambitious first day objectives of 6,000 yards and initial progress was good against weakly held German front lines especially in the north from the Yser Canal and Boesinghe up onto the Pilckem Ridge. The French and Guards divisions made 4,000 yards behind effective creeping and standing barrages before they were attacked by specialist German Eingrief (counter-attack) units who drove them back with 70 per cent losses. Further south on the critical Gheluvelt Plateau gains were poor, the four assaulting infantry divisions had been unable to keep pace with the creeping barrage and had run into strong German defences, pill boxes, machine-gunners and increasingly powerful German artillery firing shrapnel and mustard gas. On top of that now began a three-day rainstorm that turned the ground into a muddy swamp where a man could die as likely from drowning as from gunfire. British tanks and artillery struggled to move whilst the Royal Flying Corps struggled to ascertain what, if any, progress had been made. On 2 August the assault was halted, Gough launching another on 10 August at Westhoek and, while the heaviest August rain for thirty years continued, on 16 August at Langemarck, British advances again heavily countered-attacked with both sides suffering in turn from defensive artillery fire. As the fighting degenerated into the attritional warfare so detested by Lloyd George, Haig replaced Gough with Plumer. Three weeks of preparation then allowed additional artillery to begin a series of successful 'bite and hold' attacks in better weather on the Menin Road Ridge, Polygon Wood and Broodseinde where Germans massing in forward positions for their own attack suffered grievously at the hands of the British artillery.

As the rain began to fall once more Lloyd George failed to intervene whilst Haig continued to believe the German Army was ever closer to collapse. He would attack again in October at Poelcapelle on the Passchendaele Ridge.

August

"Do not send to me so long as my son lives, let the boy win his spurs, let the day be his."

KING EDWARD III OF ENGLAND,
CRÉCY, 1346

1 August 1759

Seven Years' War
Battle of Minden

THE SEVEN YEARS' War had broken out in Europe in 1756, consuming the French and Indian War across the Atlantic in North America and reaching as far east as India. Britain sided with several smaller German states but principally with King George II's ancestral homeland Hanover and new ally by the 'Diplomatic Revolution' of 1756 Prussia against all other major European powers, including yet again of course, France.

Initially Britain honoured the alliance with cash rather than men and arms, leaving the Prussians and Hanoverians to fight on the defensive whilst the British Army and the Royal Navy enforced a blockade of the European Atlantic coast and pressed British colonial ambition globally – a strategy that had paid in India but not as yet in North America. After the 1758 Prussian victory over the French at Krefeld, Emden, the British Government of William Pitt 'the elder' sent 9,000 men to assist Prince Ferdinand of Brunswick protect Hanover (King George particularly anxious they do so) and if possible force a decisive victory against a still largely intact French Army. The French, however, were of similar mind, reinforcing the junior Marshal of France Victor Francois, Duke de Broglie (who had won the honour in April by defeating Ferdinand at Bergen) with the senior Marshal of France Louis Georges, Marquis de Contades, bringing French strength up to 45,000 men with 162 guns. In July 1759 Contades took the town of Minden on the south-north flowing River Weser against which Ferdinand, commanding the 38,000, 181-gun-strong Anglo-Prussian-Hanoverian Army, now advanced from north-west of the Weser and its tributary, the River Bastau, many of the Anglo-Prusso-Hanoverians plucking roses from the hedgerows as they went.

The main French Army was in a strong position south of the marshy Bastau but on 31 July Contades, believing the allies to be over extended, began moving his troops forward across five pontoon bridges to attack what they perceived to be vulnerable Germans under General Georg von Wagenheim but who in fact had been specifically placed north of Minden as bait. East of the Weser Broglie crossed through Minden to join the attack whilst Ferdinand moved British and Germans south to attack the French in the flank and rear. The Anglo-Prussian-Hanoverians moved out of camp at dawn on 1 August 1759 but without the British cavalry of Lord George Sackville who were nowhere to be found.

The Battle of Minden began with Saxons under Allied Lieutenant General Prince Karl von Anhalt, assisted by accurate British artillery but not by the late arriving Sackville, taking the village of Hahlen on the right of the Allied line. Two British and Hanoverian infantry brigades under Lieutenant General Friedrich von Sporcken then prematurely moved forward on Anhalt's left having misread an order to advance 'on the beat of drum' as 'to the beat of drum'. As drummers drummed a disaster looked certain but instead one of the great advances of the British Army unfolded as the single line of infantry delivered a series of devastating volleys into the massed centre of Contades' army who repeatedly counter-attacked with artillery support. As the French panicked in the face of the relentless British advance Ferdinand ordered a coup de grace from Sackville's cavalry, not just once but on four occasions, Sackville failing to move on each request. In desperation Ferdinand then ordered the cavalry of Lieutenant General John Manners, Marquess of Granby to support Sporcken who was now also coming under attack on his right as French counter-attacks on Hahlen forced Anhalt to retreat. Granby, however, was halted by his superior, Sackville. Meanwhile, the battle continued, on the left of the allied line, Wagenheim repulsed Broglie whilst in the centre Germans under Lieutenant Generals Heinrich von Wutginau and Johann von Scheele advanced to support Sporcken, driving the French back to the Bastau. At the bridges on the Bastau, French casualties mounted as British guns moved within range to deadly effect. The French lost over 7,000 men, the Anglo-Prusso-Hanoverians just 2,700.

Minden is a celebrated British victory but the Seven Years' War would still run for another four. The British would gain greatly from the 1763 Treaty of Paris whilst in the meantime Lord George Sackville demanded his own Court Martial to clear his name. Despite being declared 'unfit to serve his Majesty in any military capacity whatsoever' Sackville would become Secretary of State for the Colonies on the eve of the American War of Independence, it would prove a costly appointment.

1 August 1798
French Revolutionary War
Battle of the Nile

BY 1797 REVOLUTIONARY nationalism and a levée en masse called by the Committee of Public Safety had increased the French Army to over one million men. The Declaration of the 'Rights of Man and the Citizen' was the central ideology of the French revolutionary cause which the ruling National Constituent Assembly wished this army to spread throughout the whole of monarchic Europe. Austria, Prussia, Spain, Great Britain, the Dutch Republic and Sardinia had formed the First Coalition to fight French military aggression but had been systematically defeated on all fronts from Italy to the Low Countries with the exception of Great Britain which, not for the last time, now fought on alone. The eight million British population could not hope to match the strength of the French Army but the Royal Navy was harassing French interests globally and blockading the entire enemy coast which after the 1797 Treaty of Ildefonso included a turncoat Spain. Admiral John Jervis and Commodore Horatio Nelson had defeated the Spanish off Cape St Vincent in February 1797 before Nelson lost an arm five months later attacking Santa Cruz de Tenerife. Whilst Nelson recuperated the brilliant twenty-nine-year-old French Corsican General Napoleon Bonaparte, who had defeated the Austrians and Sardinians before crushing a Royalist revolt in Paris, was gaining influence with the ruling French Directory and Foreign Minister Charles Talleyrand. The pair decided that in regard to any invasion of Britain, the French Navy, even if combined with that of the Spanish (but not the Dutch/Batavian fleet which had been defeated at Camperdown in October), was not powerful enough to defeat the Royal Navy (it quite possibly was) and instead looked to target British interests in the Eastern Mediterranean, Egypt and British India where they speculatively hoped to spark an uprising by Tipu, Sultan of Mysore.

Napoleon sailed from Toulon on 19 May 1798 with 400 transports carrying 40,000 troops protected by seventeen warships. After forcibly taking the strategic island of Malta from the Knights of St John, Napoleon's fleet sailed on to Crete and Alexandria, Egypt eluding an increasingly frustrated Rear Admiral Horatio Nelson (promoted after St Vincent) aboard HMS *Vanguard* who had reentered the Mediterranean to give chase with twelve other British ships of the line and two others.

Nelson arrived off Alexandria before Napoleon but with no sign of the enemy had then sailed on to Anatolia, returning on 1 August 1798 only to find that Napoleon and his Armée d'Orient had already disembarked. French Vice Admiral Francois-Paul Brueys d'Aigalliers had, however, remained at Aboukir Bay at the mouth of the River Nile to protect Napoleon's bridgehead with a line of warships close to shore joined by ropes. Despite having been at sea for weeks and with night fast approaching Nelson attacked immediately giving French sailors ashore little or no time to reach their posts. As they approached the French defences the line of British ships split into two when Captain Thomas Foley, aboard HMS *Goliath*, realised Brueys had left too much room on his landward side. Followed by half the British fleet, Foley raked broadsides down the inside of the sandwiched French whilst the other half of the British fleet raked their outside. The French predicament was soon desperate, blasted by superior British gunnery amidst a ferocious exchange of broadsides, Brueys' flagship *L'Orient* fighting on despite being increasingly engulfed in flame with Brueys, wounded in head and arm by musket and cannonball, refusing to surrender. The British in close proximity to *L'Orient* then disengaged, Nelson badly wounded above the eye returning to the quarterdeck just as the French flagship's magazine exploded tearing the ship apart with the loss of her entire crew. The fighting, however, continued on into the night, just two French ships surviving the battle, nine captured. French casualties are estimated at 5,000 men with another 3,000 captured whilst the British suffered losses of 1,000.

With no transport home Napoleon and the Armée d'Orient marched on Acre. From Aboukir Bay Nelson alerted the British Governor General of India, Richard Wellesley who would send Lieutenant General George Harris and his brother, Colonel Arthur Wellesley, to besiege Seringapatam, home of the troublesome Tipu Sultan. Rear Admiral Pierre de Villeneuve survived the Battle of the Nile to command the Franco-Spanish fleet seven years later at Trafalgar where he would be up against what was now the world's most powerful naval force as well as its greatest commander.

2 August 1649

English Civil Wars, Ireland
Battle of Rathmines

IN 1641 ULSTER'S Catholics had rebelled against ever increasing numbers of English and Scottish settlers and a coerced conversion to Protestantism, the revolt spreading over all Ireland with many thousands of Protestants losing their homesteads if not their lives. Led by Phelim O'Neill, the Irish organised themselves into the Irish Catholic Confederation and, being more fearful of the Presbyterian and Protestant Puritans of the English Parliament than King Charles I, claimed allegiance to the Crown. Although potentially a source of military assistance and despite being married to a Catholic himself, King Charles was, however, initially unwilling to be associated with the Confederates in light of previous Parliament accusations regarding his Catholic sympathies. Indeed Charles' army was about to crush the Confederate rebellion when the outbreak of Civil War in England forced a recall of forces leaving the Royalist James Butler, Earl of Ormonde, Governor of Dublin and an uncommitted Protestant to balance an uneasy three-way relationship between Royalists, Parliamentarians and the Irish Catholic Confederation.

In 1643 Ormonde defeated the Confederates at New Ross before the war in Ireland degenerated into a series of skirmishes with Charles, his fortunes waning in England, giving absolute credibility to previous Parliament suspicion by urging Ormonde to entreat with the Confederates for military assistance. Ormonde not only failed but King Charles' subsequent defeat in England left the Confederates to believe themselves strong enough (with Vatican support) to conquer the whole of Ireland and they consequently advanced by a series of sieges toward still Royalist Dublin (Cork was Parliamentarian). In Dublin, Ormonde held off the Irish rebels before handing over his post to a Parliament army under Michael Jones (victor of Rowton Heath 1645) who then inflicted a series of devastating defeats on the Confederates, including Dungan's Hill where half the 6,000 Irishmen were wiped out. Jones' fellow commander in Cork, Murrough O'Brien, did likewise in

Munster where, on top of a scorched earth policy which starved the population, he massacred the garrison and clergy at Knocknanauss. The Confederates, Ulster apart, only now entreated with Ormonde's Royalists just as the Royalist cause was receiving a short lived boost from uprisings in England and Scotland. It would prove to be another catastrophic miscalculation.

In June 1649, five months after the Independents of the Westminster Parliament had executed King Charles I and the coming into being of the Commonwealth of England, Ormonde led Royalists (in support of King Charles II) and his former enemy turned ally, the Irish Catholic Confederation, in a military campaign to recover Dublin and rid Ireland of the English Parliament menace. Ormonde advanced with 11,000 infantry and 3,000 cavalry, taking and garrisoning Drogheda and Dundalk confident that Jones' army in Dublin, suffering desertion, was far from full strength. Jones, however, received Parliament reinforcements in late July which allowed him to take the offensive just as Ormonde was preparing to assault the city, Ormonde anxious to do so before the arrival of Oliver Cromwell and the New Model Army.

On 2nd August 1649, the Irish Confederates moved forward from their camp at Rathmines to take and rebuild the largely destroyed castle at Baggotrath outside the walls of Dublin but Jones contested possession with an advance of 1,200 Parliament cavalry and 4,000 infantry who comprehensively overran the Confederate vanguard. Jones then pushed on toward Rathmines where the Munster Confederate infantry desperately tried to hold his advance. Ormonde, who had been asleep in his tent, then arrived to rally his men but they were already being outflanked by Jones' cavalry. The only Irish hope was for Thomas, Lord Dillon, who was besieging Finglas north of Dublin, to attack Jones from across the River Liffey but Dillon would not move. Having lost all his artillery and baggage, 1,500 men dead with another 2500 captured, Ormonde fled to Kilkenny.

Ormonde's failure left the Port of Dublin in Parliament hands, facilitating the arrival of 130 ships carrying Cromwell and 12,000 largely Puritan Protestants of the New Model Army intent on righting the perceived wrongs of the previous decade. The next three years in Ireland would herald unprecedented misery.

3 August 1692
Williamite Wars
Battle of Steenkerque

KING LOUIS XIV of France had invaded the Spanish Netherlands in 1667, 1672 and again in 1688. The third attempt had been combined with a war of annexation (reunions) across the borders of France, north into the Rhinelands of Germany and in the south into the Duchy of Savoy and Catalonia. Louis was taking advantage of a distracted Leopold I, Emperor of the Holy Roman Empire (Germany, Austria, Bohemia, Hungary, Croatia) who with Victor Amadeus, Duke of Savoy was in the middle of a sixteen year war halting Ottoman (Turkey) advances in Eastern Europe. At one point Louis had taken the Rhineland south of Mainz as far as Switzerland but the German Princes of Saxony, Hesse, Hanover and Brandenburg then combined their resources with Bavaria to take the war back to the French King. William III, King of England and Stadtholder of the Dutch Republic, also resisted French advances in 1689 with a decisive victory at Walcourt before putting down Jacobite risings against his and his Queen Mary's rule in Scotland and Ireland.

Fighting then concentrated in the Rhinelands as Louis held off the Grand Alliance of now Austria, Bavaria, Denmark, Dutch Republic, Holy Roman Empire, Palatinate of the Rhine, Savoy, Saxony, Brandenburg, Spain, Scotland, Ireland and England. To break the deadlock Louis resolved to launch a two-pronged attack on William by invading England in support of the deposed Catholic King James II (who had fled to France after defeat to William at the 1690 Battle of the Boyne) and an advance north into the Spanish Netherlands to the town of Namur at the confluence of the Rivers Meuse and Sambre. The invasion of England, however, ended before it began when the French fleet under Admiral Anne Hilarion de Constantin, Count of Tourville and James himself were defeated by a superior Anglo-Dutch fleet under Admiral Edward Russell, Earl of Orford and Philips van Almonde at Barfleur and La Hogue in May/ June 1692. Undeterred, a French army of 60,000 under Marshal Sebastien de Vauban supported by another of 60,000 under Francois de Montmorency, Duc de Luxembourg, then took Namur on 30 June 1692 leaving William to march at the head of an 80,000-strong Anglo-Dutch-Scottish-Danish Grand Alliance Army for a surprise counter-attack.

At 05.00 on 3 August 1692, William's advance infantry under Ferdinand Willem, Duke of Wurttemberg discovered the French, now also 80,000-strong, near Steenkerque. Luxembourg was unprepared with his main French Army still some distance to the rear but he began rushing infantry and cavalry forward as soon as he became aware of Wurttemberg's proximity. Wurttemberg did not, however, press an immediate attack, instead opening an artillery barrage while waiting for the rest of the Grand Alliance Army to march up in column. Any element of surprise had been completely lost by 12.30 when a full attack was finally launched but Wurttemberg's men, with musket and bayonet, nevertheless made short work of the French front line before meeting heavier resistance behind. Luxembourg's second and third lines came under severe pressure, giving ground but crucially holding while their commander formed up behind with far greater efficiency than was William behind the Grand Alliance. As indeed confusion reigned in the rear of the Grand Alliance, increasing numbers of French fell upon Wurttemberg's beleaguered vanguard and other Grand Alliance regiments that had made their way onto the field. General Hugh Mackay, a faithful servant of William since the Glorious Revolution, urged withdrawal against what were now overwhelming French forces only to be ordered to hold his position, Mackay philosophically accepting his fate to die with the rest of his regiment. The Alliance position was lost once Louis Francois, Duc de Boufflers joined the French counter-attack from the west, William only now ordering a retreat covered by Master of the Horse Henry de Nassau, Lord Overkirk but already the Grand Alliance had lost 10,000 men, the French 8,000.

Defeated again by Luxembourg a year later, William only regained Namur in 1695 after a two month siege. The Nine Years' War dragged on until 1697 and the Treaty of Ryswick. In November 1700 the death of the childless Habsburg King Charles II of Spain would precipitate another European War of similar alliances for a preservation of the balance of power, the War of the Spanish Succession.

4 August 1265

Baron's War
Battle of Evesham

AS HAD HIS father King John, the extravagant Henry III of England had incurred the wrath of many English barons who were now principally led by the French born Simon de Montford, Earl of Leicester. De Montford and the barons had become exasperated at Henry's fanciful ambitions, their associated demands for money and the king's at best reluctant, often dismissive recognition of Magna Carta. De Montford had once been a favourite at Henry's court before secretly marrying the king's sister, Eleanor, an act that soon had the happy couple fleeing to France. After a spell in exile, De Montford returned only for his relationship with Henry to plumb new depths when Henry's demands for tax revenues increased. De Montford and his fellow barons then introduced the Provisions of Oxford which, for good measure, were superseded by the Provisions of Westminster, both attempting to limit Henry's spending and his power to make ministerial appointments. Backed by Pope Urban IV, Henry threw out the Provisions sparking a downward spiral toward the Second Baron's War (the first had been against King John) which, against a backdrop of social upheaval, exploded in violence at Lewes in May 1264.

Largely due to the negligence of his son Prince Edward (future King Edward I) Henry was soundly defeated at Lewes but survived the resultant bloodbath by hiding in the local priory which the pious De Montford's 'Army of God' declined to attack. Edward was taken prisoner as a guarantee for his father's future behaviour although once he had sworn allegiance to the Provisions of Oxford and Westminster he was held in a fairly relaxed manner within De Montford's entourage.

During the year of his reign following Lewes, so too did De Montford become increasingly power hungry whilst his family, ever more desiring of wealth and privilege, alienated many of their former allies including Gilbert de Clare, Earl of Gloucester. England was still in social turmoil with a resumption of the war inevitable when Edward, with Gloucester's help, escaped De Montford's knights at Hereford by bolting on a fresh horse. At large Edward began to make amends for

492

his performance at Lewes with a successful campaign for the king's cause that took the town of Gloucester by siege in June and surprised the army of De Montford's son (also Simon) at Kenilworth Castle. On 4 August 1265, Edward then led an army near twice the size of De Montford's onto the field outside Evesham. Returning from Wales De Montford crossed the River Severn trying in vain to join with his son's army which was desperately trying to move west to support him. The son Simon was too late, leaving De Montford trapped by Edward in a loop of the River Avon from which there would likely be no escape. Indeed on seeing Edward's force, De Montford gloomily remarked 'may the Lord have mercy on our souls for our bodies are theirs'.

Edward drew up the Royal Army of 10,000 men in three battles on Green Hill to the north of Evesham which De Montford approached from the town at about 09.00. The Baronial Army was formed in column with cavalry to the front followed by English infantry and Welsh spearmen with the intention of driving a wedge through the Royal Army. As the two armies met De Montford's cavalry were initially successful in forcing back much of Edward's centre but when the Royal infantry held and then counter-attacked De Montford and most of his men became outflanked before eventually becoming surrounded. A desperate fight raged for the next two hours, many of the baronials fleeing if given the chance but with De Montford's knights doggedly fighting on until De Montford heard that his eldest son Henry had been slain. The aged baron exclaimed that it was 'now time to die' before charging into the fray himself, becoming unhorsed but fighting to the bitter end. No quarter was given to his men, the wounded finished where they lay and any that managed to flee chased into Evesham where they were mercilessly slaughtered in the streets and even in the abbey.

The Battle of Evesham did not finish the Baronial War which continued for another two years and included a five month siege of Kenilworth Castle. Henry III celebrated his restoration to the throne by finishing the shrine of Edward the Confessor at Westminster Abbey. Prince Edward became King of England on 16 November 1272 when on Crusade in Palestine, returning in 1274 to become one of England's most fearsome warlords.

5 August 1388

Anglo-Scottish Wars
Battle of Otterburn

AFTER THE ENGLISH victory at the 1346 battle of Neville's Cross the Scottish King David II was imprisoned in the Tower of London whilst much of Scotland was subjugated by Edward III, King of England. Scotland remained deeply divided, many Scots happy to maintain their wealth and status under English rule whilst others supported France during the Hundred Years' War, notably William, Earl of Douglas at Poitiers 1356. Spiteful raids across the Anglo-Scottish borders ceased in 1357 with the signing of the Treaty of Berwick in which David was released on payment of a £100,000 merk (Scottish currency) ransom to be paid in ten installments. Only two payments were made, however, before David suggested Edward inherit the Scottish Crown should he, as was likely, die without issue in return for a cancelling of the debt. Rejected by the Scottish Parliament, the suggestion was pressed continuously by Edward who still ruled large parts of Scotland until his death in 1377. By then King David was also dead and Robert Stewart, Robert II had ascended the throne of a Scotland still inhabited by many lords paying fealty to the English king. Robert only had to look across the Irish Sea to witness the attempted anglicisation of Ireland (the 1367 Statutes of Kilkenny) and he now looked to take advantage of English misfortune in France with a gradual escalation of Scottish aggression across the border. His task was boosted on Edward's death by the fact that Edward's formidable eldest son, Edward, the Black Prince had pre deceased him leaving not Edward's third son, the equally formidable John of Gaunt, Duke of Lancaster, but his ten-year-old grandson Richard of Bordeaux to become king. England was therefore now run by a series of councils lacking decisive leadership at a time when social change following the Black Death had been dramatic, Wat Tyler leading a peasants revolt in 1381 over dissatisfaction with the introduction of all things, a poll tax. Just fourteen-years-old, Richard put down the revolt personally at Smithfield. As Richard then began to take more control of his affairs he relied on a small court, diminishing the influence of many, including the Earls of Arundel, Warwick and Gloucester who formed the 'Lords Appelant' questioning the king's excesses and impeaching his favourites. The developing row was settled at Radcot Bridge in December 1387 and by the subsequent 'Merciless Parliament' which conducted a clearance of the Royal Household.

The Scots were rarely slow to take advantage of England's problems and it was James, Earl of Douglas (son of William) who assembled 3,000 Scots in the Forest of Jedburgh intent on ridding Scotland of English influence. The main Scottish Army marched into Cumbria whilst Douglas and 1,200 men marched into Northumberland pillaging their way toward Durham and Newcastle. Henry Percy, Earl of Northumberland was responsible for the defence of the region and responded to this pincer threat by sending a similar sized English Army under his sons Ralph and Henry Percy (aka Harry Hotspur).

The initial clash between the two forces was a skirmish outside Newcastle in which Douglas and Hotspur met in hand-to-hand combat, Hotspur's pennon captured by Douglas who boasted that he would carry it back to his castle at Dalkeith and 'set it on high'. Chased by an indignant Hotspur, Douglas then marched the Scottish Army north, continuing his destructive work before besieging Otterburn Castle where Hotspur caught up with him on 5 August 1388. Despite the long march north, Hotspur attacked immediately in failing light and without giving his tired army any chance to get its full strength on the field. Douglas on the other hand responded by sending men forward to hold a ridge in front of his camp giving the rest of his force time to organise. He then led another force along a depression below the ridge to attack Hotspur's right flank. Hotspur reeled backwards and was not helped when Sir Thomas Umfraville on the English left outflanked Douglas' right under John Dunbar, Earl of Moray to attack the Scottish camp rather than supporting the beleaguered Hotspur in the main mêlée. So bloody was the fighting that the death of Douglas only became apparent the following morning after the Scots had won a magnificent victory. Both Hotspur and his brother Ralph were captured and shortly after ransomed.

Douglas had temporarily achieved his aim, England would stay out of Scotland but for only for a few years. Hotspur would seek his revenge in 1402 at Homildon Hill.

6 August 1915

The Great War
Battle of Sari Bair

AS STALEMATE GRIPPED the Western Front from late 1914 on into 1915, the British War Cabinet turned their attention to the Eastern Mediterranean where Turkey had entered the Great War on the side of the Central Powers (Germany, Austria Hungary). Turkey intended to regain territories previously lost to Britain's Triple Entente ally Russia and in March 1915 had been successful in defeating a plan devised by First Lord of the Admiralty, Winston Churchill – a forcing of the Dardanelles Straits leading from the Mediterranean Sea to Constantinople (Istanbul) and the Black Sea. Undeterred, Secretary for War Horatio Kitchener then ignored the concerns of First Sea Lord John 'Jackie' Fisher by agreeing to send large numbers of troops, the Mediterranean Expeditionary Force, under General Ian Hamilton for a clearance of Turkish defences on the Gallipoli Peninsular. The April landings on the southern tip of Gallipoli at Cape Helles and subsequent advances barely beyond the beaches had come at a terrible price whilst twenty miles north at Anzac Cove, similar meagre gains had come with losses even more fearful.

The next three months delivered increasing misery as dysentery and swarms of 'corpse flies' added to increasing casualties, 6,000 in just a day at Krithia. Hamilton wrote 'the beautiful battalions of 25 April are wasted skeletons now' but the British High Command had become fixated on Gallipoli. Indeed, Hamilton now received another five infantry divisions much to the outrage of several generals on the Western Front who considered the venture a sideshow. These reinforcements encouraged a revisit of Lieutenant General William Birdwood's plan for a breakout from Anzac Cove, attacking the Turkish right on the central high ground of the peninsular at Sari Bair with the consequently exposed British left flank protected by a simultaneous landing further north at Suvla Bay. South at Helles, Hamilton would also attack again to prevent the Turks from moving men north. The essence of both advances from Suvla Bay and Anzac Cove was speed.

At 14.30 on 6 August 1915, the British VIII Army Corps attacked at Helles but Brigadier General Harold Street needlessly lost half his 4,000 force in fruitless assaults on Achi Baba and Krithia. At 17.30 Australians at Anzac Cove, exhausted after a Turkish attack on their own positions, crossed one hundred yards of no-man's-land to take Lone Pine in heavy close quarter tunnel and cave fighting, winning seven Victoria Crosses in the process. The following morning the 3rd Australian Light Horse moved forward on foot in four waves of 150 men each to cross sixty yards of open ground on the Nek from Lone Pine to Hill Baby 700 against forty Turkish trenches defended by interlocking machine-gun fire. Urged on by the optimistic Colonel John Antill the Australians lost 435 men, half of them left lying wounded under the burning sun. To their left two columns then approached the Sari Bair after a night march, Australians and Indians halting under the cautious Brigadier General John Monash and Major General Charles Cox while New Zealanders under Brigadier General Francis Johnston pressed on to reach Chunuk Bair, their stop for breakfast allowing thousands of Turks to contest the position. Nevertheless, joined by Gurkhas under Major Cecil Allanson the New Zealanders took the heights with assistance from Royal Navy artillery, temporarily holding the key to the entire Gallipoli campaign but no support was forthcoming from below and worse, they were now fired upon by their own artillery.

To the north at Suvla Bay the landing of the British IX Corps had gone without incident since the sixty-one-year-old, Lieutenant General Frederick Stopford, who had never before commanded in battle, did not understand the urgency of his task. Indeed neither did his staff who had not been party to plans shrouded in such secrecy that they were in fact a mystery. As Stopford watched from HMS *Jonquil*, leaving decisions to his commanders ashore, Hamilton arrived to enquire into the delay, Kitchener also cabled from London suggesting the assault be 'gingered up' whilst thousands of Turkish reinforcements led by Mustafa Kemal Ataturk now attacked the Gurkhas and New Zealanders on Chunuk Bair, driving them off with the bayonet despite defensive flanking fire from ten machine-gun crews. After four days of savage fighting 30,000 men lay dead or wounded on the battlefields.

Hamilton sacked Stopford and would now try to unite the Suvla Bay and Anzac Cove forces with an attack on Scimitar Hill and Hill 60.

7 August 1826

Anglo-Ashanti Wars
Dodowa

 HENRY THE NAVIGATOR, the Infante of Portugal, great-grandson of England's King Edward III, led the Age of Discovery sponsoring oceanic voyages that beyond Cape Bojador (Morocco) braved huge sea monsters and of course, the edge of the world. Initial voyages crept around the coast of West Africa, Henry seeking to trade directly with the gold and slave rich economies that transported goods to the Mediterranean by the Trans Saharan trade routes. On Henry's death, Fernao Gomes then advanced into the Gulf of Guinea to discover a lucrative gold trade at 'A Mina', the town renamed Sao Jorge da Mina (Elmina) in 1481 by King John II of Portugal. Whilst their intrepid seafarers sailed further, Bartholomew Diaz reaching the Cape of Good Hope in 1488, Vasco da Gama India in 1491 and Ferdinand Magellan the Pacific Ocean in 1520, the Portuguese Gold Coast (Ghana) continued to ship predominantly gold, ivory and slaves for 150 years but other nations were following the Portuguese including the Dutch Republic and Great Britain.

The Dutch, the world's premier sea power, built their own trading posts and captured Elmina in 1637, paying a tribute to the Denkyira and later, as they became the dominant native power, the Ashanti. The Dutch and British, the latter represented by the African Company of Merchants, then successfully attacked each others forts as part of the Fourth Anglo-Dutch War (1780–84) but by the 1784 Treaty of Paris ownership of all forts returned to the pre-war status quo. Untouched by the Napoleonic Wars both Britain and the Dutch Republic then collectively increased their ambition to rid West Africa of the slave trade. The suppression was not, however, immediate and so the Ashanti remained on good terms until the British Gold Coast was taken over by the British Government of Robert Jenkinson, Earl of Liverpool, the Gold Coast becoming a dependency of Sierra Leone. The subsequent strangling of the slave trade infuriated the Ashanti's Asantahene Osei Bonsu who had profited from it, the peoples from his vassal states now theoretically protected by the British Governor Charles MacCarthy. With tension high a British patrol was then ambushed on its way to negotiate the release of a Royal African Corps soldier to which MacCarthy retaliated by leading 3,000 men north in two columns, his own of just 500 men ambushed by 12,000 Ashanti at Nsamankow in January 1824, MacCarthy saving a bullet for himself before having his heart eaten.

Osei Yaw inherited the Ashanti Golden Stool shortly after and looked to punish the Ashanti's disloyal former vassals but two years of sickness and disease meant the new Asantahene could manage only a destruction of property which gave Lieutenant Colonel Edward Purdon time enough to recruit from several local tribes including the Fante, Banta, Akwamu and Dwaben. Purdon was also reinforced when new Governor Major General Charles Turner arrived with 500 Royal African Corps and West Indians. On Turner's succumbing to sickness, the next Governor, Major General Neil Campbell then arrived with another 60 Royal Marines complete with artillery and Congreve rockets. Campbell and Purdon now learnt of Osei Yaw's intention to attack Cape Coast Castle with an army of 25,000 Ashanti warriors.

On 7 August 1826 Purdon advanced with at least 12,000 men but possibly many more to take up a four-mile -wide position on the open plains of Dodowa, south of the Ashanti camp. As a mark of honour, Osei Yaw chose to concentrate his attack on the centre of the British line where Purdon had positioned his best troops, many Ashanti falling on their rapid approach but many delivering musket volleys before joining a soldier's battle, close and personal. For several hours the battle, the greatest in West African history, raged hand-to-hand, the Ashanti flanks forced back but not their centre which was nearing success when Purdon delivered his rockets to devastating effect. Adding to the casualties, the sight and sound of the assault shattered the surviving Ashanti who fell back in their entirety.

Osei Yaw's army remained in tact but he would not prosecute the war. A Second Anglo-Ashanti War would break out in 1873, this time the British invading Ashanti. Happily, cocoa has replaced slavery and ivory as chief Ghanaian exports.

8 August 1918
The Great War
Battle of Amiens

 THE WINDOW OF opportunity for German Quarter Master General Erich Ludendorff and Chief of General Staff Paul von Hindenburg to win the Great War on the Western Front after the withdrawal of Russia and before the arrival in force of the United States had disappeared with the failure of their 1918 Spring Offensive. Germany had nevertheless come close to achieving a victory that only a year before even they had believed impossible. In desperate times Field Marshal Douglas Haig Commander in Chief of the British Expeditionary Force had stated to all ranks in his Special Order of the Day 'There is no other course open to us but to fight it out. Every position must be held to the last man: there must be no retirement'. His men, British, Irish, Australian, New Zealanders, American, Canadian, South African, Indian, Portuguese and Chinese with help from the French had done just that, defeating the final German offensive of the Great War, Operation Marne-Rheims, on 17 July 1918.

The Supreme Allied Commander Generalissime Ferdinand Foch now planned a Franco-British counter-offensive against the exhausted German 2nd Army of General Georg von der Marwitz before Amiens. Haig had already planned for just such on firm ground around the River Somme, a massed tank attack with supporting infantry under a sudden artillery storm. On the right of the British Fourth Army (formed from the remnants of General Hubert Gough's shattered Fifth Army and reinforcements from Palestine and Mesopotamia) of General Sir Henry Rawlinson however the French 1st Army had few tanks and would lose surprise by employing the overused tactic of a prolonged artillery barrage. Haig was reluctant to use them at all but agreed to a delayed French support attack. The Indian Expeditionary Force had fought alongside the British to halt the German offensives of 1914–15 and now the elite Australian Corps of Lieutenant General John Monash and the Canadian Corps of Lieutenant General Arthur Currie would fight alongside the British III Corps and Cavalry Corps under Lieutenant

Generals Richard Butler and Charles Kavanagh respectively to decisively turn the war with an all arms attack involving over 500 tanks and 2,000 aircraft.

After a carefully concealed build up, the size of Rawlinson's attack caught the Germans completely by surprise in heavy fog at 04.20 on 8 August 1918. As 75,000 men climbed out of the trenches to cross a no-man's-land 500 yards wide in places, 700 guns using 'predicted fire' techniques struck 504 of the 530 German guns before forming a brief creeping barrage. The German front lines were also hit by 600 aircraft dropping phosphorus bombs leaving the vastly outnumbered defenders to crumble as the spearhead of Australian Corps swept over them toward Bray with the Canadian Corps advancing to their south toward Lihons. Previously thought, unimaginable gains of three miles were made in five hours as mobile warfare at last returned to the Western Front. Rawlinson brought up reserves and cavalry to exploit the breakthroughs, extending Canadian gains to eight miles and Australian to six by the day's end. To the north of their colonial Allies, however, the British III Corps struggled having suffered from disruption to their own build up by a German attack two days previous and a lack of armour, gaining only their first objectives before German resistance stiffened. To the south the French 1st Army followed an intense artillery bombardment by making five mile gains by the days end. On the first day alone the German 2nd Army suffered losses of 30,000 men, many taken prisoner indicating a collapse in morale – Ludendorff described the 8 August 1918 as 'the Black Day of the German Army'. Rawlinson continued the offensive but with infantry outrunning the support of their artillery and almost the entire tank force spent by 12 August Haig called off the offensive in favour of switching the point of attack north to Albert with Julian Byng's Third Army. On 22 August Fourth Army resumed the offensive on the Somme and on 26 August General Sir Henry Horne's First Army attacked at Arras. The Germans fell back to the formidable defences of the Hindenburg Line.

Amiens was the decisive victory of the Great War, starting the Hundred Days Offensive and a series of Entente victories that would ultimately lead to the Armistice. Before then Haig would need to gain positions at Havrincourt and Epehy for an assault on the Hindenburg Line.

9 August 1757

French and Indian War
Battle of Fort William Henry

BY 1757 THE French and Indian War in North America had ignited the still burning embers of distrust left over from the War of the Austrian Succession which had ended nine years previous. The players of the now Seven Years' War were the same bar the Dutch Republic who would not side with France but neither did they fancy Britain's chances. Neither were the major alliances the same, in a 'Diplomatic Revolution' the British suspected the Habsburg monarchy in Vienna ruling the Holy Roman Empire was now a spent force and instead sided with King Frederick 'the Great' of Prussia, several smaller German states and Portugal against all other powers of consequence in an attempt to maintain the European balance of power.

In Britain the Whigs had been governing since 1715 with William Pitt 'the Elder', Earl of Chatham now Leader of the House of Commons. Pitt's determination to defeat the rival powers of France and Spain would ultimately lay the foundations for the development of the British Empire, his strategy leaving Prussia to do most of the fighting in Continental Europe whilst he directed the new Commander-in-Chief of the Thirteen Colonies (British America) General John Campbell, Lord Loudoun to attack Louisbourg in French Canada (now Cape Breton Island, Nova Scotia). Whilst Loudoun was sailing for Louisbourg, where he would be repulsed by a larger French fleet, the French Brigadier General Louis Joseph de Montcalm focussed his attention on a determined advance into the Hudson Valley from Fort Carillon (Lake Champlain) and in particular an attack on the British Fort William Henry at the southern end of Lake George around which French troops and their American Indian allies had been harassing the British since the beginning of the year.

On 3 August 1757 Montcalm cut the road between Fort William Henry and Fort Edward fifteen miles further south, surrounding the former with 7,000 men and artillery before demanding the surrender of British Commander, Lieutenant Colonel George Monro. Monro had 2,500 men, regulars, militia and frontiersmen, to man a defence of the fort which was naturally protected on three sides by a dry moat and on the fourth by Lake George. Fort William Henry, however, could not hold all these troops leaving many housed outside the walls in an entrenched camp that probably provided better cover than the fort itself. On receiving Monro's negative response, Montcalm began an artillery bombardment on 5 August 1757 that soon began to wear down the British defences. Monro's gunners answered with spirit but the British guns were no match for the French, the British troops and their camp followers suffering accordingly. Monro sent messengers desperately requesting Colonel Daniel Webb at Fort Edward come to his assistance but, to the disgust of the Fort Edward garrison, Webb would not move, instead urging Monro to negotiate terms. Montcalm intercepted Webb's reply, delivered it to Monro and again demanded the British surrender. Monro again declined but after another heavy bombardment he bowed to the inevitable, negotiating that his men keep their muskets, albeit devoid of ammunition, and that the French provide an escort back to Fort Edward.

On 9 August 1757 Monro's battered army and its followers marched out of Fort William Henry but Montcalm failed to provide adequate protection. The column was attacked by Ottawa, Potawatomi, Abenaki and Huron American Indians eager for plunder, plunder they had been promised as a reward for their services by Montcalm who had in fact already relieved the British of most of their valuables before leaving Fort William Henry. The result was a massacre of possibly 500 men, women and children, killed and scalped or taken captive by the furious Indians while the French turned a blind eye. Others fled into the forest for Fort Edward including Monro who died three months later.

Montcalm destroyed Fort William Henry and belatedly rescued some of the American Indian captives. Webb was relieved of his command. The British would take the attack back to the French at Fort Carillon the following year. The siege and massacre at Fort William Henry is depicted in the 1992 Morgan Creek Productions film *Last of the Mohicans*, an adaptation of an 1826 James Fenimore Cooper novel.

10 August 991

Viking
Battle of Maldon

 VIKING RAIDS ON the north and east coasts of the British Isles had come to prominence in 793 with a ferocious sack of the Holy Island of Lindisfarne that shocked the whole of Europe. Largely Norwegians and Danes, the raids continued with brutal terror for over half a century into southern England and northern France, isolated Anglo-Saxon settlements easy pickings for the pagan Norsemen who showed no regard for the pious, indeed the wealth of monasteries, cathedrals and churches were often their chief targets. As poor land failed to support a growing population in Scandinavia, the Viking threat then went beyond plunder toward territorial conquest so that by 871 almost all Britain north of the River Thames was in Viking hands as a 'Great Heathen Army' roamed the country from the Viking capital of England, Jorvik (York).

An effort by the ambitious Guthrum to add the southern Anglo-Saxon Kingdom of Wessex to Viking East Anglia, Mercia and Northumbria had, however, met with the dogged King of Wessex, Alfred the Great. Alfred's victory at Edington and Guthrum's consequent surrender at Chippenham gave Alfred's son, Edward the Elder, a platform to bring Mercia and East Anglia back under Saxon control before Edward's son Aethelstan consolidated the conquest of Northumbria at the bloody 937 Battle of Brunanburgh to unite England into a single Kingdom. England now enjoyed peace for over forty years but in 980 the dreaded Viking longboats once again appeared off the English coast, their lightning raids supported from across the English Channel by old Norse ancestors who had remained in Normandy all along. The King of England, Aethelred the Unready (ill advised), had the choice of fighting the new Viking menace or buying them off, Danegeld.

Earl Byrhtnoth, Ealdorman of Essex was the most powerful Ealdorman in England. A huge man for his time, around 6 feet 9 inches in height, Byrthnoth had formed a strong allegiance with Athelwine, Ealdorman of East Anglia. He was in Maldon not just as an Essexman but for the whole of the eastern seaboard and wanted to pursue a decisive battle rather than buy off the Danish 'sea robbers' who were likely commanded by the Norwegian Olaf Trygvasson (according to the Anglo-Saxon Chronicle) or the Dane Sweyn Forkbeard, father of the future King Cnut (Canute). The Viking longboats sailed up the River Blackwater towards the town of Maldon where Byrhtnoth met them with his huscarls (personal bodyguards), theyns (lords) and the local Saxon *fyrd* (Saxon militia). The Vikings landed on Northey Island but the two armies of 3–4,000 men were separated by the Blackwater since the narrow causeway to the mainland was submerged at high tide. The Danes requested gold and armour to hasten their peaceful departure but instead of the usual meek acquiescence Byrhtnoth suggested they first be reconciled with spear point and sword edge.

As the tide receded Danes began crossing onto Northey Island's causeway but blocking the exit were three of Byrhtnoth's toughest warriors, Wulfstan, Ælfhere and Maccus. The Vikings could make no headway against this trio and requested they retreat so that they could advance on to the mainland. Byrthnoth has been heavily criticised for granting this request but if he had not the longboats would merely have departed to attack elsewhere depriving him of a fight. The Saxons retreated to form a shield wall on which the 'wolves of slaughter fell' for a hand-to-hand fight of considerable ferocity. The battle's direction is unclear but it seems at some point Byrhtnoth recklessly stepped out of the shield wall to attack a particular Dane only to be instantly cut down by another three. His death prompted a shameful flight from the field by his theyn Godric which in turn prompted other parts of the *fyrd* to flee. Though now heavily outnumbered but true to the Saxon feudal system Byrhtnoth's huscarls and many of his other theyns fought on, dying where they stood when the tide of battle inevitably turned against them.

The Viking victory precipitated a fearful sacking of Maldon. King Aethelred was now advised to buy off the Vikings with 10,000 Roman pounds of silver, Danegeld had returned with interest. What is known of the Battle of Maldon is largely based on an incomplete Anglo-Saxon poem likely written by one of the monks of Ely Cathedral where Byrhtnoth's headless torso now lies.

11 August 1673 o.s

Anglo-Dutch Wars
Battle of Texel

CHARLES STUART HAD become King Charles II of England on the Restoration of the monarchy in 1660, eleven years after his father's execution. Ever since, the king had championed the cause of his nephew, Prince William of Orange, as rightful Stadtholder to the Dutch Republic. Dutch government officials controlling the wealth generated by the nation's expansive global trading empire had been reluctant to relinquish their grip but in 1673 the republic had been invaded by French and German armies while the Royal Navy, to the English Protestant Parliament's disgust, supported Catholic France rather than the Protestant Dutch. From a commercial standpoint Charles reasoned, as he had eight years earlier at the beginning of the Second Anglo-Dutch War, that if England was to take a side more was to be gained capturing Dutch trade than French.

The Third Anglo-Dutch War started badly for the Royal Navy and Lord High Admiral James, Duke of York (Charles' brother) when suffering a defeat at Solebay trapped against the Suffolk coast – York was only spared total disaster because the wind dropped. King Charles also suffered an unexpected blow when the Dutch populace, in panic at the French occupation of all but the Province of Holland, murdered Grand Pensionary of the States General, Johan de Witt. Though William did indeed now become Stadtholder, Charles expected his nephew to become an ally on payment of a one off gratuity and an annual payment for fishing rights. William, however, furiously declined – the Third Anglo-Dutch War consequently now setting uncle against nephew.

In 1673 the French, unable to cross the defences of the Hollandic Water Line, planned an amphibious landing with Royal Navy assistance but first Vice Admiral Prince Rupert would have to reckon with the Dutch fleet of Lieutenant Admiral Michiel de Ruyter anchored in the protective shoals of the River Shelde. De Ruyter, however, dealt Rupert a double blow within a week off Schooneveld causing significant damage but Rupert remained in tact for another effort in July, again Rupert's combined Royal Navy/French fleet of 122 ships looking to land troops in Holland north of Rotterdam and on Texel Island. De Ruyter sighted Rupert on 20 July 1673 but declined battle knowing that the highly experienced Rupert would not risk the planned landing with stiff resistance in front of him onshore and a powerful Dutch fleet behind him at sea. De Ruyter's hand was forced, however, by a returning fleet of Dutch East Indiamen loaded with valuable spices requiring his protection.

The Dutch Fleet of 105 ships sailed up the Dutch coast sighting Rupert again on 10 August but avoided battle until the following day, 11 August 1673, when the wind changed to an easterly. De Ruyter attacked with his vanguard under Admiral Adriaen Banckert trying to separate the French vanguard of Jean D'Estrées from Rupert in the English centre and Sir Edward Spragge in the rear. Initially Banckert struggled with only a dozen ships against D'Estrées thirty, Banckert nearly surrounded but in fierce exchanges of cannon eventually succeeding in forcing D'Estrées out of the battle. Banckert then joined De Ruyter, the Dutch now splitting Rupert who was in danger of being overwhelmed by continuous broadsides of shot and canister before retrieving his situation by joining with Spragge. The two English squadrons now became involved in bitter fighting with De Ruyter and the Dutch rear under Cornelis Tromp, the battle confused by an ever changing wind. Fighting continued until evening when D'Estrées brought the French back into the fray, De Ruyter retreating back into the shallow waters off Texel having inflicted heavy damage and over 2,000 casualties, including Spragge, on the heavy troop laden decks of the Anglo-French ships.

De Ruyter escorted his spice fleet into the Republic and the Dutch later signed an alliance with old enemy Spain to force a French withdrawal. Increasing English discontent at fighting the Dutch then forced their own withdrawal but by the 1674 Treaty of Westminster gained the return of New Amsterdam, renaming the city after their Lord High Admiral – New York. In 1677 William of Orange married his cousin Princess Mary, James' daughter. Though the marriage would bring the two nations closer it would drive James and Mary apart.

12 August 1969

The Troubles
Battles of Bogside, Derry
and Belfast

THE COMPROMISE OFFERED by British Prime Minister David Lloyd George to end the 1913–22 Anglo-Irish War was supported by Irish Republican Army (IRA) leader Michael Collins but not by President of the Republic, Eamon De Valera. The successful vote to partition Ireland, Ulster remaining under British governance, led to De Valera's resignation and an all Irish Civil War in which British armed, pro treaty government forces prevailed. By 1956, however, Lloyd George's belief that the six counties of Protestant dominated Northern Ireland would be consumed on economic grounds by the twenty-six counties of the Catholic dominated Republic of Ireland had not materialised – indeed De Valera, who had returned as President of the Republic in 1932 (Taoiseach), had given the Catholic Church a 'special position' whilst the North's Prime Minister James Craig had described his nation as having a 'Protestant people and a Protestant Parliament'. The two entities were now so sectarian that the North's pro British loyalists such as the Orangemen and the Apprentice Boys of Derry were ever more determined to maintain partition and for Catholic rights to be restricted.

Consequently the IRA began attacking soft Unionist targets across the border but the Ulster Unionist Government of Basil Brooke, Lord Brookeborough so successfully prevented their fellow loyalists from retaliating that the IRA campaign achieved little. On Brookeborough's resignation in 1963, however, his work began to unravel, the fiery Reverend Ian Paisley leading rioters into Divis Street to remove a Republican tri colour that resulted in three days of unrest. The IRA's Sean Garland was then arrested in Dublin in 1966 with documents implicating Republican infiltration of social reform movements, so that when the Northern Ireland Civil Rights Association (NICRA) began a series of marches through Protestant areas in 1967 tension again soon reached boiling point. In Derry, where NICRA certainly had a point concerning Unionist gerrymandering, Catholics formed the Derry

Citizens Defence Association in response to increasing sectarian violence in time for the 12 August 1969 parade of the Apprentice Boys of Derry – a Protestant association dedicated to the memory of those that defended Derry in 1688 for Protestant William of Orange against the Catholic forces of King James II.

Just four weeks after United States President Richard Nixon had noted in a telephone conversation with Astronauts Neil Armstrong and Buzz Aldrin on the moon's Sea of Tranquility, that 'for one priceless moment in the whole history of man, all people on this Earth are truly one' (the US were themselves fighting a twenty-year war in Vietnam), the Apprentice Boys were marching along the perimeter of Bogside with missile exchanges escalating. By the time the parade reached a barricaded Rossville Street the Royal Ulster Constabulary (RUC) which had entered Bogside were losing control, flooding the area with CS gas as they struggled against Catholic residents whose arsenal now included petrol bombs and who were joined by IRA gunmen. Prime Minister of the Republic Jack Lynch further antagonised the RUC and Apprentice Boys as rioting continued in Derry throughout the night, the next day and in Belfast where those returning were greeted by piped bands. In Belfast, the Apprentice Boys marched down the Shankill Road singing loyalist ballads as Catholics called for armed risings throughout the province, 2,000 of them launching a petrol bomb attack on the Hastings Street RUC station before armoured RUC vehicles intervened.

The rioting in Belfast now surpassed Derry, cars set ablaze in a defence of Catholic areas with the RUC additionally hit by grenades and gunfire. In London the following day, 14 August, Home Secretary James Callaghan agreed to send in the British military but was concerned as to when he would be able get it out again, thirty-eight years later would be the answer, Operation Banner being the longest campaign in British military history. The fighting raged on in Hastings Street, the Falls Road and Dover Street, Catholic areas now entered by Protestant loyalists, RUC armoured cars and the Ulster Special Constabulary (USC); homes, businesses and cars ablaze; IRA gun fire returned by RUC Browning machineguns. On 15 August an RUC retreat then allowed loyalists to rampage through Cupar, Bombay and Kashmir Street exchanging gunfire and setting housing ablaze before the Royal Regiment of Wales arrived to barricade Catholic areas in both Belfast and Derry, assisted in Ardoyne by fifty stolen buses – eight people were already dead.

The Official IRA called a ceasefire but the paramilitary Provisional IRA would go to war against the paramilitary Ulster Volunteer Force (UVF), the Ulster Defence Association and, very soon, the British Army. The violence of the Anglo-Irish and Irish Civil War had moved to Ulster with interest.

13 August 1704 n.s

War of the Spanish Succession Battle of Blenheim

IN 1700 THE House of Habsburg King of Spain, Charles II, died without issue but in his will indicated that House of Bourbon Philip, Duke of Anjou, grandson of Bourbon King Louis XIV of France, should succeed to the throne of Spain. Worse for the enemies of France, Louis would not remove Philip from the line of the French succession creating the spectre that at a future date France and Spain could become one. Even before then Louis would no doubt have considerable influence not just in Spain but also in Spanish European and American possessions. To preserve the balance of power England (ruled by Queen Anne I following the 1702 death of King William III), the Dutch Republic and the Duchy of Savoy formed a Grand Alliance with Leopold I, Holy Roman Emperor backing Archduke Charles of Austria (Leopold's son) for the Spanish throne, both Leopold and Charles belonging to the House of Habsburg.

Initial encounters went well for the Grand Alliance but in 1703 Louis had been victorious at Friedlingen and Maximilian Emanuel, Elector of Bavaria had declared for the House of Bourbon. Vienna was now in acute danger from French and Bavarian forces to the west and a Hungarian uprising to the east – should Austria be knocked out of the war the Grand Alliance would no doubt fall apart leaving Louis and a huge Franco-Spanish empire to dominate Europe. The Commander of the Grand Alliance, John Churchill, Duke of Marlborough therefore resolved to march an army from the Dutch Republic down the River Rhine to threaten Bavaria. Since Marlborough knew the Dutch would never agree to expose their own territories he convinced them that he would march only as far as Moselle although, once there of course, he intended to go back on his word and continue toward the River Danube. Having successfully deceived both the Dutch and the enemy, Marlborough marched 250 miles in five weeks but despite burning much of Bavaria was unsuccessful in bringing Maximilian and

French Marshal Ferdinand de Marsin to battle before they were reinforced by Marshal Camille d'Hostin, Duke of Tallard. At Donauworth on 12 August 1704, following a series of counter-marches, Marlborough was himself reinforced by Prince Eugene of Savoy for a concentration in force.

Despite protests from his fellow commanders that the Franco-Bavarians were in too strong a position Marlborough deemed that 'bravery and discipline would make amends for our disadvantages'. At 02.00 on 13 August 1704, forty Grand Alliance cavalry squadrons advanced with the main force following an hour later. The Franco-Bavarians were unaware of the advance until sighting the Alliance two miles distant, 52,000-strong, in nine columns on a front four-miles-wide. The Franco-Bavarians, 56,000-strong but with Tallard and Maximilian openly at odds, hurried to form up before opening fire on Marlborough's main body of 36,000 men on the Alliance left. On the Alliance right Eugene was having difficulty getting his 16,000 Prussians and Danes into position leaving Marlborough to endure a three hour wait prostrate under cannon fire before at 13.00 the whole Alliance line was at last in position. Immediately restarting the advance, Lieutenant General John, Lord Cutts led part of the main Alliance attack towards Blenheim on the Alliance left where he was killed but where supporting Hessians succeeded in tying down numerous French forces. On the Alliance right Eugene's Savoyards were firmly repulsed twice but only after Maximilian had out of necessity inspirationally rallied his wavering Bavarians. Looking to split Tallard and Maximilian, Marlborough also moved forward the Alliance centre, his cavalry to the front charged by their French counterparts, the Gens d'Armes. Disciplined British volley fire from supporting infantry sent the French horse into retreat with De Marsin unable to reinforce them since he was tied down on both flanks. Marlborough then requested Count Hendrick Fugger and his cuirassiers attack the village of Oberglau on the Alliance right while he waited for Eugene to prepare another general advance. At just after 17.00 the whole Alliance front moved forward behind a murderous artillery bombardment. The French made a determined stand but eventually broke and fled, many cut down by pursuing Alliance cavalry or drowning in the Danube. Behind them Blenheim burned, surrounded by the Alliance the remaining French held out until 21.00 before surrendering.

Queen Anne rewarded Marlborough with Woodstock Park and £240,000 to build Blenheim Palace. The War of the Spanish Succession was far from over, however, since Marlborough could not fully press his Blenheim victory until 1706 when he suddenly encountered a Franco-Bavarian-Spanish Army at Ramillies.

14 August 1352

Hundred Years' War
Battle of Mauron

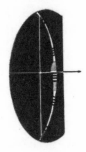

ENGLAND'S STAGGERING RUN of military victories during the first decade of the Hundred Years' War had left King Philip VI of France reluctant to contest a set piece battle. Much of the nobility of France had been killed at Crécy in 1346 whilst Philip's candidate for the post of Duke of Brittany, Charles, Count of Blois had been defeated at La Roche Derrien and was now keeping company with King David II of Scotland in the Tower of London (both were allowed to compete in English tournaments). Philip was spared further military misery by the Truce of Calais and the onset of the Black Death, the financial consequences of which rather than the loss of recruits prevented England's King Edward III from aggressively prosecuting the war. Philip was not, however, spared personal misery as his wife, Joan of Burgundy succumbed to the pestilence. The fifty-six-year-old French king did not mourn for long, marrying the nineteen-year-old Blanche of Navarre just forty eight days later, strengthening his allegiance with Navarre (North Spain) but alienating many of his own nobles including his son John who had previously been betrothed to the lady. The new queen's tenure as Queen Consort of France would in fact have been a lot longer had she remained with John as Philip followed his first wife to the grave just seven months later.

With France in wretched turmoil the struggle for Brittany continued despite Blois' enforced absence and his rival, John de Montford's death. Edward continued the campaign as part of his wider ambition for all of France, possibly holding De Montford's resolute wife Joanna of Flanders against her will in England where she was reputed to have gone mad. Since La Roche Derrien the war in Brittany had seen just small scale skirmishing and a series of minor sieges amongst which the English commander in Brittany, Thomas Dagworth, had been murdered by the Breton traitor Raoul de Cahours. At sea, however, King Edward had swept away Spanish privateers in person at the 1350 Battle of Winchelsea allowing him to counter the aggressive intent of the jilted new French King John II who was

At Saint-Jean-d'Angelys, however, De Nestlé suffered a reverse, becoming an irritating extra expense on being captured by John de Beauchamp who ransomed him back to the French king. In Brittany Du Guesclin was more successful, capturing the town and castle of Fougères before Dagworth's replacement, William Bentley, countered and retook the town for the English leaving in command the uncompromising Robert Knollys. Bentley returned to England for reinforcements but, since the Black Death was only now abating, he returned with pitifully few, relieving the besieged Fougères regardless after several months of grim resolution on the part of Knollys. The French returned once again to Brittany in August 1352 with De Nestlé looking to redeem himself at the head of 5,000 men intent on first taking Rennes and then Brest in the far south west. Meanwhile Bentley, Knollys and 2,500 Anglo-Bretons were at Ploermel and moved north to intercept. De Nestlé could easily have side stepped but instead eagerly turned south for an inevitable clash and possible redemption.

On 14 August 1352 the English, all dismounted, occupied the high ground east of Mauron but on an extended front with every man available in the line. Archers formed herces on the flanks where they could cover most of the front but they could not cover all of it. The French also dismounted apart from a body of cavalry which moved to their left. As the whole French line advanced up the slope they overlapped the English on the English right so that there was a danger of encirclement, additionally so when the English archers on the right broke under attack from the French cavalry (Bentley had thirty of them beheaded afterwards). This in turn forced the men-at-arms in the English centre to retreat but the archers on the left flank, with the benefit of better defensive ground, halted the French men-at-arms to their front and then, regardless of their own lack of armour, charged them. Inspired, the English men-at-arms who had retreated to a wood behind returned to join the counter-attack, forcing the French centre back down the slope. Near exhaustion in the summer heat, the French were left trapped at the bottom of the valley where they were mercilessly shot down by thousands of goose feathered English arrows.

Mauron had proved another crushing English longbow victory, De Neslé among the dead. Bentley was badly wounded but Brittany was now firmly in English hands. King Edward could, henceforth, look forward to offensives ever deeper into Normandy and Southern France.

15 August 1416

Hundred Years' War
Battle of the Seine

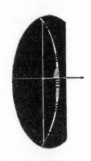

FOLLOWING THE 1415 siege of Harfleur and the near miraculous English victory at Agincourt, the King of England Henry V had returned to joyful scenes in London. Te Deums had been sung for Henry was a pious man who firmly believed that his cause was just. His cause was the French Crown (he believed unjustly denied his great-grandfather King Edward III) and the conquest of France, Harfleur adding to the longterm English possessions of Calais in the North and Bordeaux in the South. Bordeaux had been an English possession for centuries and was relatively secure whilst Calais, being across only twenty miles of water, was easily defendable. Harfleur was neither. The new French Constable Bertrand, Count of Armagnac immediately realised the English garrison's predicament and moved to isolate the town, nearly destroying its Captain Henry Beaufort, Earl of Dorset and a large part of the garrison in March 1416 at Valmont. Simultaneously, the French Navy began to both blockade Harfleur and harass the English south coast; commanded by Guillaume de Montenay, French naval strength was complimented by oared galleys sailing from the Mediterranean, carracks from Navarre (Spain) and eight bigger carracks from Genoa (Italy) – the world's finest. The French grip around Harfleur consequently began to tighten, leaving Dorset to send desperate pleas to Henry for supplies and naval reinforcement. After an unsuccessful attempt to run the blockade by Walter, Earl of Hungerford it became clear that if Henry was to hold Harfleur let alone begin a conquest of Normandy he would require an immediate break of the blockade and achieve mastery of the English Channel.

Since Henry was involved in peace negotiations led by Sigismund, Holy Roman Emperor, his brother John, Duke of Bedford was appointed to command a 100-strong fleet that collected under himself off Southampton and under Hungerford off Winchelsea. The first attempt to unite the two squadrons off Beachy Head was thwarted by a French blockade of the Solent but a second attempt proved successful, the combined English fleet reaching the mouth of the River Seine on the evening of 14 August after a day's sailing.

The following morning 15 August 1416, following a reconnaissance the night before, the blowing of trumpets signaled the start of Bedford's simple plan, the English Navy sailing into the Seine Estuary for a full frontal attack. Anchored in tightly packed lines across the estuary from Harfleur to Honfleur the French fleet seems to have been less than fully prepared with many sailors ashore scrambling to crew their ships but they did have superiority in numbers and size, 150 ships with both the galleys and Genoese carracks towering above the smaller but more agile English carracks. English intent was standard of the medieval period, to ram, board and fight the French hand-to-hand across decks in a typical bloody mêlée but whilst still at some range from the French line they began taking heavy casualties from a furious onslaught of cannon and ballista balls. As the distance shortened, arrows and crossbow bolts fired from men on the fighting decks and top sails of the French, Spanish and Genoese vessels joined the incoming debris. The English archers desperately tried to suppress this fire before the English carracks rammed into the French line, the archers now clearing the enemy rails so that their men-at-arms could grapple and clamber aboard their opponents to begin the real business of the day with swords, axes, halberds, maces and daggers. Once aboard the physically more powerful English (due to the strength required to pull a longbow) were difficult to dislodge, ship after ship succumbing to a storming party during a seven hour fight, four giant Genoese carracks captured and a fifth grounded. Other smaller dispirited French ships then fled for Honfleur as the battle turned decisively in Bedford's favour.

Bedford lost twenty ships and was badly wounded but England was once again the dominant naval power in the English Channel, indeed with her captured prizes now more powerful than ever. Harfleur was relieved and Dorset made Duke of Exeter. On hearing the news King Henry rode from Hythe to Canterbury Cathedral for another Te Deum. There would be no peace, Sigismund had become an ally. Henry could now launch the English Conquest of Normandy.

16 August 1780
American War of Independence
Battle of Camden

BRITISH FORTUNES IN North America had taken a turn for the worse in 1777 and 1778 but in 1780 Secretary of State for the Colonies George Germain, Lord Sackville and his Commander-in-Chief, General Sir Henry Clinton, had changed the point of attack south, initially on Savannah, Georgia before delivering a crushing defeat on the rebel cause of independence with a successful siege of Charleston, South Carolina complete with over 6,000 prisoners of war.

Clinton personally benefited very nicely from the wealth of Charleston and departed back to New York City which was still in British hands. Left to tame a huge hinterland believed to harbour significant loyalist support and advance north through South Carolina, North Carolina and possibly Virginia against the Southern Continental Army, Clinton left Lieutenant General Charles, Lord Cornwallis with several thousand Redcoats and a growing local militia. Cornwallis immediately sent the aggressive Colonel Banastre Tarleton with just 300 men up to the North Carolina border where on 29 May 1780 he routed 400 Americans under Colonel Abraham Buford at Waxhaws amidst claims of a murderous massacre. Any claims of British atrocities were a rally call for American Patriots and under Major General Horatio Gates, the 1777 American hero of Saratoga, they would now attempt to counter-attack from Charlotte, North Carolina.

Gates recognised the road junction at Camden, 100 miles north of Charleston, to be the key to controlling the back country of the Carolinas. The British had 2,000 men stationed there under Major General Francis Rawdon-Hastings but reinforcements under Cornwallis moved inland to support them against the advance of Gates and his reputed army of over 5,000. Temperatures were stifling and both sides were suffering from various fevers, particularly dysentery. For many of Gates' army the march south from Charlotte was just the end of their trek, they had already slogged many hundreds of miles from Virginia or from even further north and were now suffering to such an extent that when Gates reached Rudgeley's Mill, north of Camden, only near half his men were fit for battle. Even if he had been at full strength it would have been an extraordinary gamble to march and confront the professionals of the British Army on such an extended line of supply but on the morning of 16 August 1780 that is exactly what Gates did, 3,500 Patriots facing Cornwallis' 2,000 Redcoats and militia who had marched out of Camden.

Gates had hoped to take up a strong position overlooking Sanders Creek which would act as an obstacle to any British advance and in turn trap them should they manage to ford it but Cornwallis' early departure meant the British were already across the creek before Gates arrived. Gates realised that although he outnumbered his enemy, the British position was a lot stronger than he had envisaged – since many of his own men including the Continental regulars were inexperienced, Gates figured he needed every advantage available. A deeply concerned Gates called counsel but there was no chance of disengaging from the likes of Cornwallis and Tarleton.

The British and the Americans both formed up with their best troops on their right in the traditional European fashion based on honour. This meant that as the lines approached each other the battle-hardened British volley fired into the American militia before routing them with a bayonet charge. On seeing his left disintegrate Gates ordered his right under Bavarian Johann de Kalb to advance on the less reliable British left, loyalist militia under Rawdon-Hastings. De Kalb's regulars inflicted heavy casualties but crucially the British militia held, urged to do so by Cornwallis. Gates on the other hand, instead of rallying his own militia or supporting his advancing troops on the right, turned tail for the exit leaving De Kalb to be additionally attacked on his left by British Redcoats and on his rear by Tarleton's cavalry. The Americans broke and fled, chased by Tarleton for over twenty miles, suffering 2,000 killed, wounded and captured. Shot eleven times, De Kalb died shortly after the battle which had lasted just an hour.

By evening Gates was having dinner back in Charlotte sixty miles to the north – disgraced he was replaced by Nathaniel Greene. Cornwallis and the British Army would fight their way across McCowan's Ford, North Carolina before eventually meeting Greene at Guildford Court House.

17 August 1424

Hundred Years' War
Battle of Verneuil

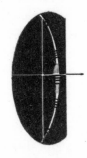 THOMAS, DUKE OF Clarence had been killed at Baugé in 1421 and was followed to the grave a year later by his brother King Henry V of England. The two younger brothers, John, Duke of Bedford and Humphrey, Duke of Gloucester and a multitude of counsellors then governed England and France on behalf of the ten-month-old King Henry VI, born to Henry V's French Queen Catherine of Valois. Bedford governed England only when home but not so in France which he governed as regent, continuing the Hundred Years' War against Catherine's brother, the Dauphin Charles who had been disinherited by his parents at Troyes in 1420 but who nevertheless now proclaimed himself King Charles VII of France.

Bedford took the offensive in France with an advance by Thomas Montagu, Earl of Salisbury into Dauphinist Champagne, besieging Montaiguillon. The Dauphin relieved pressure on Montaiguillon by launching his own advance into Burgundy whose Duke Philip was allied to the English. Besieging Cravant, the Dauphin's strategy worked perfectly until Salisbury crushed his largely Scottish Army outside the town walls in July 1423, John Stewart, Earl of Buchan, the man who had killed Clarence, captured but shortly after exchanged back to the Dauphin to become the Constable of France. With almost all northern France now under English or Burgundian control Bedford began gathering forces in Rouen, 10,000 men for a push south into the Dauphin's heartlands. The Dauphin too called a levy in southern France under Jean D'Harcourt, Count of Aumâle and received another 6,500 Scots under Archibald, Earl of Douglas whilst mercenaries, including Milanese cavalry, increased French strength to 15,000 men.

The focus of attention was the siege of Ivry thirty miles west of Paris where the previously rampaging French garrison had retreated to the castle in the face of William de la Pole, Earl of Suffolk. The Dauphinists moved to relieve Ivry whilst Bedford and Salisbury marched to Suffolk's assistance, both armies arriving within proximity of each other on 13 August. As the senior French commander

Aumâle resisted impetuous Scottish demands for an immediate attack on Bedford's prepared defensive position and instead marched to Verneuil, taking the town by deceit. Bedford reinforced the garrison at Ivry and inexplicably released his Burgundians before following Aumâle, arriving outside Verneuil on 17 August 1424 to find the Dauphinist Army in front of the town, drawn up for battle. Aumâle, it seemed, had at last been over ruled, his Frenchmen formed his left, Scots the right with the Milanese cavalry, whose state of the art plate armour could supposedly resist English bodkin arrows, on both flanks. Bedford marched onto the plain to deploy his 9,000-strong English Army, himself on the right opposite the French, Salisbury on the left opposite the Scots with herces of archers to the front and on the flanks plus a reserve of archers to protect the baggage. The two armies then eyeballed each other, the Scots grimly but confidently declaring no quarter to be asked or given.

At 16.00 both armies simultaneously advanced, initially the English suffering what could have been a disastrous blow when the Milanese cavalry charged through a hail of arrows to ride down the archers on the English right. Bedford's men-at-arms were now left dangerously exposed on their flank but fortunately the Milanese were more interested in looting the English baggage train. Bedford was consequently able to fight the French unhindered in a murderous melée, himself wielding a two-handed battle axe as the English began to gain the upper hand, the French giving ground before breaking and fleeing. Against Salisbury's battle on the English left the Scots, however, continued to fight on fanatically, completely undeterred by the loss of the French on their left or the Milanese cavalry on their right who had also departed to join their compatriots attacking the English baggage train. Not only had the Scots been deserted but the English archers defending the baggage had made short work of both Milanese attacks and now entered the main affray on the English left. Bedford's battle had pursued the French back to the walls of Verneuil but now returned to assist Salisbury, attacking the Scots in the rear. Bereft of allies the surrounded Scots did indeed receive no quarter and were slaughtered to a man. Never again would a Scottish Army take the field during the Hundred Years' War.

An incredible victory, Verneuil has been termed the 'Second Agincourt'. Bedford now overran Maine and Anjou with the Dauphin's cause seemingly lost but in 1429 a French peasant girl would arrive in Orléans to decisively turn the war.

18 August 1417

Hundred Years' War
Sack of Caen

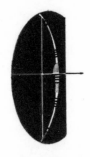

THE SAME DAY as John, Duke of Bedford defeated a numerically and physically larger French fleet at the mouth of the River Seine, his brother King of England Henry V signed the Treaty of Canterbury with Sigismund, Holy Roman Emperor. Both events opened the way for the English king to further his claim for 'just rights and inheritances' (the Kingdom of France) denied his great-grandfather King Edward III nearly ninety years before. The English towns of Bordeaux in the south, Calais in the north and Harfleur in Normandy meant Henry could launch an invasion against an enemy that would have to spread their forces so thinly that it would not be able to effectively defend anywhere (Nazi Germany would have the same dilemma 527 years later). The Constable of France Bertrand, Count of Armagnac guessed the likely landing place to be Harfleur but Henry did not want to be confined by the River Seine and landed south at what is now Trouville, immediately sending his brother Thomas of Lancaster Duke of Clarence, John Holland Earl of Huntingdon and Thomas Montagu Earl of Salisbury out to threaten any towns and castles in the area which might oppose the English Army – many including the formidable Bonneville Castle surrendered without a struggle. Clarence moved further southeast to prevent any attack from the direction of Rouen before turning back west to Caen, appearing before the walls on 14 August 1417. The town of Caen, burial place of Henry's forefather William the Conqueror, had been sacked by an English Army under King Edward III in 1346, now, seventy-one years later on 18 August 1417, another English Army 10,000-strong under King Henry V arrived to join Clarence and again summon the town surrender or suffer the same shocking fate. Henry's summons was declined.

With help from a Monk, Clarence had captured the two fortified but vacated abbeys, Abbey aux Dames to the east and Abbey aux Hommes to the west, and had prevented a demolition of housing outside the walls that would serve to protect the besiegers. In the years since Edward, however, the walls around Caen had been reinforced and were now seven feet thick with thirty-two towers and twelve gates which were themselves protected by the River Orne and other defensive ditches. The Orne, however, also served Henry who transported upon it a large number of cannon. He also built a bridge across the river connecting his two camps, the eastern under Clarence and the western under himself. Mining accompanied the immediate bombardment which was directed from the two Abbeys and continued until 4 September when two practicable breaches had been made at either end of the New Town. The pious Henry then heard three masses before blowing a trumpet to signal simultaneous attacks on both breaches, Clarence leading that on the eastern, himself on the western.

The king, however, made little headway against determined defenders who rained down crossbow bolts, stones, boiling fat, incendiaries and quicklime but Clarence was having more success across town, his vanguard eventually climbing over the rubble down into the streets after a fierce fight. Once inside the walls Clarence's force headed across town shouting 'á Clarence! á Clarence! Saint George!' killing everyone in their path before attacking the rear of the defenders at the west gate. It was too much, French resistance crumbled allowing Henry to advance through the breach to meet up with Clarence as another fearful sack commenced. The king had insisted women and priests be spared and churches left unscathed but this was a medieval army exacting revenge for the 'rebellion' of the inhabitants, the streets running with blood as 1346 was repeated.

Henry made no attempt to storm the castle which agreed to surrender on 19 September if not relieved. There was little chance, the French King Charles VI was now besieged in Paris by Duke John 'the Fearless' of Burgundy, and with fourteen other towns, including Bayeux, the castle duly capitulated on generous terms. Many of the terrified inhabitants of Caen had already fled to Falaise, the birthplace of William the Conqueror, it would not be long before the English Army caught up with them.

19 August 1942

Second World War Raid on Dieppe

THE FOLLY OF Russian General Secretary Josef Stalin's trust in the 1939 Molotov-Ribbentrop Pact of Non-aggression had been cruelly exposed two years later by his ideological enemy, German Chancellor Adolf Hitler. Operation Barbarossa then witnessed three million German troops accompanied by over 3,000 tanks and 2,700 aircraft crossing into Soviet territory, the Wehrmacht sweeping all before them until, on the point of emulating Napoleon's capture of Moscow 129 years previous, they had been halted by the extreme cold of the Russian winter. Better prepared for a winter war, Russian counter-attacks under General Georgy Zhukov removed the immediate threat to Moscow but by April 1942 the German High Command was already planning another massive offensive for June, this time Case Blue, an advance into southern Russia to capture the oil fields of the Caucasus and the iconic city of Stalingrad. By mid August the German 6th Army of General Friedrich Paulus was already on the outskirts of Stalingrad, an embattled Stalin sending Foreign Minister Vyacheslav Molotov to plead with his Ally by a common enemy, British Prime Minister Winston Churchill, to relieve pressure on the Red Army by opening a new front in the west. On the retreat himself against Germans and Italians under Lieutenant General Erwin Rommel in North Africa and the Japanese all over the Far East (particularly Lieutenant General Shojiro Iida's 15th Army in Burma), Churchill could do little but continue bombing raids into Germany and keep open supply routes to Russia via the Barents Sea and the Persian Corridor. He was, however, determined to maintain an offensive spirit in the west with limited objective raids across the English Channel with Combined Operations Headquarters now under Vice Admiral Lord Louis Mountbatten. The success of the March raid on St Nazaire, France and a desire to show a commitment to Russia prompted both men to plan another raid, this time of dubious strategic value on the defended port of Dieppe, France, Operation Rutter, later Jubilee.

On 19 August 1942, 1,000 British commandos and fifty US Rangers crossed the English Channel followed by 5,000 Canadians of the 2nd Infantry Division under Major General John Roberts. The Canadians had been in Britain for two years and were anxious to fulfill the expectation of their Prime Minister William Mackenzie King by replicating the gallant deeds of their forebears during the Great War. Two hundred and thirty-seven Royal Navy vessels under Vice Admiral John Hughes-Hallett accompanied the troops who were to land with armoured support from fifty-eight tanks of 14th Army Tank Regiment (Calgary) on six beaches Yellow, Blue, Red, White, Green and Orange, the main attack centred on the middle four. Any element of surprise was already forfeit by repeat cancellations, German reconnaissance and at the very last minute when the fleet encountered a German coastal convoy.

On landing at Yellow the British commandos scaled the cliffs to knockout the 'Goebbels' gun battery at Berneval whilst their colleagues at Orange did the same with the 'Hess' gun battery at Vasterival. The central four beaches and Dieppe itself were then approached through a smokescreen by Canadian landing craft protected from above by an artillery barrage from British destroyers and fifty-six squadrons of British and American aircraft. Despite their losses at Yellow and Orange German artillery along the developing 'Atlantic Wall' fired with considerable intensity before interlocking machine-gun fire from their pill boxes inflicted catastrophic casualties on the Canadians. The Canadian tanks then landed, just twenty-nine of them struggling to cross the pebble beach as the whole operation lurched toward disaster. Devoid of information, Roberts nevertheless sent in his reserve at 07.00, commandos and French Canadian fusiliers sailing into a maelstrom from the German guns before Lieutenant Colonel Joseph Picton-Phillips ordered his landing craft back, himself mortally wounded in the process. Hughes-Hallett and Roberts now ordered a withdrawal, just 300 men returning from the beach leaving 3,369 killed, wounded and captured. The RAF had also lost 106 aircraft, the Royal Navy a destroyer.

Dieppe had been a disaster to add to several other British disasters but crucially lessons were learnt for a much bigger landing two years later on the defining day of the twentieth century, D-Day. Indeed Mountbatten would later put the successes of Normandy down to the failures of Dieppe.

20 August 1710 n.s

War of the Spanish Succession
Battle of Zaragoza

THE WAR OF the Spanish Succession had dragged on for nine years with both sides becoming increasingly battle weary and economically impoverished yet unwilling to concede anything of consequence. The Grand Alliance of Britain, the Dutch Republic, Portugal and the Holy Roman Empire had hoped the 1709 Battle of Malplaquet would at least force France back to the negotiating table willing to comply with demands that the Bourbon Philip, Duke of Anjou, who was already sitting on the throne of Spain, could not at some future point also inherit the throne of France – Philip being a grandson of French King Louis XIV. Although Malplaquet had been a victory, so heavy were Grand Alliance losses that division created both between the member nations and within their respective governments meant the prosecution of the war became less resolute. Louis knew it, so too Marshal Claude Louis Hector de Villars commanding the French at Malplaquet who claimed 'if it please God to give your Majesty's enemies another such victory, they are ruined'. Morale within France therefore increased in the belief that any Alliance advances would now be at a cost too painful to sustain. To bolster his own defences though Louis had crucially to weaken his forces in Spain just when Joseph I, Holy Roman Emperor and father to Philip's adversary, the Habsburg pretender Archduke Charles of Austria, was able to reinforce Anglo-Portuguese-Catalan armies in the Iberian Peninsular. The Grand Alliance therefore sought to settle the issue by defeating Philip in Spain itself.

In May 1710 Philip marched on Balaguer, Catalonia, which was the only region in Spain (it was virtually an independent state) to show any support for Charles. Alliance forces under Austrian Guido Starhemberg and the British James, Earl of Stanhope stopped Philip at the River Segre before inflicting a sharp defeat at Almenara, Philip then retreating to Zaragoza where he appointed the

French Alexandre Maître, Marquis de Bay, hero of La Gudina to command his 20,000 men.

Starhemberg and Stanhope advanced on Zaragoza with 30,000 men, skirmishing for several days before the two armies faced each other by the River Ebro on 20 August 1710. The battle began with an obligatory exchange of cannon balls, this time of four hours duration before Stanhope attacked the Bourbon left with Catalan, Portuguese and Walloons but the Spaniards held firm, counter-attacking themselves to yet again put the Portuguese to flight. The Spaniards, however, continued pursuing the Portuguese allowing Stanhope another opportunity, counter-attacking in turn to force the Bourbon left back but unable to make any headway on the centre and right. As Austrians then entered the battle, the whole front erupted in violence, Spanish cavalry to the fore but facing disciplined volley fire from Alliance infantry. Gradually the Spaniards were forced back and by 15.00 were in full retreat leaving behind 6,000 casualties and a similar number prisoner.

Zaragoza's catastrophic losses left Philip no choice but to leave Madrid which Archduke Charles entered for a second time on 28 September 1710. There was no one there to greet him, the people of Madrid had spoken with their feet and once again Charles' position soon became untenable, he departed a few months later never to return. Stanhope would be isolated and defeated at Brihuega on 9 December, Starhemberg at Villavicosia the very next day. Archduke Charles left Spain altogether in April 1711 on the death of his father to take up his hereditary role as Holy Roman Emperor, ruling over the huge Habsburg Empire of Austria, Germany, Italy, Bohemia, Hungary, Croatia and Belgium. Both the Grand Alliance as well as France wanted peace, the protagonists generally achieving it at Utrecht in 1713 where Philip was offered a choice of Kingdoms, France or Spain, he chose the latter (he would have had a nervous wait for France). Unfortunately, however, Charles was not ready to give up and the war dragged on largely siege by siege for two more miserable years until Catalonia (1714) and Majorca (1715) surrendered to Philip. After fourteen years, hundreds of thousands of deaths and economic misery across Europe the War of the Spanish Succession was finally over. Philip was still the King of Spain, now for the first time, in her history, a united country that apart from a seven year period in the 1930s would remain so until today.

21 August 1808

Napoleonic Wars
Battle of Vimeiro

SINCE 1793 REVOLUTIONARY France and the Emperor of the French, Napoleon Bonaparte had carried all before them on European soil. Four opposing coalitions had come and gone, each member bar Great Britain, defeated, occupied or suing for peace so that by the end of 1807 Napoleon was at the zenith of his power ruling over an empire from his ally Spain to the Low Countries, Russia and Italy. At sea though it was King George III of Great Britain's Royal Navy that reigned supreme, defeating Napoleon's Franco-Spanish fleet in 1805 at Trafalgar to make the British Isles safe from French invasion. Britain and France had constantly been stifling each other's European and global ambition for over a century and now was no different, Napoleon unable to bring his stubborn foe to heel by force and now trying to do so by the 'Continental System', an enforced embargo on all British trade throughout Europe. Britain, however, was a vibrant economy in the early stages of the industrial revolution and was producing goods that were in high demand. Consequently the system leaked, particularly in Russia, Spain and long term British ally, 'neutral' Portugal.

After the Battle of Friedland, Napoleon coerced Russia into the system by the 1807 Treaty of Tilsit before looking to Portugal where the Prince Regent, John VI of Braganza, ruling in place of his mother Maria the Mad, refused to cooperate. General Jean Junot marched through Spain to enter Lisbon unopposed as the Portuguese Royal family fled to Brazil but Napoleon was not content and looked to gain the whole of the Iberian Peninsular by taking advantage of a rift between Spain's King Charles IV, his chief advisor Manuel Godoy (who was also the lover of Queen Maria Luisa) and Charles' son, Crown Prince Ferdinand.

Initial Spanish opposition to the French revolutionaries had been followed by an unhappy twelve year alliance between the nations with relations disintegrating completely when French forces crossed the Pyrenees to occupy fortifications in North Spain. As internal Spanish strife prevented any resolute resistance Napoleon sent Marshal Joachim Murat with 120,000 troops to Madrid where they forced the abdications of both Charles and Ferdinand in favour of Napoleon's brother, Joseph Bonaparte. Bloody riots in Madrid led to further chaos across Spain, militias and armed *guerrilas* attacking French troops despite the absence of their own elite troops serving France in northern Europe. Napoleon now increased French strength to a massive 280,000 but, viewed from London, he was over extended, a perfect opportunity therefore to send the British Army back onto European soil in force.

As Spaniards joined the *guerillas* in their thousands, French communications across the Pyrenees became tenuous forcing the *Grande Armée* to retreat behind the River Ebro. Junot was consequently left badly isolated in Lisbon facing a 15,000-strong British Army which landed at Mondego Bay under Lieutenant General Arthur Wellesley, a man anxious for an accomplishment before another 15,000 Redcoats under Lieutenant General Sir Hew Dalrymple caught up with him. Wellesley marched south, achieving a minor victory at Rolica before being frustratingly ordered to halt, delighted therefore to learn that Junot and 12,000 French were advancing from Lisbon to meet him. On 21 August 1808, on the hills outside Vimeiro, with his back to the Atlantic, Wellesley was attacked by Junot on his left flank which he reinforced only to be attacked in the centre. The French attack, however, lost impetus on crossing a large ravine against British skirmishers and artillery. The seasoned French grenadiers continued up the hills regardless into volleys of musket from a double line of British infantry that had been screened on the reverse slopes from French artillery, the French then driven back in a vicious hand-to-hand fight of sword, bayonet and musket. A reserve French grenadier counter-attack then reignited the fighting but was again driven off, Wellesley looking to press a pursuit before again being ordered to halt. Junot had lost 2,000 men and thirteen guns – now totally isolated he asked for terms.

Dalrymple agreed the scandalous Convention of Cintra with Junot, sailing the French Army home to Rochefort fully armed. Wellesley was recalled but exonerated at the resultant enquiry whilst Dalrymple never again held a command. Lieutenant General John Moore now arrived in Portugal for an advance into Spain.

21 August 1915

The Great War
Battles of Scimitar Hill
and Hill 60

THE WAR OF movement on the Western Front in Autumn 1914 had been replaced in 1915 by trench warfare that, by the technology, transportation and communication of the age, heavily favoured the defending army. The failure of the German Schlieffen Plan had led to a reversal of tactics by the Central Powers of Germany and Austria Hungary who now defended in the west whilst attacking Russian armies in the vast spaces of the east where movement was still possible. As the British Expeditionary Force under Field Marshal Sir John French struggled to grasp the implications of trench warfare, embarking on costly offensives that would develop in complexity over the next three years, the British Secretary of State for War, Field Marshal Horatio Kitchener and particularly First Lord of the Admiralty, Winston Churchill looked to the alternative theatre of the Eastern Mediterranean where Turkey had joined the Great War on the side of the Central Powers. The initial British naval bombardment of the Dardanelles Straits had, however, failed dismally and follow up landings by British, Indian, Australian and New Zealand (Anzac) troops on the Gallipoli Peninsular – defended by Turks under Mustapha Kemal Ataturk – had resulted in fearful casualties. Advances too had been poor, indeed troops had advanced barely beyond the beaches at both Cape Helles on the southern tip and Anzac Cove twenty miles north on the west coast.

By the end of May Lieutenant General William Birdwood commanding the Anzacs planned an attack on the Turkish right flank at Sari Bair with a breakout from Anzac Cove supported by a simultaneous landing north at Suvla Bay. On receipt of a further five infantry divisions, infuriating commanders on the Western Front, General Ian Hamilton commanding the Mediterranean Expeditionary Force had put the plan into operation on 6 August when the British IX Army Corps under the out-of-retirement Lieutenant General Frederick Stopford landed at Suvla Bay whilst Anzacs and the British 13th Infantry Division under Major General

Alexander Godley attacked at Anzac Cove. In desperate fighting over rock and scrub and in ferocious heat New Zealanders and Ghurkhas had almost unlocked the door to the Gallipoli campaign but had been unsupported particularly from Suvla Bay where Stopford had not understood the battle plan and was replaced by Major General Beauvoir de Lisle. Hamilton, who had previously claimed frontal attacks to be absurd, now planned the biggest single day attack of the campaign, a frontal attack on Scimitar Hill and Hill 60 linking Suvla Bay with Anzac Cove.

On 21 August 1915, having transferred from Helles, the badly depleted British 29th Infantry Division advanced on Scimitar Hill, the 11th Infantry Division advanced on the W Hills and a British and Anzac force made for Hill 60, all initially under the protection of an artillery barrage. The 29th's attack on Scimitar Hill was checked by Turkish machine-gun fire before the Yeomen of the 2nd Mounted Division were called up. Despite suffering from artillery fire on the approach the Yeomen succeeded in pushing through to take Scimitar Hill only to find Turks still held the surrounding high ground, they were consequently driven back suffering staggering casualties. At Hill 60, which had not been fully scouted, the British artillery barrage was even more desultory, alerting the defenders to an imminent attack by the 13th and 14th Australian battalions who were wiped out in a hail of fire with burning scrub increasing the agony of the wounded. The New Zealanders following were more successful as Turks vacated their front trenches but on the left the Indian 29th Brigade met tough resistance as did the right, the Australian 4th and Hampshires. Connaught Rangers then supported the New Zealanders overnight, grimly holding the lower slopes as the newly arrived Australian 18th Battalion of 750 men were ordered to attack with bombs and bayonets only. Lacking bombs it was bayonets only as they duly suffered 50 per cent casualties in minutes.

Fighting at Hill 60 raged for nine days, Hamilton unaware of the scale of his losses due to Birdwood's false reporting. It would prove to be the last offensive of a Gallipoli campaign that had cost over 200,000 men. Even before a miraculous evacuation in December, Churchill had resigned for the trenches of the Western Front. Ataturk went on to become the First President of the Republic of Turkey in 1923.

22 August 1485

Wars of the Roses
Battle of Bosworth Field

THE FEUD BETWEEN Richard Plantagenet, Duke of York and Edmund Beaufort, Duke of Somerset had left both dead within six years but York's son, Edward, Duke of York had continued the struggle for the Crown of England to become King Edward IV in 1461 after Britain's bloodiest ever battle at Towton. Only Edward's favouritism toward the family of his wife, Elizabeth Woodville, at the expense of Richard Neville, Earl of Warwick had led to any significant threat when Warwick defected to the House of Lancaster, making his peace with Queen Margaret, (wife of King Henry VI) before temporarily hounding Edward from England. The 'Kingmaker' Warwick was, however, defeated and killed by a returning Edward at Barnet in 1471 but Edward had no time to celebrate as Margaret then landed at Weymouth. Gathering loyal Lancastrians she was, critically, unable to join with Jasper Tudor, Earl of Pembroke before Edward caught up with her at Tewkesbury, her only son, Edward mercilessly executed after the battle. When King Henry, a prisoner of seven years then suspiciously died shortly after in the Tower of London only one Lancastrian pretender remained and then only by a claim so tenuous that most Englishmen had forgotten about him – in exile in Brittany, the grandson of King Henry V's widow Catherine of Valois by her second marriage to Owen Tudor, son of their son Edmund Tudor, Henry Tudor.

The premature death of King Edward IV in 1483 left his twelve-year-old son as King Edward V but a struggle for power between the Woodvilles and the young king's uncle Richard, Duke of Gloucester led to a coup, Gloucester becoming Lord Protector with the king in his custody. With designs on the Crown himself Gloucester then removed a likely opponent, his long term Yorkist ally William, Lord Hastings who was beheaded after dubiously being accused of treason by way of sorcery. Later that same year Edward and his younger brother Richard, Duke of York then both disappeared from the Tower shocking all England before Gloucester was crowned King Richard III in July 1483. Unsurprisingly the new King's popularity plummeted whilst from the sanctuary of Westminster Abbey the missing boy's mother, Elizabeth Woodville, promised Yorkist support if the twenty-six-year-old Lancastrian Henry Tudor would marry her seventeen-year-old daughter Elizabeth – he would. After uncoordinated uprisings and an aborted landing Henry landed at Milford Haven on 7 August 1485 for a march through Powys to Shropshire where support joined in earnest but still no match for Richard. Henry badly needed the support of Thomas, Lord Stanley, a former Yorkist supporter but now married to Henry's mother, Margaret Beaufort. Stanley and his brother, William Stanley, were compromised since they had already been summoned by Richard to march against Henry!

On 22 August 1485, King Richard III's vastly superior army of 10,000 men stood ready to give battle on Ambion Hill, Bosworth. In the vanguard were archers under John Howard, Duke of Norfolk with a huge force of cavalry and infantry behind and cannon on the flanks. Richard and his own knights were further back with Henry Percy, Earl of Northumberland in the rear. Possessing just 5,000 men Henry Tudor sent desperate requests to the Stanley brothers who were spectating from the side declining requests to join Richard also. John De Vere, Earl of Oxford, commanding Henry's Army, began the battle by advancing his entire force uphill toward Norfolk's archers, a fierce exchange of arrows ensuing before Norfolk charged Oxford for a bloody mêlée of hand-to-hand fighting. As Oxford stood firm, Norfolk was killed by an arrow to the throat dispiriting his men before Richard ordered Northumberland to advance. The earl refused, possibly due to his position, the terrain or treachery but it was immaterial since Richard had spotted his adversary Henry riding across the field toward the Stanleys. Realising a swiftly executed charge could save a lot of fuss Richard led his knights down Ambion Hill, killing Henry's Standard bearer with his lance and another with his battle axe. It was indeed now that the battle was decided when William Stanley and 3,000 horsemen counter-attacked on behalf of Henry, annihilating Richard's household knights leaving the King to shout 'treason! treason!' before likely being killed by a blow from a halberd.

Henry was crowned King Henry VII on 30 October 1485 beginning the Tudor period, 118 years dominated by religion and religious wars but the Wars of the Roses were at an end, the Houses of Lancaster and York united under the Tudor Rose in January 1486 when Henry married Elizabeth.

23 August 1914

The Great War
Battle of Mons

BY 1871 CHANCELLOR Otto von Bismarck had united the independent German States under the Crown of Prussia, creating a new European power that had defeated Austria in 1866 and France in 1871. Bismarck and the new Germany initially remained content with their new territories of Alsace and Lorraine, Bismarck promoting peace in Europe whilst developing colonies in Africa. However, when Kaiser (Emperor) Wilhelm II, grandson of the United Kingdom's Queen Victoria, ascended the German throne in 1888 he immediately sacked Bismarck losing Germany her leading statesman. It was no accident, often considered partially insane, the Kaiser ruled Germany much as a medieval monarch with a close court rather than as a democracy and was far from content with the status quo. Instead the Kaiser wished to compete with France and Britain for territory and power both in Europe and across the globe, openly supporting Boer resistance against British aggression before the turn of the twentieth century. Additionally the Kaiser's failure to renew an alliance with Russia, drove the Russians into an alliance with France who in turn signed a 1904 *Entente Cordiale* with Britain, the three forming a Triple Entente in 1907. In 1912, after years of investment developing a navy to rival that of his cousin King George V, the Kaiser and his military advisors seemed to have planned in detail for the outbreak of a war in which they sought to gain land from a weak Russia and extend German hegemony in Europe.

The German *casus belli* arrived when Archduke Ferdinand of Austria Hungary was assassinated in June 1914, Austria then serving impossible demands on the main suspect, Serbia. Though the Serbians nevertheless agreed, Austria, backed by Germany, declared war anyway. Allied with Serbia, Russia then declared war on Austria, leaving Germany as planned to declare war on Russia. Realising that Russia would be defeated leaving them to face Germany alone, France then declared war on Germany (the Russians would not reciprocate in 1939). By the *Entente Cordiale* and the Triple Entente Great Britain was only morally obliged to step forward but that soon became a strategic necessity when Germany invaded 'poor little Belgium'. Having not wanted to fight the British too soon, the Germans were astonished when British Prime Minister Herbert Asquith declared war on 4 August 1914.

The German attack in the west came by way of the Schlieffen Plan, a right hook by 750,000 Germans through Belgium towards Paris. The British Expeditionary Force (BEF) had landed in Calais on 9 August, just 80,000 men in six infantry and one cavalry division under Field Marshal Sir John French, to take up a position on the left of an enormous French Army under General Joseph Joffre. Advancing to Mons and under instructions from Secretary of State for War, Field Marshal Horatio Kitchener, not to expend the professional soldiers of the BEF, French learnt that the 5th French Army to his right was heavily engaged at Charleroi and so agreed to defend the Mons-Conde canal on their left. He then received Royal Flying Corps reports that the German 1st Army (160,000 men, 600 guns) of General Alexander von Kluck was to his front. Von Kluck began an artillery bombardment at first light on 23 August 1914, following up with concentrated infantry attacks on the bridges across the canal contested by the British II Corps of General Horace Smith-Dorrien (a survivor of Isandlwana, 1879) who inflicted heavy casualties with artillery, machine-gun and rifle fire at long range before Von Kluck extended his line into open order. Outnumbered the BEF then began taking heavy casualties themselves, winning the first three Victoria Crosses of the war, but held the bridges under cover of their own artillery fire until mid afternoon when they began to fall back to a defensive line from Boussu to Frameries. As the Germans poured over the Mons-Conde canal in strength the French 5th Army retreated leaving French and the BEF little choice but to retreat further themselves, fighting three days of rearguards back to Le Cateau where Smith-Dorrien again stood his ground attempting to deliver a 'smashing blow'.

Both Entente Armies continued retreating for a fortnight before counter-attacking on the River Marne. The BEF had lost 8,000 men already but an army for which the Kaiser had little respect had shown that it knew how to fight. Lessons learnt in the Boer War were, however, just a precursor.

24 August 1346

Hundred Years' War
Battle of Blanchetaque

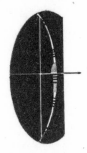 ENGLAND WAS A comparatively young nation, the Anglo-Saxon nobility had been replaced with a new Norman ruling class in 1066 and French had been their first tongue ever since. But as a series of English kings had chafed at paying homage to their French counterparts for their French possessions, predominantly Aquitaine, they also began consolidating power over their lands in Britain. By the turn of the fourteenth century King Edward I had crushed Welsh revolts and was now in the process of bringing Scotland to heel, campaigns that had been fully revived in 1333 at Halidon Hill by his grandson King Edward III after his son Edward II had been defeated in 1314 at Bannockburn by Robert the Bruce. Even in Ireland there was growing concern that the old Anglo-Norman classes had become more Irish than the Irish themselves but the anglicisation of Ireland would have to wait. Amidst deteriorating relations with England, King Philip VI of France had directly threatened Edward III by moving his fleet from the Mediterranean to the Normandy coast in support of his alliance with Scotland, the final straw in a succession of mutually antagonistic acts that included French refuge for King David of Scotland and English refuge for Robert of Artois. With a claim to the French throne at least as good as that of Philip, Edward decided on war, gaining allies in Flanders and the Holy Roman Empire before taking sides in the Breton War of Succession. In 1346, he then invaded northern France once again, landing on the Cotentin Peninsular before brutally sacking the town of Caen.

Following Caen, the English Army and their king ignored pleas from the Pope in Avignon and continued their chevauchée of destruction, marching north-east to link up with an Anglo-Flemish Army under Hugh Hastings and Count Henry of Flanders. In response Philip had collected the sacred Oriflamme from the Abbey of St Denys and marched to Rouen in an attempt to block the English advance only for Edward to side step him to the east before turning north to cross the River Seine. Conscious of French numerical superiority Edward required favourable ground and a line of retreat before entertaining any thought of battle but with all crossings well defended or destroyed his tiring army was again forced east, this time along the south bank of the Seine almost to the outskirts of Paris. Panic swept the French capital, the walls of which could be seen in the distance but Philip's army was shadowing the English menacingly from the north bank. Edward then took advantage of Parisian fears by sending his son Edward, Prince of Wales, the Black Prince further east to burn the village of St Cloud. In response Philip hurried east himself across several bends of the Seine only to find the whole exercise had been pure deception, simultaneously Edward's engineers had rebuilt the bridge over the river at Poissy which the English Army now crossed to continue north to the River Somme. Edward made Airaines in just five days but amazingly Phillip was soon just twenty miles behind him at Amiens. Pressing on along the west bank of the Somme the English were again unable to seize a bridge or ford, their morale also suffering from the French scorched earth policy. In desperation Edward offered a reward for knowledge of a crossing, a bribe accepted by a French traitor, Gobin Agache, who told of a 1.5 mile wide ford at Blanchetaque which was traversable at low tide.

Early on 24 August 1346 the English Army marched the six miles to Blanchetaque again pursued by the French, Philip confident that he had blocked the ford on the north shore with a force of 3,500 men-at-arms and Genoese crossbowmen under Godemar du Foy. After waiting four agonising hours for the tide to recede the English vanguard of one hundred archers under Hugh Despenser and one hundred knights and men-at-arms under Thomas de Beauchamp, Earl of Warwick entered the ford. Two hundred yards from the north shore the English archers came within range of the Genoese but unable to return fire suffered accordingly. Doggedly they pressed on into shallow water where they removed their bow strings from their hats to begin a superior fire that had the Genoese suffering in turn. The English knights and men-at-arms then moved up to engage their French counterparts in a violent mêlée fought half in the water and half up the sloping bank opposite. Covered by intense archery a bridgehead was created into which more English men-at-arms rushed breaking the French who were pursued by Sir Reginald Cobham and William de Bohun, Earl of Northampton.

The English Army moved north searching for the Flemings but Hastings and Count Henry had been badly bruised at the Siege of Bethune and had retreated. Outnumbered but with morale now high the English king turned to face Philip in battle two days later at the village of Crécy-en-Ponthieu.

25 August 1689
Williamite Wars
Battle of Walcourt

KING LOUIS XIV of France had invaded the Spanish Netherlands (Belgium, Luxembourg) and the Dutch Republic in 1672 but when England withdrew their support amidst public anger at King Charles II's decision to side with Catholic France rather than the Protestant Dutch the war turned against France. The Dutch had all but been defeated in 1672 but in alliance with their former enemy Spain and the Holy Roman Empire, their position was further strengthened in 1677 when Mary, the Protestant daughter of Charles' brother James, Duke of York (by his first marriage) married her Protestant cousin Prince William III of Orange, Stadtholder (Head of State) of the Dutch Republic. Now defensively minded, Louis sought to strengthen French borders by annexing the territories (Reunions) just beyond before taking the opportunity to again invade the Spanish Netherlands whilst the Habsburg Holy Roman Empire was distracted by a 1683 Turkish invasion of Austria.

Then in 1685 hundreds of thousands of French Protestant Huguenots fled France for the Dutch Republic and England where James, a devout Catholic now married to a devout Catholic, (Mary of Modena) with a Catholic son (James Stuart), had succeeded his officially childless brother Charles (unofficially Charles had sired many children) to the throne. Huguenot tales of Catholic French brutality increased fear in both England and the Dutch Republic so that James, who appointed Catholics to his military and his court and was a friend of Louis, was also deemed a danger to Protestants. By July 1688, the patience of former Admiral Arthur Herbert, leading Members of Parliament and the clergy had broken, they requested William overthrow his father-in-law, the king. Blessed by the Dutch States General and crucially England's leading military commander John Churchill, William did just that by landing 450 ships at Torbay loaded with 40,000 men. James fled first to France then Catholic Ireland without firing a shot, this 'Glorious Revolution' leaving William ruling the Three Kingdoms of England,

Scotland and Ireland jointly with his queen, Mary. Protestant England now joined the Dutch against Bourbon King Louis XIV of France in a 'Grand Alliance' with the Habsburg Holy Roman Empire on condition they also back Habsburg King Leopold I against Bourbon Phillip of Anjou (grandson of Louis XIV) as King of Spain should the current king, Habsburg King Charles II, die without issue – they would and did fourteen years later in the War of the Spanish Succession.

Louis had been concentrating his reunion efforts in the Rhineland where individual German states had formed stiff resistance but now sent Louis de Cravant, Duc de Humières and 24,000 men into the Spanish Netherlands. Although busy consolidating power in his newly acquired Three Kingdoms, William opposed Humières with 27,000 Dutch under the sixty-nine-year-old Field Marshal Prince Georg of Waldeck and 8,000 English and Scots of dubious quality under the formidable Churchill, now Earl of Marlborough. The army of the Grand Alliance then spent two months in a game of chess with Humières trying to gain an advantage before the French suddenly attacked Alliance foragers near Walcourt (now Belgium) on 25 August 1689. The French vanguard began swarming into the area south of Walcourt whilst Waldeck and Marlborough formed up to the north, a single infantry regiment under Colonel Robert Hodges holding the French advance for nearly two hours while they did so. Under increasing pressure Hodges was ordered to retreat east allowing the French to attack Walcourt over difficult ground against a defence of Dutch and Germans. French attempts to break into the town became ever more desperate, shelled from the flanks by Alliance guns Humières swung his left around the town only to meet Dutch under General Frederick van Baer, Duke of Slangenburg. Waldeck then ordered Marlborough forward against the French right with two infantry regiments and the cavalry of the Life Guards and the Blues. Exhausted by their efforts the French reeled back under the onslaught from both flanks but were spared total annihilation by the cavalry of Claude Hector de Villars. The adversaries then shelled each other for two days before Humières retreated, he had lost 2,000 men against the Alliance's 600.

The victory at Walcourt bolstered morale within the Grand Alliance but for two years William's main concern would be in Scotland (the ancestral home of James' House of Stuart) and Catholic Ireland where James was attempting to raise support in an effort to reclaim his throne.

26 August 1346

Hundred Years' War
Battle of Crécy

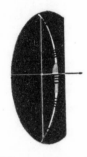

THE REASONS FOR the 1337 outbreak of hostilities between England and France were varied but not least because of King Philip VI of France's posturing in support of his ally Scotland against renewed English aggression and belatedly King Edward III's claim to the throne of France through his mother Isabella of France. The English king began in earnest what would become over a century of conflict in July 1346 with an invasion of Normandy and a trail of destruction that led from St Vaast La Hogue to Caen. In this ancient Normandy town, burial place of Edward's ancestor William the Conqueror, between 2,500–5,000 inhabitants were slain by an English Army in a bloody five day sack. The chevauchée of violence, an accepted tactic of medieval warfare designed to demonstrate the impotence of the French king or force him to a decisive encounter on the battlefield, then continued when Edward marched out of Caen. Philip, however, had collected the sacred Oriflamme from the Abbey of St Denys and marched west with a French Army, twice the size of Edward's to intercept his foe at Rouen. Whilst Edward also sought battle he did, however, require ground of his choosing and hopefully a link up with an Anglo-Flemish Army under Hugh Hastings and Henry, Count of Flanders marching south from Ypres, Flanders. To this extent Edward marched north, deceiving Philip at Poissy to cross the River Seine before miraculously forcing his way across a 1.5 mile wide tidal ford at Blanchetaque on the River Somme. With no sign of Hastings and the Flemings and with Philip still in close pursuit the English Army, with morale high in the belief that God was on their side, turned to give battle on 26 August 1346 on the ridge above the Vallée aux Clercs outside the village of Crécy-en-Ponthieu.

In pursuit Philip mistakenly believed the English to be near the burning Le Crotoy and so turned north only late in the day, his 25–30,000 somewhat disordered men advancing into the Vallée aux Clercs at around 16.00 below the banners of the 12–13,000 strong dismounted English Army. Commanding from a windmill, Edward had drawn up into three battles, the right commanded by his sixteen-year-old son Edward, the Black Prince, the left by William de Bohun, Earl of Northampton whilst his own remained in reserve. At the ends of each battle protruded massed herces of longbowmen whose counterparts in the French Army, 6,000 Genoese crossbowmen, were forced by the crush and impatience of the men behind to attack immediately without their protective palliasses. Edging up the hill with only a desultory fire the Genoese were within 150 yards of the English line when they were struck by a torrent of white goose-feathered death from English and Welsh longbowmen who could fire at least twice as fast, with greater range and were also accompanied by the deafening crash of cannon being fired on a battlefield for the first ever time. The Genoese reeled backwards under this onslaught only to be accused of treachery and ridden down by furious French mounted knights under Philip's brother, Charles, Count of Alençon. Alençon's horsemen continued up the slope only for many to be brought down by another storm of arrows (full plate armour was not common in 1346) and slit trenches dug in front of the English line but many also closed to engage in hand-to-hand fighting with the battle of the Black Prince. As more Frenchmen approached the battlefield they swung up the slope to engage Northampton on the English left so that fighting now raged along the entire line. Making no headway French bodies piled up but they continued to press attacks relentlessly, more men-at-arms waiting in turn to assault the hated English who remained in position to receive each attack. The Black Prince's battle in particular was coming under heavy pressure, concerning Godfrey Harcourt and Thomas de Beauchamp, Earl of Warwick to such an extent that Richard FitzAlan, Earl of Arundel was requested to conduct a flanking counter-attack whilst Harcourt also sent to the king for reinforcements. Arundel duly counter-attacked but the watching Edward merely retorted 'do not send to me so long as my son lives, let the boy win his spurs, let the day be his'.

The bloody murder continued until after dark but the French could not break the English and fell back beaten. A wounded Philip hurriedly retreated back to Amiens leaving behind 10,000 French dead including Alençon and much of his nobility. Edward had lost just a few hundred men, only a few of them men-at-arms. Wishing to facilitate a conquest of France, Edward refrained from marching immediately on Paris, instead he fell back to claim a prize that would remain English for over two hundred years, Calais.

27 August 1776

American War of Independence
Battle of Long Island, New York

SINCE AMERICAN DISSATISFACTION at British rule had broken into organised violence in May 1775 the British Army had been besieged in Boston and Charlestown. In a miserable and ultimately untenable position Commander-in-Chief, North America, General William Howe finally evacuated Boston in March 1776 for a retreat to Halifax, Nova Scotia to repair and reinforce. In London a few months before, the Government of Prime Minister Frederick, Lord North had appointed Lord George Germain, Viscount Sackville as Secretary of State for America – a man who at his own Court Martial following the 1759 Battle of Minden had been declared 'unfit to serve His Majesty in any military capacity whatever'. With the obvious difficulties caused by two months of delay between events and their news, Sackville and North would over the course of the next few years completely fail to grasp the political and military situation across the Atlantic and lose all thirteen of King George III's American colonies. For the time being though, Sackville confidently claimed 'these country clowns cannot whip us'.

In July 1776, Howe resumed the contest with an assault on New York City but General George Washington, the architect of Howe's Boston defeat, had second guessed him, moving the bulk of the Continental Army south in preparation for a defence of the city and its port. On 2nd July 1776, the same day that Congress in Philadelphia voted for Independence, an undeterred Howe began to unload redcoats (regulars) on Staten Island across The Narrows from Manhattan. So great was the British fleet and army, 130 ships carrying 20,000 men, that American regulars fled and the local militia changed sides. After negotiations failed (as a former colonel in the British Army, the British refused to address Washington as a general) a full scale amphibious invasion became inevitable, at that point the greatest in history. Even with 19,000 men himself Washington could not defend everywhere in strength and yet Howe was still receiving reinforcements including Hessians, soon totalling 32,000 men supported by seventy-three Royal Navy ships of the line in New York Bay. Washington decided to risk dividing his force between Lower Manhattan and Long Island, those on the latter defending the Guan Heights before making a tactical retreat to the Brooklyn Heights. The three passes through the Brooklyn Heights would be strongly defended so that British casualties would leave Howe little option but to discontinue his advance on Manhattan.

At 21.00 on 26 August, 10,000 British redcoats under Howe and Major General Charles, Lord Cornwallis marched east of the American Patriot left flank looking for the Jamaica Pass which they knew to be virtually undefended whilst another 4,000 men under General James Grant moved simultaneously toward the Patriot centre and right flank in the west of Long Island. In the early hours of 27 August 1776 Grant attacked up the Gowanus Road where fierce fighting broke out at the Red Lion Inn on what is now Battle Hill. Meanwhile, Howe's flanking army to the east took William Howard, a tavern landlord, and his son hostage, forcing them to act as guides along an Indian trail through the Jamaica Pass. At 09.00 two cannons were fired as a signal to Grant's Hessians below to begin a frontal holding assault. Washington then arrived from Manhattan realising he was involved in a major battle and began to reinforce but his centre and right were coming under increasing pressure from Grant's Hessians whilst his left was being outflanked by Howe. General John Sullivan, commanding the Patriot centre, left a guard to defend the Hessians and turned left to fight Howe but the pressure was too great, many Patriots surrendering as others ran for the Brooklyn Heights behind. Washington's right also now began to collapse, 400 brave Marylanders desperately holding off the swarming redcoats as the remainder also retreated to the Heights, the Marylanders wiped out bar a dozen.

Howe, however, no doubt aware of Bunker Hill the year before, failed to press an attack on the Brooklyn Heights, instead beginning preparations for a siege. Washington reinforced and bombarded British positions before conducting an evacuation across the East River under the cover of darkness and fog, much to the embarrassment of the Royal Navy. The Continental Army had escaped to fight another day, it would come at Harlem on Manhattan Island.

27 August 1979

The Troubles
Mullaghmore and Warrenpoint

 RELIGIOUS SECTARIANISM ON both sides of the Irish border had become so entrenched that Protestant Loyalists in Northern Ireland were prepared to commit outrages on their own soil, blaming them on the Irish Republican Army (IRA), to prevent further Catholic concessions and Ireland's unification. Violence steadily increased before exploding into open street violence, gunfire, petrol bombs and CS gas, in Derry and Belfast in August 1969. The British Army had restored order but associated with the Protestant dominated Royal Ulster Constabulary (RUC), any goodwill was soon lost when loyalist violence continued. The IRA now took the offensive, attacking soft targets from bases often in the Republic of Ireland, bombings, ambushes and assassinations of anyone defending unionism, specifically the RUC and the Army including the Ulster Defence Regiment (UDR). The IRA had won the Anglo-Irish propaganda war fifty years previous and so they did again despite specific British Army 'Rules of Engagement' that permitted the use of firearms only if lives were threatened. Fourteen unarmed civilians, however, had been killed by the Parachute Regiment in Derry, January 1972 sparking international condemnation, a burning of the British Embassy in Dublin and a flood of recruits to the IRA who carried out 1,200 operations that year, twenty-two bombings alone on 21 July in Belfast.

The now 30,000 strong British Army (including UDR) then removed all barricades in Catholic areas bringing the streets back under control but the IRA merely retreated across the border continuing as before with increasingly sophisticated and powerful Improvised Explosive Devices. British counter-insurgency, including the use of Special Forces, then began to degrade the IRA who resorted to high profile attacks including the murder of Shadow Northern Ireland Secretary Airey Neave (the first British officer to escape from Colditz, 1942) by the republican Irish National Liberation Army. The opportunity for the IRA to attack another high profile individual and the Parachute Regiment both presented themselves on 27 August 1979.

Lord Louis Mountbatten of Burma, Admiral of the Fleet, Supreme Allied Commander South East Asia Command (WWII) and last Viceroy of India was a second cousin to Queen Elizabeth II. He was holidaying as usual with low security at Classiebawn Castle in Mullaghmore, Sligo, Republic of Ireland, just twelve miles from the Northern Ireland border when, against the advice of the Garda Siochana (Police), he and several of his family decided to go lobster-potting in his 30 foot boat *Shadow V*. The boat, however, unguarded overnight, had been compromised by a radio controlled fifty-pound bomb which was detonated at 11.30 when the party was 200 yards offshore, killing Mountbatten, his grandson, the local boat boy and Doreen Knatchbull, Lady Brabourne.

The day was far from over, five hours later across the other side of Ireland, A Company, 2 Para was heading through Warrenpoint, County Down in two four-ton lorries and a Landrover toward Newry, Armagh when a half-ton fertiliser bomb aboard a parked hay lorry was detonated killing six and wounding two paratroops. The paratroops in the front lorry and Landrover immediately halted to seal the area and aid their comrades, believing perhaps mistakenly that they were still under fire. Within minutes Lieutenant Colonel David Blair of the Queen's Own Highlanders flew in by Gazelle helicopter, taking command as a Westland Wessex helicopter flew in to pick up the wounded. The IRA bombers, however, had been closely watching how the British Army reacted to an ambush and were still watching now from across the River Newry, exploding a second bomb twenty minutes after the first at the Gate Lodge to Narrow Water Castle where ten paratroops were taking cover together with Blair and his signaler. The blast destroyed the building, killed all twelve men and almost brought down the departing Westland, the worst loss in a single action suffered by British Forces during the 'Troubles'.

More bombings, hunger strikes, ambushes and assassinations followed but ultimately 27 August 1979 led to improved British and Irish dialogue. British Prime Minister Margaret Thatcher, the IRA's No. 1 target, and Taoiseach Garret Fitzgerald assisted by US President Ronald Reagan opened the path to a peace process that led to a loyalist ceasefire in 1994, a final IRA ceasefire in 1997 and a British Army withdrawal from Ulster in 2007.

28 August 1914

The Great War
Battle of Heligoland Bight

THE NINETEENTH CENTURY unifying of the independent German states under the Prussian Crown had resulted in a new global power that was initially prepared to maintain the status quo in Europe whilst competing with France and Great Britain for colonies in Africa but when Kaiser Wilhelm II sacked his Chancellor Otto von Bismarck in 1888 a very different Germany began to emerge. The Kaiser wanted to increase German hegemony in Europe, annex lands to his east and west and increase German naval power to rival that of his grandmother, Queen Victoria of Great Britain. Between 1898 and 1912 the Kaiser's Naval Secretary, Grand Admiral Alfred von Tirpitz began an impressive programme to increase the German Navy to forty-one battleships, fifty-eight cruisers, 144 torpedo boats and seventy two submarines. The British could not mistake the German threat to their global sea power and duly signed the Triple Entente with Russia, their foe throughout the nineteenth century and France, their foe through time immemorial. The Royal Navy meanwhile under First Sea Lord Sir John 'Jacky' Fisher truly ignited the arms race by building huge battleships of their own, dreadnoughts – by 1914 the Royal Navy's forty-two outnumbering Germany's twenty-six. Fisher also reorganised the Royal Navy with the Channel Fleet stationed in the English Channel, the Grand Fleet soon to patrol the North Sea from Scapa Flow, and the Atlantic Fleet at Gibraltar able to move north, west or into the Mediterranean as necessity required.

When the Kaiser received news that Archduke Franz Ferdinand of Austria Hungary had been assassinated, he was already fully prepared for war, ideally with just France, intent on defeating them before turning to defeat a slow mobilising Russia. He was therefore somewhat shocked when Britain declared war immediately over Germany's infringement of Belgian neutrality. The British Expeditionary Force (BEF) was soon being shipped to France by Fisher's Channel Fleet and although not yet directly threatened by German submarines, German destroyers and cruisers were operating to the north in the Heligoland Bight.

On 28 August 1914 having observed the pattern of German destroyer patrols, Commodore Roger Keyes commanding the British 8th Submarine Flotilla and Commodore Reginald Tyrrwhitt commanding thirty-two destroyers and two cruisers out of Harwich attacked German shipping in the Heligoland Bight. Keyes and Tyrrwhitt received additional support from six light cruisers under William Goodenough and later five battlecruisers under Vice Admiral David Beatty sent by the Commander of the Grand Fleet at Scapa Flow, Admiral John Jellicoe. Keyes, aboard HMS *Lurcher*, had ordered his submarines to attack any German ships heading back to port in an attempt to force them back out to sea where they could be attacked by the Royal Navy surface fleet. At 07.00 the leading British destroyer, Tyrrwhitt's newly built HMS *Arethusa*, which had been sent to sea in the knowledge that her guns would likely jam, sighted and attacked the German destroyer G-194 in the mist off Heligoland. G-194 radioed in to Rear Admiral Franz Hipper who immediately ordered six cruisers to support the other German destroyers who were also coming under attack and were requesting support from German coastal artillery. A confused mêlée developed, the German destroyers considerably outnumbered but the low tide preventing their dreadnoughts sailing from Wilhelmshaven – the German fleet was, however, somewhat aided by British submarines mistakenly firing on British cruisers. Smaller German ships were able to leave port and joined the fray but before the rising tide allowed the departure of the German dreadnoughts, the British fleet broke off. Eight hours of battle had left six German warships sunk with six badly damaged. HMS *Arethusa* somewhat unsurprising had also been badly damaged after her guns did indeed jam.

Tirpitz received notice from British First Lord of the Admiralty Winston Churchill, that his son had been rescued from SMS *Mainz*. The German losses were too much for the Kaiser who, going forward, was content merely to maintain a fleet in being. Royal Navy staff work and communications had been poor, a situation Jellicoe would need to rectify before a greater opportunity presented itself two years later off Jutland.

29 August 1350

Hundred Years' War
Battle of Winchelsea

KING EDWARD III of England's quest for the throne of France had begun with a failed advance into France in 1337 but a more encouraging intervention in the War of the Breton Succession in 1342. Edward began what would be come known as the Hundred Years' War in earnest in 1346, burning his way through Lower Normandy to sack Caen before devastating the numerically superior French Army of King Philip VI at Crécy. Calais then became an English town after a siege of almost a year, during which the Scots (allies of France) were defeated at Neville's Cross, Durham and Charles of Blois, the rival claimant for the Duchy of Brittany, was defeated and captured at La Roche Derrien, Brittany.

By now the Black Death had reached European shores from the Far East via trading ships from the Levant (Middle East). Originally arriving at Messina, Sicily the bubonic plague then appeared in Venice and Genoa before landing in Marseille spreading north through France. The shortage of funds hampering Edward's war effort then paled into insignificance when the Black Death arrived in England in 1348 ravaging the four million population by as much as half. The pestilence left Edward desperately short of money and manpower to garrison his recent conquests in Brittany and Normandy whilst even the long term English possession of Gascony, Aquitaine, South West France became vulnerable – the king's difficulties were further exacerbated by the new pastime of football which he promptly banned in 1349.

Philip and his August 1350 successor King John II failed to take advantage of Edward's predicament with a more vigorous prosecution of the war even though supplying Calais by land and from the sea was becoming more difficult. So too the English held territories in Brittany and Gascony where Spanish allies of the French were constantly terrorising English ports and merchantmen with acts of piracy and murder. Edward had to remove this Spanish menace or face losing his lands and conquests in France, he therefore increased his fleet and parked it off Sandwich waiting for an opportunity to punish the Spanish. In August 1350 a Castillian fleet under Don Carlos de la Cerda, a relative of the French king, had sailed up the French coast to Flanders intercepting several English merchants to confiscate their cargo and in the time honoured fashion murder their crews by throwing them overboard. Edward looked to retaliate by repositioning his fifty ships, mainly cogs, off Winchelsea where he boarded the *Cog Thomas* with his ten-year-old son, John of Gaunt. The Black Prince had his own command whilst also present were several of England's finest knights, Henry of Grosmont, Duke of Lancaster (second only to the Black Prince in his election to the Order of the Garter formed by Edward around 1348) William de Bohun Earl of Northampton, William Montagu Earl of Salisbury, Thomas de Beauchamp Earl of Warwick, Richard FitzAlan Earl of Arundel, Sir Reginald Cobham, Sir John Chandos and Sir Walter Manny.

The Castillian fleet soon sailed out of Sluys into the English Channel, De la Cerda confident his forty-four ships including several galleons could out run or overpower any English cogs sent against them. At 16.00 on 29 August 1350 the Spanish came into sight of the English who had been patiently tacking back and forth across the Channel just off Dungeness. The English Admiral Robert, Lord Morley now sailed his ships directly in front of the Spanish galleons, putting their helms up to run on the same course but shortening sail so that his enemy could overtake but only very slowly. Several of the giant Spanish galleons crashed into the smaller English cogs including the *Cog Thomas* which immediately began taking on water. Staying in the fight, however, archers aboard the *Cog Thomas* sent a barrage of arrows against the next Spaniard keeping the Spanish crew off the deck rails to allow a boarding – naval warfare in medieval times meant no cannon but bowmen, grappling and boarding followed by hand-to-hand combat. English men-at-arms climbed onto the galleon to begin a ferocious fight on deck, an exercise that was repeated down the line whilst thousands of their compatriots roared them on from the cliff tops above and from the harbour of Winchelsea. The *Cog Thomas* soon sank but the King had safely transferred as did the Black Prince when his own vessel went down. At least seventeen Spanish ships were captured, De la Cerda escaping later to be made Constable of France.

For the time being the sea routes to France were clear but it would be two years yet before Edward could restart hostilities in earnest, again in Brittany.

29 August 1778

American War of Independence
Battle of Rhode Island

BY MID 1778 the American War of Independence had swung decisively in favour of the home side with the British bottled up as they had been at the onset of the war but now in New York City rather than Boston. The escape route by sea was, however, now obstructed by a French naval fleet under Admiral Count Charles Henri D'Estaing consisting of twelve ships of the line including two massive triple decker, eighty-gunners all firmly on the side of American Independence. D'Estaing though could do little against the Royal Navy protective screen of seven ships of the line under Admiral Richard, Lord Howe (brother of the recently resigned General William Howe) and after eleven days of inactivity he sailed north to join his new American friends in blockading the British naval base on Rhode Island.

The British fleet at Rhode island was no match for the powerful French and to prevent it falling into the wrong hands was torched virtually at first sight of the enemy. The British garrison therefore isolated on the island was 5,000-strong commanded by Major General Robert Pigot but it was not strong enough to defend the whole fourteen mile length, the five regiments in the north in danger of being cut off from those in the south should the Americans and French attempted a landing. On 8 August D'Estaing, with eight ships of the line headed north between Newport Harbour and Conanicut Island trading cannonballs with British defences that were woefully outgunned. This show of force immediately caused Pigot to bring in his northerly regiments but although the move allowed Americans to cross onto the island Pigot was not yet required to make a concerted defence since Howe was approaching from the south to assist. Howe's ships were older, less well-gunned and had been short of hands until a flood of English merchantmen and soldiers, bristling with indignation at French involvement in the Anglo-American dispute, had volunteered. D'Estaing was forced to put to sea to meet Howe's challenge when, as far as the British were concerned, divine providence struck in the form a storm. The French had by far the worst of it with D'Estaing's flagship *Languedoc* being completely dismasted. Howe took advantage, pounding his disabled enemy for nearly two hours before D'Estaing veered off to the south-west. A week later the French fleet limped back toward Rhode Island but refused to support the 10,000 Americans now in the north ready to besiege the British in the south. The now vulnerable D'Estaing instead departed for Boston amid American accusations of treachery.

The Americans began to withdraw from Rhode Island but Pigot had been alerted to their intentions by deserters and moved forces up to attack the American defensive cover line. On 29 August 1778, two Hessian infantry regiments under Lieutenant General Friedrich Wilhelm von Lossberg advanced up the western side of the island whilst two British under Major General Francis Smith advanced up the eastern. Lossberg's Hessians attacked aggressively and pushed American light troops under Colonel John Laurens back onto their main force behind under Quartermaster General Nathanael Greene. Musket volleys and cannon raked the Americans who were then also bombarded from the sea by three British warships. Smith's attack on the American left was met with stronger resistance by Lieutenant Colonel Henry Livingston with both sides being reinforced throughout the battle until Livingston began to give way, retreating back to Quaker Hill. Smith and his flanking Hessians then forced Livingston all the way back onto the main American defences but declined to press on. Back on the American right Greene had begun returning the cannon fire of the three British warships and with Livingston returning to action, now launched a counter-attack on Lossberg. Greene's Rhode Islanders and the Massachusetts Militia began to outflank Lossberg who began his own withdrawal under cover of an all night artillery bombardment. The British had lost 260 men killed and wounded but had again failed to trap a sizable American Army which evacuated over the following two days.

With enemies on all sides it was difficult to see how and where Great Britain could carry on the war. An invasion of South Carolina would go into effect in 1780.

30 August 1942
Second World War
Battle of Alam El Halfa

THE JUNE 1941 Second World War entry of the Soviet Union had been followed six months later by that of the United States of America giving British Prime Minister Winston Churchill two powerful allies against the Tripartite Pact forces of Germany, Italy and Japan (the Axis) but it would still be almost another year before American forces would land in North Africa. Coinciding with Japanese advances at the end of 1941, the German invasion of Russia had been stopped by bad bad weather before Moscow but another German offensive, this time into southern Russia, began in June 1942 toward the iconic city of Stalingrad on the River Volga. The vast Soviet Red Army, shorn of much of its leadership by General Secretary Josef Stalin's 'Great Purge' of 1936, again crumbled, Stalin pleading for Churchill to open another front in the west. The British though could do little beyond the night bombing of German cities and limited objective raids on the German 'Atlantic Wall'. British and American supplies to Russia continued, however, through the Barents Sea and the Persian Corridor – a journey around the Cape of Good Hope through Iran and Soviet Azerbaijan. Protecting this Corridor as well as Egypt and the Suez Canal against the German Afrika Korps and Italians of Generalleutnant Erwin Rommel was now the British 8th Army including Australians, New Zealanders and South Africans under Lieutenant General Neil Ritchie.

In May 1941 the forerunner of the 8th Army, the Western Desert Force of General Richard O'Connor, had been on the verge of victory over the Italians in North Africa before being stripped of troops for an ultimately futile defence of Greece. On his and the Afrika Korps arrival, Rommel had taken full advantage, counter-attacking back to the Egyptian border, capturing O'Connor and besieging Tobruk. Lieutenant General Alan Cunningham then launched several unsuccessful British counter-attacks before being replaced by Ritchie who succeeded in forcing Rommel back to El Agheila, Libya. At the end of long supply lines Ritchie was then counter-attacked and defeated in a series of flanking manoeuvres at Gazala, Libya and Mersa Matruh, Egypt. Commander-in-Chief Middle East, General Claude Auchinleck sacked him and retreated back to El Alamein, both men unfortunate that the Royal Navy had temporarily lost control of the Mediterranean and had not been able to prevent Axis supplies reaching North Africa. Despite taking Tobruk, for which he was promoted to Field Marshal, Rommel's advance now stretched his own supply lines, oil particularly scarce as Auchinleck halted him at El Alamein just sixty miles from Alexandria. Not satisfied, Churchill was desperate for a great victory before the Americans arrived to dominate the war and replaced Auchinleck as CIC Middle East with General Harold Alexander, Lieutenant General Bernard Montgomery taking command of the British 8th Army.

Rommel needed a quick victory to prevent a build up of British armoured strength which would render impossible Axis objectives in Egypt and the Middle East. Unable to attack too far south through the Qattara Depression (impassable for Tanks), Rommel attacked with two Panzer Divisions and the 90th Light Division across southern British minefields which Montgomery, who was accessing enemy plans via Ultra intercepts, had deliberately left weakly defended. At night on 30 August 1942 over 400 German Panzer and Italian tanks advanced only to be caught in the British minefields by British bombers and the British 7th Armoured Division which then withdrew east. By midday on 31 August, German armour was through the minefields and, as expected, swung north to cut British supply lines. Waiting on the Alam El Halfa Ridge, however, were 170 British tanks including ninety-two brand new American built General Grant M3s of the British 22nd Armoured Brigade along with the British 44th and New Zealand 2nd Infantry Divisions. A fierce armoured battle developed with the British tanks ordered not to leave their positions behind the ridge whilst anti-tank units halted a German flank attack further east. With casualties mounting (Montgomery's heavier but Rommel's less affordable) the shortage of fuel added to the Afrika Korps difficulties and they began to withdraw, again harried by British aircraft and tentative British and New Zealand counter-attacks, Montgomery not prepared to incur heavy losses just yet.

Alam El Halfa was Rommel's last Desert offensive, he now dug in behind five miles of minefields attempting to hold down the British 8th Army. Montgomery continued to plan for Churchill's desired offensive that would drive the Axis out of North Africa. It would come at El Alamein on 23 October 1942.

31 August 1813
Napoleonic Wars
Storming San Sebastian

GENERAL SIR ARTHUR Wellesley, Marquess of Wellington, Commander-in-Chief of the 80,000-strong Anglo-Portuguese Army in the Iberian Peninsular also became Commander of Spanish forces in late 1812 with 160,000 Spaniards under his command spread across the entire country. It had been quite a turn around since the 1809 battle of Talavera where the Spanish performance had been so poor, particularly their command, that Wellington had refused to enter into any further cooperation with them at all. Spanish resistance through guerilla warfare (the term has its origins here) against almost overwhelming French forces had been impressive but the resolute British general had little time to wield them into an effective battlefield force. Wellington's 1813 offensive into northern Spain had begun with 25,000 Spaniards under his immediate command, taking advantage of French difficulties following Emperor Napoleon Bonaparte's disastrous 1812 invasion of Russian to defeat Joseph Bonaparte and Marshal Jean Baptiste Jourdan at Vitoria- the decisive battle of the Peninsular War. In Russia, Napoleon and the *Grande Armée* had lost half a million men but after crossing the River Berezina in November 1812 the Corsican General had swiftly returned to Paris to raise a new army, astonishingly putting 170,000 troops in the field in May 1813 at Lutzen against the Russians and the now suddenly emboldened Prussians.

French strength in Spain had again been tapped for this army as it had been the year before, all French forces now marching north having already abandoned the thirty month siege of Cadiz in August 1812. Following Vitoria 100,000 Frenchmen under Marshal Jean de Dieu Soult were left to defend the passes over the Pyrenees into France and the strategic Basque fortress towns of Pamplona and San Sebastian on Spain's north coast. Wellington could not advance through the Pyrenees without first eliminating these threats to his rear, blockading Pamplona whilst besieging San Sebastian on 11 July 1813 with 10,000 men under Lieutenant General Thomas

Graham. Wellington also maintained his main force close by ready to counter any Soult advance from the Pyrenees.

At San Sebastian the Royal Navy anchored offshore as an initial British bombardment destroyed a convent outside a large defensive hornwork protecting the southern walls. The convent ruins were then occupied before another 4-gun battery across the River Urumea to east of the town began a ten day bombardment to create two breaches. A drain leading to the hornwork was also discovered and mined. On 25 July, an assault was launched to coincide with the explosion of the hornwork mine but poor timing and a lack of artillery left the assaulting troops decisively repulsed at the breaches if not exposed in no-man's-land. The siege was then postponed since Soult was indeed attempting to force the passes at Maya and Roncesvalles, succeeding at the latter with 30,000 men to head for Pamplona. Wellington intercepted and defeated him with a force of 24,000 Anglo-Spanish-Portuguese at Sorauren.

Soult limped back to France whilst Wellington resumed the siege of San Sebastian, the garrison of which under General Louis Emmanuel Rey was down to 2,700 effectives due to several recent sorties but who were now at least behind freshly repaired walls. A five-day bombardment restarted with sixty-three heavy British guns testing Rey's handiwork, opening a 200 yard breach in the south-east wall and another in the east wall. At 11.00 on 31 August 1813, San Sebastian was stormed from the south-east by the 5th Infantry Division of the returning Lieutenant General James Leith and from the east across the low tide Urumea by Portuguese Cacadores. Intense volleys of musket from defenders behind inner walls effectively trapped the now dispirited Anglo-Portuguese, stalling the attack for over two hours before Major General Alexander Dickson began an artillery bombardment just a few feet over the heads of his own terrified men. Dickson's gunners succeeded in destroying the inner walls, however, allowing the British assault to recommence, the French defenders fighting bayonet to bayonet back through the burning town to the Urgull Hill Fortress where they surrendered on 8 September.

As had Ciudad Rodrigo and Badajoz so now did San Sebastian witness a brutal sacking. Wine found in the cellars enflamed British violence that today is remembered by an annual candlelit ceremony. The town was completely destroyed and explains why it is now neatly laid out in squares. Wellington had lost another 2,300 men but at last French soil beckoned.

September

"Out of Ammo, God Save the King."

LIEUTENANT COLONEL JOHN FROST,
ARNHEM, 1944

1 September 1880

Afghan Wars
Battle of Kandahar

THE SECOND ANGLO-Afghan War came about in 1878 for exactly the same reasons as had the first forty years before, namely the threat of Russian expansion toward British India. Major General Frederick Roberts invaded the country initially in early 1879 commanding one of three columns that headed into Afghanistan through the Kyber Pass, the Kurum Valley and the Pisheen Valley to depose the ruling Emir, Sher Ali Khan, in favour of his more compliant son Mohammad Yakoub Khan. Roberts had then withdrawn but returned again in September 1879 commanding a much smaller British Indian Army to crush an uprising after the British Representative in Kabul, Louis Cavagnari and his mission had been murdered. Roberts decisively defeated a 50,000-strong Afghan force under Mohammad Jan Khan Wardak outside Kabul before Ayub Khan, Yakoub's brother and the Governor of Herat in Western Afghanistan, launched another rising on Yakoub's abdication, angry at the appointment as emir of his cousin Abdur Rahman Khan. Ayub advanced with 25,000 tribesmen and regular Afghan troops toward the British Bombay Army garrison at Kandahar 300 miles south of Kabul. From Kandahar Major General James Primrose despatched a force of 2,500 British and Indians under Brigadier General George Burrows who attempted to intercept Ayub at Maiwand in July 1880 but with disastrous consequences that shook Victorian Britain every bit as much as had defeat to the Zulu at Isandlwana the year before.

The British Prime Minister William Gladstone, a reluctant imperialist, and his Foreign Minister Granville Leveson-Gower, Lord Granville had been in office for just three months and from the start had been pressing for a withdrawal of all British forces from Afghanistan. Any show of weakness following Maiwand, however, could well lead to a similar apocalyptic disaster as that visited on Major General William Elphinstone's 1842 retreat from Kabul. On 8 August, as Ayub's rebellious Afghans reached Kandahar hot on the trail of Burrows' few survivors, Roberts and 10,000 troops of the Kabul garrison (and 8,000 followers) began the grueling 300 mile march south through the burning heat of the Afghan summer to the city's relief. To the east in Quetta, India Major General Robert Phayre would also march with a reserve of the Bombay Army whilst Lieutenant General Donald Stewart, with support from Emir Abdur Rahman Khan, evacuated the remainder of the Kabul garrison back to India through the Khyber Pass.

Roberts' Kabul Field Force completed their celebrated march in just twenty days, Roberts himself struck with fever riding into Kandahar to order Brigadier General Hugh Gough conduct a reconnaissance of Afghan positions and plan an attack without Phayre. At 09.30 on 1 September 1880 British artillery opened the battle of Kandahar with a bombardment of the village of Baba Wali Kotal to the north-west accompanied by infantry assaults from Highlanders, Punjabis and Gurkhas on the line of Afghan defences further south at Gundimullah Sahibdad and by Highlanders and Sikhs further south still on Gundigan. The opposing armies were similar in strength 11,000 British and Indian against 13,000 Afghans with thirty-two guns a piece but the superior discipline of the British Bengal and Bombay Armies soon began to tell as Roberts' main assault successfully took Gundimullah in fierce hand-to-hand fighting before pressing onto Pir Paimal behind the Afghan defenders at Gundigan. Aware of the imminent trap, the Afghans at Gundigan began to retreat, soon becoming total flight as they accompanied the last defenders of Pir Paimal (minus their entire artillery) in a desperate escape up the Argandab River Valley pursued by Gough's cavalry. Roberts had routed Ayub Khan in a matter of hours, ending the Second Anglo-Afghan War.

The British Indian Army retreated from Afghanistan six months later, Roberts returning to Britain a national hero and becoming Lord Roberts of Kandahar. He later served in the Second Boer War and is celebrated by statues in Kelvingrove Park, Glasgow and Horse Guards Parade, London. Emir Abdur Rahman Khan ruled Afghanistan for the next twenty years but Britain retained control of Afghan foreign policy until the 1919 Third Anglo-Afghan War. The British again invaded Afghanistan in 2001 as part of an ongoing global war on terrorism.

2 September 1807

Napoleonic Wars
Battle of Copenhagen

PRUSSIA HAD WITHDRAWN from the First Coalition against Revolutionary France in 1795, secretly acknowledging French acquisitions west of the River Rhine. Over the next decade, whilst his former partners Austria and Great Britain fought on, King Frederick William III of Prussia pursued peace with France, invading Hanover in 1801 at the behest of Napoleon Bonaparte even though Prussia was, at the time, a member of the League of Armed Neutrality. Though the Elector of Hanover, King George III of England and his Prime Minister William Pitt had no choice but to ignore the incursion, being in no position to resist.

Five years later, however, Napoleon formed the Confederation of the Rhine, sixteen smaller German states that included Hanover, under his direct control rather than that of the defeated Holy Roman Empire (Austria), making him a direct threat to Prussian 'independence'. On the advice of his charming but more aggressive Queen Louisa, Frederick's peace policy was then ditched when he declared war on France that same year as part of the Fourth Coalition formed with the remnants of the third – Britain, Russia and Sweden. An unmitigated disaster, Prussia suffered devastating defeats at the hands of Napoleon at Jena-Auerstadt and his Marshals Joachim Murat and Jean Bernadotte at Erfurt, Halle, Prenzlau and Lubeck, leaving Frederick and his family to flee east. Since the British Army was still no threat to his rear, Napoleon pushed on further east to defeat Russia at Friedland in June 1807, forcing both Tsar Alexander I and King Frederick William to sign the Treaty of Tilsit. Napoleon now had complete control of Europe with only a defensive Sweden and as ever, the United Kingdom of Great Britain and Ireland left to oppose him.

Napoleon, however, had no means of crossing the English Channel to finish off this 'nation of shopkeepers' having suffered several disastrous defeats at the hands of the Royal Navy in 1805–06 and so sought to destroy the British economy with a Europe wide trade embargo on all goods – the Continental System. All Napoleon's conquered and allied states were compelled to employ the system albeit highly inefficiently since most were without a navy. In exchange for French support against Turkey, a complicit Tsar Alexander then began applying pressure on neutral Denmark to cede her sizable naval fleet to France. Though no match for the Royal Navy despite having recovered from Vice Admiral Horatio Nelson's attack in 1801, the Danish fleet could nevertheless potentially severely hamper British seaborne trade, particularly boat building timber. Whilst assembling a fleet of over fifty ships under Admiral James Gambier and 25,000 troops under General William, Lord Cathcart the increasingly concerned British Government of William Cavendish-Bentinck, Duke of Portland insisted Crown Prince Frederick VI of Denmark hand over his navy, promising a return after the war and British protection in the meantime. Also under severe pressure from French diplomats and an approaching French Army, Frederick refused.

On 16 August 1807 Major General Arthur Wellesley landed on the Baltic Island of Zealand with 6,000 infantry, cavalry and artillery, advancing two weeks later on Koge to comprehensively defeat a force of 7,000 Danish militia. Wellesley then advanced on Copenhagen defended by 13,000 men under General Ernst Henrik Peymann who had already evacuated most of the population. Wellesley and Gambier surrounded Copenhagen by land and sea but had no intention of storming the city, instead on 2 September 1807, beginning a three day artillery bombardment with over 5,000 shells fired on the first night alone. Wellesley had recently returned from India where, along with Sir William Congreve, he had been impressed by Mysorean rockets at the 1799 siege of Seringapatam. Congreve had developed them further at Woolwich and had tested them at Boulogne, now employing 300 which, along with a total of 10,000 shells, set Copenhagen ablaze and caused 5,000 casualties. Peymann surrendered but failed to scuttle the Danish fleet, Gambier sailing home seventeen ships of the line, eleven frigates, fourteen brigs and sloops and three gunboats wealthier.

In Britain the bombardment of Copenhagen was highly controversial but justified when Denmark then allied themselves with France. A month later, accused of trading with the British, Portugal was invaded by a French Army marching through Spain. The extension of French forces in the Iberian Peninsular would provide an opportunity for the British Army to begin a liberation of Europe.

2 September 1898

Mahdist Wars
Battle of Omdurman

THE ANGLO-EGYPTIAN reconquest of the Sudan had been ongoing for nearly three years under the meticulous eye of the Sirdar of the Egyptian Army Horatio Herbert Kitchener, a man intent on avenging the 1885 murder of Major General Charles Gordon. Everything had gone to plan, the purpose built Sudan Military Railway now stretched from Wadi Halfa on the Egyptian border to Fort Atbara 175 miles north of Khartoum allowing Kitchener to reinforce at will. Meanwhile the Mahdist leader Khalifa Abdullahi had been nervously sweating in Khartoum all summer, missing opportunities to counter-attack but now prepared to gamble all in a full scale battle on the Kerreri Plains outside Omdurman.

Kitchener's Army consisted of 8,200 British and 17,600 Egyptian infantry including loyal Sudanese and an artillery train of eighty guns and forty-four Maxim guns. The whole force was now transported up the remainder of the Nile in gunboats and steamers (which had been reassembled above the fifth cataract) or by 2,469 horses, 896 mules, 3,524 camels and 229 donkeys along the west bank before concentrating into fighting formation on leaving Royan Island. On 1 September, the 21st Lancers crested the top of the Kerreri Hills to view Khartoum and Omdurman now just four miles away, among them a young Winston Churchill watching in awe when the magnificent spectacle of the Khalifa's *Ansar*, 50,000 spearmen, swordsmen and riflemen wearing the patched jibbah of the Mahdi appeared across a four mile front. Churchill trotted down behind the Jebel Surgham, reporting to Kitchener before being invited to lunch by the confident British staff. Meanwhile the British gunboats steamed further on up the Nile toward Khartoum and Omdurman, blasting the mud forts along the banks before a howitzer began blasting the walls of Omdurman itself, a shell crashing through the domed roof of the Mahdi's tomb. Kitchener wanted to provoke an attack on his defensive position within a Zeriba (thorn bush camp), his gunboats behind on the

Nile but suddenly with seemingly a single command the *Ansar* stopped to a man.

The following morning 2 September 1898 the *Ansar* was again on the move, coming into view of the Zeriba an hour after dawn. The British field guns were joined by the guns and howitzers on the boats behind as 16,000 Mahdists under Osman el Din and Osman Azrak charged the Anglo-Egyptian position. At 2,000 yards the Mahdists were hit by concerted volley fire and then by the Maxim guns, not one of them reaching the British lines. Kitchener did not wait for a second attack despite another 30,000 Mahdists lurking somewhere behind the hills, instead wheeling left he sent the Lancers out to scout ahead as the march to Omdurman resumed. Kitchener was anxious to prevent a street fight but the Khalifa had already detached a force to protect his line of retreat and he now began reinforcing it. The Lancers believed they were faced by 1,000 men whom they resolved to attack with what would be the last full scale cavalry charge in the history of the British Army but in cantering forward beyond the point of no return they realised too late that they faced more than double that number. Accelerating the Lancers smashed into the packed body of men, fighting their way through to the other side before turning to charge back, a desperate hand-to-hand fight raging before a carbine scattered the Mahdists. British losses were unnecessarily heavy but Churchill had survived.

In the meantime the front two Anglo-Egyptian brigades had marched swiftly on creating a gap between them and the rear brigade of Sudanese under Brigadier General Hector Macdonald. The Mahdists, 35,000 of them under the Khalifa himself, now fell upon Macdonald who maintained discipline to parry the poorly coordinated attacks whilst requesting assistance. Kitchener merely ordered him to follow on but then wheeled right to shore up Macdonald's flank and inflict further heavy Mahdist casualties. It had been the Khalifa's last throw of the dice, already perhaps 28,000 of his faithful lay dead or wounded on the Kerreri Plains.

Kitchener marched into Omdurman to destroy the Mahdi's tomb, reputedly keeping the skull as an ink stand – Queen Victoria was not amused and ordered a respectful reburial at Wadi Halfa. Two days later a memorial service was held at Gordon's Palace, Khartoum, the flags of Britain and Egypt raised, the Khedival anthem and *God Save the Queen* sung. For perhaps the only time in his life Kitchener wept, he had avenged Gordon.

3 September 1651

English Civil Wars
Battle of Worcester

THE FIRST ENGLISH Civil War ended on 6 May 1646 when King Charles I handed himself in to Scottish Covenanters besieging Newark. The king had gone to the Scots for protection from the hardline Independents of the Westminster parliament who now felt only an abolition of the monarchy would achieve their objectives. Charles had only to sign the Covenant for safe passage to Scotland but, obduracy had largely been responsible for bringing Charles to this point and it did not fail him now, once he refused and once the Scots had been paid for their military services the king was handed over to the English. Parliament was divided, Presbyterians argued the case for maintaining the monarchy but it was the New Model Army that possessed the real power and the New Model Army was ideologically firmly in the hands of the Independents. Royalist uprisings were crushed in Wales, Kent, Essex and North England as part of the Second Civil War before Charles, having refused to answer in court, was beheaded in Whitehall on 30 January 1649 by an unknown but highly paid executioner. The tearful crowd present groaned as the fateful stroke was delivered suggesting that the populace was not entirely content with the Three Kingdoms of England, Scotland and Ireland becoming a Republic. In Scotland, horrified Covenanters went further, immediately declaring Charles' son to be their new king, Charles II, starting the Third Civil War.

In Ireland the Catholic Confederation, also in fear of the English Independents, then catastrophically allied themselves with the Royalists but in attempting to take Dublin they had been defeated by Michael Jones at Rathmines before Oliver Cromwell and 15,000 Puritans of the New Model Army brutally began to restore English Protestant rule. Meanwhile in Scotland, the guilt-racked Covenanters welcomed Charles II back to British soil in the summer of 1650. For his part Charles attempted to play off the Covenanters with the once formidable James Graham, Marquess of Montrose but when Montrose was defeated at Carbisdale, hanged, drawn and quartered, Charles threw in his lot with the Covenanters, signing the Covenant and becoming head of their army.

Cheered through the streets on his return to London from Ireland, Cromwell then marched for the Scottish Borders with 5,000 men to brilliantly destroy Charles' 23,000-strong army at Dunbar on 3 September 1650. The Covenanters retreated into Scotland, Cromwell following despite the harsh winter to cross the Forth at Stirling deliberately leaving the huge armed camp that was England open to invasion. Charles and 14,000 Covenanters took the bait, marching on a westerly route but with English Parliament garrisons primed to crush all local Royalist uprisings. Cromwell followed on an easterly route, reinforcing and blocking any Royalist advance on London so that by the time Charles arrived at Worcester on 22 August all his lines of retreat and escape were blocked by 28,000 men of the New Model Army.

On 3 September 1651, Parliamentarians under Charles Fleetwood crossed the River Teme south of Worcester against fierce resistance from Highlanders under Colin Pitscottie. On Fleetwood's left Richard Deane attempted to force Powick Bridge but failed dismally leaving the Parliament attack in a stall until Cromwell moved south from the east side of Worcester to launch a flank attack on the Highlanders from across the River Severn. The Highlanders gave ground exposing their colleagues at Powick Bridge who now had no option but to fall back. Watching the battle from Worcester Cathedral, Charles had seen Cromwell's withdrawal from the east of the city and responded with his own attack toward Red Hill with William, Duke of Hamilton attacking toward Perry Wood driving the weakened Parliament infantry back until Cromwell returned to decisively turn the battle. The Royalists were now forced back into Worcester, Charles desperately trying to rally his men as Parliament troops overran the gun battery at Fort Royal and turned it on the city. A running street battle now raged as the Scots tried to escape, 3,000 of them killed and 10,000 captured – the Royalist defeat was total.

Captured Scots were deported to the Caribbean and North America but Charles had escaped. The future king hid in an Oak tree (after which Royal Oak public houses are named) before making an incredible escape to France. Worcester was Cromwell's 'Crowning Mercy' but Republicanism would not work for Britain. Charles restored the monarchy in 1660, two years after Cromwell's death in bed amidst the greatest storm in living memory.

4 September 1346

Hundred Years' War
Siege of Calais

IN JULY 1346, King Edward III of England had invaded Normandy, France claiming the French throne by virtue of being a grandson of King Philip IV of France through his mother Isabella of France. Salic Law, however, which prevented female inheritance, had led to Edward being passed over in favour of Philip of Valois, now Philip VI of France, a grandson of Philip III of France through the male line. Though Edward was a closer relative to the recently deceased King Charles IV of France, it was judged that he could not inherit a claim through his mother which his mother had not possessed herself. Such were the intricacies of medieval politics that would contribute to a century of warfare.

After burning and pillaging his way from St Vaast La Hogue to Caen which he ruthlessly sacked, Edward wrong-footed Philip to cross the Rivers Seine and Somme before turning at Crécy-en-Ponthieu. Against a French Army twice the size the English Army had inflicted a defeat so decisive that much of the nobility of France had been left dead on the field. Of the two options that now lay open to the king, advancing on Paris or retreating to Calais, both entailing a lengthy siege, Edward chose the latter where his fatigued army could be resupplied by sea and a base be established for a future English conquest of all France.

On 4 September 1346 the English king and his victorious army arrived outside the formidable walls of Calais with no siege engines but with orders sent to the Tower of London for all cannon to be shipped across the English Channel. Since he was intent on using the town for his own purposes Edward was highly reluctant to reduce it and consequently prepared for a lengthy blockade to starve the inhabitants into submission. The blockade, however, was not in the slightest effective despite the destruction of hundreds of French vessels along the Normandy coast only months earlier – the inhabitants of Calais received supplies for almost the entire year long duration of the siege. Additionally the garrison commander John de Vienne rid himself early of his *bouches inutiles* (useless mouths), 1,700 of them leaving the walls who Edward, unlike Philip II of France besieging the English at Chateau Gaillard in 1203 and King Henry V of England besieging the French at Rouen in 1418, allowed to pass. Indeed the English king fed them.

As winter approached the English Army was prevented undue suffering in the marshy land around the town by the construction of a wooden town including a market place at which locals could trade but the inhabitants inside Calais also fed well as ships continued to run the blockade. The French King Philip, however, was struck with paralysis, doing no more than tempt the Flemings into reneging on their alliance with the English and imploring the King of Scots, David II, who had spent seven years in exile in France following the 1333 battle of Halidon Hill, to invade North England. An English Army defeated the Scots at Neville's Cross in October 1346 with the hapless David now imprisoned in the Tower of London.

Outside Calais Edward renewed his efforts, reinforcing the spit overlooking the entrance to the port with cannon and increasing the size of the English fleet patrolling the sea entrance. Again De Vienne sent out another 500 *bouches inutiles* but this time the English king's patience would not stretch, condemning them to a miserable existence between the walls and the siege lines. At last, in the summer of 1347, the French king raised himself and a sizeable army, perhaps 40,000 strong to march to the relief of Calais, Philip arrived west of the city on 27 July after half hearted easterly approaches had been repulsed in Flanders by emboldened Flemings. The morale of the beleaguered but heroic garrison soared but Philip's problem was that from the west his army could do nothing, trapped between the English fleet on his left, the well defended marshland on his right and the River Hem to his front the French king had little option but to retreat, Philip challenging Edward to single combat, an offer reputedly accepted by Edward only for Philip to reconsider.

Calais surrendered on 3 August 1347, Edward demanding six of the towns Burghers, including De Vienne, appear before him bareheaded, barefooted, with ropes around their necks and with the keys to the town. Following considerable disagreement they were, however, spared and are commemorated by an 1889 Auguste Rodin sculpture that now stands in Calais town square and in eleven other cities around the globe including the Victoria Tower Gardens, London. Calais would remain an English town for the next 211 years.

5 September 1781
American War of Independence
Battle of Chesapeake Bay

BY EARLY 1781 a few German mercenaries apart, Great Britain was friendless. Having benefited from empire building during the Seven Years' War two decades previous whilst they left the bulk of the fighting to their European allies, the British now faced not only General George Washington and the American Continental Army but also France and Spain. The two latter had been impressed by American resistance and had seized the opportunity to diminish British influence in North America, reclaim territories previously lost (including Gibraltar and several Caribbean Islands) and even threaten an invasion of Britain. In North America, after the disasters of 1777, British Commander-in-Chief Henry Clinton favoured a war of attrition but at the behest of King George III and his Secretary of State for the Colonies George Germain, Lord Sackville, who desired a more vigorous prosecution of the war, the attack had been switched to the southern states of Georgia, Virginia and the Carolinas.

Initially the small British Army of Lieutenant General Charles, Lord Cornwallis seemed to be restoring some degree of hope, 1780 successes at Charleston and Camden were followed in March 1781 with another at Guildford Court House. The latter and the campaign itself, however, had been conducted in a difficult climate and had come at a price Cornwallis could not afford. Additionally hampered by extensive lines of communication, Cornwallis now had little option but to leave the Carolinas to his enemies, retreating south to Wilmington on the North Carolina coast before sailing north to Petersburg, Virginia, where he joined forces with 2,500 men under the American deserter Brigadier General Benedict Arnold and Major General William Phillips. Cornwallis arrived in May to find Phillips dead and assumed command, almost trapping French troops and the Virginia Militia under Gilbert du Motier, Marquis de Lafayette at Richmond before receiving an order from Clinton in New York requesting him to construct a deep water port through which he could be supplied. In July 1781 against Arnold's advice, Cornwallis began building at Yorktown, Chesapeake Bay.

Washington favoured an American attack on New York City but was dissuaded by the Commander of French forces in America Marshal Jean Baptiste Donatien de Vimeur, Comte de Rochambeau and instead made the 'Celebrated March' south to besiege Cornwallis in Yorktown. Meanwhile the entire French fleet under Admiral Francois Joseph Paul de Grasse with additional reinforcements sailed from Saint Domingue (Haiti) to Virginia. In New York, British Admiral Thomas, Baron Graves became aware that French Admiral Jacques Melchior Saint Laurent, Comte de Barras was also sailing from Newport, Rhode Island, assuming correctly that he was to rendez-vous with De Grasse at Chesapeake. Graves departed New York with nineteen ships of the line and arrived off Chesapeake Bay on 5 September 1781 to find the French fleet at anchor. Hurriedly De Grasse sent twenty-four ships of the line, most of them undermanned, out to give battle but on exiting Chesapeake Bay he was south of Graves on the opposite tack. The British Admiral then turned his whole line east to sail on converging lines with De Grasse and opened fire at 16.00 when the van of HMS *Intrepid* and HMS *Shrewsbury* came within range of their French counterparts. The French, however, initially had the advantage of firing broadsides with superior gunnery whereas *Intrepid* and *Shrewsbury* were firing only from their bow guns. The British fire was also limited due the north-easterly wind forcing the closure of their lower gun decks but having the weather gage they quickly closed to begin broadsiding – the French, as usual, aiming for the British rigging in a contest where the ships of both sides were almost at boarding distance. After an hour the French van began to pull away leaving the centre of each line to come into action but with hardly the same ferocity and the rear barely at all. For a week the two fleets then shadowed each other without coming into any serious action before De Grasse turned back for Chesapeake where he combined with Barras to continue the blockade of Cornwallis in Yorktown.

Badly damaged, Graves sailed back to New York leaving Yorktown surrounded by 19,000 French and American troops and thirty-six French ships of the line. On 19 October 1781 Graves would sail again with 7,000 reinforcements in twenty-five ships in a last desperate bid to save King George's America.

6 September 1814

American War of 1812
Battle of Plattsburgh

NAPOLEON BONAPARTE'S DETERMINATION to defeat Great Britain by way of a trade embargo, the Continental System, had led to an 1807 French invasion of the Iberian Peninsular and a disastrous 1812 invasion of Russia which resulted in the virtual destruction of his once invincible *Grande Armée*. Britain's efforts against France at the outset of the French Revolutionary and Napoleonic Wars had been almost entirely confined to sea where the Royal Navy blockaded the French coast. The blockade and Britain's retaliation to the Continental System impacted across the Atlantic where United States of America shipping was prohibited to trade with France (their ally from the American War of Independence) and American sailors were impressed into the service of the Royal Navy as British deserters. Whilst these transgressions were enough to anger an aspiring nation that was just thirty years old, American ambition to expand west was also impacted by British support for the Indian Confederacy of Tecumseh, Chief of the Shawnee. By June 1812 the United States could tolerate British intimidation no longer and declared war for the first time in her history but, with few muscles to flex and too few dollars forthcoming from the Banks of New England, were immediately defeated in their attempt to annex Upper Canada (South Ontario).

In return the small British forces defending Canada could make few inroads into US territory especially when Tecumseh was defeated and killed at the 1813 Battle of the Thames, effectively ending the participation of the Indian Confederacy. On Napoleon's abdication in April 1814, however, 16,000 battle-hardened British troops headed from the Iberian Peninsular across the Atlantic, 4,500 of them under Major General Robert Ross landing in Chesapeake Bay to attack Washington DC. After routing 6,500 American militia under Brigadier General William Winder in front of a spectating President James Madison at Bladensburg the British then, for good measure, burnt much of the city including the White House.

A week later Lieutenant General George Prevost, British Governor General of the Canadas, and 12,000 troops marched south down the Richelieu River to Lake Champlain and the town of Plattsburgh, Upper New York, where they hoped to restore British naval supremacy. The inhabitants of Plattsburgh fled leaving the defence to 1,500 American regulars and 2,000 untrained militia under Brigadier General Alexander Macomb. On 6 September 1814, Macomb's forward unit of 450 regulars and 700 militia encountered the British, fighting a delaying action back to Plattsburgh and a defensive position across the Saranac River where an artillery exchange ensued for the next few days. Prevost waited for the British fleet of the Frigate HMS *Confiance*, three other warships and twelve gunboats, hoping to trap the American fleet in Cumberland Bay whilst he simultaneously attacked Macomb on land. At last on 11 September with a north-east wind the British fleet under Captain George Downie rounded Cumberland Head and entered the bay, heading toward where the outgunned Master Commandant Thomas Macdonough had anchored the prevocatively named American flagship *Saratoga* alongside *Ticonderoga, Preble* and *Eagle*. Downie attacked immediately, stunning the Americans with broadsides before he was killed as soon as the US ships returned fire. Macdonough now completely outmanoeuvred the British forcing *Confiance* to strike her colours. Meanwhile Prevost's land attack was running late. After a dismal artillery duel Major General Thomas Brisbane led a brigade in a frontal feint attack over the Saranac which was easily repulsed while Major General Frederick Robinson's and elements of Major General Manley Power's brigades advanced over a ford three miles further upstream against the American left flank. When Prevost received news of Downie's defeat in Cumberland Bay, however, he called off the attack, Brisbane retreating but leaving Robinson's advanced light companies isolated. The debacle cost the British over 700 men and four warships.

Prevost was relieved of command in Canada and returned to a Court Martial in England. The defeat at Plattsburgh lessened Britain's bargaining power at the Treaty of Ghent but the war would continue until news of that treaty could reach the United States.

6 September 1914

The Great War
Battle of the Marne

 PRUSSIA HAD COME to the rescue of Great Britain in 1815 on the field of Waterloo but a century later, having unified the previously independent German states under her Crown, she had become an aggressive military nation under Kaiser Wilhelm II intent on European hegemony accompanied by territorial gains in both east and west. The June 1914 assassination of Archduke Franz Ferdinand of Austria Hungary had given the Kaiser the *casus belli* he required but it also invoked a domino effect of alliances that threw the whole of Europe into war, all parties selling their cause as one of defence but it was German troops marching into Belgium as much as a Triple Entente with France and Russia that brought Great Britain into the conflict.

The British Expeditionary Force (BEF) had sailed for northern France on 7 August, initially just four infantry and one cavalry division, followed shortly by another two infantry, 80,000 men, all of them highly trained professional soldiers that with a Lee Enfield rifle could hit a man sized target at 300 yards, fifteen times a minute. On their right was the larger conscript army of France, initially seventy-two infantry and cavalry divisions, 825,000 men that would soon grow to three million but the allies of the Entente were soon on the retreat. The German Schlieffen Plan required a giant right hook through Belgium, down through north-west France encircling Paris, the French Army and the BEF from the west and south. Meanwhile French General Joseph Joffre who knew only of offence proposed to attack the German Army through Alsace and Lorraine failing to understand that this tactic would aid the completion of the Schlieffen Plan through a 'revolving door' effect, in turn exposing the French rear. Speed was of the essence for German General Feldmarschall Helmuth von Moltke for he would shortly need to deal with the Russians on the Eastern Front but by keeping his left strong he neutralised Joffre's attack in the 'Battle of the Frontiers' to force the whole French Army and the BEF into a retreat from Mons to the outskirts of

Paris. Critically, however, Moltke had not yet defeated them. Approaching Paris, the German 1st and 2nd Armies of General Alexander von Kluck and Karl von Bulow then mistakenly swung south-east across the north of the city rather than the south, still attempting to encircle the French but in doing so too early exposed their right flank to the BEF and the new French 6th Army of General Michel Manoury. It was the end of the great retreat, sensing his opportunity the decisive Joffre moved up General Franchet D'Esperey's French 5th Army and General Ferdinand Foch's French 9th Army for a counter-attack but Field Marshal Sir John French commanding the BEF, upset at French failures over the past few weeks, initially would not move.

On 6 September 1914, French, in tears at fearing the worst, promised Joffre 'All a man can do our fellows will do' and advanced with D'Esperey's 5th French to drive a wedge between Von Kluck's German 1st Army fighting Manoury's 6th French in the west and Von Bulow's German 2nd Army fighting Foch's 9th French further east. By 8 September both Von Kluck and Von Bulow had fallen back to the River Marne but still hoped to defeat Manoury's 6th French until 600 bright red Parisian taxicabs reputedly arrived with the reinforcing French 7th Infantry Division. The BEF and D'Esperey's 5th French continued to press the attack widening the gap between Von Kluck and Von Bulow with Moltke in Luxembourg too far back to coordinate the battle. For four days the fighting raged unabated over the fields north of Paris, both sides of more than a million men attacking with little thought of digging for cover and consequently suffering the highest daily casualty rates of the entire war (each 250,000 in total). On 9 September Von Kluck and Von Bulow could hold no longer and began a 50-mile fighting retreat back to the River Aisne. For the Entente the 'Miracle of the Marne' had been completed.

The Germans began to dig in on the high ground north of the Aisne repulsing waves of mainly French attacks but Joffre and French had defeated the Schlieffen Plan. Now facing a war on two fronts Moltke had a nervous breakdown and was replaced by General Erich von Falkenhayn who would try to outflank Joffre and French in a 'Race to the Sea' that would culminate in October at Ypres.

7 September 1191
Third Crusade
Battle of Arsuf

IN 1095 POPE Urban II called for a Christian military offensive in Anatolia (Turkey) and the Holy Land (Lebanon, Israel, Palestine, Syria and Jordan) where the Byzantine Empire was under threat from Muslim Seljuk Turks migrating from the east. Urban's main objective was to end 461 years of Muslim rule in the city of Jerusalem but also unite Christianity following the 1054 'Great Schism' between the Catholic and Orthodox Churches. This First Crusade successfully took Jerusalem after a one-month siege and a bloodbath of a sacking but in 1147 a Second Crusade was ordered by Pope Eugene III after the fall of the Crusader State of Edessa to Imad ad-Din Zengi. French and German armies met at Jerusalem but a siege of Damascus proved a step too far and although gains were made some years later in Egypt these merely introduced a new enemy, the Sultan of Egypt, Salah ad-Din Yusuf ibn Ayyub (Saladin). In 1183 Saladin defeated the Zengids in an all Muslim conflict to unite Egypt and Syria before his Saracen Army defeated a Crusader Army at Hattin. As another fifty-two towns fell to Saladin including Beirut, Acre, Nablus, Jaffa, Ascalon and Jerusalem, Pope Gregory VIII issued a papal bull, *Audita Tremendi* calling for a Third Crusade. This call was answered by King Henry II of England whose 1170 murder of the Archbishop of Canterbury, Thomas Becket, had been giving him no end of trouble and no doubt still weighed heavily upon his conscience. Henry died, however in 1189, recognising his third son as King of England, Richard I 'the Lionheart' who honoured his father's papal pledge by joining his English Army with that of Philip II of France, the pair travelling east by sea whilst that of another ally, Frederick Barbarossa, Holy Roman Emperor, marched overland.

Philip reached the Holy Land where he joined Conrad of Montferrand, Guy Lusignan (who both claimed the throne of Jerusalem) and Leopold V, Duke of Austria (Barbarossa having died en route) who were besieging Acre whilst they themselves were besieged by Saladin. Richard, however, had stopped in Limassol,

Cyprus to rescue and marry Berengaria of Navarre as well as take control of the island from Manuel and Isaac Komnenos. On his belated arrival at Acre Richard successfully concluded the siege before a row saw Philip and Leopold head home. Undeterred, the Lionheart and Saladin conducted a civilised exchange of gifts and a less civilised execution of prisoners before the Lionheart marched his estimated 20,000-strong Crusader Army through the August heat south toward Jaffa, from there intending to advance on Jerusalem. Supported by a 200-strong fleet offshore the Crusaders maintained a strict defensive formation, French and English infantry to the outside, Knights Templar in the vanguard and Knights Hospitaller in the rear fending off attacks from Saladin's mounted bowmen and missile throwers.

On 7 September 1191 the Crusaders were only a seven-mile march from Arsuf but Saladin was about to increase their discomfort with a full-scale attack on the plain beyond the Forest of Arsuf. On exiting the forest the Crusaders came under attack for several hours once again from Saracen mounted bowmen until Saladin began concentrating his attacks on the rear, the Hospitallers holding the Saracens with crossbow and spear as they marched backwards. Soon beginning to lag behind the centre, however, Garnier de Nablus, Grand Master of the Knights Hospitaller, concerned at his position, losses and especially his honour, pleaded for a counter-attack but was refused by the Lionheart who was waiting for the Saracen horsemen to tire before delivering a decisive blow. Nablus could not wait and led his own knights and the French into the Saracen right. A furious Richard now had no choice but to commit there and then, ordering Richard de Sable, Grand Master of the Knights Templar to attack the Saracen left. As both Saracen flanks reeled backwards under the sudden onslaught Richard attacked the centre with Englishmen and Normans. It was too much, the Saracens broke and fled, pursued for a mile by the victorious Crusaders.

Although Saladin had lost several thousand men (Richard several hundred) he quickly recovered to harass the Crusaders on to Jaffa. Richard never attempted a capture of Jerusalem but instead agreed a treaty that allowed Christians to visit the sacred city. Of nine Crusades (against heretics as well as Islam) only that of Richard the Lionheart was predominantly English. Though Richard's coat of arms featured one or two lions passant for most of his life, he added a third shortly before his death – the original three lions passant of todays royal coat of arms and the emblem of the England football and cricket teams – they represent the Kingdom of England and the Duchies of Normandy and Aquitaine.

8 September 1755

French and Indian War
Battle of Lake George

THE TRUCE CREATED by the 1748 Treaty of Aix-la-Chapelle at the end of the War of the Austrian Succession had been broken in 1754 thousands of miles to the west in the North American hinterland of the Ohio Valley. Anxious to protect their fur trade French settlers and their American Indian allies had forced British settlers migrating into disputed territories from the east coast back whence they had come. The British Colonial administration reacted by sending a small force under Colonel George Washington to rectify the situation only for Washington to be victorious at Jumonville Glen but then surrender at Fort Necessity. Ironically Washington had started a conflict fighting for the British against the French that would ultimately end nearly three decades later with him defeating the British with the French. With Washington's rise to fame still some distance in the future Major General Edward Braddock planned four invasions of the disputed areas south-east of the St Lawrence River, Lake Ontario and Lake Erie but within months Braddock was dead, dying from a gunshot wound incurred at the disastrous July 1755 Battle of Monungahela, the survivors of his column spared having their scalps nailed to a tree only down to the leadership of Washington. In August 1755 another British invasion force of 1,500 colonial militia under Major General William Johnson and 200 Mohawks under Hendrick Theyanoguin then marched up the River Hudson into Upstate New York to attack the French Fort Saint Frederic at Crown Point on Lake Champlain. Having limited military experience Johnson had only recently been promoted to Major General but he had previously been the British agent to the Iroquois League, spoke Mohawk and had been adopted as an honorary chief – the British had failed to win American Indian allies in the Ohio Valley, they were not going to fail in the Hudson Valley.

On reaching Lac Saint Sacrament, south of Champlain, Johnson renamed the lake after his king, George II, forming camp at Fort Edward before an intended advance north up the lakes to attack the French Fort Saint Frederic. The French, however, were well warned of Johnson's intentions and had sent General Jean Erdman, Baron Dieskau with 600 Canadiens, 600 Caughnawagas, Mohawks, Abenaki American Indians and 200 French regulars to oppose the advance. Dieskau took an easterly route for Fort Edward while Johnson was already camped fourteen miles to the north of it but the two forces turned toward each other when Johnson became aware of Dieskau's threat and Dieskau's Indians refused to attack Fort Edward's cannon.

Johnson sent Colonel Ephraim Williams back to Fort Edward with 1,000 Massachussets and Connecticut Militia and his 200 Mohawks but they were stopped short, marching into a French ambush set by Dieskau on 8 September 1755. The French and Indian fire was overwhelming, Williams and Theyanoguin were killed almost immediately but a desperate British retreat covered by Lieutenant Colonel Seth Pomeroy and the surviving Mohawks inflicted heavy casualties on the pursuing French including Jacques Legardeur de Saint Pierre, the French equivalent of the British Johnson. Pomeroy retreated back to Johnson's camp closely followed by Dieskau but once again Dieskau's Indians refused to assault an entrenched position, especially one which contained many of their Mohawk brethren. The infection spread to the Canadiens who also refused. Dieskau now led by example, marching his French regulars in close order straight for the camp where they were blasted by grapeshot before delivering several volleys of musket. Johnson and Dieskau were both wounded before the French retreated. Those French and Indians that chose not to fight soon had their own problems, retreating only to encounter a 120-strong British ambush set by Nathaniel Folsom's New Hampshire and New York provincial militias who had sortied from Fort Edward.

Johnson had won an important victory in stopping the French advance down the Hudson Valley. Although his own advance had faltered he built Fort William Henry on Lake George, forming part of a chain of forts west to Lake Ontario. One of these, Fort Bull, would come under attack the other side of winter in March 1756.

9 September 1513

Anglo-Scottish Wars
Battle of Flodden

BY THE EARLY sixteenth century Venetian power had spread across North and East Italy to such an extent that a concerned Pope Julius II countered the threat to his own Italian interests by excommunicating the republic and forming the League of Cambrai with Spain (Aragon), the Holy Roman Empire and France who also possessed significant territory in Italy. After the 1509 Venetian defeat at Agnadello the Pope then considered King Louis XII of France rather than the Doge Leonardo Loredan, to be a greater threat and changed sides, forming a Holy League in 1511 against France in conjunction with the Doge, Maximilian I Holy Roman Emperor, King Ferdinand II of Aragon and by way of the latter's daughter, Catherine of Aragon's husband, King Henry VIII of England. Though the relationship between the Vatican and Henry would eventually breakdown, adding to the 1054 Great Schism of the Christian Church with the 1529 Reformation, Henry's motives to side with the Pope included his ambition to retake Aquitaine, a long time English territory lost at the end of the Hundred Years' War over half a century previous.

Attacked by England, Louis followed a succession of French kings by invoking the 'Auld Alliance' with Scotland and the King of Scots, James IV who although Henry's brother-in-law needed little encouragement to attack England after two decades of poor relations and the more recent English murder of his Sea Captain Andrew Barton, a privateer of dubious morals. Henry disregarded a Scottish ultimatum to continue his siege of Therouanne but accused James of treachery in his absence and warned that any Scottish invasion of England would be strongly resisted. In turn, James disregarded the King of England's ultimatum and invaded Northumberland in August 1513 with an army of 30,000. The English regent, Queen Catherine was, however, had already prepared for such an eventuality. Thomas Howard, Earl of Surrey, who had been levying soldiers in the Northern Counties received the banner of St Cuthbert (for centuries carried against the Scots) from Durham Cathedral to join with Thomas Lovell at Newcastle who had been similarly levying in the Midlands. The English Army was additionally augmented by the arrival from France of Surrey's son Thomas Howard, Lord High Admiral and another 1,000 men, 26,000 in total.

After marching to Wooler, Northumberland, Surrey discovered that the Scots had moved from Ford to Flodden Hill, a defensive position of enormous strength which Surrey declined to attack. Instead he marched north leading many to believe he was about to invade Scotland but on 9 September 1513 his English Army was in fact marching to attack James' rear at Flodden. James left his position on Flodden Hill for a march of a mile north to the equally strong Branxton Hill and formed into five battles, the left under Alexander Gordon, Earl of Huntly, left centre John Lindsay, Earl of Crawford and William Graham, Earl of Montrose, right centre himself, and right Archibald Campbell, Earl of Argyll and Matthew Stewart, Earl of Lennox with one behind, Adam Hepburn, Earl of Bothwell, all separated by cannon. The English were in four battles, another of Surrey's sons Edmund Howard, on the right, the Lord High Admiral in the centre and Surrey on the left, a true family effort supported from behind by Thomas, Lord Dacre.

An artillery duel began at about 16.00 with the more experienced English gunners getting the better of their Scottish counterparts whose more powerful cannon largely flew too high. The English cannon fire sufficiently agitated Huntly on the Scottish left to break ranks, running down the hill to attack Edmund, the majority of whose battle immediately fled. Those that did stand, however, were quickly supported by Dacre's mounted reserve whilst the rest of the Scottish Army were now following Huntly's example with an advance down through the cannon fire to join battle along the whole front. James initially forced back Surrey on the English left before being halted in bitter hand-to-hand fighting. The battle then turned with the late arrival of Edward, Lord Stanley and his longbowmen on the extreme English left, sending Argyll and Lennox to flight and consequently leaving James' centre badly exposed. The fighting continued for several hours with the English archers and billmen gradually overcoming the Scottish pikemen. King of Scots James IV, hit by an arrow, died with 5–10,000 of his countrymen.

North Italy remained under part French, part Venetian rule. Italian Wars would lead to more Franco-Scottish-English conflict three decades later.

10 September 1547

Anglo-Scottish Wars
Battle of Pinkie Cleugh

THE 1542 SCOTTISH defeat at Solway Moss and subsequent death of King James V of Scotland had given King Henry VIII of England an opportunity to secure his border with Scotland. The Scots, however, were encouraged by King Francis I of France to enact the 'Auld Alliance' against Henry who had allied himself with Charles V, Holy Roman Emperor against France in the Italian Wars (a long running dispute over ownership of the Duchy of Milan). Henry now proposed a 'Union of the Crowns' by marrying his son Edward by his deceased third wife Jane Seymour to Mary, Queen of Scots, grand-daughter of James IV of Scotland (killed at Flodden 1513) and his Queen, Henry's sister, Margaret Tudor. The proposal was not unacceptable to all Scots and the Treaty of Greenwich was duly signed on 1 July 1543 by James Hamilton, Earl of Arran, the Protestant Regent of Scotland – Edward was five years old and Mary just one. Following the signing, however, Henry insisted that Mary be raised in Protestant England rather than remain under the influence of her pro Catholic French mother, Mary of Guise (who had once spurned Henry's marriage proposal) but pro Catholic, pro French Scots under Cardinal David Beaton moved Mary to Stirling Castle under a 3,500 strong guard. Arran, who had previously opposed Beaton, then embraced Catholicism and repudiated the Treaty of Greenwich by consenting to Mary's betrothal to Francis, Dauphin of France (later King Francis II), destroying Henry's ambitions altogether.

Pained by Scottish treachery and a continuously weeping leg sore suffered jousting in 1536, a furious Henry then began bullying the Scots with violent raids across the border, the 'Rough Wooing'. The Scots would not submit and took advantage of an English invasion of France to prevail in battle at Ancrum Moor in 1545. Henry was more concerned about an imminent French invasion of England and defeated a French fleet in the Solent that same year although with the loss of his flagship Mary Rose. In January 1547 after years of poor health, clinical obesity to the extent he required a cart to be moved, Henry died leaving Edward to become

King of England aged just nine. Edward's uncle, his mother Jane's older brother, Edward Seymour, Duke of Somerset then became Lord Protector of England for the remainder of Edward's minority.

A supporter of the 'Union of the Crowns' Somerset took up Henry's cause, marching across the border on 1 September 1547 with 12,000 infantry and 4,000 cavalry whilst eighty warships under Edward, Lord Clinton sailed up the east coast of Scotland into the Firth of Forth. Skirmishing ensued until on 9 September Somerset reached the River Esk on the far side of which were 25,000 Scots, the left under George Gordon, Earl of Huntly, left centre Highlanders under Archibald Campbell, Earl of Argyll, centre Arran, centre right Archibald Douglas, Earl of Angus and the right Alexander, Earl of Home. Home's cavalry then foolhardily crossed the Esk to provoke an English attack, succeeding so absolutely that they were decisively routed with substantial losses.

The following day, 10 September 1547, Somerset advanced on Inveresk Hill, south of the Scottish line, from where his field artillery could combine with the English fleet on the Forth for a massive bombardment. Devoid of Home's cavalry, Arran could not match or attack the English artillery and his infantry were too close to disengage. He therefore took the only other option available which was to form a massed phalanx of pikemen (as had Robert the Bruce at Bannockburn over two centuries before) and advanced to deliver a knockout blow before the English could fully deploy. It nearly worked but the advancing Scots came under a terrible fire from Clinton's fleet as well as from mercenary Spanish arquebuses to their front. Somerset's heavy cavalry then charged, halting the Scots for a bloody battle of pikes, bills and battle axes with their English counterparts before the latter disengaged. The Scots miraculously held the field but were again pounded by English offshore and onshore artillery, massed bowmen and the Spanish arquebuses who could not miss the densely packed pikemen. The Scots broke and fled with Somerset's cavalry instantly in hot pursuit. Between 5–10,000 men lost their lives.

Mary sailed for France becoming French Queen Consort in 1559 but on Francis' death returned to Scotland in 1561. Her troubled reign would culminate in the 1568 Battle of Langside. It would be a Scottish king that would eventually unify the Crowns, James VI of Scotland, James I of England.

11 September 1297

Anglo-Scottish Wars
Battle of Stirling Bridge

IN 1291 KING Edward I of England had been appointed by the Scots to arbitrate on who should be King of Scotland. After a ceremony in which Edward was recognised as the direct Lord of Scotland he elected John Balliol from the thirteen possible candidates to take the Crown. The task completed, Edward duly returned to his own realm but still considered himself Lord Paramount of Scotland and that, as such, Balliol owed him fealty. The idea of having their king pay homage to an English king was as appetising for most Scots as it was for the English to have their king pay homage to a French king despite many of them owning lands in each others realms. As did a succession of English kings, however, Balliol begrudgingly submitted but on his weakness Scots rebelled to form a council of twelve who signed a treaty of alliance with France just as Edward was ordering them to raise an army against France.

In 1296 an apoplectic Edward marched north with a 25,000-strong English Army to mercilessly sack the then Scottish port of Berwick, reducing the town to rubble as the blood of over 7,000 inhabitants ran through the streets. Edward then defeated the Scots in a mounted battle at Dunbar, imprisoned Balliol in the Tower of London and confiscated the Stone of Scone on which all Scottish kings had previously been crowned, fitting it under a wooden chair in Westminster Abbey (it was returned in 1996). By 1297, however, Scotland was in open revolt against English garrisons, in the north led by Andrew Moray and at Lanark by William Wallace who murdered Sir William Haselrig, the English garrison commander. Large numbers of Scots rallied to the cry of independence which then gained additional spiritual impetus when the bishop of Glasgow, Robert Wishart joined. The rebels also began attracting nobles including William the Hardy, Lord Douglas who had only recently sworn an oath of fealty to Edward to save his own skin at Berwick. Edward, campaigning in France, ordered Robert the Bruce, Earl of Carrick and Governor of Carlisle (himself a strong candidate for the Scottish throne) to attack Douglas whilst Sir Henry Percy and Robert, Baron de Clifford marched against Wallace and Moray. Bruce had supported Edward against the Welsh a decade earlier but now defected to the Scots before the two armies met across Loch Irvine on 9 July 1297. So great was Scottish internal strife, however, that several nobles then defected in the opposite direction to the English including the vacillating Bruce and Douglas.

Wallace and Moray still controlled Scotland north of the River Forth apart from Dundee which they now besieged. John de Warenne, Earl of Surrey and Sir Hugh de Cressingham, a man despised by the Scots, were sent to relieve Dundee with 2,000 cavalry and 7,000 infantry but would first have to cross the Forth by the narrow wooden bridge at Stirling Castle, the other side of which, on Abbey Craig, were camped Wallace and Moray with a further 10,000 Scots. Arriving on the 10 September the English camped south of the river and opened fruitless negotiations with the defiant Wallace advising that he had come not to make peace but to do battle. The next morning, 11 September 1297, instead of fording the Forth lower downstream, Cressingham inexplicably led the English just two horsemen abreast across Stirling Bridge as Wallace and Moray watched and waited on Abbey Craig. After about two hours the two Scots launched their attack with much of the English Army still on the south bank of the Forth, the English heavy cavalry reacting to protect the bridgehead by charging the oncoming spearmen but held by the sheer weight of Scottish numbers. As the Scots continued to surge forward they gained control of the east side of the bridge, cutting off the line of retreat to those English knights and bowmen trapped to the north. A desperate battle for survival now raged with many Englishmen attempting to swim the river. After an hour of fierce fighting all resistance had disintegrated, 5,000 Englishmen had been butchered or drowned including Cressingham who was reputedly flayed alive by his captors, his skin used by Wallace as a baldrick for his sword.

Surrey burnt the bridge and abandoned the garrison at Stirling Castle before retreating back to Berwick. Moray was mortally wounded in the battle and died two months later. King Edward returned from France to address the situation in Scotland himself. He would face Wallace at Falkirk the following year.

11 September 1709 n.s
War of the Spanish Succession
Battle of Malplaquet

THE WAR OF the Spanish Succession had rumbled on for eight years bringing economic despair to the majority of the participants, particularly France. The harsh winter of 1708–09, the Royal Navy blockade of the French coast and the capitulation of Pope Clement XI in Italy, freeing thousands of Austrians to fight in the Low Countries, had eventually brought King Louis XIV of France to the negotiating table. Louis, however, could not agree to Holy Roman Empire (Austria, Germany) and British demands that he remove his grandson, the Bourbon King Philip V from the Spanish throne. Philip though, was far more popular in Spain than the Habsburg pretender Archduke Charles of Austria and far more secure after Anglo-Dutch-Portuguese armies of the Grand Alliance had been heavily defeated at Almansa in 1707 and La Gudina in May 1709.

Though himself struggling Louis still had a large military presence in the field but was content to maintain a defence along his northern borders with the Spanish Netherlands and on the River Rhine much to the frustration of his Marshal Claude Louis Hector de Villars. Unable to bring the Bourbon French and Bavarians to a decisive battle the equally frustrated Captain General of the Grand Alliance John Churchill, Duke of Marlborough instead besieged Tournai and Ypres. Tournai fell in time but Marlborough then moved east to Mons rather than remain at Ypres, a decision that would have been greatly appreciated at the nadir of human conflict 208 years later. Louis realised that Marlborough's move, if successful, could expose his eastern flank and accordingly ordered Villars to support the French garrison at Mons.

In August 1709 the French Marshal moved up to Malplaquet where he was reinforced by the sixty-five-year-old Louis Francois, Duc de Boufflers, the Franco-Bavarian Army now close enough to Mons to threaten the besieging forces of the Alliance. Marlborough could not ignore this threat and after a delay due to the caution of his fellow generals resolved to attack Villars' 75,000 men. The delay, however, had been put to good use by Villars whose flanks enjoyed the natural protection of the Forests of Lagnières on the right, Taisnières on the left and a series of man made redoubts to the front. Villars held his cavalry behind the three mile front, ready to move wherever required once Marlborough committed the 86,000 men of the Grand Alliance.

At 07.30 on 11 September 1709 the bloodiest battle of the eighteenth century began with the obligatory artillery duel before General Johann Matthias von der Schulenburg advanced with Prussian, Austrian and British infantry against French positions in Taisnières whilst General Henry Withers moved around the same French left flank. Bitter fighting raged with Villars requesting reinforcements from Boufflers before a musket ball shattered his knee. Boufflers on the French right could not comply because he was now under attack himself from Dutch and Scots under John William Friso, Prince of Orange who had inherited the principality on the death of England's King William III. Orange had been ordered only to hold the French but instead he pressed a full attack which, though severely distressing the defenders, also resulted in horrific Alliance casualties from French cannon and disciplined volley fire. As the Alliance attack was held on the French right, Marlborough launched another 30,000 man attack on the French left, the wounded Villars desperately moving men from his centre which was in turn attacked by George Hamilton, Earl of Orkney. The French centre then gave way as Orkney's infantry stormed into the redoubts allowing British and Prussian cavalry to gallop through on to their French counterparts beyond. The whole front now descended into a bloody mass of men and horse fighting with bayonet and sword, the brave French cavalry, the *Maison du Roi*, driving their British and Prussian counterparts back several times only to repeatedly run into concentrated Grand Alliance volley fire from Orkney's men in the redoubts.

Having exacted a price of 20,000 Alliance casualties Boufflers ordered a retreat, Villars claiming 'if it please God to give your Majesty's enemies another such victory, they are ruined'. Villars himself had lost 10,000 men, the butchers bill shocking the whole of Europe. Marlborough would receive no letter of thanks from Queen Anne this time. Malplaquet strained relations within the Grand Alliance but the misery would go on, mainly in Philip's Spain.

12 September 1899

North West Frontier
Battle of Saragarhi

FOLLOWING THE SECOND Anglo-Afghan War (1878–1880) the British Indian Army withdrew from Afghanistan leaving Abdur Rahman Khan as emir but with Britain retaining control over Afghan Foreign policy. The 'Great Game' between Britain and Russia had already lasted over half a century but still British concerns over the security of India remained especially since very little was known of the topography north of Afghanistan. Not until 1895 were spheres of influence defined by the Pamir Boundary Commission which left Afghanistan a buffer state between Russia and British India. The mountainous boundary between Afghanistan and British India, the North West Frontier, had been defined two years earlier by the Durand Line, cutting through Pashtun tribal areas in Afghanistan and what is now Pakistan but many Pashtuns were already unwelcoming of British developments, specifically roads which had opened up their previously remote lands. Rebellions became increasingly common, the fort at Chitral besieged in 1895 requiring a British relief expedition from Peshawar before in July 1897 an uprising of Swati Pashtuns led by the 'Great Fakir' Saidullah invested Malakand and Chakdara, the relief of which required a 10,000-strong Malakand Field Force under Brigadier General Bindon Blood and included Lieutenant Winston Churchill. An uprising further south of Afridi and Orakzai Pashtuns who had been paid by the British since the Second Anglo-Afghan War to maintain the safety of the Khyber Pass then overran all their own forts before advancing against a line of six British forts built by Sikh Maharaja Ranjit Singh in the Samana Mountains of the Hindu Kush commanding the Tirah Valley. Since two of the forts, Lockhart and Gulistan, could not communicate with each other a communication post complete with heliograph had been built in between on a rocky ridge at Saragarhi. After an early September Pashtun attack on the western most Fort Gulistan had been repulsed by the Kohat Field Force from Fort Lockhart, the communication post at Saragarhi was reinforced to bring its defence up to just twenty-one men of the 36th Sikh Regiment under Havildar Ishar Singh.

At 09.00 on 12 September 1897, with the Kohat Field Force having withdrawn, Forts Gulistan, Sangar and Dar were again attacked, this time by over 20,000 Afridi and Orakzai Pashtuns at least half of whom were determined to knock out the post at Saragarhi in order to isolate Fort Gulistan. Ishar Singh immediately ordered his nineteen-year-old heliographer Sepoy Gurmurkh Singh to request reinforcements only to be informed by Lieutenant Colonel John Haughton commanding the 36th Sikhs from Fort Lockhart that none were available. Ishar and his detachment then decided to hold the position rather than allow the whole defensive line to collapse even though it meant certain death, opening fire with their .303 breech loading Martini Henry rifles at 250 yards. Desperate mountain warfare, much of it close quarter hand-to-hand, raged for the next three hours, the Sikhs soon down to just ten men but still inflicting heavy casualties on the Pashtuns who several times gave Ishar the opportunity to surrender, each time rejected. The Pashtuns then broke into the walled compound of Saragarhi despite a last suicidal bayonet charge by Ishar to stop them. The survivors were soon forced back inside the heliograph tower, firing from loop holes, Haughton watching on from Fort Lockhart below, powerless to act but given accurate detail of the fighting by Gurmurkh Singh who continued to signal from the tower. After seven hours of fighting the last defender, Gurmurkh, sent his final message before being killed screaming the Sikh battle cry *Bole So Nihal, Sat Sri Akal!*

The Sikhs of Saragarhi had inflicted near 200 casualties on the Pashtuns and delayed their full attack on Fort Gulistan long enough for reinforcements to hold the position and the line of forts. The Pashtun rising was eventually put down three months later by the Tirah Expedition. Saragarhi Day is remembered both in the Indian and British Armies and by an epic Sikh poem *Khalsa Bahadur*. All twenty-one Sikhs were awarded the Indian Order of Merit by Empress of India Queen Victoria, at the time the highest possible award for gallantry for an Indian soldier.

13 September 1759

French and Indian War
Battle of the Plains of Abraham, Quebec

THE SEVEN YEARS' War in Europe had flared as a result of the unsatisfactory 1748 Treaty of Aix-La-Chapelle, the outbreak of the French and Indian War in North America and King Frederick II of Prussia's paranoia at forthcoming Russian and Austrian aggression. The Leader of the House of Commons, William Pitt 'the Elder' had initially pursued a naval policy in Europe, the Royal Navy preventing Austria's allies, France and Spain, from reinforcing their global colonies whilst on land Britain financially subsidised Prussian and Hanoverian (King George's ancestral homeland) military efforts. By 1758, however, neither the French and Indian War nor the Seven Years' War had been auspicious for British interests but in 1759 Pitt at last sent a modest number of troops into Europe to assist the Prussians who had been defeated at Emden but who now with the British achieved a famous victory at Minden, a victory that would have been a rout had Lord George Sackville, commanding the British cavalry, obeyed orders. Sackville had called for and was awaiting a Court Martial to clear his name but across the Atlantic two near neighbours of his family seat of Knole, Sevenoaks, were in the process of changing North American history. On 26–27 July 1759, just a few days before Sackville's Minden disgrace, Major General James Amherst, Commander-in-Chief North America, defeated the French at Fort Carillon (renamed Ticonderoga) on Lake Champlain and on 29 June Major General James Wolfe had landed at Point Levis on the south bank of the St lawrence River, opposite the French city of Quebec, on which he had been training his artillery ever since.

Wolfe had 8,000 troops and forty-nine ships under Admiral Sir Charles Saunders while Quebec Governor Pierre de Rigaud, Marquis de Vaudreuil and General Louis Joseph de Montcalm garrisoned 3,500 men in Quebec itself with a further 12,000 defending a six-mile-line of earthworks and redoubts to the east between the Rivers Saint Charles and Montmorency. Steep cliffs to the west made a landing seemingly impossible so Wolfe duly attacked and failed at the Montmorency Line on 31 July. The British commander then began burning French settlements up and down the St Lawrence in an attempt to draw Montcalm out from his defences but Montcalm stayed put. As sickness spread and morale dropped in the British ranks, Wolfe considered a landing much further up river (west) but here once alerted Montcalm would surely have time enough to alter his defence. Indeed the French general was already alert to the danger, preemptively moving 3,000 troops under Louis Antoine de Bougainville eight miles upriver to Cap Rouge. Acting on new information, Wolfe then decided to land at L'Anse au Foulon just two miles upriver where his men could scale the 175-feet-high cliffs through a ravine leading up onto the Plains of Abraham before Quebec. Should there be any determined French resistance on the climb, however, it would likely prove catastrophic.

On the night of 12 September, Saunders began a diversionary naval bombardment on the Montmorency Line whilst Wolfe and 3,300 British Redcoats began landing and ascending the cliffs at L'Anse au Foulon. An advance guard of light infantry led by Lieutenant Colonel William Howe cleared a small group of French militia under Louis de Vergor, allowing Wolfe to deploy onto the Plains of Abraham above, two ranks deep and nearly a mile across. A shocked Montcalm had three options: abandon the city and fight a guerrilla war; wait for an advance from Bougainville to trap the British between the two French forces; or attempt to immediately throw Wolfe back himself. He chose the latter, advancing at 10.00 on 13 September 1759 with 3,500 men, almost all of them infantry, marching out onto the Plains. The British infantry, muskets double shotted, had been lying down during an initial artillery duel but rose as the French infantry approached to within 30 yards before delivering a weak volley. In contrast the British reply was devastating, hundreds of French falling and those still standing left to face an equally devastating second volley as the British second rank stepped through the first. The fighting was over in minutes with 2,000 casualties, mainly French but also Wolfe, killed by balls to the stomach and chest. Montcalm had also been hit and died the following day.

Bougainville arrived too late to assist his compatriots and retreated leaving the British to take Quebec. They would have to fight for it again seven months later a mile upstream at Saint Foy. Wolfe is remembered by statues in his home towns of Westerham and Greenwich.

13 September 1882

Egypt
Battle of Tel-El-Kebir

ISMAIL PASHA HAD been the Khedive of Egypt since 1863, transforming Egypt into a more modern state based on European models of urbanisation, commerce, transportation, education, culture and entertainment. Ismail's influence had also been felt in the Sudan where, with British help, he strived to halt slave trading and in Ethiopia where he unsuccessfully attempted to expand Egyptian territory at the expense of Emperor Yohannes IV. Ismail, who lavishly entertained his guests and business partners, had, however, run up some serious debts exercising his ambitions for Egypt and was now paying ever increasing interest rates on bonds partially backed by Egyptian holdings in the new Suez Canal Company.

Light canal traffic and a global depression during the 1870s, however, negatively impacted Egyptian finances so much so that the Governments of France and Great Britain stepped in with financial controllers to protect their bondholders. Anti-imperialist British Prime Minister William Gladstone also agreed to replace Ismail with his son Tewfiq but no more than that whereas French President Leon Gambetta sensed an opportunity to replace 1871 French territorial losses to Prussia with gains in North Africa. An 1881 French invasion of Tunisia then sent a clear warning to Egypt's Colonel Ahmed Arabi who, upset at Tewfiq's tolerance of foreign intervention, had led a military coup that same summer. Although holders of Egyptian bonds fretted, Arabi and the now powerless Tewfiq still intended to honour their financial obligations. To press the point that they should do so France insisted on a joint show of naval strength with the Royal Navy off Alexandria, a reluctant Gladstone acquiescing, mindful of recent debacles in South Africa but wanting to contain French ambition. The consequent arrival of four British and French warships off Alexandria, however, sparked violence against Europeans caught in Egypt and prompted the construction of onshore gun batteries. The faint-hearted French now departed leaving Admiral Edward Seymour to issue Arabi a warning before the Royal Navy levelled Alexandria, a furious Arabi responding by declaring a Holy War. Since Britain now held all Egyptian shares in the Suez Canal, war it would be as the hero of the 1873–74 Ashanti War General Sir Garnet Wolseley was sent with 40,000 troops, including Indians, to overthrow Arabi. Gladstone's nightmare had become a reality,

Arabi had been led to believe that the neutrality of the Suez Canal would be honoured but instead Wolseley seized it at both ends, Suez and Port Said, before steaming to Ismailia in the middle. Arabi prepared to make a stand a days march away from the British landing at the Fort of Tel-El-Kebir which Wolseley decided to approach by a risky night march, hopefully achieving surprise, a quick victory and a cavalry dash on Cairo. The British advance began on the afternoon of 12 September, 13,000 men including kilted Highlanders, marching in silence across flat desert. Frequent stops maintained order but Wolseley believed he was well behind schedule when the sky suddenly began lighting up. Relieved that the phenomenon had been caused by the Great Comet of 1882 the advance then continued, arriving at dawn on 13 September 1882 to be greeted by an Egyptian artillery barrage and a crash of musketry from trenches 600 yards to his front. The British infantry, 2nd Brigade on the right and Highlanders on the left, replied by instantly charging through the smoke with accurate, fast-firing, breech-loading Martini Henry rifles. Almost immediately Arabi's Sudanese and Egyptian troops gave ground, 2,000 of them then massacred during half an hour's bloody work with the bayonet and rifle shot, the remainder fleeing. The British cavalry were then duly ordered to make haste for Cairo where Arabi and his nationalists surrendered, Wolseley arriving two days later to take up residence in the Abdin Palace.

Tewfiq remained Khedive as Egypt remained an Ottoman territory under British suzerainty. A jubilant Gladstone welcomed Wolseley home but though he planned to get Britain out of Egypt he had also inherited responsibility for the Sudan where another threat was appearing in the form of an Islamic leader, Muhammad Ahmad – the Mahdi. A furious France reacted to British Egypt by henceforth vigorously prosecuting their own imperial quests, Gladstone had unwittingly started the Scramble for Africa in earnest.

14 September 1402

Anglo-Scottish Wars
Battle of Homildon Hill

 IN 1399 HENRY of Bolingbroke, Earl of Derby had taken advantage of his cousin King Richard II's absence in Ireland to usurp power and become King Henry IV. On his return Richard was imprisoned in the Tower of London and died in mysterious circumstances, likely dehydration, a year later. News of his death was slow to reach the far corners of the kingdom and even when it did it was not entirely believed – despite having alienated much of the nobility during his reign Richard still had significant support.

Both Richard's and Henry's reigns were typified by resurgent Scottish and Welsh aggression, the Scots often under the earls of Douglas, rarely hesitating to take advantage of English difficulties with regular raids into the northern English shires in an effort to rid Scotland of English influence. One such in 1388 under James, 2nd Earl of Douglas had even resulted in a shock Scottish victory at Otterburn over Henry Percy (aka Harry Hotspur), a member of the foremost family in northern England. In Wales too, Owain Glendywr, who had supported Richard in Scottish border conflicts, then rebelled against Henry with good reason, winning a significant victory in 1402 at Bryn Glas, capturing Sir Edmund Mortimer, the Earl of March (Wales) who was not only a brother-in-law of Hotspur but also possessed a stronger claim to the English throne than King Henry himself. Suspecting foul play, the suspicious Henry would not pay Mortimer's ransom.

Whilst Glendywr was rebelling in the Welsh Marches several Scottish nobles launched an army of 12,000 looting, pillaging and burning into northern England. On the very same day as Bryn Glas a small force of 400 Scots was annihilated at Nesbit Moor by 200 archers under George Dunbar, the Earl of March (Scotland) who had defected to serve King Henry following a row with the now deceased Archibald, 3rd Earl of Douglas. This action prompted Archibald's son Archibald, 4th Earl of Douglas together with Murdoch Stewart of Fife and 10,000 men to march through Northumberland to Newcastle on yet another trail of destruction.

Dunbar now joined with Henry Percy, Earl of Northumberland, father of Harry Hotspur, in an effort to protect northern England and the Scottish Marches from further raids and strike a blow against the troublesome Douglas family. After recent events the Percys were hardly inclined to help King Henry but they would protect their own interests and besides, the valiant Hotspur was anxious to avenge his Otterburn loss.

On 14 September 1402, Northumberland came upon Douglas' camp at Millfield, alert Scottish sentries, however, warned of the approaching danger allowing Douglas to retreat to Homildon Hill where his army formed a defensive schiltrom, a densely packed body of men, spears, lances and wooden stakes to defend against charging cavalry. Percy's English Army was possibly double that of the Scots and it moved forward onto Harewood Hill facing the enemy. True to form Hotspur was eager to charge immediately but Dunbar pointed out that plenty of archers were available and that it would be wasteful not to employ them. They therefore moved to the bottom of the hill to begin a rerun of the 1298 Battle of Falkirk, an archery duel over a ravine and up Homildon Hill with their Scottish counterparts. It was a one sided contest, even with the advantage of higher ground the Scots were completely outclassed by the physically more powerful English who rained down such a volume of arrows that Douglas himself was hit five times at the cost of an eye. The first Scot to lose patience was Sir John Swinton, a man who had fought for the English in France on the understanding he would never be required to fight against his own kin. Now Swinton charged down the hill toward his former employers with 100 Scottish knights all of whom were mown down by more white goose-feathered death without making contact. Shortly after, a now desperate Douglas repeated Swinton's tactic with similar results, himself captured along with many of his Lieutenants leaving those who had survived to make a run for the River Tweed. Eventually 1,500 Scots lay dead.

A paranoid King Henry would again turn the situation against himself. Fearful of the growing power of the Percy's and the wealth of their captives, he forbade them to be ransomed. On top of being prevented from paying Mortimer's ransom the restraint of trade was too much to bear, now the Percys revolted, they would meet their king and his formidable son at Shrewsbury in July the following year.

15 September 1940

Second World War
Battle of Britain

GERMANY HAD ATTACKED western Europe in May 1940 with staggering success, Holland surrendering after four days and Belgium after eighteen just as the British Expeditionary Force and the French First Army were trying to escape from the beaches of Dunkirk. British Prime Minister Winston Churchill urged France to fight on but, on 16 July 1940, the incoming French Prime Minister Marshal Phillippe Petain asked for an armistice with Germany. As Britain now stood alone the additional threat of Italy's modern Navy, the *Regia Marina*, then entered the war forcing Churchill to estrange French relations further by impounding French vessels in British ports and attacking them at Mers El Kebir lest they fall into the hands of the enemy. British bases in the Mediterranean at Alexandria, Egypt and Gibraltar were highly vulnerable, linked only by the Island of Malta which now came under intense bombardment from aircraft of the Italian *Regia Aeronautica*. Meanwhile the population of Great Britian had their own developments to worry about as German Chancellor Adolf Hitler issued a directive preparing for an invasion of Britain, Operation Sea Lion, and a 'final appeal to reason' for the British to surrender. His appeal resoundingly rejected by the BBC, Hitler resolved to deal with the Royal Air Force and the Royal Navy, the former prepared for four years by Air Vice Marshal Hugh Dowding, the latter the world's largest though ageing Naval fleet.

German High Command could not possibly contemplate towing barges and pleasure craft loaded with assault troops across the English Channel against the Royal Navy without Reichsmarshal Herman Goring's *Luftwaffe* first gaining total air superiority. Initially attacking British shipping and the radar stations of RAF 11 Group commanded by Air Vice Marshal Keith Park, Goring needed better weather to begin attacking RAF airfields further inland. That day, *Adlertag* (Eagle Day), came on 13 August, Goring believing the RAF to have just 200 Hurricanes and Spitfires remaining but who, thanks to Max Aitken Lord Beaverbrook, Minister for Air Production, were in fact stronger than ever. German attacks failed but continued on into September, Dowding using fighters in packets, needing just to remain in the battle to achieve victory. A frustrated Hitler then began bombing London, crucially allowing the now suffering RAF time to recover. Goring, however, again believed the RAF to be near extinction and looked to finally overwhelm them.

At 11.00 on 15 September 1940, as Churchill paid a surprise visit to RAF Uxbridge, radar warnings were received indicating the approach of twenty-seven Dornier bombers and twenty-one Messerschmidt 110 fighter bombers protected by sixty Messerschmidt 109 fighters. Park judged it another attack on London and put up all his available forces, 250 Spitfires and Hurricanes. As the attackers crossed the Kent coast twenty Spitfires from 72 and 92 Squadron, Biggin Hill engaged the 109s before two squadrons of Hurricanes from Kenley forced three Dorniers out of the battle, the remaining Germans forming a tight defence hit by another twenty-four Hurricanes from 229 and 303 Squadrons. As the battle raged above the Garden of England the German fighter bombers continued on to drop their cargoes on South London, the main body following with dwindling fighter escort, incredulous at being hit by another six fighter squadrons and a 'Big Wing' of five squadrons from Air Vice Marshall Trafford Leigh-Mallory's 12 Group, Duxford. Six Dorniers went down with eighteen limping back to France, machines and morale in tatters but another, larger attack was already forming, 114 Heinkel and Dornier bombers protected by 300 Messerschmidt 109s. Park again put up everything, twenty squadrons from 11 Group with reinforcements including the Big Wing, 276 Spitfires and Hurricanes attacking from the south coast to the Royal Victoria Docks. A terrific dog fight raged to the north of Maidstone as *Jagdgeschwader* 26 under Adolf Galland intercepted the reinforcing RAF 10 and 12 Groups, the sky a mass of machines and tracer. Churchill remarked on the absence of reserves but there were none. Still one hundred German bombers emerged from the mêlée to drop their cargo before turning to fly the gauntlet of angry Spitfires and Hurricanes back to France.

Fighter Command claimed 185 kills though the actual total was sixty, enough to shatter *Luftwaffe* morale but at a cost to the RAF of twenty-nine fighters and twelve aircrew. Hitler had just suffered his first defeat, he postponed Sea Lion indefinitely though he maintained the Blitz, mainly the night bombing of British cities. 'The few' had just won the Battle of Britain.

16 September 1776
American War of Independence
Battle of Harlem Heights

THE SMALL BRITISH Army present in North America at the onset of the War of American Independence were soon distinctly on the back foot having been harried from Concord and Lexington back in to Boston, there enduring a miserable ten month siege under attack not just from American Patriots but also smallpox and consumption. Following a humiliating evacuation in March 1776 the British Army repaired at Halifax, Nova Scotia before returning south with massive reinforcements in both troops (32,000 men) and naval strength to attack New York. General George Washington, a former Colonel in the British Army during the French and Indian War (1754–63) was ahead of them however, moving the American Continental Army down the east coast to defend the city but failing to prevent General William Howe commanding British and Hessians from taking Long Island in August 1776. Washington had brilliantly managed to extricate his army from Long Island's Brooklyn Heights under cover of darkness and fog and from under the noses of the all powerful Royal Navy, retreating to Manhattan Island, but his difficulties were far from over. Faced with over 400 British ships in the waters around Manhattan, including seventy-three ships of the line in the Narrows between Staten Island & Long Island and on the Hudson River he had no option but to retreat further north to the Harlem Heights, evading Howe's attempts to trap him by only a whisker.

By 15 September Washington was despairing at the fighting spirit of some of his units after a British landing at Kip's Bay, West Manhattan had prompted his Virginia Militia to turn tail and flee at first sight. On the morning of 16 September 1776, however, Washington sent Lieutenant Colonel Thomas Knowlton and 120 Connecticut Rangers to cover British movements to his south. It was not long before Knowlton clashed with 300 advancing British light infantrymen under Major General Alexander Leslie, a sharp skirmish developing for half an hour as more Redcoats joined Leslie and attempted to outflank Knowlton. Knowlton retreated, his men goaded by British buglers derisively blowing fox hunting signals since Leslie wanted the Americans to stand and fight. The fighting was reported back to Washington by his adjutant Joseph Reed who urged him to support Knowlton. The old fox himself, Washington now showed some steel and ingenuity by sending 150 volunteers forward to lure British Redcoats into Hollow Way inbetween Manhattan's southern and northern plateaux before reinforcing the 150 with another 800 under Colonial General John Nixon who would indeed stand and fight, stopping the British advance in the hollow. Knowlton's Connecticut Rangers and the Virginians, perhaps 600 in total, were also sent back into the fray making their way around the eastern, right flank of the British in an attempt to isolate them in Hollow Way. Fierce fighting raged as the British engaged the Americans to their front, Washington's plan essentially working until Knowlton's flank force attacked the British right instead of the rear alerting Leslie to the imminent peril, he too now began a retreat. In a more defensive position further south the British began receiving their own reinforcements bringing their strength up to 5,000 as Americans, gaining in confidence, pushed forward. Knowlton was mortally wounded during several hours of bitter fighting before the British disengaged short of ammunition. Washington called off the pursuit anxious not be drawn into a similar trap and outflanked in turn by Howe.

Harlem was the first battlefield victory for the Continental Army and American morale consequently soared but Washington was aware that he was still in a perilous situation as the numerically superior British began to land further north at Westchester. Washington evaded another trap, vacated Manhattan and retreated further north to Whiteplains where he would meet Howe in open battle a month later. The British had at least for the time being atoned for Boston and secured a significant port from which to launch military operations but the tone for the war had been set. The British dominant in men and firepower chasing an elusive foe in a big country, a fox hunt against a cunning fox who would before long prove to have a nasty bite.

17 September 1944
Second World War
Battle of Arnhem

THE JUNE 1944 British, American and Canadian Normandy landings had been an unmitigated success but were followed by bitter fighting through the hedgerows and sunken lanes, *le bocage*, of Normandy. The British and Canadians then turned hard left up the Channel coast while the Americans made a wider turn trapping 100,000 Germans in the Falaise Pocket, half of whom escaped. In mid August the United States 7th Army then landed on the south coast of France between Marseilles and Cannes, German Chancellor Adolf Hitler withdrawing north rather than fighting. The US sweep east from Normandy then liberated Paris on 25 August (German Military Governor General Dietrich von Choltitz mercifully ignoring Hitler's instructions to destroy the city) before linking with the 7th Army advance from the south to reach the borders of Germany.

Supreme Headquarters Allied Expeditionary Force General Dwight D. Eisenhower was, however, fighting a continuous battle on a broad front, a policy that stretched Allied logistics much to the frustration of 21st Army Group commander General Bernard Montgomery. Promoted to Field Marshal on 1 September Montgomery now requested a daring attack through the Dutch polders along the sixty mile corridor of Highway 69. Paratroops would capture eight river crossings from Eindhoven to Arnhem (Market) while the armour of XXX Corps under Lieutenant General Brian Horrocks would make a two day dash up the corridor to consolidate the gains (Garden). An encircling of the German Industrial Ruhr would then follow finishing the war by the year end. Eisenhower agreed, allowing 'Monty' the use of the 1st Allied Airborne Army.

Ignoring intelligence that the 9th and 10th SS Panzer Divisions were refitting near Oosterbeek, the largest airborne operation in history, 5,000 aircraft including 2,023 gliders, carrying nearly 35,000 paratroops began at 13.30 on 17 September 1944, Operation Market Garden. After widespread bombing, the US 101st Airborne Division dropped north of Eindhoven to take crossings over the

Wilhelmina Canal and the Dommel & Aar Rivers whilst to their north US 82nd Airborne Division captured bridges over the River Maas at Grave and Heumen but critically failed to cross the River Waal at Nijmegen. At the final objective, Arnhem, the British 1st Airborne Division of Major General Roy Urquhart dropped west of the city but with only half their strength having dropped with the first lift were halted at Oosterbeek. Lieutenant Colonel John Frost with just 700 men, however, evaded German defences to attack the north end of Arnhem Bridge on the River Rhine. In terrific street fighting Frost was holding off attacks from the German 9th Panzer Division whilst, further south, Horrocks was delayed by unexpected German resistance, a failure at the Son Bridge and jubilant Dutch crowds in Eindhoven. Worse, a copy of the Allied plans had fallen into German hands, so complete that Field Marshal Walter Model doubted the authenticity. As fighting raged in Arnhem, fog covered England leaving just the glider section of the reinforcing Polish 1st Independent Parachute Brigade to fly in, sadly to be decimated by expectant defenders. At Arnhem Bridge meanwhile, Frost was still holding out against German artillery, panzer and mortar fire, Dutch citizens piling up walls of dead in the streets to obstruct the German armour. Horrocks at last reached south Nijmegen only to find the bridge now defended by the German 10th Panzer Division. Brigadier General James Gavin commanding US 504th Infantry then outflanked the position by boat to successfully assault both ends of the bridge, Horrocks racing across only to be halted by heavy German counter-attacks in the eight mile corridor between Nijmegen and Arnhem. It was too late for Frost, after four days of fighting, his message was picked up only on German radio 'Out of Ammo, God Save the King'. British Paratroops still held out at Oosterbeek, however, and Polish Paratroops now dropped south of the Rhine near Driel to be supported by Horrocks' lead units. The Poles crossed the Rhine at night in rowing boats as German artillery pounded Allied positions but by 25 September it was clear the objectives of Market Garden could not be reached. Those troops at Oosterbeek withdrew south protected by their own artillery barrage whilst further south the corridor was reinforced to hold over the winter. Montgomery had lost 10,000 men including almost the entire British 1st Airborne Division.

The battle is celebrated in the 1977 Richard Attenborough directed, United Artists Film *A Bridge Too Far*. Frost survived the war, the new bridge at Arnhem is named after him.

18 September 1918

The Great War
Battle of Épehy

THE 80,000 PROFESSIONAL soldiers of the British Expeditionary Force (BEF) that had originally landed in France on the August 1914 outbreak of the Great War were allegedly described by German Kaiser Wilhem II as a 'contemptible little army' but after four years of bloody conflict in which over five million men had served in the BEF the Kaiser was under no illusion as to who represented his main threat. Since the defeat of the Schlieffen Plan in 1914, the Central Powers (Germany, Austria Hungary, and Turkey) had fought mainly on the defensive against France, Britain and Italy on the Western Front whilst taking the offensive against Russia on the Eastern Front. Successive French and British Commander-in-Chiefs had endeavoured to relieve pressure on Russia by maintaining offensive pressure on Germany in the west but by early 1918 Russia had withdrawn from the war, consumed by a Bolshevik Revolution that in July 1918 saw Tsar Nicholas II and his family executed. The French Army had also come close to mutiny after the 1916 Battle of Verdun and the 1917 Nivelle Offensive but despite equally appalling losses which continued throughout 1917 never once had British morale wavered. The United States of America had by now declared war in response to German unrestricted submarine warfare but the majority of American troops were still to arrive in France when German Quarter Master General Erich Ludendorff seized his opportunity to win the war by launching a Spring Offensive, transferring Eastern Front divisions to the Western Front in a desperate gamble to defeat the BEF. The BEF had held but only just, often holding positions as ordered by Field Marshal Douglas Haig 'to the last man', suffering fearful casualties but inflicting nearly a million on Germany in a four month defensive effort that finished with the Battle of Rheims in July 1918. Generalissime of the Allied Armies Ferdinand Foch and Haig had then immediately returned to the offensive with the British Fourth Army of General Henry Rawlinson supported by the French 1st Army counter-attacking at Amiens. As Australian and Canadian troops supported by British artillery, tanks and aircraft made spectacular gains using all the technological advances of the time and battle tactics learnt at such cost over the preceding four years, German morale collapsed. By early September Haig had forced the shattered German Army back to the formidable defences of the Hindenberg Line but even his unshakeable resolve now wavered having suffered 180,000 casualties in just six weeks. Only a German collapse at Havrincourt convinced him to press on again at Épehy.

At 05.20 on 18 September 1918, with few tanks available all three corps of Rawlinson's Fourth Army advanced in torrential rain along a five mile front behind a 1,488-gun creeping barrage against the German 2nd Army of General Georg von der Marwitz. On the right flank French support failed to materialise leaving IX Corps facing tough resistance and struggling accordingly. On the left III Corps also struggled against strong German defences at Quennemont and Guillement Farms despite possessing numerous machine-guns and support from V Corps of Third Army on their left. In the centre, however, the 1st and 4th Divisions of Lieutenant General John Monash's Australian Corps followed up their feats at Amiens with gains of up to three miles through several belts of defences as again German morale crumbled, near 12,000 surrendering.

Épehy was far from a decisive victory but indicated further collapses in German morale and allowed Foch and Haig to directly attack the Hindenberg Line. The British First and Third Armies would penetrate the line at Canal du Nord and Fourth Army at the St Quentin Canal before taking Beaurevoir village on 6 October completely breaking the line. Even before then Ludendorff had informed the Kaiser the war was lost.

Fighting continued up to the Armistice at 11.00 on 11 November 1918. After four years of war the British had won a great victory but at a cost of 2.5 million casualties with another 600,000 suffered by their Imperial forces amongst global totals of thirty-eight million. The Kaiser abdicated but the war to end all wars would not live up to its billing, twenty years later a second major global conflict would stem directly from the Treaty of Versailles that concluded the first.

19 September 1356

Hundred Years' War
Battle of Poitiers

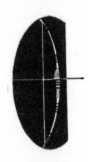

THE PURSUIT OF King Edward III's claim to the French Crown had led to a decade of English battlefield victories since 1337 but the English conquest of France then stalled against the onslaught of the 1348 Black Death which halved the population of England and the potential number of English recruits. As the pestilence relented Sir William Bentley secured Brittany for his king at Mauron in 1352 with another astonishing longbow victory against a French force twice the size under the Marshal of France, Guy de Nestlé. By 1355 Edward was also prosecuting the war in southern France, his son, the Black Prince, leading 5,000 men on a *Grand Chevauchée* from Bordeaux inland as far as Narbonne and back again. The Prince was trying to bring to battle John, Count of Armagnac who had previously been menacing English held territories in Aquitaine but Armagnac refused to come out and fight despite the Prince burning everything in his path in a show of strength toward the peasant population. Rather than fight, Armagnac in fact retreated to Toulouse leaving the prince to return again in 1356 simultaneous to a 2,500 strong *Chevauchée* into Lower Normandy led by Henry of (Grosmont) Lancaster as part of an English three-pronged assault on exterior lines. Hearing that the son of the French King John II, the Dauphin Charles, was at Tours, the Black Prince headed north to besiege the city and hopefully join up with Lancaster. On reaching Tours, however, the prince found the walls strongly defended, the fast flowing river uncrossable and an enemy appearing in ever larger numbers. Since there was no sign of Lancaster he decided to retreat. More forthright than his father, King John had resolved to deal with the troublesome english prince and had gathered the main French Army at Chartres, an army including Scots under Sir William Douglas that was now crossing bridges along the River Loire on both sides of the isolated English. A series of marches followed south to Poitiers (brutally sacked ten years previous by Lancaster) where the English Army was finally outflanked. Envoys from the Pope in Avignon tried to avert bloodshed but the Black Prince soon lost patience, fearing further delays would be to his detriment he chose to stand and fight.

Far from safety the 6,000-strong English Army was drawn up on high ground in three battles, William Montagu Earl of Salisbury on the right, Thomas de Beauchamp Earl of Warwick on the left and the Black Prince behind with a mounted unit under the loyal Gascon, Jean de Grailly, Captal de Buch, each battle flanked by herces of archers. They faced a French Army over 20,000-strong drawn up in four columns but on the morning of 19 September 1356 the French king failed to advance immediately, prompting the Black Prince to attempt a getaway on Warwick's left, a move spotted by the French mounted vanguard who only now attacked. Initially Warwick's archers made little impression on the approaching French horsemen but on moving further left still they fired into the exposed flanks and rears of the enemy with deadly results. The French vanguard defeated, the Dauphin Charles' column advanced on foot surviving a barrage of arrows to engage in a murderous hand-to-hand fight across a hedge in front of the English position. The battle raged for some considerable time before the exhausted Dauphin disengaged leaving the equally exhausted English to await the next French column under Philip, Duke of Orléans. Whilst the English repaired weapons and collected arrows, panic seems to have overcome Orléan's men after hearing the fate of the first two attacks. Additionally unaware of the whereabouts of King John's column they fled east to Chauvigny without engaging. A concerned John advanced regardless, his huge column cresting a ridge to sight the English many of whom required reassurance from the Black Prince to maintain their position 'thou liest thou knave, if thou sayest we can be conquered as long as I live!'. The Prince then advanced his men-at-arms half way down the slope simultaneous to a mounted attack from the Captal de Buch on the French king's left and rear. Bloody fighting again raged until the French crumbled, many fleeing for Poitiers but leaving their king an English prisoner.

After dining with the Black Prince, King John was held in Bordeaux before, in May 1357, crossing to London where he was paraded through streets adorned with longbows and armour, a jubilant spectacle celebrated by many thousands. Allowed to hold his court in the Savoy Palace, John would now follow his ally, the Scottish King David II, as an English prisoner attempting to raise an enormous ransom. The subsequent Treaty of Bretigny saw Edward's gains in France consolidated into an enlarged Aquitaine (Gascony, Poitou), Ponthieu and Calais, areas no longer under French suzerainty. The peace would not last.

20 September 1643
English Civil Wars
Battle of Newbury

ELEVEN YEARS OF personal rule meant answering a long list of grievances when King Charles I of England, Scotland and Ireland finally called a Parliament. It was the opposite of what Charles had been looking for, rather than being granted a tax levy to quell insubordination in Scotland instigated by his new Book of Common Prayer he instead now had a full scale civil war on his hands. Charles believed firmly in his divine right to rule the Three Kingdoms and in peace negotiations with his Parliament over the 1642–43 winter had maintained a hard line. No doubt the king was confident of victory on the battlefield but with a limited supply of money and many men fighting out of personal loyalty rather than for a cause, he would need that victory to be quick. The first year of the war had indeed gone well for the king, the 'Royalist Summer' of 1643 had increased Charles' territories in South West England, captured the port of Bristol in July whilst, in the Midlands, Prince Rupert harried the roads into London from the king's court at Oxford. The Parliamentarians were in disarray, Robert Devereux, Earl of Essex commanding the Parliament Midlands Army was threatening to resign and Sir William Waller's Army of the South West had been destroyed. Kentishmen too had risen, rioting in the name of the king from Tonbridge to the Thames. Although the Parliament army of the Eastern Association under Edward Montagu, Earl of Manchester and Oliver Cromwell were strongly resisting Royalists under William Cavendish, Duke of Newcastle in Lincolnshire the Parliament cause nevertheless looked hopeless. Nervous Londoners protested outside Parliament, expecting Charles to advance at any moment.

Heavy casualties, however, meant the Royalist Army was not fit to march on London. The alternative, to besiege Parliament-held Gloucester, was readily accepted, a decision which bought Parliament time and provided a figure of outstanding courage who served to rally men to the Parliament cause, Edward Massey the twenty-three year old Governor of Gloucester. Charles summoned

Massey to surrender on 10 August but the governor and his Puritan citizens stood firm despite any relief being weeks away if at all. A classic siege developed, unwilling to storm after losses incurred at Bristol, Charles began a continuous bombardment, mining the walls and severing all supplies including the water. In London meanwhile, the Trained Bands signed up in their droves to march with Essex across the Cotswolds undeterred by Rupert's cavalry, relieving Gloucester and her brave governor on 5 September 1643. Having congratulated and resupplied Massey, Essex then took advantage of the king's indecision, feinting north before making for London. On 18 September, however, Rupert caught him at Aldbourne Chase but was held before, a day later at Newbury, 17,000 Royalists blocked the road to London. Essex now had no option but to fight.

At 07.00 on 20 September 1643, 14,000 Parliamentarians advanced between the Rivers Kennet and Enborne onto Wash Common with Essex immediately sending forward infantry under Major General Philip Skippon to take Round Hill dominating the centre of the field which Rupert had inexplicably left weakly defended. Parliament cavalry under John Middleton and infantry under John, Lord Robartes advanced on Skippon's left against Royalist infantry under Sir William Vavasour but over difficult ground, lanes and hedgerows, the battle there became a musket contest. In the centre Rupert then contested Skippon's initiative at Round Hill, Royalist musketeers under Thomas, Lord Wentworth and George Lisle now additionally facing Skippon's artillery which inflicted heavy losses before Rupert aggressively renewed the attack with the cavalry of Nicholas and John Byron. Again the Royalist's suffered as Skippon further reinforced the Hill. Meanwhile to the south, Parliament cavalry under Philip Stapleton advanced to initially gain an ascendancy over Rupert's charging cavaliers which allowed an advance of Parliament infantry. Rupert attacked a second time, driving off Stapleton's cavalry but not the pikemen or, remarkably, the barely-trained Trained Bands, both sides then bombarding each other before, after fighting all day, the Royalists withdrew short of gun powder. Possibly 3,500 men lay dead or wounded.

Newbury was inconclusive but marked a turning point in fortunes. Essex marched back into London on 28 September, his success plus those of Massey, Manchester and Cromwell had given Parliament new resolve. The following year, 1644, would see Scots and Irish on the battlefields as the dispute engulfed the entire British Isles.

20 September 1854

Crimean War
Battle of the Alma

THE OTTOMAN EMPIRE (Turkey) had been in decline since the mid eighteenth century but by the mid nineteenth century still stretched west into the Balkans and the River Danube. Orthodox and Catholic Christians living within this predominantly Islamic Empire had two external powers claiming to watch over their interests, France and Russia. The latter had been fighting wars with the Ottomans intermittently since the sixteenth century and continued doing so in the nineteenth century at the behest of Tsar Alexander I and his brother, Tsar Nicholas I. Russian expansion into South and Central Asia had already caused Great Britain considerable concern at the security of British India, the 'Great Game' leading directly to the 1839 First Anglo-Afghan War before, in 1853, the Russians advanced through the Ukraine to directly threaten the Ottomans across the River Danube and the Black Sea. Russian ambition was now seen by France and Britain as a threat to the Eastern Mediterranean and again as far as Britain was concerned the trade routes to India. When the Russian Navy attacked and destroyed a squadron of Ottoman frigates at Sinop, Turkey and ignored an allied ultimatum to withdraw from the Danube, Britain and France declared war.

Initially an Anglo-French naval force entered the Black Sea to support Ottoman forces on the Danube but in June 1854 Anglo-French forces began landing at Varna (Bulgaria). The Russians retreated satisfying the original allied demands but still remained a considerable threat. Despite the retreat the British Government of George Hamilton-Gordon, Lord Aberdeen and French Emperor Napoleon III resolved to cross the Black Sea, invade the Crimean Peninsular and destroy the Russian fleet at Sevastopol, a move they believed would decisively end Russian ambition in the Black Sea and by extension the Mediterranean.

Landing in Kalamita Bay, thirty-five miles north of Sevastopol, the allies met no immediate resistance but faced five river crossings to reach their objective, cholera and dysentery soon becoming rife. At the second crossing, the River

Alma, the Russian General Alexander Menshikov had decided to make a stand in formidable defensive positions on the 300 foot high coastal cliffs and further inland at Kourgane Hill and Telegraph Height with near 40,000 troops and 120 guns. On 20 September 1854 the allies with 60,000 men at their disposal attacked the Russian block. On the right the French under General Jacques de Saint Arnaud initially made some progress up the cliffs before their advance stalled completely on Telegraph Height whilst on Kourgane Hill and on the left the British launched a full frontal assault with light infantry under General Sir George Brown, the 2nd Infantry Division under General George de Lacy Evans and the 3rd Infantry Division under Sir George Cathcart. The British commander, Field Marshal Fitzroy Somerset, Lord Raglan, a veteran of the Peninsular War, showed none of his former commander Arthur Wellesley, Duke of Wellington's élan by attempting to turn a flank. Instead the British infantry advanced downhill in close shoulder-to-shoulder order, crossing the river to march up the other side into round shot fired from Russian gun batteries in low level redoubts. As the Russian guns began to find their target order was somewhat lost in the British ranks but the advance continued, forcing the Russians into a bayonet attack. This attack was stopped before a point had been landed largely because the British were armed with new Minié Rifles, accurate to a range of up to four times that of the old Russian muskets. The British now fired on the run as many Russians fled the redoubts and defensive positions after a fruitless attempt to remove their guns. A concerted Russian counter-attack, however, initially had some success before being routed by another devastating display of British firepower.

The Russians were in full retreat and the road to Sevastopol open but the British cavalry under George Bingham, Lord Lucan and his subordinate James Brudenell, Lord Cardigan was fatefully held back by the cautious Raglan. The opportunity to storm Sevastopol was lost and a painful siege would now have to be endured. The Russian Army retreated but under General Pavel Liprandi would return to attack the British port at Balaclava a month later when Raglan, Lucan and Cardigan would have their infamous day in history.

21 September 1745

Jacobite Rebellion
Battle of Prestonpans

 THE 1714 SUCCESSION of the 57th in line, German-speaking, King George I to the throne of Great Britain and Ireland had caused widespread riots and a short uprising in support of the House of Stuart. The Stuarts were headed by Catholic James Francis Edward Stuart, whose father King James II had been deposed in the 'Glorious Revolution' of 1688 by the Protestant William III of Orange. The Jacobite rising (*Jacobus* – James) of 1715 was short-lived and bar a couple of skirmishes, fully extinguished at Glenshiel in 1719. In 1727 George was succeeded by his son George Augustus, Prince of Wales now King George II. The two Georges had not had an easy relationship but the consistency of their reigns was the development of Parliament under the Whigs of Robert Walpole. The Whigs supported the Hanoverian Succession and Protestantism, ruling without interval from 1715 to 1760, Walpole presiding over the economic shock wave of the 1720 South Sea Bubble but largely successful in avoiding wars on any significant scale. British stability meant any return of the House of Stuart and with it, Catholicism, to the British monarchy would now require an event of some magnitude, an event which duly materialised at the Favorita Palace (*Palais Augarten*), Vienna on the death of the Habsburg Charles VI, Holy Roman Emperor, beginning the War of the Austrian Succession (1740–1748).

Protestant Great Britain was once again at war with Catholic France, George, who spent much of his time in Europe anyway, leading the British on the battlefield at Dettingen in 1743 to become the last British monarch to do so. The French, however, then defeated British, Austrian, Dutch and Hanoverians under George's youngest son William Augustus, Duke of Cumberland at Fontenoy in 1745 and sought to maintain pressure on the fully stretched British Army by supporting the claims of James Stuart and his son, the Italian-speaking Charles Edward Stuart, Bonnie Prince Charlie, by sparking another Jacobite Rebellion.

In February 1745 King Louis XV of France launched an invasion of Britain with 10,000 troops but not for the first or last time did a storm wreck an approaching Catholic armada. Louis then cancelled the venture but continued to support Bonnie Prince Charlie who was receiving encouraging words from the largely Catholic Scottish Highlands that if he could land with just 3,000 French troops the clans would rally. Charlie set off with two frigates, *Du Teillay* and *Elizabeth*, which were intercepted off Cornwall by the 64-gun HMS *Lion*, *Elizabeth* returning to France with most of Charlie's ammunition whilst *Du Teillay* succeeded in delivering Charlie and his army of seven men to the Hebrides. One can imagine the Macdonalds and Macleods were hardly impressed but Charlie persevered and within a month had raised 1200 men (many though were poorly armed and were only obeying their feudal overlords). The Jacobite Army marched for Perth, still gaining in strength but unwilling to fight a Government force led by Lieutenant General Sir John Cope who continued north to Aberdeen before returning by ship down the east coast of Scotland to Dunbar, failing to beat Charlie to Edinburgh.

From Dunbar Cope marched his 2,500 men west toward Edinburgh coming into contact with the Jacobite vanguard at Prestonpans on 20 September. Now in similar numbers the Jacobites held the high ground but Cope was protected by a marsh to his front and the walls of Preston House to his right. Lord George Murray commanding for Bonnie Prince Charlie, believed the Jacobites only hope was to attack Cope's left flank and having been advised by a farmer of the Riggonhead defile through the marshland, marched at 04.00 on 21 September 1745 around Cope to attack his rear. Cope had stationed 200 dragoons and 300 infantry as pickets but even so had little time to wheel into position to receive the oncoming Highlander threat. Most of Cope's gunners then fled leaving the Jacobite charge to crash into both wings of the government position from where the dragoons now also fled. Cope's isolated infantry in the centre were therefore assailed from three sides and collapsed. In just fifteen minutes 300 government troops lay dead with 1,500 captured.

With the victory Bonnie Prince Charlie also gained £5,000 and a large stock of weapons from Cope's baggage train. The Young Pretender advanced into England but there were no new adherents to be gained there. Cumberland would catch up with him on his return to Scotland the following April at Culloden.

22 September 1415

Hundred Years' War
Siege of Harfleur

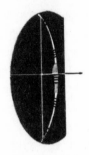

IN 1413 HENRY V was crowned King of England at the age of twenty-six and immediately resurrected the English claim to the French Crown of which his great-grandfather King Edward III had been deprived eighty five years before. To avoid bloodshed Henry offered to marry Catherine of Valois, daughter of Charles VI, King of France but romance joined peace on the casualty list when relations broke down over the size of Catherine's dowry.

War was again inevitable but the portents for Henry to succeed where Edward had failed were good – Charles' House of Orleans (Armagnac) were involved in a bitter long running dispute with Duke John 'the Fearless' of Burgundy and Charles himself was often prone to bouts of insanity. After recent rebellions at home against his father, Henry also knew that nothing galvanised the English and Welsh nations like war with France. Any doubts regarding the magnitude of the undertaking disappeared on 11 August 1415 when a flock of swans joined the English fleet of 1,500 ships headed by Henry's own 500-ton carrack, the *Trinity Royal*.

Only now did Henry reveal his destination to the 2,000 men-at-arms and 8,000 longbowmen aboard – Harfleur at the mouth of the River Seine, a town specifically chosen to compliment the English possessions of Calais in the north and Bordeaux in the south. After two days at sea Henry disembarked to begin construction of a camp one mile north of Harfleur but the French defenders had been aware of a likely attack and had taken extensive measures. As well as Harfleur's natural defences of the River Lezarde and a moat, the valley north of the town had been flooded, chains had been placed across the Lezarde where it exited the town, bridges had been destroyed, entrenchments and earthworks had been dug and a two mile wall complete with cannon, quicklime and oil surrounded the town. The garrison of 200 men-at-arms and crossbowmen under Jean D'Estouteville were then reinforced by another 300 men-at-arms under Raoul de Gaucourt but a further French supply column was intercepted by Thomas of Lancaster,

Duke of Clarence (Henry's brother) who was completing the English investment east of the town. Henry then invested the west and south-west leaving Charles D'Albret, the Constable of France, south of the Seine separated from Harfleur by the English Navy.

Henry initially tried to bring down the walls by mining but the French defenders were equal, counter-mining effectively and causing heavy casualties in bitter underground fighting. Henry now turned to a method that would eventually spell the end for castle building, artillery. Possessing up to a dozen guns, three of which were heavy, 'Messenger', 'London' and 'the King's Daughter', a cannonade began around the clock aimed mainly at the walls and towers around the main gates but also into the town. The defenders worked tirelessly at night to repair the damage so that by early September the English besiegers had made frustratingly little headway. Worse, the 'bloody flux' (dysentery) was now depleting the English ranks, the lack of sanitation and hot weather causing misery for the besiegers as well as the besieged. His campaign already in trouble, Henry now concentrated his efforts on the south-west gate, 'the Bulwark', by mining, concentrated cannon fire and the filling in of the moat with fascines. The Bulwark and surrounding towers were soon in ruins forcing the French to sortie but incendiary artillery and an English counter-attack across the fascines forced them back behind an inner wall. As the Bulwark burnt furiously Henry continued the bombardment but prepared for a general assault, De Gaucourt, however, aware that few townsfolk would survive an English sack, asked for terms, agreeing to surrender on 22 September 1415 if not relieved before. In Paris, Charles remained impassive, De Gaucourt duly surrendering for seventy-six of Harfleur's notables to appear before Henry with a rope around their necks. They handed over the keys to the town and spent the next ten years in an English gaol.

Henry now looked to anglicise Harfleur as Edward III had Calais sixty-eight years before. It was to that town that an English Army of just 6,000 would now make one of the most ill-judged yet glorious marches in English military history.

23 September 1568
Anglo-Spanish Wars
Battle of San Juan de Ulua

IN 1492 THE Italian Christopher Columbus had sailed west across the Atlantic Ocean reaching not the East Indies but the West Indies and ultimately the even greater treasures of South America. By virtue of Columbus sailing under the flag of Spain not only did Italy fail to benefit but also Portugal, a loss partly offset by Bartholomew Diaz' discovery four years earlier of the passage to India via the Cape of Good Hope. A 1493 papal bull and the 1494 Treaty of Tordesillas with Portugal granted Spain a trade monopoly in the west but their incoming wealth soon attracted unwanted attention from French corsairs and men who cared little for a papal bull, Protestant Englishmen. England was also looking to expand trade, William Hawkins following the Portuguese to the Gulf of Guinea before in 1562 his son John, sponsored by notables including Queen Elizabeth I, began sailing from West Africa to the West Indies where he sold slaves to the Spaniards. The Spaniards and Portuguese, however, believed Hawkins was selling not just his own slaves but those seized from other vessels through acts of piracy, their complaints to a profiting Elizabeth coinciding with Spanish orders to their colonies not to trade with Hawkins. The Englishman, however, knew the Spanish required more slaves not less. Since Hawkins was forbade to sail by Elizabeth a three ship fleet sailed in 1566 under John Lovell, this time with a young blood relative of Hawkins aboard, Francis Drake. The expedition was a disaster, unable to sell slaves at Rio de la Hacha, Colombia, Lovell returned to find England and Spain on the verge of war. King Philip II of Spain (former Jure Uxoris of England by his wife Queen Mary I), the self-declared defender of the Catholic faith whose hand in marriage had previously been spurned by Elizabeth, was using military force to put down a Protestant revolt in the Spanish Netherlands (Belgium, Luxembourg), the faith to which Elizabeth owed her very existence.

On 2nd October 1567 six English carracks sailed from Plymouth, Hawkins aboard his flagship *Jesus of Lubeck* for an Atlantic voyage that soon had his crews praying for deliverance. After repairing at Santa Cruz de Tenerife a tribal feud was exploited to capture slaves at Conga, Liberia, Hawkins then crossing the Atlantic only to be denied a trading licence at Borburata and Rio de la Hacha. Resorting to force at the latter, Hawkins sold 200 slaves before repeating the exercise at Santa Marta. An eight day storm off Cuba then forced the fleet to make for San Juan de Ulua, Mexico, Hawkins taking the deputy governor and treasurer hostage who had mistaken him for the new Viceroy of Mexico, Don Martin Enriquez, whose arrival from Seville was imminent. On 17 September 1568 Enriquez, eleven Spanish merchantmen and two warships under Don Francisco de Luxan arrived early off San Juan de Ulua leaving Hawkins to hastily seize all the town's gun batteries but allowing the Spanish fleet to enter the harbour only after three days of negotiation and an exchange of hostages.

Enriquez, however, had no intention of keeping his word and stealthily began packing his ships with reinforcements from Vera Cruz. On 23 September 1568, a Spanish trumpeter prematurely signaled the attack, rowing boats filled with armed Spaniards appearing from all parts of the port as the larger moored Spanish vessels were hauled closer to the English *Minion*. Hawkins, however, had sensed treachery afoot, an alert defence successfully fighting off boarders on the gunwales as both the *Minion* and *Jesus of Lubeck* cut their moorings. An exchange of point-blank broadsides followed, the two Spanish warships suffering from the power of the English guns which then turned on the merchantmen but the Spanish shore batteries were also doing terrible work, the *Angel, Swallow, Gratia Dei*, a captured Portuguese slaver, all overwhelmed and the *Jesus of Lubeck* soon crippled. Drake's *Judith* braved the Spanish shot to draw alongside Hawkins' flagship, taking off men and stores before the *Minion* did likewise, pulling away only as a Spanish fireship approached. Hawkins jumped for his life but his overcrowded, severely under provisioned surviving ships still faced a grueling four month voyage home.

Half of Hawkins men asked to be set ashore rather than brave the journey, many dying painfully at the hands of American Indians or the Spanish Inquisition. Deteriorating Anglo-Spanish relations would suit Drake, a devout Protestant, he would spend his life fighting Spaniards whilst Hawkins would quit slaving to begin a development of the English Navy. The ultimate test for all three would come twenty years later off the south coast of England.

23 September 1803

India
Battle of Assaye

THE 1802 TREATY of Amiens had provided a temporary respite between the French Revolutionary Wars and the beginning of the Napoleonic Wars but by 1803 Russia, now under Tsar Alexander I, had altered her stance forming the Third Coalition with Britain against Napoleon Bonaparte who had made his intentions clear by displaying the Bayeux Tapestry whilst gathering a 100,000-strong French 'Armée d'Angleterre' at Boulogne. As 400,000 Britons answered a national call to arms for the defence of the mother country the 19th Light Dragoons and just two infantry battalions of Scottish Highlanders with significant local assistance were about to bring an area of India, ten times the size of Great Britain, under British suzerainty.

The British East India Company already controlled Bengal, Mysore, Madras, Hyderabad and Bombay but remaining independent were the five Hindu Maratha chiefdoms of Nagpur, Baroda, Poona, Gwalior and Indore stretching from the Indian east coast across Central India and north-west to the Punjab. Internal strife, however, led to the Holkar of Indore, Yashwant Rao, defeating the Peshwa of Poona, Baji Rao II, at Poona in 1802, the defeated Peshwa placing his lands under British suzerainty in return for military protection. To restore Baji Rao, the British Governor General of India, Richard Wellesley, Lord Mornington ordered his brother Major General Arthur Wellesley (future Duke of Wellington) with troops of the British Madras Army reinforced by Hyderabadis, to advance from Mysore to Poona.

The Scindia of Gwalior, Daulut Rao, immediately realised the consequent threat to Maratha independence created by Baji Rao's British alliance and attempted to form a coalition with the other Maratha chiefdoms. Yashwant Rao, however, remained indifferent and the Gaekwad of Baroda, Anand Rao, followed Baji Rao into British protection. This left only Daulut Rao and the Bohnsale of Nagpur (Rajah of Berar), Raghoji II, to face a two-pronged British invasion, Lieutenant

General Gerard Lake defeating a French led Gwalior Army at Delhi and Colonel James Stevenson, under Wellesley but acting independently, successfully assaulting Jalna over 600 miles to the south.

Believing the Marathas to be withdrawing, Wellesley gave chase urging Stevenson to march north with due haste. As Wellesley's 9,500 British and Indian sepoys advanced toward Assaye they found the European trained Maratha Army of 50,000 (mainly cavalry) and over 100 guns under Hanoverian Anthony Pohlman drawn up in position north of the River Kaitna. On 23 September 1803, Wellesley resolved to attack but declined a full frontal advance across the Kaitna instead turning right toward the villages of Peepulgaon and Waroor where his infantry crossed an unguarded ford at extended range from Pohlman's cannon. Now between the Kaitna and the River Juah Wellesley deployed into two lines of infantry with cavalry behind as Pohlman turned the Maratha Army ninety degrees left. The British infantry advanced with casualties mounting under intensifying Maratha canister, grape and round shot, Wellesley unable to compete with his inferior artillery but increasing the pace of his advance before stopping at fifty yards to execute a devastating musket volley and a bayonet charge that routed the Maratha gunners. On Wellesley's right, however, Lieutenant Colonel William Orrocks had mistakenly marched toward Assaye leaving Wellesley's right exposed to an oncoming Maratha cavalry charge and himself dangerously isolated. Wellesley ordered a cavalry charge of his own into the gap, light dragoons and the Madras Native Cavalry under Colonel Patrick Maxwell successfully repulsing the enemy. Maratha gunners who had earlier feigned death then began firing into the British rear but were annihilated whilst the Maratha infantry were assaulted on their left by Maxwell's cavalry and to their front by Wellesley's Infantry. Maxwell was amongst the 1,580 British casualties but it was too much for the Marathas, they fled north across the Juah leaving 5,000 casualties on the field.

Wellesley, who had two horses killed from under him and would soon be recalled for momentous campaigns in Europe, later described Assaye as his greatest achievement. Fifteen years of consolidation would give Britain control of all India south of a resurgent Sikh empire in the Punjab.

24 September 1645
English Civil Wars
Battle of Rowton Heath

IN 1643 KING of England Charles I had been unable to vigorously prosecute the English Civil War against his Parliament just when he most needed and had been paying the price ever since. Badly defeated at Marston Moor in July 1644, the King had then suffered an even more decisive defeat at Naseby in June 1645 at the hands of Parliament's New Model Army, professional soldiers committed to their cause and faith led by professional commanders. The king had lost all his infantry and cannon but had at least managed to escape himself. Unfortunately his private papers had not, the subsequent damning exposition of his efforts to rally support from Irish and European Catholics damaging his cause beyond repair. Even now the king, still held several important towns, including Bristol and Chester, with which to bargain but refused to entreat for peace. Instead he made for Raglan Castle, South Wales, separating from his Commander-in-Chief and nephew Prince Rupert who crossed to Barnstable where the fifteen-year-old future King Charles II held his court.

The King's South West Army under George, Lord Goring was in poor health, desertion rife and victim to local 'clubmen' who took every opportunity to punish Royal troops for their previous misdemeanors. Sir Thomas Fairfax, commanding the New Model Army, was in pursuit, defeating Goring at Langport forcing Rupert to rush to the defence of Bristol. In the North of England the king's garrisons had fallen following Naseby, immediately Leicester and now Carlisle and Scarborough but further north still, in Scotland, James Graham, Marquess of Montrose and his Highlanders had been all conquering giving Charles a distant hope that a combined Scottish and Irish Army might just redeem all his past failures. Charles therefore moved north raising die-hard Royalists even in Cromwell's East Anglia but not in anything like enough numbers. Back south Fairfax indeed moved to besiege Bristol imploring Rupert to surrender. With cannon aplenty but lacking manpower Rupert continued to resist the committed assaults of the New Model Army until, with no cards left to play, he asked for terms on 10 September 1645. Treated with the utmost respect by Fairfax, Rupert was atrociously accused of betrayal by his uncle and initially exiled.

Chester now remained the only seaport still in Charles' hands. Crucial to the shipment of the king's supposed Irish recruits, it was, however, in dire straits, inconsistently besieged by Parliament forces since 1644 but now vigorously so by 1,500 men and cannon under Michael Jones. John, Lord Byron commanding the garrison advised Charles that immediate relief was required to prevent the town's fall. To that effect but pursued by 3,000 Parliament cavalry under Sydnam Poyntz, Charles arrived on 23 September leaving 3,000 of his own cavalry under Marmaduke Langdale five miles south whilst he evaded the Parliament siege lines with another 600 to enter the town. Byron and the king then hatched a plan to attack the besiegers with a joint effort from Langdale's Horse and a sortie from the town garrison.

In the early morning of 24 September 1645, Langdale advanced toward Chester onto Hatton Heath apparently only becoming aware of Poyntz' proximity at 07.00 when he lined the hedgerows with dragoons who opened fire with muskets and carbines on the Parliament vanguard. The two sides exchanged fire for half an hour before the Royalists began to retreat, Langdale sending to Chester for reinforcements. Several hours later Langdale had retreated himself to Rowton Heath where he was attacked by Jones' Parliament forces from Chester, an event which now prompted a Royalist sortie from the town. The Royalist sortie, however, failed to break through leaving Langdale trapped between Poyntz and Jones with his king watching in horror from what is now Phoenix Tower. Outnumbered and outflanked, hit by volleys of musketry on both sides Langdale desperately charged before his men made a break west for Holt Bridge over the River Dee and Chester. In the battle and crush at the gates of Chester, Charles had lost another 1,500 men.

Byron held Chester for another four months before surrendering on 3 February 1646. Any Irish reinforcements would require a different port to save the king who escaped to Newark, one of his last remaining strongholds in England but still in hope that Montrose could yet provide salvation.

25 September 1066

Viking
Battle of Stamford Bridge

ON 5 JANUARY 1066 the King of England, Edward the Confessor died with no issue and no clear indication as to his succession but the very next day Harold Godwinson was crowned king igniting a dispute that would be settled in considerable bloodshed before the year was out. A Saxon, Harold's father Godwin had been made Earl of Wessex in 1018 by the Viking King Canute and had likely been instrumental in the ascension to the English throne of Edward on the sudden death, in 1042, of King Harthacnut (son of Canute). During Edward's reign Harold's own influence grew, in particular ending the Welsh Revolt of Gruffydd ap Llywelyn whose widow, Edith, he married for good measure bringing peace to Wales and improved relations with the northern English earldoms for Edith was the sister of Edwin, Earl of Mercia and Morcar of Northumbria.

As Earl of Wessex, the most powerful man in England behind the king, it is conceivable that it was to Harold that the throne was promised on his deathbed by Edward but the immediacy of Harold's coronation increased suspicion and anger across the English Channel where Edward's first cousin, once removed, William the Bastard, Duke of Normandy also claimed the throne through blood ties and similarly, an Edward promise which William claimed Harold had supported in 1064 under oath whilst a 'prisoner'. Regardless, Harold believed Edward's deathbed wish superseded all those that had gone before leaving William no option but to promote his own cause with the use of force.

In 1065, however, another threat to Harold had begun to develop in Northumbria when a rebellion of theyns against the harsh rule of Harold's brother Tostig Godwinson, Earl of Northumbria saw Tostig outlawed from York and replaced by Morcar. The new earl met up with his brother Edwin to march on London and make their case to the ailing King Edward but were intercepted at Northampton by Harold who no doubt, anxious to avoid a civil war, found in their favour against his brother. Edward consequently deposed a furious Tostig who initially tried to ally himself with William, raiding the South and East of England before spending the summer of 1066 in Scotland. At some point, he made contact with the King of Norway Harald Hardrada, perhaps the most feared individual in the whole of Europe, who also had a claim to the English throne just as poor as both William's and Harold's, an even older agreement with Harthacnut.

Hardrada, Tostig and 300 ships carrying a 9,000-strong Viking Army sailed up the Humber Estuary and the River Ouse destined for York but were opposed on 20 September by 5,000 Saxons under Edwin and Morcar at Fulford. In a bitter fight the brothers were defeated by the sheer weight of Viking numbers leaving the former Viking capital of England, York open to a sack but instead Hadrada rallied the populace to his cause, ensuring their commitment did not waver by arranging to receive hostages outside York at Stamford Bridge. On 25 September 1066, Hardrada and Tostig left 3,000 men with their fleet at Riccall and headed to Stamford Bridge to collect their hostages but much to their dismay were greeted by thousands of helmets and weapons shining in the morning sunlight 'looking like a sheet of ice'. Harold's huscarls (personal guards) had incredibly marched 185 five miles in just five days to join Edwin and Morcar's *fyrds* from Mercia and Northumbria. Surprise was complete but Hardrada was not one to retreat, forming a defensive circle on the east bank of the River Derwent, while thousands of his men desperately tried to cross the bridge from the west. The Saxons attacked, killing all before them on the west bank of the river but in the bottle neck at the bridge were held up by a colossus of a Viking who took down possibly forty of them with his battle axe before a Saxon floating in a barrel underneath delivered a painfully fatal blow. The Saxons then crossed the river, both sides forming a shield wall to commence battle in earnest with the Viking decision to leave their armour behind at Riccall soon proving catastrophic. In a desperate fight the Vikings began to give way despite fully armoured reinforcements arriving from Riccall who initially checked the Saxon push but ultimately could not hold it. Hardrada and Tostig were both slain, the former with an arrow through the throat, whilst their army was virtually wiped out.

The remaining Vikings at Riccal swore never to attack England again but Harold would have little time to celebrate his victory. Three days later in Pevensey Bay on the south coast William would arrive with a similar sized threat to claim his inheritance.

25 September 1915

The Great War
Battle of Loos

THE 1914 FAILURE of the Schlieffen Plan
condemned the Central Powers of Germany, Austria
Hungary and latterly Turkey to simultaneously fight a
war on two fronts, against Russia in the east, France,
Great Britain (the Entente) and Belgium in the
west. Kaiser Wilhelm II and Chief of German General
Staff Erich von Falkenhayn reversed German priorities, driving the Russians out
of Poland whilst now defending in the west. Fearing the defeat of Russia in early
1915 French General Joseph Joffre determined to pin down German troops on
the Western Front with continued offensives in Champagne and Artois. The role
of the British Expeditionary Force (BEF), reorganised into the First and Second
Armies, had, however, been compromised by the 1914 slaughter of its professionals
(including a high percentage of officers) and a shortage of ammunition. But,
thanks largely to the foresight of the Secretary for War Horatio Kitchener the
shortage of manpower had been resolved by Territorials, the Indian Corps and
more recently the first of Kitchener's Volunteer Army recruits who had signed
up at the outbreak of the conflict. The increase in numbers meant British officers
at all levels were now commanding formations for which they had not been
trained with German defensive tactics and modern weaponry adding severely to
their problems. Consequently 1915 had so far been a series of disasters, Neuve
Chapelle, Aubers Ridge and Festubert whilst fifteen British divisions were still
fruitlessly fighting in Gallipoli. Despite these consecutive setbacks, Joffre again
requested the now twenty-eight division strong BEF on the Western Front (up
from the original six) to support a 450,000 man French offensive in Champagne
by combining with a 50,000 man French offensive in Artois. By moral duty to the
Triple Entente (Britain, France and Russia) that obliged the BEF to fight at times
and on ground not of its own choosing, Kitchener ordered an unhappy Field
Marshal John French to commit the 75,000-strong British First Army of General
Douglas Haig to attack with the French 10th Army on a twenty mile front over

the featureless landscape of Loos against the German 6th Army of Crown Prince Rupprecht of Bavaria.

At 03.00 on 25 September 1915, as a four-day artillery bombardment continued, Haig ordered two mines to be exploded under the German lines at La Bassée. Chlorine gas was then released at 05.50 and a diversionary infantry assault launched on Givenchy but unfortunately the gas barely reached the German front line, instead settling across no-man's-land through which the main body, the 9th and 15th (Scottish) Infantry Divisions advanced to *Scotland the Brave* into machine-gun and artillery fire, the 15th surging on to take the German front line and the town of Loos before heading beyond Hill 70 only to retreat under heavy artillery fire. The 9th too advanced to take Fosse 8 and the formidable Hohenzollern Redoubt, a few units even pressing on to the German second line but increasing German artillery annihilated British support troops. On the right the 47th (London) Infantry Division, some kicking a rugby ball before them, made initial gains, capturing the Loos Double Crassier slag heap despite heavy machine-gun fire but on the left the 1st Infantry Division suffered from their own gas drifting back into the trenches. Those that did manage to go forward were then cut down by German machine-gunners except for the 1st Brigade who achieved their initial objectives. By midday the advance had stalled, reserves called up by Haig at 08.45 were only now arriving at the front lines but were exhausted after a march of sixteen miles. Meanwhile Rupprecht remained on the defensive, meeting French attacks in the south and British again when Haig renewed his attacks the following day. In poor weather and due to French failures the British were again checked by German reserves arriving in strength that now began a desperate week long fight to regain the Hohenzollern Redoubt. Fighting continued until 13 October when Haig launched a 430-gun bombardment around the Redoubt, Fosse 8 and the Chalk Pits, followed by another gas attack and finally massed infantry assaults which again foundered in fields of barbed wire with horrific casualties. The three week battle had cost the BEF another 60,000 casualties.

Though almost a victory Loos had ended as another fiasco in a year of fiascos. Again initial opportunities had not been exploited, Haig blaming the positioning of the reserve. In December French was replaced with Haig whose chance to do better would come the following year on the Somme. Rudyard Kipling's poem *My Boy Jack*, although naval, relates to the loss of his own son John 'Jack' Kipling at Loos.

26 September 1916

The Great War
Battle of Thiepval Ridge

THE STAGGERING CASUALTY rates of 1914 and 1915 continued into 1916 nowhere more so than on the Eastern Front where Russian losses approaching 5,000,000 men were leading the country toward a Bolshevik Revolution. German Chief of Staff Erich Falkenhayn, with huge territorial gains in the east as well as in France and Belgium, was, however, alone amongst the German High Command in considering a negotiated peace. Tsar Nicolas II of Russia, though he may have been tempted, also promised his Triple Entente allies Britain and France that he would not negotiate a separate peace deal while they fought on to expel Germany from French and Belgian soil.

Falkenhayn had then sought to destroy the Anglo-French alliance on the Western Front by drawing the French into a costly defence of the historically and spiritually important town of Verdun. Indeed it was not long before French morale began to waver under mounting losses, General Joseph Joffre requesting British Chief of Staff Douglas Haig relieve pressure on Verdun by attacking astride the River Somme. Haig had little choice if the Triple Entente was to remain intact but on 1 July 1916 the first day of the offensive led by the British Fourth Army of General Henry Rawlinson had been only partially successful in the south whilst an unmitigated disaster in the north, recording the highest casualties in British Army history. Despite the losses Haig was duty bound to maintain pressure on the Germans, suffering further casualties in piecemeal attacks that achieved little before the Fourth Army again launched a major effort on 14 July with tactical changes in artillery and objectives to capture Bazentin Ridge. It was now Germany who were drawn into an attritional battle, bringing in reinforcements from Verdun and Ypres but with growing air superiority as intense fighting continued particularly in Delville Wood and High Wood near Longueval. As poor summer weather continued, Haig launched more offensives further north at Fromelles and again back on the Somme at Pozières, Guillemont and Ginchy in preparation for a final push to Thiepval and the Ancre Heights, a position that would overlook German defences to the north and likely force their withdrawal.

At Flers-Courcelette on 15 September, just as they lost control of the war in the air to the superior new machines of the *Luftstreitkräfte* (*Die Fliegertruppe* before October 1916), the British introduced for the first time on a battlefield a new weapon, twenty-one 30-ton MK I tanks. Whilst another twenty-seven broke down their attack alongside the infantry of Fourth Army succeeded in capturing two miles of ground from the stunned German ground troops of General Fritz von Below's First Army. Switching the focus of his attack further east on 25 September Rawlinson, assisted by the French Sixth Army on his right, then attacked Morval behind a creeping barrage in an effort to prevent potential German reinforcements from any move west to Thiepval. Perhaps with Von Below now wrong-footed but still facing considerable resistance the key to the whole campaign, the Thiepval Ridge from Courcelette to Thiepval, was then attacked in turn on 26 September 1916 by the British Reserve Army of Lieutenant General Hubert Gough. Gough's men were working uphill against three lines of German trenches guarded by three Redoubts that had originally been a 1 July objective. The 1st and 2nd Canadian Divisions on the right advanced north of Courcelette to take the German first line and part of the Kenora Trench whilst on their left the British 11th (Northern) Infantry Division was resisted in fierce fighting at Mouquet Farm before taking more heavy casualties in an advance on the Zollern Redoubt. On the left the British 18th (Eastern) Infantry Division under the enlightened Major General Ivor Maxse ran into heavy resistance from German machine-gunners and artillery at Thiepval before Maxse outflanked the defenders and brought up two tanks capable of at least two miles per hour to break the deadlock. Maxse cleared Thiepval the following day before tackling the formidable Stuff and Schwaben Redoubts behind. It would require another three weeks of bitter fighting to fully reduce them.

The September successes of the British Fourth and Reserve Armies were down to limited objective, highly planned assaults but it would not last, the mistakes of old would soon reappear on the Ancre Heights.

27 September 1810

Napoleonic Wars
Battle of Bussaco

IN 1809 NAPOLEON Bonaparte, Emperor of the First French Empire, ruled almost all Europe bar his perennial foe Great Britain and a now rebellious Spain. The War of the Fifth Coalition arose in support of these two from an Austrian Empire in financial difficulty, the shortage of funds likely to prevent any further resistance once a disbanding of the 340,000-strong Austrian Army had occurred. Field Marshal Archduke Charles, brother of King Francis II, therefore sought another confrontation with France before any demobilisation of his own forces and duly took the offensive calling for supporting British offensives in Germany, Italy or Spain. Before the British Government of William Cavendish Bentinck, Duke of Portland could get what would be a disastrous expedition to the Netherlands under way, however, Austria had been catastrophically defeated at Wagram with 40,000 casualties. Fearing the ancient Holy Roman Empire ruled from Vienna was about to be crushed, Francis and Charles were happy to be given the opportunity to sign a peace deal with Napoleon despite many French commanders urging Napoleon to take a far stronger line. On Austria's capitulation, Napoleon then consolidated French gains in Italy, including a French annexation of Papal territories which earned him an excommunication from Pope Pious VII. For his troubles, Pious was then captured and imprisoned for the next six years.

Meanwhile in Spain, British Lieutenant General Arthur Wellesley defeated a French Army double his strength at Talavera but heavy casualties had forced a retreat to Lisbon, Portugal where thousands of Portuguese began a one-year-project building fortifications around the city from the River Tagus to the Atlantic Ocean, the Lines of Torres Vedras. Meanwhile Wellesley, now Viscount Wellington, was so disgusted with the Spanish and their leadership that he refused 'to enter into any system of cooperation' instead spending the next year in Portugal with General William Beresford training his British and Portuguese troops. The Spanish, however, continued to resist French rule with battlefield victories at

Alcaniz and Tamames before the consequences of Austria's capitulation, 325,000 French troops now concentrating in the Iberian Peninsular, left them routed at Ocana, Alba de Tormes and Gerona. Both Spanish held Ciudad Rodrigo and Badajoz, controlling the north and south passages respectively into Portugal, were then besieged, Wellington covering both and another passage along the Tagus by splitting his forces, himself with 32,000 Anglo-Portuguese on the ridge at Bussaco across which he believed would be the likely route of a French advance. When Ciudad Rodrigo and Almeida, Portugal fell to Marshal André Masséna's 65,000 plus strong French Army in July 1810 Wellington summoned General Rowland Hill and his 20,000 men covering Badajoz to join him in forming a 52,000 man defence on the Bussaco Ridge.

At 05.45 on 27 September 1810, French General Jean Louis Reynier sent three divisions in column up the ridge toward the centre of the Anglo-Portuguese line led by Major General's Thomas Picton and Brent Spencer. Most of the Anglo-Portuguese were hidden on the reverse slope protected from French artillery and were quickly transferred where needed along a road specifically prepared over the preceding weeks. The French were initially repulsed with volleys of musket and cannon but General Maximilien Foy renewed the attack to rout Picton's Portuguese militia. Wellington realised his right was not under attack and ordered Major General James Leith to support Picton, in turn driving Foy back. Further north, two hours after the initial assault, Marshal Michel Ney sent two French infantry divisions under Generals Jean Marchand and Louis Loison up the Mortagua-Bussaco Road toward Wellington's command post outside the Bussaco convent. Against heavy skirmishing, Loison and Marchand reached the convent but were repulsed by a close range musket volley, cannon and a bayonet charge from hidden British and Portuguese infantry under Brigadier Generals Denis Pack, Robert Craufurd and Major General Lowry Cole. The battle then degenerated into skirmishing.

Wellington retreated to Lisbon and the Lines of Torres Vedras of which Masséna as yet had no knowledge. The next few months would be the most miserable suffered by a French Army since the beginning of the Revolutionary and Napoleonic Wars eighteen years before.

28 September 1652 o.s

Anglo-Dutch Wars
Battle of the Kentish Knock

THE DUTCH REPUBLIC (United Provinces) and England had much in common. Both largely Protestant, they had been fighting Catholic Spain for many years, the English intermittently, the Dutch more or less continuously for eighty, and were both energetically developing overseas trade. In 1585 the Dutch had offered their Crown to England's Queen Elizabeth I who declined only for Oliver Cromwell to return an offer of Protestant unification between the Dutch and the now Commonwealth of England in 1651. Cromwell's offer was barbed, however, for the English Rump Parliament was bitter. England had supported the Dutch in their struggle for independence from Spanish Habsburg rule yet when England, Scotland and Ireland had been torn apart by civil war, the Dutch, Royalist supporters during and after (Prince William II of Orange was the son-in-law of King Charles I of England), had taken full advantage by dramatically increasing their global trade and more recently the power of their navy. They now spurned Cromwell, even to the extent of abusing the English envoys as they journeyed back to England. It was too much, Parliament passed the Navigation Acts prohibiting Dutch shipping from entering English ports and insisted that when in the presence of an English vessel the Dutch lower their colours in respect.

Off Dover in May 1652 Dutch Lieutenant Admiral Maarten Tromp failed to do so, offending General-at-Sea Robert Blake whose warning shots initiated a sixty-four ship battle. Tromp then sailed north to Shetland two months later to battle Blake once again but weather thwarted his efforts leaving the previously immensely respected Dutch Admiral facing censure at home. Tromp was replaced by the brave but divisive Vice Admiral Witte de With who himself had faced a Court Martial adjudicated by Tromp twelve years earlier. Bitter enemies of opposing loyalties, the pair disagreed on everything from discipline to tactics, the popular Tromp content to protect the large Dutch merchant convoys whilst the detested De With favoured direct aggression against the English. Now in command the latter sailed from Schooneveld on 25 September 1652, joining Vice Commodore Michiel de Ruyter to attack Blake and the English fleet at anchor in the Downs. As with many fleets that have sailed to England's harm, De With was hit by a storm but being a man of conviction and despite being outnumbered in ships 68–62, guns 2,400–1,900 and men 10,000–7,000 and against De Ruyter's advice he decided to ride it out.

By the morning of 28 September 1652 the Dutch fleet had been badly scattered and Blake looked to take full advantage. Transferring to the faster 88-gun *Resolution* Blake sailed north to surprise De With at the Kentish Knock, east of the Thames Estuary. Coincidentally, De With was also attempting to transfer ship, specifically to the 54-gun *Brederode*, Tromp's old flagship, but in a sign that the provinces were becoming less united, the crew would not allow him on board. Without waiting for his rear and now short of daylight hours, Blake attacked from the south-west. Sailing west De With then tacked to face south-east engaging Blake and Vice Admiral William Penn in the English van with two of the English ships, the 106-gun *Sovereign* and the 66-gun *James*, running aground on the Knock. Meanwhile, De Ruyter in the Dutch rear swung south to attack the English rear under Rear Admiral Nehemiah Bourne who soon faced the additional onslaught of De With sailing on from battle with Blake. The exchange of broadsides continued furiously and to the English favour when the *Sovereign* and *James* were finally freed from the Knock to add their formidable gunnery to the battle. The smaller Dutch ships simply could not stand up to the firepower of the English and began to suffer a fearful battering. De With's *Prins Willem* was dismasted before the battle began to fade near 19.00 when several Dutch vessels broke off to return to port. De With wanted to fight on but his dispirited sailors refused, the entire Dutch fleet then retreating to Hellevoetsluis.

The English believed they had won a decisive victory at Kentish Knock and made the dubious decision to send a twenty ship fleet to reinforce the Mediterranean. The Dutch began to build bigger, more heavily gunned ships and immediately replaced De With with his old rival Tromp. Two months later the returning Dutch hero would fight Blake in the Straits of Dover off Dungeness.

29 September 1364

Hundred Years' War
Battle of Auray

DESPITE AN INCREDIBLE run of victories through twenty-three years of war that saw both the Scottish and the French kings imprisoned in the Tower of London, King Edward III of England had still not accomplished his ultimate ambition of succeeding to the French throne. This ambition had initially been secondary to a king of England no longer having to pay homage to a French king for his lands in France, specifically Aquitaine which had been inherited by a succession of English Kings since 1152 when Eleanor of Aquitaine had married King Henry II. Following the 1356 English victory at Poitiers and in his subsequent confinement (with his son Philip) the King of France John II began negotiating the 1360 Peace Treaty of Bretigny. From such a weak position John would have little option but to free the English monarchy from maintaining their French possessions under French suzerainty but on the plus side he might just remain King of France.

Across the English Channel meanwhile, France plunged into chaos, armed gangs, English and French, roamed the countryside at will with the teenage Dauphin Charles, who had fled Poitiers, attempting to restore law and order against opposition led by Etienne Marcel and the Great Ordinance of 1357 which sought to limit French monarchic excesses. In contrast to the French Revolution of 1789 Marcel was defeated and assassinated leaving the Dauphin to rule but the peace negotiations with the English king were dragging on. In 1359 an exasperated Edward launched his sixth invasion of France, a massive army of at least 15,000 advancing on Rheims but just when it really mattered the French at last stood firm and Rheims held out. Edward then roamed through Burgundy burning and pillaging the duchy before advancing to the walls of Paris but the French retaliated with a seaborne attack on Rye. Exhausted, both sides at last signed the Treaty of Bretigny – John would remain king (he still had a ransom to pay) whilst Aquitaine, Calais and Ponthieu were ceded to England. In Brittany, however, the tinderbox that had twice before reignited the Hundred Years' War, the peace would last just four years.

Captured at La Roche Derrien in 1347 Charles, Count of Blois had raised his huge ransom and returned to Brittany in 1356 on the understanding he observe an alliance in perpetuity with England. Blois' rival for the Dukedom, John de Montford IV, son of the original contestant and widower of Edward's recently deceased daughter, Mary of Waltham, then returned to Brittany in 1362 on the understanding he was not to remarry without Edward's permission – the English king was not about to lose his hard won influence in Brittany. The English alliance with Blois, however, would not last – Don Carlos de la Cerda, the Constable of France who had negotiated it in 1354 was dead and although De Montford agreed a division of Brittany with Blois, the Count's wife, Jeanne de Penthièvre (who actually held the claim), would not countenance it.

In 1364 De Montford and John Chandos with 3,500 men were besieging the south coast Breton town of Auray with the stricken Bloisian garrison agreeing to surrender if no relief was forthcoming before 29 September. Arrive it did though on the west bank of the River Auray in the form of the discredited Blois himself and Bertrand Du Guesclin. Wary of being trapped between Blois and the garrison, Chandos departed the town for high ground on the east bank of the Auray over to which Blois crossed with 4,000 men before advancing through a marsh with himself in the centre, John de Chalon, Count of Auxerre on the left and Du Guesclin on the right. Despite the diplomatic efforts of the French knight Jean de Beaumanoir both sides were intent on a decisive outcome, grimly agreeing that no quarter was to be asked or given. A short duel between French crossbowmen and English archers was then followed by the two armies clashing in earnest, Blois going against Du Guesclin's advice by attacking the English head on. Chandos held the English centre, the Anglo-Breton Olivier de Clisson the right and the formidable Robert Knollys the left with a reserve behind under a disgruntled Sir Hugh Calveley (more honour was to be had in the front line) that restored order wherever and whenever necessary. In a desperate fight with lance and battle axe rather than longbows the French right collapsed with Du Guesclin extremely fortunate to be taken prisoner. Blois' centre fought on but when his left collapsed as well, Auxerre just as fortunate as Du Guesclin, the end was nigh for the Count who did indeed receive no quarter.

After twenty-three years the Breton War of Succession was at an end but subsequently the English backed John de Montford would play a delicate political game, paying homage to King Charles V of France for Brittany whilst continuing to maintain an English military presence in the peninsular.

30 September 1342
Hundred Years' War
Battle of Morlaix

SINCE THE REIGN of King Henry II (1133–89) a succession of English kings had begrudgingly paid homage to the kings of France for their extensive lands in France. Indeed in 1324 such was King Edward II's reluctance that his lands were declared forfeit by King Charles IV of France before Edward's Queen Isabella, Charles' sister, the 'she-wolf of France' negotiated a settlement. Amidst deteriorating relations, King Edward III then paid homage to King Philip VI of France only at the second time of asking before being threatened by Philip sailing his Mediterranean Fleet to Boulogne in honour of France's Auld Alliance with Scotland. Philip's refuge for the defeated nine-year-old King David of Scotland (Halidon Hill, 1333) and Edward's refuge for Philip's arch enemy, Robert of Artois, did little for diplomatic relations and led to Philip confiscating Aquitaine in 1337. It was the final straw, Edward looked for allies in the Low Countries, tempting Flemings with cash and an impressive longbow display at Cadsand before gaining the support of Louis IV, Holy Roman Emperor who also backed Edward's claim to the Crown of France as a grandson of Philip IV of France.

Edward invaded France but initially achieved only a staring match with Philip's army at La Flamengerie before his fragile but expensive allies deserted. In 1340 Edward then returned to destroy the French fleet at Sluys before, again with his fickle allies, besieging Tournai. The siege dragged on, Edward finally evading a relieving French Army and his creditors (he was bankrupt) when the resolution of his allies again wavered. The Hundred Years' War looked to be over after just four but a chance to resume hostilities then arose in Brittany when the death of Duke John of Brittany sparked the Breton War of Succession between his niece Jeanne de Penthièvre and his half brother John de Montford. Jeanne was married to Charles, Count of Blois, a nephew of King Philip whilst Edward backed De Montford in return for De Montford backing Edward as the rightful King of France. In regard to their own claims for the French throne, both Philip and Edward were therefore backing the wrong side.

In 1341 the pious Blois advanced against De Montford at Nantes, catapulting the heads of thirty captives into the town on his arrival that sufficiently rattled the inhabitants to surrender. De Montford was condemned to a Parisian jail leaving his forthright wife, Joanna of Flanders, to pursue his cause but Joanna was soon besieged in well-defended Hennebont with Edward sending Sir Walter Manny and only a token English force as a gesture of support. After two months of delays, Manny then excelled to such a degree that the arrival in Brest of reinforcements under William de Bohun, Earl of Northampton presented an opportunity to capture the north coast port of Morlaix, a success that would facilitate the arrival of further reinforcements under King Edward.

A short distance away at Guincamp, Blois gathered 15,000 Bloisian Bretons to trap the 4,000 English besiegers but the astute Northampton smartly departed Morlaix to meet Blois in front of a wood on high ground astride the Morlaix-Lanmeur Road. On 30 September 1342, after arranging his army in three battles each bigger than the entire English Army, Blois approached from Lanmeur at 15.00. Struggling up the hill toward the English, Blois' first column of dubious quality was sent reeling back by a storm of arrows from Northampton's archers grouped in herces at either end of the English line. The display of archery sent Blois into immediate consultation with his fellow commanders before a second French column of mounted men-at-arms was ordered forward. Thousands of horsemen led by Geoffrey de Charni charged up the hill but most were brought down by camouflaged trenches and traps dug earlier by the defenders that Blois' first column had not reached. The agony of the prostrate horses and their riders was increased further by another storm of arrows, just 200 riders reaching the English line where they were slaughtered or taken prisoner, De Charni included. Blois and his command now entered another more protracted consultation before the third column, mainly infantry, began moving forward so numerous that Northampton withdrew into the wood behind to form a hedgehog. Blois surrounded the wood but could not outflank or break the English position, suffering heavy losses in the attempt. As night fell the disheartened French began to desert but it would be two days before Northampton could resume the siege of Morlaix.

Though Morlaix did not fall, Northampton was nevertheless reinforced by King Edward, siege by siege conquering south and west Brittany. A two-year-truce then followed by the end of which De Montford was dead and Joanna mad but Edward took up the struggle on behalf of their son John as part of his ambition for the whole of France. In 1347, at La Roche Derrien, the Breton War of Succession would erroneously appear to reach a decisive conclusion. Before then Edward would invade France in strength.

October

"Here goes the last of the Brudenells."

MAJOR GENERAL JAMES BRUDENELL, LORD
CARDIGAN, COMMANDING THE LIGHT BRIGADE,
BALACLAVA, 1854

1 October 1916

The Great War
Battle of the Ancre Heights and
Transloy Ridge

THE FEBRUARY 1916 German attack on Verdun had, as planned, drawn in huge numbers of French for its defence. At 303 days, the longest battle of the Great War produced possibly as many as one million casualties, mostly to artillery fire, and forced France's partner by the political straight jacket of Allied warfare, Great Britain and Ireland, to launch an offensive of their own astride the River Somme. For two months since the initial July attack, Commander-in-Chief of the British Expeditionary Force Douglas Haig had achieved little in the way of territory but had suffered casualties at least as high as those of 1914 and 1915. Haig would earn the sobriquet 'the Butcher of the Somme' but in fairness, as well as his commitments to France, he could not have countenanced near 30 per cent of his shells being duds, nor that the summer weather would deteriorate quite as it did. Beyond that the British Army, used to a century of smaller scale colonial battles, was still at the bottom of a steep learning curve with all its professionals already dead or incapacitated. The men that replaced them, the Pals battalions, though fearlessly brave, were not much more than a militia commanded by men untrained to manage them. It should also be remembered that the British were not losing this battle, several times a break through had seemed tantalisingly close as the resources of the Central Powers (Germany, Austro Hungary) were stretched to breaking point not just by French and British efforts but simultaneously by Russia's Brusilov Offensive, their biggest of the Great War. If an uncommitted Romania had joined the war two months earlier it may just have cracked the German High Command but nevertheless their frayed nerves were clearly evident when, in August 1916, their Chief of Staff Erich von Falkenhayn was sacked.

Whilst Falkenhayn would head east to ultimately defend Palestine, Haig, the British Fourth Army of General Henry Rawlinson and the Reserve Army of General Hubert Gough continued the fighting with a series of limited objective September attacks toward the key to the whole battle, the Thiepval Ridge, introducing tanks at Fleurs Courcelette before attacks on Morval and Thiepval Ridge itself. These successes, achieved in bitter fighting but with more enlightened tactics, were now to be followed by further attacks on the reverse side of the Thiepval Ridge, the Ancre Heights, and further east on the Transloy Ridge, an advance that if successful would at least force the Germans into a large scale retreat.

On 1 October 1916, the British 25th and Canadian 3rd Division attacked the German First Army of Fritz von Below from Courcelette toward Grancourt immediately north of Thiepval but made little ground after an unsatisfactory artillery barrage. To their right, however, the Canadian 2nd Division fared better, capturing the main German front trench whilst further east still the Canadian 4th Brigade and British 23rd Division made 1,000 yards towards Le Sars, penetrating the German front line trenches. But once again the rains returned to make life difficult for the British artillery and tanks, Gough now struggling to break a determined German defence with attritional attacks that were opposed by machine-gunners with clear fields of fire, particularly from the bright chalk of the Butte de Warlencourt, too far back to be targeted by British artillery. Again the Canadians attacked at Courcelette, this time the 4th Division benefitting from an effective creeping barrage to capture the Stuff Redoubt before holding off furious German counter-attacks. Though the British 39th Division finally captured the Schwaben Redoubt on 14 October the offensives were becoming more and more painful, the fighting ending only on 19 November.

More than four months (141 days) of British and French effort on the Somme ultimately succeeded in forcing the German High Command into a forty mile winter retreat to the Hindenburg Line. It had cost 400,000 men but German losses were no doubt catastrophically higher, according to Captain von Hentig of the German Guards 'the Somme was the muddy grave of the German Field Army'. Difficult to quantify as a victory the Somme laid the foundations for the British victory of 1918 but at the time peace seemed as distant as ever. Small shrines in memory of the fallen began appearing on British street corners and in an attempt to raise national morale, a poem by William Blake was put to music by Sir Hubert Parry – Jerusalem.

2 October 1649
English Civil Wars, Ireland
Siege of Wexford

THE ENGLISH AND Scots had been settling confiscated lands in Ireland since before the turn of the seventeenth century in an effort to convert native Irish Catholics to Protestantism. The Catholic Spanish had tried to intervene but Spanish naval power had suffered a serious decline following defeat at the 1639 Battle of the Downs against a Dutch Republic that had been revolting against Spanish rule for seventy years already. Regardless of Spain's demise but in fear of the growing power of the Protestant led Parliament in London, Irish Catholics rebelled in 1641 whilst also declaring an unhealthy allegiance to King Charles I. Uprisings spread from Ulster across the country causing the deaths, by murder or by eviction from their homes, of many thousands of Protestant settlers before, in 1643, the Irish Catholic Confederation suffered a defeat against English Royalists at New Ross (politically King Charles had no choice but to put down the Irish uprising). The reversal at New Ross and the intensification of the Civil War in England led to a three year stalemate but fighting again erupted in Ireland toward the end of the Civil War with Irish Catholic Confederate victories over English Parliamentarians and Scottish Covenanters at Duncannon and Benburb respectively. Still fearful of growing English Parliament ambition, and with ambitions to govern Ireland themselves, the Confederates again aligned themselves with the failing fortunes of King Charles, their cause boosted in 1648 when the Cork Parliamentarian commander Murrough O'Brien, Lord Inchiquin also declared for the king. Inchiquin's defection left the English Parliament with just one port capable of landing an army and even that was soon under threat from a combined Royalist/ Irish Catholic Confederate Army intent on ridding Ireland of Protestant influence for good – Dublin. The Governor of Dublin, Michael Jones, had, however, been recently reinforced and led a surprise attack on the Confederates and Royalists at Rathmines, routing them with heavy losses to secure the landing on 15 August 1649 of Oliver Cromwell, Henry Ireton and 15,000 committed Puritans of the New Model Army.

Mindful of atrocities committed in the rising of 1641, Irish allegiance to the recently executed King Charles I and recent combined Royalist/Confederate offensives, Cromwell then began his own brutal offensive to capture ports on the east coast. First, Drogheda was bombarded for a week before Cromwell summoned the garrison commander Arthur Aston to surrender. Despite an ammunition shortage Aston declined leading to near 12,000 men of the New Model Army storming the town on 11 September, mercilessly massacring the entire 3,000 man garrison and likely several hundred civilians, Aston included.

The New Model Army then marched 160 miles south to Wexford from where Irish privateers and Dunkirkers had been operating against Parliament shipping for the past six years. Arriving on 2 October 1649, the Irish garrison at Rosslare was overrun by dragoons under Jones whilst Cromwell, with naval support, began the siege of Wexford itself. Commanding the garrison of initially 1,500 men, David Synnot declined to surrender despite lenient terms and against the wishes of many of his understandably terrified civilians. As Confederate reinforcements filtered into Wexford, Synnot continued negotiating with an increasingly vexed Cromwell until on 10 October a bombardment of the town saw Synnot agreeing to Cromwell's terms. No sooner had Synnot agreed, however, did he renege, requesting that his garrison be allowed to withdraw fully armed; that privateers blockaded in the harbour be allowed to sail out; and that the Catholic clergy be protected. Amidst these ongoing negotiations Cromwell's bombardment continued throughout the following day with two breaches being made in the walls of Wexford Castle (the Castle Captain James Stafford surrendered) through which New Model Army troops stormed in to the town. The Irish Confederates fell back in panic, mixing with civilians desperately trying to escape across the River Slaney as Cromwell's Puritans rampaged through the streets, burning the town, harbour, housing and churches whilst massacring 2,000 of the garrison including Synnot and several of the clergy. As many as 1,500 civilians also died in the rush to escape.

According to seventeenth century military custom the sackings of Drogheda and Wexford can not be considered exceptional but they were no doubt extreme. Cromwell has been held responsible for both although there is no evidence he ordered the assault at Wexford. Neither did he prevent it, however, and did not punish any troops afterward. Prince Rupert's Royalist fleet at Kinsale was now dangerously vulnerable. He fled to Portugal.

3 October 1594

Scottish Religious War
Battle of Glenlivet

 THE PROTESTANT REFORMATION had taken hold not only in England but also in Scotland where outrage at the behaviour of the Catholic Mary, Queen of Scots, had forced her 1567 abdication in favour of her baby son James. Under four regencies and the strict tuition of George Buchanan, King James VI of Scotland was then raised as a Presbyterian Protestant. In an age of extreme religious intolerance, howeve, both the maturing James and his southerly neighbour, Queen Elizabeth I of England (James was Elizabeth's heir by descent from King Henry VII of England), pursued a lenient policy towards Catholics despite Elizabeth in particular living in constant fear of Catholic plots and invasion by Catholic Spain. By the 1586 Treaty of Berwick, Elizabeth, now Supreme Governor of the Church of England, began paying James, nominally the head of the Church of Scotland (Kirk), subsidies which assured James' allegiance against Spain, notably the 1588 Spanish Armada with which King Philip II of Spain had not only hoped to restore heretic England to Catholicism but also avenge Elizabeth's 1587 execution of James' Catholic mother. His mind no doubt fixed upon his future English inheritance, James was seemingly less upset about his mother's gruesome fate than Philip.

Catholic threats to James existed none more so than from George Gordon, Earl of Huntly who had framed the last of James' regents, James Douglas, Earl of Morton for the 1567 murder of James' likely father Henry Stuart, Lord Darnley and had opposed the 1582–83 Ruthven Plot which had abducted James to impose fiscal discipline and restrict Catholic influence. By 1588 Huntly had openly converted to Protestantism but was in fact working covertly to support a planned Spanish invasion. Once his duplicity had been exposed, Huntly was remarkably pardoned by James who was hedging his bets should Elizabeth rewrite her will. Huntly then murdered his bitter rival James Stewart, Earl of Moray but was confined for only a week despite public outrage before in 1592 he was implicated for treason yet again when the 'Spanish Blanks' were found signed amongst others by himself and Francis Hay, Earl of Errol – Errol had already been denounced in 1589 when letters swearing his allegiance to Spain had been unearthed. James yet again excused both men of treason but ordered them to formally renounce Catholicism or leave Scotland. They did neither, instead they fled to their Catholic support in the Highlands.

In pursuit James sent Archibald Campbell, Earl of Argyll who collected at least 6,000 Protestant Highlanders to do battle in a clash of the clans with Huntly and Errol's 2,000 Catholics on the slopes of Balrinnes at Glenlivet. On 3 October 1594, having sprinkled holy water on their weapons and painted the white cross of Christ on their armour the Catholic Highlanders were likely already in position when Argyll began deploying on the hillside opposite. Despite their geographical and numerical disadvantage both Huntly and Errol agreed to attack immediately since they held an advantage in cavalry and possessed six cannon. Argyll, with no cavalry or artillery, initially suffered desertions when his vanguard was softened up by Huntly's cannon. Argyll's arquebusiers in the front lines then desperately fired into Errol's initial cavalry charge before Huntly's infantry closed for a fight with the Protestant pikemen. As the fighting raged across the slopes, Errol's cavalry then charged for a second time into Argyll's flank. It was too much, the Protestant clans broke and fled, losing several hundred men including Robert Fraser, the king's herald, whose distinctive armour attracted three spears. Huntly and Errol's casualties were light, those wearing the white cross miraculously untouched.

A furious James swore vengeance, ordering Huntly and Errol's castles to be destroyed. The two rebels fled Scotland but returned the following year to sign a confession of faith to the Kirk. Huntly was yet again restored to James' favour, even to the point of being granted a Marquisate but was required twice more to sign a confession of faith to the Kirk before on his deathbed finally declaring himself a Catholic.

In 1603 James became King of England, uniting the Crowns of England, Ireland and Scotland. He survived the 1605 Gunpowder Plot and oversaw the initial British colonisation of North America. His largely peaceful reign would turn out to be in sharp contrast to that of his son, King Charles I.

4 October 1777

American War of Independence
Battle of Germantown

AT THE END of 1776 the American Continental Army under General George Washington had violently jumped started back into life after almost a year on the run. General William Howe and the massively reinforced British Army had seemingly ended hope of American independence by chasing Washington out of New York City and across New Jersey but crucially had not managed to bring him to a decisive battle. Indeed once British supply lines had been extended Washington had stung them so badly at Trenton and Princeton that they retreated back whence they had come for the rest of the winter, New York.

In London, the Secretary of State for the Colonies, Lord George Germain, Viscount Sackville had hatched an ambitious plan for 1777 with General John Burgoyne which involved three separate columns converging along exterior lines on Albany. The subsequent British domination of the Hudson Valley from New York to Quebec would in theory isolate strong American Patriot support in New England from the other twelve colonies allowing Howe to bottle up the perceived hot bed of rebellion and crush further resistance. To this end Burgoyne led 8,000 men south from Quebec who by September 1777, having defeated General Horatio Gates at Freemans Farm, were only twenty-five miles from Albany. With a much stiffer test ahead of him at Bemis Heights, Burgoyne now received the news that the support he was supposed to receive from a 2,000-strong column approaching down the Mohawk Valley under Brigadier General Barrimore St Leger had turned back after a siege of Fort Stanwix. Worse, Howe himself had failed to understand the importance of his own role in approaching Albany from New York and would not be making an appearance either. Instead the British Commander-in -Chief was advancing on Philadelphia having decided the seat of Congress was key to the whole war regardless of the fact that it was in the exact opposite direction to that which the strategic objective suggested he ought to have been marching. Whether

Sackville had not been specific with his orders or Howe had cynically hatched his own plan is not clear but the result was that Burgoyne was now alone in enemy territory, a long way from home, facing a daunting proposition.

Howe had transported his army of 15,000 men down the east coast of America by ship before sailing up Chesapeake Bay to land fifty-five miles south of Philadelphia. All communication with Burgoyne had consequently been impossible but Howe did leave a garrison in New York albeit too small to march north should Burgoyne require assistance, which he certainly did. On 11 September, Howe defeated Washington at Brandywine and at Paoli with a bloody bayonet attack before out manoeuvring him to enter Philadelpia on 26 September 1777. The victory was hollow, Congress had completely evacuated the city whilst Washington was still in good shape outside. Howe therefore left 3,000 men in Philadelphia while moving 9,000 out to Germantown. Once advised of Howe's divided force, Washington resolved to attack him.

At first light but through heavy fog on 4 October 1777, the Americans attacked in four columns desperate to avenge the massacre at Paoli. The British troops were to a large extent still asleep but surprise was not complete since most of them acted as light infantry and were already fully armed. The British were immediately in some discomfort, however, as they hastily formed up to resist the American charge, fighting over broken ground, fences and copses but taking heavy casualties, Howe instrumental in rallying his men. The fighting continued for three hours in the fog, at times becoming highly confused with instances of troops firing on their own men but eventually visibility improved to allow the more disciplined British to counter-attack with supporting artillery. The poorly coordinated American columns began to disintegrate before a withdrawal began – their losses over 1,000 killed, wounded or captured.

British losses were similar but although Howe had held Washington's attack it would be the cause of American Independence that gained from the battle. Forsaken by Howe, Burgoyne would now fight alone at Bemis Heights while worse still, Charles Gravier, Comte de Vergennes, the French Foreign Minister had been so impressed by American resolve that he was about to send France into the fight.

5 October 1804

Napoleonic Wars
Battle of Cape Santa Maria

THE SIGNING OF the 1802 Treaty of Amiens by France and the United Kingdom of Great Britain and Ireland marked the end of the French Revolutionary Wars and more specifically the War of the Second Coalition but the peace lasted just fourteen months. In the belief that the French Consul for Life, Napoleon Bonaparte, had violated the treaty in several areas ranging from interfering in international affairs, to taxing British trade, to cynically using the interlude to strengthen both the French Navy and the *Grande Armée* (aided by the sale of Louisiana for eighty million Francs to their old allies the United States of America) the patience of British Prime Minister Henry Addington's Government broke. Across the English Channel at Boulogne 200,000 French troops had been training for a likely invasion of Britain whilst Napoleon had also put the Bayeux Tapestry on public display for the first time. The message from France was clear, a message Haddington replied to in May 1803 with a British declaration of war – the Napoleonic Wars.

The Royal Navy blockade of the French coast was quickly back in place and, after Haddington's Parliamentary majority and been trimmed to breaking point, William Pitt 'the Younger' was back in office as Prime Minister calling a Defence of the Realm Act – 800,000 men joining the British Army, the Royal Navy and the National Defence. Napoleon, however, believed that if he could be master of the English Channel for six hours he would be master of the world since it initially appeared Britain would once again have to fight France alone. These fears were quickly allayed, however, when Napoleon murdered Louis Antoine, Duc d'Enghien of the House of Bourbon, shocking the aristocracy of Europe who were further alienated in May 1804 when Napoleon titled himself Emperor of the French. After the many executions and battlefield casualties of the previous fifteen years revolutionary France had moved merely from a king to an emperor, Napoleon now more than justly viewed as an usurper.

The War of the Third Coalition against France was an alliance principally between those of the Second, Russia, Austria and Great Britain, Napoleon soon having to reckon with Russian and Austrian armies to his east with his only allies, the conquered territories of the Low Countries and Italy apart, being Bavaria and Spain. Spain was, however, not at war with Britain, although an ally of France since the now not so secret 1796 and 1800 Treaties of Ildefonso, the Spaniards had opted to pay France an annual subsidy of seventy million Francs rather than fight. Now under pressure from Napoleon, that situation was likely to change and in the knowledge of a four frigate treasure fleet under Rear Admiral Jose de Bustamante y Guerra departing Montevideo, Uruguay for Cadiz carrying £100 million (today's equivalent) Pitt and Vice Admiral Cuthbert Collingwood ordered Captain Graham Moore aboard the 44-gun HMS *Indefatigable* (to be joined three days later by the 38-gun HMS *Lively*, 38-gun *Medusa* and 32-gun *Amphion*) to intercept.

At 07.00 on 5th October 1804 Bustamante on the *Medea* sighted Moore's squadron off Cape Santa Maria, Portugal and formed line astern preparing for battle as the British sailed up alongside. Moore explained his orders and requested Bustamante surrender but, considering any use of force an act of piracy, Bustamante declined. The Spanish third in line, *Nuestra Senora de las Mercedes*, then broadsided the *Amphion* at close range, igniting a frenetic ten minute exchange of broadsides when the whole of Moore's line replied. The superior British gunnery outperformed that of the Spanish who suffered fearfully under a hail of metal and splinters before the *Mercedes* exploded killing almost her entire crew. The *Medea* and *Clara* then surrendered but the *Fama* made a break for Cadiz pursued by *Lively* and *Medusa*, striking her colours three hours later.

The three Spanish ships were towed to Gibraltar and pressed into Royal Navy service, each English Captain profiting to the tune of £1 million (modern equivalent) by the sale of their cargoes. Two months later a furious Spanish Government declared war on the British. A year later their fleet would be combined with that of the French for a major confrontation with the Royal Navy off Cape Trafalgar.

6 October 1421

Hundred Years' War
Siege of Meaux

THE FRENCH ROYAL family had been torn asunder by the King of England Henry V's 1415 resumption of the Hundred Years' War. France itself was also divided, the French King Charles VI enjoying considerable support from Orléanists, a faction that had supported his nephew Charles, Duke of Orléans in a bitter internal dispute against John 'the fearless', Duke of Burgundy, now an English ally by a common enemy. The 1415 English victory at Agincourt and subsequent conquests throughout Normandy had by 1418 left the Orléanists (now Armagnacs) under Bernard, Count of Armagnac vulnerable to attack in pro Burgundian Paris, Duke John murdering Armagnac on entering the city only to be murdered himself a year later by King Charles VI's son and heir, the Dauphin Charles. Any chance of uniting the two French factions against the English had now disappeared, a predicament that drove Charles' Queen Isabelle of Bavaria (Charles having gone mad) to disinherit her son in favour of King Henry upon her husband's death. The disinheritance of the Dauphin provided opportunity for Isabelle's daughter, Catherine of Valois, for the French queen also granted Henry's desire to wed her. Henry then returned to England with his queen, confident that his Normandy garrisons could withstand Scottish reinforced Dauphinist attacks and that Philip, the new Duke of Burgundy could punish the defection of Jacques D'Harcourt, Sire de Tancarville north-west of Paris. In March 1421, however, it was the turn of the English Royal family to suffer when Henry's brother Thomas, Duke of Clarence was killed at Baugé when suicidally charging a Scottish Dauphinist army without his archers. Henry returned to France in June, restoring calm before relieving Chartres and successfully besieging Dreux. Continuing south to Beaugency Henry fruitlessly attempted to bring about a decisive battle only for the Dauphin to retreat further south still over the River Loire to Bourges. Since the English Army was suffering from smallpox and dysentery, Henry did not follow but turned north-east for Meaux, a strategically important Dauphinist stronghold east of Paris.

After waiting at some distance for a vast array of cannon and siege engines to join him, Henry began the siege of Meaux on 6 October 1421, sending his uncle Thomas Beaufort, Duke of Exeter on a raid to burn down all the buildings outside the town walls. It was just a start, Meaux was protected by the River Marne, a moat, walls, a canal that cut across the Marne's meander and was defended by desperate men who knew their likely fate if captured – English deserters, Scots, Irish and French outlaws under the highly unpleasant Louis de Gast, the Bastard of Vaurus. A massive bombardment continued into December but deteriorating weather, heavy rain, flooding and amphibious sorties by the spirited garrison hampered the English. Over the winter months sickness returned to the English besiegers but Henry resolutely maintained the siege. In March a reinforcement of the garrison by Guy de Neslé, Sire of Offement failed when De Neslé fell into the moat, the failure persuading Vaurus to abandon the town for the more heavily fortified Market but in doing so allowing the majority of the inhabitants to surrender. To reach the Market across the Marne, Henry had a beffroi built with a drawbridge to replace that destroyed by the retreating defenders and under cover of cannon fire began landing men in between the Marne and the north wall of the Market. To the south Richard Beauchamp, Earl of Warwick did likewise across the canal and to the west Walter Hungerford built footbridges. As desperate hand-to-hand fighting continued on three sides of the Market, the English king had another beffroi built to the east, this time on barges to be floated across the fast flowing river with its drawbridge landing on the wall. As construction of the wooden monstrosity progressed in front of them, the morale of the defenders plummeted, after a six month siege they sued for terms on 9 May 1422, the castle following the next day.

The Bastard of Vaurus was hanged on his own execution tree outside Meaux but the cost of the siege only now became apparent. After a reunion with his Queen Catherine who had born him a son, the English court set out for Senlis, north of Paris, Henry so ill he was soon reduced to being carried in a litter. On returning to Bois de Vincennes King Henry V died on 31 August 1422 aged thirty-six. The son he never saw, the ten-month-old King Henry VI of England and the nineteen-year-old Dauphin Charles (VII of France) were both proclaimed King of France seven weeks later on the death of the French King, Charles VI.

6 October 1879

Afghan Wars
Battle of Charasiab

GREAT BRITAIN HAD been concerned at Russian expansion into the Eastern Mediterranean and south central Asia for over four decades. The First Anglo-Afghan War began in late 1838, Russian influence won from the Ottoman Empire in the Caucasus and Persia and by extension closer Russian ties with Afghanistan, led to a British Indian Army crossing through the Bolan Pass to overthrow the unreliable Afghan ruler Dost Mohammed Khan, replacing him with a British puppet, the former Emir of Afghanistan, Shuja Shah Durrani. The British occupation of Afghanistan, however, ended in disaster in 1842 when increasing Afghan opposition persuaded Major General William Elphinstone to make a winter retreat from Kabul. Harassed by tribesmen under the treacherous son of Dost Mohammad, Wazir Akbar Khan, Elphinstone's column was finally massacred at Gandamack with just one man, William Brydon, reaching Jalalabad. The Governor of India George Eden, Lord Auckland suffered a stroke at the news and returned to England but the 'Great Game' between Russia and Britain continued when Anglo-French forces invaded the Crimean Peninsular in 1854 to prevent Russian expansion into the Eastern Mediterranean at Turkish expense. Russian hostilities again resumed with Turkey in 1877, this time in the Balkans, the settlement of which a year later by the Treaty of Berlin left the Russians disappointed – a disappointment that would lead to near armageddon in 1914.

For their part the arch imperialist British had not been idle expanding their governed territory, in 1848 taking advantage of Sikh dissension to annex the Punjab up to the borders of Afghanistan, in 1852 consolidating British rule in Burma and in the mid 1870s beginning a 'Scramble for Africa' that would immediately increase British influence in West and South Africa.

Russia meanwhile again turned her attention to Afghanistan, sending an envoy to another of Dost Mohammad's many sons in Kabul, Emir Sher Ali Khan. Although Sher Ali regarded the Russians with suspicion he failed to dismiss them and increased British paranoia further by refusing to admit the British envoy, Neville Bowles Chamberlain. The Governor General and Viceroy of India, Lord Robert Bulwer-Lytton consequently invaded Afghanistan with a 50,000-strong British Indian Army, starting the Second Anglo-Afghan War. Sher Ali fled seeking Russian assistance leaving his son Mohammad Yakoub Khan as emir under the control of British Representatives throughout the country. Sher Ali's death in May 1879 and Russian ambivalence seemingly lessened the threat to the British who, failing to learn lessons of 1842, then withdrew their forces. In September the Afghans again duly rebelled, killing the British Representative Pierre Louis Cavagnari and his staff to initiate a second British invasion this time by Major General Frederick 'Little Bobs' Roberts and 7,500 men of the British Indian Army. Roberts advanced through the Kurrum Valley to reach Charasiab on 5 October with Yakoub denying any involvement in the rebellion. Roberts intended to wait for his full force and supplies to catch up before proceeding through the Sang i Nawishta defile on the River Logar but the following morning, 6 October 1879, 8,000 regular troops of the Afghan Army under Yakoub's uncle, Nek Mohammad Khan, appeared on the high ground west of the defile across a three mile front blocking Roberts' advance while 4,000 tribesmen threatened his rear. Roberts with just 4,000 Highlanders, Punjabis and Gurkhas and just five guns sent Brigadier Thomas Baker to attack Mohammad Khan's right whilst a force of Pioneers and Highlanders under Major George White advanced to attack his left above the Sang I Nawishta. Although heavily outnumbered Baker drove the Afghans back onto their second line where they also now faced the British forces under White moving west from the Sang i Nawishta. It was too much, the Afghan centre and right broke leaving their left isolated before they too shortly collapsed.

Roberts marched into Kabul on 9 October but within two months another rising of 50,000 Afghans under Mohammad Jan Khan Wardak had him besieged. White's tactical acumen at Charasiab would desert him twenty years later at Ladysmith, Natal.

7 October 1777

American War of Independence
Battle of Bemis Heights

THE BRITISH ARMY of General William Howe had the American Continental Army of General George Washington on the run for most of 1776 and had been looking to finish off 'the old fox' in early 1777, in doing so restoring King George III's colonies firmly back to British rule. By autumn, however, an ambitious plan to isolate rebel support in New England (devised by General John Burgoyne and Lord George Germain, Viscount Sackville in London in December 1776) had begun to unravel. Sackville, who had been cashiered after the 1759 battle of Minden and declared 'unfit to serve his majesty in any military capacity whatever' and particularly Howe, who clearly did not grasp the strategic objective, had failed to support Burgoyne's advance from Quebec, down Lake Champlain and the Hudson Valley to Albany as had been agreed.

Leaving General Henry Clinton in New York with a garrison to small to be of any offensive value, Howe had incredibly decided to march in the exact opposite direction, attacking the Continental Army in New Jersey and Pennsylvania to take the Seat of Congress in Philadelphia where American independence had been declared in 1776. Howe had defeated Washington in battle at Brandywine, Piola and Germantown but even with Philadelphia had gained nothing of value. Indeed Washington's determined resistance had so greatly impressed France and Spain that they were now on the point of championing the American cause themselves. Burgoyne would hardly have been inclined to worry about French and Spanish involvement for he had also been failed by another British column under Barrimore St Leger which had failed to emerge from the Mohawk Valley. Alone, Burgoyne's column had fought its way successfully to Saratoga on the Hudson River but was now about to come up against more formidable American resistance for Washington had made no mistake. Although concerned at the British presence in New York City, the American Commander-in-Chief had sent reinforcements north to Major General Horatio Gates who had recently taken command of the

Northern Department of the Continental Army, amongst them the dynamic Major General Benedict Arnold and Colonel Daniel Morgan accompanying riflemen from Maryland, Virginia and Pennsylvania.

Gates occupied Bemis Heights which dominate the Hudson Valley, blocking Burgoyne's advance to Albany. As per the original plan Burgoyne was requesting reinforcements from Clinton in New York but by mid September there was still no news of any approaching British column. On 19 September Burgoyne attacked at Freeman's Farm but was met by Morgan's riflemen who initially took a considerable toll before Burgoyne's main force followed up to drive them back. This pyrrhic British victory had, however, come at a cost in officers and men Burgoyne could ill afford, losses exacerbated by vigorous American skirmishing. At the end of huge supply lines Burgoyne forlornly waited in vain for Clinton to move north but by October time had run out, he would have to make an assault on the American positions at Bemis Heights.

On 7 October 1777, Burgoyne advanced against the American left, grenadiers under Major John Acland led the attack but their bayonet charge was halted by Patriot riflemen under Enoch Poor. Brigadier General Simon Fraser also attacked the American left further to the west but his attempt to outflank them was stopped, this time by Morgan's riflemen. In a fierce firefight the British officer was highlighted by Benedict Arnold and eliminated by an American marksman decisively turning the battle. Burgoyne now fell back to his own defences, in particular two large redoubts, the first of which was assaulted by Poor and Arnold but the redoubt held out in another desperate fight under the command of Major Alexander Lindsay, Earl of Balcarres. Arnold then recklessly exposed himself to British fire by transferring across the line to join Ebeneezer Learned for an assault on the second redoubt. Learned succeeded in another fierce fight which saw the defending Hessian commander Heinrich von Breymann reputedly attacking his own men in frustration at their performance before being killed. Arnold too was shot in the leg for the second time in eighteen months but survived.

Burgoyne was unable to retake Breymann's redoubt forcing a British retreat to Saratoga Springs where they surrendered to Gates on 17 October. For the victory Washington proclaimed the first ever American National Day of Thanksgiving. Saratoga was the major turning point in the American War of Independence as France and Spain now entered into an alliance with their new friends against their old enemy.

8 October 1951

Korean War
Battle of Maryang San

 IN 1950 KIM Il-Sung, Supreme Leader of the Soviet backed Democratic Peoples Republic of Korea (North) had taken full advantage of the US backed Republic of Korea's (South) poor defences with a full scale invasion across the 38th Parallel, a border agreed upon only five years previous between the US and the Soviet Union. The North Korean People's Army (NKPA) had come within fifty miles of the south-eastern port of Pusan where they were halted by United Nations-backed Americans under General Douglas MacArthur. As troops from several more nations arrived to reinforce the Americans, MacArthur then outflanked the NKPA by landing at Inchon west of Seoul before advancing into North Korea as far as the Chinese border. People's Republic of China Chairman Mao Zedong, however, now feared an American attack on China and preemptively counter-attacked (with some justification since when MacArthur later retreated across the 38th Parallel he recommended US President Harry Truman employ nuclear weapons. Truman sacked him).

Lieutenant General Matthew Ridgway initially stabilised the UN position but Chinese Marshal Peng Dehuai then launched a two-pronged Spring Offensive across the Imjin River and further east toward Kapyong. The United Nations Forces countered Peng's vast numbers with pockets of troops supported by massive artillery and air strikes that exacted a terrible price in Chinese lives for every yard gained toward a UN defensive position north of Seoul. Mao had been involved in the Chinese Civil War since 1927, the war against Japan 1931–45 and a resumption of the Chinese Civil War in 1946, he was acutely aware of his losses and pressurised Kim Il-Sung to enter peace talks which began at Kaesong in July 1951. The fighting, however, continued, at Bloody Ridge 20,000 casualties, the Punchbowl 10,000 casualties and Heartbreak Ridge 30,000 casualties before General James Van Fleet commanding UN Forces sought to advance to a new defence, the Jamestown Line, using the US I Corps which included the 1st Commonwealth Division (formerly 27th British Commonwealth Brigade) mainly British and Canadians but also

Australians, New Zealanders and Indians under General Officer Commanding Archibald Cassells, an Egypt cricket international.

Operation Commando began on 3 October 1951 and required Cassells to take Kowang San (Hill 355, Little Gibraltar) and Maryang San (Hill 317) defended by two Chinese infantry regiments. Advancing to the west of the Imjin River, Hill 199 north-east of Kowang San was taken under cover of dark by the Royal Australian Regiment (RAR) of Lieutenant Colonel Francis Hassett allowing both they and British Centurion tanks to fire on Kowang San which was assaulted with a classic pincer movement from the south by Scottish Borderers and from the north-east by C Company of the RAR, the two eventually overrunning the defenders in fierce fighting. Cassells now turned his attention north to Maryang San which was being reinforced by the Chinese. Royal Northumberland Fusiliers attacked from the south-west as the RAR assaulted Chinese positions along the ridge immediately to the south-east and east before working westward. The Fusiliers were taking heavy casualties but the RAR, with support from Royal New Zealand artillery, brilliantly took the Victor, Whisky and Uniform Chinese defensive positions against determined opposition. Hassett now moved C Company RAR up for an assault on Tango which was taken in heavy fighting before launching a successful assault on Maryang San itself. The Chinese still held formidable positions on the western slope, Hill 217, Sierra and the Hinge, the Fusiliers attacking the former but repulsed at Sierra before the RAR attacked from the east, C Company successfully taking the position where they withstood ferocious Chinese counter-attacks for over twelve hours. Hassett prepared a final assault to clear the Hinge and Hill 217, B and C Companies assaulting the Hinge after an intense artillery bombardment before again holding off determined Chinese counter-attacks and heavy artillery. Their position now untenable on Hill 217 the Chinese withdrew so that at dawn on 8 October 1951 the whole of the Maryang San was in UN hands.

The success of Maryang San and Operation Commando allowed Van Fleet to occupy the Jamestown Line for the duration of the Korean War. The war degenerated into trench warfare before an armistice was agreed in 1953. No peace treaty has yet been signed.

9 October 1917

The Great War
Battle of Poelcapelle
(Third Ypres)

AT LOGGERHEADS, BRITISH Prime Minister David Lloyd George regarded recent casualties suffered assaulting German defences on the Western Front as disastrous whereas Field Marshal Douglas Haig, Commander-in-Chief of the British Expeditionary Force, believed them to be unavoidable and that the Great War could only be won right there, in the main theatre. After French General Robert Nivelle, backed by Lloyd George, had failed so miserably in early 1917 Haig had asserted himself ever more surely, believing intelligence that reported Germany to be close to collapse whereas Lloyd George believed his own intelligence that reported German divisions transferring from the Eastern Front already likely gave the Central Powers a numerical superiority in the west and that Haig's proposed Flanders offensive would receive scant support from the mutinous French. When, however, First Sea Lord, Admiral John Jellicoe stated the success of German submarine warfare meant the Royal Navy could not continue on into 1918 Lloyd George acquiesced despite both he and Haig considering Jellicoe sensational.

Haig looked to use massive concentrations of artillery for an advance in the Ypres Salient which would relieve the poor strategic situation (British troops had been shelled from three sides since 1914) and allow a British amphibious attack on the Belgian coast which harboured the troublesome German submarines. For the offensive, Haig appointed, not the recently victorious architects of Arras or Messines, Generals Edmund Allenby or Herbert Plumer, but an ex-cavalryman General Hubert Gough whose over ambitious objectives of 31 July 1917 (Third battle of Ypres) had meant a dilution of artillery with initial advances consequently being pulverised by German artillery and *Eingreif* (counter-attack) units. In liquid mud produced by the wettest August for thirty years, Lloyd George's fears of an attritional battle were soon being fully realised but he did not intervene. On 25 August Plumer eventually replaced Gough, delaying for additional artillery for three limited 'bite and hold' attacks in temporarily better weather on Menin Ridge Road, Polygon Wood and Broodseinde creating a 'crisis in the German command'. On 7 October, however, the weather once again turned for the worse but there was no turning Haig who now brought forward an assault on Passchendaele Ridge centred around the remains of Poelcappelle.

At 05.20 on 9 October 1917, the British Second Army launched the assault over an eight mile front against the German 4th Army of Crown Prince Rupprecht of Bavaria but in conditions so bad that Plumer was not able to bring all his artillery to bear and those guns which he could were on such poor platforms that any accuracy was impossible. Many of the British, Irish and Anzac troops moving up to the jump off were also exhausted after a ten hour plus journey across duckboards and waist deep mud. The 1st Australian Division, attacking to the south, soon waded into heavy resistance following initial 1,200 yard gains whilst to their north the 2nd Australians, 66th Lancashires and 49th West Ridings were late in arriving to lead the main attack and could not keep pace with the 100 yards per six minutes creeping barrage that moved toward the Passchendaele Ridge. Against increasing German artillery the West Ridings were stopped by the swamp that was once the Ravebeek stream – heavy German machine-gun fire and counter-attacks from the Bellevue pill boxes then added to their difficulties with any support from British tanks out of the question once they had become stranded on the heavily shelled Poelcappelle Road. Desperate fighting raged as the British and Anzacs struggled against the formidable defences of the German Flandern I Line but with communications now collapsing more troops advanced only to be mercilessly pinned down in the killing ground by German machine-gunners and artillery firing with improved visibility before *Eingrief* divisions drove the British back to their original positions. To the north the British Fifth Army struggled against lightly shelled German positions around Poelcappelle but the Guards did make advances toward the Houthoulst Forest against determined *Eingrief* units.

Ignorant that none of his objectives had been gained Plumer would prosecute a further attack on Passchendaele on 12 October, the two battles producing little for estimated losses of 25,000 men on both sides. Haig would push for a second time at Passchendaele on 26 October 1917.

10 October 1914

The Great War
Battle of La Bassée

AS ENGLAND SLOWLY emerged from the 1066 Norman Conquest she had flexed her nationalist medieval muscle with aggressive invasions of Wales, Scotland, Ireland and most notably France. So too the French, emerging from monarchic absolutism in the late eighteenth century, had flexed her republican muscle with Napoleonic conquests of all Europe bar Great Britain. The trend continued in the 1870's after the unification of the independent German States under the Prussian Crown but their conquests in north-east France and a handful of African Colonies under Kaiser Wilhelm I and Chancellor Otto von Bismarck were of nothing compared to the ambition of Kaiser Wilhelm II. Almost two decades of arms building and a *casus belli* when Archduke Ferdinand of Austria Hungary was assassinated in Serbia saw the Kaiser and his senior military advisers confident of victory against a series of adversaries ranged against them and their own alliances (Austria Hungary with Turkey to follow – the Central Powers).

The German blueprint for victory, the Schlieffen Plan, was in fact a big right hook through Belgium into North West France and was immediately successful in forcing the British and French *Entente* back to the outskirts of Paris, speed of the essence since Field Marshal Helmuth von Moltke would also soon face a mobilising Russia on his eastern flank. But as Thomas Montagu, Earl of Salisbury had blundered at Orléans in 1428, Napoleon had blundered in Russia in 1812, Generals Alexander von Kluck and Karl von Bulow blundered now, turning east to the north of Paris rather than encircling the French and British from the south. The decisive French General Joseph Joffre had then seized his opportunity, dragging with him Field Marshal Sir John French commanding the British Expeditionary Force (BEF) to counter-attack on the River Marne, driving both Von Kluck and Von Bulow back to the River Aisne. On the Aisne, however, the pursuing *Entente* realised within 48 hours that the war here had suddenly become very different to that on the Marne and began to dig in but it was not the end of all movement on the Western Front as both the Germans and French now tried to outflank each other northward in a 'Race to the Sea'.

Whilst Moltke suffered a nervous breakdown believing the war to be already lost, the German 6th Army of Crown Prince Rupprecht of Bavaria continued to hold an advantage over the French 2nd Army of General Edouard Castelnau as the fighting moved to Albert and Arras. Further north still the Belgians were still bravely defending Antwerp with support from British reinforcements arriving from across the English Channel. While the German Chief of Staff Erich von Falkenhayn finally tried to reduce the port city – the Belgians holding him to the task until 6 October – the BEF at Aisnes entrained for the north, the British II Army Corps of General Horace Smith-Dorrien, III Army Corps of Lieutenant General William Pulteney and I Army Corps of Lieutenant General Douglas Haig disembarking the railway at St Omer for the front between La Bassée, Armentières and north of Ypres (Flanders) respectively while the IV Army Corps of General Henry Rawlinson marched south from Antwerp to Ypres between Haig and Pulteney.

On 10 October 1914, at La Bassée, hussars and lancers of Smith-Dorrien's British II Army Corps were immediately engaged on arrival at the still fluid front in encounter battles with their Prussian Uhlan and Saxon hussar counterparts from the German 6th Army. The fighting intensified on 12 October as the British 3rd Infantry Division advanced across flat ground north of the La Bassée Canal with Germans contesting every feature, natural and man made, their machine-gun concentrations taken out by British artillery. The British, however, could not take La Bassée, surrounded as it was by canals protecting the fledgling German trenches, leaving Smith-Dorrien to wheel north towards Givenchy and Lille. As the British approached Lille, however, two German Army Corps with four divisions of cavalry arrived to force Smith-Dorrien back, the British position only restored by a remarkable ten day stand by the Royal West Kents.

The British II Army Corps had suffered appalling losses at La Bassée with French now calling upon the Indian Corps, the Lahore and Meerut Infantry Divisions consisting of Britons, Gurkhas, Sikhs, Hindus and Muslims. By the end of October fighting was also raging to the north, at Ypres and Gheluvelt.

11 October 1776

American War of Independence
Battle of Valcour Island

THE ONSET OF the War of American Independence had provided General George Washington with an opportunity to drive the small British Army from North America altogether but, although successful in New England, a December 1775 attempt by General Benedict Arnold and Richard Montgomery to defeat British General Guy Carleton at Quebec failed. Montgomery had been killed during the battle and a wounded Arnold, after continuing a pointless siege, was soon forced to retreat in the face of imminent large scale British reinforcements sailing down the St Lawrence River the following spring. Arnold retreated south to Lake Champlain where an American council of war chaired by Major General Philip Schuyler decided to abandon Fort Crown Point and retreat further to Fort Ticonderoga at the southern end of the lake.

Carleton knew that if he could take Lake Champlain and link up with an advance of British forces moving north from New York under General William Howe, the British would control the Hudson Valley and split the American Continental Army in two, facilitating a systematic crushing of the rebellion in New England. The Americans had only very light shipping on Champlain but in Arnold they possessed a master ship builder who assumed overall command and immediately set to work constructing a fleet that could put up a fight, the first American naval fleet in history. Carleton was aware of Arnold's industry but for the British there was no rush or shortage of men and material that could be brought to Lake Champlain. Twelve prefabricated gunboats and the 180-ton HMS *Inflexible* carrying eighteen 12-pound cannon were assembled at Fort St Jean, Quebec to join eight other gunboats, two schooners and a gondola which were dragged overland from the St Lawrence River. To further increase firepower a Radeau floating gun platform named *Thunderer* carrying twelve 24-pounders, six 12-pounders and two howitzers joined the British fleet which sailed out of Fort St Jean under Lieutenant Thomas Pringle for the journey down the Richelieu River to Lake Champlain. Arnold meanwhile had increased the American fleet to sixteen ships, three schooners, a sloop, four row galleys and eight gondolas, all smaller and capable of attaining only half the British firepower.

Arnold knew he could not possibly succeed with an attack against such an overwhelming force and instead, in an effort to reduce his enemy's concentration of fire, formed a defensive line in the narrows to the west of Valcour Island, thirty-five miles north of Crown Point. On 11 October 1776, the British fleet sailed down the east side of the island initially completely unaware of Arnold's position behind it. At 11.00 one of Arnold's schooners, the *Royal Savage*, was spotted, the British turning back into the wind to attack. The *Royal Savage* was immediately pounded and ran aground but the rest of Arnold's fleet put up a terrific fire, putting the British Schooner *Carleton* out of action and sinking three gunboats. As the afternoon wore on, however, the superior British firepower began to take effect, the gondola *Philadelpia* sinking after being holed below the waterline, before near sunset HMS *Inflexible* entered the battle after a struggle in confined water against the wind. The effect was devastating, Arnold's fleet was quickly silenced and began to retreat but now against the wind themselves in the narrow channel they were effectively trapped. Since the light was fading Pringle and Carleton decided to wait for morning to finish them off.

As the morning of the 12 October broke the two British commanders were dismayed to find no enemy in front of them. What was left of the American fleet had rowed through them in the fog and was now eight miles up Lake Champlain making for Crown Point a further twenty-seven miles distant. An embarrassed Pringle gave chase sighting the Americans still twenty-miles short and successfully forced many of them to surrender or beach. Arnold burnt his flagship *Congress* and made for Crown Point overland with 200 men. Carleton and Pringle were in possession of Lake Champlain but winter was coming on and the snow already falling, they retreated back to Quebec.

Just five of Arnold's ships survived but it was enough, crucially he had maintained a toehold in the Hudson Valley. The Continental Army would decisively fight the British there the following year.

12 October 1428
Hundred Years' War
Siege of Orléans

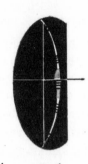

THE ENGLISH CONQUEST of France had been continued after the 1422 death of King Henry V by his brother John Duke of Bedford, Thomas Montagu Earl of Salisbury and their ally Philip, Duke of Burgundy who, by 1428, had control of all northern France to within fifty miles of the River Loire. The cause of the Dauphin Charles, King Henry VI's uncle, looked to be lost, dispossessed by his parents at Troyes in 1420 the Dauphin's armies, based largely on Scottish reinforcements, had been wiped out at Cravant and Verneuil whilst even the defection to his cause of John, Duke of Brittany had been reversed by an outrageous feat of arms at St James by Thomas Rempston. Bedford now favoured an advance to Angers in Anjou whilst Salisbury preferred to attack Orléans on the Loire just sixty miles from the Dauphin's court at Bourges. Salisbury won the argument, immediately taking a number of towns including Chartres and Janville just fifteen miles from Orléans which he then isolated by taking Meung-sur-Loire and Beaugency downstream before William de la Pole, Earl of Suffolk took Jargeau upstream. The 5,500 strong Anglo-Burgundian Army then moved across the Loire to advance on Orléans from the south for the decisive siege of the Hundred Years' War. A French loss here would expose the South of France to further English advances but although the Dauphin's forces were close to collapse, Orléans was at least well defended, from the south by the 400 yard wide Loire, massive walls lined with towers and over seventy cannon, a garrison and militia of 5,000 and a population of 30,000 all under the command of Raoul, Sire de Gaucourt.

On 12 October 1428, Salisbury began his investment of Orléans but was not strong enough to complete it, instead commencing a bombardment of *Les Tourelles*, a fortified barbican at the southern end of a nineteen arch bridge spanning the Loire. After several days cannonading Salisbury assaulted *Les Tourelles* but was caught in a crossfire from St Augustin's Friary and a determined defence of *Les Tourelles* itself. The English then resorted to mining, sending De Gaucourt immediately back across the river breaking down arches as he went. Now looking into Orléans from *Les Tourelles* Salisbury was then mortally wounded by a cannon ball, his death leaving the more cautious Suffolk to take command. Suffolk failed to increase pressure on the demoralised defenders before the forty-six-year-old 'English Achilles' John Talbot arrived to begin building a series of forts and trenches to the north and a fort at St Loup to the east. De Gaucourt meanwhile was also reinforced – 1,400 men under La Hiré, Jean Poton de Xaintrailles and John, Count of Dunois, the Bastard of Orléans arriving with Dunois assuming French command. Mining and artillery duels continued throughout the winter with the town garrison launching several sorties but with supplies reaching Orléans the only really significant development occurred at the Dauphin's court in Chinon. Here in March 1429, an illiterate seventeen-year-old peasant girl from Domrémy calling herself *La Pucelle* (the maid) arrived after hearing voices telling her to go to the relief of Orléans. Just as the Burgundians deserted the English, the Dauphin put *La Pucelle* at the head of a 4,000-strong relief army led by the clergy – amidst much celebration Joan of Arc entered Orléans on 30 April 1429. Having warned Bedford, Suffolk and Talbot by post Joan initially only traded insults until woken one night to hear a French sortie against St Loup was being overwhelmed. Joan arrived to rally her comrades and secure the first major French success of the siege. The Bastard then decided upon an amphibious attack of *Les Tourelles* and St Augustin but De Gaucourt crucially hesitated in the face of the English at St Augustin. A furious Joan and La Hiré then charged on horseback followed by their men-at-arms to take the Friary in a bitter hand-to-hand fight. Isolated in *Les Tourelles* were now 500 English archers and men-at-arms, Joan attacking the next morning to receive a bodkin arrow in the shoulder for her troubles. Battered by cannon, fireship, frontal assaults and militia advancing across the hastily repaired bridge, the English garrison was soon overwhelmed, its commander William Glasdale drowning in the Loire.

Defeat south and east of Orléans prompted Talbot and Suffolk to lift the siege, silently parading their army outside the gates of the city in hope of provoking a set piece battle before marching away. The Bastard and the Maid, who had reputedly pulled out the bodkin herself, now went on the offensive.

13 October 1812

American War of 1812
Battle of Queenston Heights

FOR TWO DECADES the United Kingdom of Great Britain and Ireland had been fighting Revolutionary France and the Emperor of the First French Empire, Napoleon Bonaparte. By 1812 Napoleon had defeated five European coalitions but a decisive 1805 defeat inflicted at Trafalgar by Vice Admiral Horatio Nelson had left him with no means to invade the British Isles. Napoleon had then sought to defeat the British by way of a trade embargo, the Continental System, which prevented any country, allied, occupied or neutral, in short all of Europe from trading in British goods. The Royal Navy in turn enforced an embargo on the French, specifically targeting ships sailing from the United States of America, a now self-governing nation that had benefited enormously from French support just a quarter of a century previous during the American War of Independence. Not only did the Royal Navy hamper American trade but in the search for British deserters also regularly stopped American ships, a policy that led to as many as 10,000 Americans being pressed into the service of the Royal Navy.

As the British blockaded both the French and the American seaboards so too did they obstruct Americans migrating across the north-western frontier by arming the Indian Confederacy led by Tecumseh, Chief of the Shawnee but including Iroquois, Cherokee, Potawatomi, Huron and others. Americans were further outraged in 1807 when HMS *Leopard* under Captain Salusbury Humphreys fired on USS *Chesapeake* after the latter refused to hand over deserters. As Americans bristled with indignation at the actions of their former colonial master, the British remained oblivious, busy prosecuting the Napoleonic Wars in the Iberian Peninsular whilst US President James Madison, leading a powerful Republican party, called on the House of Representatives to deliberate on American grievances. On 18 June 1812, for the first time in her short history, the United States of America made a declaration of war... on the United Kingdom of Great Britain and Ireland.

Madison thought British Canada would fall easily but with New England Banks refusing finance just 1,000 US militia crossed the Detroit River in July 1812 only to make a hasty retreat before surrendering to Major General Isaac Brock and Tecumseh. The cautious British Lieutenant General George Prevost then negotiated an armistice during which American forces east of the Niagara River were reinforced under Major General Stephen van Rensselaer, Brock powerless to intervene although aware of an intended American crossing. Sure enough at 04.00 on 13 October 1812, 4,000 Americans in seven lifts began landing at Queenston Village, Ontario under fire from British muskets and artillery, Colonel Solomon van Rensselaer (cousin) wounded whilst leading the attack. US artillery returned a covering fire but in the light of day the troop laden American transports were hit by British cannon which also pinned down those still on the beaches. The wounded Solomon Rensselaer then ordered a flanking attack on the Queenston Heights which had been denuded by Brock for the defence of the village. The Americans took the heights before Brock led a doomed British counter attack in which he was killed by a musket ball. As more Americans arrived a second British counter-attack led by Lieutenant Colonel John Macdonnell then also failed; Queenston now open to further US advances though the invaders were still under fire from a British gun battery at Vroomans Point. British reinforcements then arrived from Fort George including Mohawks (Iroquois) who scaled the heights only to be driven off but who succeeded in unnerving American militiamen still waiting to cross the Niagara. Major General Roger Sheaffe now led an 800-strong fourth British attack up the heights, 450 Americans under Brigadier General William Wadsworth retreating before being charged with the bayonet by the whole British line screaming Mohawk war cries. Wadsworth surrendered before discovering another 500 of his men hiding in the undergrowth.

US forces continued to struggle in and around the Great Lakes and Upper Canada until defeating and killing Tecumseh in 1813, breaking British native support. Following Napoleon's 1814 abdication in Paris, stronger British forces would begin to arrive in North America.

14 October 1066

Norman Conquest
Battle of Hastings

THE YEAR OF 1066 had already seen two major battles at Fulford and Stamford Bridge but still the dispute for the English throne raged on, indeed it was now time for the main event. The vacuum left by Edward the Confessor's lack of direction as to his succession had seen Harold Godwinson crowned the day after Edwards death, a coronation violently contested eight months later in North England by a 9,000-strong Viking Army led by the Norwegian King Harald Hardrada and Harold's estranged brother Tostig. Hardrada defeated the brothers Edwin, Earl of Mercia and Morcar, Earl of Northumbria at Fulford on 20 September but then suffered a crushing defeat when surprised by Harold at Stamford Bridge five days later. Just another three days, however, and William the Bastard, Duke of Normandy was mooring on the south coast outside the derelict Roman fort above what is now Pevensey cricket ground, intent on pressing his claim that Edward, his cousin once removed, had promised him the throne and not Harold.

After celebrating his Stamford Bridge victory in York and at news of William's arrival Harold marched back to London with the elite of his Saxon *fyrd* (army) – the huscarls. Much of the remainder of his force, however, including the Northumbrian and Mercian elements of Edwin and Morcar remained north. After the week long march and another week recuperating in London, Harold, no doubt brimming with confidence, resolved not to wait for reinforcements, of which he could have called upon many thousand, but advanced to confront William at the earliest opportunity. For his part William had moved around the coast to Hastings and was living off the local land to the obvious discomfort of the local population, Harold's own people from Wessex. After leaving London the Saxon *fyrd* marched through the *Andredsweald*, the great forest that stretched from Blackheath to a 'hoar apple tree' at Caldbec Hill, just north of what is now Battle. The English king did not require a decisive victory, it would be enough just to keep the Normans in the marshes and headlands of Kent and Sussex (the geography was then very different) where they would suffer over an English winter.

On 14 October 1066, Harold planted his standard of the fighting man on Senlac Hill, he was accompanied by 3,000 huscarls, his personal guards wielding huge double handed battle axes and another 3–4,000 more lightly armed local levies with just a few archers. Meanwhile William had moved his 8,000 strong Norman Army up from his Hastings castle (he had brought his own) to take up a position on the hill opposite Harold who was clearly going to fight on the defensive. Beginning proceedings William sent forward his archers followed by infantry and cavalry none of whom could make any impression on the interlocked Saxon shield wall. The Norman cavalry were not mounted on the big destriers of latter medieval times but on smaller horses that would only be able to charge up the steep Senlac Hill so many times and by midday the shield wall still stood firm. The prospects for William were looking bleaker by the moment when yet another charge, this time by Bretons on the Norman left, was repulsed with such vigour that it tumbled back down the hill in total disarray. Confidence was never higher in Harold's ranks and against orders many Saxons now broke ranks, pursuing the Bretons down the hill to complete the rout but in so doing presenting William with his opportunity. Raising his helmet to allay fears that he had been killed amidst the Breton debacle, William rallied his men to encircle Harold's undisciplined troops who paid the price to a man. William then renewed his efforts back up Senlac Hill, gradually reducing the Saxon shield wall with a storm of arrows and spears in a six-hour hand-to-hand fight before Harold was struck in the eye by an arrow, falling with his brothers Leofwine and Gyrd, his loyal huscarls fighting on regardless to the bitter end.

The Battle of Hastings marked the end of Anglo-Saxon Britain. William was crowned on Christmas Day 1066 and began a ruthless conquest of the realm, replacing all Saxon nobles with Norman. Security he reinforced with castles and strongholds in the major towns, including the Tower of London, and in 1086 compiled an audit of England's possession's for taxation purposes – the Domesday Book. According to the twelfth century Benedictine Chronicler Orderic Vitalis, on his deathbed William confessed 'to making my way to the throne of that kingdom by so many crimes I dare not leave it to anyone but God alone'.

15 October 1810
Napoleonic Wars
Battle of Fuengirola

AFTER A THREE year absence the Austrian bid to resurrect concerted opposition against Napoleonic France as part of the Fifth Coalition had lasted just three months until Archduke Charles, brother of King Francis II of Austria, was decisively defeated at Wagram. The pair then signed the 1809 Treaty of Schönbrunn which saw Austria hand over territory, a large percentage of her population, an annual indemnity and the hand in marriage of Francis' eldest daughter Marie Louise, Duchess of Parma to Napoleon. Once Napoleon had finished consolidating his new territories in Italy, including those of Pope Pious VII, the only active Napoleonic theatre of war was the rebellious Iberian Peninsular, all of Europe otherwise being under French control. In Spain, Napoleon was now able to reinforce the French armies leaving the disunited Spanish and Anglo-Portuguese to face 325,000 Frenchmen. Determined Spanish resistance at Alcaniz and Tamames ultimately gave way to French strength at Ocana, Alba de Tormes and the siege of Gerona but when the neighbouring border towns of Ciudad Rodrigo, Spain and Almeida, Portugal fell the 65,000 strong French Army of Marshal André Masséna advanced into Portugal for a determined effort to rid the European continent of the British. The Anglo-Portuguese Army of Lieutenant General Arthur Wellesley, Viscount Wellington successfully fought Masséna at Bussaco in late September but heavy casualties forced Wellington into an uncomfortable retreat to his well prepared siege lines of Torres Vedras outside Lisbon. Further south the well fortified Spanish held port of Cadiz had withstood a siege since February against perhaps the largest siege guns of the Napoleonic Wars while outside in Andalusia Marshal Jean de Dieu Soult skirmished with Spanish *guerillas* under Francisco Ballesteros.

In the neighbouring Costa del Sol resistance to French occupation was slight, Marbella excepted which was also besieged by the French. The Anglo-Spanish under Lieutenant Governor Colin Campbell in Gibraltar wished to relieve pressure on Cadiz and Marbella by attacking the 3,500-strong French garrison of General

Horace Sebastiani in Malaga, Major General Andrew Thomas, Lord Blayney deciding on a remarkably simple but ambitious plan to attack the small garrison in French service at the Castle of Fuengirola –150 Polish infantry from the Duchy of Warsaw under Captain Franciszek Mlokosiewicz with eleven French dragoons and three Spanish gunners. Blayney hoped Sebastiani would quit Malaga to relieve Mlokosiewicz whilst he, Blayney, would reembark his force and sail for Malaga.

At midday on 14 October 1810, Blayney landed with 1,700 men at Cala Moral Bay for a march along the beach to find Fuengirola Castle much stronger than imagined but nevertheless requesting Mlokosiewicz surrender. When Molokosiewicz declined, Blayney's fleet of two frigates and five gunboats opened fire causing the Spaniards manning the Polish guns to flee. The Poles then returned fire destroying a gunboat before Blayney launched an assault with the 89th Regiment of Foot, 'Blayney's Bloodhounds', who were repulsed in a sharp engagement. Overnight the wounded Mlokosiewicz received sixty Polish reinforcements as Sebastiani indeed hurried from Malaga. Blayney's plan was seemingly working but so close was Sebastiani that Blayney could only reembark at the cost of abandoning his own guns. On 15 October 1810 with the approach of the British 74-gun HMS *Rodney* and 1,000 reinforcements of the 82nd Regiment of Foot Blayney instead chose to stand and fight, his bombardment resuming with additional support from the Rodney and a Spanish warship. As the 82nd Foot began making for the shore, however, Mlokosiewicz and the eleven French dragoons successfully charged the British gun battery on Fuengirola Hill which had been left in the hands of a small contingent of Spaniards. The guns were then turned on the stricken 82nd Foot still approaching the beach, Blayney reacting by leading his Bloodhounds back up the hill in a determined counter-attack but now also opposed by the arriving Sebastiani, Blayney unsure who he was. Blayney realised soon enough and charged once again but he and his Bloodhounds were overwhelmed by Sebastiani's numbers, the 82nd Foot unable to recover the fiasco as Blayney was abandoned to a French jail for the next four years.

Mlokosiewicz was awarded the Legion d'Honneur for his defence of Fuengirola. Malaga was still in French hands but equally Cadiz was still in Anglo-Spanish hands. The fighting would intensify there the following March.

16 October 1781

American War of Independence
Capitulation at Yorktown

ON 16 OCTOBER 1781 General Charles, Lord Cornwallis called a meeting of his fellow officers, all day they had been under a terrific artillery bombardment just as they had been for the past fortnight. American 24-pounders, 18-pounders, howitzers and mortars had smashed British defences still manned by 8,000 brave British Redcoats and loyalists. Beyond the defences the wooden houses of Yorktown had been ripped apart by cannonballs, many of the soldiers preferring to sleep in the relative safety of their trenches but never daring to venture out to repair the disintegrating earthworks to their front. Earlier on in the day Cornwallis had thrown the dice one last time in a desperate attempt to evacuate as much of his army as possible across the River York to Gloucester Point but this time poor weather had conspired against the British and the operation had been cancelled. Cornwallis and his officers knew the game was up, vastly outnumbered and outgunned by American Patriots and their French allies outside the town and with no knowledge that Admiral Thomas, Baron Graves was about to sail from New York on a final desperate relief mission, they had no alternative but to surrender. After six years of fighting America would have her independence from British rule.

Such had been the length of his casualty list at Guildford Court House the previous March and so long his lines of communication in a country of few friends that Cornwallis had become dangerously isolated in North Carolina. He had marched south-east to the coast and sailed north to Virginia where he had received reinforcements from New York. A series of conflicting orders from Commander-in-Chief Henry Clinton, however, saw the British Army arrive in Yorktown on the Virginia Peninsula in May 1781 to build fortifications for a new naval base. Meanwhile to the north, French General Jean Baptiste de Vimeur, Comte de Rochambeau had met with General George Washington commanding the American Continental Army, Washington wanting to attack the British garrison in New York but Rochambeau pointing out that Admiral Francois Joseph Paul de Grasse was preparing to sail from the Caribbean to combine with Admiral Jacques Saint Laurent, Comte de Barras sailing from Rhode Island for attacks on British coastal interests, particularly in Chesapeake Bay. The combined Franco-American Army therefore made the 'Celebrated March' south to Yorktown, arriving in late September just after De Grasse had defeated Graves at the naval battle of the Chesapeake. Blockaded by the French at sea and by 19,000 Continental regulars, militia and French regulars by land, the British Army was hopelessly trapped in Yorktown.

Cornwallis had attempted to hold on by tightening his defence lines but in so doing allowed American and French artillery to come close enough to shell the British redoubts. A week of artillery exchanges raged, both sides leading spirited sorties until a Franco-American trench had been dug from where they could also indiscriminately shell British shipping and Yorktown itself. The shelling was incessant but worse was to come on 14 October when the two main British redoubts fell to a Franco-American bayonet charge that allowed Washington to direct accurate cannon fire directly into the town and harbour. His attempt to evacuate to Gloucester Point having failed, Cornwallis sent out a drummer on 17 October to signal for a parley, officially surrendering on 19 October 1781.

The honours of war were denied the British since Clinton had denied them to the Americans at Charleston. A sick Cornwallis left Brigadier General Charles O'Hara to present his sword, the honour of its acceptance given by Washington to Major General Benjamin Lincoln. As the British Army marched out of Yorktown little love was lost for their foes immemorial opposite who had come to liberate America, the French. It would be just a decade before those same men had liberated themselves and would face the British again in a conflict of hitherto unimaginable scale that would see no final British surrender. De Grasse would not have to wait anywhere near that long, his masters in France wanted him to take British Jamaica.

The British Empire would still have a sun that never set but it had just lost, in terms of future prosperity, and mineral wealth, its greatest ever colony. The Jewel in the Crown of Empire would now be in the east.

17 October 1346

Anglo-Scottish Wars
Battle of Neville's Cross

ENGLAND'S KING EDWARD III had sponsored Edward Balliol's efforts to reclaim the Scottish throne (originally awarded to Balliol's father John in 1292 by Edward's grandfather, Edward I) even though his adversary, at the time, the six-year-old King David II, was married to Edward's sister Joan. Scottish internal strife and the ambition of Robert the Bruce had left the Balliols exiled in France since 1299 but even after Bruce had gained independence from England at Bannockburn in 1314 Scotland had remained a deeply divided nation containing many 'disinherited' nobles' previously loyal to the English Crown, particularly Balliol and the ancestors of Bruce's old adversary, John Comyn.

In 1332 Balliol had succeeded in defeating the Guardian of Scotland Domhnall II, Earl of Mar on Dupplin Moor but was then surprised at Annan, Dunfries by further supporters of David and fled back to England seeking further support from Edward. The English king obliged, marching north himself to besiege Berwick before routing the new Guardian of Scotland, Archibald Douglas outside the town on Halidon Hill. Balliol was reinstated but his reign would again be short, deposed in 1336 with King David II returning from exile in France in 1341. By now Edward's attentions were fixed on gaining the throne of France as a grandson of King Philip IV of France, intervening in the Breton War of Succession before invading northern France in 1346. After burning most of Lower Normandy including Caen the English king had then delivered a crushing defeat on the French at Crécy in August 1346, killing or capturing most of the French nobility. With France suddenly facing ruin, King Philip VI of France looked to the Auld Alliance with Scotland, pleading for the now twenty-two-year-old David to invade North England. Since Edward and the main English Army were largely tied up at the siege of Calais, David, according to the Scottish Chronicler Andrew Wyntoun, was 'right jolly' to oblige.

On 7 October King David crossed into Cumberland with 12,000 Scots burning everything in their path, including the Priory of Lanercost, as they marched toward Durham. The destruction continued with the sack of Hexham before halting at Beaurepaire where David was paid not to destroy the town. King Edward was, however, well prepared to meet the Scottish challenge having deliberately not recruited for his French exploits in the far North of England where William de Zouche, Archbishop of York had been left to raise an army. Numerically only half that of the Scots but led by two formidable soldiers in Henry Percy and Ralph Neville, the English marched north from Richmond, Yorkshire for yet another Anglo-Scottish confrontation.

In Durham David was seemingly unaware of Percy and Neville's approach until 17 October 1346 when William Douglas suffered heavy casualties in a surprise encounter, David reacting by moving his army to high ground above the city at Neville's Cross. The English Army followed to form up in three battles of men-at-arms, the left under Sir Thomas Rokeby, the centre under Ralph Neville and the right under Henry Percy whilst in between and forward of each were herces of archers. As at Crécy the English preferred to fight on the defensive and consequently remained motionless waiting for the Scots to attack. The Scots, however, also remained motionless with the stalemate lasting well into the afternoon before the English archers advanced to begin raking the Scots at maximum bowshot range. The torment succeeded in forcing the Scots into advancing themselves, David leading the centre, John Randolph, Earl of Moray and Douglas the right, Robert Stewart (future Robert II of Scotland) and Patrick Dunbar, Earl of March the left. Things went badly for the Scots immediately, with ditches, fences and rocky outcrops slowing their approach they duly suffered as the English archers mowed them down. Rokeby then attacked the Scottish right which broke and fled leaving Moray dead, Douglas captured and allowed Rokeby to turn on David's centre which was fighting Neville to its front. Only on the left did the Scots have any success but only until the English reserve counter-attacked, the Scottish position soon beginning to crumble before the left departed altogether. For some time the Scottish centre bravely fought on, David distinguishing himself before finally fleeing with his men.

Covering twenty miles the English pursuit left 1,000 Scots dead and their king an english prisoner for the next eleven years (after being paraded through the streets of London he was later held at Odiham Castle). King Edward now subjugated Scotland and reinstated Balliol whilst concentrating his efforts at the Siege of Calais preparatory to an English conquest of France.

18 October 1016

Viking
Battle of Assandun

THE STRUGGLE AGAINST Viking raiders and the subsequent Viking conquest of Britain had continued for over two centuries since the 793 sack of Lindisfarne. The over population of poor Scandinavian soil led to Danes and Norwegians settling across the British Isles and northern France during the mid ninth century but the seizure of all England bar Wessex would prove to be the height of the Viking conquest for another 140 years. The resolute Alfred the Great, his son Edward and grandson Aethelstan had fought back to release England from Viking rule, Aethelstan becoming the first king of the English in 927. The peace that followed the Saxon heroics, however, was not to last, Viking longboats again appeared off the coast in 980 accompanied by violent sacks of isolated towns and villages. The achievements of Alfred had not been lost on Byrhtnoth, the Ealdorman of Essex, however, who had sought to again rid East Anglia of the Viking menace on behalf of his King, Aethelred the Unready (ill-advised) but, on confronting a Danish Viking fleet at Maldon in 991, Byrthnoth had been slain whilst those of his Saxon *fyrd* who had not fled were slaughtered to a man. The violent sack of Maldon which then followed sufficiently shocked Aethelred into paying Danegeld, partially pacifying the Norsemen, particularly Olaf Trygvasson who returned to Norway to spread Christianity only for Viking raids to continue anew in 997. Once again Viking influence spread across the East and North of England which came under the Danelaw whilst Aethelred ruled only Wessex (an area south of the Thames) the West and the West Midlands. The great feats of Alfred and his boys had unravelled almost entirely.

In 1013 Sweyn Forkbeard, King of Norway and Denmark, seized the throne of England after landing at Sandwich to conduct a rampaging march throughout the country culminating in a Saxon capitulation of Lundenburh (London) that forced Aethelred and his sons to flee to France. Sweyn died in 1014 leaving his son Cnut (Canute) ruling all England but the Saxon *Witangemot* (really just a council of 'wise men' with vested interests in various parties, usually blood related) was unwilling to acquiesce. The divisive Aethelred sensed his opportunity to return and forced Canute back to Denmark where he assembled another Viking Army, returning in 1016 with 10,000 Scandinavians aboard 200 longboats who would receive considerable support in the old Viking North and also from anti-Aethelred Saxon nobility. If, however, Canute believed the reconquest was to be a formality he reckoned without Aethelred's formidable eldest son, Edmund Ironside.

Edmund was hardly at one with his father either but he was determined that Canute would not deprive him of his inheritance (succession in Anglo-Saxon England was not necessarily a birthright). A series of battles raged around the country with much of Aethelred's and Edmund's traditional support failing to muster or worse, declaring for Canute. Edmund had his father's poor rule to blame for undermining his efforts but on Aethelred's death in April 1016 and in the light of Edmund's admirable valour, Wessex at last began to unite against the Viking invaders. Edmund broke up Canute's siege of Lundenburh and won battles at Brentford and Otford forcing Canute to retreat north into Mercia (Midlands) ravaging the countryside as he went before returning to Essex. On 18 October 1016, Edmund caught up with him at Assandun.

King of the English, Edmund Ironside, set up his army on Ashingdon Hill whilst King of Denmark, Canute the Great, did likewise two miles away on Canewdon Hill. By this time Edmund had been 'reinforced' by the treacherous Eadric Streona, Ealdorman of Mercia, who had defected from Canute having already defected from Edmund. It would prove a colossal mistake to welcome him back. What is known of the battle is provided by the Anglo-Saxon Chronicle and the less reliable Encomium Emmae Reginae. It seems Edmund moved his army forward to meet the Danes but Eadric lagged behind, a fierce bloodbath raging for several hours but with Eadric playing no part. Eventually Eadric and his men deserted the field 'betraying his natural Lord and all the English nation'. The Viking victory was decisive, Edmund and the remnants of his army fled back to Gloucestershire where he submitted to Canute. Canute allowed Edmund to continue to rule Wessex whilst he himself ruled the rest of England but on Edmund's mysterious death that same year Canute became King of all England, a united Kingdom, part of the Danish Empire.

19 October 1914

The Great War
First Battle of Ypres

 IN 1888 KAISER Wilhelm II had inherited a far more powerful nation than any of his forefathers largely due to the efforts of his Chancellor Otto von Bismarck who in 1871 had formed the German Empire by uniting the previously independent twenty-six German states under the Prussian Crown. Cousin of Great Britain's King George V through his grandmother Queen Victoria, the Kaiser then sacked Bismarck, failed to renew a treaty with Russia and initiated an arms race determined to achieve German hegemony in Europe. On the June 1914 assassination of Archduke Franz Ferdinand of Austria Hungary, Austria, strongly backed by Germany (the Central Powers), declared war on Serbia causing a domino effect of alliances that left the Triple Entente of Russia, France and Great Britain ranged against them. Perhaps surprised that Great Britain entered the fray so quickly, Germany had nevertheless already prepared for such a war by way of the Schlieffen Plan, an invasion and defeat of France with a right hook through Belgium before turning east to defeat a slow mobilising Russia.

Schlieffen had worked perfectly at the outset of war in August 1914 as ninety-eight German divisions, 1.4 million men, pushed seventy-two French and eight British Expeditionary Force (BEF) divisions back to the outskirts of Paris but here, in early September, directed by Field Marshal Helmuth von Moltke commanding from Luxembourg, the plan faltered when the German right wing of General Alexander von Kluck's 1st and Karl von Bulow's 2nd Army turned east to the north of Paris rather than from the south-west, a move that exposed their right flank. The decisive French General Joseph Joffre seized his opportunity with a determined counter-attack from the French 5th, 6th and 9th Armies and the BEF under a reluctant Field Marshal Sir John French, the bold strike forcing the Germans back fifty miles to the River Aisne where they dug in on the high ground of the north bank, successfully halting the Entente advance. Deadlocked, both sides then tried to outflank each other to the north-west in a 'Race to the Sea', Joffre moving French

Armies as well the BEF from the east whilst Chief of General Staff Erich von Falkenhayn, replacing Moltke, likewise moved the German 4th and 6th Armies of Generals Albrecht, Duke of Wurttemberg and Crown Prince Rupprecht of Bavaria toward the Ypres Salient whilst the 3rd Reserve Corps of General Hans von Beseler reduced Antwerp further north still.

On the fall of Antwerp, French and Belgians continued fighting with Royal Navy support along the Yser River whilst the BEF, reinforced by the Territorials and the Indian Corps, were in the process of forming a thirty-five mile defensive front at Ypres, Falkenhayn moving Beseler south in an attempt to deny the BEF access to Dunkirk and Calais. On 19 October 1914 Wurttemberg's German 4th Army began engaging the British around Ypres when Major General Thomas Capper's British 7th Infantry Division advanced toward Menin only to be immediately forced back. The following day German artillery attacks increased followed by infantry assaults north-east of Ypres, Lieutenant General Sir Henry Rawlinson's IV Corps resisting doggedly to exact a heavy toll on the massed German advances before I Army Corps under Lieutenant General Douglas Haig arrived to counter-attack around Langemarck. To the north, however, Falkenhayn had been forced to divert his drive south when King Albert of Belgium, who had personally fired the last shot in the defence of Antwerp, flooded Nieuport in a desperate attempt to hold the German advance. The new German approach then ran straight into Haig's I Army Corps with the British professionals inflicting enormous casualties on the German conscripts, many of whom were students. As the German advance staggered, French strengthened his line around Ypres before on 29 October Wurttemberg's 4th Army again attacked directly north of Ypres. The French resisted strongly but they could not now support the British to their south who were about to face a massed attack from the German XXIV Corps and Army Group Fabeck directly down the Menin Road through Gheluvelt.

The Battle of Gheluvelt would continue the First Battle of Ypres but already the British Expeditionary Force of August 1914 had all but been wiped out.

20 October 1899

Second Boer War
Battle of Talana Hill

BY 1899 THE fiercely independent Boer (Afrikaner) Republics of the Transvaal and the Orange Free State had been partially surrounded by British South Africa for more than twenty years. The former Dutch settlers had fought since the Great Trek of 1835 to preserve 'their' lands from the Pedi and particularly the Zulu before fighting the British in the First Boer War of 1880–81 when a series of British fiascos had culminated in defeat at Majuba Hill, Major General George Pomeroy Colley paying the expected Victorian price.

In 1886 the discovery of gold on the Witwatersrand in addition to previous diamond discoveries at Kimberley, North Cape Colony increased political tension in the Transvaal with Afrikaners protecting their rights by restricting those of the *Uitlanders* (foreigners). Also of concern to Britain was the growing imperial ambition of Germany extending from German South West Africa (Namibia) and South East Africa (Rwanda, Burundi, Tanzania). Also expanding was the British South Africa Company of Cecil Rhodes, founder of De Beers, who had sent a pioneer column north in 1890 bringing by coercion, Royal Charter and force, Matabeleland and Mashonaland (now Zimbabwe) under British control. In 1995/96 Rhodes then attempted to gain further control of the Transvaal mining industry by initiating a *Uitlander* uprising in Johannesburg through what turned out to be a disastrous raid launched from Bechuanaland (Botswana) by Leander Starr Jameson and 520 Rhodesian Police. The problem of Afrikaner treatment of *Uitlanders* and Britain's own African imperial ambition would, however, not disappear with the demise of the Jameson Raid despite British embarrassment. By 1899, with the Boer Republics now fully surrounded by British colonies bar Portuguese Mozambique, tension was so high that Transvaal President Paul Kruger issued Britain a warning that unless troop reinforcements be removed from the Natal/Transvaal Border a state of war would exist between the two nations. It was a political gift to British imperialists such as Alfred Milner, High Commissioner for South Africa and Governor of the Cape Colony who had long been searching for a *casus belli*. *The Daily Telegraph* called it 'a grotesque challenge' adding that 'Mr Kruger has asked for war and war he must have'.

British General Sir Redvers Buller left Southampton for South Africa to the tune of 'for he's a jolly good fellow' but he was well aware that the Boer commandos, though merely a militia, presented a threat far greater than that of previous African adversaries and that this would be a war reported daily in Britain and Europe where interested parties included an armament building Kaiser Wilhelm II, Alfred von Schlieffen and Helmuth von Moltke. Taking no chances Buller issued strict orders to his 13,000-strong forces already in Natal 'do not go north of the Tugela [River], do not go north of the Tugela'.

In Natal, however, Lieutenant General Sir George White had split his force, himself at Ladysmith whilst the far more confident Major General William Penn Symons commanded 4,000 men at Dundee, thirty-five miles north of the Tugela. Ignorant that 20,000 Boers were now descending on Natal Penn Symons forsook the heights around the town allowing 3,500 Boers under General Lucas Meyer to begin shelling him on 20 October 1899 with German Krupp guns. Aggrieved at his breakfast being interrupted Penn Symons returned fire with his eighteen field guns while three British infantry battalions in close order began climbing Talana Hill against Boer marksmen using German Mauser magazine loading rifles. Simultaneously the 18th Hussars and mounted infantry under Lieutenant Colonel Bernard Moller rounded Talana Hill to prevent a Boer retreat. On the forward slope the British infantry were pinned down until rallied in the traditional Victorian fashion by Penn Symons who ultimately paid the same price as had Colley. Under cover of suppressing fire and now in more open order Penn Symons men finally crested the hill, fixed bayonets and charged only to be cut down by their own artillery who had not seen the attack go in. The Boers disengaged, retreating to their mounts courtesy of Moller who had been unable to bring himself to shoot them and who only now realised the danger, pursuing Meyer north straight into a further 2,500 Boers under General Hans Erasmus.

With 250 casualties and Moller's hussars and mounted infantry now captive, Talana Hill had been every bit as bad as Majuba Hill. Immediate British prospects were not about to improve.

21 October 1805

Napoleonic Wars
Battle of Trafalgar

INTENT ON SPREADING the seemingly noble ideology of the 'Rights of Man and of the Citizen' Napoleon Bonaparte was crowned Emperor of the First French Empire on 2 December 1804. Already a more powerful autocratic ruler than ever had been King Louis XVI, Napoleon now ruled in alliance with Bavaria and Spain from the Low Countries to Italy having previously defeated or brought to a favourable peace all members of the First and Second Coalitions bar the United Kingdom of Great Britain and Ireland. Domination of world trade from the the West Indies to the Far East now lay before France once they had defeated the 'wooden walls' of Great Britain, the Royal Navy. To this extent Napoleon had cynically taken advantage of the 1802 Treaty of Amiens to increase French forces, 200,000 of whom were now outside Boulogne as part of the *Armée d'Angleterre* ready to cross the English Channel. In response British Prime Ministers Henry Addington and William Pitt 'the Younger' introduced the Defence of the Realm Act, raising 800,000 armed volunteers and building defensive Martello Towers as a Third Coalition formed with Russia and Austria both of whom were angry at Napoleon's recent self-appointment and his murder of the Bourbon Duc d'Enghiens.

Despite the threat of Russian and Austrian armies approaching from the east, Napoleon continued planning for the invasion of Britain by the combining, in the Caribbean, of the French Mediterranean Fleet with that of the Spanish who would then return to break the Royal Navy blockade of Brest, potentially giving France a total force of fifty-nine ships of the line. British Vice Admiral Horatio, Lord Nelson, commanding the Royal Navy Mediterranean Fleet, was evaded off Toulon by French Vice Admiral Pierre Villeneuve but gave chase across the Atlantic and back again. After fighting an indecisive battle off Cape Finisterre, Villeneuve, however, sailed for Cadiz rather than Brest, much to the chagrin of the *Armée d'Angleterre* which now marched in the opposite direction to Ulm, Germany to confront the Austrians before they could unite with the Russians. Napoleon nevertheless ordered Villeneuve back to sea, the vacillating Frenchman departing Cadiz on 18 October with a forty-one strong Franco-Spanish fleet. Aboard the 104-gun HMS *Victory* loosely blockading Cadiz, Nelson caught Villeneuve twenty miles north-west of Cape Trafalgar on 21 October 1805. Drawing up his twenty-seven ships of the line, four frigates, a schooner and a cutter in two parallel lines sailing at right angles toward the Franco-Spanish, the Vice Admiral signaled 'England expects that every man will do his duty'.

At noon the French *Fougueux* opened fire at the fastest British ship HMS *Royal Sovereign* but the line of approach left the commanders of the two British lines, Nelson and Vice Admiral Cuthbert Collingwood, to endure an hour under bombardment unable to bring their own guns to bear before cutting the single inter mixed Franco-Spanish line. Once amongst the Franco-Spanish the British ships would broadside to left and right into the undefended bows and sterns of the enemy, indeed on reaching the Franco-Spanish line HMS *Victory*, steered from below decks, opened fire with a double-shotted 50-gun broadside on the rear of Villeneuve's *Bucentaure* before a mêlée developed in which Nelson placed his trust in the superiority of his more highly practiced gun crews, the French and Spanish having been blockaded in harbour for most of the previous decade. After the initial broadsides *Victory* now became locked in point-blank exchanges with *Redoutable* whilst *Bucentaure* was assailed by HMS *Temeraire, Conqueror* and *Neptune* again in an exchange of broadsides at point-blank range, musket fire and hand-to-hand fighting raging across decks. At 14.00 disaster then struck on the quarterdeck of HMS *Victory* when Nelson was hit by a musket ball fired from the rigging of *Redoutable*, the greatest hero of his day carried below decks as the battle raged on above. Attacked on both sides by *Victory* and *Temeraire, Redoutable* soon surrendered, later sinking whilst Villeneuve's *Bucentaure*, the massive four-deck, 140-gun, *Santisima Trinidad* and many of the Franco-Spanish fleet followed, the damage done in a four hour fight primarily by the first dozen British ships to engage. Villeneuve had lost twenty ships and suffered 6,000 casualties whilst another 2,000 men would be imprisoned in hulks off Portsmouth. Nelson lived just long enough to witness the greatest victory in Royal Navy history, repeatedly thanking God he had done his duty. On the news his crews wept.

Nelson was given a state funeral, 10,000 infantry and cavalry escorting his coffin for a four hour service at St Paul's Cathedral. Today Nelson's Column towers over Trafalgar Square in Central London, his statue looking south to Trafalgar whilst the immaculately restored HMS *Victory* lies in a Portsmouth dry dock. The victory at Trafalgar not only prevented a French invasion but enabled Britain to become the dominant world power for the next century.

22 October 1764
India
Battle of Buxar

RATHER THAN DIRECT involvement in Indian politics the British and French East India Companies had always exerted influence by giving military support to local Mughal Nizams and Nawabs in return for advantages trading in Indian spices, tea and textiles. Events in Europe, however, began change in India when the 1740–48 Austrian War of Succession pitched France against Britain once more, the fighting spreading to southern India in 1746. Then, in 1755, four years after the Battle of Arnee, where he had successfully promoted Muhammad Ali Khan as Nawab of the Carnatic, the now Lieutenant General Robert Clive returned to India to soon find himself once again in a global war with France on the outbreak of the Seven Years' War (Third Carnatic War in India). That France's architect of expansion on the sub continent over the past three decades, Joseph Dupleix, had returned home just a year earlier would prove much to both Clive's and British advantage.

The focus of the Third Carnatic War moved north twice, in 1756 and 1757, when the Nawab of Bengal, Siraj-ud-Daulah successfully assaulted the British Fort William in Calcutta. Clive and Vice Admiral Charles Watson relieved the city on both occasions before making their own statement by flattening the French settlement at Chandannagar further up the River Hooghly. Clive then resolved to replace the unreliable Siraj with his uncle Mir Jafar, a feat he achieved in June 1757 by defeating Siraj at Plassey having bribed Mir Jafar not to fight.

Instead of mere trading posts the British now effectively controlled Bengal via a puppet Nawab, placing at his court a 'Resident', the de facto ruler. Such heavy taxation was required, however, from the Bengalis to compensate the British East India Company for their military expenses that before long Mir Jafar also sought to rid Bengal of British imperialism by employing Dutch military assistance from Batavia (Jakarta). In 1759 at Chinsurah it was the turn of the Dutch to be crushed by the British East India Company this time under the command of Colonel Francis Forde with Mir Jafar subsequently replaced as Nawab by his son-in-law, Mir Qasim.

Unfortunately the new Nawab's reign soon followed a similar path to that of his predecessors, Mir Qasim eventually rebelling against British taxes by abolishing them. Considerably less well off, the British became even more irate when Mir Qasim sacked the company offices at Patna, slaughtering 170 Britons in the process whilst on the way to Allahabad where he combined forces with Mughal Emperor Shah Alam II (Ali Gauhar) and the Nawab of Awadh, Mughal Grand Vizier, Shuja-ud-Daulah.

On 22 October 1764, a 40,000 strong Mughal Army with 140 cannon advanced to Buxar on the River Ganges where it was confronted by Major Hector Munro with 7,000 men, mainly Indian sepoys but including the 89th Highland Regiment and thirty cannon. Discord had been a characteristic of both camps, Mir Qasim did not want to fight at all and Shuja-ud-Daulah was openly at odds with Shah Alam. Neither was there content in the British Army, Munro having just crushed an Indian mutiny by executing the ringleaders in the old Mughal way, blowing them from the mouth of a cannon. After brushing aside skirmishers at Kalwa Ghat and Banas Nala, Munro arranged his force in two lines, his Indian sepoys on the flanks, the Highlanders in the centre. An artillery duel then commenced with the faster firing British at least holding their own against the numerically superior Mughal before the Mughal cavalry attacked the sepoys on the British left. In heavy fighting the sepoys rate of musket fire supported by artillery repulsed the Mughal attack before Munro advanced both his lines volley firing. Unable to compete with the British musketry, the Mughals were routed, Shuja-ud-Daulah prematurely quitting the field leaving Shah Alam to make his own peace with Munro when Mir Qasim fled north.

Munro lost 800 men at Buxar but the Mughals lost considerably more, not only 2,000 dead but the end of a near two and a half century empire as the British East India Company gained the Bengal Diwani (license to raise tax) by the Treaty of Allahabad – Mir Jafar returning as a more compliant Nawab. By furthering influence into North India the British would have to deal with the Marathas whilst in South India the troublesome Sultan of Mysore would in time align himself with Napoleon Bonaparte. On hand to defeat them both would be one of Britain's greatest generals, Arthur Wellesley, the future Duke of Wellington.

The Seven Years' War ended in Europe with the 1763 Treaty of Paris. British global gains won relatively cheaply did not go unnoticed. When American colonists revolted in 1775 they would find willing allies in France and Spain, the former anxious to rid North America of British influence.

23 October 1642

English Civil Wars
Battle of Edgehill

IN 1603 KING James VI of Scotland (I of England) united the Crowns of Scotland and England to enjoy a largely peaceful reign once he had survived the 1605 Catholic Gunpowder Plot. The same could not be said for James' son, King Charles I, who inherited the throne in 1625 before arousing the suspicion of nervous Protestants by marrying the Catholic Henrietta Maria of France; failing to call a Parliament during 'Eleven Years of Tyranny'; implementing his own taxes and introducing High Anglicanism, a move seen by many, especially Puritans, as the beginning of a return to Catholicism. In 1637 Charles then incurred the wrath of his ancestor's old kingdom with a new *Book of Common Prayer* inducing rioting in Edinburgh that spread throughout Scotland. The Presbyterian Church of Scotland was in favour of religious freedom and the abolition of the Episcopal (with Bishops) Church whereas Charles desired exactly the opposite. In need of funds for an invasion of Scotland, Charles at last recalled Parliament in 1640 but headed by John Pym this 'Short Parliament' (three weeks) instead took advantage of their long overdue assembly by drawing up a long list of grievances which included the king's economic record, poor civil liberties and his peace dealings with Catholic Spain with whom the Puritan Pym believed England and Scotland should be at war. No money forthcoming, Charles was consequently defeated by the Scots and again recalled Parliament. This 'Long Parliament' (twenty years) then began dismantling all aspects of the king's rule, a policy deeply unedifying for many since Charles was a mild man who resolutely believed in his divine, God given right to rule. When Irish Catholics then revolted against the consequent growing power of the English Protestant Parliament, Pym and his supporters voted through the Grand Remonstrance, taking command of the army (Trained Bands) away from the monarchy and moved to prevent bishops from voting in the House of Commons. His patience broken Charles sought to finally crush the Parliament threat to his authority, arriving in person at Westminster to arrest Pym and four other members only to find them absent, remarking 'all my birds have flown'. Civil War was now inevitable between the shaven headed apprentices, 'Roundheads', who formed Parliament's Trained Bands and the King's loyalists, derisively named after Spanish horsemen (Cabelleros), 'Cavaliers'.

In October 1642, Charles raised the Royal Standard at Nottingham and marched south on London. Robert Devereux, Earl of Essex, commanding the Parliamentarians advanced to meet him, awaking on 23 October 1642 to find the Royalist Army behind him at Edgehill above the Avon Valley, blocking his return to London. Although holding the advantage of high ground, there was, however, considerable disagreement amongst the Royalists especially when Charles delegated command to his nephew, Prince Rupert of the Rhine. It was calmer in the Parliament ranks on the hill opposite, both sides with about 2,000 cavalry and 12,000 infantry, many poorly armed and trained, some carrying muskets or pikes but most just farmyard tools, scythes, pitch forks and axes. In the cold morning both sides traded insults amidst a half-hearted artillery duel after several hours of which Prince Rupert and his Cavaliers charged down the hill and up the other side against the cavalry on the Parliament left and partially into the infantry in the centre. The defending Parliamentarians showed their inexperience and fled, gleefully pursued for several miles by Rupert's undisciplined Cavaliers. When Royalist General Henry Wilmot's Horse charged on the opposite flank the story repeated but the Parliament infantry in the centre bravely stood their ground when the Royalist infantry closed for a push-of-pike. Kept in reserve by Essex, Sir William Balfour's cavalry now fell upon the abandoned and consequently exposed Royalist infantry who in turn also bravely stood firm in a fearful mêlée of bloody hand-to-hand fighting. Fortunately for Charles, Captain John Smith managed to restrain some of the Royalist cavalry from further plunder (many were there only for profit) and returned to attack the Parliament centre in the flank. Essex disengaged whilst the Royalists were also reluctant to continue.

Both armies remained on the field overnight claiming victory amidst 4,000 dead and dying. Essex would block the Royalist advance on London with barely a blow landed at Turnham Green in November before fighting resumed in the New Year in the Royalist stronghold of Cornwall.

23 October 1942

Second World War
Battle of El Alamein

BRITISH PRIME MINISTER Winston Churchill travelled to Moscow in August 1942, stopping en route in Cairo, Egypt with Commander-in-Chief Middle East and British 8th Army General Claude Auchinleck. Churchill explained the forthcoming Operation Torch (Anglo-American landings in Morocco and Algeria) and that a decisive British victory in Egypt was imperative against the German Afrika Korps and Italians commanded by the newly promoted Field Marshal Erwin Rommel. Having only recently managed to halt Rommel's advance into Egypt at the First Battle of El Alamein, Auchinleck was adamant that any British offensive would have to wait. Churchill sacked him, appointing General Harold Alexander as C-in-C Middle East and Lieutenant General Bernard Montgomery to command the British 8th Army. On reaching the Kremlin, Churchill was then subjected to suffocating hypocrisy when Soviet Secretary General Josef Stalin, conveniently forgetting that it was his own diplomacy which had ultimately left Britain to fight alone for a year, claimed that by not opening a new front on the European Atlantic coast, the British were afraid of Germany. Churchill detested Bolshevism almost as much as Nazism – he had already told the British public that he 'would make a pact with the devil if Hitler invaded hell' – but he now explained to Stalin the British bombing tactics and forthcoming offensives in North Africa that would expose the soft under belly of the Third Reich, Italy.

Having stopped Rommel at Alam El Halfa in August, Montgomery was, however, as per his predecessor, not to be rushed into an offensive, aware that the British had already been twice up to Libya and back. The 8th Army now underwent intensive training as American Grant and Sherman tanks arrived in Egypt. The Afrika Korps on the other hand were hampered by supply shortages on extended supply lines (Malta grimly withstanding the most intense bombing of the war) and suffered further when their inspirational leader returned to Germany sick after more than two years of continuous fighting. In his absence at 21.40 on 23 October 1942, the inevitable British counter-attack, the Second Battle of El Alamein, erupted with the 'Devils Orchestra' lighting the night sky, 882 British guns firing 100,000 shells per hour for five and a half hours joined by Wellington bombers from above.

Aptly codenamed Operation Lightfoot 200,000 infantry, British, Australians, New Zealanders, South Africans, Indians, Greeks, Czechs, Free French and Poles led the advance through five miles of German minefields, the 'Devils Gardens', clearing a path for 1,100 tanks. By the morning, however, the tanks had not exited the minefields and came under German artillery fire which destroyed 200 over the first two days. Rommel arrived back at the front as bitter fighting, much of it hand-to-hand, stretched from the coast forty miles south to the Qattara Depression. With casualties rising amongst his 116,000 men and with just 540 tanks Rommel ordered a counter-attack in the north led by the 15th Panzer and the Italian Littorio Division before opting to defend across the whole front. After four days of fighting, superior numbers and total air supremacy, Montgomery had still not broken through but had created a salient toward the Aqqaqir Ridge. The battle for the ridge, Operation Supercharge, developed between 260 tanks of the British 2nd and 8th Armoured Brigades supported by British and New Zealand infantry against 150 Axis tanks. Pounded additionally by British aircraft Rommel, down to just fifty tanks by 2nd November, requested permission from Berlin to withdraw. Denied by his Fuhrer Adolf Hitler, Rommel withdrew regardless, the delay leaving thousands of unmotorised Italians to be captured. Down to 600 tanks, Montgomery resumed the British advance after a 24-hour delay, now sending Rommel into full retreat toward Libya. In Britain, church bells rang out for the first time in over two years but the battle would continue for another 1,200 miles past Mersa Matruh, Sidi Barrani, Benghazi and El Agheila, again capturing Tobruk on the way.

In January 1943 Montgomery captured Tripoli to give Churchill and the British nation their great victory, Churchill describing the achievement as 'the end of the beginning'. The British advance and the launch of Operation Torch in November would squeeze the Axis back into Tunisia whilst in southern Russia, the German 6th Army was also on the point of surrender at Stalingrad. The Second World War was suddenly looking very different.

24 October 1899

Second Boer War
Battle of Rietfontein

GREAT BRITAIN'S AMBITION to form a confederation of South African states under the Union Jack again became a distinct possibility in 1899 when just for once Transvaal President Paul Kruger lost his political acumen by threatening the British with military force. For Prime Minister Robert Gascoyne-Cecil, Lord Salisbury, Colonial Secretary Joseph Chamberlain and High Commissioner for Southern Africa Alfred Milner the opportunity to avenge the 1881 Battle of Majuba Hill and annex the mineral rich Boer Republics of the Transvaal and the Orange Free State was just too good to be missed.

British reinforcements were steaming south almost immediately including, aboard the RMS *Dunottar Castle*, Commander-in-Chief of British Forces in South Africa General Redvers Buller and a young *Morning Post* journalist Winston Churchill, all those aboard concerned that the fighting would be over before they arrived. Buller, however, had fought alongside the Boers twenty years earlier against the Zulu and was well aware of their hunting and shooting prowess even if they were not fully disciplined in military science. He therefore issued orders accordingly to his commanders already in Natal, Lieutenant General Sir George White, twice a recipient of the Victoria Cross, and Major General William Penn Symons not to venture north of the Tugela river but he had been ignored. Penn Symons had 'defeated' the Boers at Talana Hill, Dundee thirty-five miles north of the Tugela on 20 October but at the price of a bullet in his guts and 260 further casualties before on the following day at Elandslaagte, still fifteen miles north of the Tugela, Major General John French and his talented staff officer Major Douglas Haig had defeated the Johannesburg commando of General Johannes Kock but again with similarly heavy casualties.

As intelligence suggested there were now 25,000 Boers descending on isolated British positions in Natal the consequences of the failure to adhere to Buller's Tugela order began to increase in gravity. Major General James Yule, commanding in place of Penn Symons in Dundee, requested reinforcements from White in Ladysmith but White was concerned for his own safety and that of Natal itself. Yule realised he was about to be cut off but sought to take advantage of French's Elandslaagte victory by retreating in haste from Dundee to Ladysmith, in the process abandoning all his wounded (including Penn Symons who was later buried with full military honours by the Boers), tents, medics and forty days worth of supplies to the enemy. Although still commanding 3,000 infantry the absence of his cavalry, which had been captured at Talana Hill, left Yule's march dangerously exposed to pursuing mounted Transvaal Boers behind him and Orange Free State Boers threatening his line of retreat from the west. Yule's retreat, however, was fully endorsed by White who planned to use his entire available force for a future opportune strike out of Ladysmith, defeating the Boers with a single decisive 'knock down blow'. First he had to secure Yule's passage back to Ladysmith and consequently advanced north to prevent the Free State Boers from forming a deadly trap between they and their Transvaal comrades.

On 24 October 1899 White, with a brigade of infantry and a strong force of cavalry (3,000 men) supported by three artillery batteries (eighteen guns), advanced toward the Elandslaagte-Ladysmith railway line where 1,500 Boers under General Martinus Prinsloo, Adries Cronje and Christian De Wet were dug in on the Inyoni Hills extending toward Rietfontein. Initially the British cavalry met heavy fire from Cronje's commando before two Boer guns opened fire from the hills behind. The superior British artillery suppressed that of the Boers with White happy just to hold the enemy advance but he began suffering much heavier casualties when Lieutenant Colonel Edmund Wilford inexplicably advanced his Gloucesters up to attack De Wet. The Gloucesters were soon duly driven back by heavy Boer rifle fire, Wilford amongst the dead. The Natal Carbineers and the British artillery then successfully held off Cronje until at 15.00, after a five hour artillery duel, White learnt that Yules' retreat from Dundee had gone well and was now clear of danger.

White called off the attack and fell back on Ladysmith from where he expected to deliver that single, knock down blow. He would be there for some time.

25 October 1415

Hundred Years' War
Battle of Agincourt

IN AUGUST 1415 King of England Henry V restarted the Hundred Years' War with France after a twenty-six year truce during which both Kingdoms had been racked by internal strife. Sailing with a vast fleet to the River Seine the English king added Harfleur to Calais and Bordeaux amongst English towns on French soil but only after a frustrating six week siege. On 8 October a garrison of 2,000 men under Thomas Beaufort, Earl of Dorset was then left in Harfleur whilst the English fleet returned home and Henry, ignoring the advice of his fellow commanders, set out for Calais nearly 200 miles to the north with an army of just 6,000. It was very late in the season for campaigning and Henry gambled the French King Charles VI would not challenge an impudent English show of strength.

Somewhat ominously, however, the march soon began to resemble that of Henry's great-grandfather King Edward III sixty eight years before, destroyed bridges over the River Somme, fords defended and a French scorched earth policy forced the English Army to trek inland to Voyennes where they at last managed to cross the Somme. The whereabouts of the French Army then became evident when three heralds arrived in the English camp at Peronne, Henry advising them that 'if our adversaries seek to disturb us on our journey it shall be at their utmost peril and not without harm to them' before resuming his march directly toward Calais. Any optimism amongst the exhausted English troops crossing the River Ternoise at Blangy that the French had thought better was short lived, to their right blocking the road to Calais was the terrifyingly impressive sight of 25–30,000 armed Frenchmen.

That night the English Army slept out in the rain, few expecting to live another day. After receiving mass the next morning, 25 October 1415 they drew up for battle, just 1,000 men-at-arms in the centre between two herces of archers to be addressed by their king. Opposite them 1,500 yards away were three lines of French, each line bigger than the entire English Army consisting of dismounted men-at-arms and mounted knights eager to run down the detested low-born English longbowmen. Flanked by the Agincourt and Tramecourt woods the two armies stood at opposite ends of the field eyeballing each other for four hours. Time was on the French side, however, Jean le Maingre, Marshal Boucicaut and Charles D'Albret, Constable of France, commanding but as history dictated, hesitant to attack an English defensive position.

At 11.00 Henry ordered 'Advance banner!' and the whole English line moved forward to within 300 yards of the French. It is debatable whether the 5,000 archers then gave birth to the two-fingered salute but they certainly opened fire at extreme range. Short of bowmen the French could not return and their patience quickly snapped under a barrage in which up to 25,000 arrows were fired in the first minute alone. Boucicaut and D'Albret could not maintain order and the French horsemen charged on both flanks but suffered in the continued arrowstorm, those that reached the English line impaled on sharpened stakes and finished off with a dagger. The French front line of men-at-arms in heavy plate armour was now advancing across the deepening mud but hemmed in by the woods and the continued concentrated fire of the English longbowmen could barely raise their weapons in defence. The lightly armed English archers ran forward to take full advantage, firing deadly bodkin arrows at point-blank range before again finishing fallen Frenchmen trapped under the weight of bodies with the dagger. The French second line only added to the press, many men dying from drowning and suffocation. In the midst of this slaughter several Frenchmen made a desperate bid to slay Henry, landing a blow on the king's helmet before all were killed. The third French line meanwhile had remained in position, this threat combined with a late attack on the baggage train leading to a summary execution of prisoners on Henry's orders – such was the disparity in numbers no chance could be taken. After three hours, the French had lost near 10,000 men including D'Albret, three Dukes, ninety Lords, 1,560 knights and many captured including Boucicaut. Light English losses included Prince Edward, Duke of York.

The greatest English victory of the Hundred Years' War, Agincourt left France open to the King Henry but it would be nearly two years before he began a conquest, instead he now returned to London and a great pageant. 'This story shall the good man teach his son', William Shakespeare's St Crispin's Day Speech celebrates Henry's Agincourt address.

25 October 1854

Crimean War
Battle of Balaclava and the
Charge of the Light Brigade

BRITISH AND FRENCH armies had landed on the Crimean Peninsular in September 1854 for an advance on Sevastopol and the elimination of the Russian Black Sea Fleet, neutralising the threat to the Ottoman Empire and by extension the Eastern Mediterranean posed by Tsar Nicholas I. The Russian Army of Prince Alexander Menshikov had been decisively defeated at the River Alma but British Field Marshal Fitzroy Somerset, Lord Raglan had failed to allow a pursuit by his Light Brigade (cavalry) concerned at the possible presence of Russian cavalry. Consequently a loose siege of Sevastopol now began with the British holding the allied right flank supplied through the inadequate port of Balaclava.

On 25 October 1854, General Pavel Liprandi and 25,000 Russians then crossed the River Chernaya to occupy the Fedioukine Heights before attacking southward across the North Valley to the Causeway Heights where British redoubts and gun batteries were under construction. On taking the Causeway Heights against weak Turkish defences the Russian cavalry pressed on into the South Valley and Balaclava itself. The main Russian attack was successfully repulsed by the Heavy Brigade (cavalry) led by Lieutenant General George Bingham, Earl of Lucan whilst a detachment which headed directly for the port was repulsed by 'the thin red line' of the 93rd Highlanders. The bruised Russians then retreated behind their Don Cossack gunners at the eastern end of the North Valley whilst those still on the Causeway Heights began carrying off the British guns. From the Sapoune Heights facing the western end of the North Valley, Raglan saw the chance to counter-attack the Causeway Heights, dictating an order to Captain Louis Nolan 'to prevent the enemy carrying off the guns'. Nolan duly delivered the order to Lucan and the commander of the Light Brigade, Major General James Brudenell, Earl of Cardigan. The view from the valley floor, however, was very different to that of Raglan, the only guns visible being the Don Cossack Battery at the far end of the North Valley at which Nolan vaguely waved his arm. Both Lucan and Cardigan could have requested confirmation but, although brothers-in-law, were bitter enemies with communication between them at a minimum.

At 11.10 lancers leading light dragoons and hussars, collectively 666 men of the Light Brigade, started at a walk toward the 8-gun Don Cossack Battery over a mile away to their front. As the brigade entered the valley, still a full seven minute ride from their objective, the Russian guns on the Fedioukine Heights opened fire with Nolan the first to be hit as he rode across the line perhaps only now aware of the misunderstanding. The brigade increased to a trot, coming under fire to left and right from further Russian gun batteries and rifles but maintaining order in classic knee-to-knee formation with Raglan and his officers watching in horror as Cardigan, mounted on his favourite charger *Ronald*, failed to swing right, up the Causeway Heights. The Heavy Brigade led by Lucan followed behind taking fire from the left but was somewhat spared when the Chasseurs d'Afrique reacted by charging the Russian guns on Fedioukine. The Light Brigade continued, Cardigan still leading by the rule book but now fired upon from the Causeway Heights, round shot and shell depleting the ranks which closed up again and again. Worse, they were now on their own, Lucan seeing the imminent destruction of the Lights opting to save the Heavies and retreating. The Light Brigade trotted on fighting the urge to speed up as casualties mounted when at 250 yards from the Cossack guns Cardigan's Trumpeter, Billy Brittain, gave the order to gallop. The Cossack guns continued to fire devastating volleys in a desperate bid to stop the oncoming tide but at 30 yards Brittain sounded the charge, lances and sabres lowered as the Light Brigade crashed through the Cossacks killing all in their path. For several minutes a disorganised mêlée raged behind the guns before the Russian cavalry launched a counter-attack, only now the survivors of the charge realising the Heavy Brigade had abandoned them. Back into 'the valley of death' rode the Light Brigade, running the gauntlet of the Russian guns and sharpshooters once again, regaining their own lines having taken 278 casualties.

Previously reviled by the British public (largely due to his behaviour in Ireland during the potato famine), Cardigan would return to Britain a hero, even making fashionable a knitted article of clothing he had been wearing on campaign. In the meantime the Crimean War still had to be won, Menshikov would attack again ten days later at Inkerman.

'Honour the charge they made!' *The Charge of the Light Brigade* is famously commemorated in verse by Alfred, Lord Tennyson.

26 October 1917

The Great War
Battle of Passchendaele
(Third Ypres)

APPALLED AT BRITISH casualties on the Western Front Prime Minister David Lloyd George had been an advocate for a push north from Italy. Italian reluctance and the contrasting view of British Expeditionary Force Commander-in-Chief Field Marshal Douglas Haig that the Great War could only be won in Flanders and France, meant Lloyd George's worst fears were again being realised at the Third Battle of Ypres. Believing Germany to be close to collapse after the attritional battles of Verdun, Somme, Aisne and Arras despite transfers of German divisions from the Eastern Front (where Russia was being consumed by revolution) Haig had appointed the aggressive General Hubert Gough for an Ypres offensive which had minimal French assistance and failed to achieve any day one objectives. The ground then deteriorated during the wettest August for thirty years, the shell-shattered Ypres Salient becoming a sea of mud, almost impassable to tanks and massed artillery but since the British strategic position was poor Haig opted to push on to the Passchendaele Ridge rather than face the political consequences of a complete withdrawal. Gough was replaced by the architect of the previously successful attack on the Messines Ridge, General Herbert Plumer who, in better Autumn weather, then launched three 'bite and hold' attacks on the Menin Ridge Road, Polygon Wood and Broodseinde causing Crown Prince Rupprecht of Bavaria commanding the German 4th Army to contemplate a complete German retreat. Another hammer blow may well have broken Germany but in the mud at Poelcappelle, Plumer just could not establish the same concentration of artillery against determined German resistance on the formidable Flandern I Stellung.

British communications were collapsing, cables shattering, runners drowning in the mud whilst from above, the Royal Flying Corps could not distinguish friend from foe. Mistakenly thinking he had made gains south toward the Ridge (he had to the north) Plumer launched the First Battle of Passchendaele from the same start lines as Poelcapelle, achieving more but at a shocking price in British, Australian, New Zealand and German lives. A GHQ conference then halted the offensive and Haig withdrew the shattered II Anzac Corps but the Passchendaele Ridge was still to be assaulted, this time by the Canadian Corps of Lieutenant General Sir Arthur Currie.

Currie prepared for a Plumer style offensive, patiently moving up massed artillery whilst Gough's British Fifth Army attacked to his north toward Westroosebeke and Plumer's British Second Army with the French attacked to his south toward Malmaison. In ominous signs of what lay ahead Gough's Fifth Army immediately suffered in driving rain across the flat muddy swamps. Concentrated British artillery barrages on the Wallemolen and Bellevue spurs of the Passchendaele Ridge were met by German counter-battery fire that hampered Currie's own preparations but when the Canadians assaulted at 05.40 on 26 October 1917 they prospered from their own barrage in a two-pronged attack around the swamp created by the shattered Ravebeek Stream. On either side of them, however, the British struggled, the Fifth Army attacked again across the same ground as before and again suffered in the mud from German machine-gunners and artillery in what used to be the Houthulst Forest. Likewise the British Second Army suffered on the Gheluvelt Plateau. After a four day consolidation the Canadians attacked again against rows of pill boxes and machine-gun nests on the Meetcheele Spur but reached Passchendaele village, in desperate close quarter fighting holding on with virtually all officers and NCO's dead but assisted by massive British artillery bombardments. The poor Fifth Army was yet again ordered forward on the left, yet again with disastrous casualties as the relentless bombardment on Passchendaele Ridge continued, the Canadians finally clearing the north end on 10 November.

Haig closed Third Ypres, better known by its final objective Passchendaele, on 20 November, the same day as massed armour opened another British offensive at Cambrai. The capture of Passchendaele Ridge was the climax of a four-month, seven-mile gain costing 250,000 casualties, near half of them in October alone. Tyne Cot Cemetery at Passchendaele is the largest Commonwealth Cemetery in the world containing 11,956 graves, 8,369 of them are unnamed.

27 October 1644
English Civil Wars
Second Battle of Newbury

KING OF ENGLAND Charles I had required an early victory over his rebellious Parliament on the 1642 outbreak of the English Civil War. Within a year it seemed the king would get exactly that but heavy casualties and a Parliament galvanised by the Puritan citizens of Gloucester meant the king's advances had ground to a halt. Worse still, in 1644, a defeat at Nantwich, Parliament's recruitment of Scottish Covenanters and the successes of Parliament's Eastern Association under Edward Montagu, Earl of Manchester and Oliver Cromwell left Charles' strongholds in North England highly vulnerable. On Marston Moor outside York, in early July 1644, Charles' Commander-in-Chief Prince Rupert had then suffered a shattering defeat, in the aftermath of which York itself had surrendered followed by all Royalist northern strongholds bar Liverpool which by October was in the extremity of a siege. Charles' problems increased further with the self-imposed exile of William Cavendish, Marquis of Newcastle who was disgusted that his months of effort defending York had been rendered void in a matter of hours by Rupert. In the Midlands also Charles himself had created difficulties when failing to heed Rupert's defensive advice to find himself hunted throughout the countryside by the Parliament Army of Sir William Waller. Fortunately for the king, Waller had been abandoned by Robert Devereux, Earl of Essex who instead attempted to relieve Lyme and capture Queen Henrietta Maria (who had just given birth to a daughter, Henrietta) in Exeter.

Essex' absence gave Charles the opportunity to inflict a sharp reverse on Waller at Cropredy Bridge in late June which drove many of Waller's recruits to desert in fear of continued campaigning so far from London. As Waller licked his wounds back to London, Charles moved south-west in search of Essex who, by August, was retreating into Lostwithiel after an unsuccessful Parliament foray into Cornwall. A three-week siege ensued with Essex' cavalry breaking out on 31 August 1644, Essex himself escaping on a fishing boat but not 6,000 Parliament infantry who surrendered two days later, Charles graciously allowing them to march out without their weapons. In the south Parliament was suddenly again in total disarray, the Eastern Association were coming to assist but despite their success at Marston Moor, even Manchester and Cromwell were bitterly at odds with each other. Charles took full advantage by again marching east toward London, relieving several garrisons including Donnington Castle, whilst also hoping to join with Rupert moving south from Cheshire. The Parliament commanders, anxious to attack Charles before Rupert's arrival and with information from a deserter that the Royalists (8,500) were not as strong as thought, put their differences aside to trap Charles at Shaw House and on Speen Heath, Newbury.

Cromwell, Essex and Waller with 12,000 men including Cromwell's 'Ironsides' (Cavalry) made a wide detour north to Winterbourne before turning south to attack Charles from the west side of the Heath whilst Manchester's 7,000 made ready to simultaneously attack from the east, a cannon to signal the start of the battle. At Shaw House, however, Manchester attacked before dawn on 27 October 1644, several hours before Waller and Cromwell were in position and was thrown back with bruising losses. In mid afternoon when the Parliament attack eventually went in from the west, Royalist musketeers lining the hedges and lanes hampered their advance. Cromwell's Ironsides on the left and Sir William Balfour's cavalry on the right were making little headway but Essex's infantry led by Philip Skippon began breaking into the Royalist positions to recapture a number of guns lost at Lostwithiel. As darkness began to fall Manchester again attacked at Shaw House but it was too little too late, the Royalists withdrew north to leave Parliamentarians fighting each other in the dark.

Charles retreated to Donnington Castle but his army was not fit to fight the next day and retreated further over the Rivers Lambourne and Thames, returning two weeks later to relieve Donnington when Parliament refused to fight. The king had finished a dismal year on a better note but in June 1645 at Naseby he would have to fight the decisive battle of the war against a more professional and more committed Parliament Army, one based on a New Model.

28 October 1776

American War of Independence
Battle of White Plains

THE BRITISH ARMY had spent nearly a year bottled up in Boston but after evacuating, significantly reinforcing and launching a new offensive further south in New York had begun to make count their advantage in numbers, materials and firepower. General George Washington commanding the American Continental Army was under no illusion as to the strength of the British Army and Navy in relation to his own dispositions and although having nearly been trapped twice had managed to avoid an all out confrontation. Washington knew his enemy well having formerly been a colonel in the British Army, his brilliance wrong-footing the more ponderous British General William Howe illustrated by slipping out of Long Island from under the nose of the Royal Navy and again at Harlem Heights on Manhattan Island. Having had the better of the latter battle, Washington fell back north aware that he was in danger of being outflanked by a Royal Navy advance up the River Hudson, Howe again attempting to trap the rebels with an amphibious landing at Throgs Neck, a move which was beaten off by the Americans only for Howe to make a second attempt three miles further north at Pelham. The Battle of Pell's Point saw 750 American Patriots led by John Glover oppose a 4,000 strong mainly Hessian force as they landed before conducting a fighting retreat that exacted such heavy casualties the British/Hessian advance was halted. Glover had done just enough, buying time for Washington who, save leaving a garrison behind to defend the forlorn hope that was Fort Washington, retreated from Upper Manhattan ten miles further north to White Plains, east of the River Bronx.

Howe with 10,000 British Redcoats and Hessians followed on Washington's heels still looking for that elusive but decisive battle. On 28 October 1776, the two came into contact once again, the Continental Army holding the advantage of high ground on the west bank of the River Bronx but Washington still unwilling to risk all on a single battle. As Howe approached, Washington ordered Brigadier

General Joseph Spencer and his Connecticut Regiment to attack the Hessians under General Leopold Philip von Heister on the British left whilst he reinforced Chatterton Hill on the front right of his own position. The Connecticuts poured a galling fire into the Hessians but could not hold them. General Henry Clinton's British 2nd Infantry Brigade then pushed forward on the right of the Hessians exposing the Connecticut's flank which forced them back onto Chatterton Hill, Hessian artillery adding panic to the American retreat with a ferocious barrage of the hilltop. Spencer's dispirited Patriots were now on the verge of departing but order was restored by the arrival of long time anti-British political agitator Brigadier General Alexander McDougall and an infantry brigade of New Yorkers.

Howe decided to take Chatterton Hill and in the old medieval style of keeping costs down again sent in the Hessian mercenaries to do the dirty work. Hessian battalions under Colonel Johann Rall and Colonel Carl von Donop attacked the American right and centre respectively whilst British light infantry under General Alexander Leslie assaulted the left. Leslie's lights engaged the Americans before Donop arrived and were held but Rall sent the American militia on the right to flight. This left Washington's Maryland and New York Regiments exposed but under covering fire from the Delaware Regiment to their left they began a fighting retreat back into the hills behind. Both sides had suffered over 200 casualties.

Washington prepared his army to slip away once again whilst the ever cautious Howe reinforced Chatterton Hill. It was only two days later that Howe followed up his tacit victory by which time the Continental Army was marching west to cross the River Hudson. General Charles, Lord Cornwallis now began a long pursuit of Washington through the Jerseys to Philadelphia whilst Howe returned to Manhattan to take Fort Washington. A furious Clinton was ordered to take Newport, Rhode Island for the benefit of the Royal Navy. In the New Year the British would attempt to isolate the hot seat of rebellion, New England, with an advance down the Hudson Valley, the Saratoga Campaign.

29 October 1914

The Great War
Battle of Gheluvelt (First Ypres)

PRUSSIA HAD BEEN an inconsistent member of the seven Coalitions that had opposed Napoleon Bonaparte a century before but having been united with the other twenty-five previously independent German kingdoms, Duchys, Principalities and Free territories, a new force had emerged when the cousin of King George V of Great Britain, Kaiser Wilhelm II, succeeded to the Crown. The Kaiser was intent on developing German military strength to dominate Europe and rival British global power, sacking the man responsible for the forming of the German Empire, Otto von Bismarck, to begin a naval programme that caused such alarm at the British Admiralty that 25 per cent of Britain's GDP was spent on shipbuilding. Defeat in the Heligoland Bight, the first naval encounter of the Great War, had, however, led the Kaiser to confine his precious new fleet in Wilhelmshaven (much to the fury of his Grand Admiral Alfred von Tirpitz) but it mattered little for on land the German Army under Generalfeldmarshal Helmuth von Moltke had, so far, executed the nine-year-old Schlieffen Plan perfectly.

Driving through Belgium the Germans had driven the armies of France and the British Expeditionary Force (BEF) back to the outskirts of Paris but here Moltke's right flank turned east to the north of Paris rather than executing an encirclement from the south. On the River Marne French General Joseph Joffre had counter-attacked the consequently exposed German right flank, driving the invaders back to the River Aisne where movement was lost leaving both sides to attempt a series of flanking moves to the north-west and Belgium. The final failure of Schlieffen had broken Moltke but his successor as Chief of German General Staff, Erich von Falkenhayn, captured Antwerp before advancing on Ypres with the German 4th and 6th Armies against a badly depleted BEF that was already being reinforced with Territorials and the Indian Corps via the French channel ports – Falkenhayn's ultimate targets. At Ypres the British IV Army Corps of Lieutenant General Henry Rawlinson with French and Belgian support had held German assaults before counter-attacking upon the arrival of the British I Army Corps under Lieutenant General Douglas Haig. Falkenhayn had then thrown in the inexperienced conscripts of General Albrecht, Duke of Wurttemberg's 4th Army Reserve but suffered such shocking losses at the hands of Haig's professionals that the German Chief of Staff looked to renew the German offensive south-east of Ypres on Gheluvelt.

On 29 October 1914, Wurttemberg's German 4th Army attacked again to the north of Ypres holding the French whilst the German 6th Army of Crown Prince Rupprecht of Bavaria and the newly formed Army Group Fabeck under General Max von Fabeck made preliminary attacks further south along both sides of the Menin Road. The German attacks successfully captured the crossroads before Gheluvelt as Brigadier General Charles Fitzclarence (a VC winner at the 1899–1900 siege of Mafeking) hastily brought up British reinforcements to hold the village itself. The main German assault followed the next day, supported by artillery Fabeck again attacked in almost overwhelming numbers along the Menin Road and south toward the Messines Ridge but in desperate fighting the Indian Corps and Rawlinson's IV Army Corps held out with help from the British 5th Infantry Division. To their north, however, Zandvoorde fell exposing the British flank at Gheluvelt, Fabeck then launching his biggest attack yet across a twelve mile front from Messines to Gheluvelt. German infantry broke into Gheluvelt for a ferocious hand-to-hand fight with just 1,000 British troops holding the ruins, taking the village by midday to create a catastrophic gap in the centre of the British line directly before Ypres. In a desperate last throw of the dice, Fitzclarence called up the 370 men of the 2nd Worcestershire Regiment from Polygon Wood for an almost suicidal counter-attack back into Gheluvelt over 1,000 yards of ground exposed to German artillery. Here the surviving Worcesters surprised the German defenders to link up with South Wales Borderers still holding out. The British 7th Infantry Division with French support then arrived to fully restore the line.

Joining the 100,000 casualties at Ypres was Fitzclarence, tragically killed in another heroic defence at Nonne Bosschen Wood just as Falkenhayn called off the German offensive. Gheluvelt Park, Worcester is named in honour of the regiment's feats at Ypres. Both sides now dug in for the winter, 400 miles of trenches stretching from the English Channel to Switzerland.

30 October 1899

Second Boer War
Battle of Ladysmith

THE AFRIKANER REFUSAL to grant civil rights to *Uitlanders* (mainly British immigrants taking advantage of the huge mineral discoveries in the Transvaal) and of course British imperial ambition had led directly to the outbreak of a Second Boer War. Naked aggression did not sit comfortably with Victorian Britain but their *casus belli* had been provided by the Transvaal President Paul Kruger himself when for once his usual infallible diplomacy had failed him. 'Kruger has asked for war and war he must have' reported the *Daily Telegraph*.

As British reinforcements mustered in India and Britain those already in Natal were ordered by General Sir Redvers Buller, aboard ship en route for the Cape of Good Hope, not to go north of the Tugela River but by the end of October 1899 battles had been fought at Talana Hill, Elandslaagte and Rietfontein, all well to the north of the Tugela, with the British claiming victory in all. Indeed immediate British defensive objectives had been achieved but at the cost of an alarming casualty list, high officer fatalities and losses of equipment that led to a retreat of all British forces, 13,000 men, back to Ladysmith, a small railway junction town of tin-roofed houses on two dusty streets still twelve miles north of the Tugela. It was here though that Lieutenant General Sir George White believed he could deliver a decisive single 'knock down blow' with a set piece battle in which the 20–25,000 Boers now encircling him in the Drakensberg Mountains would be catastrophically defeated. White's gamble was huge, fail and Ladysmith would at the very least be besieged if indeed Boer Commander Piet Joubert did not advance to take the whole province of British Natal.

White's plan was ambitious, a four-mile night march north-east where Colonel Geoffrey Grimwood's 8th Infantry Brigade would attack Long Hill. The victorious Grimwood, in conjunction with Colonel Ian Hamilton's 7th Infantry Brigade, would then execute a pincer movement on Pepworth Hill, both actions fought simultaneously to Lieutenant-Colonel Frank Carleton leading a separate attack four miles further on at Nicholson's Nek. On the rack, the Boers would then be routed by the British cavalry of Major General John French. Somewhat understandably White's senior officers were sceptical.

On the night of 29 October Carleton led his 1,100 men out towards Nicholson's Nek but he was so late in departing that by daybreak on 30 October 1899 he faced being caught in the valley in front of his objective. Preempting the danger Carleton wisely decided to instead climb the nearby Tchrengula Hill only for his unhappy mules to stampede, taking with them the British guns and ammunition. Instead of retreating back to Ladysmith, however, Carleton continued up to the southern end of the plateau where his men built defensive 'sangars' amongst the rocks. Meanwhile, Grimwood arrived at Long Hill to find the enemy absent along with half of his own force and French's cavalry who had all lost their way in the darkness, Grimwood's predicament taking a further turn for the worse when he came under fire from Boers under General Louis Botha on the neighbouring Lombard Kop and Pepworth Hill. The Boers main gun, a Creusot 'Long Tom', for good measure also began shelling Ladysmith itself. Realising Grimwood was in difficulty and would be unable to support, Hamilton then postponed his attack on Pepworth Hill. Grimwood's artillery at least temporarily silenced the Boer 'Long Tom' giving the British infantry some respite but after several hours had produced little or no progress, White ordered a retreat 'as opportunity offered'. The sight of the British retiring onto the open plain below, however, merely served to intensify Boer rifle fire, with only disciplined fire on the retreat from the British artillery (including six naval guns arriving from Durban) and Joubert's reluctance to pursue, saving Grimwood. Carleton would not be so lucky, as the sun rose over Tchrengula Hill he had faced the dreadful reality that his southern end was overlooked by Boers flooding onto the northern end and from the neighbouring summits. A fierce firefight raged, the British firing disciplined volleys against the skirmishing Boers but after suffering 150 casualties and on becoming aware of Grimwood's retreat behind him, Carleton surrendered his entire force, the biggest British military capitulation for nearly a century.

White's gamble had failed dismally, too late to cross back over the Tugela River he was trapped in Ladysmith. Now was Joubert's big chance to take Natal before British reinforcements could make the Durban quayside.

31 October 1917

The Great War
Battle of Beersheba

GERMAN AND TURKISH (Ottoman) ambition in the Middle East had retreated since the summer of 1916 when British General Archibald Murray commanding the Egyptian Expeditionary Force (EEF) had counter-attacked at Romani, twenty miles east of the Suez Canal. Murray had then forced the Ottoman Army back across the Sinai Peninsular to southern Palestine (now Israel/Gaza) where his subordinates, Australian Major General Harry Chauvel and British Lieutenant General Philip Chetwode, were again victorious at Magdaba and Rafa. The run of victories ended, however, when Murray suffered two successive defeats at Gaza with casualties he could not afford, a stalemate of trench warfare then developing through the stifling summer heat from Gaza inland to Beersheba on the edge of the Negev Desert. Better news came from the south though where Colonel Thomas Lawrence (aka of Arabia) and Bedouin Irregulars under Auda ibu Tayi of the Huweitat and Sharif Nasir of Mecca had taken Aqaba, removing the Ottoman threat to the EEF's extended right flank. Ottoman forces were also under pressure in Mesopotamia (Iraq) where Lieutenant General Frederick Maude had taken Baghdad to force an additional Ottoman retreat from Persia (Iran).

The Ottoman Army was now reorganised under German General Erich von Falkenhayn (sacked as German Chief of General Staff the previous year) and Turkey's hero of Gallipoli, Mustafa Kemal Ataturk. After the double disasters of Gaza, Murray was also replaced by General Edmund Allenby (transferring from the British Third Army on the Western Front) who reorganised the EEF into three Corps, XX, XXI and the Desert Mounted Corps but had no instruction for the Palestine Campaign beyond that of his Prime Minister David Lloyd George who, anxious to cheer a dispirited Britain, wanted Jerusalem taken by Christmas (British command was occupied with Third Battle of Ypres in which Allenby had just lost his son).

Allenby decided to make a flank attack on the eastern end of the Ottoman trench system at Beersheba which itself was defended by additional redoubts and outposts further east in the Judean Hills. As British reinforcements arrived Allenby's main problem was one of supply, especially the water required by over 60,000 troops and their horses but by the end of October hurdles had been overcome and preparation was complete, German intelligence confident the British attack would fall on Gaza. Adding to the deception the Royal Navy began bombarding Gaza on 27 October before British, Australian and New Zealand divisions moved up toward Beersheba three days later.

At 05.55 on 31 October 1917, British artillery began bombarding the 4,000 entrenched Turkish troops at Beersheba with the Turkish gunners replying in kind. At 08.20 the bombardment intensified as the EEF XX Infantry Corps moved up west and south-west of the town whilst the 7th Mounted Brigade moved up on their right and the Anzac Mounted Division on the extreme eastern right flank. As the infantry attack developed into a fierce fight with the British gaining the advantage, the mounted divisions moved around to the east and north-east of the town to cut the Beersheba-Hebron-Jerusalem Road. The New Zealand Mounted Rifles then moved to attack Ottoman positions on the high ground of Tel El Saba but immediately ran into a determined defence against which they made little headway until reinforced by Australians and mountain batteries which enabled them to take their objective in mid afternoon. The delay meant the capture of Beersheba before nightfall was now seemingly impossible but Chauvel called up 800 men of the 4th Australian Light Horse under Brigadier William Grant for a charge against incomplete Ottoman defences to the south-east of Beersheba. In their own charge of the Light Brigade, the Australians crossed four miles of open ground under artillery fire from Turks who additionally engaged with rifle and machine-gun fire as the attack drew closer. The Australians armed with just hand-held bayonets with rifles on their backs crossed the first defensive line before dismounting for a close quarter firefight which allowed the supporting 12th Australian Light Horse to ride on, crucially capturing the wells of Beersheba in tact. More mounted brigades then followed up to secure victory and an Ottoman retreat.

Allenby also forced an Ottoman retreat from Gaza two days later. Allowed little respite, the Turks would be charged again at El Mughar Ridge in November.

November

"They are not here."

"They are sitting uncommonly tight if they are, Sir."

MAJOR GENERAL HENRY COLVILLE REPLYING
TO LIEUTENANT GENERAL LORD PAUL
METHUEN, MODDER RIVER, 1899

1 November 1893

Matabele Wars
Battle of Bembesi

THE IDEA OF a Cape to Cairo British-African Empire surfaced in 1888 under Prime Minister Robert Gascoyne-Cecil, Lord Salisbury. A three-pronged advance into Central Africa was required, one south from Egypt, another west from British East Africa (Kenya) and another north from Bechuanaland, British South Africa but although the Mahdi of Sudan was dead, strong Mahdist forces still threatened Egypt making the use of British troops unviable even though threats from German South West Africa (Namibia) and German East Africa (Tanzania) were mounting. Salisbury therefore had no option but to leave the conquest to private enterprise under Royal Charter with potentially willing participants in East Africa, William Mackinnon the head of the Imperial British East Africa Company, and in South Africa, a gold and diamond mining magnate, Cecil Rhodes head of the British South Africa Company. Sending an emissary, Charles Rudd, to Matabeleland (South Rhodesia/Zimbabwe) to obtain land and mining rights by deceit from King Lobengula of the Ndebele gave Rhodes the chance to begin mining and farming further north in Mashonaland. The giant Lobengula was no fool, however, and on realising he had been defrauded sent a deputation to London and Queen Victoria in protest. Under pressure from the Missionary Society, the Colonial Office refused Rhodes the Royal Charter he needed to settle Mashonaland but by financial inducement and persuasion that he could deliver David Livingstone's three Cs, of Christianity, Commerce and Civilisation to Central Africa, Rhodes eventually won over his detractors.

In June 1890, whilst Mackinnon appeared to have lost the game in East Africa (he hadn't) to German Carl Peters, Rhodes sent a pioneer column led by big game hunter Frederick Selous from Bechuanaland into Matabeleland. Shadowed by Ndebele warriors the column then continued on further north into Mashonaland and Mount Hampden where Selous established Fort Salisbury (Harare). Lobengula's warriors refrained from attacking Rhodes' column since the Ndebele chief was well aware of the fate of his Zulu cousins further south eleven years prior and sought to avoid war with the British at all cost. He did not, however, hesitate to attack his vassals, the Shona, whenever a chief refused to pay him tribute, refusals that became more prevalent as supposed British protection emboldened the Shona. In 1893 Rhodes' pioneers were at last prompted to act when the violence – Ndebele burnings, murder and abduction of the Shona – entered their own homes near Fort Victoria. Indeed it now suited Rhodes to destroy Lobengula since his new colony, South Zambezia (Rhodesia from 1895, Zimbabwe from 1879), was already near bankrupt and greater security was required to attract more investors.

In October 1893 700 men of the British South African Police commanded by Major Patrick Forbes trekked south from Salisbury and west from Victoria to combine at Iron Mine Hill for an attack on Lobengula's Royal Kraal at Bulawayo whilst another under the pro British Khama III of the Bamangwato (Bechuanaland) approached from the south. Lobengula sent 3,500 warriors to intercept Forbes at the Shangani River but their assault on 25 October cost 1,500 casualties at the barrels of the Forbes' five new Maxim guns. Forbes continued his advance south to reached the vacated Ndebele camp at Bembesi where, anticipating another attack, he formed two defensive wagon laagers, Salisbury and Victoria. Just after midday on 1 November 1893 6,000 Ndebele warriors of the Ngubi, Mbezu and Nsukamini Regiments began to sweep around the Salisbury laager firing from 2,000 Martini Henry rifles. A stampede of horses briefly threatened to decimate the defences before Major Allan Wilson moved three Maxims and a Hotchkiss gun from the Victoria laager to support his colleagues in Salisbury who had been fully stretched holding off the heightening attacks but now possessed overwhelming firepower. The next hour of fighting produced 3,000 casualties, the bravery of the Ndebele no match for Forbes' industrially produced death.

Lobengula torched his Bulawayo Kraal, ammunition, gold and ivory all destroyed before making for the River Zambezi. Forbes would soon make a three week pursuit through heavy rains, his flying column under Wilson crossing the Shangani River in early December for a fateful contact.

2 November 1914

The Great War
Battle of Tanga

THE SCRAMBLE FOR Africa developed after the celebrated 1871 meeting of Henry Stanley and Doctor David Livingstone at Ujiji. Germany had only come into being as a nation state that same year and was consequently late to join 'the Scramble' but by 1885 the explorer Carl Peters had signed treaties in East Africa with assistance from the German Navy who had silenced the protesting Sultan of Zanzibar, Barghash bin Said Al-Busaid. At the 1885 Berlin Conference Britain and Germany agreed to split East Africa, Britain administering what is now Kenya and Uganda, Germany what is now Tanzania, Rwanda and Burundi, both spheres with access to Lake Victoria. Germany's leading diplomat, Chancellor Otto von Bismarck was, however, sacked in 1890 by the incoming Kaiser Wilhelm II whose far more ambitious plans for the German Empire would initiate an arms race in Europe whilst in Africa Livingstone's three Cs, Christianity, Commerce and Civilisation were now being imposed largely by the Maxim gun as Britain, France, Belgium, Portugal and Germany brought white rule to black Africa. The British then fought the Boers of the Transvaal and Orange Free State in a conflict where the combatants were almost exclusively white (though far the greater number of casualties were black) but when, in 1914, the consequences of the Kaiser's ambition spread to East Africa, the longest theatre of the Great War, both Britain and Germany would use Indians and Africans to do most of the fighting for them.

From British East Africa Major General Arthur Aitken resolved to attack German East Africa with a simultaneous two-pronged invasion on both ends of the Usambara Railway, in the west on Mount Kilimanjaro by 4,000 men of Indian Expeditionary Force 'C' commanded by Brigadier General 'Jimmie' Stewart and in the east on the Port of Tanga by 8,000 men of Indian Expeditionary Force 'B' commanded by himself. At dawn on 2 November 1914, Aitken arrived off Tanga, Captain Francis Caulfield commanding HMS *Fox* requesting the town surrender but District Commissioner Dr Auracher declining. Unwilling to alienate the locals,

Aitken did not immediately instigate a bombardment but instead planned for a landing that night three miles to the east at Ras Kasone. Meanwhile, General Paul von Lettow-Vorbeck, Commander-in-Chief of German East Africa was in the process of moving 700 Askari (native) reinforcements by rail from Moshe to Tanga, a journey of 190 miles.

On landing at Ras Kasone at 22.00, 1,200 British Rajputs and Pioneers under Brigadier General Michael Tighe silenced a token volley of resistance before advancing in torrential rain on Tanga without waiting for reinforcements to land behind them. On the outskirts, Tighe came under fire from two German machine-guns in the railway cutting, the Rajputs and Pioneers forming line to outflank the 300 defenders but now clashing with Lettow-Vorbeck's arriving Askaris on Auracher's right. The Rajputs were decimated before being driven back with the Pioneers to Ras Kasone where Tighe requested another four infantry battalions. Aitken, however, fatally delayed another attack for over twenty-four hours allowing Lettow-Vorbeck to organise his defences around no less than fifteen machine-guns. On the afternoon of 4 November Lancashires, Grenadiers, Rajputs, Palamcottahs, Mahrattas, Hyderabadis and Kashmiris then advanced slowly through spiked-pit booby-traps in the rubber plantations to assault Tanga with a bayonet charge whilst assaulted themselves by swarms of angry african bees. In Tanga a ferocious street fight developed, the Rajputs taking the Kaiserhof Hotel before the German Askaris counter-attacked whilst HMS *Fox* and the *Bharratta* shelled from offshore. To the south, the British Grenadiers moved west potentially outflanking a right hook of six machine-guns Lettow-Vorbeck was about to deliver from the railway yard but when the Grenadiers turned north too early the German right hook produced the biggest sting of the day with devastating consequences. As their left disintegrated, Aitken's troops fighting in Tanga had no option but to retreat, Aitken then later withdrawing altogether despite reports that the town had been vacated.

Since Stewart had also been defeated at Kilimanjaro, Aitken remained on the defensive in British East Africa until 1916 when South Africans arrived under Jan Smuts. Before then Lieutenant Commander Geoffrey Spicer-Simson would make a daring attempt to gain control of Lake Tanganyika.

3 November 1883

Mahdist Wars
Battle of El Obeid

GREAT BRITAIN AND France had become involved in Egypt largely through financial necessity in 1879. In developing Egypt the ruling Muhammad Ali dynasty had borrowed heavily from Europe but without the expected economic results was now struggling to repay. Despite Egypt being an Ottoman (Turkish) territory the British took control of Egyptian finances and the Suez Canal with a more capitalist approach which alienated the chief beneficiary of the original debt, the Egyptian Army. The Khedive of Egypt, Tewfiq Pasha sacked his Prime Minister and fled to Alexandria where nationalist violence amidst a military coup led by Colonel Ahmed Arabi erupted. The British were then coerced into a show of naval strength off Alexandria by the French (also holders of Egyptian debt) which descended into the British shelling the city once the French had departed and Arabi had failed to heed British warnings. Arabi then declared a Holy War only to be defeated in September 1881 at Tel-El-Kebir by 13,000 British troops sent by the reluctant anti-imperialist British Prime Minister William Gladstone.

Under British suzerainty Tewfiq was back in control of Egypt but not the Sudan where a political and religious revolt was gaining momentum under a Sudanese religious leader, Muhammad Ahmad, the Mahdi (guided one) who sought to replace the European style rule of previous Khedives with Islamic law. Hunted by Egyptian authorities the Mahdi had escaped into Kordofan in Central Sudan where his followers, the *Ansar* (dervishes), gained from Baggara, Ta'aisha and Hadendoa tribesman. When tribes from western, southern Sudan and the Bahr-al-Ghazal joined, the *Ansar* became a national movement which threatened the security not only of the Sudan but Egypt, the Suez Canal, British ports on the Red Sea and, consequently, the route to India. In January 1883 El Obeid (North Kordofan) fell to the Mahdi whose emissaries were now appearing in cities throughout the Middle East (the Mahdi sought to overthrow the entire Ottoman Empire), concerning Egyptian authorities that active Mahdist support could spread north. The British, however, were unconcerned, doubtful of Mahdist strength whilst confident the vast empty expanses of the Sudan were ungovernable. They did, however, permit Colonel William Hicks (Hicks Pasha) to lead a punitive Egyptian force into Kordofan that according to Winston Churchill was 'perhaps the worst army that has ever marched to war'.

Since his recruits were imprisoned ex-Arabi troops, released specifically to serve in the Sudan, Hicks himself was less than confident but with a high reward both professionally and financially for securing the Sudan he pressed on, achieving a victory that settled his nerves somewhat in April 1883 against 4,000 *Ansar* at Jebelein. Setting off again from Omdurman, Khartoum in early September Hicks, his British staff, 8,000 Egyptians, 1,100 Bashi-Bazouks, 1,000 Irregulars, artillery, machine-guns and 5,000 camels marched 110 miles in twelve days through 50°C heat down the White Nile River to Dueim. After recuperating another grueling fifty day march followed across the desert to El Obeid, the well informed Mahdi sending 3,000 dervishes to harry Hicks' rear, fill in water holes and leave religious proclamations along the route frightening Hicks' Egyptians whose morale plummeted. On 3 November 1883 Hicks formed his army into a defensive square to approach a densely wooded area thirty miles short of El Obeid where he was attacked by large numbers of dervishes. Many of the Egyptians hit the ground in terror but the British officers rallied them, fighting off the attack with machine-guns red hot. After a night under fire Hicks then formed up in three squares to make for the water hole at Fula al Masarin only to find he had been beaten to it by the Mahdi who resumed hostilities by making a direct frontal assault in strength through thick forest. The Egyptian guns opened up but Hicks' force was also hit by surprise attacks from within the squares, hundreds of dervishes having hidden in holes over which the squares had marched. As the fire turned inward both dervish and Egyptian fell, Hicks trying to fight his way out on horseback, first with revolver then with sword but against overwhelming numbers both he and his army were massacred, Hicks' head delivered to the Mahdi.

The Mahdi would now advance on Khartoum where a Briton would disobey orders to defy him, Major General Charles Gordon.

4 November 1805
Napoleonic Wars
Battle of Ortegal

AFTER A DECADE of warfare the self-appointed Emperor of the First French Empire, Napoleon Bonaparte had defeated all his major European adversaries bar one. The Dutch Republic, Prussia, Austria, Sardinia, Spain and Russia had all either been occupied, sued for peace, withdrawn or in Spain's case, changed sides. Only Great Britain remained a constant wartime thorn in the side of Napoleon's plans for the domination of Europe and global trade, countering French expansionist campaigns in the Ottoman Middle East and blockading the French and Spanish coastlines, Atlantic and Mediterranean. By 1804 the British blockade was already ten years old, the dogged resistance on Europe's periphery now encouraging further resistance from within as Austria and Russia, angry at Napoleon's ruthless murder of the Bourbon Duc d'Enghiens and at his perceived usurpation of the French throne, mobilised the Third Coalition with Britain.

In 1805 Napoleon's 200,000 strong *Armée d'Angleterre* was in Boulogne poised to invade Britain but it required a fleet capable of protecting transports across an English Channel patrolled by the world's most powerful maritime force, the Royal Navy. Napoleon sought to combine the French Mediterranean and Atlantic fleets with that of the Spanish under the overall command of Vice Admiral Pierre Villeneuve but off Cape Trafalgar on 21 October 1805 Villeneuve had been routed by Vice Admiral Horatio, Lord Nelson. The defeat of their navy at least left the *Armée d'Angleterre* to instead consolidate a victory over Austria at Ulm two days earlier before advancing against the Russians.

Meanwhile off the Spanish Atlantic coast a seven day storm of biblical scale battered the heavily damaged ships of both Trafalgar fleets causing as many deaths as the battle itself. Just four of the nineteen captured Franco-Spanish vessels made Gibraltar along with the shattered HMS *Victory* carrying the body of the heroic Nelson. Still at sea, British squadrons searched for those Franco-Spanish ships that had escaped, particularly the French vanguard of Rear Admiral Pierre Dumanoir le Pelley who could threaten a returning East India convoy transporting Major General Arthur Wellesley.

After attempting to assist the *Redoutable* and the *Santisima Trinidad* at Trafalgar Dumanoir had made a break for the Straits of Gibraltar without realising they were strongly defended by Rear Admiral Thomas Louis. Turning back north-west into the storm Dumanoir's vanguard had reached the Bay of Biscay heading for Rochefort, France when his four ships were spotted by HMS *Phoenix* captained by Thomas Baker. Dumanoir pursued Baker who fled south where he knew there to be a Royal Navy squadron under Captain Richard Strachan, into the middle of which the Frenchmen sailed. Strachan's squadron, however, was scattered over a wide area, himself on the 80-gun HMS *Caesar* now chasing Dumanoir back north-west whilst Baker gathered in HMS *Hero, Courageux, Namur, Bellona, Santa Margarita* and *Aeolus*. After losing Dumanoir, Strachan's squadron managed to reform additionally with HMS *Revolutionaire* before again sighting French sails early on 3 November off Cape Ortegal. A twenty-hour chase led into 4 November 1805 when the faster British frigates, *Phoenix* and *Santa Margarita* caught Dumanoir, the pair attacking *Scipion* in the French rear before *Caesar* joined them from windward three hours later. Dumanoir now attempted to turn his line past *Ceasar* only to find Strachan had doubled his line, frigates on one side and ships of the line on the other raking the French with broadsides on both starboard and port. After a three hour exchange of cannonballs, the outnumbered Dumanoir's *Formidable* and *Scipion* surrendered leaving the *Duguay-Troulin* and *Mont Blanc* to again attempt an escape but surrendering half an hour later.

Ortegal completed the British victory of Trafalgar but a month later, in a tactical masterpiece at Austerlitz, Napoleon defeated the Russians so completely that British Prime Minister William Pitt commented on a map of Europe 'Roll up that map, it will not be wanted these ten years'. The captured Dumanoir was released back to France in 1809 where he faced two Courts Martial, one each for Trafalgar and Ortegal.

5 November 1854

Crimean War
Battle of Inkerman

IN 1854 BRITISH and French armies had invaded the Crimean Peninsular to remove the Russian naval threat to the Ottoman Empire and the trade routes to India and the Far East (overland) via the Eastern Mediterranean. The allied army under Field Marshal Fitzroy Somerset, Lord Raglan had moved south from Kalamita Bay, defeating a large Russian army under General Prince Alexander Menshikov at the River Alma but by failing to pursue had condemned his troops to a siege of the Russian port city of Sevastopol. The siege lines, with the French on the left and British on the right had stretched around Sevastopol from the southeast to the heights in the east, the British supplied through the inadequate port of Balaclava. On 25 October General Pavel Liprandi and 25,000 Russians had crossed the River Chernaya to attack Balaclava with some success, gaining positions on the Fedioukine and Causeway Heights whilst, and largely due to British incompetence, virtually wiping out the Light Brigade of the British cavalry.

On 5 November 1854, Menshikov would again attack, this time against extended British positions on Home Hill at the northernmost extremity of the siege line. Lieutenant General F.I. Soimonoff with 20,000 Russians marched east out of Sevastopol along the Careenage Ravine whilst Lieutenant General P. Pavlov and another 20,000 approached from the north-east against a defensive wall, the Barrier, manned by 2,700 men and twelve guns of the British 2nd Infantry Division. At dawn British pickets in the valley below Home Hill engaged Soimonoff's approaching columns alerting Major General John Pennefather above that a large scale assault was developing. Pennefather immediately committed his units forward to engage on the slopes with the advantage that when the Russian artillery on Shell Hill opened up on the British positions there was no one at Home. Also, as Russians emerged from the Careenage Ravine they struggled to deploy presenting an easy target for the oncoming British infantry who immediately began inflicting heavy casualties. With their new Minié rifles far superior to the old

Russian muskets, especially in the damp fog that enveloped the battlefield, the 2nd Division halted the Russian advance before driving them back with a bayonet charge. Soimonoff himself led the next Russian assault against the left of the 2nd Division but after successfully capturing three guns was again driven back, himself dead. Further north Soimonoff's Russians were attacking up towards the Barrier but similarly met intense British rifle and artillery fire before also retreating with heavy casualties.

Pavlov then approached the north-east slope of Home Hill again advancing toward the Barrier and the Sandbag Battery further east. Only several hundred British were on hand to hold the oncoming Russian tide before the supporting British 41st Infantry Regiment drove the attackers back to the Chernaya. The Russians regrouped under General Peter Dannenberg who led yet another assault, this time with improved results as the British line began to falter against the sheer weight of Russian numbers. In a bitter hand-to-hand fight the 2nd Division held just long enough for the 4th Infantry Division under General George Cathcart to join the fray checking Dannenberg's advance before Cathcart himself paid the ultimate price. Once again the British position became tenuous as the Russians attacked on three sides but reinforcing French Zouaves counter-attacked the Russian flank, again driving them off Home Ridge. Two heavy British guns then supported the field guns by pounding the 100 Russian field guns on Shell Hill. Devoid of reserves and with morale fading, the Russians began a retreat, they had taken 12,000 casualties, the British and French 3,000.

Although the Russian attack at Inkerman had failed, the British had lost a not inconsiderable part of their force whilst a ferocious storm just over a week later would cost them a huge quantity of supplies, weakening the siege of Sevastopol. The next two winters would be bleak, the only heroes to be found in the hospitals, Mary Seacole and Florence Nightingale being the most notable. The 1856 Treaty of Paris would end the war but new alliances were created that fifty-eight years later would lead to a calamitous European conflict.

6 November 1706 n.s

War of the Spanish Succession
Battle of Santa Cruz de Tenerife

THE DISPUTE OVER who was to be King of Spain had rumbled on for over five years, splitting Europe apart in an effort to maintain the balance of power both in Europe and the Americas. As it stood the House of Bourbon Philip, Duke of Anjou, grandson of King Louis XIV of France and grand-nephew and nominated successor of the House of Habsburg King Charles II of Spain, would collect his Spanish inheritance and, just as long as he outlived his grandfather, his father Louis (the Grand Dauphin), his elder brother Louis, Duke of Burgundy and Louis' male issue, he would at some future date unite the Kingdom of Spain with the Kingdom of France. The threat of such a seemingly unlikely event, however, occurred in an age when life was a lot more fragile and was enough to send the whole of western Europe into conflict, the Habsburgs of the Holy Roman Empire in Vienna led by Emperor Leopold I promoting the cause of Leopold's son, Archduke Charles of Austria by forming a Grand Alliance with Prussia, England, Dutch Republic and Portugal. Bavaria then declared for the Bourbons, becoming an obvious threat to Austria before John Churchill, Duke of Marlborough defeated them and the French in 1704 at Blenheim. Marlborough then went on to defeat another Franco-Bavarian army in May 1706 at Ramillies forcing the Bourbons out of the Spanish Netherlands (Belgium, Luxembourg) almost entirely. Despite both King Louis and the Queen of England, Scotland and Ireland, Anne I, now desiring peace Marlborough, however, could not significantly press his advantage.

Whilst the war was going well for the Grand Alliance on the European continent, so it was also at sea. An Anglo-Dutch fleet under Admiral George Rooke (who had fought against the Dutch in 1672–74) had, after a 1702 defeat at Cadiz, inflicted devastating losses on the Spanish at Vigo Bay in 1702, Gibraltar in 1704 (it has remained British ever since) and had strategically defeated a Bourbon fleet off Malaga in 1704. With the Spanish Navy now on the defensive, Rear Admiral John

Jennings, who had fought with Rooke in all four of the above battles and had been knighted for his efforts by Queen Anne, sailed for the West Indies via the isolated Spanish islands of Tenerife following in the wake of a 1657 attack by General-at-Sea, Robert Blake, the 'Father of the Royal Navy'. Instead of treasure seeking, however, Jennings was seeking to cripple Spanish shipping.

Jennings approached Santa Cruz, Tenerife on 6 November 1706 in his flagship, HMS *Binchier* and twelve other ships of the line. A formidably defended port, Santa Cruz possessed a sea wall, overlooking high ground, and three forts – Castillo San Juan to the south, Castillo San Cristobal in the centre and Castillo de Paso Alto to the north – all defended with numerous cannon by over 4,000 Spanish militia who were given plenty of warning from lookouts in the Anaga Mountains on the northern tip of the island. Jennings sailed into Santa Cruz Bay at first light flying the Blue Flag of the Royal Navy and began to disembark his men into rowing boats. It was not clear whether they intended to storm the town but the acting Spanish Commander Corregidor Jose de Ayala y Rojas was taking no chances and opened a furious artillery barrage. Jennings immediately recalled his troops and replied with his own guns which numbered over 800. After a two hour gun battle had caused considerable damage and heavy casualties onboard, Jennings sent a delegation ashore under a flag of truce rather lamely claiming they had not come to wage war but to request that the Spanish support the Habsburg Charles rather than Bourbon Philip. Ayala answered definitively that if his King Philip should lose all his peninsular, the islands of Tenerife would remain faithful to him. Jennings retreated back from the harbour and cruised off the coast for a day. Since any attack on Santa Cruz would be futile, he continued on to Jamaica.

Santa Cruz was attacked again by the Royal Navy in 1797 when Rear Admiral Horatio Nelson suffered his greatest defeat and the loss of an arm. The flag of Santa Cruz de Tenerife has three lion heads on its central coat-of-arms representing the three 'British' battles of 1657, 1706 and 1797.

7 November 1900
Second Boer War
Battle of Leliefontein

AS THE BRITISH Army marched into Pretoria on 5 June 1900 Field Marshal Lord Frederick Roberts believed the Second Boer War to be 'practically over'. Just hours before Roberts' arrival, however, Winston Churchill, in his dual role as a reporter for the *Morning Post* and a cavalryman for the South African Light Horse, had witnessed a train steaming out of Pretoria loaded with heavily armed Boers not yet ready to throw in the towel. The war had been a catalogue of British mistakes and Roberts had just made yet another. Believing he had fought a 'Gentlemans war' Roberts had waited since the 30 May Johannesburg armistice for the surrender of General Louis Botha but during the week that had followed Boer fighting men, artillery and ammunition had taken advantage of the British failure to cut the railway line and, after emptying the bank at gunpoint, had headed out of Johannesburg and Pretoria for the Eastern Transvaal. It had been Martinus Steyn, President of the Orange Free State in a telegram to his Transvaal counterpart, Paul Kruger, who had rallied the cause to which Botha, Jan Smuts, Koos De La Rey, Christiaan De Wet, Martinus Prinsloo and, over the next two years, near 50,000 Boers would flock – the *bitter-einders*. Five days later Roberts realised his error and sent the British Army back out onto the veld to hunt them down.

Within a month Roberts' army that had advanced on Pretoria through the Free State was joined by the Natal Field Force under General Sir Redvers Buller that had advanced from Ladysmith up through the Drakensberg Mountains. The British commanders now combined tactics to burn the farms off which the Boer commandos lived whilst converging columns conducted wide sweeps to trap them. By the end of July, five columns under Lieutenant General Archibald, principally converging on De Wet, had success in trapping a dispirited Marthinus Prinsloo and 4,000 Boers in the Brandwater Basin. The chase for the elusive De Wet, however, continued, by mid August 12,000 men under Lieutenant General Horatio Kitchener, General Lord Paul Methuen and Major General Horace Smith-Dorrien were then in a position to trap him if Lieutenant General Ian Hamilton and 7,600 men could block Olifants Nek. Hamilton needed only obey orders but instead he tried to cut off De Wet on the rand. Too slow, Hamilton allowed De Wet to escape again, the Boer continuing to strike British outposts with terrifying violence. Botha's main force was then defeated at Belfast in August, the 3,000 fugitives pursued north by Buller, east by Hamilton and finally toward the Komati River and Mozambique by Major General Reginald Pole-Carew where they surrendered to the Portuguese. Boer attacks on the Pretoria/ Delagoa Bay Railway (used by Winston Churchill to escape Boer imprisonment the previous December) were then left to the Carolina Commando commanded by General JC Fourie based at Leliefontein.

Smith-Dorrien left Belfast with 250 cavalry, 900 infantry, eight guns and a Maxim, crossing undulating ground to attack Fourie on 6 November but it was Fourie's ouposts who opened proceedings before executing a retreat to prepared defensive positions on the Komati River. Smith-Dorrien followed for a frontal assault and a flanking move that forced Fourie back further. The following day 7 November 1900 Fourie, now reinforced by the Ermelo Commando, looked to counter-attack but Smith-Dorrien, unnerved by Boer strength the previous day, had decided to make a retreat of his own back to Belfast. As the Carolina Commando moved back up the west bank of the Komati, the Ermelo Commando looked to land a left hook which, due to Smith-Dorrien's retreat, missed. Both Commandos therefore turned to attack the British rear of Canadian Mounted Rifles, Royal Canadian Dragoons and two 12-pounders under Lieutenant Colonel Francois-Louis Lessard across a two mile front with increasing intensity, the exceptionally well drilled Canadians holding off the Boer attacks which included a desperate charge led by Fourie and Hendrik Prinsloo on Lieutenant Richard Turner's guns in the centre – both Fourie and Prinsloo were killed.

Smith-Dorrien made his way back to Belfast with minimal losses thanks to his Canadians who earnt three Victoria Crosses during the engagement, Turner included. In respect for his enemy Smith-Dorrien later paid for a memorial to Prinsloo and Fourie which now marks the site of the battle.

8 November 1944

Second World War
Battle of the Scheldt

THE SUCCESS OF the June 1944 Allied amphibious invasion of Normandy had rivalled the greatest in history, including Julius Ceasar's invasion of Britain in 54 BC and William, Duke of Normandy's invasion of the same in 1066. Supreme Headquarters Allied Expeditionary Force commander General Dwight D Eisenhower had then continued with a broad front strategy keeping the German Wehrmacht under pressure in the west (450,000 German dead, wounded and captured) whilst they were also under pressure in the east defending the Soviet Operation Bagration (another 450,000 casualties). Eisenhower's strategy, however, was causing the Allies serious supply problems, US 3rd Army General George Patton exclaiming, 'I'll shoot the next man who brings me food. Give us gasoline', but the nearest Allied port was far away Cherbourg. Eisenhower could keep no one happy, least of all Bernard Montgomery who had been replaced as Commander of Allied Ground Forces by Eisenhower on 1 September but retained as commander of 21st Army Group (mainly British and Canadian). Though the British public was mollified by 'Monty's' promotion to Field Marshal, he himself was not, his attitude afterward tantamount to insurbordination.

The port of Antwerp, Belgium was the answer to Allied supply problems and though the city and port were taken on 4 September no Minesweeper could enter the sixty-mile Scheldt Estuary until General Gustav von Zangen's 100,000-strong German 15th Army had been defeated. To this end Admiral Bertram Ramsay, Commander-in-Chief of Allied Naval Expeditionary Forces tackled Montgomery. Instead 'Monty' ordered Canadian General Henry Crerar to capture Le Havre and Boulogne, ports big enough to supply his 21st Army but not the Americans. 'Monty' also pushed for a concentrated thrust through Holland over the Rhine at Arnhem, the failure of which resulted in a weakening of the Canadian II Corps under Lieutenant General Guy Simonds who were poised for an assault on the Scheldt. Well supplied from Le Havre and Boulogne Montgomery still favoured an advance into North Germany and failed to support Simonds when the Battle of the Scheldt opened on 2 October 1944. Ramsay then insisted Eisenhower force Montgomery to prioritise the Scheldt where the Canadians were soon suffering heavy casualties on the flat marshes of Breskens to the south and South Beveland to the north. When Montgomery finally acquiesced British, Canadians and Poles cleared Breskens and South Beveland in a series of flanking manoeuvres and frontal assaults but still the Island of Walcheren and its concrete gun emplacements needed clearing before any Minesweeper could enter the Estuary.

To increase Allied difficulties Simonds believed the German defenders would partially flood Walcheren and so he decided to go one better by completely flooding it himself, smashing the Westkapelle Dyke with a bombing raid. The tactic ruined the Walcheren economy but gave the Canadians mobility with the use of a variety of amphibious landing craft. On 1 November Scots of the 52nd Lowland Division attacked west across the causeway from South Beveland in conjunction with a battalion from No. 4 Commando attacking north from Breskens to Flushing (Vlissingen) and 4th Commando Brigade (three battalions 41, 47 and 48 Royal Marines) attacking from the west (seaward). The German defenders put up determined resistance, their guns seemingly untouched by an earlier softening up from the Royal Air Force. The bigger British landing craft guns then moved in to shoot it out at close range with the German batteries allowing those British commandos already ashore to take up assault positions. Their follow up troops suffered, however, as twenty-one of the twenty-five landing craft tanks carrying both they and their transport were put out of action. In bitter fighting across minefields and difficult under foot conditions the commandos cleared the island position by position in close quarter fighting, machine-guns, bayonets and flamethrowers backed up by artillery from Breskens and RAF Hawker Typhoons. The towns of Westkapelle, Dishoek, Domburg, Zoutelande and Flushing all fell within a week of fighting as 40,000 Germans retreated into North Walcheren – Von Zangen having escaped north into Holland with the remainder. On 8 November 1944 they surrendered.

After two weeks of minesweeping the Port of Antwerp opened. His supply problems solved, Eisenhower prepared to invade the Third Reich.

9 November 1337

Hundred Years' War
Battle of Sluys and Cadsand

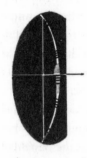

IN 1152 HENRY Plantagenet, Count of Anjou by his father Geoffrey of Anjou and Duke of Normandy, married Eleanor of Aquitaine adding the Province of Aquitaine (South West France) to his lands. His estate dramatically increased again only two years later when he became Henry II, King of England by his mother Matilda (daughter of Henry I) and by the grace of her cousin Stephen I, King of England (Stephen had himself snatched the throne from Matilda after previously agreeing under oath to support her). Henry now governed not only England but also almost half of France for which he paid homage to the King of France, Louis VII, none other than his wife's former husband. This state of affairs no doubt chafed just a little bit on Henry, he and Louis having a difficult relationship. The reluctant English payment of homage then continued through the Crusades into the late thirteenth and early fourteenth century when Edward I and his son, Edward II, managed either to avoid the matter altogether or at least perform only under duress whilst waging war on Scotland, a nation supported by their 'Auld Alliance' with France. However, when Charles IV became King of France in 1322 and did not receive the required homage, Edward II's lands in France were declared forfeit. Edward's wife Isabella of France, Charles' sister, then reached a partial settlement but just a few years later with her lover Roger Mortimer, Earl of March was involved in Edward's abdication and brutal murder at Berkeley Castle (in 1330 the seventeen-year-old Edward III, now King of England executed Mortimer for the crime but pardoned his mother). When Charles then died in 1328 with no male issue, the throne of France passed (after a nervous wait to see if his pregnant wife gave birth to a son) to his first cousin Philip of Valois, dubiously passing over a closer relative, a nephew, who happened to be King of England, Edward III. Edward was not concerned at the time, rather intent on securing his French possessions and in particular annexing Scotland. Meanwhile Philip did not stand idly by his Scottish alliance, encroaching into English Aquitaine and raiding the English south coast before moving his fleet, including oared galleys from Genoa, from the Mediterranean to Normandy.

The French provocation was too much for Edward who looked to the Low Countries for allies, Flanders in particular – an unhappy fiefdom of France whose economy was heavily reliant on high quality English wool – but also Brabant and Hainault, fiefdoms of the Holy Roman Empire. These small nations were, however, understandably reluctant to join the four million populace of England against the ten million of France despite financial inducements from Edward's fast emptying treasury via Italian banks. To convince his allies, Edward sent Sir Walter Manny, a Hainaulter, to begin the Hundred Years' War with a show of strength by an English Army no longer feudal but indentured – containing professional, highly trained soldiers where even the common man wielded a weapon not possessed by any other nation and of devastating power, the longbow.

Manny and his 3,700 men arrived off the then Port of Sluys (Sluis, now connected to the sea only by the Damse-Vaart Canal), Flanders on 9 November 1337 but failed to make any impression on the garrison commanded by Guy, the Bastard of Flanders, who drove them off. Undeterred Manny then landed across the waters of the River Zwin on the marshy island of Cadsand, home to a few fishing villages where, over the next few days, he proceeded to burn, rape and pillage everything in sight in an attempt to draw Guy out to battle. The half-brother of the pro French Louis I, Count of Flanders, Guy hurriedly gathered forces and crossed the Zwin to find Manny's numerically smaller army drawn up in a defensive position, most likely a line of men-at-arms with herces of archers at either end. No accounts of the battle survive but we can assume Guy attempted to charge the English only to be met with devastating volleys of arrows before Manny counter-attacked, routing the Flemish Army. Only a few Flemings escaped back over the Zwin, the noblemen, including Guy, captured and ransomed while the remainder were put to the sword. Manny then abandoned the island.

Rather than appall Edward's show of strength impressed the rest of Europe including Philip who carried out reprisals against 'traitors' in Flanders. Edward also won a valuable ally in Louis IV of Bavaria, Holy Roman Emperor who would support Edward's claim to the French throne the following year. Having added the French Fleur-de-Lis to the Royal Coat of Arms (it would remain there until 1801 when King George III decided being a French King no longer held the attraction it once had), Edward gained a great naval victory over the French at Sluys in 1340 before Manny would take the war to France in Brittany.

10 November 1813
Napoleonic Wars
Battle of Nivelle

NAPOLEON BONAPARTE, EMPEROR of the French had, at differing times, controlled Europe including satellite states and allies from Cadiz, Spain to Moscow, Russia and from Kiel, Germany to Otranto, Italy. Just one nation had been a permanent fixture in all six coalitions that had opposed him, at times fighting alone when the rest of Europe had been subjugated, the United Kingdom of Great Britain and Ireland. France had failed to defeat Britain in a decisive battle, indeed except at sea where they had been catastrophically defeated at Trafalgar in 1805, they had not been able to bring the British to battle at all except on ground and at times of Britain's own choosing and even then always with an available line of retreat.

Napoleon's determination to bring the philosophies of the French Revolution to Britain by forcing all his conquered and allied territories to employ a Europe-wide trade embargo on British commerce, the Continental System, had led to an anti French armed Spanish uprising in the Iberian Peninsular and a catastrophic French invasion of Russia, the former supported by the British Army and their greatest General of the day, Sir Arthur Wellesley, Marquess of Wellington. Nevertheless Napoleon's genius had him create another army in the wake of his Russian disaster, putting 170,000 men in the field in May 1813 to defeat the Russo-Prussian Army of Peter Wittgenstein and General Gebhard von Blucher at Lutzen and Bautzen before suffering defeat in October 1813 against the Russo-Prusso-Austro-Swedish Army of Tsar Alexander I, Blucher, Karl Philipp, Prince of Schwarzenberg and Crown Prince Charles John respectively, who were augmented by a defecting Saxony and Bavaria in a three day, 600,000-man, 2,200-gun, 150,000-casualty bloodbath at Leipzig.

Meanwhile across France's southern border, Wellington's Anglo-Portuguese-Spanish Army had decisively defeated Joseph Bonaparte and Marshal Jean Baptiste Jourdan at Vitoria, captured the Port of San Sebastian and repulsed Marshal Jean de Dieu Soult's attempts to maintain French territory in Spain. On 7 October

Wellington then defeated Soult at the River Bidassoa by outflanking the French right at low tide before pressing on into France, Soult falling further back to the River Nivelle. Then on 31 October the French garrison that had been left behind at Pamplona finally capitulated leaving Wellington free to prosecute the invasion of France with ever more vigour. As Napoleon and the survivors of the *Grande Armée* fled back into northern France from Leipzig, Wellington's 80,000-strong army was well established in southern France, advancing to the Nivelle where Soult's 60,000 men defended a twenty mile line from the Atlantic coast up into the Pyrenees past the dominating peak of the Greater Rhune.

On 10 November 1813 Wellington's entire army advanced upon the French front, the British 1st and 5th Infantry Divisions under Lieutenant General Sir John Hope on the left, the 2nd and 6th Infantry Divisions with Spaniards and Portuguese under Lieutenant General Rowland Hill on the right whilst the main attack would be led in the centre by the Light Division supported by the 3rd, 4th and 7th Infantry Divisions under Marshal William Beresford. In the darkness before dawn, Beresford's Lights had found the Greater Rhune to be deserted and therefore continued unnoticed down into a ravine below the well-defended Lesser Rhune. On the firing of a cannon from Mount Atchubia the Lights stormed the Lesser Rhune in overwhelming force with Soult's overstretched defences taken completely by surprise and consequently routed. Wellington's main central assault then forced Soult's whole line to give ground despite the presence of several French forts and redoubts along the line of the hills. The 3rd Division then captured the bridge at Amotz separating the French left from the right. Consequently Soult was forced to retreat to the River Nive and Bayonne to avoid an encirclement.

Wellington would be victorious again at the Nive a month later but the Peninsular War would drag on as Soult began receiving reinforcements retreating from Catalonia under Marshal Louis Suchet, both sides claiming victory at Toulouse in April 1814. It mattered little, in Paris three days later Emperor of the French Napoleon Bonaparte abdicated to be subsequently exiled to the island of Elba by the Treaty of Fontainebleau. The British refused to ratify Fontainebleau primarily because Elba was a French territory close to mainland France and because the treaty recognised Napoleon not as an usurper but as Emperor of the French. Indeed, it would not be the end of him, not by a hundred days.

11 November 1940

Second World War
Raid on Taranto

ON 10 JUNE 1940 Italy's founder of Fascism, *Il Duce* (The Leader) Benito Mussolini, opportunistically declared war on a beaten France and a Great Britain that had only just retreated back across the English Channel. Formerly a Socialist, Mussolini had become more nationalist during the Great War believing only a powerful dictator could unite Italy and end the country's economic and political chaos. In 1922, with Italy yet again gripped by industrial action, Mussolini had threatened to march on Rome with his black shirted *fasci di combattimento* (fighting group) should the Government of Luigi Facta fail to respond to the unrest. The Italian Army at Facta's disposal was far stronger than the disaffected *fascisti* but King Victor Emmanuel III refused to sign a decree of Martial Law leaving Facta little alternative but to resign. The King then invited pro monarchist Mussolini to form a Government, the Italian coming to power a full eleven years before his more powerful northern neighbour, German Chancellor Adolf Hitler. King Victor however, now stood aside while the Fascists formed an increasingly authoritarian regime following their victory in the fraudulent 1924 Italian general election and the assassination of their Socialist rival Giacomo Matteotti.

Geographically, Mussolini was looking to re-establish a Mediterranean Empire similar to that of his Roman ancestors, initially demanding territory for Italian Libya from British Sudan before expanding his empire in 1935 with a merciless invasion of Abbyssinia (Ethiopia). Mussolini's conquest exacted sanctions from the League of Nations with the only country seemingly at ease with *Il Duce's* gas attacks on Africans being Nazi Germany, the pair forming a 'Pact of Steel' in 1939 after Mussolini had invaded Albania. Hitler's stunning 1940 victories in Europe then prompted the Italian dictator to up his game, in successive months from August 1940 Italy invaded British Somaliland, British Egypt (advancing from Libya to Sidi Barrani threatening Cairo and the Suez Canal) and Greece. In response Admiral Andrew Cunningham commanding the British Mediterranean Fleet implemented plans drawn up in 1935 by First Sea Lord, Dudley Pound for a night attack by the Fleet Air Arm on the powerfully modern Italian Navy (*Regia Marina*) at anchor in Taranto, Operation Judgement.

The Task Force, commanded by Rear Admiral Lumley Lyster, consisted of two heavy and two light cruisers, four destroyers and the new aircraft carrier HMS *Illustrious* carrying twenty-four Fairey Swordfish biplanes (Stringbags) for the attack and Fairey Fulmars for a defence. A Short Sunderland flying boat confirmed the *Regia Marina* to be in port (the Italians maintaining a fleet in being) on the evening of the 11 November 1940 before the first wave of twelve Swordfish took off from near Kefalonia, Greece at 21.00 later followed by another nine. At 23.00 the first wave, now just eight Swordfish after four had lost their way, three carrying bombs and five torpedoes, flew into a hail of fire from Taranto's 100 anti-aircraft guns, 200 machine-guns and twenty-three warships at Mar Grande and Mar Piccolo. Dodging barrage balloons two Swordfish bombed the oil tanks whilst three lined up for a torpedo attack over the centre of the harbour on the battleship *Conte di Cavour*, putting her out of service until after the 1943 Italian surrender but in the process losing Lieutenant Commander Kenneth Williamson. The two surviving Swordfish continued on to unsuccessfully attack the battleship *Andrea Doria* whilst the other three, not previously engaged, torpedoed the battleship *Littorio*, sinking her bow but missing the flagship *Vittorio Veneto*. The 'lost' bombers then arrived hitting two cruisers and destroyers. The second wave led by England rugby international Lieutenant Commander John Hale, now just eight strong, arrived from the north at 23.35, again attacking the oil tanks, torpedoing the stricken *Littorio* and the battleship *Caio Duilio*, putting her out of action for five months but for the loss of another Swordfish. Three Swordfish also bombed the cruiser *Trento* and the destroyers *Libeccio* and *Pessagno*.

The *Regia Marina* had lost six capital ships and moved many of the remainder north handing Cunningham temporary control of the Mediterranean, safeguarding Alexandria, Malta, Suez and isolating Italian forces in North Africa where they would soon be counter-attacked. The Fleet Air Arm attack on Taranto was studied by both Japan and the United States prior to the former's attack on the latter at Pearl Harbor, Hawaii in December 1941.

12 November 1944

Second World War
Sinking of the Tirpitz

THE 1919 TREATY of Versailles imposed severe restrictions on the German Wehrmacht (Armed forces) but the rise to power of Adolf Hitler and the negotiation of the 1935 Anglo-German Naval Agreement gave Admiral Erich Raeder, Commander-in-Chief of the Kriegsmarine, the chance to develop a surface fleet primarily to oppose the Bolshevik threat of the Soviet Union rather than that of the Royal Navy. Content with their naval superiority the British mistakenly believed the treaty would limit German naval ambition but Raeder immediately added to his Versailles permitted pocket battleships by building the impressive battleships, *Scharnhorst, Gneisenau, Bismarck* and *Tirpitz*. Shipbuilding in Britain also accelerated primarily to protect the huge quantities of imported food from the United States, Canada, South Africa, Australia and New Zealand but whilst nine British battleships were under construction in 1939 so too were six aircraft carriers, twenty-five cruisers and forty-three destroyers. None of them, however, could match the firepower of any of the German big four, the most fearsome of which was *Tirpitz*. Completed in 1941 and named after Grand Admiral Alfred von Tirpitz, architect of Kaiser Wilhelm II's Great War High Seas Fleet, *Tirpitz* was the biggest battleship ever built by a European nation. Displacing 52,600 tons fully loaded, protected by belts of armour up to 14 inches thick with eight 15-inch, twelve 6-inch and forty-four anti-aircraft guns she was capable of 30 knots.

Following the 1941 German invasion of the Soviet Union *Tirpitz* remained in the Baltic Sea guarding against the Russian Fleet at Leningrad. By this time her sister ship *Bismarck* had been sunk in the Atlantic but at a cost to the Royal Navy of HMS *Hood* and 1415 men. The British Admiralty and Prime Minister Winston Churchill were therefore acutely aware of the 'beast' *Tirpitz* and requested Bomber Command destroy her but by the end of 1941 six bombing raids had failed to record a scratch. As the Eastern Front moved toward Moscow the threat to Germany from Russia diminished but Russian armies were being supplied by British and American convoys sailing around the North Cape to Archangel and Murmansk. Raeder therefore sent *Tirpitz* to threaten these convoys from the natural protection of the Norwegian fjords additionally opposing any potential Allied invasion of Norway. To contain *Tirpitz,* British Combined Operations Headquarters then destroyed the 'Normandie' dock at St Nazaire in March 1942 denying her an Atlantic port. Bomber attacks continued but *Tirpitz* remained damage free until in September 1943 when Australian Lieutenant Henty Henty-Creer led four midget Submarines, X-craft, into Kaafjord that succeeded in causing extensive damage. Bomber attacks, however, continued to fail until 15 September 1944 when twenty-three Lancasters from No. 9 and 617 'Dambusters' Squadron took off from Yagodnik, Russia, seventeen of them carrying a Barnes Wallis invention, the 12,000 lb 'Tallboy' earthquake bomb. Just one hit destroyed *Tirpitz*' bow with near misses damaging the hull and bulkheads. Now fit only as a static battery the once great ship was towed to Tromso where a follow up RAF attack merely served to increase Focke Wulf protection from the nearby Bardufoss airfield.

On 12 November 1944, RAF 9 and 617 Squadron under Wing Commander James Tait, took off again on Operation Catechism, thirty-two adapted Lancasters carrying one 'Tallboy' each flying at maximum range from Lossiemouth to Tromso. Despite being picked up on radar Major Heinrich Ehrler commanding *Jagdgeschwader* 5 at Bardufoss failed to intercept the bombers who were now flying at 16,000 feet. Approaching over the mountains from the south-east and with no smokescreen *Tirpitz* was in clear view. On the ship Kapitan zur See Robert Weber ordered intense anti-aircraft fire from his forward guns and batteries around the fjord but two, possibly three Tallboys slammed into *Tirpitz*' decks, the first ripping a sixteen metre hole in her hull and killing almost everyone on deck. Listing to port *Tirpitz* was rocked minutes later by a huge explosion capsizing her completely, it had taken twenty-six attempts. Weber lost his life with almost half his 2,000 crew, eighty rescued later when the upturned hull was cut open.

Tirpitz was the last of his battleships but Hitler had other concerns, Operation Watch on the Rhine, a last gasp 450,000 man German gamble through the Ardennes.

13 November 1917
The Great War
Battle of Mughar Ridge

BRITISH PRIME MINISTER David Lloyd George had been under unimaginable pressure since coming to office in December 1916. At odds with the tactics of his own generals, he had in early 1917 subordinated British command to that of French General Robert Nivelle. The failure of the April Nivelle offensive, however, personally empowered Field Marshal Douglas Haig Commander-in-Chief of the British Expeditionary Force who was arguably commanding the technically most advanced army in the field and was confident of a German collapse provided he maintain pressure in the theatre that really mattered, the Western Front. Lloyd George, however, was desperate to achieve victory in any way that avoided further slaughter but the high casualty rates of the Great War continued throughout 1917 at Arras, Aisne, Messines and the four month, 250,000 casualty, Third Battle of Ypres which now continued in appalling conditions for a final British and Canadian assault on the Passchendaele Ridge. One of the casualties of the very first day of Third Ypres had been the son of General Edmund Allenby who four days beforehand had arrived in Cairo, Egypt to take command of the Egyptian Expeditionary Force (EEF). The news had nearly broken Allenby but with unwavering resolution he now went about attaining the 'Christmas present' Lloyd George so desired for the despairing British nation, the capture of Jerusalem.

Allenby was succeeding General Archibald Murray after the EEF had suffered two costly defeats at Gaza but benefited from Murray having laid a railway, road and water pipe across the Sinai Peninsular and the efforts of Colonel Thomas Lawrence (aka of Arabia) and Bedouin Irregulars to his south who had defeated the Turks (Ottomans) at Aqaba. Further east Lieutenant General Frederick Maude had also advanced up the River Tigris to take Baghdad, Mesopotamia (Iraq) causing a general retreat of Ottoman forces across the Middle East. Allenby saw no strategic value in taking Jerusalem but nevertheless resumed the British offensive with a reorganised 100,000-strong EEF attacking Beersheba where a successful Australian equivalent to the Charge of the Light Brigade captured the precious wells. Allenby followed up at Gaza, Sheria, Hareira and Tel El Khuweilfe forcing the Turks into a retreat from the whole Gaza/Beersheba line, maintaining pressure on the Turkish 8th Army immediately to his north on the coastal plain whilst the Australian Mounted Division protected his right flank from the Turkish 7th Army in the Judean Hills.

On 11 November, the Australian Mounted Division came under pressure from increasingly strong Turkish 7th Army counter-attacks but, reinforced by New Zealanders, crucially held the line. As the Turkish counter-attacks weakened on 13 November 1917 Allenby launched another attack of his own toward the strategically important Junction Station where the east-west Jerusalem-Jaffa railway connects to the north-south Gaza and Beersheba lines. The 75th and 52nd British Infantry Divisions attacked the southern end of the strongly defended Mughar Ridge at Mesmiye but Turkish machine-gunners swept the open ground to slow the advance before falling back to another defensive position a mile to the north. The Australian Mounted Division then moved up on the British right and the Yeomanry Mounted Division the left whilst further left still the 8th Mounted Brigade moved on toward Ramla, all with the Anzac Mounted Division in reserve. As the infantry attack in the centre on Mughar Ridge stalled at midday, the Royal Buckinghamshires and Queens Own Dorsets were called forward from the Yeomanry for a joint charge with the 52nd Division across two miles of open ground under covering fire from the Royal Horse Artillery. The 750 men and horses gained the Turkish positions with 130 casualties and the loss of 265 horses, the Turks retreating except at El Mughar and Qatra until the Yeomen dismounted to join the 52nd Division for another successful two hour battle.

The EEF captured Junction Station the following day, cutting communications between the Turkish 7th and 8th Armies and opening the way for an advance north-west to Jaffa and east to Jerusalem. Allenby still had plenty of time to deliver his Christmas present.

14 November 1940
Second World War Bombing of Coventry

SINCE 22 JUNE 1940 Britain had fought on alone against the military might of a resurgent Nazi Germany led by Chancellor and *Fuhrer* Adolf Hitler. The Germans had been belatedly joined in war by Fascist Italy led by Benito Mussolini but whilst British Prime Minister Winston Churchill wished to maintain an aggressive defence in the Mediterranean and Middle East, particularly British Egypt and the Suez Canal against the Italians, the British Armed Forces at home were hard pressed just to deny the Germans a crossing of the English Channel. Two Operations, 'Dynamo' from Dunkirk and 'Ariel' from the French Atlantic coast, had been required to save the British Expeditionary Force but once the battle of France was over, the battle of Britain had begun. In fear of the Royal Navy, however, the German High Command could not contemplate the initiation of Operation Sea Lion, the German invasion of Britain, until Reichsmarschall Herman Goring's *Luftwaffe* of 2,500 medium bombers and fighter aircraft had achieved complete air superiority. Initially Hitler and Goring had been intent on targeting military installations only but Royal Air Force resistance and British bombing raids over Germany had increased over the summer, culminating on 25 August in an eighty-one bomber raid on industrial and consequently residential targets around Berlin. In retaliation the *Luftwaffe* ignored British airfields by bombing London from 7 September onwards crucially allowing the RAF some respite to deliver a shattering reverse on 15 September 1940 (Battle of Britain Day). Hitler now postponed Sea Lion indefinitely but the *Luftwaffe* continued bombing British cities at night, fifty-seven consecutively on London but also on Liverpool, Hull, Bristol, Portsmouth, Plymouth, Southampton, Swansea, Cardiff, Birmingham, Belfast, Glasgow, Manchester, Sheffield and Coventry.

On 9 November a downed German airman revealed the imminence of a massive raid on either Birmingham or Coventry, information seemingly confirmed three days later by an intercepted *Luftwaffe* 'Brown' Enigma decrypt which revealed a raid on a major city in the Midlands, the code word 'Korn' indicating which city was, however, undecipherable. Early on 14 November 1940 Churchill was then advised by codebreakers at Bletchley Park that the size of the raid indicated the likely target as London but as he returned to the capital it became clearer that Coventry, a city originally manufacturing automobiles, tools and machinery but now also munitions was the target. It is not absolute that Churchill was fully aware but he was nevertheless in a shocking position, with just four hours to evacuate Coventry, an impossible task, bring in additional fighters to attack the bomber formations, a difficult task, or bring in additional anti-aircraft guns (they had already been strengthened), another impossible task, he would almost certainly reveal to the German High Command that the *Luftwaffe* Enigma Code had been broken. It was also possible that at any time the German attack could be cancelled, the Enigma 'prize' thus revealed for no reason.

At 19.20 on 14 November 1940, the first Henkel 111's of Kampfruppe 100 guided by navigation radio beams began dropping flares around Coventry in Operation Mondsheinsonate (Moonlight Sonata). The city's twenty -four anti-aircraft and twelve Bofor guns began a spirited defence when just minutes later the first of 515 German bombers began dropping 500 tons of high explosive, rupturing water pipes, electricity cables, gas mains, buildings and roads. Having shattered the infrastructure of Coventry, incendiary bombs and incendiary petroleum mines then fell, igniting buildings including the fourteenth century Coventry Cathedral (St Michael's) with the Fire Brigade virtually helpless to prevent the flames from hundreds of fires spreading. The raid intensified as the night progressed, 558 citizens killed, over 1,200 injured and 4,500 homes destroyed as a firestorm tore through the centre of the city, melting lead roofing and gutters. Coventry's seventy-nine air raid shelters, however, held firm sparing over 30,000 inhabitants.

The ruins of Coventry Cathedral remain in the city centre. Coventry is twinned with her German equivalent, Dresden.

15 November 1899
Second Boer War
Chieveley Train Ambush

ON 30 OCTOBER 1899 a spectacular British gamble at Nicholson's Nek had ended in abject failure with the loss of 1,200 men dead, wounded or captured. The defeat added to three hollow British victories at the very start of the Second Boer War which had left Lieutenant General George White to retreat with 13,000 troops, the vast majority of British troops in Natal, to Ladysmith where they were bottled up by 20–25,000 Boers under General Piet Joubert. Reinforcements were, however, steaming south for South Africa from the Mother Country and India including Commander-in-Chief General Sir Redvers Buller and *Morning Post* journalist Winston Churchill, both aboard RMS *Dunottar Castle* which docked in Cape Town just as White was blundering. Buller assessed the situation with High Commissioner for Souther Africa Alfred Milner, a longtime advocate of a British annexation of the Boer Republics of the Transvaal and Orange Free State but who now faced Boer invasions of the Cape Colony and Natal with accompanying Afrikaner uprisings from within. Buller had also to consider Kimberley and Mafeking in North Cape Colony which were both besieged by Boer commandos.

In Ladysmith, White, who had so far ignored Buller's instructions, was calling for a relief column whilst in Kimberley mining magnate Cecil Rhodes, instigator of the disastrous Jameson Raid three years previous, was also frantic for assistance. In Mafeking, however, the ingenious Lieutenant General Robert Baden-Powell, future founder of the Boy Scouts, had the situation under such control that he was able to arrange cricket matches and theatrical performances. Buller decided to restore order everywhere but the nearest infantry brigade was still at sea and would only dock in Durban in mid November. Meanwhile just two battalions, 2,500 men, based at Estcourt, stood between the Boers and the whole of Natal but the cautious Joubert, instead of striking aggressively, instead merely sent out a reconnaissance in force.

On his arrival in Cape Town, Churchill had made his way by train to East London (the last before the Boers cut the line), where he took a boat to Durban (through an Antarctic gale) before again catching a train to Estcourt. Anxious to report on the situation in Ladysmith, Churchill offered a reward for anyone who would guide him through enemy lines. He duly received an offer from Captain Aylmer Haldane who, on 15 November 1899, was taking an armoured train 'Hairy Mary' (due to her protective rope covering) north on reconnaissance with 120 men of the Dublin Fusiliers and Durban Light Infantry. Churchill had taken Hairy Mary as far as Colenso a few days before and now at Frere, just across the Blaauw Krantz River, he urged on Haldane when the Captain cabled his commander Colonel Charles Long for information. Haldane did not wait for Long's reply warning of Joubert's patrols in the area, one of which, consisting of 500 Boers from the Kruggersdorp and Wakkerstroom Commandos under General Louis Botha, Hairy Mary now steamed past en route for Chieveley. At Chieveley Haldane received Long's order to return to Frere but two miles short of the town Botha's Boers opened fire with three field guns and a Maxim gun panicking the driver into increasing speed. As Boer rifles joined their artillery, Hairy Mary raced around the next bend crashing into a boulder, derailing all three of the front three trucks but not the engine in the centre or the three rear trucks. The British field gun behind the engine then began returning fire but was soon knocked out leaving the Dubliners and Durbans desperately seeking cover beneath the trucks. Churchill, a non-combatant and oblivious to the incoming fire, organised nine men to partially drag the trucks away from the track, the engine smashing its way past but unexpectedly leaving her rear three trucks behind, the coupling having been destroyed by shellfire. As Maxim fire intensified men ran forward from the rear for the cover of the engine as she steamed back toward the Blaauw Krantz. On approaching the river, Churchill jumped off to help stragglers but ran straight into two mounted Boers levelling their rifles at 100 yards. Scrambling up the nearest bank as the Boer horsemen closed to 40 yards Churchill surrendered for a Pretoria jail.

Haldane had lost thirty-two dead and wounded with fifty-six captured. Churchill, however, would soon make a daring escape through the Transvaal to Portuguese Mozambique.

16 November 1776

American War of Independence
Battle of Fort Washington

THE AMERICAN WAR of Independence had begun with a humiliating British fighting retreat from Lexington and Concord followed by a miserable ten month siege of Boston from where the British evacuated in March 1776. General William Howe had then switched the British fightback south, sailing the British Army from Halifax, Nova Scotia to New York while his opponent General George Washington marched the Continental Army overland to resist. Howe was immediately successful, defeating the Americans on Long Island before Washington checked him at Harlem Heights on Manhattan Island. The overwhelming numbers of men and material possessed by the British Army in conjunction with the world's most powerful navy controlling the River Hudson meant Washington could not hold Manhattan and he retreated north evading British landings designed to cut his line of retreat. Howe had given chase, bringing Washington to battle once again at White Plains but had again been unable inflict a decisive defeat and had again allowed the Continental Army to continue their retreat west and south through New Jersey for Philadelphia.

As Washington started south the likelihood of American independence from Great Britain was fast disappearing, desertion from the Continental ranks consequently rife. Howe, however, rather than pursue, turned his attention to the American garrison left behind at Fort Washington on Manhattan Island. Garrisoned by 1,200 men under Colonel Robert Magaw, the fort had been barely hampering the Royal Navy or threatening Howe's rear as the British had advanced on White Plains since Major General Hugh Percy had been left to cover any threatening American sorties. Percy was no friend of Howe's and had conducted his own offensives on the fort in late October and early November 1776 both of which had ended in minor American victories. An emboldened Magaw therefore believed he could continue to hold Fort Washington indefinitely despite heavy numbers of British Redcoats now heading his way while Washington wanted to abandon the site. Since Congress and Major General Nathanael Greene insisted that the fort was worth holding to hinder the launching of further British offensives into New Jersey, Washington and 2,000 reinforcements interrupted their retreat to march on Fort Lee, on the opposite bank of the River Hudson before crossing to join Magaw in Fort Washington.

On 16 November 1776, after Magaw had declined to surrender, Howe, armed with information from American deserter William Demont, launched the British attack from the east across the River Harlem with a Hessian artillery barrage on Laurel Hill on the north-east side of the Fort, a naval barrage on the west and his own barrage on the south. The barrage effectively silenced the American guns before the Hessians in the north under Lieutenant General Wilhelm von Knyphausen advanced against determined resistance from Marylander and Virginian riflemen. In the south, Percy also advanced with 3,000 British and Hessians in conjunction with 800 Highlanders under Lieutenant Colonel Thomas Stirling who had crossed the Harlem to the south-east. Seeing his left flank threatened Lieutenant Colonel Lambert Cadwalader had 150 American Patriots to resist Stirling's advance yet more British were already beginning to land east of the Fort from across the Harlem. Assaulted on three sides Magaw's outer perimeter soon disintegrated, Patriots falling back to inner defensive positions except Cadwalader who had no option but to retreat to the fort itself. Washington had seen enough and took the opportunity to escape back across the Hudson to Fort Lee but requested Magaw hold out until nightfall when an evacuation could be attempted. It was too late, guns jamming and ammunition low, Magaw's men were charged with the bayonet by Knyphausen who then offered the Americans another chance to surrender. This time Magaw accepted, he had lost 150 dead and wounded (the British 450) with nearly 3,000 Americans marching into captivity. Add the loss of thirty-six guns and equipment and the battle had been a disaster for the American cause.

General Charles, Lord Cornwallis now began a pursuit of the retreating Continental Army through the freezing North American winter, across New Jersey and the River Delaware River to Trenton. The war had taken a very different turn and it would soon take another.

17 November 1942

Second World War
Battle for Tunisia

THROUGHOUT THE 1930's United States President Franklin D. Roosevelt had led a nation emerging from the Great Depression that wanted no active part in a European or Asian war. The American public, however, did sympathise with the Republic of China's fight against Japanese expansion and also now with Great Britain who in 1940–41 stood alone against Germany and Italy (Japan, Germany and Italy had formed the Axis in 1937). Roosevelt determined to assist both China and Great Britain with military supplies yet still preserve US 'neutrality', the US becoming 'an Arsenal of Democracy'. Though Roosevelt never actually expected repayment the 'Destroyers for Bases' Agreement and the Lend-Lease Act would nearly bankrupt Britain (the loan was paid off in 2006) and consequently contributed to her losing an empire but at the time British Prime Minister Winston Churchill was hardly in a position to bargain. In June 1941 Roosevelt extended the 'Arsenal of Democracy' to the autocratic Soviet Union whilst also placing an oil embargo on an enraged Japan, the President nevertheless stunned when the Imperial Japanese Navy (IJN) attacked the US Pacific Fleet in Pearl Harbor, Hawaii on 7 December 1941. To Churchill's delight German Chancellor Adolf Hitler and Italian Prime Minister Benito Mussolini then supported their Axis partner with their own somewhat unnecessary declarations of war on the United States.

By October 1942 the US Navy had retaliated by crushing the IJN at Midway and had landed on Guadalcanal, Solomon Islands. In Europe the US Army Air Force began bombing Germany whilst Anglo-American landings in Morocco and Algeria against pro German Vichy French forces were imminent, Operation Torch. Lieutenant General Bernard Montgomery commanding the British 8th Army had also counter-attacked Axis forces in Egypt under German Field Marshal Erwin 'the Desert Fox' Rommel, sending them into full retreat across North Africa. The success of Torch then encouraged North African Vichy French forces to defect, Germany responding by immediately invading the South of France and rushing 15,000 troops with 170 Panzer tanks for a defence of Tunisia. In response Lieutenant General Kenneth Anderson and the British First Army then began a 'Run for Tunis' and Bizerte from Algiers with two columns comprised of the 11th and 36th Infantry Brigades under Major General Vyvyan Evelegh (78th Division) and Armoured support (Blade Force) from 17th/21st Lancers under Colonel Richard Hull with some US and French units, all under aerial attack from the *Luftwaffe* and *Regia Aeronautica*.

On 17 November 1942 the advancing 36th Brigade ran into seventeen German Panzers and 400 Axis infantry on the North Road at Djebel Abiod (Nefza) beginning the fight for Tunisia. A fierce battle raged in which the British destroyed half the Panzers but with support scarce could not push on. Evelegh resumed the attack on 24 November, the 11th Brigade on the Southern Road running into heavy resistance at Medjez before General Walther Nehring commanding Axis forces withdrew to a defensive line running twenty miles west of Bizerte and Tunis. Attempts to outflank the Axis positions, including commando raids and paratroop drops, failed before Nehring launched his own counter-attack spearheaded by the newly arrived 10th Panzer Division. The Allies were pushed back to the River Medjerda, Blade Force virtually destroyed by new German Tiger tanks and Stuka dive bombers. On 22 December another Allied attack on Tunis with increased Anglo-American forces then also failed before Commander-in-Chief Dwight D. Eisenhower changed tactics. Now additionally opposed by the German 5th Panzer Division at Bizerte and Rommel retreating from Libya, Eisenhower transferred troops from Morocco and Algeria to fight on a much wider front. In February 1943, the final showdown in North Africa initially swung in favour of the Axis with a collapse of American defences at the Kasserine Pass before British General Harold Alexander joined Eisenhower to better coordinate Anglo-American strategy. Montgomery's British 8th Army with the help of Bletchley Park intelligence intercepts then beat off a desperate German counter-attack south at Medenine leaving Rommel to propose an evacuation. He was declined and placed on sick leave. In bitter weather the fighting continued, Tunis and Bizerte eventually falling to the Allies on 7 May 1943. The following week 230,000 Axis troops surrendered in Tunisia adding to the similar loss of the entire German 6th Army at Stalingrad three months earlier.

Victory in North Africa opened the way for an Allied invasion of Italy via Sicily. Soon it would not be just Vichy France defecting from the Axis.

18 November 1857

Indian Mutiny
Relief of Lucknow

BY 1850 ALL of India from the Punjab east to Bengal and south to the Madras Presidency & Ceylon (Sri Lanka) was under the control of the British East India Company. As British influence spread the arrival of families joining British officers had created more enclosed British communities which led to a decrease in social interaction between those officers and their Indian sepoys. In turn further insensitivity and intolerance to longstanding Indian traditions and a reluctance to engage in local language and dialect beyond abuse created a further disconnect between the British and the native Indian population. The Governor General of India (1848–56) James Broun-Ramsay, Lord Dalhousie had been determined to modernise India but this policy, including that great Indian success, the railway system, actually exacerbated the problem by aggravating Hindu fears over the caste system. So too Dalhousie's final act before returning to Britain which was to annex the state of Avadh between Bengal and the Punjab, inflaming Muslim resentment in Avadh which spilled over into the Bengal Army, 40 per cent of sepoys being recruited from Avadh. On 10 May 1857, an Indian uprising sparked into life at Meerut when Muslim and Hindu sepoys refused to use a new rifle cartridge rumoured, not without some foundation, to be greased with pig and cow fat. The offending sepoys were then insensitively sentenced to ten years hard labour before being paraded in leg irons in front of their outraged comrades who rose in rebellion, released the sentenced men and burnt the housing of, or killed any European they happened to come across. In the absence of British Indian regiments fighting in Persia (Iran) the Indian Mutiny spread across Bengal and Avadh but no further – the Bombay and Madras Armies as well as the Sikhs in the Punjab remained loyal to the British.

In Lucknow, Brigadier Sir Henry Lawrence recognised the danger, calling 1,300 British civilians in to the Residency under the protection of loyal sepoys and the 32nd (Cornwall) Regiment of Foot, 1,700 men with supplies to endure a siege. Meanwhile forty miles south in Cawnpore, sepoys did not initially rebel until the Maratha Prince, Nana Sahib, bribed them with better pay to initiate a three week siege. Ignorant that a 1,500 strong relief force under Major General Henry Havelock was coming to his assistance, Major General Sir Hugh Wheeler commanding the British in Cawnpore, was persuaded to surrender against his own better judgement having been assured by Nana Sahib of free passage to Allahabad. Treacherously Wheeler was then attacked by the rebels who took 200 women and children prisoner before later murdering them at Bibighar. On 16 July the relieving Havelock recaptured Cawnpore before crossing the River Ganges for Lucknow where Brigadier John Inglis was leading a spirited defence but with supplies now running low and too many non combatants to force a breakout. Havelock was reinforced by Lieutenant General James Outram who assumed command (both men had just returned from Persia), the pair fighting through the narrow streets of Lucknow to reach the Residency but in the process losing a quarter of their 2,000 men. Although now significantly reinforcing the garrison, Outram felt he was still too weak to force an evacuation and on discovering two months of supplies opted to prolong the siege. The new Commander-in-Chief in India Sir Colin Campbell, reinforced by troops from Hong Kong and naval gunnery, then began the relief of Lucknow on 14 November by marching from the east through the Dilkusha Park and Martinière School, thus avoiding the street fighting endured by Havelock and Outram. Nevertheless, fortified strongholds in the walled garden of Secundra Bagh and at the Mosque Shah Najaf still had to be taken in bitter hand-to-hand fighting, twenty-four Victoria Crosses awarded at Secundra Bagh alone. When Campbell then took the Moti Mahal Palace with the bayonet he was left with another 400 yards of open space to cover but successfully cleared out determined snipers to reach the Residency on 18 November 1857.

Campbell successfully evacuated Lucknow before returning in March 1858 to recaptured the city. The Indian Mutineers did not find the support for which they had hoped, even from the nominal Mughal Emperor Bahadur Shah II and the uprising was over by July 1858. Nana Sahib was never captured. The Indian Mutiny spelled the end of British East India Company rule, henceforth India would be ruled by the British Crown, Queen Victoria becoming Empress of India in 1876.

19 November 1917

The Great War
Battle for Jerusalem

BRITISH ATTEMPTS TO break the deadlock on the Western Front in 1917 had made some headway at Arras and Messines but the sheer scale of losses at the Third Battle of Ypres (Passchendaele) made any description of success difficult. Field Marshal Douglas Haig Commander-in-Chief of the British Expeditionary Force believed the Great War could only be won on the Western Front and that high casualties were consequently unavoidable whereas his Prime Minister David Lloyd George had grasped for alternatives, later describing Passchendaele as 'one of the greatest disasters of the war'. As another desperate year had unfolded Lloyd George had sent Lieutenant General Edmund Allenby to command the British and Colonial troops of the Egyptian Expeditionary Force (EEF) in Egypt and Palestine with intent to deliver, from German commanded Ottoman forces, a Christmas present for the British people, Jerusalem.

Allenby had benefited from his predecessor General Archibald Murray's logistics across the Sinai Peninsular, Colonel Thomas Lawrence's (of Arabia) Arab Irregular victory at Aqaba and large British and Anzac reinforcements to decisively renew the British offensive in Palestine. The now 100,000 strong EEF had forced the whole Turkish (Ottoman) Gaza to Beersheba defensive line into a fighting retreat that after the Battle of Mughar Ridge formed a broken line from the coastal plains around Jaffa (Tel Aviv) to the Judean Hills before Jerusalem, Allenby initially on the defensive at the former but the offensive at the latter. Neither Allenby, his Central Power counterpart Field Marshal Erich von Falkenhayn of the Ottoman Yildirim Army Group nor Turkish 7th Army commander, Maresal Fevsi Cakmak were, however, willing to fight in or close to Jerusalem conscious of the city's historical and religious significance. Allenby therefore looked to isolate Jerusalem by cutting the road to Nablus with a left hook, the 75th British Infantry Division advancing up the Jaffa-Jerusalem Road whilst over difficult ground on their left advanced the 52nd (Lowland) Infantry Division, further left still advanced the more mobile Yeomanry Mounted Division. Meanwhile the 53rd (Welsh) Infantry Division would advance on extended lines of communication from the south up the Beersheba-Jerusalem Road to take Hebron and Bethlehem

On 19 November 1917, after the Australian Mounted Division had cleared a Turkish outpost at Latron, the main advance began with the 75th Infantry fighting through the well defended pass at Bab el-Wad, the narrow defiles and rocky ground favouring the Ottoman defenders in fierce close quarter fighting while deteriorating weather turned the hard tracks into quagmires impassable for heavy artillery. Nevertheless the 75th made good progress, the following day taking advantage of heavy fog at Abu Gosch to launch a bayonet charge before moving to attack Nabu Samuil (Samuel's Tomb) on 21 November again in fierce fighting. On their left the 52nd Infantry, bereft of artillery, and the Yeomanry struggled over the difficult ground against more determined resistance since most of the Turkish 7th Army had retreated north of Jerusalem. The British advance, now fully on extended lines and in bitter weather, stalled when Falkenhayn ordered Ottoman counter-attacks along the front particularly in the five mile gap between EEF positions in the hills and those on the plain. The 7th Mounted Brigade and the Australian Mounted Division were pressed back into action, successfully holding the line in desperate hand-to-hand fighting, the Turks suffering heavy casualties as Allenby reinforced his fronts with greater numbers of infantry, 10th Irish, 60th London and 74th Yeomanry Divisions. On 8 December to the south of Jerusalem, the 53rd Welsh advanced to Bethlehem to link with 60th Infantry Division on their left, cutting the road east to Jericho but just a day later Falkenhayn retreated further north, effectively surrendering Jerusalem.

On 11 December, Allenby rode up to the Jaffa Gate and dismounted before humbly walking into the holy city. He was the first Christian to govern Jerusalem for 673 years, making the oft quoted speech that his 'army had come not as conquerors but as liberators' (the British remained in Palestine for thirty-one years). Watching on, Lawrence felt it 'was the supreme moment of the war'. Allenby had delivered his Christmas present early but he was not finished, he would next attack Ottoman forces over the River Auja at Jaffa.

20 November 1917

The Great War
Battle of Cambrai

FIELD MARSHAL DOUGLAS Haig's Third Battle of Ypres (Passchendaele) offensive had cost 250,000 British and Commonwealth casualties and a similar number of German. Since coming to office eight months earlier Haig's Prime Minister David Lloyd George had been deeply uneasy at the prospect of further high casualties but had consented to the offensive only after First Sea Lord, John Jellicoe had sensationally claimed that due to German submarine warfare the Royal Navy would not be able to continue the Great War on into 1918. Lloyd George would later claim Passchendaele to be one of the 'great disasters of the war' but at the time, having retained the option of halting the battle when objectives had not been met, he had failed to intervene. Haig had believed the German army close to collapse and indeed General Herbert Plumer's hammer blows at Menin Road Ridge, Polygon Wood and Broodseinde had brought them to the verge of defeat, Crown Prince Rupprecht of Bavaria considering a general retreat before the German 4th Army had stood firm at Poelcappelle. As conditions in the Ypres Salient tested the limits of human endurance, Haig had centred his offensive around Lieutenant General Arthur Currie's Canadian Corps who fought on with Plumer's British Second Army and General Hubert Gough's now devastated British Fifth Army to secure the Passchendaele Ridge before winter. Additionally Currie's, Plumer's and Gough's efforts would hold German troops in Flanders whilst an innovative British offensive was about to be launched by Lieutenant General Julian Byng's British Third Army on the Hindenberg Line at Cambrai, France.

Byng embraced the combined operations ideas of Staff Officer John Fuller who believed tanks, which had performed poorly since their appearance the previous year, should be used on suitable ground, en masse, with infantry support, aircraft and of course surprise. Byng's assault would also be supported by another innovation, a 'predicted artillery bombardment' mastered by Major General Henry Tudor where precise mapping, wind speed and direction, gun barrel calibration and ammunition variation were all calculated in advance so that a target would be hit with the first shell. British Tank Corps Brigadier General Hugh Elles thought Cambrai not perfect but at least the ground was comparatively lightly damaged and lightly defended.

At 06.20 on 20 November 1917, 1,003 British guns began picking off German targets as 476 Mark IV tanks rumbled forward at 2mph across a six-mile front supported by six infantry divisions with cavalry in reserve ready to exploit any breakthrough. On reaching the German 2nd Army front line the tanks crushed barbed wire and dropped wooden fascines to cross the trenches. German 2nd Army commander General Georg von der Marwitz was not completely taken by surprise, however, German intelligence had indicated an attack at Havrincourt but he was certainly taken aback by Byng's execution and both British flanks made good ground. In the west the West Ridings almost reached Bourlon Wood whilst on their left Ulstermen reached the Bapaume Road. In the east the 20th Light Division reached the St Quentin Canal at Masnières but any crossing was forfeit when the bridge collapsed under the weight of a 30-ton tank. British cavalry coming up in support pushed on north to Noyelles but were repulsed when the attack began to lose impetus. In the centre at Flesquières, Highlanders were held by much stronger German defences including an anti-tank battery which knocked out forty British tanks alone. By nightfall 179 British Tanks had been lost mostly to mechanical failure but the battle resumed the following day toward the ridge at Bourlon Wood on which Marwitz had retreated after recovering from the initial shock. Pressed on three sides the West Ridings were now relieved by the 40th Infantry Division who attacked with one hundred tanks and 430 guns to reach the ridge in bitter fighting against reinforced German positions. As the British dug in they were hit by intense German artillery before Marwitz launched a massive twenty division counter-attack from the north and east. In desperate fighting the British were pushed back to their start lines, both sides having suffered near 50,000 casualties over seventeen days of fighting.

Cambrai heralded a new era in all arms warfare, indeed Fuller's theories would be studied and employed by General Heinz Guderian of the German World War II Panzer Army. Germany had suffered huge losses throughout 1916 and 1917 but it would be they who would try to win the war in the Spring of 1918.

21 November 1920

Anglo-Irish War
Dublin, Bloody Sunday

 THE 1798 DEFEAT of the Society of United Irishmen signaled the end of an Irish Parliament in Dublin and, it seemed, any hope of an independent Ireland. The calls for a return of Home Rule for Ireland, however, would not go away, Irish nationalism was boosted not least by the 1845–52 Potato Famine before in the second half of the nineteenth century the Irish Parliamentary Party (IPP) twice held the balance of power at Westminster for William Gladstone's Liberals in return for the introduction of what would be failed Home Rule Bills. For the same price the IPP again held the balance of power for Herbert Asquith's Liberals in 1911, this time the Bill passing the House of Commons three times to override the House of Lords. A civil war in Ireland between Catholic and Protestant paramilitary organisations was then averted when Kaiser Wilhelm II and the Central Powers of Germany, Austria and Turkey caused a four year delay in the Bill's implementation. While 200,000 Irishmen, both Catholic and Protestant, fought in the trenches for 'King and Country' between 1914–18 paramilitary nationalist Irish Volunteers sponsored by the Kaiser took advantage of Britain's distraction by seizing the centre of Dublin in 1916 to declare an Independent Ireland.

Despite executing only eleven of the 108 Irishmen found guilty of treason and leniently treating another 1800 the 'ruthless' crushing of the 'Easter Rising'; the destruction of central Dublin; the continued failure to implement Home Rule; and the extension of conscription further polarised Irish politics and the law enforcing organisations – the Royal Irish Constabulary (RIC), the Dublin Metropolitan Police (DMP) and the British Army. Consequently the IPP all but vanished in the 1918 General Election, replaced by the nationalist Sinn Fein under Eamon De Valera which refused to take its seats at Westminster (instead calling an Irish Parliament, the Dail Eireann) and which had close ties to the paramilitary Irish Republican Army (IRA) of Michael Collins. Easily building an arsenal at the end of the Great War, the IRA then led a campaign against the British Army and the RIC, destroying 366 barracks whilst murdering or intimidating anyone who worked or associated with them. For their part the British Army and the RIC launched reprisals. As attacks mounted across the country, the IRA lost seventy five men in a shoot out at the Dublin Custom House but made huge gains in intelligence, Collins infiltrating the DMP G-Men to gain identities, addresses and knowledge.

On the morning of Sunday 21 November 1920, just days after British Prime Minister David Lloyd George announced he had 'murder by the throat', Collins launched an attack on the 'Cairo Gang', a crack British intelligence cell in Dublin. Fifteen Britons, most of them involved in intelligence, were assassinated delivering a devastating blow to the British military. That afternoon as military and constabulary families flooded into their barracks for protection, the RIC, its Auxiliary Division (ADRIC) and the unforgiving Temporary Constables (Black and Tans), 100 men with emotions running high descended on Croke Park where 5,000 Gaelic football fans had gathered to watch Dublin play Tipperary. At 15.25 the match had already kicked off when the security forces reached the stadium with orders to announce that the ground had been surrounded and that all males would be searched or, if they resisted, shot. On the arrival of the military lorries ticket sellers outside the ground, believed to be IRA pickets by the security services, ran into the ground and were fired upon. On hearing the shots all order within the stadium was then lost as crowds of spectators rushed to the far side of the ground. Major Edward Mills lost control of the RIC who fired 114 rifle rounds and an unknown amount of revolver ammunition into and over the crowd for ninety seconds killing thirteen people (including a ten- and an eleven-year-old boy), wounding over another sixty, with two more dying in the stampede to avoid the gunfire to which was added machine-gun fire from an armoured car outside the ground.

Three of that morning's IRA assassins had indeed been at Croke Park but escaped in the chaos. Two others were later arrested and with another were shot that night in dubious circumstances at Dublin Castle. The 'Bloody Sunday' shootings handed a propaganda gift to the IRA whose cause had been bolstered by the brutality of the British security forces. The event is incorrectly depicted in the 1996 Warner Bros film *Michael Collins*.

22 November 1739

War of Jenkins' Ear
Raid on Portobello

ALTHOUGH FIGHTING FINISHED only in 1715 (Siege of Majorca), the War of the Spanish Succession had mainly been concluded two years previous by the Treaty of Utrecht. The conditions gave Britain access to trade with Spanish colonies in South America and the Caribbean particularly in the trafficking of slaves from West Africa to work on the lucrative sugar plantations. Strict limits were placed on this trade with the Spanish constantly suspicious that Britain was exceeding its quotas in an age where any meaningful regulation was almost impossible. To add to the difficulties, vast numbers of sailors left unemployed after the cessation of hostilities fuelled a 'Golden Age of Piracy' in the Caribbean and off North America creating the legends of Calico Jack, Edward Teach (Blackbeard) and in the Pacific the tale of Robinson Crusoe, really Alexander Selkirk. The situation did not improve once Britain and Spain were back at war in 1718–20 by the War of the Quadruple Alliance and again between 1727–29 the Anglo-Spanish War, the latter including a failed one year British blockade of Portobello (Panama) and a failed Spanish attempt to regain Gibraltar.

Following the Anglo-Spanish War, Spain was allowed to board and inspect the cargoes of British vessels which they did with particular zeal. One such boarding, of the British brig *Rebecca* off Florida in 1731, resulted in the Captain, Robert Jenkins, being accused of smuggling by Captain Julio Leon Fandino who executed summary justice by cutting off one of Jenkins' ears. When relations between Spain and Britain deteriorated further in 1738 Jenkins reputedly produced his ear to a horrified Houses of Parliament, the indignant house (Britain's first Prime Minister Robert Walpole excepted) backed enthusiastically by a public who enjoyed nothing better than a quarrel with Spain, thus began the War of Jenkins' Ear.

Rather than directly attack Spain, Vice Admiral Edward Vernon sailed to the Caribbean on the orders of King George II and the Admiralty. On arrival in Antigua, Vernon initially ordered Captain Thomas Waterhouse with three warships to attack Spanish shipping operating between Venezuela and Panama but Waterhouse decided to add the fort at La Guaira, Venezuela to his shopping list, coming up with the cunning plan of flying the Spanish flag when he entered the harbour on 22 October 1739. Waterhouse's plan, however, fooled no one, Brigadier Don Gabriel Jose de Zuloaga treating the British to three hours of heavy cannon fire once they had sailed well within range. Considerably damaged, Waterhouse then limped back to Jamaica to explain the debacle.

Vernon now considered an attack on Portobello where he had previously failed in 1726/27, this time with a mere six ships of the line but planning a sharp, robust effort. Despite the added presence of two large forts at Portobello and against the advice of his fellow commanders who believed a much larger force to be required, Vernon anchored offshore on 20 November. The following dawn the British squadron sailed into Portobello Harbour to engage the Fort of Todo Fierro on its port side. So devastating was the British gunnery and so damp the Spanish powder that the Todo Fierro battery of near 100 guns was unable to put up sustained resistance and surrendered after just a couple of hours. Vernon then moved swiftly on to the head of the harbour where the town itself lay defended by the Castillo Santiago. Once again Vernon's guns put down a tremendous fire that failed to do much damage to the Castillo but caused havoc within the town. By the morning of 22 November 1739, the Spanish were in total disarray, the surrendering Governor Francisco Javier de la Vega y Retes requesting Vernon protect the inhabitants of Portobello from their own mutineering troops. The British then robbed the Spanish of 10,000 pesos, destroyed the Castillo Santiago and helped themselves to a multitude of Spanish cannon before returning to Jamaica.

For his feats of daring Mount Vernon in Virginia is named after the Vice Admiral, so too the Portobello Road, London and the Portobello areas of Dublin, Edinburgh and Virginia but Vernon was not finished. In 1741 he would lead a disastrous attack on Cartagena, Colombia before the war was consumed by the wider War of the Austrian Succession. Portobello only recovered with the building of the Panama Canal 175 years later.

23 November 1899

Second Boer War
Battle of Belmont

THE MAIN CONCERN for British troops heading to South Africa at the end of 1899 was that the Second Boer War would be over before they arrived but worry they need not for hollow British victories had left 13,000 British troops bottled up in Ladysmith whilst Boer Commandos freely menaced Natal. Even the *Morning Post*'s reporter Winston Churchill was now languishing in a Pretoria jail. British garrisons were also besieged at Kimberley and Mafeking in North Cape Colony leaving the recently arrived General Redvers Buller to make some tough decisions. Fearful of Boer advances further into British territory and of Afrikaner uprisings from within, Buller was consequently obliged to divide his forces in an effort to restore order everywhere. The Boers meanwhile, despite possessing highly mobile forces and well aware of gathering British strength, were content to maintain the investment of the British garrisons whilst building a strong defensive line in the Drakensberg Mountains on the north bank of the Tugela River, Natal. Only on the open Highveld of the Orange Free State and the Transvaal were the Boers more flexible.

For the relief of the diamond mining town of Kimberley, Buller sent Lieutenant General Lord Paul Methuen with 7,000 infantry, 1,000 cavalry and twelve field guns up the railway line from Cape Town to the Orange River for an advance across the stony desert. In case Methuen was in any doubt as to the magnitude of his task, his arrival at the Orange River coincided with that of a badly worsted reconnaissance patrol under Colonel George Gough. Disgraced, Gough would shoot himself in Cape Town but his problem out on the veld was just one of those now facing Methuen, a lack of any meaningful intelligence. The Boers were mobile, camouflaged and armed with German Mauser rifles (accurate up to nearly a mile) making it impossible for a British scout to get close. Additionally, a lack of transport (no oxen), poor maps and no water except that brought up by train meant Methuen's line of approach would have to be up the predictable line of the railway. The general could only guess where he was likely to find Boers whilst they knew his position virtually to the last detail. On 21st November 1899 Methuen's advance began toward the railway station at Belmont with the scouting Rimington's Tigers and 9th Lancers to his front spotting Boers ascending kopjes (hills) east of the town. A couple of miles south of Belmont Methuen's vanguard began to receive incoming fire which was silenced by the British field artillery as night fell. The following day Methuen attempted to gain more information on the Boer positions but with a shortage of cavalry had scant success and so decided to make a silent night march on the handful of kopjes running in two lines parallel to and east of the railway line, all of which he correctly believed to be well defended (by General Jacobus Prinsloo and 2,000 Boers).

At 03.00 on 23 November 1899, the British 9th Infantry Brigade advanced on Table Mount whilst the Guards Brigade advanced on Gun Hill both on the western edge of the Boer defences, closest to the railway line. Table Mount was taken after a short action but the Guards' approach to Gun Hill faltered when the supporting Grenadier Guards were not only late in departing but lost their way in the darkness. As the sun came up the grenadiers were caught on the open plain to the front rather than on the flank of the Boer defences, Lieutenant Colonel Eyre Crabbe holding his nerve to attack in open order, taking Gun Hill with the bayonet but with heavy casualties. Methuen now attempted to bring his artillery up to pound the Boer trenches on Mount Blanc further east but without the necessary horses could only manage light, ineffective shrapnel fire. Boers were also still resisting on the far slopes of Table Mount whilst others were putting down a heavy fire from Razor Back and Sugar Loaf Hill. Methuen responded by sending two infantry battalions to assault Razor Back and Sugar Loaf while heavier naval guns bombarded Mount Blanc from the valley floor. The 9th Brigade finally cleared the Boers from the slopes of Table Mount before advancing on Mount Blanc which was now the scene of a mass Boer retreat.

As Methuen took Mount Blanc, Boers could be seen galloping away across the veld ready to fight a similar battle two days later further up the railway line at Graspan and five days later at the Modder River. Methuen had already lost 300 men at Belmont, the thought of just a repeat appalled him but it would get worse.

24 November 1542

Anglo-Scottish Wars
Battle of Solway Moss

IN 1513 KING James IV of Scotland had been killed in battle at Flodden Field fighting against the army of his brother-in-law King Henry VIII of England. Flodden had been rather an unnecessary battle fought over the vacillating interests of Pope Julius II, the Doge Leonardo Loredan of Venice and King Louis XII of France. Henry had been happy to support the Pope early in his reign but by 1534 their relationship was very different. Seeking an annulment of his marriage to Catherine of Aragon Henry had broken from Rome by the 1534 Act of Supremacy which declared him 'the only supreme head on earth of the Church of England' – the English Reformation. Henry was, however, now potentially isolated against the rest of Catholic Europe, the threat from whom increased when Pope Paul III sought an alliance between the Holy Roman Empire, France and Scotland.

Attempting to regain French territories lost during the Hundred Years' War Henry had been in conflict with France thirty years earlier but on this occasion was contemplating a largely defensive effort, increasing his naval power and coastal defences accordingly. He also attempted to prize his nephew, King James V of Scotland, away from the Catholic Church and the 'Auld Alliance' with France. As James pondered, Henry showered him with gifts whilst northern English barons menacingly raided Scottish border territories as a gentle taste of what might happen should he falter. Conversely Pope Paul sent James a blessed sword and a hat to protect him from English heresy. Indeed, James had persecuted Protestants earlier in his reign and he did not change direction now. When his mother, Margaret Tudor, Henry's sister, died in 1541 any civility between the two kings was lost when Henry invited James to meet him at York, a meeting endorsed by James' Treasurer James Kirkcaldy but not by his clergy. Not that anyone told Henry who was humiliatingly left waiting for twelve days as James failed to make an appearance. The furious English king was now convinced James was in league with his two prime enemies, the Pope and King Francis I of France.

Henry, no doubt sore at the recent revelations and execution of his fifth wife Catherine Howard, increased his raids into Scotland, sacking Kelso and Roxburgh, to which James retaliated by mustering a Scottish Army of 18,000 men which crossed through the Western Marches into England on 24 November 1542 heading for Carlisle. Sir Thomas Wharton commanded just 3,000 Englishmen in Carlisle since the vast majority of the English Army were at Berwick waiting for a Scottish attack through the Eastern Marches. A supreme military tactician, Wharton nevertheless advanced into the wetlands near Solway Moss to meet the Scots who had fallen into disarray. James had been taken ill at Lochmaben and the Scottish Warden of the West Marches Robert, Lord Maxwell had assumed command, an assumption contested by Sir Oliver Sinclair, a courtier of James, who disputed Maxwell's authority and insisted that he was the Scottish king's chosen commander.

Division and dissent had long been common themes in Scottish politics and warfare and as they quarreled yet again, Wharton, watching from Hopesike Hill above, saw his opportunity. An impressive English cavalry charge fell upon the disorganised Scots who were immediately put to flight across marshy ground back to the River Esk. The battle did not last long, unable to move in the mud and trapped by the Esk the Scots surrendered after a sharp fight in which far more men drowned than were killed by enemy action. The English took 1,200 prisoners including Sinclair and Maxwell, 3,000 horse and twenty cannon.

James V of Scotland died just twenty days later at the age of thirty, a fever said at the time to be caused by the defeat at Solway Moss and because on 8 December his wife had born him a daughter – Mary (Queen of Scots) – and not a son. Henry VIII again tried to make peace with the Scots, proposing a Union of the two Crowns by the marriage of Mary to his five-year-old son Edward, Prince of Wales under the Treaty of Greenwich. The proposal was accepted by the Protestant Regent of Scotland James Hamilton, Earl of Arran but Catholicism and the pro France faction remained strong – the Scots rejected the treaty a year later. An apoplectic Henry increased his bullying of the Scots (the 'Rough Wooing') but it would merely encourage the French to invade England. The ships and men to perform it would sail into the Solent in July 1545.

25 November 1759

India
Battle of Chinsurah

THE BRITISH HAD been behind the Dutch, French and Portuguese in developing trade with the various Emperors, Nizams and Nawabs that ruled India but had gradually extended influence through the British East India Company, avoiding direct confrontation with native rule until 1757. At war with France as part of the Seven Years' War in Europe (Third Carnatic War in India), Colonel Robert Clive and Vice Admiral Charles Watson had flattened the French settlement at Chandannagar before Clive marched north to Plassey where he defeated the duplicitous Mughal Nawab of Bengal, Siraj-ud-Daulah. Clive consequently regained control of Bengal for the Company through the new Nawab of Bengal, Mir Jafar Khan (who he had bribed before Plassey) and by his own promotion to Governor of Bengal in 1758. Mir Jafar, however, found his new office came at a heavy price, ongoing British taxation of the populace was bad enough but Mir Jafar was also to hand Clive and the East India Company vast sums paid in jewels, rupees, gold and silver in compensation for their military expenses. The costs inflicted considerable hardship on the local Bengali population who thus became increasingly hostile to Mir Jafar, so much so that the Nawab was initially thankful for British protection. Caught between a rock and hard place, however, it was not long before Mir Jafar looked to free himself and his people from the British yoke.

The Dutch had been present at Chinsurah north of Calcutta, close to the Hooghly residence of the Nawabs of Bengal, before the arrival of the British but rather than compete with the French, British and Portuguese had concentrated on their near monopoly of trade in the Spice Islands of the East Indies. No strangers to warfare against Britain having fought three purely naval wars in the English Channel and North Sea during the second half of the seventeenth century and having ignominiously kicked the British out of the East Indies in 1682 it was to them that Mir Jafar turned for assistance. Whilst the British held a huge naval advantage in the Bay of Bengal, the Dutch had notable strength at Batavia, capital of the Dutch East Indies, now Jakarta, Indonesia.

Mir Jafar turned in earnest to his Dutch solution after using Clive to protect him from Mughal rival Ali Gauhar but a suspicious Clive had already received intelligence that the Dutch garrisons in Bengal were to be reinforced. In August 1759, just a few days apart, two Dutch warships loaded with Malay soldiers destined for Chinsurah were detained by Clive in the River Hooghly only for another two to arrive in October. Downriver in Calcutta, Clive again denied them permission to proceed but was compromised by Mir Jafar's noticeably more friendly welcome. Another five Dutch warships followed, sailing upriver to unload 1,500 troops (Dutch and Malays) complete with field artillery to add to the 150 troops who already garrisoned Chinsurah. Clive was no fool but since Britain was not at war with the neutral Dutch Republic (Britain was at war with France, Austria and Spain) he could do nothing. The predicament was solved, however, when the Dutch attacked British shipping on the Hooghly River and the Governor's House at Fulta. Clive sent out for assistance in the Bay of Bengal, three East Indiamen, *Duke of Dorset*, *Calcutta* and *Hardwicke* responding for an attack on the Dutch defensive line across the Hooghly at Melancholy Point. On 24 November the British East Indiamen routed the Dutch fleet in a two-hour battle to cut off the Dutch Army from the Bay of Bengal. Colonel Francis Forde then drove the Dutch further north before he was reinforced by Captain Richard Knox. Given permission to engage at the earliest opportunity, Forde formed up his now 1,200 British and Indian sepoys behind a ditch across the Chandanagar-Chinsurah Road with four guns and fifty cavalry in a mango grove to his left. Though still hoping for a Dutch victory, Mir Jafar also sent Forde another 150 cavalry to hedge his bets. At 10.00 on 25 November 1759 the Dutch under Colonel Jean Baptiste Roussel suffered heavy losses while advancing into Forde's guns but pressed on in the need to break the British line. At the ditch, however, an hour of purgatory was delivered in the form of disciplined British volleys of musket and grapeshot before British infantry and cavalry charged to decisively complete the rout.

Clive allowed the Dutch to remain at Chinsurah as British dependants. Mir Jafar was forced to abdicate as Nawab for Mir Qasim but the British would have a similar problem with the new incumbent who would turn to the Mughal Emperor Shah Alam II for support. Matters would come to a head in 1764 at Buxar.

26 November 1645

English Civil Wars
Siege of Newark

FIRST YEAR FORTUNES of the English Civil War could hardly have been better for the King of England, Charles I. The struggle for the king's divine right to rule, however, could not be prosecuted just when Parliament's problems were at their greatest and by the autumn of 1645 the greater resources of his enemy had turned those fortunes decisively against him. Heavily defeated at Naseby by professional soldiers of the New Model Army committed to the 'Good Old Cause', Charles had taken refuge at Raglan Castle in still loyal South Wales. Around the country the king's garrisons fell, most notably Bristol leaving Chester as his only sea port, vital to his dream of invading England with a combined Irish and Scottish Army. Charles therefore raced to Chester on reports of the town's imminent capitulation but although demoralisingly defeated on Rowton Heath the effort had bought Chester time and the town was still in Royalist hands. By a series of night marches, Charles then moved on to his stronghold of Newark where he hoped to join with James Graham, Marquess of Montrose who was until recently the all conquering commander of Scottish Royalist forces. Further Royalist capitulations at Devizes, Winchester and Basing House though were nothing compared to the news of Montrose's Highlanders who, in an attempt to raise the Lowlands, had been decisively defeated at Philiphaugh. The distraught king was then abandoned by his nephew Prince Rupert who had eventually been cleared of wrongdoing at the siege of Bristol but who now protested at replacing the Governor of Newark Sir Richard Willys with John, Lord Belasyse, commander of the King's Lifeguard.

As the 9,000-strong Parliament Army of the Northern Association under Sydnam Poyntz (victor of Rowton Heath) approached Newark, Charles departed for Oxford leaving Belasyse to endure the third and final siege of Newark. To his advantage Belasyse was behind massive medieval walls, protected by the River Trent and a series of forts (including the two massive King's and Queen's Sconces to the east) connected by earthworks, ditches and palisades that would break up

Parliament attacks. Initially Poyntz resolved to attack the outlying Fort at Shelford, twice summoning the garrison commander Sir Philip Stanhope to surrender only to be refused. Stanhope's professions of loyalty to the Crown ensured little quarter would be forthcoming whilst his additional boasts that he was prepared to die in a defence of Shelford were duly realised when Poyntz stormed the fort on 3 November 1645, massacring 140 defenders.

Poyntz then moved on to Newark itself, joining Scottish Covenanter forces under Alexander Leslie, Lord Leven on 26 November 1645. Leven immediately stormed Muskham Bridge, allowing his 7,000 Scots to advance onto the island created by the Trent west of the town but to the east Poyntz was unable to complete the investment, condemning his forces to endure repeated attacks from Royalist sorties throughout the freezing winter. In Spring 1646 Poyntz then created lines of circumvallation to the east and south, earthworks through which no supplies could pass. On the island too, Leven built his own Fort Edinburgh before capturing the Sandhills Sconce immediately west of the town which placed Belasyse's forces within range of Parliament musketeers and artillery. Conditions in Newark were deteriorating miserably, typhus and plague now rife but still Belasyse resisted.

In February 1646, King Charles lost the loyal South West of England after defeat at Torrington and in March he was defeated at Stow-on-the-Wold in the last battle of the First Civil War. In May Oxford was besieged but a disguised Charles had already departed for Newark. His cause hopeless, on 5 May 1646, the king handed himself in to acting commander David Leslie at the Scottish Covenanter headquarters at Southwell, west of Newark. Belasyse was ordered to surrender Newark the following day.

King Charles I was put on trial by the Rump Parliament on 1 January 1649, only half the appointed judges presented themselves, the rest being unwilling to adjudicate against their king. After refusing to recognise the court or defend himself Charles was sentenced to death but on the day of his execution, 30 January 1649, a huge sum of money (£100) was required to find a willing executioner. The Monarchy was abolished a week later, England becoming a republic for the next eleven years but the fighting was not over.

27 November 1940

Second World War
Battle of Spartivento

THE TIMING OF Italian dictator *Il Duce* Benito Mussolini's 10 June 1940 declaration of war on an already beaten France and a retreating Great Britain had not been lost on German Chancellor Adolf Hitler. Mussolini had initially been unwilling to wage war, recognising that Italian armed forces, though sizable, were not fully prepared but he did not want to miss out on the opportunity to rebuild a Roman Mediterranean Empire in the wake of what seemed an imminent total German victory. Parts of southern France, Corsica, Malta, Tunisia , Algeria, French and British Somaliland, British Egypt and the Sudan were all on Mussolini's radar to add to his previous conquests of Libya and Abyssinia (Ethiopia) whilst Hitler, with ambitions to the east of Germany, was for the time being content to allow his 'Pact of Steel' partner a free reign. Hitler would come to regret his decision but at the time Mussolini held the upper hand in the Mediterranean and North Africa, invading British Somaliland and British Egypt from Italian Libya as far as Sidi Barrani. Greece too was invaded on 28 October 1940 although Greek Prime Minister Ioannis Metaxas had responded to Italian surrender demands with a resolute *Oxi* (now a Greek public holiday) before launching a series of counter-attacks.

The British at Alexandria, Egypt were now isolated 2,200 miles from Gibraltar with only the tiny but gallant island of Malta linking the two. Already under intense bombardment from the *Regia Aeronautica Italiana* (Italian Air Force) if Malta could not be held Egypt could only be supplied via the far greater journey around the Cape of Good Hope. In Britain's favour, Fascist Spain, exhausted by civil war, could not be tempted into the fight and the French Navy had so far not fallen into enemy hands (determined that it should not do so British Prime Minister Winston Churchill had ordered a confiscation of French shipping in the Mediterranean which had required the use of force at Mers El Kebir, Algeria). With supremacy maintained in the Mediterranean but wary of the *Regia Marina* (Italian Navy) Churchill urged Admiral Andrew Cunningham commanding the British

Mediterranean Fleet and Archibald, Lord Wavell Commander-in-Chief of the British Army Middle East to take the war to the Italians, Cunningham attacking the *Regia Marina* at anchor in Taranto whilst Wavell prepared to counter-attack at Sidi Barrani. Following the destruction at Taranto, Ultra intercepts from Bletchley Park indicated that Mussolini had dropped his naval policy of a fleet in being and Vice Admiral Inigo Campioni had put to sea.

Campioni's twenty-four battleships, heavy cruisers and destroyers had previously successfully disrupted a Malta bound British convoy. Campioni was again targeting the same convoy, three merchant vessels now protected by Gibraltar's Force H commanded by Vice Admiral James Somerville aboard the aircraft carrier HMS *Ark Royal* and from Force D approaching from Malta. At 09.56 on 27 November 1940, south of Cape Spartivento, Sardinia, Somerville was informed that Italian warships had been spotted fifty miles to his north. Sending his merchantmen south-east with an escort, Somerville combined the remainder of Force H with the approaching Force D, the battleship HMS *Renown* with five cruisers and destroyers in the vanguard under Vice Admiral Lancelot Holland followed by the battleship *Ramillies* with seven destroyers. Minutes earlier Campioni had also been advised by a floatplane that Gibraltar Force H was to his south and, in the belief his fleet was stronger, advanced to attack in three groups before becoming aware of Force D. Under instruction to engage only if in a favourable situation and with little faith in his shore based aircraft, Campioni altered course but his vanguard including the battleship *Vittorio Veneto* was already within extreme twenty mile range and exchanged fire. As indecisive shelling continued *Ark Royal's* Swordfish torpedo bombers and Blackburn Skua dive bombers arrived overhead only to be met by determined anti-aircraft fire from Campioni's destroyers. Italian bombers from Cagliari then joined the battle in two waves, narrowly missing *Ark Royal* which had rejoined the main fleet. Unable to stay with Campioni, Somerville withdrew south, the three merchantmen safely reaching Malta and Alexandria.

A Board of Inquiry in Gibraltar cleared Somerville for failing to press his attack. Campioni, however, was sacked two weeks later but continued to serve until the 1943 Italian armistice when he was arrested by Mussolini, imprisoned and finally executed by firing squad in Parma.

28 November 1899

Second Boer War
Battle of Modder River

ON ARRIVAL IN Cape Town Commander-in-Chief of British Forces in South Africa, Sir Redvers Buller had divided his forces to relieve both Ladysmith in Natal and Kimberley in North Cape Colony. Mafeking, to the north of Kimberley, would have to wait and anyway, the town was in the more than capable hands of Lieutenant General Robert Baden Powell. Although the steadfast Lieutenant Colonel Robert Kekewich commanding the Kimberley garrison was also comfortable unbeknown to him Cecil Rhodes, owner of diamond mining giant De Beers, was sending out messages screaming for relief. Since Buller was also about to take command of the Natal Field Force, leaving no one in charge of overall strategy in South Africa, he sent General Lord Paul Methuen with two infantry brigades, one cavalry and twelve guns to relieve Rhodes. Due to a lack of transport and water in the stony desert, however, Methuen, out of necessity, had to take the predictable path up the Cape Town–Bulawayo Railway from the Orange River leaving General Martinus Prinsloo of the Orange Free State Commando all too aware of British dispositions whilst the Boer's long range German made Mauser rifles kept British reconnaissance at a distance and consequently British intelligence at a minimum.

At Belmont on 23 and Graspan on 25 November Methuen had successfully launched what were virtually full frontal attacks on Boer defensive positions at the cost of 300 casualties on each occasion. Boer casualties had conversely been light since they had simply galloped away once their position had been compromised, Methuen unable to pursue them in the light of British deficiencies in cavalry. Methuen was appalled at his casualty lists but was obliged to push on to within twenty-five miles of Kimberley where the Modder River Railway Bridge crosses the confluence of the Riet and Modder Rivers. In defensive positions on the kopjes of the north bank were Prinsloo's Free Staters, General Koos De La Rey of the

Transvaal Commando (which had fought at Graspan) and yet more Transvaalers under General Piet Cronje who had ridden south from Mafeking, 3,000 Boers in total facing an approaching 8,000 British.

At Graspan, De La Rey had been upset that his men had given up their positions too easily, dug in on the hill tops they had turned tail under incoming artillery fire and on the approach of Methuen's infantry but now De La Rey ordered his commandos to dig in on the lower slopes – Prinsloo's Free Staters in the west, De La Rey's Transvaalers in the centre and Cronje's Transvaalers in the east. All were invisible to Methuen's approaching infantry and all were ordered to withhold fire until the last moment for maximum effect. Indeed as Methuen approached he remarked to Major General Henry Colville 'they're not here' but within seconds and still at over 1,000 yards range some of Cronje's Transvaalers opened fire, a mistake that allowed the Scots Guards to go to ground losing De La Rey all chance of landing a decisive blow. The battle now erupted in full fury as the British infantry tried to rush forward for some cover only to become pinned down on the veld, noses in the sand, covered with ants, not daring to raise their heads. The twelve British 15-pounder guns began to reply with an additional four 12-pounders soon joining but generally crashing into the hillside above the Boer positions whilst Boer artillery continuously moved to stay in the fight. After three hours lying prostrate under the hot sun part of the British 9th Infantry Brigade under Major General Reginald Pole-Carew began to move forward in a series of rushes toward Rosmead Drift in the west of the Boer defensive line. Prinsloo's Free Staters there gave way allowing Pole-Carew's Lancashires and Highlanders to cross the Riet River where they began a flank attack on De La Rey's centre, the Lichtenburg Commando driving the British back to the drift but not back over the river. After ten hours of fighting darkness fell, the wounded Methuen then reinforcing Pole-Carew's bridgehead before recommencing an artillery bombardment the next morning. By then De La Rey had vanished.

Furious at Prinsloo's Commando (Transvaal President Paul Kruger accused them of cowardice) and in the knowledge Methuen would reinforce, De La Rey had had no option but to retreat, his misery completed with the loss of his son Adriaan amongst eighty Boer casualties. Methuen's campaign had already suffered losses of over 1,000 men and there were more defended kopjes blocking his path at Magersfontein and Spytfontein.

29 November 1900

Second Boer War
Battle of Rhenosterkop

 BY JUNE 1900 the British Army had taken both Bloemfontein, capital of the Orange Free State and Pretoria, capital of the Transvaal, but the Second Boer War which British Commander-in-Chief Field Marshal Lord Frederick Roberts had recently believed to be 'practically over', was very much on going. Martinus Steyn, President of the Free State, had taken over from Transvaal President Paul Kruger as the standard bearer for Afrikaner independence against British rule, a cause to which thousands of despairing Boers now flocked joining commandos out in their natural home, the South African Veld. That they had been allowed to do so had been down to Roberts' mistaken belief that the Johannesburg armistice of May 1900 had been a precursor for the full surrender of Boer forces by General Louis Botha.

Roberts soon realised his mistake, sending British forces, including his own army which had advanced from the Cape Colony and the Natal Field Force under General Sir Redvers Buller which had advanced from Ladysmith, back out onto the veld to respond with a policy of burning 30,000 Boer farmsteads, native black homesteads, small towns and raiding suspected store houses in an attempt to starve the enemy into submission. Under the command of Roberts' Chief of Staff Lieutenant General Horatio Kitchener, the British would go on to build over 8,000 blockhouses whilst their army, now almost as mobile as the Boers themselves, attempted to trap enemy forces by conducting great sweeps of land with converging columns of mounted infantry. In military terms the results of the policy were initially mixed but already by the South African spring of late 1900 the consequences of the Boer guerrilla war were being heavily borne by their own women and children left on the farmsteads, food now scarce and the rule of law disintegrating. The dilemma whether or not to continue the patriotic struggle prompted the Boer command of Steyn, Botha, Jan Smuts, Christiaan De Wet and Koos De La Rey to consider attacking Cape Colony and the mines of the rand before on 6 November Steyn's and De Wet's

Free State Commando was routed by Major General Charles Knox at Bothaville, 100 miles south-west of Johannesburg. Also in acute danger were 1,200 Boers of the Johannesburg and Boksburg Commandos and the Johannesburg Police under General Benjamin Viljoen who had been raiding British outposts at Balmoral and Wilges River Station north-east of Johannesburg. Viljoen had retreated back to his defensive laager at Rhenosterkop but in pursuit were two British columns totaling 5,000 men under Major General Arthur Paget and Lieutenant Colonel Guy Carleton.

Viljoen held a strong position on the high ground of the Rhenosterkop and the crescent shaped ridge that ran along it and was initially shelled by Paget on 28 November. The battle well and truly began at 07.00 on the 29 November 1900 as Paget, learning nothing from the previous year's fighting, opted for a full frontal attack on a well defended position that consisted of Boers light on artillery but, of course, well versed with the Mauser magazine loading rifle. Under cover of British artillery, Australians moved up on the British left but were soon stopped by heavy Boer rifle fire. Paget then moved New Zealanders up to support the Australians whilst the West Riding Regiment moved up in the British centre with Munster Fusiliers to their right. A fierce close quarter firefight raged along the line all morning with British artillery raining overhead. Rather than launch a flank attack on the Boer line of retreat, however, Paget continued to push the frontal attack throughout the heat of the afternoon and evening taking predictably heavy casualties but unable to break Boer resistance. Eventually British field artillery moved forward to increase pressure on the Boer lines until, after fifteen hours of fighting, a last desperate charge was repulsed by a Boer 15-pounder and a pom-pom which until then had been out of action all day.

As darkness fell Viljoen slipped away in the time honoured Boer fashion to fight another day. Despite over a hundred casualties Paget claimed victory but realistically had gained nothing. The increasing misery of the Boer civilians would continue for some time yet.

30 November 1652 o.s

Anglo-Dutch Wars
Battle of Dungeness

DUTCH ORANGIST SYMPATHY for their relatives amongst the dispossessed English monarchy and fury at the opportunistic advances of Dutch global trade throughout the English Civil War had been the driving force behind the outbreak of hostilities between the Commonwealth of England and the Dutch Republic in May 1652. The former Protestant allies for almost eighty years against Catholic Spain had considered unification twice, in 1585 and as recently as 1651 when Oliver Cromwell's offer was seen for what it was by the Dutch States General, an attempt to exploit the politics of their provinces to form powerful Protestant trading and naval fleets capable of dominating global trade, including the Baltic, the Mediterranean, Spanish South America, North America, the Levant and the Far East, all governed and administered in London by the Rump Parliament of the Commonwealth – the Dutch declined. Anger and tension increased as the English, upset at the treatment of their envoys and aware of recently increased Dutch naval strength, began strangling Dutch trade by imposing draconian restrictions on Dutch shipping which resulted in a five hour exchange of broadsides off Dover in May 1652. The Dutch Admiral that day, Maarten Tromp, who had finished Spain as a major naval power in 1639, was then replaced after weather wrecked his next offensive effort off Shetland against English General-at-Sea, Robert Blake. Tromp's unpopular successor, Vice Admiral Withe De With, was then defeated by Blake at the Kentish Knock in early Autumn, his leadership of the Dutch Navy having witnessed a fiasco of discipline and desertion. De With subsequently suffered a breakdown and was replaced by non other than Tromp.

The English believed Kentish Knock to have so severely damaged both Dutch morale and their shipping that Blake somewhat complacently sent ships to assist the English Mediterranean Fleet. Dutch morale, however, had in fact soared with Tromp's return whilst that of many English, with pay in arrears and desertion rife, had dropped. Worse still, several of England's most powerful ships were still in port repairing when on 23 November 1652 Tromp and ninety-three Dutch warships put to sea to protect a 270-ship merchant fleet. After weather delays Tromp left his merchantmen off Flanders before sailing west looking for Blake's forty-two strong fleet anchored in the Downs. Heavily outnumbered and wary of becoming trapped between the North and South Forelands of the Kent coast as had the Spanish in 1639, Blake sailed south and west before the Dutchman into the Dover Roads.

At first light on 30 November 1652, proceedings resumed, the fleets sailing parallel with the English to shore separated from the Dutch further out by the Varne Sand Bank but with the hour of reckoning soon approaching as Blake neared the Dungeness promontory. Making a southerly turn Blake's flagship, the 60-gun *Triumph* sailed between the Varne Bank and Dungeness exchanging broadside's with Tromp's 56-gun *Brederode* before *Brederode* was rammed by the 44-gun *Garland*, the Dutch crew immediately assaulting the *Garland* whose Captain blew up his own upper deck in an attempted defence. The *Brederode* was then blasted with canister on its port side by the 36-gun *Anthony Bonaventure* but was assisted by Vice Admiral Johan Evertsen in the *Hollandia*. As the battle raged across the decks of all four ships Blake attempted to turn the *Triumph* about but was engaged by further Dutchmen joining the battle. The 60-gun *Victory* and 58-gun *Vanguard* then came to Blake's aid but they could not prevent the loss of the *Garland* or the *Anthony Bonaventure*. A devastating English defeat was likely had darkness not intervened allowing Blake to disengage, Tromp reputedly sailing back to his merchant convoy with a broom tied to his mast indicating that he had swept the sea of the English.

Blake threatened to resign believing failures of administration had led to the poor performance of his fleet, six of his captains were dismissed. Sir Henry Vane, who had led the development of Parliament's New Model Army nine years before now set his hand to reforming the Navy. The Dutch would have free passage in the English Channel until the two fleets met again off Portland in February 1653.

December

"Hart has got himself into a devil of a mess down there, get him out as best you can."

COMMANDER-IN-CHIEF BRITISH FORCES IN
SOUTH AFRICA, REDVERS BULLER TO MAJOR
GENERAL NEVILLE LYTTLETON, COLENSO, 1899

1 December 1417

Hundred Years' War
Siege of Falaise

IN AUGUST 1417 Henry V King of England launched a conquest of France in pursuit of 'just rights and inheritances' that ninety years before had been denied his great-grandfather, King Edward III. The invasion of Normandy from Touques (now Trouville) had been timed to coincide with Edward's new ally John 'the Fearless', Duke of Burgundy advancing on Paris from his lands in Flanders and Burgundy itself. Duke John had been involved in a bitter dispute for over a decade with Louis, Duke of Orléans, brother of King Charles VI of France, both men vying for favour from a king often prone to bouts of insanity including the belief that he was made of glass.

Although both suspicious of the others sincerity, Henry and John had a common target of grievance and also formed a further convenient alliance with Sigismund, Holy Roman Emperor, who had previously been negotiating a peace between England and France as well as attempting to put an end to the papal schism of 1378. In 1407 the dispute between Duke John and the House of Orléans escalated when John murdered Louis before reaching a head in 1415 when the Duke and his retinue failed to fight against the detested English at the Battle of Agincourt. Louis' son, also Charles, the new Duke of Orléans was now languishing in England having been captured at Agincourt leaving his father-in-law Bernard, Count of Armagnac to become de facto head of the Orléanists (now read Armagnacs).

Following Agincourt, Armagnac, as the Constable of France, had immediately set about recovering the French king's shattered forces, marching north with a French Gascon Army to narrowly fail in recapturing Harfleur, wounding Henry's uncle, Thomas Beaufort, Earl of Dorset in the process at Valmont. Since Duke John's Burgundians were now taking advantage of King Charles' weakness to advance on Paris, Armagnac had little choice but to defend the city and the king's' court, consequently giving the English Army a near free hand in Normandy. Henry took full advantage, following in Edward III's footsteps with a brutal sack of Caen but magnanimously allowing anyone who had survived the experience to retain their property and enjoy his protection upon a sworn oath of allegiance. Not only that but the one thousand souls who refused to take the oath were given three days safe conduct, many of them joining those that had already fled heading for the nearby town of Falaise. Henry began campaigning once again on 1 October 1417 leaving Gilbert Talbot to guard the marches around Caen from Brittany, Gilbert Umfraville to command at Caen, John Assheton at Bayeux and Richard Wydeville further east at Lisieux. Meanwhile Henry himself moved south capturing Argentan, Exmes, Sees and Alencon where he signed a truce with John 'the wise', Duke of Brittany and Yolande of Aragon, Duchess of Anjou. Only then did the English King turn back to deal with Falaise.

On 1 December 1417, with his brothers Thomas, Duke of Clarence and Humphrey, Duke of Gloucester Henry arrived at Falaise, birthplace of his ancestor William the Conqueror. The town was and still is dominated by the white walled castle, Chateau de Falaise, sitting on a rocky outcrop with additional protection from a thick surrounding wall. It would be no easy task to reduce but Henry was in no hurry and was anxious not to waste the lives of his men unnecessarily. He also possessed an impressive siege train consisting of siege engines and cannon capable of projecting 20-inch diameter balls at the defences and the inhabitants incessantly for the next month whilst miners burrowed beneath. To house his besieging army the English king also had his engineers construct purpose built winter lodgings. By 2 January 1418, the combined English efforts had created a breach in the wall forty yards wide, the town immediately surrendering but not the castle which held out for another month. On their capitulation, the stubborn defenders of the castle paid for their resolution by being put to work repairing and upgrading the walls whilst those inhabitants who had failed to swear allegiance at Caen only to again resist at Falaise paid the traditional medieval price.

Henry then sent Gloucester and John Holland, Earl of Huntingdon to capture the Cotentin Peninsular, eventually reducing Cherbourg after a five month siege but failing at Mont St Michel whilst he, Clarence and Beaufort, now the Duke of Exeter marched north-east toward the River Seine and France's second city, Rouen. It would be another tough assignment, all the tougher because the Armagnacs had been betrayed in Paris, Burgundians taking the city as Parisians, not for the last time, rose against their King. The Count of Armagnac had been murdered, King Charles and Queen Isabelle held but their son, the Dauphin Charles (heir) had escaped. Likely as not the treacherous John, Duke of Burgundy would make his peace with the French king and now defend Rouen and France against the English.

2 December 1943

Second World War
Attack on Bari

FOLLOWING THE MAY 1943 defeat of the Axis Powers (Germany and Italy) in North Africa, Great Britain and the United States of America disagreed strongly as to where the major assault of Continental Europe should take place. Russia was just anxious there should be one. A compromise was reached where an immediate invasion of Italy, the choice of British Prime Minister Winston Churchill, would precede a 1944 invasion of France, the choice of US President Franklin D. Roosevelt.

The attack on Italy commenced with Operation Husky, an invasion of Sicily, which failed to destroy Italian and German field forces but coincided with Italian King Victor Emmanuel III's dismissal of the Italian Prime Minister Benito Mussolini. Mussolini was arrested by the Carabinieri and replaced by Marshal Pietro Badoglio, both Badoglio and the king determined to pull Italy out of the war. As the political situation in Italy disintegrated, Allied Force Headquarters increased their ambitions in the Mediterranean with Operation Baytown, 3 September 1943 landings in Calabria (Italy's toe) by British XIII Corps, part of General Bernard Montgomery's British 8th Army, followed by Operation Avalanche, 9 September landings at Salerno by the US Fifth Army of General Mark Clark. Badoglio surrendered the moment Montgomery's troops landed but German Chancellor Adolf Hitler had been well aware of a potential Italian defection. Also with little trust in his Commander-in-Chief South, Albert Kesselring, Hitler sent Field Marshal Erwin Rommel and General Kurt Student with heavy reinforcements who began to disarm Italian troops often with atrocities, particularly on Kefalonia, Greece, La Spezia, Italy and at Genoa when the Italian Navy defected.

Despite having been undermined Kesselring nevertheless demonstrated he was determined to fight, in anticipation of the main Allied attack at Salerno he had withdrawn north the German 10th Army of Generaloberst Heinrich von Vietinghoff. With Royal Navy fire support, Clark held Vietinghoff's counter-attacks on 13 September while Montgomery pushed up from Calabria through Bari to concentrate east of the Apennine Mountains. With Kesselring's agreement Vietinghoff then withdrew again to form a defensive line on the River Volturno before being forced further back to the reinforced natural defences of the Winter Line, a combination of the Bernhardt, Hitler and Gustav Lines stretching across Italy, hinged on the town of Monte Cassino. As Clark and the US Fifth Army prepared to assault the Bernhardt Line, Royal Air Force Air Marshal Sir Arthur Coningham announced that Germany had lost the air war. Unknown to Coningham, however, a reconnoitring Messerschmidt 210 was at the time flying over the lightly defended Bari Harbour observing the large build up of Allied supply ships. On receipt of the consequent report, Kesselring ordered Field Marshal Wolfram von Richthofen (cousin of Manfred, the Red Baron) commanding Luftflotte 2 to attack.

On 2 December 1943, Richthofen's 105 Junkers Ju 88 bombers flew a detour out across the Adriatic Sea to approach Bari from the east. The British tactic of Hamburg was employed, the dropping of tin foil blinding the Allied radar defences before Pathfinders dropped flares, the latter somewhat unnecessarily since the harbour, in line with Coningham's complacency, was brightly illuminated. The Junkers lined up at 19.30 for a twenty minute visit of destruction on the tightly packed, unsuspecting shipping below. Soon the harbour was a mass of blasted metal and fire, munition ships exploding with exceptional violence and petroleum leaking across the water from a shattered pipeline before igniting. Amongst the desperate scene an even more deadly menace lurked aboard the Liberty ship *John Harvey* which had sailed from the US. When the ship caught fire her crew, mostly ignorant of their own cargo, fought to save her but in vain, *John Harvey* exploded releasing 100 tons of mustard gas into the burning Bari night.

A thousand lives were lost at Bari, the Pearl Harbor of the Mediterranean. Shipping losses totalled twenty-seven sunk and twelve badly damaged with the port only returning to full capacity three months later, severely hampering preparations for the Allied assault of Monte Cassino. The cargo of *John Harvey* was subject to a cover up but Doctors working in Bari's many hospitals soon realised that of the 1,000 patients flooding in many were victims of a chemical agent, their suffering only exaggerated by the lack of disclosure. Bari was the only instance of battle casualties through gas during the Second World War.

3 December 1751

India
Battle of Arnee

SINCE VASCO DA Gama had reached India by rounding the Cape of Good Hope in 1498 European traders had sought favour with the local rulers for a license to trade. In 1608 Englishman William Hawkins arrived in Agra, capital of the Mughal Emperor Jahangir, where his perseverance led to the British East India Company gaining trading rights. Sir Thomas Roe continued Hawkins work, increasing factories and trade whilst advising his government not to resort to force. Francis Day then built a factory at Fort St George (later Madras (Chennai)) in southern India and in 1661 King Charles II's marriage to the Portuguese Catherine of Braganza delivered Bombay by way of the bride's dowry. Growing commerce in the Ganges Delta at Fort St William then led to the development of Calcutta as the capital of British India. In the late seventeenth century British influence again increased in North India with successive Mughal Nawabs of Bengal requiring military assistance against Afghan and Mahratta (Maratha) incursions. Meanwhile the French East India Company was trading mainly from Pondicherry in South East India until the 1715 arrival of Joseph Dupleix saw an ambition to expand, both they and their British equivalent having survived an early 18th Century onslaught from the Pirates of Madagascar. The 1740 outbreak of the Austrian War of Succession therefore meant a violent clash of interest in India between Britain and France, inaugurating the First Carnatic War. Fighting was confined to the south-east until the 1748 Treaty of Aix-la-Chapelles resumed the status quo but an increased Royal Navy presence in the Bay of Bengal ensured ongoing Anglo-French distrust, both now seeking favour from local rulers in return for the provision of protection against Marathas and each other, particularly the rival claimants for the Nawabship of the Carnatic – the British East India Company supporting Muhammad Ali Khan, the French, Chanda Sahib.

At the 1749 Battle of Ambur (Second Carnatic War) Anwaruddin Muhammad Khan, Nawab of the Carnatic had been killed by Chanda Sahib, leaving his son,

Muhammad Ali Khan to flee to Trichinopoly (Tiruchirappalli). Under threat himself from Maratha incursions Chanda Sahib was unable to immediately besiege Trichinopoly but in July 1751 eventually marched from Arcot. Robert Clive of the British East India Company then returned to Madras from Bengal to join a relief of Trichinopoly that failed dismally but sufficiently encouraged Clive to lead another British attack on vacated Arcot. With just 200 British and 300 Indian sepoys, Clive succeeded in taking Arcot which he then prepared to defend from a 4,000-strong relief force sent by Chanda Sahib under the command of his son, Raju Sahib. On arrival Raju was immediately attacked but such was the cost to Clive that the British immediately retreated back behind the fort walls on which Raju trained his cannon. The resultant breach and the Delhi Gate was then assaulted, Raju using elephants as battering rams but Clive held firm and indeed benefited when injured elephants ran amok amongst their own men.

A dispirited Raju marched away but Clive, reinforced by a Madras column under Captain James Kilpatrick, set off in pursuit now with 200 British, 700 sepoys and 600 Marathas. On 3 December 1751, Clive caught up with Raju's now 4,800 troops (including 300 French) at Arnee who turned to confront him. Outnumbered the British had taken up a defensive position around a rice paddy, Maratha horse on the left in a palm grove, sepoys on the right in a village and British infantry and cannon in between. On crossing the River Kamandala Naaga, Raju's cavalry and some French sepoys attacked the Marathas who were fought back to the palm grove whilst the French infantry and a further 1,500 French sepoys approached the village along a causeway, taking cover in the adjacent rice paddies when the British cannon opened fire. Clive sensed his opportunity, reinforcing the village with two guns and fifty British to attack the stricken men in the paddies whilst similarly the Marathas sent Raju's cavalry reeling backwards with a series of musket volleys. Raju's position now collapsed, the French desperately trying to rescue their guns as Clive advanced on both sides of the paddy routing Raju and capturing his treasury.

Arnee and the April 1752 relief of Trichinopoly by Major Stringer Lawrence and Clive were the first steps in the forthcoming British domination of India. Also in 1752 a Hindu mutiny executed Chanda Sahib leaving Muhammad Ali Khan as Nawab of the Carnatic.

4 December 1370

Hundred Years' War
Battles of Pontvallain

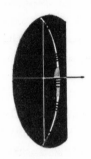

TWENTY-THREE YEARS of English battlefield success had been enshrined in the 1360 Treaty of Bretigny. In his own right King Edward III of England now ruled the Duchy of Aquitaine for which his predecessors had always paid fealty to the Kings of France (he also owned the Calais Pale and Ponthieu) and in Brittany, for the Dukedom of which he had backed John de Montford, the Breton War had also ended successfully. Though De Montford would recognise Charles V, King of France as his liege Lord rather than Edward he would still maintain an English military presence in the Peninsular. Things began to unravel, however, in 1367 when Edward's son, the Black Prince became involved in the Castilian Civil War, backing in return for money and territory Pedro the Cruel against his bastard brother, Enrique of Trastamara. In 1367 the Black Prince had destroyed Enrique at Najera but the treacherous Pedro then reneged on his commitments leaving the Prince in a dire financial position, difficulties he looked to address by increasing taxation on the population of Aquitaine. Since France had already suffered over a decade of ruin unrest was soon evident, dissatisfaction spreading as far as the Prince's own commanders, notably the Constable of Aquitaine, John Chandos.

The consequences of Najera soon reached Paris when a representation of Gascons requested Charles intervene despite the French king now having no jurisdiction over Aquitaine. Charles summoned the Black Prince to his court only for the invitation to be met with derision by the prince who claimed he would go to Paris only 'with helmets on and 60,000 men behind him'. Military activity again increased, the French besieging outlying English Gascon towns whilst the prince's brother John of Gaunt, Duke of Lancaster reinforced by Thomas de Beauchamp, Earl of Warwick led a chevauchée from Calais to Harfleur in an effort to draw French forces away from the south. Disaster struck Gaunt, however, in 1369 when Warwick died of the plague and Chandos was killed in a skirmish at Lussac les Chateaux. In 1370 Sir Robert Knollys and Sir Hugh Calveley then began another chevauchée from

Calais to Paris whilst the Black Prince marched north from Bordeaux to besiege Limoges which, under Bishop Jean de Cros, had treacherously defected to Charles. Though the French Chronicler Jean Froissart claims the Prince murdered 3,000 men, women and children in an afternoon on the fall of Limoges more recent evidence would suggest just 2–300 perishing. Certainly though tension was high.

Tension there was none more so than within Knollys 6,000-strong force which had moved south from Paris to the Loire Valley intending to continue either into Poitou or Normandy as the situation dictated. The French under the Constable of France, Bertrand du Guesclin, were, however, looking to attack Knollys from Caen to his north whilst Louis de Sancerre, the Marshal of France was also looking to attack from Chatellerault to his east. Knollys was aware of the two threats and proposed retreating to Brittany but his subordinates, Sir Thomas Grandison, Walter, Lord Fitzworth, Sir John Minsterworth and Calveley all disagreed, preferring to stay put, even dividing their forces when Knollys departed. When Du Guesclin then caught up with Grandison near Pontvallain on 4 December 1370, the latter was wiped out in a brutal hand-to-hand mêlée when his archers failed against French armour. The massacre of Englishmen was also replicated at the fortified Abbey of Vaas to which Sancerre had chased Fitzwalter. Minsterworth too was pursued through Brittany by Olivier de Clisson (who had fought for the English in 1364 at Auray) whilst Calveley was pursued into Poitou by Du Guesclin. Though Calveley himself escaped his men were wiped out at Bressuire whilst in Brittany, Minsterworth regained contact with Knollys only to find just two ships on hand to facilitate their evacuation from Saint Mathieu. The bulk of the abandoned English Army was subsequently also massacred by De Clisson. After thirty-three years the French had at last defeated the English in battle.

On his return to England Knollys was stripped of his lands whilst Minsterworth later defected to France. Two years later an English fleet was defeated off La Rochelle to leave English possessions in France once again in peril, a situation worsened by the deaths of the Black Prince (1376) and King Edward III (1377). Since King Richard II and Henry IV (Bolingbroke) would have domestic issues aplenty, not until 1415, during the reign of one of England's greatest warrior kings, would the Hundred Years' War restart.

4 December 1893

Matabele Wars
The Shangani Patrol

GOLD AND DIAMOND magnate Cecil Rhodes had become Prime Minister of the Cape Colony in 1890 but had been carving out his own country, South Zambezia (North Rhodesia/Zimbabwe) since 1888. The private annexation of territory in Central Africa suited the British Government of Robert Gascoyne Cecil, Lord Salisbury which was concerned at encroaching German imperialism toward the mineral riches of the rand potentially dividing British South Africa. After Charles Rudd, an emissary of Rhodes, had initially duped King Lobengula of the Ndebele into signing away mining rights in Mashonaland, Rhodes then either bought off or persuaded his doubters (principally the Missionary Society) that his intentions were good to obtain a Royal Charter. The Charter then enabled Rhodes to settle Mashonaland before Ndebele attacks on the Shona gave him the excuse to also invade Matabeleland (First Matabele War), crush Lobengula and clear the way for further investment.

In October and November 1893 the bravery of nearly 10,000 Ndebele had been no match for the Maxim guns of Major Patrick Forbes and just 700 British South African Police at the Shangani River and Bembesi. Lobengula, who had always sought to avoid war, then went on the run after burning his Kraal at Bulawayo but was requested by Leander Starr Jameson, an official of Rhodes' British South Africa Company, to return and put an end to the war, additionally Jameson safeguarded the king's life. As the proud Lobengula stalled, however, Jameson assembled 470 Police from Mashonaland, Bechuanaland and Rangers with three Maxim guns again commanded by Forbes to pursue the Ndebele north towards the Shiloh Mission Station and Inyati.

Although delayed by heavy rains, Forbes was soon upon Ndebele stragglers before continuing with a Flying Column of 160 men which, on 3 December, caught up with an Ndebele Impi across the Shangani River. Believed to now be within touching distance of Lobengula, Forbes sent Major Allan Wilson with twenty men, the Shangani Patrol, across the river to reconnoitre while he formed a defensive laager 200 yards further back. After several hours Wilson sent back two men to report that he had followed Lobengula for five miles and that he would remain on patrol overnight. Another three men then arrived back to inform Forbes that Lobengula's wagon had been discovered. Wilson was no doubt hoping for a reinforcement in strength for an attack at first light but Forbes was concerned about his own position which he thought could be subject to an Ndebele attack at any time. The paralysis meant that just twenty-one men arrived to support Wilson, too small to defeat an Ndebele Impi and too large to be merely a reconnaissance. Nevertheless, the Shangani Patrol bravely if somewhat foolhardily advanced upon Lobengula's camp at first light on 4 December 1893 calling for a surrender only to hear the ominous sound of rifle bolts clicking amongst the still trees. Lobengula had departed but 3,000 of his warriors were about to spring a deadly trap.

As the Ndebele began firing Wilson signaled a retreat back to his camp of the previous night. Though a few horses were shot down all thirty-seven men successfully arrived to begin returning fire. The Ndebele then began to encircle, increasing their fire to leaving Wilson ordering a further retreat back through the forest towards Forbes, still five miles away across the Shangani. Hundreds of Ndebele warriors flanked the retreat which after a mile was blocked by hundreds more, three of Wilson's men escaping across the river whilst the other thirty-four retreated to a clearing where they declined to surrender, instead forming a defensive position, back-to-back, firing continuously at the overwhelming numbers encircling them. The firefight went on for several hours before Wilson and the Shangani Patrol ran out of ammunition, Ndebele reports suggest the British then shook hands and sang 'God Save the Queen' before being slaughtered to a man.

The First Matabele War was over when Lobengula died shortly after but three years later the Ndebele would again rise when Jameson led a raid into the Transvaal which left Rhodesia defenceless. Wilson and his men were buried in the Great Zimbabwe before later being moved to the Matopos Hills alongside Rhodes. In Victorian Britain *the last stand of the Shangani Patrol* was theatrically portrayed in front of large crowds around the country for two years.

5 December 1777

The American War of Independence
Battle of White Marsh

BRITISH COMMANDER-IN-CHIEF North America General William Howe had escaped Boston in 1776 to open a new front against rebelling American Patriots further south in New York City. Though the American Continental Army and Commander-in-Chief General George Washington had then been harried through New York State by Howe and through New Jersey by Lieutenant General Charles, Lord Cornwallis they had avoided fighting a decisive battle. Even when Cornwallis believed Washington to be trapped at Trenton, the 'old fox' had eluded him once again to record such a sharp reverse at Princeton that Cornwallis retreated for the winter. British strategy, directed from London by George, Lord Sackville and General John Burgoyne now attempted to isolate American Patriot support in New England with an advance from Quebec down the Hudson Valley by Burgoyne himself supported by an advance north from New York by Howe. Howe, however, either did not understand his role or was not appraised of it, not only failing to support Burgoyne but heading in the exact opposite direction by sea to Chesapeake Bay and the River Delaware in an effort to capture the seat of American Congress, Philadelphia. That Philadelphia was deserted on Howe's arrival left the achievement somewhat meaningless whilst also, despite defeats at Brandywine and Paoli, the Continental Army outside remained in tact, confidently counter-attacking Howe at Germantown the moment the British General split his forces. As thick fog lifted, the disorganised American attack had been firmly repulsed by disciplined British musket volleys but any satisfaction gained was to be short-lived when just three days later in the Hudson Valley, Burgoyne was defeated at Bemis Heights, surrendering at Saratoga on 17 October 1777.

That Howe was at least part to blame for Burgoyne's demise was not in doubt, recriminations rife as he set about securing British supply lines on the Delaware,

774

clearing American forts from Chesapeake Bay to Philadelphia whilst Washington summoned American reinforcements south from the Hudson Valley. The fallout from Saratoga was only to get worse, however, as France and Spain now championed the cause of American independence at the expense of British colonial power won in North America just two decades earlier. Howe would soon resign his post but first he wanted one last crack at his nemesis camped just fourteen miles to the north-west on the Shuylkill River.

By 5 December 1777, 10,000 British Redcoats had marched forward to White Marsh, light infantry under Lieutenant Colonel Robert Abercromby successfully inviting and defeating an attack from a thousand Americans at Chestnut Hill on Washington's right, in the process capturing American Brigadier General William Irvine minus three fingers. Howe similarly declined to attack the American right in the hope that Washington would attack again but both commanders spent the next day observing each other across the heavily wooded countryside. On 7 December Howe then feigned a retreat, marching back to Germantown burning everything in his path before doubling back toward Jenkintown in an attempt to outflank the American left. Sending Major General Charles Grey with a force of light infantry and chasseurs to hold the American centre, Howe swung further right leaving Grey instructions not to attack before he was in position. Grey's impetuosity, however, got the better of him when he ran into American riflemen under Quarter Master General Daniel Morgan at Edge Hill, men who just two months earlier had been instrumental in Burgoyne's defeat at Bemis Heights. After initial fierce resistance Morgan retreated, narrowly avoiding becoming a casualty as Grey took control of Edge Hill giving him a view of the American position. Holding off strong American counter-attacks Grey was at last reinforced by two battalions of Hessians but already the ever cautious Howe was having doubts. Perceiving Washington's right and centre to be as strong as the left with an easy line of retreat and with any British attack having to negotiate difficult terrain in deteriorating weather he declined to press the attack.

The British retreated to Philadelphia for the winter, it had been a terrible year. Howe would be replaced by General Henry Clinton but British offensives in New Jersey were at an end. The Continental Army retreated to Valley Forge from where they would emerge a more professional force the following year. It would be another year yet before another British offensive could begin again, this time in Georgia and the Carolinas.

6 December 1649
English Civil Wars, Ireland
Battle of Lisnagarvey (Lisburn)

IN FEAR OF the growing power of the English Parliament at Westminster the Irish Confederate War had erupted in 1641 with violent Catholic rebellions against Protestant English and Scottish settlers spreading from Ulster across Ireland. A heavy defeat to Royalist government forces in 1643 at New Ross then checked the Confederates before an escalation of the English Civil War intervened, the Confederates claiming allegiance to King Charles I without ever providing him with military assistance. At the conclusion of the Civil War the Confederates then sought to benefit from rifts between Independents and Presbyterians within the English Parliament with another drive to rid Ireland of English Protestant influence.

Their advance on Dublin was, however, halted by James Butler, Earl of Ormonde, the Royalist Governor of Dublin who then resigned his post to Michael Jones at the head of English Parliament reinforcements. The Confederates again renewed their allegiance to the Crown (the future King Charles II was in exile in France and the Dutch Republic), now siding with Ormonde for another effort against their common foe, the Independents of the English Parliament. The Royal allegiance divided the Confederates, many of them fighting intransigent Ulstermen led by Owen Roe O'Neill whilst, across the Irish Sea, English Parliament forces were occupied putting down Royalist uprisings in Wales and North England. Only when an invasion of Ireland by the New Model Army (the property of the Independents) become imminent did the Confederates and Ormonde's Royalists advance once again on Dublin. The disastrous early August 1649 Royalist/Confederate defeat at Rathmines with losses to match was bad enough but worse, their impudence had merely hardened the resolve of Oliver Cromwell and 15,000 battle-hardened, religiously committed Puritan professionals of the New Model Army who were arriving to finally bring Ireland to heel.

The Cromwellian Conquest of Ireland began on 15 August 1649, Cromwell investing Drogheda on 3 September with 12,000 men, siege guns and a naval blockade. The garrison commander, Royalist Arthur Aston, however declined to surrender, Cromwell then storming the town, massacring the entire garrison including Aston as well as several hundred civilians with a ferocity designed to deter further Royalist/Confederate resistance. Too late, Owen Roe O'Neill now realised the preservation of Irish rule and Catholicism in Ulster lay in an alliance with the Confederates but his sudden death meant his Ulster army remained inactive. After Drogheda, Cromwell turned for Wexford but sent Robert Venables, a veteran of Nantwich, Chester and Rathmines, north to join with Sir Charles Coote who had so far held Londonderry only by virtue of an alliance with O'Neill. Venables marched up the east coast taking Dundalk, Carlingford, Newry and Belfast with minimal opposition while Coote advanced east to Coleraine. Protestants opened the gates to Coote who perpetrated another massacre, this time on the Royalist-Scottish Presbyterian garrison. Venables and Coote then united in Belfast intending to march on Carrickfergus to the defence of which two Royalist Scottish armies (also containing Catholic Irish) under George Munro and James Hamilton, Lord Clandeboye (3,000 men) were advancing from southern Ulster. Venables and Coote learnt of the Royalist approach and moved south with 5,000 men to give battle at Lisnagarvey. On 6 December 1649 the Royalist vanguard clashed with that of the Parliamentarians and, low on morale, put up scant resistance before turning tail. When the main Parliament Army arrived the rout had already been completed, Coote and Venables pursuing for ten miles leaving half the Royalists dead.

Royalist resistance in Ulster collapsed. The Royalist garrison at Cork then defected (it had originally been Parliamentarian) adding to further Confederate defeats when Cromwell pushed west. The Royalist-Confederate alliance then collapsed completely when Charles Stuart (King Charles II) abandoned them in favour of the Scottish Covenanters, Cromwell returning from Ireland to crush the Covenanters at Dunbar in September 1650. By 1653 the population of Ireland had suffered around 600,000 dead with many transported to English colonies in the Caribbean and North America. Catholicism was banned and Catholic land ownership dropped to 8 per cent. Unsurprisingly Catholic Irish would flock to support the Catholic King James II forty years later in his bid to regain the throne of England, Scotland and Ireland from the Protestant William of Orange, King William III.

7 December 1942

Second World War
Raid on Bordeaux

AS BRITAIN WAS withstanding the 1940 onslaught of the German *Luftwaffe*, British Prime Minister Winston Churchill had determined to maintain an offensive spirit by creating the Special Operations Executive under the Minister of Economic Warfare Hugh Dalton and Combined Operations Headquarters under Admiral of the Fleet Roger Keyes. In October 1941 Lord Louis Mountbatten replaced Keyes to command what was now fifteen highly trained commando units in Britain with another five in the Middle East (a further eight had also been formed by the Royal Marines for their own purposes). By the end of November 1942 the commandos had executed no less than thirty raids on the developing defences of the German Atlantic Wall, mainly in France and Norway often with a hundred men or less but almost always creating chaos out of all proportion to their strength. German Chancellor Adolf Hitler, driven to distraction by recent raids, notably St Nazaire in March 1942, Dieppe in August 1942 and Sark in October 1942, then reached another low by issuing an infamous 'Commando Order' stating that all Allied Commandos falling into German hands were to be executed immediately without trial. The raids continued regardless, four in November 1942 each with barely a dozen men while over 200,000 British and Commonwealth troops counter attacked in Egypt, over 100,000 British and Americans landed in Morocco and Algeria and over one million Russians counter-attacked at Stalingrad. The Second World War was turning and the now Minister for Economic Warfare Roundell Palmer, Lord Selborne wished to turn it further by devastating German shipping in Bordeaux Harbour, shipping that was successfully running the Allied blockade of the Atlantic coast particularly in the delivery of rubber. Since aerial bombing would incur high French civilian casualties and Bordeaux was too far inland for a Naval bombardment Selborne turned to Mountbatten who, in turn, turned to Major Herbert 'Blondie' Hasler of the Royal Marines Boom Patrol Detachment, much, much more than protectors of the Portsmouth Harbour boom and all expert canoeists to a man.

At 19.17 on 7 December 1942, the Royal Navy submarine HMS *Tuna* surfaced ten miles off the Gironde Estuary to unload six two-man collapsible canvas canoes, Cockles. Leading the raid (Operation Frankton) Hasler immediately lost the canoe *Cachalot* damaged in passing through *Tuna*'s hatch leaving five to continue toward the estuary. *Coalfish* was then lost in the strong currents, Sam Wallace and Robert Ewart picked up and shot four days later under Hitler's commando order, before disaster again struck when *Conger* capsized. *Conger*'s canoeists George Sheard and David Moffat, were towed towards shore by the others before making a desperate swim, both perishing from hypothermia. The bad luck then continued when *Cuttlefish* hit an underwater obstacle, John Mackinnon and James Conway making the shore for an overland dash through Vichy France before also being apprehended by the Gestapo and shot. Undeterred and with little option, the two remaining canoes *Catfish* and *Crayfish* continued up the River Garonne, by night, paddling up to twenty-two miles against the current whilst by day hiding in thick reeds away from the shore. On the night of 11 December, having covered seventy miles, the four men prepared their sixteen Limpet mines and paddled into Bordeaux Harbour, Hasler and Bill Sparkes in *Catfish* placing their mines on four vessels including a Minesweeper on the western side whilst Albert Laver and William Mills in *Crayfish* placed theirs on two vessels on the eastern side. Both crews then paddled back down river to the Isle de Caseau before independently making for neutral Spain on foot. Laver and Mills were picked up by the Gestapo and shot but Hasler and Sparks were fortunate to be assisted by English born, Mary Lindell, Comtesse de Milleville, reaching Spain, Gibraltar and finally Britain in April 1943.

All six ships attacked sank in the shallow water of Bordeaux Harbour, Churchill believing the raid shortened the war by six months. Mary Lindell survived the war despite internment at Ravensbruck concentration camp. Herbert Hasler went on to compete in the first solo Transatlantic Yacht Race in 1960. Operation Frankton is the subject of the 1955 fictional Warwick film *Cockleshell Heroes*.

8 December 1914

The Great War
Battle of the Falkland Islands

PRUSSIAN SHIPPING HAD been operating in South East Asia long before 1871 when Chancellor Otto von Bismarck united the independent German states to form the German Empire. The German East Asia Squadron, however, lacked a permanent base until finding a *casus belli* in 1897 when two German missionaries were murdered in Tsingdao (Qingdao), China. An agreement with the Chinese then allowed Germany, already with considerably naval ambitions under Kaiser Wilhelm II, to develop the port and infrastructure of Tsingdao (including a brewery) but when the Great War broke out in August 1914 the German Squadron, now under Vice Admiral Maximilian von Spee, was left badly isolated. To escape Allied shipping, especially Japanese, Spee sailed from the Caroline Islands (where he had been monitoring events) across the Pacific for Chile. On arrival off Coronel, Spee then advanced on what he thought was the lone HMS *Glasgow* but was in fact almost the entire British West Indies Squadron under Rear Admiral Christopher Cradock which was specifically searching for Spee along the west coast of South America. Nevertheless Spee's five cruisers, headed by SMS *Scharnhorst* and *Gneisenau*, completely overpowered Cradock's four near obsolete cruisers who accepted battle without the dreadnought HMS *Canopus* which had been left behind in the Falkland Islands. Both HMS *Good Hope* and HMS *Monmouth* were sunk with the loss of all 1,500 hands including Cradock, Spee awarded the Iron Cross though barely sustaining a scratch.

The British public had been surprised by several land battle losses over the previous half century but a naval loss such as Coronel was so inconceivable that First Sea Lord, Admiral Sir John 'Jackie' Fisher withdrew the battlecruisers HMS *Inflexible* and *Invincible* from the Grand Fleet at Scapa Flow to sail south under Vice Admiral Doveton Sturdee, join with three armoured and two light cruisers patrolling off the east coast of South America including the escaped HMS *Glasgow* and destroy Spee. Sturdee made a leisurely pace, conserving coal for a lengthy voyage whilst, following Coronel, Spee had put in at Valparaiso before making a run around Cape Horn for an Atlantic dash home, en route and against the advice of his senior commanders, deciding to raid the British coaling station at Port Stanley, Falkland Islands.

On the morning of 8 December 1914, Spee was steaming north along the east coast of East Falkland, his progress reported to the already well-informed Sturdee by Mrs Muriel Fenton from her sheep farm at Fitzroy. When Spee then turned west to attack Port Stanley he was checked by heavy fire from the grounded and concealed HMS *Canopus* as the rest of Sturdee's fleet steamed out of Port Stanley. Completely surprised Spee immediately realised he was heavily outgunned and steered north with just a fifteen mile head start. After a three hour chase, Spee could hold off the British battlecruisers no longer, ordering his three light cruisers to make their escape while he held off *Invincible* and *Inflexible* with his armoured cruisers *Scharnhorst* and *Gneisenau*. To eradicate the range deficiency of his guns Spee closed the distance between he and Sturdee, staying to leeward so that smoke from the British ships would obscure their targets. Spee was initially successful in scoring two hits on *Invincible* as he outmanoeuvred Sturdee but the superior 12-inch guns of both *Invincible* and *Inflexible* soon began finding their mark, inflicting heavy damage on both German ships, *Gneisenau* attempting to disengage while *Scharnhorst* desperately tried to launch her torpedoes. At 16.15 *Scharnhorst* sank with all hands including Spee before the British fleet turned to sink *Gneisenau*. Of his light cruisers, *Leipzig* and *Nurnberg* were also sent to the bottom after a further five hour chase. *Dresden* escaped but was scuttled after being cornered in March 1915 off San Fernandez.

The Second World War German heavy cruiser *Admiral Graf Spee* was named after Maximilian but also sank in South American waters in 1939. Muriel Fenton received an OBE for her services. Tsingdao fell into Japanese hands and was only returned to China in 1922. In 1993 Tsingdao Brewery became the first Chinese Company to be listed on the Hong Kong Stock Exchange.

9 December 1940

Second World War
Battle of Sidi Barrani

ITALIAN IMPERIAL AMBITION had begun in Libya during the Italo-Turkish War of 1911–12 but in 1919 fierce Libyan resistance to Italian rule led to an area around Tripoli declaring independence from the rest of Italian Libya- the Tripolitanean Republic. After the 1922 rise to power of the Italian Fascist dictator Benito Mussolini, Italian Libya and particularly the Senussi of Cyrenaica (North East Libya) then underwent a brutal pacification from General Rodolpho Graziani and the Italian military, again consolidating Italian power across the whole of Libya by 1934. Wishing to recreate a Mediterranean Roman Empire for his present day Italy, Mussolini was not content, invading Somaliland and Abyssinia (Ethiopia) as well as demanding further territory from British Egypt and Sudan especially south of Libya where the Aouzou Strip was intended to form the basis for a link between the Italian north African conquests.

Mussolini, then invaded Albania in April 1939 before, emboldened by signing the 'Pact of Steel' with Nazi Germany a month later and subsequent German victories a year later, beginning a September 1940 invasion of British Egypt in which Graziani intended to capture the Suez Canal. Lieutenant General Archibald Wavell commanding British forces in the Middle East had at his disposal just 36,000 troops and sixty-five tanks of the Western Desert Force under Major General Richard O'Connor supported by 205 mainly obsolete Royal Air Force aircraft to defend against ten divisions of the Italian 10th Army (150,000 men) and over 300 aircraft of the *Regia Aeronautica*. Though Graziani's 10th Army was hardly well-equipped and suffered from Royal Navy domination of the Mediterranean which increased their hardships at the end of extended supply lines through the inhospitable Libyan and Egyptian desert, O'Connor had little option but to fall back. After an Italian advance of sixty-five miles, still 300 short of Cairo, Graziani stopped at Sidi Barrani, building fortifications of dubious strength whilst sending units forward as far as Mersa Matruh. As British destroyers bombarded the Italians from offshore, O'Connor planned a limited counter-attack.

On 9 December 1940, Operation Compass began with an artillery bombardment and a simultaneous attack by the 11th Indian Infantry Brigade supported by forty-seven heavy Matilda tanks of the Royal Tank Regiment on the coastal town of Nibeiwa, surprise so complete that General Pietro Maletti commanding the Italian defence was killed in his pyjamas. Immediately the British 7th Armoured Brigade and 6th Royal Tank Regiment backed up by infantry attacked Tummars and Maktila. A day later Sidi Barrani was then targeted by an artillery bombardment whilst the 16th and 11th Indian Infantry Brigades trapped the Italian 1st Libyan Division against the 7th Royal Tank Regiment. Italian resistance began to collapse, large numbers surrendering (38,000) with those that retreated along the coastal roads back to Halfaya Pass having little respite from British armour and bombarding British warships. O'Connor then found the capture of Italian supplies allowed him to expand his offensive, the 6th Australian Infantry Division replacing the 4th Indian to continue along the coast to capture Bardia and Tobruk. Since Italian Enigma Codes had long been cracked by Bletchley Park, O'Connor became aware that Graziani was now retreating south of Benghazi and consequently ordered the British 7th Armoured Division (the Desert Rats on account of their insignia) under Major General Michael Creagh to cut across the desert to Beda Fomm, Lieutenant Colonel John Combe leading a flying column of 2,000 men and light tanks to hold off desperate Italian attacks until the remainder of the 7th Armoured arrived to complete the trap. On 7 February 1941, 130,000 Italians surrendered complete with 400 tanks and 1,300 artillery pieces.

Mussolini's imperial designs appeared to be in tatters but with Tripoli in British sights the Desert War altered dramatically when British Prime Minister Winston Churchill withdrew two Australian divisions for the defence of Greece. Within days Lieutenant General Erwin Rommel's Afrika Korps began arriving in North Africa and within a few days of that, the Western Desert Force was back in Egypt, O'Connor in a German prisoner of war camp.

10 December 1899

Second Boer War
Battle of Stormberg

BY DECEMBER 1899 Commander-in-Chief South Africa Redvers Buller and the biggest overseas force that Great Britain had ever sent to war had restored some order to British South Africa. The first month of the Second Boer War had begun rather grimly, in the far North of Cape Colony Mafeking had been besieged and would have to wait for relief but was at least in the resourceful hands of Lieutenant General Robert Baden Powell. Kimberley, also in North Cape Colony was also besieged but an 8,000-strong British Army under General Lord Paul Methuen had at least advanced from the Orange River to the Modder River forcing Free State and Transvaal Boers back to within just twenty-five miles of the objective. British reinforcements had also been arriving in Natal since mid November for an effort to relieve Lieutenant General George White and 13,000 British troops besieged in Ladysmith. For the relief of Kimberley, Methuen was about to assault tough Boer defences at Magersfontein whilst for the relief of Ladysmith, Buller was about to assault extensive Boer defences on the north bank of the Tugela River at Colenso in the foothills of the Drakensberg Mountains.

In between the two theatres, in Eastern Cape Colony, Field Commandant JH Olivier had led approximately 2,000 Free State Boers south with the intention of igniting an Afrikaner uprising within the Cape Colony, an event which so far had not happened. At the beginning of hostilities a half battalion of British troops had been stationed at the strategic railway junction of Stormberg but despite the protection of fortified defences had withdrawn without firing a shot when approached by Olivier's advance along the Aliwal North/East London Railway – having been gifted Stormberg Olivier then also took Dordrecht. The task of halting Olivier was given to Major General William Gatacre, a veteran of the Indian North West Frontier and Omdurman (Sudan) who was highly respected by his men who nicknamed him 'Backacher' for the tireless duties he set both they and himself. Gatacre's orders were largely defensive, hold Queenstown and protect East London but they also gave him the latitude to attack Olivier if the opportunity arose. In early December reinforcements and the wishes of his senior officers prompted Gatacre to take advantage of this freedom of movement with a counter-offensive on Stormberg. A lack of intelligence and maps, however, had been Methuen's problem further west and would now be Gatacre's, himself patrolling the area around Stormberg before gathering in 2,600 men from various outposts for a six-hour march east to the Kissieberg kopje.

Led by local guides, Gatacre set off from Molteno at 21.00 on 9 December to attack the western slope of the Kissieberg on which he was informed was the main Boer laager (camp). In the pitch dark the guides lost their way but Gatacre nevertheless pressed on, arriving at the bottom of the western slope of the Kissieberg only to march right past to the north-west slope. At dawn on 10 December 1899 the British assault initially surprised the Boer defenders on the crest of the Kissieberg but a steady stream of bullets soon began felling Royal Irish Rifles and Northumberland Fusiliers struggling up the stony slopes. British artillery then supported their infantry by firing at the top of the Kissieberg, successfully suppressing Boer resistance only for it to resume from a neighbouring kopje across the valley where 500 Boers joined the shooting match. Gatacre's inaccurate ascent of the Kissieberg now had deadly results in that the steep rocky upper north-west face prevented a bayonet charge of the crest, the Irish and Northumberlands now trapped in a crossfire between the two Boer held kopjes. Some of the Northumberlands began to retreat, a retreat spotted by the British artillery who assumed it to be general and lowered their guns to cover it, unintentionally firing on their own men still on the upper slopes.

Since the whole assault was fast becoming a fiasco, Gatacre ordered a withdrawal to Molteno where the customary roll call revealed nearly 800 dead, wounded and missing. It transpired that the order to retreat had not been received by many of Gatacre's men who were left to join a growing British Army in Pretoria prison camps. It had been a black day for the British Army and it would soon become a 'Black Week'.

11 December 1899

Second Boer War
Battle of Magersfontein

SINCE THE OCTOBER 1899 outbreak of the Second Boer War the fortunes of Transvaal and Orange Free State Boers had benefited largely from British incompetence. Boer advances into Natal had outnumbered and outmanoeuvred the 13,000 British troops under Lieutenant General Sir George White who was now besieged in Ladysmith whilst further Boer advances into Natal and particularly upon Durban were a distinct possibility. Indeed the arriving Commander-in-Chief Redvers Buller and thousands of British reinforcements had only the high moral character of Boer General Louis Botha to thank for landing on the Durban quayside at all (Botha would not invade foreign territory) – though they would still need to break heavily defended Boer positions on the Tugela River to rescue White. Meanwhile at Mafeking, west of Pretoria, Colonel Robert Baden Powell was besieged as too was Lieutenant Colonel Robert Kekewich further south at Kimberley where former Prime Minister of the Cape Colony Cecil Rhodes was making his life more difficult than the besiegers. It was here along the line of the Cape Town-Bulawayo Railway that General Lord Paul Methuen had made some progress but across the open plains of the veld against kopjes defended by both Transvaal and Free State Boers, was paying for his hollow gains in blood. After the November Battle at the Modder River, Methuen had little choice but to rest his fatigued troops, await reinforcements and repair the railway before assaulting the last line of kopjes before Kimberley at Magersfontein. Boer General Koos De La Rey, however, used the delay to good effect, digging into the stony desert a staggering twelve-mile-line of defences, all of it camouflaged.

The main problem that had plagued Methuen's entire advance was a lack of intelligence, no accurate maps and an inability to get within a rifle shot of the Boer lines to discern their positions, the exact same problem which had beset Major General William Gatacre before suffering a shambolic defeat on 10 December 1899 south-east of Methuen at Stormberg. To alleviate intelligence difficulties a reconnaissance balloon was in transit but Methuen was not prepared to wait an extra twenty-four hours despite Kekewich in Kimberley being amply supplied. Instead just hours after Gatacre's albeit at the time unbeknown Stormberg shambles, Methuen sent the newly arrived Highland Brigade under Major General Andrew Wauchope behind five batteries of artillery toward the Boer defences at Magersfontein. About three miles distant the Highlanders bivouacked whilst the artillery began a visually impressive but tactically naive bombardment of the Magersfontein kopje. Just after midnight on 11 December 1899 the Highlanders then began a night march though a thunderstorm in densely packed quarter column straight toward an unreconnoitred trap, Methuen believing De La Rey could be dislodged with a well-timed, dawn bayonet attack but in reality being totally ignorant of his enemy's positions. Wauchope was understandably not so confident, comforted only by the reserve of the 9th Infantry Brigade and the Guards, he advanced with serious doubts.

The Boers meanwhile had learnt from their mistakes at the Modder River and remained silent until the Highlanders, still in quarter column, were within a few hundred yards at which point the lower ground of the Magersfontein lit up with the muzzle flashes of 8,000 Mauser rifles. Too late Wauchope gave the order to extend into open order, himself dead within minutes as the Highlanders went to ground either dead, wounded or seeking cover where there was none. As the Scots Guards had been for three hours at the Modder River so now were the Highlanders for nine hours at Magersfontein, raked by rifle fire in the scorching heat of the desert whilst eaten by insects, their only cover provided by British artillery which included a naval gun 'Old Joey' (after Joseph Chamberlain) and several Maxims. Boer General Piet Cronje then led his Transvaalers to attack the Highlanders' right flank temporarily leaving a wide gap in his defences that Methuen may have been alerted to had he been in possession of all things, a balloon. Cronje's attack was, however, halted by the British reserve of Grenadier and Coldstream Guards. As Cronje retreated many Highlanders seized the opportunity to make a retreat of their own but in so doing left their artillery dangerously exposed until Gordon Highlanders and the Scots Guards covered the danger. By the time a truce was signaled Methuen had suffered another 1,000 casualties.

De La Rey had ended his string of retreats and remained in position, the British relief of Kimberley would have to wait for a new British Commander-in-Chief, Field Marshal Frederick Roberts. The black day at Stormberg was fast becoming a 'Black Week' at Magersfontein, could Buller do better at Colenso?

12 December 1941
Second World War
Battle of Jitra

JAPAN HAD SUFFERED during the economic depression of the 1920s and 30s but had recovered quickly. A land of meagre resources the nation was reliant on raw materials from North China to the Dutch East Indies (Indonesia), materials controlled by the western powers, primarily Great Britain, Holland and the United States of America. The Japanese believed this order needed to be overturned for both herself and South East Asia to flourish and in frustration with China (seen as complicit to Great Britain after suffering defeat in the Opium Wars seventy years previous) invaded Manchuria in 1931. Violence increased with a series of small incidents before the Second Sino-Japanese War erupted in 1937 with Japan taking control of almost all coastal China with shocking brutality – notably in the then capital, Nanking. The Chinese Government of Chang Kai Shek had little choice but to retreat inland. In 1940 with the Imperial powers of Holland and France overrun by Germany, Britain besieged and the United States reluctant to involve herself in any war, the opportunity was ripe for Japan to extend her plan for the new order across South East Asia. French Indo-China (Vietnam) was forced to accept Japanese troops but the Dutch refused any trade concessions over oil. At last perceiving the Japanese threat the United States then reacted with an economic embargo before, in 1941, freezing all Japanese assets in the US. For Japan the critical hour had come, Prime Minister Hideki Tojo ordering an air attack on the United States Pacific Fleet in Pearl Harbor, Hawaii on 7 December 1941 simultaneous, albeit the following day in Asia, to air attacks on Hong Kong and Singapore accompanied by invasions of the Philippines, the Dutch East Indies, Thailand and British Malaya.

The Japanese invaded Malaya at Kota Bharu on the north-east coast and through southern Thailand with the 25th Army of Lieutenant General Tomoyuki Yamashita. The 9th Indian Infantry Division initially put up fierce resistance at Kota Bharu supported by RAF Lockheed Hudson bombers whilst three columns of Punjabis were sent north into Thailand by General Officer Commanding

Lieutenant General Arthur Percival specifically to delay the advance of the Japanese 5th Infantry Division heading for the road junction at Jitra in North West Malaya. Aircraft of the Imperial Japanese Navy then sank the battleship HMS *Prince of Wales* and battlecruiser HMS *Repulse*, shattering the defence strategy of Singapore as Percival responded by withdrawing all his aircraft from North Malaya. Now devoid of air cover Major General David Murray-Lyon commanding the 11th Indian Infantry Division at Jitra sent forward more Punjabis and Gurkhas to delay the Japanese armoured vanguard of Lieutenant Colonel Shizuo Saeki. Immediately in a perilous position with the 18th Division of the Japanese 25th Army also flooding into Malaya to his south-east, Murray-Lyon requested Percival grant him a retreat to Gurun but was denied.

On 12 December 1941, Saeki reached the British fourteen-mile front at Jitra and immediately attacked Jats east of the Singora Road. Before long Leicesters to the west of the road were also engaged but Saeki was already beginning to outflank the Jats through the thick jungle. The Japanese attacks intensified after dawn with the Jats forced back in the centre exposing a gap a mile wide over the Bata River up into which the British reserve of Gurkhas moved. Punjabis now counter-attacked on the British right (east) holding Saeki's flank attack as the Leicesters retreated to form a new defensive line centering on Jitra but by late afternoon the Punjabis were struggling to hold. Fearing that he was about to be outflanked Murray-Lyon withdrew East Surreys from his left to flank guard the railway line before again, after fifteen hours of ferocious close quarter jungle fighting, requesting permission to withdraw, this time granted by Percival.

Murray-Lyon's difficulties were just beginning as communications in the jungle completely broke down. Many companies left behind in the confusion were either wiped out or hiked across country to escape by sea, regaining their units at Gurun. The 11th Indian Division had taken heavy losses and would again be defeated at Gurun, losing virtually the entire 6th Infantry Brigade before checking the Japanese at Kampar. Outflanked by Japanese landings on the east Malaya coast the British then withdrew to the Slim River.

13 December 1939

Second World War
Battle of the River Plate

THE GREAT WAR Armistice of November 1918 saw the abdication and exile of German Kaiser Wilhelm II. The Kaiser's cousin, Great Britain's King George V, called him 'the greatest criminal in history' but disagreed with his Prime Minister David Lloyd George that Wilhelm should be hanged. Disagreements continued over Germany's future, France, pricing her losses at 209,000 million gold Francs, insisting 'the Boche' (Germany) must pay whereas Britain was concerned that an impoverished Germany would be vulnerable to Russian Bolshevism. Following German debt defaults, France then occupied the German Rhineland (an area they had been nowhere near occupying during the Great War) in an attempt to force payment but in so doing added to the increasing polarisation of German politics between extreme left and right. The Great Depression then halted American loans, increasing German unemployment and yet further political polarisation that created enough support for the Nationalsozialistische Deutsche Arbeiterpartei (Nazi Party) and its leader (*Führer*) Adolf Hitler to democratically gain control of Germany, Hitler becoming Chancellor.

Establishing a totalitarian regime intent on restoring German prestige Hitler began with his own military reoccupation of the Rhineland, France reacting by doing nothing. The French inaction, however, scared King Leopold III of Belgium into immediately declaring neutrality, a move that instantly destroyed Franco-Russian defence strategy since France was now effectively trapped behind Belgium and her own impressive but purely defensive fortifications, the Maginot Line. As Germany rearmed, Hitler then annexed the nation of his birth and old German ally Austria (*Anschluss*) before repeating the dose of strong arm diplomacy to annex the Sudetenland, Czechoslovakia. France and Great Britain abandoned the Czechs at Munich for 'peace in our time', the folly of which was not lost on Conservative backbencher Winston Churchill who prophetically accused his Prime Minister Neville Chamberlain of having 'the choice between war and dishonour. You chose dishonour and you will have war'.

The defence policy against German aggression then finally collapsed completely in August 1939 when Bolshevik Russia, also concerned that France could and would now fight only on the defensive, signed the Molotov-Ribbentrop Non-Aggression Pact with her ideological enemy Nazi Germany. A reading of Hitler's 1925 *Mein Kampf* renders the pact folly since, as had the Kaiser in 1914, Hitler was always intent on creating *Lebensraum* (living space) in the east. Russians and Belgians would both come to regret the diplomacy of their politicians but for now Hitler's rapidly expanded Wehrmacht (Armed Forces), particularly the *Luftwaffe* (Air Force), were given a free hand to invade half of Poland from the west whilst a month later the Russian Red Army moved in to take the other half from the east. This time Chamberlain honoured British obligations to Poland and on 3 September 1939 declared war on Germany.

For eight months a 'Phoney War' existed in western Europe but at sea the German U-boat menace of the Great War immediately resurfaced with the sinking of HMS *Royal Oak* in Scapa Flow. In the South Atlantic Commodore Henry Harwood commanding cruisers HMS *Exeter, Ajax, Cumberland* and HMNZS *Achilles* then received news of the German heavy cruiser (the 1919 Treaty of Versailles prevented Germany from possessing battleships) *Admiral Graf Spee* off the River Plate Estuary, Argentina/Uruguay. At 06.10 on 13 December 1939, Captain Hans Langsdorff spotted HMS *Exeter* and although aware that other British cruisers were in the region turned to give battle believing British merchantmen to also be present. Too late Langsdorff realised he was up against *Exeter, Ajax* and *Achilles*, engaging within range of the British 8-inch guns when he could have comfortably stayed outside with his 11-inchers. The three British cruisers split but *Graf Spee* took them on simultaneously, *Exeter* first damaged when taking a direct hit on her B turret killing all but three crew on the bridge. *Exeter* then missed with her torpedoes before taking another direct hit on A turret and her hull causing fire, flooding and a serious list which forced her out of the battle. *Ajax* and *Achilles* continued the fight with shellfire and a sea plane but, perhaps with a fuel problem but otherwise inexplicably, Langsdorff then made for neutral Montevideo, Uruguay under a smokescreen, the shadowing British cruisers still firing continuously.

Short of ammunition and hoodwinked a large British force now awaited outside, Langsdorff enraged his Führer by scuttling the *Admiral Graf Spee* before committing suicide two days later. Compared with what was to come, it mattered little.

14 December 1814

American War of 1812
Battle of Lake Borgne

THE FRENCH REVOLUTIONARY and Napoleonic Wars had spread back and forth across the Atlantic several times but until 1812 the fighting had always involved the navies of Great Britain and France. French Emperor Napoleon Bonaparte had attempted to defeat the British with a trade embargo but the British had retaliated with an embargo of their own which merited an additional blockade of the United States eastern seaboard and a drive to man the Royal Navy, not just by impressment but also a round up of deserters in which as many as 10,000 American sailors were caught.

Additional British interference in the American Mid-West, in particular arming the Indian Confederacy, did nothing for US/ British relations and in April 1812 US President James Madison declared war on Great Britain. US financial difficulties and the British preoccupation with Napoleon, however, meant neither side achieved anything of significance for two years until in 1814 Napoleon's abdication freed 16,000 British veterans from the Iberian Peninsular. These battle-hardened troops crossed the Atlantic escalating the significance of peace talks already under way in Ghent, Netherlands (now Belgium) despite the main cause of the war, the British embargo, no longer being relevant.

To force a favourable agreement the British launched four invasions of the US while the talks were in progress, the first, to capture Baltimore, failing although Washington DC including the White House was set ablaze. A small invasion of Maine was then partially successful whilst a large scale invasion of Upper New York State was defeated at Plattsburgh on Lake Champlain, the British returning to Canada. The British Government of Robert Jenkinson, Lord Liverpool were left with few cards to play, even Field Marshal Sir Arthur Wellesley, Duke of Wellington poured scorn on British territorial claims whilst the merchants of London, Bristol, Liverpool and the West Indies were pleading for a resumption of trade. The peace talks did indeed conclude favourably in December 1814 but it was too late to stop the fourth invasion which was about to take place on New Orleans, Louisiana.

To attack New Orleans, Vice Admiral Alexander Cochrane had little chance of forcing the well defended mouth of the Mississippi River and instead looked to sail into Lake Borgne to the east where he would land an invasion force of 11,000 men. Defending Lake Borgne were just an American schooner USS *Sea Horse*, two sloops USS *Alligator* and *Tickler* and five gunboats under the command of Lieutenant Thomas Ap Catesby Jones. In Catesby Jones' favour, however, Lake Borgne is extremely shallow and was therefore inaccessible to the larger British warships, more than fourteen of which were now stranded at the entrance. Cochrane, however, amassed forty-two longboats from his fleet each armed with only a carronade but manned in total by 1,200 troops commanded by Captain Nicholas Lockyer who prepared to win a naval battle the old medieval way, grappling and boarding followed by hand-to-hand fighting. At 10.30 on 14 December 1814, following a thirty-six hour row across Lake Borgne, Lockyer's flotilla advanced in line under fire from the larger American gunboats which were becalmed short of the channel leading to Lake Pontchartrain, north of New Orleans. Unable to reply, Lockyer's men rowed hard, first their small bow cannons returning fire before being hit by musket volleys and grapeshot as they reached the first two American gunboats. A deadly battle then raged as the British attempted to board the Americans, musket balls, bayonets, swords and spikes beating them off the rails but their overwhelming numbers prevailing before fighting raged across the decks of all the American vessels, both Catesby Jones and Lockyer wounded fighting aboard the same ship. The fight did not last long before all five American gunboats and USS *Alligator* had been captured, USS *Tickler* scuttled. The battle had, however, cost Lockyer nearly a hundred casualties.

The defeated Catesby Jones had bought time for the defenders of New Orleans led by future US President Andrew Jackson who soon received news that more than 2,000 British troops were landing at Villere Plantation, seven miles south of the city astride the Mississippi. With a sailing time of several weeks from Ghent to New Orleans the biggest battle of the war and perhaps the most futile of all time was about to begin.

15 December 1899

Second Boer War
Battle of Colenso

COMMANDER-IN-CHIEF of British forces in South Africa, General Redvers Buller arrived in Frere, Natal on 6 December 1899 to take personal command of the Natal Field Force, leaving General Lord Paul Methuen and Major General William Gatacre in the Cape Colony loose directives but effectively no one in overall command of the strategic situation in South Africa. 'Poor Buller' had to make the best of a situation in Natal which he personally had strived to avoid, specifically the besieging of Lieutenant General Sir George White and 13,000 British troops at Ladysmith in the Drakensberg Mountains. Between Buller and White, on the north bank of the Tugela River outside Colenso, were 4,500 well-entrenched Boers organised in nine commandos under the overall command of General Louis Botha. Buller initially planned to outflank Botha with an attack on Potgieters Drift fifteen miles to the west, a move that would require a fifty-mile circuitous march through dangerous country, away from the railway and required a brigade to cover its rear leaving just three for the assault itself. Any defeat at Potgieters would, therefore, likely result in Buller joining White, Lieutenant General Robert Baden-Powell (Mafeking) and Lieutenant Colonel Robert Kekewich (Kimberley) on a list of British commanders besieged in South Africa.

Buller then received news from central South Africa that Gatacre, whose directive had been largely defensive, had been repulsed with heavy losses in an attack at Stormberg and that Methuen had suffered similarly at Magersfontein. With the stakes raised Buller's nerve wavered, he would not now risk the Natal Field Force at Potgieters but instead would attack Colenso directly to his front, a tougher assignment but rather negatively, with a ready line of retreat. For two days British guns pounded the upper slopes of the kopjes at Colenso, high over the heads of Botha's men who were dug in on the lower slopes. Methuen and Gatacre's problem was now that of Buller, a scant knowledge of the Boer defences and the ineffective barrage merely alerting the enemy to an impending attack.

On 15 December 1899 the largest force the British Army had put into battle for over forty years, 14,000 infantry, 2,700 cavalry and forty-four field guns marched toward the Dutch farmers (Boers) at Colenso. The assault was divided into three infantry columns with the cavalry protecting the flanks and directed at separate drifts across the fast flowing Tugela, albeit that these areas would be the most heavily defended. On the British left the Irish Brigade under Major General Arthur Hart approached Bridle Drift in close order before being misled by their African guide toward Punt Drift in a loop of the Tugela. Hart was now exposed on three sides to Boers who until now had remained silent but this was too good an opportunity to miss and they opened fire with an intensity hereto unmatched during the war. If they were not lying flat on the ground, Hart's Irishmen moved into more open order, extending left toward Bridle Drift a mile away where their commander was still determined to force a crossing.

In the British centre, two artillery batteries consisting of twelve 15-pounders, under Colonel Charles Long plus six Naval 12-pounders, moved up to support Major General Henry Hildyard's 2nd Brigade, Long inexplicably riding ahead bringing his 15-pounders within range of the Boer Mauser rifles. Again the Boers had remained silent but with another golden opportunity, opened fire to devastating effect. Long was immediately mortally wounded but his two batteries continued firing until a third of the British gunners had become casualties and the other two-thirds had fled for the cover of a nearby donga (gulley, ravine). Buller had been watching the fiasco from Naval Gun Hill and now rode down to Hildyard (who so far had not fired a shot) calling off the attack. Buller then asked for volunteers to save Long's 15-pounders and ordered Major General Neville Lyttleton's Brigade up to extricate Hart who had gotten himself 'into a devil of a mess'. Hart finally retreated with 1,200 casualties whilst of the twelve abandoned 15-pounders only two were rescued.

Buller had taken a bullet in the leg and Lieutenant Freddy Roberts, the only son of the incoming Field Marshal Lord Frederick Roberts had been killed, posthumously awarded the Victoria Cross. The black days at Stormberg and Magersfontein had become a 'Black Week' at Colenso.

16 December 1914

The Great War
Raid on Scarborough, Whitby, Hartlepool

THE SIGNING OF the 1904 *Entente Cordiale* with France and Russia's 1905 defeat to Japan eased British fears of a Franco-Russian alliance but it was soon clear that Germany presented the main threat to British global trade and colonial interests. Chancellor of the Exchequer David Lloyd George believed every Englishman would spend his last penny to preserve naval power and they very nearly had to as First Sea Lord Admiral John 'Jackie' Fisher embarked on a naval arms race with Germany's Kaiser Wilhelm II, building the worlds biggest warships, dreadnoughts, forty-two of them (including battlecruisers) by 1914. Undeterred the Kaiser, who was also expanding the German Army, and his Grand Admiral Alfred von Tirpitz built twenty-six dreadnoughts of their own, ships capable of hitting targets ten miles distant with 13–15-inch shells.

Soon after fighting broke out in August 1914 the Royal Navy, concerned at protecting British transports crossing the English Channel from German naval strength at Wilhelmshaven, defeated German Rear Admiral Franz Hipper in the Heligoland Bight. The Kaiser had then been content to maintain a 'fleet in being' but allowed Hipper to launch limited raids into the North Sea, minelaying and attacking isolated British shipping. In return the Royal Navy kept most of the Grand Fleet at Scapa Flow, Orkney Isles and the Channel Fleet off the Thames Estuary, patrolling England's east coast but not in strength, happy to allow their own minefields do most of the defensive work. News of disaster off Coronel, Chile, however, not only rattled the British public but emboldened the Imperial German Navy to launch a somewhat derisory raid on Yarmouth, Hipper, however, encouraged just enough to launch another bigger raid on the English coast. Reconnoitering with a U-boat whilst requesting nine armoured and light cruisers accompanied by eighteen destroyers supported by the rest of the German High

Seas Fleet at Dogger Bank, Hipper planned to attack shipbuilding Hartlepool, spa Whitby and tourist Scarborough.

Almost a week after the victors of Coronel, the German East Asia Squadron, had been sent to the bottom of the South Atlantic British intelligence received information of a German fleet leaving Wilhelmshaven on 15 December, Admiral John Jellicoe opting to allow the Germans to raid, though he didn't know where, and ambush them on their return home. Four British battlecruisers under Vice Admiral David Beatty, five dreadnoughts under Vice Admiral George Warrender and four light cruisers under Commodore William Goodenough departed Scapa Flow whilst forces from Harwich patrolled the east coast. Commodore Roger Keyes also posted eight submarines off Tershelling, Holland. At 06.30 on 16 December 1914, in poor North Sea weather Hipper divided his forces, sending SMS *Seydlitz*, *Blucher* and *Moltke* to Harlepool whilst SMS *Derrflinger*, *Von der Tann* and *Kolberg* headed for Scarborough, their escorts departing for home. At 07.45 the British destroyer HMS *Doon* unsuccessfully torpedoed the three German ships off Hartlepool but heavily outgunned then retreated. Fired at a range of just 4,000 yards German shells soon began to hit Hartlepool striking the gasworks, steelworks, port and housing with the Durham Royal Garrison Artillery replying spiritedly but with little effect on the giant German cruisers. Too late the British light cruiser HMS *Patrol* and the submarine HMS *C9* attempted to sally from port as terrified civilians fled in the opposite direction by road and railway. At 08.00 further south Scarborough came under fire for ninety minutes, the Grand Hotel struck as well as housing before the raid progressed on to Whitby. The two German squadrons then joined for a dash home as Warrender and Beatty moved to intercept, Keyes' submarines also moving directly into the German path in the Heligoland Bight.

Deteriorating visibility, minefields and poor communications facilitated Hipper's escape, even Keyes' submarines could not locate him. Harlepool, Whitby and Scarborough suffered nearly 700 casualties, mostly women and children. Secretary of State for War Horatio Kitchener would take advantage of public outrage by using the German raids as propaganda for his British Army recruitment drives, 'Remember Scarborough!'

17 December 1941

Second World War
Battle of the Gulf of Sirte

THE FALL OF Crete in May 1941 left all western and southern Europe bar Spain and Switzerland (both neutral) under the direct control of Nazi Germany and her ally, Fascist Italy (Axis Powers with Hungary, Romania and Japan), only the United Kingdom fought on. German Chancellor Adolf Hitler's continued bombing of Britain had, however, only hardened British resolve and his U-boat Atlantic offensives were losing effectiveness now that the Kriegsmarine Enigma Code had been broken. By June 1941 Britain was nevertheless still in no position to launch a major counter-offensive leaving Hitler to launch another of his own with three million men, 3,500 tanks and 1,830 aircraft, the greatest in military history, on Soviet Russia. Despite British warnings, Russian Secretary General Josef Stalin had mistakenly believed Hitler would honour the Molotov-Ribbentrop Non-Aggression Pact signed between the two countries just two years earlier. Russian defences had crumbled under the initial onslaught but in early December, with the Wehrmacht poised to emulate Napoleon's occupation of Moscow, freezing temperatures had abruptly halted their advance.

Meanwhile in Britain fears of immediate invasion had consequently disappeared but a threat to the British Empire had then developed in the Far East when Japan looked to establish a new order in South East Asia, specifically against communism and western influence, an order brutally confirmed on 7 December 1941 by a shock attack on the United States Pacific Fleet at Pearl Harbor, Hawaii simultaneous to invasions across South East Asia. Four days later Hitler then, unnecessarily but in support of his Axis ally, also declared war on the United States who, much to the relief of British Prime Minister Winston Churchill, returned the favour. Americans were, however, still eight months away from landing across the Pacific (Guadalcanal) and eleven months away from landing across the Atlantic (Morocco and Algeria). While British and Commonwealth troops attempted to hold the

Japanese in Malaya, so too did they continue fighting the German Afrika Korps (and Italians) of Generalleutnant Erwin Rommel in North Africa. Frustrated at a lack of progress in the Western Desert, Churchill had removed General Archibald Wavell for General Claude Auchinleck who launched Operation Crusader in November 1941. The British 8th Army under Lieutenant General Neil Ritchie had soon pushed Rommel back to El Agheila, Libya but at the end of long supply lines from Alexandria Richie struggled to maintain the British offensive whereas Rommel was now only 400 miles from Tripoli. The supply battle, the British from Gibraltar to Alexandria, Egypt, the Axis from Taranto to Tripoli centred around the besieged island of Malta.

On 17 December 1941, the Axis convoy M42 of four merchantmen arrived in the Gulf of Sirte off Tripoli protected by three Italian battleships, five cruisers, twenty destroyers and a torpedo boat. Meanwhile the British Mediterranean Fleet was escorting just one merchantman, HMS *Breconshire*, west from Alexandria to Malta protected by three cruisers and eight destroyers under Rear Admiral Phillip Vian who would receive additional protection from two cruisers and six destroyers from Force K Malta. The two British fleets met on the same day, coming under attack from *Regia Aeronautica* and *Luftwaffe* aircraft without suffering loss. Vian was under instruction from Admiral Andrew Cunningham to avoid battle but Admiral Angelo Iachino commanding the Italian Fleet believed him to be an aggressive threat with the *Breconshire* mistakenly believed to be a battleship. To protect his convoy, Iachino moved to intercept the British Fleet but Vian avoided any confrontation until again under Axis air attack. Iachino now opened fire at an extreme 35,000 yards lightly damaging several British destroyers but did not press the attack when Vian disappeared behind a smokescreen and darkness. The Italian convoy proceeded to Tripoli but several of Vian's vessels now entered a minefield, a cruiser and a destroyer were both sunk while another two cruisers were badly damaged, 830 men killed by the explosions or drowning.

From an innocuous engagement Iachino and the *Regia Marina* had suddenly gained a temporary naval superiority in the Mediterranean whilst, additionally, Italian Special Forces were about to further damage the British Mediterranean Fleet in Alexandria. His supply lines improved, Rommel would soon renew the Axis offensive back into Egypt.

18 December 1845

Sikh Wars
Battle of Mudki

FOLLOWING THE BRITISH East India Company's 1803 victory at Assaye under the then Major General Arthur Wellesley – but now Leader of the House of Lords, Field Marshal Sir Arthur Wellesley, Duke of Wellington – British control over the Indian sub continent had expanded as far north as the River Sutlej. On the north-west side of the Sutlej was the Sikh Empire centred around the rich heartland of the Punjab stretching south from Kashmir to Sindh and west from Tibet to the Khyber Pass. This empire had been built by Maharaja Ranjit Singh and his powerful army, the Khalsa, which consisted not just of Sikhs but also Muslims and Hindus trained and equipped by Europeans and Americans.

Sikh relations with the British Governors of India had been cordial for much of the nineteenth century but not so with the Emirs of Afghanistan, particularly Dost Mohammed Khan and Wazir Akbar Khan of the current ruling Barakzai Dynasty with whom Ranjit Singh had regularly been at war. When the British opened their own First Anglo-Afghan War in 1839 they had done so with tacit Sikh support (though they were not allowed to march through Sikh territory) but within a few months Ranjit Singh was on his deathbed. The iron hand with which the Maharaja had checked his own Khalsa had gone and in the subsequent power vacuum the strength of the army exploded, more than doubling in size in six years. Though different factions fought for the Sikh throne it was becoming ever more apparent that it was the Khalsa that controlled the Punjab and surrounding region rather than any one individual. Watching the internal strife of the Punjab from North India, the British began increasing their military strength along the Sutlej for the protection of British India and the opportunity, should it arise, to expand their influence across it.

The British dispositions south of the Sutlej antagonised the Khalsa who crossed the river themselves in December 1845 with 50,000 troops and 200 guns toward a

7,000 strong British garrison at Ferozepur. The British Governor General of India Sir Henry Hardinge immediately declared war but Tej Singh, commanding the Khalsa, refrained from attacking Ferozepur, a decision that bewildered his troops. Recent Sikh intrigue now played into British hands as both Tej Singh and his fellow commander Lal Singh were in thrall of Ranjit Singh's widow, Maharani Jindan Singh, whose brother Wazir Jawahir Singh had recently been murdered by the Khalsa. By seeking favour with the revenge seeking Jindan, who wanted the Khalsa destroyed, both Tej and Lal Singh have been accused of deliberate sabotage ever since.

Hardinge and British Commander-in-Chief Hugh Gough hurried to relieve Ferozepur with British Bengal troops from Ambala and Ludhiana, 10,000 arriving at Mudki on 18 December 1845. Lal Singh and 35,000 Sikhs with eighty-five guns were at Ferozeshah when they became aware of Gough's approach but Lal moved to intercept with just half that force and only twenty-two guns on the pretence that Tej Singh might need the remainder. Arriving that same evening the Khalsa opened the battle from the jungle edge with an artillery barrage on the fatigued British Bengal Army. The lighter but more numerous Bengal Horse Artillery immediately replied before Gough ordered his Bengal Light Cavalry and Dragoons to attack both flanks of the Khalsa whilst his infantry advanced in the centre. In turn the 10,000-strong Sikh cavalry then counter-attacked the flanks of the British Bengali infantry who formed squares, driving off the Sikh cavalry before resuming their own advance. The Sikh guns were overrun before the Bengalis closed for a desperate hand-to-hand fight with the outnumbered Sikh infantry. It is alleged that Lal Singh now deserted but in confused fighting, friendly units firing on each other in clouds of dust and darkness, the Sikhs doggedly fought on, earning eternal British respect. After two hours the Sikhs melted back into the jungle having suffered heavy casualties. The British had taken nearly 900 casualties themselves including Major General Sir Robert 'Fighting Bob' Sale, the hero of Ghazni and Jallalabad.

Hardinge reprimanded Gough for his tactics but the pair would be at loggerheads again just three days later when they would fight the main Khalsa at Ferozeshah.

19 December 1941

Second World War
Raid on Alexandria

ITALIAN DICTATOR BENITO Mussolini had joined the Second World War in the summer of 1940 just as Germany's Chancellor Adolf Hitler appeared to be on the verge of victory over both France and Great Britain. Hitler's Wehrmacht had already overrun Poland, Holland and Belgium and though Italian forces were not fully prepared, Mussolini's dream of creating *spacia vitale* (living space) through a Mediterranean Empire rivalling that of his Roman ancestors seemed there for the taking. The memory of disciplined, all conquering Roman Legions remained firmly in antiquity, however, as the Italian offensive from Libya was driven back out of British Egypt by Major General Richard O'Connor's Western Desert Force and back out of Greece by Field Marshal Alexandros Papagos' Hellenic Army. On the Mediterranean Sea the powerful *Regia Marina* had also been badly bruised at Taranto and Matapan as well as in numerous convoy contacts. Initially content to allow Mussolini to play his hand in the Mediterranean but then acutely concerned that his main ally was already on the verge of collapse, Hitler intervened both in the Balkans and North Africa, achieving complete victory in the former in just over three weeks. His southern flank secure, Hitler then invaded Russia in June 1941 with over 120 Axis divisions just as Generalleutnant Erwin Rommel's four division strong German Afrika Korps and Panzergroup Africa supported by six divisions of the Italian XX and XXI Corps were halted at the Egyptian border before being forced back to El Agheila, Libya by the British 8th Army now under Lieutenant General Neil Ritchie. The battle of supply across the Mediterranean, until now dominated by the British Mediterranean Fleet then began to turn when four British ships were sunk or badly damaged in a minefield off Tripoli after the somewhat innocuous, inconclusive Battle of Sirte on 17 December 1941. With millions of men in armed deadlock from the icy wastes of Russia to the arid deserts of North Africa, six Italian frogmen of the *Decima Flottiglia* MAS Special Operations Unit would attempt to turn the supply war further with a daring raid on the British Mediterranean Fleet moored behind the formidable defences of the Port of Alexandria, Egypt – Operazione EA3.

After being dropped by the submarine *Scire* before dawn on 19 December 1941 three newly invented manned torpedoes, crewed by Lieutenant Luigi de la Penne and diver Emilio Bianchi on Maiale (Pig) 221, Captain Antonio Marceglia and diver Spataco Schergat on Maiale 222 and Captain Vincenzo Martellotta and diver Mario Marino on Maiale 223, approached the Alexandria Harbour entrance through minefields and offshore patrols. The six men were fortunate to time their arrival with that of three British destroyers, quickly descending to follow while the anti-submarine nets were still open. The frogmen then separated to their respective targets, De La Penne and Bianchi to the battleship HMS *Valiant*, Marceglia and Schergat the battleship HMS *Queen Elizabeth* and Martellotta and Marino the Oil Tanker *Sagona* after failing to find the departed aircraft carrier HMS *Eagle*. All three successfully placed 600 pounds of high explosive under the unprotected hulls before attempting to escape ashore. De La Penne and Bianchi were, however, immediately apprehended by the crew of *Valiant* and held by Captain Charles Morgan directly above their own charge before De La Penne advised Morgan of the imminent danger. The Italian refused any details and was returned to his cell only for *Valiant* to be rocked minutes later by a terrific explosion. Both De La Penne and Bianchi miraculously survived to witness, minutes later, the detonation of Marceglia and Shergat's torpedo beneath the *Queen Elizabeth*. A few more minutes and the *Sagona* was then rocked by an explosion which also damaged the refueling destroyer HMS *Jervis* next door.

Marceglia, Schergat, Martellotta and Marino were all eventually picked up by the Egyptian Police. British Prime Minister Winston Churchill maintained a news blackout since both battleships were now resting on the bottom of Alexandria Harbour with only their decks above the water line. It would be eight months before they returned to service. The *Regia Marina* now took control of the Mediterranean, resupplying Rommel's North African forces for a January 1942 major Axis offensive on British Egypt. Operazione EA3 features in the opening scene of the 1958 Romulus film *The Silent Enemy*.

20 December 1880

First Boer War
Battle of Bronkhorstspruit

IN 1806 GREAT Britain had taken the Cape of Good Hope by force from the Batavian (Dutch) Republic to protect the shipping routes to India from Napoleonic aggression. The Dutch, however, were soon unhappy with the British administration and the British abolition of slavery, beginning in 1835 a 'Great Trek' into the Eastern Cape before turning north across the Orange and Vaal Rivers. These 'Voortrekker Boers' were principally farmers negotiating land treaties with local tribes, in particular the Zulu who in 1838 double-crossed and murdered a Boer delegation before massacring 500 Boers at Blaauwkrans. Later that year 500 Boers under Andries Pretorius then avenged Blaauwkrans by defeating 20,000 Zulu at Blood River, the victory and the vow to God taken beforehand giving the Boers the belief that they had been granted a divine right to build an independent nation, two in fact – the Republics of the Orange Free State and the Transvaal.

In 1867 large mineral deposits including diamonds were then discovered on the Vaal River causing the British increasing concern that large numbers of colonists would be attracted from what would become German South West Africa (Namibia) and the Portuguese Province of Mozambique. Since any future German or Portuguese annexation of the Boer Republics would split British South Africa in two, Britain annexed the Transvaal in 1877, the Boers satisfied with the protection provided against their old foes, the Pedi and the Zulu. British imperialism, however, was not satisfied and in 1879 an annexation of Zululand followed, an event which ironically increased Boer security and decreased their need for further British protection.

At the conclusion of the Zulu War the unpopular Lieutenant Governor of Griqualand West, Owen Lanyon was transferred to the Transvaal where his autocratic policies exacerbated Boer grievances. On 8 December 1880, a dispute over unpaid tax was then the catalyst for 10,000 Boers gathering at Paardekraal where they declared independence from British rule before raising their old national flag, the Vierkleur, at Heidelberg. British garrisons in the Transvaal were inadequate to deal with the Boer uprising but in Natal, Commander-in-Chief of South Eastern Africa, Major General George Pomeroy Colley had already responded to Lanyon's warnings by sending two companies of the 94th Regiment of Foot (247 troops) under Lieutenant Colonel Philip Anstruther (a Zulu War veteran with detailed knowledge of the area) for a march on Pretoria.

On 5 December, Anstruther departed Lydenburg with thirty-four wagons, reaching Middleburg ten days later where he received a warning from Pretoria that 500 armed Boers were out on the eastern veld and that all precautions should be taken. Anstruther it seems paid scant regard, his regimental band playing on whilst his column rumbled on. On 20 December 1880, British scouts then reported Boers to the front but Anstruther remained dismissive and continued on to Bronkhorstspruit where the column suddenly came to a halt. To the left was a party of 150 Boers cresting a low ridge, this time Anstruther quickly drawing in his wagons before turning to meet an approaching rider who requested the British column return from whence it had come. Given two minutes to reply, Anstruther declined, stating his intention to proceed in haste to Pretoria. Whilst the two men parleyed 250 Boers moved up to within 200 yards of the column's left across an open field of fire, the First Boer War erupting when Commandant Franz Joubert received Anstruther's reply. The British were no doubt taken by surprise since many were not in possession of their weapons though the Boers later reported that, highly visible in their red tunics, the British had taken up defensive positions during the parley. The terrific Boer onslaught lasted a mere fifteen minutes during which the rear of the British column had become surrounded and by the end of which 157 of the British troops had become casualties, Anstruther included who died from his wounds a week later. Despite total defeat but in the spirit of Anstruther the regimental band again played on, *Rule Britannia*.

Soon all British garrisons in the Transvaal were besieged. Though British Prime Minister William Gladstone was decidedly unhappy waging war against the Boers (or anyone for that matter) Colley would take up the challenge himself and attempt to fight his way through the Drakensberg Mountains on a relief mission.

21 December 1845

Sikh Wars
Battle of Ferozeshah

SINCE 1830 THE British East India Company had been concerned at Russian expansion into central and southern Asia, specifically from Persia (Iran) into Afghanistan out of which the British had been ruthlessly kicked in 1842. British concern in the region had then been heightened following the death of Sikh Maharajah Ranjit Singh, the power vacuum created in the Punjab and surrounding areas leaving the powerful Sikh European-trained Army, the Khalsa, as the dominant force but under uncertain command. Ever opportunistic to extend influence in the Indian subcontinent and anxious that the Khalsa might also now pose a threat to British India, the East India Company moved forces up to the River Sutlej, the amicable relations previously enjoyed between the two nations then destroyed when the Sikhs responded by indeed invading British India. This act of aggression was, however, also a perfect opportunity for Ranjit's widow, Maharani Jindan Singh to gain revenge on the Khalsa for the murder of her brother, Wazir Jawahir Singh. The two principal commanders of the Khalsa, Tej and Lal Singh (the latter already in correspondence with the British), were both smitten by Jindan and had performed suspiciously lamentably – failing to attack the isolated British garrison at Ferozepur before being defeated at Mudki by the British Bengal Army under Commander-in-Chief Sir Hugh Gough and Governor General of India Sir Henry Hardinge when the two Sikh commanders had committed just half their disposable force.

On 21 December 1845, British reinforcements arrived at Mudki, Gough instructing Major General Sir John Littler at Ferozepur to launch a coordinating attack whilst he marched north-west on a wide front to attack 18,000 Sikhs with 120 heavy guns at Ferozeshah. Gough arrived in the late morning urging immediate attack but Hardinge, as Governor General, pulled rank insisting he wait what would be another five hours for Littler. Gough, also with 18,000 men but only sixty-five guns, placed Littler's division on the left, the 3rd Infantry Division under Brigadier Newton Wallace in the centre and the 2nd Infantry Division under Major General Sir Walter Raleigh Gilbert on the right, a mile of artillery separating the 2nd and 3rd Divisions but all with cavalry interspersed and a reserve in the rear under Lieutenant General Sir Harry Smith, a veteran of the 1806 British invasion of South America and the Peninsular War.

In traditional fashion the battle of Ferozeshah opened with an artillery duel during which the Khalsa comfortably held the upper hand. Gough countered by moving his lighter artillery closer whilst Littler moved up to attack the Sikh right, charging at 150 yards with the bayonet only to be repulsed with heavy losses. Gilbert's 2nd Division then attacked the Sikh left in similar fashion but with more success, breaching the defences to rout the Sikh gunners in a bitter struggle before fending off repeated Sikh cavalry and infantry counter-attacks. In the centre Wallace's 3rd Division also advanced but was checked by heavy artillery and musket volleys until Smith restored the situation by moving up with his reserve before pushing on to take the village of Ferozeshah. Heavy fighting now raged along the whole front as the Khalsa grimly fought on in a desperate hand-to-hand struggle with an ammunition magazine explosion adding to the horror, Lal Singh reputedly hiding in a ditch. By midnight the fighting had subsided only to resume again at 15.00 the next day when determined Sikh counter-attacks fell upon isolated British positions. Gough and Hardinge managed to reform the British line again under heavy artillery fire before clearing Ferozeshah and the Khalsa camp of all Sikhs but still the battle was not at an end. Tej Singh and 30,000 men now began an advance against the British left, forcing back the British cavalry and bombarding Ferozeshah. British casualties mounted with confused orders causing their cavalry to retreat whilst the infantry formed squares, Tej again failing to press the Sikh advantage, weakly claiming the British move to be a ruse as he withdrew.

The Khalsa had suffered heavy casualties and pulled back across the Sutlej to Sobraon from where they would launch raids into British territory. The British had suffered nearly 2,500 casualties with Hardinge again furious at Gough's tactics. Harry Smith would be in action again a month later at Aliwal.

22 December 1917

The Great War
Battle of Jaffa

THE GREAT WAR had continued through 1917 with the same appalling casualty rates at Arras and the Third Battle of Ypres (Passchendaele) as had occurred over the previous three years. Though his Prime Minister David Lloyd George had favoured exploring other offensive possibilities, Field Marshal Douglas Haig, commanding the British Expeditionary Force, had believed there to be no alternative but to defeat the Central Powers on the Western Front with an offensive war of attrition. Caught in the technological impasse of the early twentieth century, Haig had certainly employed all the innovation available to him but so far had been unable to break formidable German defences despite continued grim fighting.

The despairing Lloyd George meanwhile had also sought to break the impasse in the Middle East, sending General Edmund Allenby to command 100,000 British and Colonial troops of the Egyptian Expeditionary Force (EEF) for an advance through Palestine that would deliver a morale boosting Christmas present to the British people, the capture of Jerusalem. Indeed on 11 December 1917, after the German Field Marshal Erich von Falkenhayn and the Ottoman (Turkish) Army had withdrawn from Jerusalem (neither army would fight in or close by, conscious of the city's significance in Christianity, Judaism and Islam), Allenby had humbly walked through the Jaffa Gate, the first Christian to govern the city for 673 years. Although Colonel Thomas Lawrence (aka of Arabia) described the scene as the 'supreme moment of the War' the war was very much ongoing as Falkenhayn halted just four miles to the north of the city, the Turks now holding a more or less continuous defensive line down to and across the coastal plains to the north of Jaffa (Tel Aviv).

On 24 November, as a part of his Jerusalem offensive, Allenby had attacked the Turkish 8th Army around Jaffa in an effort to force them back from the Nahr el Auja (River Yarkon) which would relieve pressure on British supply ships arriving at the Port of Old Jaffa. Mounted New Zealanders initially made a successful crossing of the fast flowing river and were reinforced by British infantry before strong Turkish counter-attacks under German General Friedrich von Kressenstein forced them back. By mid December 1917, Allenby, now holding Jerusalem, needed to secure EEF supply lines by forcing and holding the Nahr el Auja for good.

Late on 20 December 1917, the three infantry Divisions of XXI Corps commanded by Lieutenant General Edward Bulfin, the 52nd Lowland Division on the left by the coast, the 54th East Anglia in the centre and British, Indians and South Africans of the 75th Division on the right, began to cross the Nahr el Auja in torrential rain aiming to achieve surprise by foregoing a preliminary artillery bombardment. The Scots of the 52nd led the way in flimsy boats many of which capsized but they succeeded in gaining the opposite bank allowing engineers to build pontoon bridges. Now coming under Turkish artillery fire ever increasing numbers of Scots pushed on to take the heights at Sheikh Muwannis and Khirbet Hadra with the bayonet that same day. By 22 December 1917 the 54th and 75th supported by artillery had pushed the Turks back five miles but the 52nd on the coast had made even greater progress courtesy of gunnery provided from HMS *Grafton, Lapwing, Lizard* and three monitors. Major General John Hill then followed in the footsteps of King Richard I of England (Lionheart) and the Third Crusade, albeit from the opposite direction, by capturing Arsuf.

The attack by XXI Corps and particularly the 52nd Infantry Division had been a brilliant success allowing the Port of Jaffa to be used as a British supply base. Falkenhayn would soon counter-attack outside Jerusalem only to be repulsed. Allenby lost troops to the Western Front in 1918 but was reinforced with Indians, a Jewish Legion and Lawrence's Arabs of Prince Feisal's Sherifial Force, renewing his offensive in the Autumn of 1918 at Megiddo before capturing Damascus and Aleppo. On 30 October 1918 the Ottoman Naval Minister Rauf Bey signed the Treaty of Mudros with Admiral Somerset Gough-Calthorpe aboard HMS *Agamemnon* in Lemnos, Greece bringing hostilities in the Middle Eastern theatre to a close. The Ottoman Empire was then partitioned as per the 1916 Sykes-Picot (Anglo-French) Agreement, the ramifications of which are still felt today.

23 December 1879

Afghan Wars
Battle of Kabul

THE GREAT GAME between Russia and Britain had been ongoing for almost the entire nineteenth century. Initially British fears of Russian expansion into South Asia and the consequent threat to the security of British India had prompted an ultimately disastrous British invasion of Afghanistan in 1838 whilst fifteen years later a Russian defence of the Orthodox Church from a supposed Islamic Ottoman (Turkish) threat was perceived by Britain and France as an attempt to advance Russian imperialism into the Eastern Mediterranean, a war of misery in the Crimean Peninsular resulting.

In 1878 further Russian diplomatic approaches with the fiercely independent Afghans prompted a second British invasion of Afghanistan, this time from the Punjab, by Sikhs, Pathans, Baluchis, Gurkhas, Jats and Muslim and Hindu Punjabis of the British Indian Army. The Emir of Afghanistan Sher Ali Khan fled on the approach of the 50,000-strong British Indians leaving his son, Mohammad Yakoub Khan as emir who understandably was considered by many Afghans to be a British puppet. On Sher Ali's death and the failure to materialise of any Russian threat the British Indian Army then withdrew only to begin a return four months later after the British Representative in Kabul, Louis Cavagnari and his staff had been butchered during an anti-British, Afghan uprising. Commanded by Major General Sir Frederick 'little Bobs' Roberts, a 4,000-strong column of the Kabul Field Force defeated a much larger Afghan force of regulars and tribesmen at Charasiab before marching into Kabul on 13 October 1879. Although suspected of complicity in Cavagnari's murder Yakoub was restored as emir and given refuge in the British Sherpur Military Cantonment (built north of the city by the British soldiers of forty years previous) whilst Roberts unsympathetically rounded up and hanged many of the suspected Afghan mutineers. Unsurprisingly Roberts' actions incurred the wrath of many Afghans including Mohammad Jan Khan Wardak who, with 10,000 Afghans retaliated in turn by marching against the Sherpur Cantonment.

Roberts preemptively advanced to crush the approaching rebellion but on assessing enemy strength during several days of skirmishing on the Chardeh Plains retreated back behind the protection of the cantonment walls, a show of weakness which encouraged many thousands more to join Jan Khan. On 15 December 1879, the Afghans, now perhaps 50,000-strong, approached the five mile perimeter of the cantonment but lacked the necessary weaponry and discipline to conduct an effective siege. In the deteriorating weather of an Afghan winter their misery was magnified by over twenty Kabul Field Force guns which bombarded them from the walls, Roberts also launching several sorties whilst awaiting a relief force under Brigadier General Charles Gough from Jugdulluk. On 22 December, Jan Khan became aware of Gough's proximity and resolved to attack the Cantonment with his entire army the following day.

Before dawn on 23rd December 1879, a bonfire on the Asmai Heights south-west of Kabul signaled the 50,000-strong Afghan attack on the three accessible sides of the cantonment, the north being protected by the Bimaru Heights. The hard pressed British Indians, reinforced by Roberts withdrawing Sikhs from the Heights, volley fired under the light of star shells to keep the massed charges at bay for several hours until at 11.00 British cavalry and field guns sortied from the North Gate for a decisive counter-attack on the Afghan left flank. At midday the remaining cavalry completed the rout, pursuing the Afghans into the surrounding country giving no quarter, Jan Khan fleeing. The British Indian Army had suffered a mere thirty-three casualties but had inflicted perhaps a hundred times as many on their assailants.

Yakoub Khan abdicated as emir, vacating the throne for either his brother Ayub Khan, the Governor of Herat in west Afghanistan or his cousin Abdur Rahman Khan. Viceroy of India Robert Bulwer-Lytton preferred to negotiate the emirship with Abdur Rahman, promising a British withdrawal from Kabul but maintaining a garrison at Kandahar should he accept. Now a furious Ayub rebelled and marched on Kandahar. He would be met in July 1880 at Maiwand by Brigadier General George Burrows.

24 December 1601
Anglo-Spanish Wars, Ireland
Battle of Kinsale

THE ULTIMATE FAILURE of the Statutes of Kilkenny to anglicise Ireland had led to a Tudor Conquest prosecuted by Queen Elizabeth I against a backdrop of deteriorating relations with Philip II, King of Spain, the self appointed defender of the Catholic faith. Philip, however, failed to adequately support Catholic rebellions in Ireland led by the Fitzgeralds of Desmond and the O'Byrnes of Leinster, both of which had been ruthlessly put down by 1583. A plantation of English settlers then followed in Munster but anglicising Ulster, though sparsely populated, was much slower. Ulster's Catholic Gaelic clans were headed by 'Red' Hugh O'Donnell and Hugh O'Neill between whom little love was lost until the threat of English rule and the Anglican Church forced them into each others arms. Originally loyal to Elizabeth, O'Neill defected to defeat his former brother-in-law Sir Henry Bagenal at Clontibret in 1595 just as Anglo-Spanish hostilities were again escalating.

In 1596 the Spanish capture of Calais and the consequent threat of another Spanish invasion of England sparked an Anglo-Dutch sacking of Cadiz under Robert Devereux, Earl of Essex, a second Spanish Armada wrecked off Ireland, an English attack on the Azores and a third Armada wrecked off England. The Anglo-Spanish War then paused in 1598 on Philip's death but the Nine Years' War in Ulster continued, Bagenal again defeated at Yellow Ford, Armagh by O'Neill and O'Donnell before Munster again rebelled, the recent English settlers fleeing for their lives. Despite 18,000 troops in Ireland, Essex could only add to English disasters and was replaced by Charles Blount, Lord Mountjoy who, with George Carew, Lord President of Munster succeeded in defeating the Munster rebellion by the summer of 1601, the rebellion's leaders James Fitzthomas Fitzgerald and the duplicitous Florence MacCarthy now contemplating a lengthy stay in the Tower of London.

Success in Munster was timely for just a month later 4,000 Spaniards under Don Juan del Aguila landed at Kinsale in support of Fitzgerald and MacCarthy only to be greeted by Mountjoy and Carew. Admiral Richard Leveson opportunistically blockaded the hapless Del Aguila in Kinsale Harbour and defeated another 2,000 Spaniards reinforced by the O'Driscolls at Castlehaven. It was the critical hour for O'Neill and O'Donnell, in danger of losing Spanish support for good which would leave them isolated in Ulster, they made a 300 mile winter march south to relieve Del Aguila in Kinsale.

Whilst O'Donnell marched directly to Kinsale, O'Neill attacked Dublin hoping to draw Mountjoy's 7,500 Englishmen back north but the resolution of the English commander was greater and he forced O'Neill south. Once at Kinsale, O'Neill preferred to let the harsh winter take its toll on the English Army but not O'Donnell, the pair eventually agreeing to make a joint attack in conjunction with a Spanish sally on 24 December 1601. In darkness 12,000 Irishmen attempted to move into position north-west of the town but were badly disorganised by the time they came within striking distance of the fully expectant English cavalry. Unable to see the advancing Irish vanguard of Richard Tyrrell, Del Aguila remained in Kinsale which in turn caused O'Neill to retreat, avoiding a trap between Mountjoy's cavalry and the pro English Donogh O'Brien, Earl of Thomond. Mountjoy's cavalry charged O'Neill regardless but a stout defence from Irish musketeers and their own cavalry saw them break away only for an undeterred Mountjoy to prosecute a second assault, a full frontal attack with two regiments of infantry and reinforcements of cavalry on the flanks. This time O'Neill's cavalry broke leaving his badly exposed infantry to make a fighting retreat against withering volleys of English musket. Still Del Aguila remained motionless and O'Donnell, away to O'Neill's left, could not rouse his badly unnerved men. The defeat then turned to a rout when O'Neill's infantry finally broke, Mountjoy's cavalry pursuing to slaughter perhaps 2,000 Irishmen in total. English losses were light.

O'Donnell and O'Neill retreated north leaving Del Aguila to surrender. Though Donal Cam O'Sullivan Beare led a brave defence of Dunboy Castle and a guerrilla war continued in the north, Mountjoy had undoubtably broken the rebellion. O'Neill submitted to Elizabeth but in 1607 joined a 'Flight of the Earls', fleeing Ulster never to return. King James I of England (VI of Scotland) then began a plantation of Protestant English and Presbyterian Scottish in Ulster, the consequences of which were still being felt nearly four centuries later.

25 December 1941
Second World War
Battle of Hong Kong

THE JAPANESE ECONOMY had not fared unduly during the Great Depression. Fiscal stimulus had largely steadied the downturn but the real force in Japanese politics, the Imperial Japanese Army (IJA) already had expansionist ideas whereby Japan would no longer be hostage to the western Imperial powers, specifically Great Britain, Holland and the United States of America who effectively controlled South East Asian resources. For Coal and Iron ore Japan invaded Manchuria in 1931, suffering only a rebuke from the League of Nations which merely encouraged them to next target coastal China. Soon afraid the Japanese economy was overheating, however, Finance Minister Korekiyo Takashi began a policy of fiscal tightening largely at the expense of the Japanese military and was consequently assassinated in an attempted coup in February 1936. Though the coup was defeated IJA influence increased so that when shots were exchanged the following year between Chinese and Japanese troops near Beijing, Japan escalated the incident into the Battle of Beiping-Tianjin and by extension the Second Sino-Japanese War. Japan duly advanced into north and coastal China, capturing Shanghai and the then capital Nanking with shocking brutality whilst the Kuomintang Government of Chiang Kai Shek and much of the population fled inland.

Japanese aggression provoked trade embargoes particularly from the United States which served only to further Japanese belief in their new Asian order, a 1939 US relaxation then only serving to facilitate an increase in production for Japan's war machine. For Great Britain, whose colony Hong Kong was already surrounded by Japanese forces in China, Ambassador Robert Craigie urged a conciliatory stance but anxious to cut Allied supply lines to Chiang Kai Shek, Japan increased troops in Indo-China (Vietnam, Laos and Cambodia) to earn another oil embargo from the imperial powers. Her ambition again jeopardised, Japan signed the Tripartite Act with Germany and Italy before attacking across South East Asia and the Pacific, Hong Kong included.

British Prime Minister Winston Churchill had considered Hong Kong indefensible but belatedly believed a show of strength, an extra 2,000 inexperienced Canadians bolstering the 12,000 British and Indians already there, might just deter the Japanese. On 8 December 1941, this forlorn hope was ruthlessly shattered when 52,000 Japanese troops of Lieutenant General Takashi Sakai's Japanese 23rd Army crossed into mainland Hong Kong supported by artillery and overwhelming air power. In just twelve hours Sakai advanced twenty-five miles to attack the surprised British 'Gindrinkers' defensive line which crumbled on the loss of the Shing Mun Redoubt. All Commonwealth troops now retreated through Kowloon across to Hong Kong Island where Major General Christopher Maltby declined two invitations to surrender despite having just one Vildebeest biplane and one destroyer, HMS *Thracian*, to aid his defence. On 18 December, after a five-day bombardment, Japanese troops began landing on the north-east Hong Kong shoreline, moving inland for a fierce battle in the fortified Wong Nai Chung Gap between Mount Nicholson and Jardine's Lookout. Outnumbered and often fighting to the last man, the defenders both inflicted and suffered heavy casualties before West Brigade Headquarters was eventually overrun, Brigadier John Lawson killed. Successive British counter-attacks failed to move the Japanese who had now effectively split the Commonwealth forces and captured Hong Kong's water reservoirs. Maltby carried on fighting despite no chance of relief, many casualties hospitalised in St Stephens College, Stanley into which, on 25 December 1941, burst Japanese troops, bayoneting the wounded, executing doctors, orderlies, St John's Ambulancemen, raping and killing nurses, just one of several atrocities. Governor Mark Young surrendered Hong Kong that afternoon.

Maltby had lost 4,000 men fighting and would lose many more in Japanese labour camps. During the three and a half year occupation of Hong Kong 10,000 Chinese were executed and a million transported to labour camps in China. In 1946 Sakai was executed for war crimes but Japanese Governor of Hong Kong, Rensuke Isogai would serve only a six-year prison term.

26 December 1915

The Great War
Battle for Lake Tanganyika

THE GREAT WAR had spread almost immediately to East Africa on its August 1914 outbreak. Here British East Africa (Kenya, Uganda) directly bordered to her south, German East Africa (Tanzania, Rwanda, Burundi) but Major General Arthur Aitken's failed November 1914 assaults on the German Port of Tanga and Mount Kilimanjaro meant British forces in East Africa would remain largely on the defensive for over a year. Likewise their adversary, Lieutenant Colonel Paul von Lettow-Vorbeck, attacked the British post at Jassin in January 1915 suffering such heavy losses that he also abandoned offensive operations for a guerrilla campaign against the Uganda Railway linking Mombasa, Kenya with Lake Victoria.

The British had achieved supremacy on Lake Victoria and further south on Lake Nyasa in the first naval action of the Great War but in between, on the 420 mile long Lake Tanganyika, key to the entire East African theatre, the Germans had gained total control after sinking the Belgian steamer *Alexandre Delcommune* and badly damaging the British *Cecil Rhodes*. German raids on Lukuga, Belgian Congo (now Kalemie, Democratic Rep of the Congo) and Fife, Northern Rhodesia (now Tunduma, Zambia) also heightened fears that native Africans north of the River Zambezi would rebel against Belgian and British rule to the benefit of Germany. An invasion of German East Africa was required but both Belgian General Charles Tombeur and incoming British Brigadier General Michael Tighe agreed that any invasion could not possibly be successful until control of Lake Tanganyika had been wrested from the German steamers *Kingani* and *Hedwig von Wissman*. The logistics involved, however, would be mind boggling.

The answer arrived at Admiralty House when big game hunter John Lee advised that the Germans were about to launch a 1,500-ton steamer, *Graf von Goetzen*, armed with guns from the SMS *Konigsberg*, recently scuttled in the Rufiji Delta. Since the Royal Navy was committed off Gallipoli, Lee suggested sending two faster 40-foot gunboats overland from Cape Town, South Africa, the agreeing

Admiralty appointing to the task the eccentric, twice Court Martialled, Lieutenant Commander Geoffrey Spicer-Simson, a man who had watched the German torpedoing of his last command, HMS *Niger*, from a Deal hotel bar.

Naming the two craft *Mimi* and *Toutou* Spicer-Simson departed in June 1915 for an epic four month, 10,000 mile journey by sea to Cape Town, rail to Fungurume (Belgian Congo), porter, tractor, winch and oxen through a hundred miles of bush to Sankisia, train again to Bukama, again by the River Lualaba and Lake Kisale to Kabalo and finally Lukuga on the shores of Lake Tanganyika. By now the *Graf von Goetzen* and Hedwig von Wissman were both shipping troops the length of Lake Tanganyika at will, German Captain Gustav Zimmer concerned only at the construction of the Belgian 700 ton *Baron Dhanis*, sending Lieutenant Job Rosenthal aboard *Kingani* to investigate. Rosenthal braved crocodiles to swim inshore and instead discovered *Mimi* and *Toutou* but was discovered himself when the *Kingani* retreated from the Belgian guns.

Spicer-Simson hastened the reconstruction, testing and arming of both his gunboats so that when German Sub Lieutenant Junge then arrived offshore on *Kingani* on the morning of 26 December 1915 he was attacked by *Mimi* and *Toutou*. The surprised Junge increased speed but could not fire on his pursuers with only a forward mounted gun, the faster British gunboats closing to fire their 3-pounders, killing Junge and four crew in an eleven minute battle watched by thousands of locals ashore before the German boat struck her colours. Spicer-Simson, now the 'Great White Chief', then pressed *Kingani* into service as HMS *Fifi*.

Only in February 1916 did the *Hedwig von Wissman* arrive to investigate *Kingani's* disappearance. Spicer-Simson's now three gunboats and the Belgian *Vedette* gave chase, attacking and sinking the German steamer with seven hands who had received over forty hits from *Mimi* and *Fifi*. German domination of Lake Tanganyika was at an end despite the continued presence of the *Graf von Goetzen*, Spicer-Simson happy to maintain a stalemate threatening German troop movements.

Today the *Graf von Goetzen* is still in service on Lake Tanganyika as the passenger ship MV *Liemba*, sailing between Kigoma, Tanzania and Mpulungu, Zambia. Later in 1916 South African reinforcements under General Jan Smuts would arrive in British East Africa for another British invasion of German East Africa.

26 December 1943
Second World War
Battle of the North Cape

1943 HAD BEEN a disastrous year for the European Axis partners Germany and Italy whilst in the Far East Japan had fared little better. Already defeated at sea by the US Navy (Midway) Japan was then defeated in the jungles of New Guinea and Guadalcanal by the US Army. Adding to these reverses was the death of Marshal Admiral Isoroku Yamamoto, Commander-in-Chief of the Combined Japanese Fleet who was killed when his plane was shot down by sixteen American P-38 Fighter's flying the longest intercept mission of the Second World War, Operation Vengeance. Back over in Russia the Axis had lost the 250,000 strong German 6th Army at Stalingrad before losing another 250,000 men as well as over 1,000 tanks and almost as many aircraft (Russian losses were even greater) at Kursk. Meanwhile in North Africa they had also lost another 250,000 men before Italian Prime Minister Marshal Pietro Badoglio withdrew Italy from the war. Germany now fought on alone against Anglo-American landings in southern Italy whilst also expecting Allied landings in France. Only in the Atlantic did German Chancellor Adolf Hitler have any grounds for optimism and then only for two months between March and May 1943 when Allied shipping losses increased due to additional security incorporated into the Kriegsmarine Enigma Code.

Within weeks of the resumption of intelligence, however, Grand Admiral Karl Donitz lost 25 per cent of his entire U-boat strength, increased Allied convoy escort, air cover, technology and tactics all contributing to the dramatic turn around. Though the British would not escape rationing for another eleven years, convoys crossed the Atlantic and the Mediterranean with increasing success supplying not only their own armies but also Russian via the Persian Corridor and around the North Cape of Norway to Murmansk and Archangel. Here, as well as the U-boat, lurked another threat, the German surface fleet. After the sinking of the Bismarck in 1941, this fleet was headed by the battleships *Tirpitz*, *Gneisenau* and *Scharnhorst*, the latter two surviving the Channel Dash in February 1942. Damaged in an air raid *Gneisenau* would never again put to sea but *Tirpitz* and *Scharnhorst*, each more powerful than any single Royal Navy vessel, hid in Norwegian fjords preying on the Allied convoys. By the end of 1943, however, the power of the Bletchley Park codebreakers would again tell and a trap was set for the *Scharnhorst*.

On Christmas Day 1943, the Convoy JW55B, nineteen British merchantmen protected by ten destroyers sailing from Loch Ewe to Murmansk, was spotted for the second time by a German U-boat. Donitz ordered Rear Admiral Erich Bey commanding *Scharnhorst* and five destroyers in Altenfjord to intercept. Struggling to locate his quarry Bey then fatally sent his destroyers south in search whilst his own *Scharnhorst* sailed north alone in just a half light and appalling arctic weather on Boxing Day morning, 26 December 1943. The trap began to close as Admiral Bruce Fraser, Commander-in-Chief of the Home Fleet, closed in from the west aboard the battleship HMS *Duke of York* with the cruiser HMS *Jamaica* and four destroyers whilst Vice Admiral Robert Burnett aboard HMS *Belfast* accompanied by HMS *Norfolk* and HMS *Sheffield* closed in from the east, the three cruisers having sailed from Murmansk. Bey first encountered Burnett's force at 09.00, *Scharnhorst* turning east and then south in an attempt to outrun the British ships whilst firing several salvoes but was hit twice by HMS *Norfolk*, crucially losing her radar. Now blind in the deteriorating weather and fading light Bey turned *Scharnhorst* back north but Burnett's squadron had remained between him and the convoy and opened fire at eight miles. Despite sustaining damage *Norfolk* scored again before *Scharnhorst* broke off to flee south-east. This time Burnett's *Belfast* pursued as Fraser's *Duke of York* closed to within seven miles firing salvoes of 14-inch shells. Illuminated by star shells, *Scharnhorst* desperately zig-zagged but was hit losing a boiler room and slowed to twelve knots. *Duke of York* was now too close to fire effectively and backed off to allow broadsides and torpedoes from *Belfast*, *Jamaica* and the destroyers. Still *Scharnhorst* fought on, Captain Fritz von Hintze radioing Berlin that 'we will fight to the last shell'. *Duke of York, Belfast and Jamaica* then continued firing as more British and a Norwegian destroyer fired yet more torpedoes. The *Scharnhorst* sank with a tremendous explosion at 20.00, just thirty-six surviving from a crew of near 2,000 men.

Of Germany's great warships just *Tirpitz* remained, the Royal Air Force and Barnes Wallis would deal with her in Tromso fjord the following year.

27 December 1814
American War of 1812
USS Carolina and New Orleans

NAPOLEON BONAPARTE'S CONTINENTAL System had been designed to starve Great Britain into submission but by 1814 its prosecution had led to catastrophic French defeats in Russia, Germany and Spain, reverses that culminated in the French Emperor's abdication. The trade embargo had stirred waves of unrest not just in Europe but also across the Atlantic where the all powerful Royal Navy enforced an embargo of their own against France by blockading the eastern seaboard of the United States. The US bristled with indignation and their young national pride was further bruised when the British armed American Indians in the Midwest under Tecumseh of the Shawnee to prevent further US expansion and protect British Canada from pro Napoleon former French settlers. In 1812, US President James Madison declared war on Great Britain but, under-funded and under-manned, suffered immediate defeats in small scale invasions of Canada which emptied his treasury yet further. On Napoleon's abdication by the 1814 Treaty of Fontainebleau battle-hardened British troops began arriving in North America but though they burnt Washington and besieged Baltimore, where a Star Spangled Banner flew defiantly over Fort McHenry, they could not gain control of Lake Champlain in Upper New York State following a naval defeat at Plattsburgh. Three months later, however, in the south of the country the British gained control of Lake Borgne preparatory for an attack on New Orleans, gateway to the American Midwest via the River Mississippi.

After the Battle of Lake Borgne, General John Keane and 1,800 British troops had marched inland to the east bank of the Mississippi where they fatefully halted at Lacoste's Plantation. Future US President Andrew Jackson and 2,000 Americans seized the opportunity to launch a sharp attack from New Orleans inflicting 277 British casualties but then retreated back behind the Rodrigues Canal at Chalmette to build defensive earthworks and gun batteries, Line Jackson.

On the Mississippi, the schooner USS *Carolina* continued a bombardment of the British camp at Lacoste as General Edward Pakenham (brother-in-law to Field Marshal Arthur Wellesley, Duke of Wellington) now joined Keane. None to happy with the position, Pakenham brought up additional artillery to begin a heavy exchange with the *Carolina* on 27 December 1814, firing heated shot at the wooden schooner which soon caught fire and exploded. With both sides unaware that peace had just been declared across the Atlantic in Ghent, Pakenham resumed the British advance toward New Orleans, immediately launching a reconnaissance in force and on New Year's Day 1815, a full-scale artillery bombardment on Line Jackson. By 8 January 1815, Pakenham had gathered the whole 10,000-strong British force for a decisive attack, sending 1,500 men under Colonel William Thornton across the Mississippi to deal with the grounded USS *Louisiana* and a 20-gun American artillery battery which threatened his left flank while his main force of two infantry columns advanced directly on Line Jackson. Two brigades under Major General John Lambert were held in reserve. The British attack faltered almost immediately when Thornton was delayed by several hours in the Louisiana swamps leaving Keane's left exposed on open ground to the Mississippi batteries. As the morning mist lifted so the whole of Pakenham's massed ranks also came under fire from American grape shot and musket volleys from Line Jackson's 4,700 militia, American Indians, slaves and pirates. With the exception of a determined attack led by Colonel Robert Rennie on an American redoubt, Keane's left column, fired on from the front and left, veered to the right, their commander killed soon to be followed by Pakenham and second in command, Major General Samuel Gibbs. British casualties mounted, only now Thornton capturing the Mississippi batteries but it was too late, three major British assaults had already been repulsed with the loss of over 2,000 men. Lambert's two reserve brigades covered the British withdrawal. Jackson's losses behind the earthworks were light.

The British Fleet attacked Fort St Philip and New Orleans for the next nine days but Lambert decided against a renewed assault on Line Jackson, instead he targeted Fort Bowyer at Mobile, Alabama before news arrived from Ghent. The British had time to capture the pride of the US Navy USS *President* but they would soon have a much bigger worry when Napoleon made good his escape from Elba.

28 December 1943

Second World War
Battle of the Bay of Biscay

SINCE THE 1939 start of hostilities Nazi Germany and Great Britain had waged economic warfare as well as military. Germany's unrestricted submarine warfare of the Great War had been replicated by a determined U-boat offensive in the Atlantic on British bound shipping that at its 1941 height threatened to knock Britain out of the war. British Prime Minister Winston Churchill later admitted 'the only thing that ever really frightened me… was the U-boat peril'. Though rich in minerals Germany too was by no means self sufficient, copper, nickel, aluminium, chromium, and iron ore were all imported from Norway, Sweden, Russia and France, whilst oil was shipped from Romania, rubber, tin and tungsten via the Trans-Siberian Railway from the Far East. War with the Soviet Union in 1941 therefore threatened Germany's Romanian oil supplies and cut the Trans-Siberian Railway leaving Chancellor Adolf Hitler to invade southern Russia and ship his rubber, tin and tungsten around the Cape of Good Hope to French Atlantic ports. To reach these ports German and Japanese (Axis) merchantmen would have to run a Royal Navy blockade that in contrast to Germany's U-boats below the surface, consisted mainly of cruisers, destroyers and corvettes on the surface supported by reconnaissance and attack aircraft above it. To evade detection an Axis freighter would transfer her cargo to smaller 'blockade runners' off West Africa that would maintain radio silence whilst making a dash under cover of night for a French port, often the well defended Bordeaux, seventy miles up the Gironde Estuary. Though four Royal Marine Commandos had temporarily put Bordeaux out of service in December 1942 throughout much of the following year the 'Bordeaux Problem' had persisted. Royal Navy blockades had made decisive contributions throughout European history but it was not until December 1943 when two blockade runners, *Osorno* and *Alsterufer* carrying rubber, tin and tungsten approached the Bay of Biscay, that a concerted British inter-service effort was finally made, Operation Stonewall.

Even now the British Fleet was too late to intercept *Osorno* though the Royal

Air Force did cause her to collide with the wreck of a minesweeper in the Gironde Estuary. *Osorno* beached but her cargo was saved. Further out to sea *Alsterufer* now became the focus of attention, closed upon from all directions by five British light cruisers whilst the German 8th Destroyer Flotilla of five destroyers and two torpedo boats under Kapitan zur See Hans Erdmenger and the 4th Flotilla of four torpedo boats under Korvettenkapitan Franz Kohlauf closed to give protection. Before any of them reached their prize however *Alsterufer* was attacked and set ablaze on 27 December by a Czech crewed Liberator bomber. The German Flotillas continued unaware that their mission had already been rendered futile whilst to their south HMS *Glasgow* under Captain Charles Clark and HMS *Enterprise* under Captain Harold Grant sailed north-east to isolate them from their home ports of Brest and Bordeaux. In the early afternoon of 28 December 1943, the last North Atlantic battle of the Second World War between surface vessels began when Glasgow opened fire. Enterprise immediately joined the fray as the German destroyers returned the compliment, no one scoring in the large swells and gale force winds. As the distance between the two 'fleets' shortened both *Glasgow* and *Enterprise* came under torpedo attack before *Glasgow* was hit by a shell, damaging a boiler. Avoiding more torpedoes *Glasgow* then also came under attack from a lone Fokker Wulf 200 Condor bomber, fighting the aircraft off before the British cruisers separated. *Enterprise* then scored a hit on German destroyer *Z27* whilst likewise *Glasgow* scored against the smaller torpedo boats *T25* and *T26*, the latter assisted by a smokescreen laid by *T22* but ultimately doomed when torpedoed at close range by *Enterprise*. Meanwhile *Glasgow*, having chased *T22* north stumbled across Erdmenger's now helpless destroyer *Z27*, the Korvettenkapitan going down with his ship after *Glasgow's* shells exploded *Z27's* magazine. Finally *T25*, previously damaged by *Glasgow*, was sunk by *Enterprise*. The remaining German shipping fled.

Many of the 283 German survivors were picked up by a small Irish steamer MV *Kerlogue* after an SOS from a German aircraft, her cargo of oranges saving many lives. German blockade runners ceased though the U-boat menace remained until the end of the war.

29 December 1940

Second World War
London Blitz

HOLLAND, BELGIUM, FRANCE and Great Britain had been given ample time to prepare for the invasion of Adolf Hitler's Nazi Germany but had been overrun in just weeks. The staggering successes of the Nazi war machine had left Britain alone as former Great War ally Russia stood by, their confidence misplaced in a Pact of Non-aggression (Molotov-Ribbentrop) with Germany. Following the fall of France the German High Command believed any transport of troops across the English Channel for an invasion of Britain would be tantamount to suicide against the power of the Royal Navy until total air superiority had been gained by the *Luftwaffe* of Reichsmarschall Hermann Goring. The Germans, however, had not accounted for the resolve of British Prime Minister Winston Churchill, Minister of Aircraft Production Max Aitken, Lord Beaverbrook, Air Chief Marshal Hugh Dowding RAF Fighter Command, Air Vice Marshal Keith Park no11 Fighter Group, South East England and 'the Few' (fighter pilots). RAF Fighter Command had not only held firm but RAF Bomber Command under Air Marshal Charles Portal had taken the war back to Germany, bombing Monchengladbach in May 1940 but largely concentrating on military targets including German troop transports assembling in Dutch, Belgian and French harbours.

On 25 August, eighty-one Hampdens, Whitleys and Wellingtons then bombed munitions factories in North Berlin embarrassing Goring with Hitler promising retaliation. A bombing 'Blitz' then began on 7 September 1940 for fifty-seven consecutive nights on London, the *Luftwaffe* suffering such a serious set back on 15 September that they were now reluctant to attack in daylight. Cities across Britain were targeted with the British Air Ministry also in a battle to disrupt *Luftwaffe* navigation beams. On the ground, air raid sirens sounded night after night, women and children were evacuated, men not in military service joined the Auxiliary Fire Service, the Air Raid Precautions or Rescue Volunteers. Anderson shelters were built in gardens and many slept in communal shelters including

London Tube Stations. By December 1940 Hitler was already planning Operation Barbarossa, an invasion of Russia, but first he intended to destroy the symbol of British resistance, the Christopher Wren masterpiece built after the 1666 Great Fire of London, holding the crypts of Horatio, Lord Nelson and Arthur Wellesley, Duke of Wellington and Wren himself – St Paul's Cathedral.

At 18.08 on a freezing Sunday, 29 December 1940, sirens sounded over the British capital indicating the imminent arrival of the first wave of ten German bombers, Pathfinders dropping flares and the first of 24,000 incendiary bombs over the square mile of the City of London. A team of 200 volunteers including the Dean, the Very Reverend Walter Matthews and many architects then climbed, as they did every night, into the rafters of the cathedral. Fire fighters rushed to the area, the men on the roof of St Paul's desperately attempting to extinguish the incendiaries as they landed, climbing as high as the fragile dome itself. Hundreds of small fires were, however, breaking out below in the narrow streets and warehouses of the book and newspaper industry around the cathedral, an inferno developing as the fires joined. At 19.00 another thirty German bombers arrived dropping incendiaries and 550-pound high explosive bombs, shattering buildings and water mains. The conflagration spread rapidly, the fire services doggedly resisting urged on by Churchill who insisted the cathedral be saved at all costs. As the heat built so too a strong wind developed, the first signs of a firestorm. A third wave of bombers then arrived at 20.00 adding more incendiaries and high explosive, fire fighters moving to defend a St Paul's surrounded by fire but now without water since the raid had been designed to coincide with a low tide on the River Thames. More waves of bombers arrived, many bombing indiscriminately to spread the fires, almost the whole of the City ablaze with buildings collapsing all around but in the centre St Paul's incredibly still towered above it all. At 01.00 the final German assault was beginning to form up across the Channel but, to Hitler's fury, was cancelled due to poor weather. The fire fight in London, however, would continue all night.

By the following morning, 163 people had lost their lives including fourteen firemen with many more badly injured. The City of London lay in ruins but, thanks to the fire services, the Dean, his 200 volunteers and a miracle, not St Paul's. British morale and resistance would only get stronger.

30 December 1460

Wars of the Roses
Battle of Wakefield

BITTER RECRIMINATIONS OVER the 1453 Hundred Years' War defeat to France were never more evident than between Richard Plantagenet, Duke of York and Edmund Beaufort, Duke of Somerset. Both had been King Henry VI of England's Lieutenants in France at differing times during the previous decade, the former in favour of a stronger prosecution of the war, the latter a peace seeker who would eventually oversee England's expulsion from France, Calais excepted. Henry's own weak rule in contrast to that of his formidable father, King Henry V, then allowed a power vacuum to develop from which both York and Somerset sought to profit at the expense of the other but from their efforts to win personal favour a struggle soon developed for the Crown of England itself, the Wars of the Roses.

After York's ally Richard Neville, Earl of Warwick had defeated King Henry at Northampton in July 1460 the king had been taken prisoner and although given the respect due a monarch was imprisoned in the Tower of London. When York arrived in London from exile in Dublin, however, he amazed even his own supporters by claiming the English throne by right of descent from King Edward III's second son Lionel, reneging on his previous oaths of loyalty to Henry. Aware that York's popularity would now plummet, Warwick brokered a deal in which Henry, who had few cards to play, would disinherit his own son Edward, Prince of Wales in favour of York who in the meantime would again become Protector of the Realm.

On hearing the news of her son's disinheritance Henry's French Queen, Margaret of Anjou, a long time adversary of York, was naturally appalled and immediately set about forming an army to challenge York. In fact two Lancastrian armies formed, one in Wales against which York sent his eldest son Edward, Earl of March and one in Yorkshire against which he himself, his second son Edmund, Earl of Rutland and Richard Neville, Earl of Salisbury (father of Warwick) advanced with 6,000 men. Warwick meanwhile was left to garrison London.

York, Rutland and Salisbury headed for Sandal Castle, Wakefield where, after a skirmish at Worksop, they spent Christmas besieged by a large Lancastrian force under Henry Beaufort, Duke of Somerset (who was additionally looking to avenge his father, killed at St Albans in 1455), Henry Holland Duke of Exeter, Henry Percy Duke of Northumberland, John Lord Clifford and Sir Andrew Trollope. York and Salisbury were safe behind Sandal Castle's impregnable walls whilst no doubt Yorkist reinforcements would soon arrive in the form of March but for some unknown reason, on 30 December 1460, both ventured out. York may have been deceived by the treacherous Clifford or Trollope potentially defecting from the Lancastrians (Clifford had previously defected from the Yorkists to the Lancastrians) or that they perceived Somerset and Clifford to be vulnerable to attack unaware that additional Lancastrian forces were nearby. It is also possible that York was merely leading a foraging party when he was engaged by Lancastrians to his front. Numbers actually involved and details are uncertain but as more Lancastrians joined the fighting the Yorkists became surrounded and were annihilated in a bloody mêlée of hand-to-hand fighting, little quarter given.

Richard Plantagenet, Duke of York was killed in the fighting or executed shortly after whilst his son Edmund, Earl of Rutland was captured and executed probably by Clifford who, it was rumoured in London, took great satisfaction in avenging his own father who had also perished at St Albans. Salisbury was captured later that night and taken to Pontefract Castle where he was beheaded, both his and York's heads displayed on spikes over Micklegate Bar, York. Yorkist London now trembled as a Lancastrian Army of wild Northerners led by an unsympathetic French queen marched south sacking Grantham, Stamford and Northampton. There was still Warwick and more importantly March who had learnt of his father's death but was still in Wales where Jasper Tudor, Earl of Pembroke (King Henry's half brother by his mother) and James Butler, Earl of Wiltshire were adding Welsh Lancastrians to their French and Irish mercenaries. March could not reinforce Warwick until he had dealt with Pembroke and Wiltshire, he would get the chance in early February at Mortimer's Cross.

31 December 1775
American War of Independence
Battle of Quebec

THE 1775 OUTBREAK of the American War of Independence had immediately set the British Army on the defensive. Holed up in Boston, surrounded on three sides and supplied only by the Royal Navy the British were so well contained that General George Washington, commanding the American Continental Army looked to take advantage elsewhere before the 1776 winter set in. The British had taken Quebec City from the French seventeen years earlier when General James Wolfe had defeated Louis Joseph de Montcalm on the Plains of Abraham and it was here now that Washington turned his attention believing he could raise the French against their new masters, take Quebec and chase the British out of North America entirely.

The Continental Army had taken Fort Ticonderoga at the southern end of Lake Champlain from a token force of British Redcoats in May 1775 and from here Major General Richard Montgomery led a force north to take Fort St Jean and threaten Montreal. Almost simultaneously, Benedict Arnold commanded a second column directly north through Maine to Quebec City. In Montreal the British Governor of Quebec, General Guy Carleton, was well aware of both American advances and requested Vice Admiral Samuel Graves sail reinforcements from Boston but Graves refused in fear of winter ice trapping his fleet in the St Lawrence River. Lieutenant Governor Hector Cramahé, however, had already begun organising a loyalist militia to defend Quebec City, receiving additional militia for the task from Newfoundland, marines from HMS *Lizard* and 200 Royal Highlander Emigrants. To aid Cramahé, Carleton abandoned Montreal to Montgomery and headed to Quebec where he additionally pressed locals into a defence of the city, in total now 2,000 men.

Arnold arrived outside the city walls on 13 November but his column was in dire straits. The rigours of the march had halved his original 1,100 men and those that had survived were barely fit for service. He also had no artillery but nevertheless demanded the city surrender, a request Carleton answered with cannon fire. Isolated, Arnold waited for Montgomery who arrived from Montreal on 1 December but with a force that only doubled American strength to 1,200, he did, however, have a few artillery pieces and much needed supplies but now ran into the same problems as had Arnold. Freezing in the Canadian winter Montgomery could not seriously damage Quebec's walls and could not force a French uprising from within.

Since a lengthy siege would likely be broken by British reinforcements arriving with the spring thaw, Montgomery resolved to assault the city under cover of a snowstorm, the opportunity for which arrived on the night of 30–31 December 1775. A double feint attack on the heavily fortified Cap Diamond and the St John's Gate by Jacob Brown and James Livingston was correctly identified as such by Carleton so that when Montgomery and Arnold's main force approached the lower city Carleton's militia were ready waiting. Once Livingstone and Brown had come into action, Montgomery and Arnold who had advanced through thick snow, cut through the city's defensive wooden palisades in the belief that complete surprise had been attained. On entering Quebec, Montgomery led his men directly towards and unbeknown to him, a defensive blockhouse from which, at point-blank range, he was blasted by British muskets and cannon, Montgomery amongst the many dead with any survivors fleeing. Arnold had meanwhile led a force through the Sault au Matelot Gate on the northern side of Quebec but once inside had come under fire from the walls above. Unable to return, Arnold moved further into the city to attack a barricade where he was shot through the ankle, leaving Daniel Morgan to sustain the attack. Indeed Morgan took the barricade before the atrocious weather began to seriously hamper the ability of his men to fire their muskets. Taking refuge in some buildings, Morgan's desperate group came under increasing pressure as the British defenders on the outer walls moved in to attack them, Morgan surrendering at 10.00. American losses totalled 500 whilst British casualties were negligible.

Arnold escaped to continue an ineffective siege of Quebec before in mid-1776 withdrawing to Lake Champlain. Carleton would follow him in an attempt to split the Continental Army down the axis of the Hudson River, linking British forces in Quebec and Montreal with those soon to arrive in New York City. The pair would meet at Valcour Island in October.

Bibliography & References

Viking/Norman Invasions
BBC Radio Four, *The Battle of Stamford Bridge*, Thursday 2 June 2011. IPlayer Radio. Retrieved 9 January 2017
http://www.newadvent.org/cathen/04578a.htm. Retrieved 15 November 2015
http://www.berkshirehistory.com/articles/reading_vikings.html. Retrieved 12 January 2016
Burton, Edwin. *St Cuthbert, The Catholic Encyclopaedia. Vol 4*. Robert Appleton Company, 1908
Ford, David Nash, *Royal Berkshire History – Viking Invasion of Reading 871*. Nash Ford Publishing, ND
Lawson, M.K., *Edmund II*, Oxford University Press 2004 https://bit.ly/2Q9hh91. Retrieved 18 April 2014
Keynes, Simon. *Aethelred II*. Oxford University Press 2004–16 https://bit.ly/2yGHFjI. Retrieved 18 April 2014

Bartlett, W.B., *King Cnut and The Viking Conquest of England 1016*, Amberley Publishing 2016
Campbell, James et al, *The Anglo-Saxons*, Penguin 1991
Glenn, Jonathan (Translation transcript Elphinston, John) *Anglo-Saxon Poem, Battle of Maldon*
Jones, Gwyn, *A History of the Vikings*, 2nd Revised edition 1984, Oxford Paperbacks
Lyndon Dodds, Glen, *Battles in Britain 1066–1746*. Brockhampton Press 1999
Pollard, Justin. *Alfred the Great; The Man Who Made England*, John Murray 2006
Schama, Simon, *A History of Britain Vol 1, At the Edge of the World 3000 BC–1603 AD*. BBC Books 2000
Swanton, Michael, *The Anglo-Saxon Chronicles*, Phoenix Press 2000
Venning, Timothy, *The Kings and Queens of Anglo-Saxon England*, Amberley Publishing 2013

Third Crusade
Ashbridge, Thomas, *The Crusades: The War for the Holy Land*, Simon & Schuster 2012
Gillingham, John, *Richard the Lionheart*, Weidenfeld & Nicholson 1989

Barons Wars
Schama, Simon, *A History of England Vol 1, At the Edge of the World 3000 BC–1603 AD*, BBC Books 2000
Lyndon Dodds, Glen, *Battles in Britain 1066–1746*, Brockhampton Press 1999

Anglo Scottish Wars
Film Documentary – *Henry VIII and His Six Wives*. Oxford Film & Television and Motion Content Group. Channel 5, 2016.

Clan Sinclair. https://bit.ly/2yI4SlD Retrieved 6 November 2015
English Moncarchs. https://bit.ly/2yH8cxw Retrieved 9 October 2015
Herbert, Jim, www.berwicktimelines.tumblr.com/halidonhill. Retrieved 23 January 2017
Historic Scotland, The Inventory of Historic Battlefields – Battle of Roslin (PDF). Retrieved 6 October 2015
UK Battlefields Resource Centre. Battle of Solway Moss, 24 November 1542 https://bit.ly/2CRs3g6. Retrieved 14 October 2015
UK Battlefields Resource Centre. Battle of Pinkie, 10 September 1547. https://bit.ly/2Ronqy8. Retrieved 7 October 2016
Langside and Battlefield Illustrated Guide. https://bit.ly/2qiDdTw. Retrieved 2 October 2017
The Ballad of Balrinnes, Dalzells Scottish Poems of the Sixteenth Century. Retrieved 2 November 2016

Armstrong, Peter, *Stirling Bridge and Falkirk 1297–98: William Wallace's Rebellion*. Osprey Publishing 2003
Barbour, John, trans Higgins, James, *The Bruce*, Arima Publishing 2013
Guy, John, *My Heart is my Own: The Life of Mary Queen of Scots*, Harper Perennial

Hume Brown, P., *History of Scotland: To the Present Time Vol 2.*, Cambridge University Press 1902

Hutchinson, Robert, *Young Henry: The Rise of Henry VIII*, Weidenfeld & Nicolson 2012

Lang, Andrew, *A Short History of Scotland*, Wallachia Publishers 2016

Lawson, John Parker, *Historical Tales of the Wars of Scotland, and of the Border Raids, Forays, and Conflicts Vol. 1*, A. Fullarton 1846

Lomas, Robert, *Turning the Templar Key*, Fair Winds Press 2009

Lyndon Dodds, Glen, *Battles in Britain 1066–1746*, Brockhampton Press 1999

Mallinson, Allan, *The Making of the British Army: From the English Civil War to the War on Terror*, Bantam Press 2009

Matthews, Rupert, *England versus Scotland: The Great British Battles*, Pen and Sword 2002

Maxwell, Herbert, *A History of the House of Douglas from the Earliest Times Down to the Legislative Union of England and Scotland Vol. 1*, Freemantle & Co 1902

McNair Scott, Ronald, *Robert the Bruce, King of Scots*, Canongate Books 2014

Morris, Marc, *A Great and Terrible King: Edward I and the Forging of Britain*, Windmill Books 2009

Oliver, Neil, *A History of Scotland*, Weidenfeld & Nicolson 2009

Sadler, John, *Border Fury: England and Scotland at War 1296–1568*, Routledge 2006

Santiuste, David, *The Hammer of the Scots: Edward I and the Scottish Wars of Independence*, Pen and Sword Military 2015

Schama, Simon, *A History of England Vol .1, At the Edge of the World 3000 BC– 1603 AD*, BBC Books 2000

—, *A History of Britain 1603-1776 , The British Wars Vol. 2.*, BBC Books 2001

Snow, Dan and Peter, *Battlefield Britain: From Boudicca to the Battle of Britain*, BBC Books 2004

The Hundred Years War

The Chronicles of Sir Jean Froissart. Chapter CCXLI. https://bit.ly/2Jta8xA. Retrieved 1 February 2017

Froissart, Jean; translated by John Bourchier. The Chronicles of Froissart. etext University of Virginia Library. https://sourcebooks.fordham.edu/basis/froissart-full.asp. Retrieved 2 February 2017

Barker, Juliet, *Agincourt: The King, the Campaign, The Battle*, Abacus 2006

Barker, Juliet, *Conquest, The English Kingdom of France in the Hundred Years War*, Abacus 2009

Burne, Alfred H., *The Hundred Years War, A Military History*, Penguin Books 2002

Dunster, Rev. Henry Peter, *Stories from the Chroniclers. Froissart.* Joseph Masters 1847

Lyndon Dodds, Glen, *Battles in Britain 1066–1746*, Brockhampton Press 1999

Monstrelet, Enguerrand, translated by Johnes, Thomas, *The Chronicles of Enguerrand Monstrelet Vol. I*, George Routledge and Sons 1867

Schama, Simon, *A History of England Vol. 1, 3000 BC–1603 AD*, BBC Books 2000

Sumption, Jonathan, *Cursed Kings: The Hundred Years War, Vol. IV*, Faber and Faber 1999

—, *Divided Houses: The Hundred Years War, Vol. III*, Faber and Faber 1999

—, *Trial by Battle: The Hundred Years War, Vol. I*, Faber and Faber 1999

—, *Trial by Fire: The Hundred Years War, Vol. II*, Faber and Faber 1999

Wagner, John A., *Encyclopaedia of the Hundred Years War*, Greenwood Press 2006

Glendowyr and Percy Rebellions

Historic England, Battle of Shrewsbury, https://bit.ly/2P0XmfN. Retrieved 3 February 2017

Lyndon Dodds, Glen, *Battles in Britain 1066–1746.* Brockhampton Press 1999

Snow, Dan and Peter, *Battlefield Britain: From Boudicca to the Battle of Britain*, BBC Books 2004

Wars of the Roses

BBC. Hereford and Worcester. https://bbc.in/2CROnWV. Accessed 6 February 2017

Goodman, Anthony, *The Wars of the Roses: Military Activity and English Society, 1452–97*, Routledge & Kegan Paul 1981

Lyndon Dodds, Glen, *Battles in Britain 1066–1746*, Brockhampton Press 1999

Schama, Simon. *A History of Britain: 3000 BC – 1603 AD, Vol. 1*, BBC Books 2000
Seward, Desmond, *The Wars of the Roses*, Constable and Robinson 2002

Italian Wars
Harrison, Simon,Three Decks Forum. Battle of the Solent. https://bit.ly/2qiNfEl. Retrieved 6 October
   2016

Childs, David, *The Warship Mary Rose: The Life and Times of King Henry VIII's Flagship*, Seaforth
   Publishing 2007
Mallett, Michael Edward; Shaw, Christine,*The Italian Wars 1494–1559*, Routledge 2014
Winton, John; Bailey, Chris Howard; McMurray, Campbell, *An Illustrated History of the Royal Navy*,
   Conway Maritime Press New Edition 2005

Anglo Spanish Wars
Jamaica History, Jamaica National Heritage Trust 2011
   http://www.jnht.com/history_english.php. Retrieved 13 October 2016
Guttman, Robert, Military History Magazine, October 1991 https://bit.ly/20GH4E3. Retrieved 20
   March 2015

Arnold, David, *The Age of Discovery 1400–1600*, 2nd Edition, Routledge 2002
Bicheno, Hugh, *Elizabeth's Sea Dogs: How the English Became the Scourge of the Seas*, Conway 2013
Black, Clinton, V., *The Story of Jamaica*, Collins 1965
Childs, David, *Pirate Nation: Elizabeth I and her Royal Sea Rovers*, Seaforth Publishing 2014
Limm, Peter, *The Dutch Revolt 1559–1648*, Longman 1989
Marley, David F., *Pirates and Privateers of the Americas*. ABC-CLIO 1994
Schama, Simon, *A History of Britain 3000 BC–1603 AD, Vol. 1*, BBC Books 2000.
—, *A History of Britain, The British Wars 1603–1776, Vol. 2*, BBC Books 2001
Snow, Dan and Peter, *Battlefield Britain: From Boudicca to the Battle of Britain*, BBC Books 2004
Sugden, John, *Sir Francis Drake*, Pimlico 2006
Thomas, Graham, *The Buccaneer King: The Story of Captain Henry Morgan*, Pen and Sword 2014
Watson, Robert, T*he History of the Reign of Philip II, King of Spain, 7th Edition*, ebook. Bradbury and
   Evans 1839

Anglo Irish Wars
Ancient Clan O'Neill. http://ancientclanoneill.com/content/hugh-earl-tyrone. Retrieved 11 May 2016
Never Felt Better https://bit.ly/2yGdGZm. Retrieved 28 December 2015
An Phoblacht, Republican News. *The Battle of Ballynahinch* https://bit.ly/2ACzFBA. Retrieved 9
   November 2016
Lisburn Historical Society Volume 1, *Henry Munro, Chief of the Irish Rebels*. https://bit.ly/2JtAJdM.
   Retrieved 9 November 2016
The Irish Story John Dorney 2012. https://bit.ly/2RmgqBQ. John Dorney 2012. Retrieved 8 December
   2016

Irish Times 26 and 27 May 1921

Bennett, Richard, *The Black and Tans*, Pen and Sword 2010
Cottrell, Peter, *The Anglo Irish War: The Troubles 1913–1922*, Osprey Publishing 2006
Falls, Cyril, *Elizabeth's Irish Wars*, Constable 1950
Foley, Michael, *The Bloodied Field. Croke Park. Sunday 21st November 1920*, The O'Brien Press 2015
Holmes, Peter; Young, Peter, *The English Civil War: A military History of Three Civil Wars 1642–51*,
   Wordsworth 1999
Jackson, Alvin, *Home Rule, An Irish History 1800–2000*, Oxford University Press 2003
McGurk, John, *Elizabethan Conquest of Ireland*, Manchester University Press 2009

O'Reilly, Terence, *Our Struggle for Independence: Eye Witness Accounts from the Pages of An Cosantoir*, Mercier Press 2009

Schama Simon, *A History of Britain: At the Edge of the World 3000 BC–1603 AD, Vol. 1*, BBC Books 2000

—, *A History of Britain: The Fate of Empire 1776–2000, Vol, 3*, BBC

Townshend, Charles, *Easter 1916: The Irish Rebellion*, Penguin 2015

Wedgewood, C.V., *The King's War 1641–1647*, Classic Penguin 2001

Mckeiver, Philip Graham, *A New History of Cromwell's Irish Campaign*, Advance Press 2008

O Siochru, Dr Michael, *God's Executioner: Oliver Cromwell and the Conquest of Ireland*, Faber and Faber 2009

Sheehan, William, *Fighting For Dublin: The British Battle for Dublin 1919–21*, Collins Press 2007

English Civil Wars

BBC.Waleshistory. https://bbc.in/2SwvM8h. Phil Carradice. Retrieved 7 January 2016

Barratt, John, *Battle of Rowton Heath 1645 and the Siege of Chester*, Stuart Press 1995

Burne, Alfred H.; Young, Peter, *The Great Civil War, A Military History of the First Civil War*, Windrush Press 1998

Clark, David, *The English Civil War*, Pocket Essentials; 2nd Edition 2014

Davies, R.T., *Four Centuries of Witch Beliefs*, Routledge 2011

Gardiner, Samuel, *History of the Great Civil War 1642–49, Vol. I*, Arkose Press 2015

Lyndon Dodds, Glen, *Battles in Britain 1066–1746*, Brockhampton Press 1999

Holmes, Richard; Young, Peter, *The English Civil War: A Military History of the Three Civil Wars 1642–51*, Wordsworth 1999

Mallinson, Allan, *The Making of the British Army:From the English Civil War to the War on Terror*, Bantam Books 2011

Mckeiver, Philip Graham, *A New History of Cromwell's Irish Campaign*, Advance Press 2008

O Siochru, Dr Michael, *God's Executioner: Oliver Cromwell and the Conquest of Ireland*, Faber and Faber 2009

Schama, Simon, *A History of Britain 1603–1776. The British Wars Vol. 2*, BBC Books 2000

Wallace, David, *Twenty-two Turbulent Years 1639–1661*, FastPrint Publishing 2013

Wanklyn, Malcolm, *Decisive Battles of the English Civil War; Myth and Reality*, Pen and Sword 2006

Wedgewood, C.V., *The King's War 1641–1647*, Classic Penguin 2001

Wheeler, James Scott, *Cromwell in Ireland*, Gill and Macmillan Ltd 1999

Anglo Dutch Wars

Rickard, J. (17 August 2009), *Battle Goodwin Sands, 19 May 1652*, https://bit.ly/2SBMhjF. Retrieved 20 January 2016

—, *Battle of Kentish Knock, 28 September 1652*, https://bit.ly/2JrGTLvl. Retrieved 22 January 2016

—, *Battle of Dungeness, 30 November 1652*, https://bit.ly/2Q8gXHzl. Retrieved 22 January 2016

—, *Battle of Portland, 18–20 February 1653*, https://bit.ly/2DcDVKP. Retrieved 26 January 2016

—, *Battle of the Gabbard, 2–3 June 1653*, https://bit.ly/2JuMKzN. Retrieved 26 January 2016

—, (19 August 2009), *Battle of Scheveningen, 31 July 1653*, https://bit.ly/2DdOHjP. Retrieved 27 January 2106

—, *Battle of Lowestoft, 3 June 1665,* https://bit.ly/2QfNBGY. Retrieved 27 January 2016

—, (22 August 2009), *St. James's Day Battle/ North Foreland/Two Day's Battle, 25–26 July/4–5 August 1666*, https://bit.ly/2AD5aLW. Retrieved 28 January 2106

—, (25 August 2009), *Dutch Raid on the Medway, 19–24 June 1667*, https://bit.ly/2RnR3j9. Retrieved 29 January 2016

—, (28 August 2009), *First Battle of the Schooneveld, 28 May/7 June 1673*, https://bit.ly/2Q6TlCV. Retrieved 28 January 2106

—, *Battle of Texel or Kijkduin, 11/21 August 1673*, https://bit.ly/2PvkCBZ. Retrieved 31 January 2106

Barratt, John, *Cromwell's Wars at Sea*, Pen and Sword 2006

Grant R.G., *Battle at Sea: 3000 Years of Naval Warfare*, Dorling Kindersley 2010

Jones, J.R., *The Anglo Dutch Wars of the Seventeenth Century*, Routledge 1996

Lavery, Brian, *Empire of the Seas. How the Navy Forged the Modern World*, Conway 2009

Rodger, N.A.M., *The Command of the Ocean: A Naval History of Britain 1649–1815*, Penguin Books 2004

Rogers, P.G., *The Dutch on the Medway*, Seaforth Publishing 2017

Rommelse, Gijs, *The Second Anglo Dutch War 1665–1667: Raison d'Etat, Mercantilsim and Maritime Strife*, Hilversum Verloren 2006

Schama, Simon, *A History of Britain, The British Wars 1603–1776, Vol. 2.*, BBC Books 2001

Pirates and Privateers

Exquemelin, Alexander, *The Buccaneers of America*, Dover Publications 2000

Latimer, Jon, *Buccaneers of the Caribbean: How Piracy Forged an Empire*, Harvard University Press 2009

Marley, David F., *Pirates of the Americas Vol. 1: 1650–1685*, ABC-CLIO 2010

Thomas, Graham, *The Buccaneer King: The Story of Captain Henry Morgan*, Pen and Sword 2014

Nine Years War

Childs, John, T*he Nine Years War and the British Army, 1688–1697: The Operations in the Low Countries*, Manchester University Press 1991

Mallinson, Allan, *The Making of the British Army: From the English Civil War to the War on Terror*, Bantam Books 2011

Schama, Simon, *A History of Britain 1603–1776 The British Wars, Vol. 2*, BBC Books 2001

Williamite Wars

Clan Cameron: *The Battle of Cromdale.* https://bit.ly/2ESPKaz. Retrieved 2 February 2016

Childs, John, *The Nine Years War and the British Army, 1688–1697: The Operations in the Low Countries*, Manchester University Press 1991

Lavery, Brian, *Empire of the Seas. How the Navy Forged the Modern World*, Conway 2009

Mallinson, Allan, *The Making of the British Army: From the English Civil War to the War on Terror*, Bantam Books 2011

Schama, Simon, *A History of Britain 1603-1776: The British Wars, Vol. 2*, BBC Books 2001

Snow, Dan and Peter, *Battlefield Britain: from Boudicca to the Battle of Britain*, BBC Books 2004

War of the Spanish Succession

Laughton J.K.; Hattendorf, Rev John, *Sir John Jennings 1664–1743, naval officer*, Oxford University Press 2004 https://bit.ly/2ACTfOh Retrieved 15 December 2015

Burton, Richard, *To the Gold Coast for Gold*, Authorama 2003

Chandler, David, *Marlborough as a Military Commander*, Batsford 1979

Falkner, James, *Great and Glorious Days: The Duke of Marlborough's Battles 1704–1709*, The History Press 2003

Falkner, James, *The War of the Spanish Succession*, Pen and Sword 2015

Glozier, Matthew; Onnekink, David, *War, Religion and Service: Huguenot Soldiering 1685–1713*, Ashgate Publishing 2007

Holmes, Richard; Evans, Martin, *A Guide To Battles: Decisive Conflicts in History*, Oxford University Press 2006

Holmes, Richard, *Marlborough: England's Fragile Genius*, Harper Press 2008

Hussey, John, *Marlborough: John Churchill, Duke of Marlborough, Hero of Blenheim*, Weidenfeld & Nicholson 2004

Mallinson, Allan, *The Making of the British Army: From the English Civil War to the War on Terror*, Bantam Books 2011

McNally, Michael; O'Brogain, Sean, *Ramillies 1706 : Marlborough's Tactical Masterpiece*, Osprey Publishing 2014

Stanhope, Earl Philip Henry, *History of the War of the Succession in Spain*, Forgotten Books 2012

Jacobite Rebellions

Scotclans. *1719 Battle of Glenshiel.* https://bit.ly/2JrpWkk. Retrieved 2 November 2015

Love, Dane, *Jacobite Stories*, Neil Wilson Publishing 2011

Lyndon Dodds, Glen, *Battles in Britain 1066–1746*, Brockhampton Press1996

Mallinson, Allan, *The Making of the British Army: From the English Civil War to the War on Terror*, Bantam Books 2011

Simms, Brendan, *Three Victories and a Defeat: The Rise and Fall of the First British Empire*, Penguin 2008

Schama, Simon. *A History of Britain 1603-1776 The British Wars Vol 2*. BBC Books 2001

War of Jenkins Ear/ War of the Austrian Succession

Ruiz, Bruce C, *Admiral Vernon and PortoBello* 2002 https://bit.ly/2OhufzI. Retrieved 24 March 2015

Bartolomeo Giuliano, *la campagna militaire del 1744 nelle Alpi occidentale e l'assedio di Cuneo*, Cuneo 1967

Charteris, Evan, *William Augustus, Duke of Cumberland: His Early Life and Times 1721–1748*, Edward Arnold 1913

Cordingly, David, *Spanish Gold: Captain Woodes Rogers & The True Story of The Pirates of the Caribbean*, Bloomsbury 2011

Fortescue, Sir John William, *A History of the British Army Vol. II (1714–1763)*, Pickle Partners 2013

Landers, Jane, *Black Society in Spanish Florida*, University of Illinois Press 1999

Laughton, J.K.; Mathews, Thomas, *Dictionary of National Biography 1676–1751*, Oxford University Press 1894

Lavery, Brian, *Empire of the Seas: How the Navy Forged The Modern World*, Conway 2009

Mallinson, Allan, *The Making of the British Army: From the English Civil War to the War on Terror*, Bantam Books 2011

Marley, David, *Wars of the Americas: A Chronology of Armed Conflict in the New World 1492–1997*, ABC ClIO 1998

Mathews, Thomas, *A Narrative of the Proceedings of His Majesty's Fleet in the Mediterranean*, J. Millan, London 1744

Richmond, H.W., Rear Admiral, *The Navy in the War of 1739–48 Vol. 1*, Cambridge University Press 1920

Richmond, Theo, *The Navy in the War of 1739–48 Vol. 3*, Cambridge University Press 1920

Rodger, N.A.M., *The Command of the Ocean: A Naval History of Britain 1649–1815*, W.W. Norton & Co 2004

Schama, Simon, *A History of Britain 1603–1776, The British Wars Vol. 2*, BBC Books 2001

Stanhope, Lord Philip, *History of England from the Peace of Utrecht to the Peace of Paris, Vol. II*. Appleton & Co 1849

Thomas, David, *Battles & Honours of the Royal Navy*, Pen and Sword 1998

Tunstall, Brian, *Naval Warfare in the Age of Sail, the Evolution of Fighting Tactics*, Conway Maritime Press 2001

India, Afghanistan, Persia

Sikhchic.com. *The Saga of Saragarhi*. Jeyaganesh Gopalsamy. https://bit.ly/2AD0C8w. Retrieved 27 April 2016

Samana. *The British Empire*. https://bit.ly/2qmz8xW. Retrieved 27 April 2017

India Post. *The Battle of Saragarhi*. https://bit.ly/2Q7QpWQ. J.S. Retrieved 27 April 2017

Atwood, Rodney, *The March to Kandahar: Roberts in Afghanistan*, Pen and Sword 2008

Barczewski, Stephanie, *Heroic Failure and the British*, Yale University Press 2016

Burton, Reginald George, *The First and Second Sikh Wars: An Official British Army History*, Westholme Publishing 2008

Churchill, Winston, *My Early Life*, Eland 2000

Churchill, Winston, *The Story of the Malakand Field Force*, Rosetta Books 2013

Collett, Nigel, *The Butcher of Amritsar: General Reginald Dyer*, Hambledon Continuum 2007

Cooper, G.S., *The Anglo Maratha Campaigns and the Contest for India: The Struggle for Control of the South Asian Military Economy*, Cambridge University Press 2003

Dalrymple, William, *The Return of a King: The Battle for Afghanistan*, Bloomsbury 2013

Forbes, Archibald, *The Afghan Wars 1839–42 and 1878–80*, Book Jungle 2008

Fortescue, John William, *A History of the British Army Vol. XII*, Macmillan and Co 1927

Hernon, Ian., *Britain's Forgotten Wars: Colonial Campaigns of the 19th Century*, Sutton Publishing 2003

Hibbert, Christopher, *The Great Mutiny: India 1857*, Penguin Books 1980

Holmes, Richard, *Wellington: The Iron Duke*, Harper Collins 2003

Hunt, Captain G.H., *Outram and Havelocks Persian Campaign*, Naval and Military Press 2009

Judd, Denis, *The Lion and the Tiger, The Rise and Fall of the British Raj, 1600–1947*, Oxford University Press 2004

Macdonald Fraser, Georg, *Flashman* (Novel), Barrie and Jenkins 1969

Macdonald Fraser, George, *Flashman and the Mountain of Light* (Novel), Harper Collins 2015

Macfarlane, Charles, *Our Indian Empire*, Google Ebook

Malleson, G.B., *The Decisive Battles of India from 1746 to 1849*, First Rate Publishers, Pyrrhus Press

Mallinson, Allan, *The Making of the British Army; From the English Civil War to the War on Terror*, Bantam Press 2009

Millar, Simon, *Assaye 1803: Wellington's First and 'Bloodiest' Victory*, Osprey Publishing 2006

Navarane, Cdr M.S., *Battles of the Honourable East India Company: Making of the Raj*, APH Publishing 2006

Paget, George, Marquess of Anglesey, *A History of British Cavalry 1816–1919: 1851–71 Vol. 2*, Pen and Sword Books 1993

Richards, D.S., *Cawnpore and Lucknow: A Tale of Two Sieges*, Pen and Sword 2007

Robson, Brian, *The Road to Kabul: The Second Anglo Afghan War 1878–1881*, Spellmount 1980

Pakenham, Thomas, *The Scramble for Africa*, Abacus 1991

Saul, David, *The Indian Mutiny: 1857*, Penguin 2003

Schama, Simon. *A History of Britain Vol. 2: The British Wars 1603–1776*, BBC Books 2001

Schama, Simon, *A History of Britain Vol. 3*, BBC Books 2002

Sherry, Frank, *The Golden Age of Piracy*, Quill William Morrow (NY) 1986

Singh, Colonel Kanwaljit and Ahluwalia, H.S., *Saragarhi Battalion: Ashes to Glory*, Lancer 1987

Tyagi, Vidya Prakash, *Martial Races of Undivided India*, Kalpaz Publications 2009

Wright, William, *Warriors of the Queen: Fighting Generals of the Victorian Age*, The History Press 2014

Yorke, Edmund, *Battle Story: Maiwand 1880*, Spellmount 2013

French & Indian War/Seven Years War

Morgan Creek Productions. *Last of the Mohicans*, 1992.

Andersen, Fred., *Crucible of War: The Seven Years War and the Fate of Empire in British North America 1754–66*, Faber and Faber 2000

Borneman, Walter. *The French and Indian War.* Harper Collins 200

Brumwell, Stephen, *Redcoats: The British Soldier and War in the Americas 1756–63*, Cambridge University Press 2006

Chartrand, Rene; Courcell, Patrice, *Ticonderoga,1758: Montcalm's Victory Against All Odds*, Osprey Publishing 2000

Fortescue, Sir John William, *A History of the British Army Vol. II (1714–1763)*, Pickle Partners 2013

Macleod, Peter, *The Canadian Iroquois and the Seven Years War*, Canadian War Museum 2012

Mallinson, Allan, *The Making of the British Army: From the English Civil War to the War on Terror*, Bantam Books 2011

Nester, William R., *The Epic Battles for the Ticonderoga, 1758*, State University of New York Press 2008

Preston, David, *Braddocks Defeat: The Battle of the Monongahela and the Road to Revolution*, Oxford University Press 2015

Schama, Simon, *A History of Britain 1603–1776 The British Wars Vol. 2*, BBC Books 2001

Szabo, Franz, *The Seven Years War in Europe 1756–1763*, Routledge 2007

American War of Independence

History.com. *Battle of Quebec (1775)*. https://bit.ly/2Q8jHoj. Retrieved 11 May 2015

Lampman, Charles. *Battle of Vincennes, Victory for G.W. Clark.* Sons of Liberty Chapter. https://bit.ly/2yDyQak. Retrieved 15 October 2016

Lengel, Edward G., *Bayonets at Midnight: The Battle of Stony Point.* Military History Weider History Group, 2009. https://bit.ly/2SzohNJ. Retrieved 12 July 2015

American Revolutionary War. https://bit.ly/2qkizCH Retrieved 18 March 2017

Shipley, Robert. *The Face of Defeat*. https://bit.ly/2SvHShY. *Jersey Evening Post*, 5 January 2007. Retrieved 20 March 2017

Bruce, Anthony; Cogar, William, *Encyclopaedia of Naval History*, Fitzroy Dearborn Publishers 1998
Carbone, Gerald, *Washington: Lessons in Leadership*, Palgrave MacMillan 2010
Dearden, Paul F., *The Rhode Island Campaign of 1778: Inauspicious Dawn of Alliance*, Rhode Island Publications Society 1980
Gabriel, Michael P., *Major General Richard Montgomery: The Making of an American Hero*, Rosemont Publishing and Printing 2002
Ketchum, Richard, *Saratoga: Turning Point of America's Revolutionary War*, Henry Holt & Co 1997
Ketchum, Richard, *The Winter Soldiers: The Battles for Trenton and Princeton*, Holt Paperbacks 1999
Judd, Denis, *The Lion and the Tiger, The Rise and Fall of the British Raj, 1600–1947*, Oxford University Press 2004
Larrabee, Harold Atkins, *Decision at the Chesapeake*, William Kimber 1965
Mahan, Alfred, Captain, *Major Operations of the Royal Navy 1762–1783*, Little, Brown and Company 1898 (or Palala Press 2016)
Malleson, G.B., *The Decisive Battles of India from 1746 to 1849*, First Rate Publishers, Pyrrhus Press
Mallinson, Allan, *The Making of the British Army: From the English Civil War to the War on Terror*, Bantam Press 2011
McGuire, Thomas, *The Philadelphia Campaign: Germantown and the Roads to Valley Forge*, Stackpole Books 2007
Miller, Nathan, *Sea of Glory: The Continental Navy Fights for Independence 1775–1783*, McKay and Co 1974
Morrissey, Brendan, *The American Revolution: The Struggle for National Independence*, Salamander 2001
—, *Saratoga 1777: The Turning Point of a Revolution*, Osprey Publishing 2000
Nelson, James, *Benedict Arnold's Navy: The Ragtag Fleet that Lost the Battle of Lake Champlain but won the American Revolution*, McGraw-Hill 2006
Nelson, Paul, *Sir Charles Grey, First Earl Grey: Royal Soldier, Family Patriarch*, Associated University Presses 1996
Palmer, Michael A., *Command at Sea: Naval Command and Control Since the Sixteenth Century*, Harvard University Press 2005
Rochfort, Lieut-Colonel W.C., *The Invasion of Jersey. With the Proceedings and Sentence of the Court Martial held on Major Corbet, The Lieut-Governor. C Le Feuvre, Beresford St et al* 1852
Rodger, N.A.M., *The Command of the Ocean: A Naval History of Britain 1649–1815*, Penguin Books 2004
Schama, Simon. *A History of Britain: The British Wars 1603–1776 Vol. 2*, BBC Books 2001
Shelton, Hal T., *General Richard Montgomery and the American Revolution: From Redcoat to Rebel*, New York University Press 1994
Stanley, George F.G., *Canada Invaded 1775–1776*, Historical Publications, Canadian War Museum, Hakkert 1977
Tonsetic, Robert, *Special Operations in the American Revolution*, Casemate Publishing 2013
Urban, Mark, *Fusiliers: How the British Army Lost America but Learned How to Fight*, Faber and Faber 2008
US Department of the Interior, *George Rogers Clark and the Winning of the Old North West*, Penny Hill Press 2016
Ward, Christopher, *The War of the Revolution*, Skyhorse Publishing 2011
Willis, Sam, *Fighting at Sea in the Eighteenth Century: The Art of Sailing Warfare*, Boydell Press 2018
Unknown Wikipedians, *The New York and New Jersey Campaign*, PediaPress

French Revolution and Napoleonic Wars
The Dawlish Chronicles: Duty and Daring in the Heyday of Empire. *Duel in the Dark: Frigates Blanche and Pique 1795*. https://bit.ly/2yH0t26 Retrieved 24 February 2016
Rickard, J. (16 January 2006) *French Invasion of Egypt, 1798–1801*, https://bit.ly/2Q8I84O. Retrieved 26 February 2016
Tucker, John Goulston Price, *A Narrative of the Operations of a Small British Force under the Command of Brigadier General Sir Samuel Auchmuty Employed in the Reduction of Monte Video on the River Plate*, John Stockdale 1807. Retrieved 2 March 2016. https://bit.ly/2Sz2RR4. Retrieved 2 March 2016
Rasmussen, Jens Rahbek. *The Bombardment of Copenhagen*. https://bit.ly/2yHaTiC. Retrieved 3 March 2016

Carr, Raymond. *Pistols at Dawn. The Spectator* 26 March 2008. Retrieved 9 March 2016
   Familylifeinspain.com. https://bit.ly/2OhnZrs. Retrieved 4 March 2016
Mazowski, Krzysztof 2008. Historyczne Bitwy F*uengirola 1810 Lord Blayney's Narrative.*
   https://bit.ly/2qlJz4D. Retrieved 14 March 2016

The London Gazette No. 15747. pp. 1309–1310, 20 October 1804. https://bit.ly/2Debufd. Retrieved 29
   February 2016
—, 9 October 1805. https://bit.ly/2Q6Zcs3. Retrieved 29 February 2016

Adkin, Mark, *The Trafalgar Companion*, Aurum Press 2005
Arnold, David, *The Age of Discovery 1400–1600 2nd Edition*, Routledge 2002
Ballantyne, Ian, *HMS Rodney: The Famous Ships of the Royal Navy Series*, Pen and Sword 2008
Becke, Archibald, *1911 Encyclopaedia Britannica Vol. 28 Waterloo Campaign.* Cambridge University Press.
   Retrieved 24 March 2016
Burleigh, Nina, *Mirage: Napoleon's Scientists and the Unveiling of Egypt*, Harper Perennial 2008
Cole, Juan. *Napoleon's Egypt: Invading the Middle East.* Macmillan 2008
Conolly, S.J., *Divided Kingdom: Ireland 1630–1800*, Oxford University Press 1812
Couzens, Tim, *Battles of South Africa*, David Philip Publishers 2004
Doyle, William, *The French Revolution: A Very Short Introduction (Very Short Introductions)*, Oxford
   University Press 2001
Dubois, Laurent, *A Colony of Citizens: Revolution and Slave Emancipation in the French Caribbean,
   1787–1804*, University of North Carolina Press 2004
Fletcher, Ian, *The Waters of Oblivion: The British Invasion of the Rio de la Plata 1806–07*, Spellmount 2007
Fortescue, Hon Sir John William, *A History of the British Army Vol .VII (1809–1810)*, Pickle Partners
   2014
—, *Vol. VIII 1811–1812*, Macmillan 1917 (Pickle Partners 2014)
—, *Vol. IX (1813–1814)*, Pickle Partners Publishing 2014
—, *Vol. X (1814–1815)*, Pickle Partners Publishing 2014
Fremont-Barnes, Gregory, T*he French Revolutionary Wars*, Osprey Publishing 2001
Fremont Barnes, Gregory; Fisher, Todd, *The Napoleonic Wars: The Rise and Fall of an Empire*, Osprey
   Publishing 2004
Grainger, John D., *British Campaigns in the South Atlantic 1805–1807*, Pen and Sword Military 2015
Henderson, James, *The Frigates: An Account of the Lighter Warships of the Napoleonic Wars*, Leo Cooper (Pen
   and Sword) 1994
Herold, Christopher, *Bonaparte in Egypt*, Fireship Press 2009
Holmes, Richard, *Wellington: The Iron Duke*, Harper Collins 2003
Hughes, Ben, *The British Invasion of River Plate 1806–7: How the Redcoats were humbled and a Nation Was
   Born*, Pen & Sword 2013
James, William; Chamier Frederick, *The Naval History of Great Britain: From the Declaration of War by
   France in 1793 to the Accession of George IV, Vol. 1*, Ulan Press 2012
Judd, Denis, *The Lion and the Tiger, The Rise and Fall of the British Raj*, Oxford University Press 2004.
Lambert, Andrew, *Nelson : Britannia's God of War*, Faber and Faber 2004
Lavery, Brian, *Empire of the Seas: How the Navy Forged The Modern World*, Conway 2009.
Mackesy, Piers, *British Victory in Egypt: The End of Napoleon's Conquest*, Tauris Parke Paperbacks 2010
Malleson, G.B., *The Decisive Battles of India*, Forgotten Books
Mallinson, Allan, *The Making of the British Army: from the English Civil War to the War on Terror*, Bantam
   Press 2011
Munch-Petersen, Thomas, *Defying Napoleon: How Britain Bombarded Copenhagen and Seized the Danish
   Fleet in 1807*, The History Press 2007
Napier, William, *History of the War in the Peninsular and in the South of France from the Year 1807 to the
   Year 1814, Vol. III*, W.J. Widdleton 1864.
Navarane, Wg Cdr M.S., *The Battles of the Honourable East India Company: Making of the Raj*, APH
   Publishing 2006.

Northcote Parkinson, C., *War in the Eastern Seas 1793–1815*, George Allen & Unwin 1954

Oman, Charles, *A History of the Peninsular War Volume I: December 1807–1809*, Oxford Clarendon Press 1902

—, *A History of the Peninsular War Volume IV: December 1810–December 1811*, Greenhill Books 2004

Oman, Charles, *Wellington's Army, 1809–1814*, Greenhill Books 1993

Padfield, Peter, *Nelson's War*, Thistle Publishing 2015

Pagnet, Julian, *Wellington's Peninsular War: Battles and Battlefields*, Pen and Sword 2009

Pakenham, Thomas, *The Scramble for Africa*, Abacus 1991

Palmer, Michael A., *Command at Sea: Naval Command and Control Since the Sixteenth Century*, Harvard University Press 2005

Parkinson, Roger, *The Peninsular War*, Wordsworth Editions 2000

Pocock, Tom, *Horatio Nelson*, Thistle Publishing 2013

Rodger, N.A.M., *The Command of the Ocean: A Naval History of Britain 1649–1815*, Penguin Books 2004

Schama, Simon, *A History of Britain: The British Wars 1603–1776, Vol, 2*, BBC Books 2001

—, *A History of Britain: The Fate of Empire 1776–2000, Vol. 3*, BBC Books 2002

Watson, Bruce, *When Soldiers Quit: Studies in Military Disintegration*, Greenwood Publishing 1997

Wilson, R.T. Sir, *A Narrative of the Expedition to Egypt under Sir Ralph Abercrombie*, Google Ebooks Retrieved 28 February 2016

American War of 1812

Naval History Blog US Naval Institute. *The Battle of Lake Borgne.* https://bit.ly/2DgoGR9 Retrieved 30 October 2016

Forester, C.S. *The Age of Fighting Sail: The Story of the Naval War of 1812*, Chapman Billies 1956

Hickey, Donald R., *The War of 1812: A Forgotten Conflict*, Bicentennial Edition, University of Illinois 2012

Hitsman, J. Mackay, *The Incredible War of 1812: A Military History*, University of Toronto Press 1965

Mahon, John K., *The War of 1812*, De Capo Press 1972

Roosevelt, Theodore. *The Fire on the Ocean: Naval War of 1812.* Google ebook. e-artnow 2018. (G.P. Putnams & sons Publishers 1882)

Maori Wars

Buick, Thomas, *New Zealand's First War: Or the Rebellion of Hone Heke*, Cambridge University Press 2011

Cowan, James, *The New Zealand Wars: A History of the Maori Campaigns and the Pioneering Period*, Forgotten Books 2015

Dalley, Bronwyn; Phillips, Jock, *Going Public: The Changing Face of New Zealand History*, Auckland University Press 2001

Crimean War

Brighton, Terry, *Hell Riders: The Truth about the Charge of the Light Brigade*, Penguin Books 2005

Figes, Orlando, *The Crimean War: A History*, Picador Publishing 2012

Mallinson, Allan, *The Making of the British Army: from the English Civil War to the War on Terror*, Bantam Press 2011

Sweetman, John, *The Crimean War*, Osprey Publishing 2001

Abyssinia (Ethiopia)

The British Empire, Abyssinia https://bit.ly/2qlYuM4. Retrieved 10 April 2017

The British Empire, Abyssinia https://bit.ly/2DeEXpo. Retrieved 10 April 2017

Adejumobi, Saheed, *The History of Ethiopia*, Greenwood Publishing 2007

Henze, Paul, *Layers of Time : A History of Ethiopia*, Hurst & Co 2000

Kingston, W.H.G., *Our Soldiers: Gallant Deeds of the British Army during Victoria's Reign*, Library of Alexandria

Macdonald Fraser, George, *Flashman on the March* (Novel), Harper Collins 2005

Stanley, Henry Morton, *Coomassie and Magdala: The Story of Two British Campaigns in Africa*, Sampsom Low, Marston, Low & Searle 1874

Murrell, Nathaniel *et al*, *Chanting Down Babylon: The Rastafari Reader*, Temple University Press 1998

Ashanti Wars

Arnold, David, *The Age of Discovery 1400–1600*, Routledge 2002

Claridge, William Walton, *A History of the Gold Coast and Ashanti Vol. 1*, Forgotten Books 2015

Diffie, B.W; Winius, G.D., *Foundations of the Portuguese Empire 1415–1580*, University of Minnesota Press 1977.

Edgerton, Robert. *The Fall of the Asante Empire: The Hundred Years War for Africa's Gold Coast*, Simon & Schuster 1995

George, Claude, *The Rise of British West Africa: Compromising the Early History of the Colony of Sierra Leone, the Gambia, Lagos, Gold Coast etc.*, Frank Cass & Co 1968/ Psychology Press

Newman, James L., *Imperial Footprint: Henry Morton Stanleys African Journeys*, Brasseys 2004.

Raugh, Harold, *The Victorians at War 1815–1914: An Encyclopaedia of British Military History*, ABC CLIO 2004

Stanley, Henry Morton, *Coomassie and Magdala: The Story of Two British Campaigns in Africa*, Low & Searle 1874

Vandervort, Bruce, *Wars of Imperial Conquest*, Routledge 1998

Zulu War

David, Saul, *Zulu: The Heroism and the Tragedy of the Zulu War 1879*, Penguin 2005

Greaves, Adrian; Mkhize, Xolani, *The Tribe that Washed its Spears: The Zulus at War*, Pen and Sword Military 2013

Knight, Ian, *The National Army Museum Book of the Zulu War*, Pan Books 2004

Mallinson, Allan, *The Making of the British Army: From the English Civil War to the War on Terror*, Bantam Press 2011

Pakenham, Thomas, *The Scramble for Africa*, Abacus Books 1991.

Penn Symons, Captain William, *Rorke's Drift Diary: An Account of the Battles of Isandlwana and Rorke's Drift Zululand 22nd January 1879*, Unicorn Publishing 2018

Egypt/Sudan

Asher, Michael, *Khartoum: The Ultimate Imperial Adventure*, Penguin 2006

Callwell, Colonel C.E., *Small Wars: Their Principles and Practice*, University of Nebraska 1996

Churchill, Winston, *The River War*, Prion Books 2000

Featherstone, Donald, *Tel El Kebir 1882: Wolseley's Conquest of Egypt*, Osprey Publishing 1993

—, *Khartoum 1885: Gordon's Last Stand*, Osprey Publishing 1993

Keown-Boyd, Henry, *A Good Dusting: The Sudan Campaigns 1883–1899*, Leo Cooper, Secker & Warburg 1986

Pakenham, Thomas, *The Scramble for Africa*, Abacus 1991.

Mallinson, Allan, *The Making of the British Army: from the English Civil War to the War on Terror*, Bantam Press 2011

Nichol, Fergus, *The Mahdi of Sudan and the Death of General Gordon*, Sutton Publishing 2004

Slatin, Rudolf Carl, *Fire and Sword in the Sudan: A Personal Narrative of Fighting and Serving the Dervishes 1879–1895*, Library of Alexandria.

Zimbabwe (Rhodesia)

Burnham, Frederick Russell, *Shangani Patrol. Westminster Gazette*, 8/9 January 1895

Gale, W.D., *Zambezi Sunrise: How Civilisation Came to Rhodesia and Nyasaland*, Howard Timmins 1958

Lumb, S.V., *A Short History of Central and Southern Africa 2nd Edition*, Cambridge University Press 1962

Marston, Roger, *Own Goals: National Pride and Defeat in War: The Rhodesian Experience*, Paragon Publishing 2009

Pakenham, Thomas, *The Scramble for Africa*, Abacus 1991

Van Wyk, P., *Burnham: King of Scouts*, Trafford Publishing 2003

First Boer War

Laband, John, *The Transvaal Rebellion : The First Boer War 1880–1881*, Routledge 2014

Mallinson, Allan, *The Making of the British Army: from the English Civil War to the War on Terror*, Bantam Press 2011

Pakenham, Thomas, *The Boer War*, Abacus 1979

Pakenham, Thomas, *The Scramble for Africa*, Abacus 1991

Raugh, Harold, *The Victorians at War, 1815–1914: An Encyclopaedia of British Military History*, ABC-CLIO 2004

Second Boer War

Hawkesbury, John, Herdengkingsritte, *Witness to Rietfontein Vol. 15 No. 5*, June 2012. https://bit.ly/2zqU9f5. Retrieved 29 April 2017

Battle of Vaal Krantz. Otago Daily Times, Issue 11717, 26 April 1900. Retrieved 4 May 2017

Viljoen, Benjamin, *My Reminiscences of the Anglo Boer War*. https://bit.ly/2qiU8p8. Retrieved 7 May 2017

Ash, Chris, *The If Man : Dr Leander Starr Jameson, the Inspiration for Kipling's Masterpiece*, Helion & Co 2012

Bridgland, Tony, *Field Gun Jack Versus the Boers: The Royal Navy in South Africa 1899–1900*, Pen and Sword 1998

Churchill, Winston, *My Early Life*, Eland 2000

Conan Doyle, Arthur, *The Great Boer War: Easyread Edition*. Readhowyouwant 2008

Digby-Thomas, Roy, *Two Generals: Buller and Botha in the Boer War*, Authorhouse 2012

Grehan, John; Mace, Martin, *The Boer War 1899–1902: Ladysmith, Magersfontein, Spion Kop, Kimberley, Mafeking*, Pen and Sword 2014.

Heaton, Colin; Lewis, Anne-Marie, *Four-War Boer: The Century and Life of Pieter Arnoldus Krueler*, Casemate 2014

Hole, Hugh Marshall, *The Jameson Raid*, Philip Alan 1930

Kipling, Rudyard, *The Collected Poems of Rudyard Kipling: The Lesson 1899–1902 (The Boer War)*, Wordsworth Editions 1994

Lumb, S.V.A., *Short History of Central and Southern Africa 2nd Edition*, Cambridge University Press 1962

Mahan, Captain A.T., *Story of the War in South Africa, 1899–1900*, Lulu 1900

Mallinson, Allan, *The Making of the British Army: from the English Civil War to the War on Terror*, Bantam Press 2011

Miller, Stephen, *Lord Methuen and the British Army: Failure and Redemption in South Africa*, Routledge 2005

—, *Volunteers of the Veld: Britain's Citizen Soldiers and the South African War 1899–1902*, University of Oklahoma Press 2007

Pakenham Thomas, *The Boer War*, Abacus 1992

—, *The Scramble for Africa*, Abacus 1991

Sandys, Celia, *Churchill Wanted Dead or Alive*, Harper Collins 2000

Spiers, Edward, *Letters from Kimberley: Eyewitness Accounts from the South African War*, Frontline Books 2013

Stewart, William, *The Embattled General: Sir Richard Turner and the First World War*, McGill-Queens University Press 2015

Wessels, Andre, *The Anglo Boer War 1889–1902: White Man's War, Black Man's War, Traumatic War*, Sun Press 2011

The Great War

Film Documentary – *The Red Baron*. Questar Entertainment 1988

Muriel Felton. London Gazette supplement 30576 page 3287 12 March 1918. https://www.thegazette.co.uk/London/issue/30576/supplement/1. Retrieved 11 April 2017

Allenby, Edmund, *A brief record of the advance of the Egyptian Expeditionary Force.* https://archive.org/details/briefrecordofadv00grearich/page/n1. Retrieved 16 May 2016

Duffy, Michael. 2009. *Air Aces of World War One* www.firstworldwar.com/features/aces.htm. Retrieved 27 May 2016

firstworld war.com. *Battle of Epehy.* www.firstworldwar.com/battles/epehy.htm. Michael Duffy 2009
  Retrieved 12 June 2016
Rickard, J. (27 August 2007), *Second Battle of the Somme, 21 March–4 April 1918* http://www.
  historyofwar.org/articles/battles_sommeII.htm. Retrieved 26 May 2016
war.com/battles/epehy.htm. Michael Duffy 2009.12 June Retrieved 2016

Anderson, Ross, *The Forgotten Front: The East African Campaign 1914–1918*, Spellmount 2014
Anderson, Scott, *Lawrence in Arabia: War, Deceit, Imperial Folly and the Making of the Modern Middle East*,
  Atlantic Books 2014
Barker, A.J., *The First Iraq War 1914–1918: Britain's Mesopotamian Campaign*, Enigma Books 2009.
Bristow, Adrian, *A Serious Disappointment: Battle of Aubers Ridge 1915 and the SubsequentMunitions
  Scandal*, Leo Cooper 1995
Cameron, David. *Gallipoli: The Final Battles and Evacuation of Anzac*, Big Sky Publishing 2011
Carradice, Phil, *First World War in the Air*, Amberley Publishing 2013
Carver, Field Marshal Lord, *The National Army Museum Book of the Turkish Front 1914–1918: The
  Campaigns at Gallipoli, in Mesopotamia and in Palestine*, Pan Books 2004
Daley, Paul, *Beersheba: A Journey Through Australia's Forgotten War*, Melbourne University Press 2009
Davis, Paul K., *Ends and Means: The British Mesopotamian Campaign and Commission*, Associated
  University Press 1994
Faulkner, Neil, *Lawrence of Arabia's War: The Arabs, the British and the Remaking of the Middle East in
  WWI*, Yale University Press 2016
Foden, Giles, *Mimi and Toutou Go Forth: The Bizarre Battle for Lake Tanganyika*, Penguin Books 2005
Ford, Roger, *Eden to Armageddon: World War One in the Middle East*, Pegasus Books 2011
French, John, *Complete Despatches of Lord French 1914–1916*, Andrews UK 2012 (Digital)
Friedman, Norman, *Fighting the Great War at Sea: Strategy, Tactic and Technology*, Seaforth Publishing
  2014
Grainger, John, *The Battle for Palestine 1917*, Boydell Press 2006
Hamilton, Captain Lord Ernest, *The First Seven Divisions, Being a Detailed Account of the Fighting from
  Mons to Ypres*, Pickle Partners Publishing 2013
Harvey, Major Kenneth, *Battle of Tanga, German East Africa 1914*, Pickle Partners Publishing 2014
Hart, Peter, *Bloody April: Slaughter in the Skies over Arras, 1917*, Cassell Kindle
Hewlett, Rose, *Frampton Remembers World War One*, Amberley Publishing 2016
Holmes Richard, *The Western Front*, BBC Books 1999
Horsfall, Jack; Cave, Nigel, *Cambrai: The Right Hook: Hindenberg Line* (Battleground Europe), Pen and
  Sword 1998
Kappelmann, Major Michael Andrew, *Parallel Campaigns: The British in Mesopotamia, 1914–1920 and the
  United States in Iraq, 2003–2004*, Pickle Partners Publishing 2014
Kendall, Paul, *The Zeebrugge Raid 1918: A Story of Courage and Sacrifice Told Through Newspaper Reports,
  Official Documents and the Accounts of Those Who Were There*, Frontline Books 2016
Korda, Michael, *Hero: The Life & Legend of Lawrence of Arabia*, Aurum Press 2012
Laffin, John, *The Agony of Gallipoli*, Sutton Publishing 2005
Lake, Deborah, *Zeebrugge and Ostend Raids*, Pen and Sword 2002
Lavery, Brian, *Empire of the Seas*, Conway Publishing 2009
Liddle, Peter; Richardson, Mathew, *1914: Voices from the Battlefields*, Pen and Sword 2013
Macdonald, Lyn, *1915: The Death of Innocence*, Headline Books 1994
—, *Somme*, Penguin Books 1993
—, Lyn, *To the Last Man: Spring 1918*, Penguin Books 1998
Mallinson, Allan, *The Making of the British Army: from the English Civil War to the War on Terror*, Bantam
  Press 2011
Massie, Robert, *Castles of Steel: Britain, Germany and the Winning of the Great War at Sea*, Head of Zeus
  2013
Morrow, John Howard, *The Great War in the Air: Military Aviation from 1909 to 1921*, University of
  Alabama Press 2009
Nield, Robert, *China's Foreign Places : The Foreign Presence in China in the Treaty Port Era 1840–1943*,
  Hong Kong University Press 2015

Oldham, Peter, *The Hindenburg Line*, Pen and Sword 2000

Paice, Edward, *Tip & Run: The Untold Tragedy of the Great War in Africa*, Phoenix 2008

Pakenham, Thomas, *The Scramble for Africa*, Abacus 1992

Passingham, Ian, *Pillars of Fire: The Battle of Messines Ridge 1917*, Spellmount 2012

Richthofen, Manfred, *The Red Baron*, Pen and Sword, Aviation 2009

Sheffield, Gary, *Forgotten Victory, The First World War: Myths and Realities*, Review 2002

—, *The Somme*, Cassell 2003

Snow, Peter and Dan, *World's Twentieth Century Battlefields*, BBC Books 2007

Steel, Nigel; Hart, Peter, *Passchendaele: The Sacrificial Ground*, Cassell Military Paperbacks 2001

Strachan, Hew, *The First World War Volume One To Arms*, Oxford University Press 2003

Sutherland, Alasdair, *Somewhere in Blood Soaked France: The Diary of Corporal Angus Mackay, Royal Scots, Machine Gun Corps 1914–1917*, Spellmount 2014

Tomaselli, Phil, *The Battle of Lys 1918: Givenchy and the River Lawe*, Pen and Sword Battleground 2011

Tucker, Spencer, *The European Powers in the First World War: An Encyclopaedia*, Routledge 2013

Warner, Philip, *The Battle of Loos*, Wordsworth Editions 2000

—, *Zeebrugge Raid*, Pen and Sword 2008

Willcocks, General Sir James, *With the Indians in France*, Constable and Company 1920

Wilson, H.W.; Hammerton J.A., *The Great War: The Standard History of the All Europe Conflict Vol. 1*, Amalgamated Press Ltd 1915

—, *Vol. 2*, Amalgamated Press Ltd 1915

—, *Vol 3*, Amalgamated Press Ltd 1915

—, *Vol. 4*, Amalgamated Press Ltd 1915

—, *Vol. 5*, Amalgamated Press Ltd 1915

—, *Vol. 6*, Amalgamated Press Ltd 1916

—, *Vol. 7*, Amalgamated Press Ltd 1916

—, *Vol. 8*, Amalgamated Press Ltd 1917

—, *Vol. 9*, Amalgamated Press Ltd 1917

—, *Vol. 10*, Amalgamated Press Ltd 1918

—, *Vol. 11*, Amalgamated Press Ltd 1918

—, *Vol. 12*, Amalgamated Press Ltd 1919

—, *Vol. 13*, Amalgamated Press Ltd 1919

Woodward, David, *Hell in the Holy Land: World War I in the Middle East*, University Press of Kentucky 2006

The Second World War

Isaacs, Jeremy. Film/Documentary – The World at War: *Banzai! Japan 1931–1942*. Thames Television 1973

Isaacs, Jeremy. Film/Documentary – The World at War: *The Desert: North Africa 1940–43*. Thames Television 1974.

Osmond, Louise. Film Documentary. *The Blitz : London's Longest Night*. Darlow Smithson Productions 2005

Anderson, Charles. *WWII Campaigns, Tunisia 17th November 1942 to 13th May 1943*. https://bit.ly/2CRAOH0. Retrieved 9 September 2016

Armoured Aircraft Carriers in World War II. *Operation Excess*. https://bit.ly/2Df9vHw. Retrieved 27 May 2017

The Dambusters. *Bergen*. https://bit.ly/2zh6G4p. Retrieved 30 October 2016

The Desert Rats. *Engagements 1945*. https://bit.ly/2DdRBoJ. Retrieved 31 October 2016

Fraser, Bruce. *Sinking the German Battle Cruiser Scharnhorst. London Gazette* supplement 38038 page 3703 5 August 1947 https://bit.ly/2SvMWTw. Retrieved 12 September 2016

Garzke, William & Dulin, Robert. B*ismarck's Final Battle Part One and Two*. Warship International Nos 1994. https://bit.ly/2SzstNu Originally Retrieved 5 July 2016

Kappes, Irwin J. Historyonline.com. *Mers El Kebir*. www.militaryhistoryonline.com/wwii/articles/merselkebir.aspx. Retrieved 17 June 2016

Mackenzie, Gregory. Ahoy – Mac's Web Log. *Battle of the River Plate*. https://bit.ly/2qlgmXv. Retrieved 4 June 2016

Sinfield, Peter. Naval Historical Society of Australia 2006. *Action off Endau*. https://bit.ly/2EUPAiW Retrieved 20 July 2016

St Michaels – The Old Cathedral (Coventry) https://bit.ly/2CSKh0H. Retrieved 28 June 2016

The National Archives. *The Thousand Bomber Raids 30/31 May Cologne*. https://bit.ly/2SyEEKz. Retrieved 5 September 2016

The National Archives. *The Thousand Bomber Raids 28th July Hamburg*. https://bit.ly/2AD2ez6. Retrieved 6 September 2016

Thompson, Julian. *The Dieppe Raid*. BBC History 2011 https://bbc.in/2CQB9d6. Retrieved 5 August 2016

Tweedie, Neil. *Cockleshell Heroes: The Truth at Last*. Daily Telegraph 28th October 2010 https://bit.ly/2yJODED. Retrieved 1 September 2016

London Gazette 22 June 1948 supplement 38331 pages 3683, 3687 and 3689. *Raid on Military and Economic Objectives in the Lofoten Islands*. https://bit.ly/2OgL260 Retrieved 4 July 2016

London Gazette 27 February 1942 supplement 35474 Page 1007. *Channel Dash Eugene Esmonde* https://bit.ly/2qjk8AD. Retrieved 28 July 2016

Adams, John, *The Battle for Western Europe Fall 1944: An Operational Assessment*, Indiana University Press 2010

Addison, Paul; Crang, Jeremy, *Firestorm: The Bombing of Dresden 1945*, Pimlico 2006

Allen, Louis, *Burma, the Longest War*, Phoenix Press 2002

Allen, Louis, *Singapore 1941–1942*, Frank Cass 2005

Ambrose, Stephen, *D-DAY: June 6.1944 The Battle for the Normandy Beaches*, Pocket Books 2002

Arch Getty, John, *Origins of the Great Purges. The Soviet Communist Party Reconsidered 1933–38*. Cambridge University Press 1985

Ashdown, Paddy, *A Brilliant Little Operation: The Cockleshell Heroes and the Most Courageous Raid of WW2*, Aurum Press 2013

Backer, Steve, *Bismarck and Tirpitz*, Seaforth Publishing 2008

Bailey, Roderick, *Forgotten Voices of D-Day*, Ebury Press 2010

Banham, Tony, *Not the Slightest Chance: The Defence of Hong Kong, 1941*, UBC Press 2003

Bayly, Christopher; Harper, Timothy. *Forgotten Armies: The Fall of British Asia, 1941–1945*. Harvard University Press 2005

Beale, Peter. *The Great Mistake: Battle for Antwerp and Beveland Peninsular September 1944*, Sutton Publishing 2004

Beevor, Anthony, *Crete: The Battle and the Resistance*, Penguin Books 1992

Bell, P.M.H., *The Origins of the Second World War in Europe*, Third Edition, Routledge 2007

Bennett, David, *A Magnificent Disaster: The Failure of Market Garden, The Arnhem Operation*, Casemate Publishing 2011

Bishop, Patrick. *Fighter Boys: Saving Britain 1940*, Harper Collins 2003

Bowman, Martin, *Battlefield Bombers: Deep Sea Attack*, Pen and Sword Aviation 2014

Bradt, Hilary, *Madagascar*, Bradt Travel Guides 2011

Brickhill, Paul, *The Great Escape*, Marks and Spencer Military Classics 2003

Burleigh, Michael, *Inside the Third Reich: A New History*, Pan Books 2001

Caddick-Adams, Peter, *Monte Cassino: Ten Armies in Hell*, Oxford University Press 2013

Canwell, Diane; Sutherland, Jon, *Air War Malta: June 1940 to November 1942*, Pen and Sword 2008

Carver, Michael Field Marshal, *El Alamein*, Wordsworth Editions 2000

Chambers, Andy. *Empires in Flames: The Pacific and Far East*, Osprey 2015

Chang, Iris, *The Rape of Nanking*, Basic Books 1997

Clayton, Tim; Craig, Phil, *Finest Hour*, Hodder & Stoughton 1999

Clayton, Tim; Craig, Phil, *End of the Beginning.*, Hodder & Stoughton 2002

Coakley, Robert, *Command Decisions*, Center of Military History United States Army 2002

Copp, Terry, *Cinderella Army – The Canadians in North West Europe 1944–45*, University of Toronto Press 2007

Cox, Jeffrey, *Rising Sun, Falling Skies: The Disastrous Java Sea Campaign of World War II*, Osprey Publishing 2015

Craigie, Robert. *Behind the Japanese Mask: A British Ambassador in Japan 1937–1942*, Routledge 2009

Dildy, Doug, *Dambusters, Operation Chastise 1943*, Osprey 2012

Dorr, Robert, *Air Combat : A History of Fighter Pilots*, Penguin 2006

Dull, Paul, *A Battle History of the Imperial Japanese Navy 1941–1945*, Naval Institute Press 2007

Ellis, John, *Cassino: The Hollow Victory, The Battle for Rome January–June 1944*, Aurum Press 2003

Evans, Richard, *The Third Reich in Power*, Penguin 2005

Ford, Ken, *Run the Gauntlet: The Channel Dash 1942*, Osprey 2012

Ford, Ken, *St Nazaire 1942 : The Great Commando Raid*, Osprey Publishing 2001

Fremantle, Michael, *The Chemist's War 1914–1918*, Royal Society of Chemistry 2014

Gray, Edwyn, *Captains of War: They Fought Beneath the Sea*, Pen and Sword 1988

Greene, Jack; Massigniani, Alessandro, *The Naval War in the Mediterranean 1940–43*, Naval Institute Press 2011

Grehan, John, *Churchill's Secret Invasion: Britain's First Large Scale Combined Offensive 1942*, Pen and Sword 2013

Grehan, John; Mace, Martin, *The Battle for Norway 1940–42*, Pen and Sword 2015

Grehan, John; Mace, Martin, *Fall of Burma*, Pen and Sword 2015

Griffiths, Samuel, *The Battle for Guadalcanal*, University of Illinois Press 2000

Grove, Philip, *Midway 1942*, Brassey's 2004

Groves, Eric, *Sea Battles in Close Up* Vol. II, Naval Institute Press 1993

Guderian, Heinz, *Panzer Leader*, Penguin Books 2000

Halsey Ross, Stewart, *How Roosevelt Failed America in World War Two*, Macfarlane & Co 2006

Harris, Marshal of the RAF Arthur, *Bomber Offensive*, Greenhill Military Paperback 1990

Haskew, Michael, *Encyclopaedia of Elite Forces in the Second World War*, Pen and Sword 2007

Hastings, Max, *Armageddon: The Battle for Germany 1944–45*, Pan Macmillan 2015

Hastings, Max, *Bomber Command*, Pan Books 2010

Hitler, Adolf, *Mein Kampf (My Struggle)*, Jaico Publishing 2016

Horne, Alistair, *To Lose a Battle: France 1940*, Penguin Books 1990

Infield, Glen, *Disaster at Bari*, New English Library Ltd 1976

Jacobs, Peter, *Daring Raids of World War Two: Heroic land, Sea and Air Attacks*, Pen and Sword Aviation 2015

Jameson, William, *Ark Royal: The Life of an Aircraft Carrier at War 1939–41*, Periscope Publishing 2004

Joel, Tony, *The Dresden Firebombing: Memory and the Politics of Commemorating Destruction*, I.B. Tauris 2013

Kaplan, Philip, *World War Two at Sea: The Last Battleships*, Pen and Sword Maritime 2014

King, Benjamin; Biggs, Richard, *Spearhead of Logistics: A History of the United States Army Transportation Corps*, US Army Transportation Center 2001

Konstam, Angus, *The Battle of the North Cape: The Death Ride of the Scharnhorst 1943*, Pen and Sword Maritime 2009

Landsborough, Gordon, *The Battle of the River Plate: The First Naval Battle of the Second World War*, Frontline Books 2016

Leasor, James, *The Unknown Warrior*, House of Stratus 2001

Leasor, James, *Singapore: The Battle that Changed the World*, House of Stratus 2001

Lowe, Keith, *Inferno: The Devastation of Hamburg, 1943*, Viking (Penguin) 2007

Lowry, Thomas; Welham, John, *The Attack on Taranto: Blueprint for Pearl Harbor*, Stackpole Books 2000

Lucas Phillips, C.E., *Cockleshell Heroes*, Pan Books 2000

Lucas Phillips, CE., *The Greatest Raid of All*, Pan Books 2000

Mallinson, Allan, *The Making of the British Army: From the English Civil War to the War on Terror*, Bantam Press 2011

Meserole, Mike, *The Great Escape: The Longest Tunnel*, Sterling Publishing 2008

McKay, Sinclair, *The Secret Life of Bletchley Park: The WWII Codebreaking Centre and the Men and Women Who Worked There*, Aurum Press 2010

Middlebrook, Martin, *Nuremberg Raid: March 30–31 1944*, Pen and Sword Aviation 2015

Middlebrook, Martin; Everitt, Chris, *The Bomber Command War Diaries: An Operational Reference Book*, Pen and Sword 2014

Moffat, John; Rossiter, Mike, *I Sank the Bismarck: Memoirs of a Second World War Navy Pilot*, Bantam Press 2009

Neville, Peter, *Mussolini*, Routledge 2015

Nichol, John; Rennell, Tony, *Tail-End Charlies: The Last Battles of the Bomber War 1944–45*, Viking (Penguin Books) 2004

Niellands, Robin, *The Dieppe Raid: The Story of the Disastrous 1942 Expedition*, Indiana University Press 2005

O'Connor, Christopher, *Taranto: the Raid, the observer, the Aftermath*, Dog Ear Publishing 2010

O'Domhnail, Ronan Gearoid, *Fado Fado: More Tales of Leser Known Irish History*, Matador 2015

O'Hara, Vincent, *In Passage Perilous: Malta and the Convoy Battles of June 1942*, Indiana University Press 2013

—, *The German Fleet at War*, Naval Institute Press 2004

Orange, Vincent, *Coningham: A Biography of Air Marshal Sir Arthur Coningham*, Diane Publishing 1992

Playfair, Major General I.S.O et al, *The Mediterranean and the Middle East: Volume I – The Early Successes Against Italy*, Pickle Partners 2014

—, *Volume II – The Early Successes Against Italy*, Pickle Partners 2014

Poolman, Kenneth, *HMS Illustrious: The Fight for Life*, Cerberus Publishing 2005

Ray, John, *The Night Blitz 1940–1941*, John Ray 1996

Rees, Quentin, *Cockleshell Heroes: The Final Witness*, Amberley Publishing 2010

Richards, Denis, *Official History of the Royal Air Force 1935–1945 Vol 1: The Fight At Odds*, Pickle Partners Publishing 2013

Roberts, Geoffrey, *Stalin's Wars: From World War to Cold War 1939–1953*, Yale University Press 2006

Roberts, Jeremy, *Benito Mussolini*, Twenty First Century Books 2006

Rolf, David, *The Bloody Road to Tunis: Destruction of the Axis Forces in North Africa, November 1942–May 1943*, Frontline Books 2015

Rooney, David, *Burma Victory: Imphal, Kohima and the Chindits – March 1944 to May 1945*, Osprey Publishing 2013

Ryan, Cornelius, *A Bridge Too Far*, Simon and Schuster Paperbacks 1995

Ryan, Cornelius, *The Longest Day: The D-Day Story, June 6th, 1944*, Tauris Parke Paperbacks 2016

Schama, Simon, *A History of Britain* Vol. 3, BBC Books 2002

Sharp, Nigel, *Dunkirk Little Ships*, Amberley Publishing 2015

Shirer, William, *The Sinking of the Bismarck: The Deadly Hunt*, Rosetta Books 2014

Smith, Colin, *Singapore Burning*, Penguin 2006

Smith, Jean Edward, *FDR*, Random House 2008

Smithers, A.J., *Taranto: A Glorious Episode*, Pen and Sword 1995

Smitka, Michael, *The Interwar Economy of Japan: Colonialism, Depression, and Recovery 1910–1940*, Garland Publishing 1998

Snow, Peter and Dan, *Battlefield Britain: From Boudicca to the Battle of Britain*, BBC Books 2004

Sondhaus, Lawrence, *Navies of Europe 1815–2002*, Routledge 2014

Stern, Robert, *Big Gun Battles: Warship Duels of the Second World War*, Seaforth Publishing 2015

Sutherland, Jonathan; Canwell, Diane, *Vichy Air Force at War: The French Air Force that Fought the Allies in World War II*, Pen and Sword Aviation 2011

Sweetman, John, *The Dambusters Raid*, Cassell Military Paperbacks 2002

Sweetman, John. *Tirpitz: Hunting the Beast*, The History Press 2004

Taylor, Frederick, *Dresden 13th February 1945*, Bloomsbury Publishing 2011

Thomas, David, *Malta Convoys 1940–42: The Struggle at Sea*, Pen and Sword 1999

Thompson, Julian, *The Victory in Europe Experience: From D-Day to the Destruction of the Third Reich*, Carlton Books 2005

Thompson, Kenneth, *Winston Churchill's World View: Statesmanship and Power*, Louisiana State University Press 1983

Thompson, Peter, *The Battle for Singapore: The True Story of the Greatest Catastrophe of World War II*, Hachette 2005

The War in Pictures, Volume One, Odhams Press

The War in Pictures, Volume Two, Odhams Press

The War in Pictures Third Year, Odhams Press

The War in Pictures Fourth Year, Odhams Press

The War in Pictures Fifth Year, Odhams Press

The War in Pictures Sixth Year, Odhams Press

Walker, Angela, *From Battle of Britain Airman to POW Escapee: The Story of Ian Walker RAF*, Pen and Sword Aviation 2017

Warren, Alan, *Britain's Greatest Defeat: Singapore 1942*, Hambledon Continuum 2007
Watson, Bruce, *Exit Rommel: The Tunisian Campaign, 1942–43*, Stackpole Books 2007
Whitley, M.J., *Destroyer! German Destroyers in World War Two*, Naval Institute Press 1991
Williams, Andrew, *The Battle for the Atlantic*, BBC Books 2003
Wilmot, H., *The Second World War in the Far East*, Smithsonian Books 1999
Zabecki, David, *World War II in Europe: An Encyclopaedia*, Routledge 2015
Zetterling, Niklas; Tamelander, Michael, *Bismarck: The Final Days of Germany's Greatest Battleship*,
 Casemate Publishing 2009

Korea

Australian War Memorial. Interview with Sir Francis Hassett (*The Battle of Maryan San*) https://bit.
 ly/2qmbFwS. Retrieved 7 June 2017
Army Museum of Western Australia. *Battle of Maryang San*. https://bit.ly/2zilEY4 uploaded Ian O'Toole.
 Retrieved 7 June 2017

Breen, Bob, *The Battle of Maryang San, 3rd Battalion, Royal Australian Regiment 2–8th October 1951*,
 Headquarters Training Command, Australian Army 1994
Catchpole, Brian, *The Korean War*, Constable and Robinson 2000
Forbes, Cameron, *The Korean War, Australia in the Giants Playground*, Pan Macmillan 2010
Hastings, Max, *The Korean War*, Pan Macmillan 2010
Hutchinson, Garrie, *Pilgrimmage: A Travellers Guide to Australia's Battlefields*, Black Inc Publishing 2006
Salmon, Andrew, *To the Last Round: The Epic British Stand on the Imjin River, Korea 1951*, Aurum Press 2010
Snow, Peter and Dan, *Twentieth Century Battlefields*, BBC Books

Cyprus

Friedman, Sergeant Major Herbert; Paschalidis, General Ioannis, Cyprus 1954–59. www.psywarrior.com/
 cyprus.html Retrieved 1 November 2016

Morgan, Tabitha, *Sweet and Bitter Island: A History of the British in Cyprus*, IB Tauris 2010
Richards, Dr. Dick, *Brief History of Cyprus in Ten Chapters*, K.P. Kyriakou Books 1992
Van der Bijl, Nick, *The Cyprus Emergency: The Divided Island 1955–1974*, Pen and Sword Military 2010

Troubles

Film Documentary – *The Battle of Bogside*, BBC 2004
Film Documentary – *8 Days: To the Moon and Back*, BBC 10 July 2019

The Rt Hon The Lord Saville of Newdigate et al. *Principal Conclusions and Overall Assessment of the Bloody
 Sunday Inquiry. 2010*. https://bit.ly/2P2hEph. Retrieved 13 June 2017
Film Documentary – *Mountbatten: Return to Mullaghmore*. Below the Radar for RTE and AETN
 Television 2009.

Edwards, Aaron, *The Northern Ireland Troubles: Operation Banner 1969–2007*, Osprey Publishing 2011
Barden, Jonathan, *A History of Ulster*, Blackstaff Press 1992
Hardy, Freya, P*aratroopers: Ready for Anything, From WWII to Afghanistan*, RW Press 2013
Hastings, Max, *Going to the Wars*, Pan Books 2001
Mallinson, Allan, *The Making of the British Army*, Bantam Press 2011
McKittrick, David; McVea, David, *Making Sense of the Troubles. The Story of the Conflict in Northern
 Ireland*, New Amsterdam Books 2002
Pringle, Peter; Jacobsen, Philip, *Those are Real Bullets: Bloody Sunday, Derry 1972*, Grove Press 2000

Falklands War

Film Documentary – *Falklands Most Daring Raid*. Darlow Smithson Productions. 2012

New York Times. https://nyti.ms/2OgvIpG. Retrieved 14 June 2017

Adkin, Mark, *The Battle of Goose Green: A Battle is Fought to be Won*, Pen and Sword 1992
Anderson, Duncan, *The Falklands War 1982*, Osprey Publishing 2002
Freedman, Lawrence, *The Official History of the Falklands Campaign, Volume Two: War and Diplomacy,*
    Routledge 2005
Gustafson, Lowell, *The Sovereignty Dispute over the Falkland (Malvinas) Islands*, Oxford University Press 1996
Hastings, Max; Jenkins, Simon, *The Battle for the Falklands*, Pan Macmillan 2010
Laver, Roberto, *The Falklands/Malvinas Case: Breaking the Deadlock in the Anglo Argentine Sovereignty*
    Dispute, Martinus Nijhoff Publishers 2001
Middlebrook, Martin, *Argentine Fight for the Falklands*, Pen and Sword Military 2009
Rossiter, Mike, *Sink the Belgrano*, Corgi Books 2008
Van der Bilj, Nick, *Nine Battles to Stanley*, Pen and Sword 2014

Gulf War
Globalsecurity.org. Operation Desert Storm. https://bit.ly/2qklHhV. Retrieved 31 December 2016

Bourque, Stephen, *Jayhawk: The VII Corps in the Persian Gulf War*, CreateSpace Independent Publishing
    Platform 2015
Macgregor, Douglas, *Warrior's Rage: The Great Tank Battle of 73 Easting*, Naval Institute Press 2009
Simons, G., *Iraq: From Sumer to Post-Saddam*, Palgrave Macmillan; 3rd Edition 2003
Snow, Peter and Dan, *Twentieth Century Battlefields*, BBC Books 2007

War on Terror
Al Jazeera 2nd November 2004. *Transcript of Bin Laden's Speech.* https://bit.ly/2RsnL34 Retrieved 3
    January 2017
The Guardian. https://bit.ly/2AEfhjA. Retrieved 3rd January 2017
The Guardian. Burke, Jason & Norton-Taylor, Richard. *Allies Move into Town held by Taliban.* www.
    https://bit.ly/2ACiNeq Retrieved 3 January 2017
The Scotsman 16 December 2007. *The Taking of Musa Qala.* https://bit.ly/2EUQX14. Retrieved 3 January
    2017
Townsend, Mark. *The Guardian. Fierce Battle Rages for Taliban Stronghold.* www.theguardian.com/
    world/2007/dec/09/afghanistan.theobserver. Retrieved 3 January 2017

Grey, Stephem, *Operation Snakebite: The Explosive True Story of an Afghan Desert Siege*, Penguin Books 2009
Snow, Peter and Dan, *Twentieth Century Battlefields*, BBC Books 2007